THE GOVERNMENT OF PHILIP AUGUSTUS

The Government of Philip Augustus

Foundations of French Royal Power in the Middle Ages

JOHN W. BALDWIN

University of California Press

BERKELEY   LOS ANGELES   LONDON

University of California Press
Berkeley and Los Angeles, California

University of California Press, Ltd.
London, England

Library of Congress Cataloging in Publication Data
Baldwin, John W.
The government of Philip Augustus.
Includes index.
1. France—History—Philip II Augustus, 1180–1223.
2. Philippe II Auguste, King of France, 1165–1223.
I. Title.
DC90.B35   1986   944'.023'0924   84-23930
ISBN 0-520-05272-2

Printed in the United States of America
1   2   3   4   5   6   7   8   9

For Birgit

Contents

Illustrations and Maps

Illustrations

Frontispiece. Philip *Dieudonné*: King Louis VII and Queen Adèle receive the infant Philip from Christ in heaven. Paris, Bibliothèque Sainte-Geneviève 782, fol. 208r.

Maps

xi

Tables and Graph

Tables

Graph

A Note on Monies and Exchange Rates Employed in This Book

All *livres*, *sous*, *deniers*, and marks designate the money of Paris except when otherwise qualified.

1 mark = 2.1 *livres* in 1202/03 (*Budget* pp. 65, 66, 181, 193)

1 mark = 2 *livres* in 1222 (Nortier and Baldwin, "Contributions," 31, 32)

1 mark sterling = 0.666 pound sterling

1 pound sterling = 4 *livres angevins* in 1204 (*Actes* II, no. 844)

1 *livre angevin* = 0.68 *livre* in 1202/03 (*Budget* pp. 43, 71, 77)

1 *livre angevin* = 1 *livre tournois*

1 *livre tournois* = 0.8 *livre* in 1221 (Nortier and Baldwin, "Contributions," 6)

1 *livre provin* = 0.75 *livre* in 1202/03 (*Budget* pp. 64, 65)

Preface

The importance of the reign of Philip Augustus has been universally recognized by historians. Viewed in the overall perspective of medieval France, Philip's achievements have been rightly acknowledged as a *tournant*, indeed a quantum leap in the development of the Capetian monarchy. Not only did his celebrated conquests enrich the king with lands far more extensive than those possessed by any other baron in France, but his accompanying governmental innovations enabled the monarchy to exploit these resources and eventually to dominate both the kingdom and western Europe by the close of the thirteenth century. Despite the celebrity of these achievements, however, twentieth-century French historians have paid little attention to Philip's reign. The explanation is readily evident. In 1898 Alexander Cartellieri, professor at Heidelberg, brought out the first volume of his *Philipp II. Augustus, König von Frankreich*, which, despite the tragedies of World War I, treated the reign in four monumental tomes, comprising more than 1,800 pages by its completion in 1921. Achille Luchaire, the leading medievalist at Paris, who had devoted his Sorbonne lectures between 1895 and 1901 to Philip Augustus, prudently conceded the field to the German and proceeded to defend French honor by writing six volumes on Philip's great contemporary in the papacy, Innocent III. As Luchaire quickly recognized, Cartellieri's work was unsurpassed in collecting the contemporary chroniclers, establishing the political and military events, and arranging them in chronological sequence, year by year. Subsequent historians have neglected these volumes only at their peril. In spite of its intimidating mass and meticulous care, however, Cartellieri's study followed the lead of the medieval chroniclers by not devoting much attention to the development of government during Philip's reign. Yet it remains true that the creation of new governmental institutions was one of the chief features of the reign.

By 1970, when I completed a study on Peter the Chanter, a contemporary theological master at Paris and the king's unappreciative critic, the
moment seemed propitious to begin an investigation of Philip's government. Most of the principal documentary collections had been printed:
the Trésor des Chartes by Alexandre Teulet, the feudal inventories and
the judicial records of the Norman exchequer by Léopold Delisle,
and the accounts of 1202/03 by Ferdinand Lot and Robert Fawtier. Volume III of the *actes* of Philip Augustus had appeared in 1966, edited by
Jacques Boussard, and Michel Nortier was well advanced with the fourth
and final volume. The eight-hundredth anniversary of the king's coronation was approaching in 1979. The principal deficiency in the published
documentation, however, was the absence of an edition of the registers of
the royal chancery. These three manuscript codices, now located at the
Vatican Library and the Archives Nationales in Paris, were the first extant
registers of the French monarchy and are invaluable witnesses to the
emergence of governmental institutions. Although known and accessible
since Philip's day, they had only been mined by scholars for royal charters
and other individual items of information, but had never been fully
edited or studied as governmental documents in their own right. Thanks
to the assistance of Françoise Gasparri and Michel Nortier and to the
support of the National Endowment for the Humanities, I have been
able to complete an edition of these registers, which is presently being
published by the Académie des Inscriptions et Belles-Lettres.

Once the major documentation of Philip Augustus's reign was assembled, the next problem was how to fashion a framework for studying
royal government. Cartellieri's annalistic approach was unsuitable for
treating the emergence of institutions that produced meager documentation in their incipient stages. The prevailing mode adopted in standard
French histories is to treat the reign as a whole and to emphasize the formative influence of England and Normandy upon Capetian government,
particularly after the conquest of the duchy in 1204. Although pre-
disposed to this approach by former training, I soon discovered its deficiencies. During the forty-odd years of Philip's reign, the French monarchy passed through successive stages of development, but it soon became
apparent to me that the most important transformations had already occurred before the annexation of Normandy. The solution appeared to be
to divide the reign into four approximate decades and within each part to
identify the salient changes that dominated the period. After the decisive
transformations were identified, it was sufficient to demonstrate their

continuation with selected illustrations. By this approach I have emphasized the process of change over that of continuity.

Each decade possessed a distinguishing character. From 1179 to 1190
the young Philip sought merely to master and perpetuate the governmental legacy bequeathed by his father. Before departing on crusade in 1190,
however, he began to make fundamental transformations in the structure
of his government and to recruit new personnel to implement his program. These basic changes were effected before 1204, when he embarked
on his great conquests. The following decade, beginning with the assault
on Normandy in 1204 and concluding with the final victory at Bouvines
in 1214, provided Philip with an opportunity to test his new administrative machinery and to consolidate his gains. The years from Bouvines to
1223 merely constituted a tranquil epilogue, in which the king's lands
enjoyed repose and prosperity. To place the governmental changes of
these four decades in historical context, I have prefaced each part with a
narrative chapter that unabashedly relies on Cartellieri's work.

The state of documentation privileges the historian of Philip's reign
over those of preceding French monarchs. The study of his government
no longer depends totally on the opinions of contemporary chroniclers
or the fortuitous and ecclesiastical biases that conditioned the survival of
royal documents. Philip's administration both generated and preserved
evidence sufficient to provide clear outlines of the great transformations
that took place in his government, but not too much to exceed the grasp
of an individual researcher. Because of the leading role of documentation
in this study, a special chapter has been required to uncover the sources of
Philip's government. If this were a French *thèse*, such a chapter would be
placed at the beginning, but since it contains detailed discussion that
might discourage the general reader, it has been put at the end. It represents more than a technical appendix, however, and historians concerned
with the interplay between sources and history should consult it first.
These records were not merely testimonies to Philip's achievements but
also direct products of his government. Review of them serves both as a
methodological postscript and as an appropriate conclusion to this study.

Documents, therefore, carry the burden of the arguments throughout
the work and largely determine its character. Beyond the royal charters,
fiscal accounts, registers, inventories, and judicial rolls that illuminate administrative institutions, I have also turned my attention to political ideology, which was entrusted to court historiographers and poets. The expression of these ideological concerns culminated in the decade following

Bouvines in the chronicles and poetry of Guillaume le Breton, the king's clerk. Although they succeeded only in a fragmentary way in formulating these theoretical concerns, which had to await later generations for fuller development, Guillaume and his predecessors articulated issues that attract the interests of historians today.

Despite the size and ambitions of this book, it cannot expect to exhaust the possibilities presented by the reign of Philip Augustus. Among the issues remaining to be explored, the surveys of fiefs—to cite an example—can be more fully exploited to detect royal policies toward the feudatories both in the old royal domain and in Normandy after the conquest of the duchy. Recognizing that such questions remain as yet unanswered, I would nonetheless hope that this large book will provide a solid foundation for other, perhaps smaller, studies that will review, refine, and even reinterpret the significance of its conclusions.

From the very beginning this project has received encouragement and aid from colleagues in France with a generosity that can only be attributed to friendship. The close coordination between the edition of the registers and the study of the government has made it impossible to separate the two enterprises. My two collaborators on the edition have unselfishly made their own work available to me. In addition to her published paleographic analysis of the first register, Françoise Gasparri has allowed me to use her continuations on the succeeding codices. Michel Nortier confided to me copies of the texts of Volume IV of the *actes* of Philip Augustus before their publication and has continued to furnish the additions and corrections to appear in the forthcoming Volume V. When he discovered the new financial account of 1221, he generously invited me to participate in its publication and explication. Robert-Henri Bautier agreed to direct the publication of the registers for the Académie, thus contributing his prodigious editorial experience, and undertook to organize a colloquium on Philip Augustus in 1980 that brought into focus much useful work on the reign. At the Archives Nationales, Jean Favier and Lucie Favier made every provision to allow me access to the registers, the Trésor des Chartes, and other collections essential for my work.

In the United States, Arthur J. Lyons, Susan J. Kupper, and Peter A. Poggioli, my former students at Johns Hopkins, served as assistants on the edition. I have learned much from Arthur J. Lyons's dissertation on the Capetian conquest of Anjou and from Susan J. Kupper's dissertation on the towns under Philip Augustus. While in this country, Bernard

Guenée read and commented on an earlier version of the book, and Gabrielle M. Spiegel read and discussed the entire manuscript with me in its various stages. By their willingness to devote time and counsel they have shown true friendship. The main arguments of Part 2, which I consider to be the crux of the book, were heard and helpfully criticized by colleagues in the venerable history seminar at Johns Hopkins. Thomas N. Bisson and Charles T. Wood read the typescript for the press with patience and care and generously shared their perspectives with me. Eugenia Sipes and Ingeborg Knight deciphered the scrawl of my hand and the skein of my footnotes to provide impeccable typescripts. And Jenny Jochens, my wife, faithfully supported me with help and advice throughout more than a decade of my preoccupation with Philip. To all these and many others, too numerous to be named, my gratitude cannot be sufficiently expressed in brief words.

In January 1972 the American Philosophical Society furnished a pilot grant that allowed me to explore the potentialities of the project in Paris, and in 1982 it provided the means for a final checking of the references. Between these dates my work was supported by the National Endowment for the Humanities. In 1973–74 I received a fellowship that enabled me to spend a sabbatical year in the Paris archives and libraries. From 1974 to 1979 work on the edition of the registers was supported by a grant from the Editions and Research Tools Division of the NEH that provided for research assistance, annual trips to Paris, and other material aid necessary to a long-term and laborious project.

Finally, too often forgotten, this project is indebted to my employer, The Johns Hopkins University. Although such research is an essential condition of my employment, the university is organized to provide unusual support for such enterprises by granting sabbatical leaves, furnishing library and clerical facilities, and creating an intellectual environment highly conducive to research—all actively encouraged by the departmental chairmen and the university administration. For all of this help I make public my grateful acknowledgement.

Baltimore
May 1983

PART ONE

The Capetian Legacy,

1179–1190

Narrative:
The Struggle for Survival

The Coronation and Its Participants

Philip Augustus himself dated the official opening of his reign from All Saints' Day (1 November) 1179.[1] On that day, in accordance with Capetian practice, he was anointed and crowned at the cathedral of Reims as the legitimate king and successor to his father, who was yet alive. (See illustration no. 2.) The coronation of 1179, however, was attended by unusual anxiety. It had been originally set for two and a half months earlier, when it was clear that the old king, Louis VII, was in failing health. Prior to that date, however, Philip, Louis's only son, had been the victim of a hunting accident that had seriously threatened his life. In desperation Louis had marshalled his energies to make an arduous pilgrimage across the Channel to Canterbury, the shrine of his old friend Thomas Becket, and to implore the aid of this then-wondrous miracle worker. Although

NOTE: King Philip II of France was first called "Augustus" by the contemporary chronicler Rigord of Saint-Denis because the king was born in August and because he increased, or "augmented," the commonwealth like the Roman Caesars, in this case by acquiring the land of Vermandois (Rigord 6).

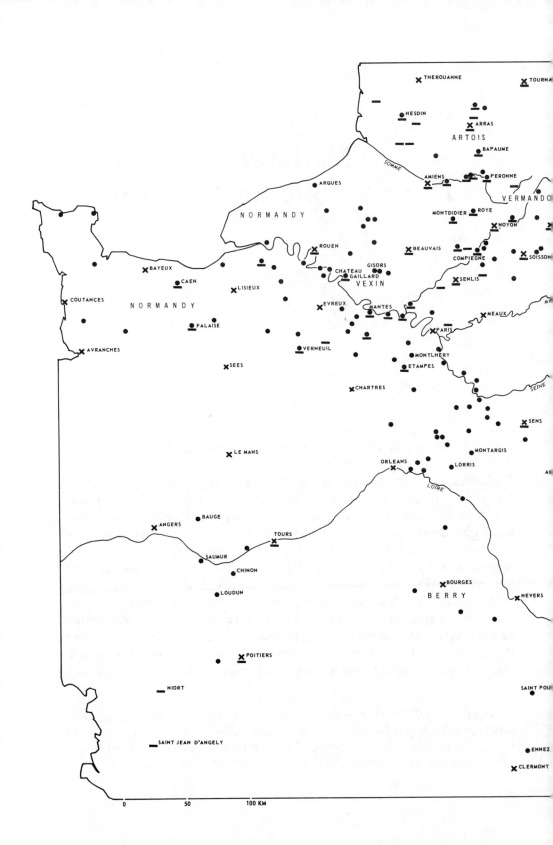

THEROUANNE   TOURNAI

HESDIN

ARRAS

ARTOIS

BAPAUME

SOMME

AMIENS   PERONNE

VERMANDO

ARQUES

NORMANDY

MONTDIDIER   ROYE

NOYON

BEAUVAIS

COMPIEGNE   SOISSON

ROUEN

GISORS

CHATEAU

GAILLARD

SENLIS

BAYEUX

CAEN

LISIEUX

VEXIN

COUTANCES

NORMANDY

EVREUX

MANTES

MEAUX

M

FALAISE

PARIS

VERNEUIL

MONTLHERY

AVRANCHES

SEES

ETAMPES

SEINE

CHARTRES

SENS

LE MANS

MONTARGIS

ORLEANS

LORRIS

A

LOIRE

BAUGE

ANGERS

TOURS

SAUMUR

CHINON

BOURGES

LOUDUN

BERRY

NEVERS

POITIERS

NIORT

SAINT POU

SAINT JEAN D'ANGELY

ENNEZ

CLERMONT

0   50   100 KM

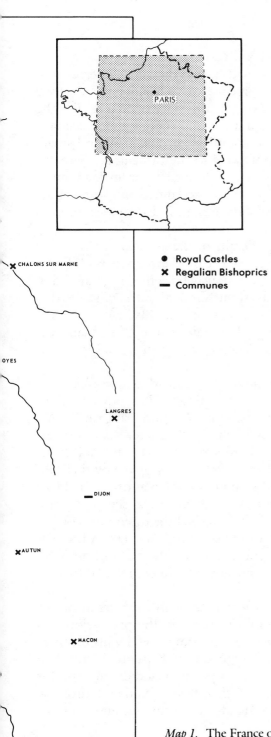

● Royal Castles
✖ Regalian Bishoprics
▬ Communes

✖ CHALONS SUR MARNE

OYES

LANGRES
✖

▬ DIJON

✖ AUTUN

✖ MACON

Map 1. The France of Philip Augustus

the old king was subsequently struck with paralysis and irrevocably confined to his bed, his appeal apparently had elicited the saint's intercession,
because the fourteen-year-old boy had recovered his health and was ready
for the coronation.[2] The great occasion filled the city of Reims with the
prelates and magnates of France—four archbishops, their numerous suffragan bishops, scores of abbots, and countless barons, great and small.
In solemn procession young Philip was led to the cathedral, where the
archbishop of Reims, newly elevated to the dignity of cardinal, anointed
and crowned him king. Afterwards the crowd acclaimed him with shouts
of *vive le roi*, and the important personages concluded the ceremonies
with a festive banquet.[3]

The chroniclers who recount the details of the occasion name three
principal parties among the participants.[4] The most evident was Philippe,
count of Flanders, who not only ceremoniously bore the king's sword in
the opening procession but also fulfilled the honored duties of steward at
the concluding banquet. His retinue was swelled by his brother-in-law,
soon to be father-in-law of the king, Baudouin, count of Hainaut, accompanied by eighty knights at Baudouin's own expense, as his chronicler complains.

The archbishop of Reims, Guillaume aux Blanches Mains, who asserted
exclusive right to perform the consecration, represented the powerful family of Champagne. Enjoying multiple ties with the monarchy, this family
consisted of three counts and the archbishop, all brothers, and a sister,
Adèle, who was King Louis's wife and Philip's mother. On the day of the
coronation the leading members of the family were notable by their absence. Henri, count of Troyes and the family's head, was off in the Holy
Land. His brothers, Thibaut, count of Blois and royal seneschal, and
Etienne, count of Sancerre, had probably avoided the ceremonies out of
opposition to the conspicuous role of the count of Flanders. Adèle was
most likely at the side of her dying husband. But the archbishop, who
played the commanding role on the occasion, was fully prepared to safeguard the interests of his brothers and sister.

Finally, the great house of Anjou was present in the person of the
young King Henry, who carried Philip's crown in the procession and
supported his head during the coronation. Accompanied by his brothers
Richard, count of Poitou, and Geoffrey, count of Brittany, Henry had
arrived with a dazzling retinue laden with precious and exotic gifts for
the new king.[5] The three brothers shared their titles with their father, the
great Henry II, who, as duke of Normandy and Aquitaine and count of

Anjou, was overlord of the western half of France as well
gland. Although these three parties were all vassals to
French lands, the splendor of their presence overshadowed the
petian even at his own coronation.

In medieval times, when ceremonial occasions betokened what was
significant, conspicuous prominence was a sure sign of the importance of
the participants. Such was the case at Reims in 1179. If we add to the
parties of Flanders, Champagne, and Anjou, recorded by the chroniclers,
the more distant figure of Frederick Barbarossa, emperor of Germany, we
have the essential elements of the political world that confronted Philip
Augustus at the outset of his reign. Within the kingdom, the houses of
Flanders and Champagne competed for domination over the young king.
To either side, east and west, Frederick and Henry II, the two great powers of the period, carefully watched the unfolding events. The German
emperor restrained himself from openly intervening during the first decade, but the English king, whose interests were more at stake, played a
direct role. Though at the outset Henry protected his young lord against
the shifting coalitions of French barons, he was himself gradually drawn
into the conflict as one of the parties, ending as the chief antagonist of
the French monarchy. Since the first decade of Philip's reign produced a
bewildering confusion of changing alliances among these four parties
and the Capetian monarchy, it will be useful to begin with an assessment
of the underlying strengths, weaknesses, and sources of contention among
the rivals.

The county of Flanders inherited by Count Philippe was one of the
two richest and best-governed principalities in the kingdom (Normandy
was its chief competitor). Occupying what are now the northeastern bor-
derlands of France and most of Belgium, Flanders consisted mainly of
flat, fertile fields. The abundance of its agriculture encouraged the highest population concentration in northwestern Europe and nourished important cities such as Ghent, Bruges, Douai, Lille, Ypres, Saint-Omer,
and Arras, which increasingly specialized in textile manufacture. Unlike
so many medieval principalities, the land, resources, and population of
Flanders were compressed into a compact entity. Over this fiefdom the
count exercised political authority unusual for his day. His central court
boasted the earliest chancery among the lay princes of France, which
produced documents essential to the increasingly complex functions
of government. The countryside had long been sectioned into well-
delimited castellanies, policed by presiding castellans. Most castles, even

those of the castellans, were in the count's own hands, thus inhibiting the independence of local lords. In recent times Count Philippe had instituted local agents, later called *baillis*, who were more responsive to his authority than the castellans. These local administrators maintained the peace and extended the count's justice throughout the countryside. In addition, the revenues from the count's rich domains were regularly collected by receivers and systematically accounted for in writing. Beyond the count's traditional rights over justice and finance, he exercised close supervision of five bishoprics and claimed to protect numerous rich abbeys, from which he increased his income and authority.

Situated at the corner of northwestern Europe, Flanders was also subject to multiple influences and allegiances. The county lay on the main route from England to the Continent, where the Channel was narrowest, and the vast sheep farms of Britain supplied the raw wool necessary for the cloth-weaving industries of the Flemish cities. Proximity and economics therefore demanded close ties between the kings of England and the counts of Flanders, expressed in treaties and feudal compacts since the early twelfth century. Moreover, whereas the counts held their southern and central lands as vassals of the French king, their eastern lands lay within the Empire. They therefore owed feudal allegiance to both the French king and the German emperor. This exposed the Flemish counts to potential intervention from both sides, as well as by neighboring imperial lords such as the marquis of Namur and the counts of Hainaut and Brabant, whose affairs were closely tied to those of Flanders. These multiple claims over the county could at times be sources of strength as well, especially when the French and German overlords were in conflict. Then one side could be played off against the other. On the whole, however, the main pressure on Flanders came from the south, and from the beginning of the twelfth century the counts reacted chiefly against the French. Because of a fortunate dynastic marriage, Count Philippe of Flanders was able to take possession in 1164 of the county of Vermandois, with its dependencies, Amiens and Valois, in the name of his wife Elisabeth. By this stroke his frontiers were advanced close to Paris and threatened the security of the royal domain. Sustained by his extensive and well-managed Flemish fiefs, Count Philippe seriously contended for hegemony over northwestern France.[6]

The rival house of Champagne presented a number of contrasts. Unlike the Flemish fiefs, its lands were widely dispersed in both eastern France, with centers at Troyes, Provins, and Meaux, and in the west, with holdings at Blois, Chartres, Sancerre, and Châteaudun. Since these territories had been slowly accumulated over two centuries by the houses of Vermandois and Blois, the organization of Champagne was largely a family affair. By the mid–twelfth century the family's leader, Henri, took the counties of Troyes and Meaux as his own and assigned Blois and Chartres to a brother, Thibaut, and Sancerre to another, Etienne. These lands, especially those in the east, were poorer and more sparsely populated than Flanders, but they were strategically located. Blois, for example, commanded the upper reaches of the Loire valley, and the count of Troyes was fortunate to possess the celebrated fairs at Troyes, Provins, Lagny, and Bar-sur-Aube, situated on the north–south overland trade route, where merchants from the Mediterranean and the north met to exchange goods. The Champagne fairs were among the count's principal sources of revenue, but the family lands were apparently less firmly governed by their counts than Flanders. Little information has survived on local officers or the administration of justice and finance. Rather, the counties were assembled as a great feudal complex in which the essential functions of government were delegated to vassals and their agents. The political situation in twelfth-century Champagne was encapsulated in a survey of fiefs executed by Count Henri at Troyes in 1172. At that time about 1,900 knights owed service to the count. Although they were divided into twenty-six castellanies, these districts were not as well defined as the Flemish castellanies.

Like those of Flanders, however, the feudal allegiances of Champagne were multiple and complex. The count of Troyes, for example, was direct vassal of the king of France only for Meaux. He held his most important fief, Troyes, from the duke of Burgundy and other large fiefs from the archbishop of Reims. Among his many overlords was the German emperor, from whom he held lands in the Empire. The great feudal complex of Meaux, Troyes, Blois, and Chartres encircled the royal domain on the east, south, and southwest, making the Champagne family the traditional enemy of the Capetians throughout the eleventh and early twelfth centuries, until the rise of the house of Anjou in the second half of the twelfth century transformed this long-standing hostility into close friendship.[7]

That the counts of Flanders and Champagne were also vassals of the German emperor points to a potential source of disturbance on the eastern borders of France. Heir to the traditions of Charlemagne and the ancient Roman emperors, the medieval emperor claimed honor and authority above all other monarchs of the west. In practice, however, he was incapable of providing effective government even for Germany. By the early twelfth century, when the great struggle between the popes and emperors had subsided, the emperor had lost the land base essential for successful authority to the German princes and prelates. Moreover, the papacy had created an irrevocable precedent for intervening in imperial affairs. In spite of these obstacles the mid–twelfth century witnessed the emergence of one of the great monarchs of medieval Germany, Frederick Barbarossa. When Frederick was elected to the imperial dignity in 1152, he not only founded a new dynasty, the Hohenstaufens, but also fashioned a new program. Like his contemporary Henry II of England, he intended to create a compact territorial state from which to draw sufficient military and financial strength to rule an extended Empire. Through inheritance, marriage, and conquest he centered this state on southern Switzerland at the source of three great rivers, the Rhine, the Rhone, and the Ticino, whose valleys formed Swabia, imperial Burgundy, and Lombardy. Preoccupied with this new base of power from the beginning of his reign, he for the most part neglected the rest of Germany. It was principally his son Henry, entitled king of the Romans, who represented imperial interests in the north of Germany.

The emperor's early attention to creating a territorial state and its later abandonment only further encouraged the great princes and prelates of Germany to strengthen control over their own localities. Henry the Lion, duke of Saxony, for example, fashioned his holdings into a compact state and supported the Guelf party of princes, who opposed the Hohenstaufens. As a sign of growing importance, he married a daughter of the English king, Henry II, who supported his son-in-law in revolts against the emperor. Likewise, Philip, archbishop of Cologne, and the most influential German prince on the northeastern frontier of France, acted independently of the emperor in that region. Although Frederick Barbarossa, as lord of imperial Burgundy and overlord of the counts of Flanders and Champagne, was in a position to intervene in eastern French affairs if he were of such a mind, absorption with his own lands in the south, conflict with the papacy in Italy, and, most important, rivalry among independent German princes and prelates in the north limited his effectiveness in French as well as German politics.[8]

Of all the rulers of western Europe, Henry of Anjou was most favored by the fortunes of inheritance and marriage. From his mother, daughter of King Henry I, he fell heir to England and Normandy, with lordship over Brittany. Anjou came to him from his father, count of the region, and with it lordship over Maine and Touraine. From his wife Eleanor, recently separated from King Louis VII of France, he gained the vast duchy of Aquitaine, whose principal center was Poitou but whose claims of lordship reached as far south as Toulouse. Styling himself with numerous titles, Henry held lands extending from the Scottish border in the British Isles down through the western half of France to the Pyrenees.

England and Normandy formed a solid nucleus within this immense conglomeration. During the century after the Norman conquest of England, the two lands were united under the same ruler over half the time. This attachment stimulated the development of similar institutions on both sides of the Channel. The countryside was clearly districted into shires in England and *vicomtés* and *baillages* in Normandy. Local officials collected regular domanial income and other occasional revenues, exercised justice, and executed royal or ducal commands. Twice a year the English sheriffs and Norman *vicomtes* and *baillis* rendered their accounts at central exchequers to report their income and deduct their expenses. Close by the exchequers at Westminster in England and at Caen in Normandy, central courts of justice staffed by permanent judges heard pleas from all over the realm. In order to make this royal or ducal justice more accessible, itinerant judges were dispatched from the central courts to hear pleas throughout the shires, *vicomtés*, and *baillages* on periodic tourneys. In both England and Normandy, knight service was extensively surveyed and recorded in inventories to keep the king and duke abreast of his military resources. In 1166 some 5,000 English knights acknowledged their service to Henry; in 1172 the obligations of almost 600 knights were recorded in Normandy. At times this knight service could be commuted into money payments that provided a kind of wartime taxation. Most of the important and strategic castles were firmly held by the king and duke, thus reducing the independence of the local nobility. Bishoprics and abbeys were closely controlled, permitting their masters to collect revenues during their vacancies and to nominate new bishops and abbots. In effect, Henry II perfected what Frederick Barbarossa had tried in vain to establish: a well-governed territorial base rich enough in financial and military resources to dominate vast continental holdings.

Apart from Normandy, Henry's French lands displayed a bewildering variety of conditions. Although his father's legacy of Anjou was held with reasonable firmness, Brittany and the fiefs south of the Loire were theaters of anarchy, where local lords acted without inhibition. Only with great difficulty could Henry force the distant count of Toulouse to acknowledge his lordship, and that to little effect. Outside of Normandy, the only castles held with any security were the Loire fortresses in and near Anjou. When one of Henry's incessant journeys brought him to a fief such as Anjou or Poitou, he acted as titular count and held court for the time he was there. In his absence his chief agent was usually the seneschal of the local court, who served in Henry's behalf, but the arrangement was to little effect or profit by comparison with England and Normandy. As in Champagne, local control and revenues were, for the most part, delegated to regional vassals. Henry's extensive French possessions outside of Normandy therefore constituted a serious weakness and a drain on his Anglo-Norman base. In an attempt to remedy this deficiency, the king enlisted the services of his sons. In 1169 the young Henry was designated the king's direct successor, with concomitant title to the heartland of England, Normandy, and Anjou. Richard was assigned the title of Aquitaine and Geoffrey that of Brittany in view of their eventual authority over these fiefs. But the young princes were impatient with mere titles. Goaded by their spirited mother, Eleanor, who was as incompatible to Henry as to Louis, they joined forces in revolt against their father in 1173. Saved by his own decisive action and the loyal support of his English and Norman barons, Henry was able to surmount the uprising and dealt generously with his unruly heirs. The following year the young Henry obtained confirmation of his former position, but Richard was conceded two castles of his own, full authority in Aquitaine, and half of its revenues. Geoffrey likewise gained two castles along with his claims to Brittany, and the youngest son, John, King Henry's favorite, was given less important lands and castles. But these settlements neither solved the underlying defects in Henry's continental landholdings nor satisfied his brood. Only the king's enormous energy and political genius held his lands together. Great personal fortune had assembled the Angevin holdings; only personal effort would guarantee their unity.[9]

In addition to Flanders, Champagne, and the Angevin holdings, the French king claimed suzerainty over a myriad of other vassals, possessing a great variety of titles and influence. Isolated in their mountains and valleys around Clermont, the distant counts of Auvergne, for example, asserted their independence against the claims to lordship of both the Capetians and the dukes of Aquitaine. To the southeast of Paris, on the other hand, the counts of Auxerre and Nevers and the dukes of Burgundy, ducal in title only, exerted relatively little influence beyond their immediate lands. Only when the Capetians themselves took the offensive did these fiefs come into play.

The resources that the young king Philip inherited from his father contrasted dolefully with those of his three chief vassals. The royal domain—

those lands and rights from which the king profited directly—were largely confined to the Ile-de-France and consisted of small scattered holdings. Orléans, Paris, and Compiègne were the chief focal points.[10] Only with difficulty had Louis VI and Louis VII subdued the major castles to permit safe travel within the domain. Both kings could easily traverse the extent of their lands, as they frequently did, in a few days. Local officials called *prévôts* were established in the clusters of royal lands to execute the king's commands, to hold courts, and, most important, to collect the domanial revenues. No financial records survive, but the *prévôts* could have delivered to the king only a fraction of what Henry received from England and Normandy and not as much as was enjoyed by the counts of Flanders and Champagne. Moreover, only a handful of castellans and minor vassals owed knight service directly to the king.

The main assets of the early Capetians were not, therefore, their financial and military resources, but rather two principal claims: the sacred character of their kingship and dynastic continuity. When the archbishop of Reims anointed the young king in 1179, he administered a ceremony that transformed Philip into a sacred personage and permitted him to rule "by the grace of God." As part of this ceremony—and, as it were, in exchange for consecration—the Capetians swore a solemn oath to defend the church from its enemies.[11] Though this patronage may theoretically have extended to all churches of the kingdom, in practice it was effective only in those that were considered "regalian"—that is, that belonged especially to the king. The Capetians claimed the right to profit from the revenues and to supervise the selection of bishops and abbots in regalian churches during their vacancies. Louis VII, for example, claimed at least twenty-five regalian bishoprics and perhaps sixty-five abbeys. With greatest concentration in the ecclesiastical provinces of Sens and Reims, these churches extended through eastern France from Tournai in the north to Le Puy in the south.[12] As a landed proprietor, the Capetian king was restricted to the tiny Ile-de-France, but as protector of the church, his influence encompassed over a third of the kingdom.

Orderly succession was likewise an asset to the monarchy because disputes over the throne inevitably vitiated effective government and despoiled the resources of the ruling house. The slow demise of the Salian dynasty in Germany during the first half of the twelfth century, for example, produced anarchy and dissolved the bases of imperial authority. It was no wonder that Frederick Barbarossa was resolved to establish a dynastic claim to the imperial succession for the Hohenstaufens by emphasizing the role of his son Henry as king of the Romans. Similarly, when the Anglo-Normans after two generations had failed to produce a male heir by the time of the death of Henry I in 1135, the resulting civil war devastated the realm on both sides of the Channel. Like Barbarossa, Henry of Anjou was determined to implant his family on the throne. He risked the fulminations of his great antagonist Thomas Becket, archbishop of Canterbury, to have his eldest son, Henry, crowned as his successor in 1170. (Since the king was at odds with the archbishop of Canterbury, he requested the consecration from the archbishop of York.) By contrast, the Capetians had not failed to produce a legitimate male heir since 987. This fecundity, combined with the practice of crowning the son before the death of the father, ensured an ordered succession for six generations. It is true, however, that Louis VII required three wives and nearly thirty years of marriage to continue the family tradition. Philip's belated birth to Adèle de Champagne in 1165 was therefore greeted with unrestrained jubilation and earned him his first sobriquet, *Dieudonné* (given by God). (See frontispiece.) Louis VII and Adèle had preserved Capetian dynastic continuity, and by consecrating Philip during Louis's lifetime, the orderly succession of the French monarchy was assured for a seventh generation.[13]

The fourteen-year-old Philip naturally fell heir to the political situation bequeathed by his father in 1179, of which the chief feature was the diplomatic revolution brought about by the gains of Henry of Anjou in the 1150s. Prior to that time, French politics had been governed by two traditional rivalries: between the Capetians and the house of Blois-Champagne because of proximity, and between Blois-Champagne and Anjou over Tours, which lay between them in the Loire valley. In the latter competition, the Angevins could usually rely on aid from the Capetians.[14] Now, however, with the union of Normandy and Anjou encircling the royal domain from the north to the southwest and the acquisition of Aquitaine through his marriage to Louis's ex-wife, Eleanor, Henry of Anjou suddenly became the unmistakable threat to the French monarchy. Unable to oppose Henry directly, Louis reacted by supporting Henry's opponents, such as Thomas Becket in the 1160s and Henry's sons in the 1170s. The hostilities that broke out intermittently in the south and in the Vexin, the buffer zone between the Ile-de-France and Normandy, were brought to a temporary halt at Nonancourt in 1177 when the two kings agreed to respect each other's lands except for the disputes over Berry and Auvergne, which were as yet irreconcilable.[15]

Against the darkening menace of Anjou, Louis VII sought new allies. Overtures were extended to his old rivals of the house of Champagne. Thibaut de Blois was granted the important office of seneschal in the royal household in 1154. Louis himself married Adèle, the youngest of the Champagne sisters, in 1160, and to strengthen the bonds between the two families, Henri de Troyes and Thibaut de Blois married the king's two daughters by Eleanor of Aquitaine in 1164. The youngest brother, Guillaume, was promoted from the bishopric of Chartres to the archbishopric of Sens and finally to the great see of Reims in 1176. In addition to this new friendship with Champagne, Louis sought support from the house of Flanders, whose position on the northern borders of Normandy tempted it to compete with Henry of Anjou. In 1159 Philippe, the heir of the count of Flanders, married Elisabeth, daughter of Raoul, count of Vermandois and a cousin of the king's. A parallel marriage was also arranged between Philip's brother Mathieu, count of Boulogne, and Aliénor, Elisabeth's sister. From his wife Philippe inherited claims[16] to the rich territories of Vermandois, Valois, and Amiens. Twenty years later this same Philippe, now count of Flanders, exercised a predominant influence over the royal court during Louis's final year, when the enfeebled king transferred authority to his young son. He was the leading French baron to accompany Louis on his desperate pilgrimage to Canterbury, and in the months before the coronation he became the prince's close counsellor, swearing an oath to the old king faithfully to protect his young charge. In 1179 the count of Flanders was not quite the king's official guardian, as Count Baudouin V had been a century earlier over the young Philip I, but he undoubtedly overshadowed the court, as indicated by his conspicuous roles at the coronation.[17]

Philippe of Flanders achieved his most striking success, however, in the spring of 1180, when he negotiated a marriage between the king and his niece. Even before the coronation, he had suggested his niece Ida, daughter of his brother Mathieu, count of Boulogne, to the old Louis, but afterwards he offered the king another niece, Isabelle, daughter of his sister Marguerite and Baudouin, count of Hainaut. With Isabelle as queen, the Flemish party would have an influential member at the royal court, just as the Champagne party had had in Adèle during Louis's last years. The marriage was celebrated at Bapaume close by the Flemish lands on 28 April 1180 by the bishops of Senlis and Laon. The magnates of the realm were summoned to the queen's coronation, not at Reims, but at Sens at the feast of Pentecost. This not only violated the archbishop of

Reims's claim to exclusive right over royal coronations but offended his sensibilities as a member of the Champagne family. The ceremony was transferred to the royal abbey of Saint-Denis, not far from the Flemish holdings of Valois, where, assisted by the bishops of Paris and Orléans, the archbishop of Sens anointed and crowned the queen and recrowned the king. Once again, the count of Flanders bore the sword in the procession. Needless to say, the Champagne party were notably absent.[18] The marriage between Isabelle de Hainaut and the king not only provided the count of Flanders with a relative at court, it also sharpened the royal interest in the Flemish region. As dowry the count assigned to his niece the important region later called Artois, with cities at Arras, Bapaume, Saint-Omer, and Aire, on condition that he be allowed its use during his own lifetime.

Shifting Alliances

The first decade of Philip Augustus's reign saw rapidly shifting alliances among the principal parties contending for influence over the French monarchy. The confusing succession of events can best be divided into three phases, distinguished by the factions that directly opposed the king: the houses of Champagne, Flanders, and Anjou. The opening phase, in which the Flemish preponderance culminated in the king's marriage, naturally challenged the ascendency of the Champagne family, especially the queen mother, Adèle. The archbishop of Reims's presence was required at the king's coronation because of his prerogatives, but none of the party was present for the humiliation of the new queen's wedding and coronation. When Adèle began fortifying her dowry lands, the king ordered them seized, forcing his mother to flee to the security of her brother, Thibaut de Blois. Whether or not Philip Augustus actively intended to replace his uncle with the count of Flanders in the seneschalship, as Gerald of Wales maintained, he nonetheless removed the royal seal from his father's disposal to prevent its use by the Champagne party during the old king's dotage.[19]

Adèle's response to these strong measures was to call for help from the king of England, who quickly arrived in Normandy. Henry, whose many years of experience had taught him to exploit such situations to his advantage, surprised everyone by offering his young sovereign a genuine peace at Gisors in June 1180, founded on the terms of Nonancourt three

years earlier. Philip Augustus, in turn, agreed to receive back into favor his mother, her brothers, Thibaut and Etienne, and other members of
the Champagne party. Adèle, who was promised the restoration of her
dowry lands after her husband's death, was granted a daily pension in the
interim. For his part, Henry assuaged the count of Flanders by renewing
an old agreement to pay him a yearly *fief-rente* of 1,000 pounds sterling
in exchange for the service of 500 knights. The English king's motives for
intervening in a French dispute at considerable expense and little profit to
himself were explained in a letter addressed to his justiciar in England.
Reaffirming continued peace between England and France, he maintained that he strove to reconcile Philip with his mother's family, presumably to eliminate a quarrel that might serve as an excuse to disturb the
peace.[20] For these services, in all likelihood, Henry hoped to obtain Capetian and Flemish support for his son-in-law, Henry the Lion, against
the emperor in Germany.[21] Three months after the treaty of Gisors, on
19 September 1180, the bedridden Louis VII finally expired, bringing to
a close the first phase of baronial rivalries.[22] Seconded by Henry II, the
young king had weathered the ascendency of Flanders and the opposition
of Champagne.

The second phase, which lasted until 1185, was less clearly defined. It
included many threats of open hostilities, but frequent truces inhibited
actual fighting. Among the shifting baronial alliances the major constant
and new development of the period was the mounting opposition of the
house of Flanders to the royalty. Apparently foiled by Henry II from ma-
nipulating the king from within the royal court, Count Philippe turned
to open defiance. His chief concern was to dominate northeastern France
by advancing the claims to Amiens, Vermandois, and Valois he had inherited from his wife. At a gathering in 1181 of the principal members
of the Champagne house at Provins, the count of Flanders negotiated a
pair of marriage agreements for his sister's children with the house of
Hainaut, thus federating the two principal baronial families against the
king and his English protector. Whereas Thibaut de Blois and Archbishop Guillaume eventually withdrew to a position of neutrality, their
brother Etienne de Sancerre joined the count of Flanders in active
opposition. On his side, Philip Augustus was supported by the sons
of Henry II.[23] The death in 1182 of Elisabeth de Vermandois, Count
Philippe's wife, placed her husband on the defensive because it weakened
his claims to her territories. Through the mediation of a papal legate and
the Champagne party, a peace was established in 1182 at La Grange

Saint-Arnoul that returned the spoils of the fighting and confirmed Count Philippe's possession, at least for the time, of Vermandois and Valois.[24]

Two years later, it was Philip Augustus who seized the initiative against Flanders. Calling an assembly of barons at Senlis in March 1184, the king placed before them his intention to divorce the queen. Motives were not revealed, but whatever the king's personal feelings, the proposal could be seen as a disavowal of the count of Hainaut and, through him, an attack on the Flemish party. Despite the political implications of the situation, the young queen took matters into her own hands. Clad in beggars' robes, she publicly sought mercy in the streets of Senlis. Apparently this dramatic gesture caused Philip to change his mind and renounce his divorce, but it did not distract him from his incursions against the Flemish party.[25]

Although Count Baudouin de Hainaut was the queen's father, he had up to this point invariably supported his neighbor and brother-in-law, the count of Flanders. In May 1184, however, at one of the frequent truces between the king and the count, Philip Augustus named the count of Hainaut among those who guaranteed the terms of the agreement on the royal side. Done without Baudouin's consent, this intimated to the count of Flanders that his former ally had gone over to the king. Baudouin repeatedly disavowed the implication, but suspicion was sown within the Flemish party.

Eventually, Hainaut was attacked from three sides by the count of Flanders, the duke of Brabant, and the archbishop of Cologne. Baudouin was forced to seek aid from Philip Augustus, but the king did little to assist his out-maneuvered father-in-law. His main goal was to split apart the Flemish coalition.[26] The two principals, however, continued their campaigns against each other, the king making incursions into Flanders, the count planning an attack on Paris, where, he boasted, he would raise his standard over the Petit-Pont. The two armies finally confronted each other across the Somme south of Corbie. For three weeks both were poised in readiness to attack, while intermediaries such as Thibaut de Blois and Archbishop Guillaume attempted to find a settlement. A peace was agreed to at Boves (near Amiens) in July 1185 that once again regulated the succession of Vermandois, Valois, and Amiens.[27] Throughout this second phase of the attack on the Flemish party, the two great monarchs to the east and west remained in neutrality beneficial to Philip Augustus. Preoccupied with his Sicilian plans, Frederick Barbarossa refused to support Flanders in its designs against the French king. As in the first phase, too, Henry II restrained himself from profiting from his young lord's difficulties, a remarkable inhibition because Philip Augustus would have been powerless against an Anglo-Flemish coalition.

Henry's advantage lay in remaining on friendly terms with the French king, but Philip Augustus never forgot his father's warning that the vast Angevin holdings to the west were the Capetians' chief danger. Only in 1185, after the ambitions of the count of Flanders had been suppressed, was the king able to turn his attention to this problem and open the third political phase of his first decade, the conflict with Henry of Anjou. Unlike the previous phases, which were principally confined to northeastern France, the third occupied a wider battlefield in western France, extending from the borders of Normandy to the distant fiefs of Toulouse. The chief centers of contention, however, were localized in the Vexin and Berry. The Vexin consisted of land in the Seine basin lying between the Ile-de-France and Normandy that served as a buffer between the two principalities. Its chief castle, which was impressively fortified by the Anglo-Normans, stood at Gisors close to an old, but flourishing, elm that served as the traditional meeting place between the French kings and the Norman dukes. Berry, centered on Bourges, whose boundaries were more extensive and less clearly defined, also acted as a buffer between the royal domain in the Loire valley and the Angevin fiefs to the south. The importance of these two regions was underscored by twin marriage agreements negotiated between the two royal houses during the previous reign. Louis VII had bestowed his daughters by Constance of Castile on two of Henry II's sons. Marguerite, the elder, brought the Vexin as her dowry to the young Henry, and Alix, the younger, brought Bourges to Richard. Because the couples were yet children, the marriages were delayed, but King Henry took immediate possession of the girls and their valuable lands. Eventually, the young Henry did marry Marguerite, but the engagement between Richard and Alix remained unfinished business between the two royal families.[28] As he had done against Flanders in 1184, Philip Augustus took the offensive against the Angevins two years later. His immediate excuse was to press for satisfaction of the unfulfilled promise of the marriage of Richard and Alix, but his overall strategy was to exploit Henry II's critical weakness in his sons. Philip sought to separate them one at a time from the family and to set them against their father.

The young King Henry's unforeseen death in June 1183, as the result of a sudden attack of dysentery, removed him from the scene at a date too early for Philip Augustus to profit from his dissatisfaction. Although Philip Augustus had supported the young Henry and had provided shelter for his half-sister Marguerite, he had not dared act overtly, fearing to offend Henry II, on whose favor he himself depended. The young Henry's death both dismantled Henry II's plans for the succession and released the Vexin, Marguerite's dowry. Henry's simple solution to the first problem was to set Richard in young Henry's place, with all of the nominal titles but none of the power, and to elevate John to Richard's former place, with authority over Aquitaine. Richard, however, obstinately refused to consent to the exchange, and in reaction Henry refused to define further the terms of succession. Though Richard continued to act as duke of Aquitaine during his father's lifetime, he was never certain that he was his father's direct heir. As regards the Vexin, Henry was more successful. At Gisors in 1186 he persuaded Marguerite to renounce her claims to her dowry for an annual rent and talked Philip into transferring the territory to Alix's dowry on condition that she married Richard. Although the marriage had not yet taken place, Henry retained hold of the valuable region that protected Normandy against the Capetians.[29]

Geoffrey, count of Brittany, was the next object of Philip Augustus's attentions. Like the young Henry, he was fiercely jealous of Richard, and he demanded the county of Anjou from his father to strengthen him against his brother. He also found consolation and friendship with the French king, who enticed him with tempting favors, including, it was rumored, the seneschalship of France. But, like the young Henry, Geoffrey disappeared before Philip could turn his friendship to advantage. In 1186 the count of Brittany, the very bloom of French chivalry, was killed in a tournament in the prime of young manhood. Philip buried him with great honor in the cathedral of Notre-Dame at Paris. So great was the king's grief, reported a chronicler, that he had to be restrained from following the count into the grave.[30] Whether his bereavement was genuine or not, he had good political reasons for regretting his friend's departure. Although Philip claimed guardianship over Brittany, in fact it was Henry who disposed of the succession of Geoffrey's wife and heirs.[31]

During the next two years (1186–1188) hostilities erupted in the areas under dispute. Richard pressed deep into the south to compel the submission of the count of Toulouse, who reacted by acknowledging the French king as overlord and appealing for aid.[32] Philip responded with two successful incursions into Berry in 1187 and 1188, which produced heavy fighting around Châteauroux and the eventual acquisition of Issoudun and Graçay.[33] In the Vexin the French undertook fortifications that threatened Gisors as early as 1186, and in 1188 Henry penetrated the Seine valley as far as Mantes.[34] The fighting was punctuated by numerous meetings between the belligerents at which little permanent was settled, but which provided short truces. At one particularly frustrating conference at Gisors in August 1188, Henry's party enjoyed the shade of the elm while Philip's suffered the full heat of the sun. After the parleys came to naught, the French precipitously cut down the venerable tree and hewed it to pieces.[35]

What Philip Augustus was unable to accomplish against the English by arms, he gained by continuing his friendships with Henry's sons. Richard and Philip renewed personal contact at the negotiations of Châteauroux in the summer of 1187. After that they became inseparable, in the words of Roger of Howden, sharing the same plate, the same food, even the same bed.[36] This gave Philip opportunity to nourish Richard's fears that his father intended to disinherit him in favor of John. When the two kings and Richard convened at Bonmoulins in November 1188, little agreement was accomplished. Finally, on the third day, Philip ventured a strategem to provoke a rupture between Richard and his father. In exchange for concessions in the Berry, he called on Henry to proceed with the marriage of Richard and Alix and to require all his barons to swear fealty to Richard as heir. Henry refused to be maneuvered into declaring the succession in this manner. Then, in turn, Richard demanded formal recognition of his succesion. When Henry's reply was evasive, Richard turned his back on his father, knelt before the French king, did homage for Normandy and Aquitaine, and asked for help if he were deprived of his rightful inheritance. Henry and Richard departed from the assembly in different directions, a sign contemporaries found ominous.[37] For the next six months, Philip and Richard combined forces to harry the now ailing English king. Driving Henry from Le Mans, his birthplace, which they reduced to ashes, they pursued him into the heartland of his Angevin patrimony. Sick both at heart and of body, Henry refused to fight back but retreated to Chinon, to Tours, and finally to the nearby Ballan, where in July 1189 he accepted his pursuers' terms. His only request was to see the names of those who had gone over to the side of Richard and the French king. That list was headed by John, Henry's beloved youngest son. This last revelation was too much for the old king. He fell into a

delirium and expired on 6 July.[38] Although Richard was largely responsible for the humiliating end of the great king, he nonetheless inherited
his father's lands and authority intact. Philip Augustus was confronted
with a new Angevin, who stepped into the place of the old. The task of
dismantling would have to start again.

As Philip Augustus directed his attention against the English holdings
throughout the third phase, the Champagne and Flemish parties attended the royal court at all critical junctures. For example, the barons
who witnessed the transfer of the Vexin from Marguerite to Alix at
Gisors in 1184 included the archbishop of Reims and the counts of Blois,
Sancerre, Flanders, and Hainaut.[39] With the exception of Sancerre, the
same group was present with the king at Déols in June 1187 during the
first campaign into Berry.[40] At no point did either party seek to profit
from Philip's struggle with the Angevins. Increasingly their influence was
directed towards encouraging peace between the two kings, an influence
certainly welcomed by Henry, who was on the defensive. In February
1187 he approached Philippe of Flanders, Thibaut de Blois, and the
archbishop of Reims to secure their good offices.[41] After the cutting
down of the elm at Gisors, the great French barons were more reluctant
to participate in the French king's campaigns. By the summer of 1189,
the last months of Henry II's life, the archbishop of Reims and the count
of Flanders served as intermediaries to bring about a peace.[42] Whatever
opposition the Champagne and Flemish houses had indulged in during
the opening years of the reign, they were as reasonably loyal as any
suzerain could expect by the end of the first decade.

Undoubtedly the barons had their own motives for urging peace, but
many voiced one argument that was irrefutable: it was scandalous for
Christian princes to fight one another while the Holy Land was in peril.
The decisive conclusion to the first decade of Philip Augustus's reign was
accomplished not by the resolution of feudal politics, but by an external
intrusion, the call for a crusade. For years the crusaders' states in the east
had been in trouble, but few in the west, except the popes, had heeded
their pleas for help. In July 1187, however, Saladin, the sultan of Egypt,
Damascus, and Aleppo, annihilated an important Christian army at the
Horns of Hattin near Tiberias and proceeded to conquer Syria and Palestine, taking the holy city of Jerusalem by October. Only Tyre, Tripoli,
and Antioch remained in Christian hands. The west received the news
with shock and disbelief. On hearing the reports in October, the old
pope, Urban III, died immediately. His successor, Gregory VIII, followed

him to the grave two months later after appealing to all Christendom to come to the aid of the Holy Land. Jocius, the archbishop of Tyre, brought to the west eyewitness accounts of the gravity of the situation.[43] The call for a crusade could no longer be ignored.

Upon hearing the news in November 1187, Richard took the cross at Tours with characteristic spontaneity. Completely absorbed by their struggle, Philip and Henry could not respond to the appeal separately without jeopardizing their respective positions. The archbishop of Tyre caught them together at Gisors in January 1188, however, and persuaded them to accept the cross in concert with the count of Flanders. The French were to wear red crosses, the English white crosses, and the Flemings green crosses. Easter 1189 was set as the date of departure. Now endowed with crusaders' privileges, the two kings took immediate advantage of their new status. Henry, followed by Philip, levied crusading taxes on laity and clergy, and Philip issued an ordinance declaring a moratorium on debts incurred by crusaders.[44] Not to be outdone by the kings of France and England, the aging Emperor Frederick Barbarossa took the cross in March 1188 and thereby asserted leadership over the western princes.

The chief problem facing Philip and Henry, however, was implementing the agreed departure time, since neither trusted the other remaining behind. At a conference between the two kings at Ferté-Bernard in April 1189, the papal legate threatened the French king's lands with interdict if he did not agree to peace. Philip replied that he neither feared the papal sentence nor admitted the church's jurisdiction in his kingdom over a matter of rebellious barons.[45] By May 1189, when the original deadline had already been passed, only the emperor had departed. The death of Henry in July 1189 further hampered the participation of the English. Richard was obliged to return to England to attend to his coronation and the administration of his lands during his absence. The departure was again postponed, this time to March 1190. Finally, after further maneuverings and negotiations, Philip received the symbolic pilgrim's staff from the archbishop of Reims at the royal abbey of Saint-Denis in June, and on the same day Richard received his from the archbishop of Tours at that place. The two kings met briefly at the abbey of Vézelay in July, recalling the origins of the preceding crusade, proceeded together to Lyon, and then took separate routes, Philip to Genoa and Richard to Marseilles, whence they continued by sea.[46] Thus began the Third Crusade, which enlisted not only the French and English kings but also their chief barons, including the counts of Troyes, Blois, Sancerre, and Flanders. After thirty years of conflict between the houses of Capet and Anjou, the lands of France could look forward to respite.

The Territorial Balance Sheet

In the Middle Ages political success was ultimately measured in terms of land. When Philip Augustus departed on the crusade in 1190 after a decade of strife, how did his lands compare with the royal domain inherited from his father? Although his Champagne, Flemish, and Angevin rivals could have taken their toll of his vulnerable lands, he in fact lost nothing and gained slightly through the permanent addition of Amiens, Montdidier, and Roye, among other acquisitions in 1185. These lands were, however, only a small part of a larger territory to the north and east of Paris that Philip Augustus eventually acquired through an inheritance set in motion during his father's reign.[47] One of the king's chief objectives during the first decade was to keep this inheritance intact. The flat, fertile lands lying between the royal domain and the county of Flanders were distinguished by neither natural boundaries nor political unity. Occasionally called by the general name of Picardie, they consisted of four loosely designated regions that ultimately came into royal hands: (1) Valois, centered chiefly on Crépy to the northeast of Paris, (2) Vermandois, consisting mainly of Saint-Quentin, Ribemont, Péronne, and Montdidier further to the north, (3) the Amiénois, centered on Amiens directly to the north, and, finally (4) Artois, composed principally of Arras, Bapaume, Saint-Omer, and Aire—all still further north on the southern boundary of Flanders. In addition, whoever held Artois and the Amiénois had suzerainty over important neighboring fiefs.

The complicated story of Philip Augustus's inheritance of the northeastern territories begins with dual marriages between the houses of Flanders and Vermandois during the preceding reign. As we have seen, Philippe, the heir to Flanders, and his brother Mathieu, count of Boulogne, respectively married Elisabeth and Aliénor, daughters of Raoul, count of Vermandois, a Capetian cousin of the royal family's. The sisters were successively heiresses to their father's lands of Vermandois, Valois, and the Amiénois. Elisabeth de Vermandois received the inheritance in 1164, but in the next decade she was forced to resign it to her husband, Philippe of Flanders, most likely as a penalty for being unfaithful to him. In 1179 Louis VII confirmed this concession, as his son did later. At the opening of the new reign, therefore, Philippe was not only count of Flanders but also count of Vermandois and Amiens and lord of Valois through his wife. Philip Augustus also had a potential claim to the latter titles, however, if his cousins Elisabeth and Aliénor died childless.[48]

The next major development came in 1180, when the king married Isabelle, daughter of Baudouin de Hainaut and Marguerite, sister of Philippe of Flanders, a marriage that was part of the latter's attempt to gain influence at the royal court. In order to make marrying his niece attractive to the king, the count provided her with a dowry of the important lands of Artois, detached from his southern borders, but on the condition that they remain in his possession during his lifetime. (It was probably in response to this dowry gift that Philip Augustus agreed to confirm Elisabeth de Vermandois's concessions to her husband.) Any hope of adding Artois to the royal domain, however, depended on the birth of an heir to Queen Isabelle.[49]

In 1182 Elisabeth de Vermandois died without children, thus depriving the count of Flanders of his original claim to the Vermandois lands. In the meantime, Aliénor had remarried. Her new husband was Mathieu, count of Beaumont-sur-Oise and chamberlain in the royal household. Freed from the domination of the count of Flanders, Philip Augustus repudiated his confirmation of Elisabeth's concession of Vermandois, Amiens, and Valois to her husband (the king asserted that he had acted under duress) and defended the claims of Aliénor de Beaumont to her sister's inheritance. The king's motives at this point are not altogether clear, but he could not help but have seen himself as a possible beneficiary, should Aliénor also die childless.[50] In all events, in the ensuing conflict, the king did, in fact, gain lands from prosecuting Aliénor's claims. In the preliminary settlement of La Grange Saint-Arnoul in 1182, the count of Flanders not only reconfirmed Queen Isabelle's dowry of Artois but renounced his ultimate rights over Vermandois and Valois, though retaining possession of these lands during his lifetime.[51] The struggle between the king and the count of Flanders culminated in the agreement at Boves (1185) by which a threefold division of the former lands of the count of Vermandois was made. The count of Flanders was permitted to hold Saint-Quentin and Péronne for his lifetime. Aliénor de Beaumont retained Valois and the rest of Vermandois including Ribemont. But in compensation for his role in the affair, the king was conceded the county of Amiens, along with Montdidier and Roye. Aliénor probably conceded these lands in the form of the relief due to a feudal suzerain when a new enfeoffment took place.[52] By 1185 Philip Augustus not only intervened as a potential heir in the succession of Vermandois, Valois, and Amiens, but had also gained actual possession of a part of the region. When a son, Louis, was born to Queen Isabelle in September 1187, his claim to Artois was also secured, provided the prince lived. In this heir the king was indeed fortunate, because three years later the queen died giving birth to twins, who also did not survive.[53] Despite the loss of Isabelle de Hainaut, Philip Augustus left the kingdom on crusade in 1190 in the company of the count of Flanders with good prospects of ultimately acquiring the northeastern territories for the royal domain.

By taking up arms against the Flemings Philip Augustus had achieved definition of the northeastern succession and even a small foothold in the area. But arms benefited him little against the Angevins. In 1190 the critical Vexin remained securely in English hands, and Richard, as king, was no more inclined to go through with the marriage to Philip Augustus's sister Alix than before. Philip was able to retain only the fiefs of Issoudun and Graçay, gained in the campaigns in Berry. From the terms of peace with the dying King Henry in 1189, he was also able to assert overlordship over the distant and turbulent county of Auvergne, an unachieved goal of his father's.[54] These southern fiefs, however, were only secure to the extent that the king was prepared to fight for them.

Although territorial gains were negligible during the first decade of his reign, the young king was able to assert his influence in the Burgundian region. Immediately after his coronation, Philip, following the example of his father, responded to calls for help from churches against the depredations of neighboring lords. The king led his first expedition, against Hebo, lord of Charenton in Berry, and then continued further to the southeast to protect the churches of Burgundy. As his father had done earlier, he imposed settlements on Humbert de Beaujeau and the counts of Chalon-sur-Sâone and Mâcon in behalf of the abbot of Cluny.[55] These early incursions were followed in 1185 by another expedition in response to Hugues de Vergy's complaints against the duke of Burgundy. After the siege of Châtillon-sur-Seine the duke himself was captured and agreed to indemnification of the churches damaged during the struggle.[56] Undoubtedly Philip Augustus's successful interventions in Burgundy facilitated his assertion of royal prerogatives in the region. When the male line of the counts of Nevers died out in 1181, the king exercised wardship over the county and took the young heiress, Agnès, into his custody at the royal court. In 1184 he married her to his cousin, Pierre de Courtenay, taking as his recompense the fief of Montargis in the Gâtinais.[57] Philip also attempted to assert rights of wardship over Brittany when Count Geoffrey died in 1186, but to no avail because of King Henry's strength in the region.[58]

The outcome of Philip's first decade well illustrates a classic situation: time favors young contenders against aged rivals. By merely defending his lands and surviving the onslaughts of the baronial coalitions of his father's generation, Philip was assured of eventual success. The anonymous author of the *Historia regum Francorum* accurately perceived the young king's confidence in his future. Depicting the dark hours of 1181, when Philip was walled up in Compiègne while the counts of Flanders and Hainaut ravaged the adjacent lands, the count of Sancerre menaced Bourges and Lorris, and the duke of Burgundy attacked Sens, the chronicler has the boy exclaim to his entourage: "Whatever is now happening, the barons will decline in men and age, but, with God's help, I shall increase in men, age, and wisdom." And, the chronicler adds, events proved him to be right.[59]

The King
and His Men

At the coronation in 1179 a fourteen-year-old youth had been over-shadowed by great vassals. But by 1190, at the age of twenty-five, Philip was able to assume leadership in the crusade. At what point did the young monarch begin to take charge of his government? Because of the poverty of governmental documentation, an answer can be found only in the records of the contemporary chroniclers, who characteristically inter-preted the king's actions from their own royal, English, or Flemish per-spectives. All the chroniclers assume that the king normally acted with the counsel of his barons. Although the court historiographer, Rigord, wished to portray Philip as a forceful monarch, he nonetheless shows the king often taking counsel. When Philip married his sister Marguerite to the king of Hungary, for example, Rigord explains that "he convoked his archbishops, bishops and major princes of the realm whose counsel and wisdom he was frequently accustomed to use in treating such affairs."[1] Similarly, the phrase *habito consilio* was characteristically employed by the English historian Gervase of Canterbury to describe the actions of all kings, including Philip.[2] To determine the point at which the king took charge of his government, therefore, one must ascertain when the barons ceased to play the predominant role and the king began to act indepen-dently of, or even against, their advice.

28

Viewed in terms of the king's actions, the period from 1179 to 1190 may be divided into two phases. The first lasted until 1184 and exhibited radical shifts between contradictory policies. At his coronation, the young king was under the tutelage of Count Philippe of Flanders, an influence that produced his marriage to Isabelle de Hainaut. This Flemish policy generated opposition from the queen mother and her Champagne family. Through the mediation of Henry of Anjou, however, the king was reconciled with his mother and uncles, which in turn provoked opposition from Philippe of Flanders—by 1181, outright warfare—and Philip's attempt to divorce the queen in 1184. The chroniclers, with one exception, agree that the king was decisively influenced by his counsellors throughout these tumultuous five years. Benedict, Gervase of Canterbury, and Gislebert de Mons all attribute the king's marriage primarily to the advice of the count of Flanders and secondarily to that of Raoul, count of Clermont. Both Benedict and Gervase declare that the king, by giving ear only to the count of Flanders, had spurned his father's counsellors.[3] Ralph de Diceto attributes the French king's designs on Normandy during the same period (which were not realized) to the persuasion of unnamed evil counsellors.[4] Benedict, however, points to the influence of King Henry in mediating between Philip Augustus and the Champagne party.[5] In this context Ralph de Diceto reports that young Philip often told his entourage of his admiration for King Henry's far-flung kingdom, which included such barbarous peoples as the Scots and the Welsh but was ruled peacefully with the counsel of Henry's advisors.[6] As to Philip Augustus's attempted divorce of Queen Isabelle, Gislebert de Mons attributes it to the urging of the Champagne party (Guillaume, Thibaut, and Etienne), seconded by Henri, duke of Burgundy, and Raoul, count of Clermont; the chronicler does not state Philip's own views on the subject.[7]

This general account of a young monarch dominated by powerful counsellors is contradicted by Rigord. As might be expected, the royal historian depicts his sovereign as fully in charge from the outset of his reign, though adhering to the convention of consulting his barons. Philip's first act as king was to despoil the Jews, a policy he had long considered but had refrained from carrying out because of the favor his father had shown them. The decision was the king's and its execution was at the royal command and "against the will of all the princes," Rigord tells us.[8] This emphasis on the king as the decisive factor was later adopted by other chroniclers.

The second phase of the decade, beginning in 1184, was characterized by Philip Augustus's initiation of personal diplomacy. Whatever the king's responsibility for the attempt at divorce may have been, in the same year he employed a pure ruse to split his father-in-law, Baudouin de Hainaut, from the Flemish party and to sow dissension within it. Philip then directed his personal diplomacy at the sons of Henry II, extending blandishments to the young Henry, Geoffrey, and Richard in succession. The campaign culminated in 1188 at Bonmoulins, where, by playing on Richard's fear of disinheritance, the French king alienated him from his father and engaged Richard's cooperation until Henry's death. Although such personal diplomacy did not exclude baronial advice, its success depended primarily on the talents of the king himself. In fact, contemporary chroniclers usually agree that the king acted contrary to the barons' advice during the second half of the decade. Benedict sees the barons as attempting to dissuade the king from aggression against Henry of Anjou. In his view, by 1187 both the Flemish and Champagne parties actively opposed Philip's war against the English.[9] He also notes the French king's defiance of ecclesiastical intervention even when the papal legate threatened Philip's lands with interdict if he did not make peace.[10] Gervase of Canterbury reports that the great French barons attempted to mediate between the English and French kings, but mistook Henry's intentions, which Philip, in contrast, rightly suspected.[11] It is Gervase who gives clearest expression to Philip's independence and decisiveness. Writing of a conversation between Philippe of Flanders and Richard at Châteauroux in 1187, the chronicler stresses the king's strength of character in the words of the old Flemish baron:

> Lord count, it seems to me and others that you are acting foolishly and without good counsel, when you war against your lord, the king of France, from whose gifts you have benefited much. . . . His youthfulness should not be despised. He may be a youth in years, but he is an old man in mind, wise and vigorous in action, ever remembering wrongs, but never forgetting good deeds. Believe those with experience. I myself contested him, but I now repent of it and at great cost.[12]

Gervase maintains this opinion of Philip in depicting the wily and experienced Henry attempting to treat the twenty-four-year-old king as a mere boy two years later. Despite the intercessions of the archbishops of Canterbury and Rouen, Philip held to his resolve to fight, "gnashing his teeth like a lion," in the phrase of the chronicler.[13] By the second half of the decade contemporary observers agreed that the young Philip was in charge.

In 1179 Philip Augustus inherited his father's government. Since the royal domain was minuscule, the framework of this consisted of two essential elements: local officials rooted in their areas of jurisdiction and an itinerant central court that by its displacements kept the king in touch with his domain. Our knowledge of the men who staffed the central court is limited to the chroniclers' accounts, because the royal charters are singularly uninformative. In the early twelfth century the royal charters had contained witness lists indicating who was in attendance at the king's court. By mid-century, however, these "subscribers" had been reduced to the traditional household officers, a practice, continuing throughout Philip Augustus's reign, that obscured all others in attendance at court.[14] The chroniclers who reported the court's activities, however, were interested primarily in political events and very little in administration. They naturally tended to notice only the men of highest station, who took part in royal decisions.[15] In attempting to identify the king's counsellors, one must identify those who were regularly in his company as distinguished from those whose presence was occasioned by particular circumstances. Philip naturally inherited his father's court personnel, a broad spectrum ranging from the powerful magnates and prelates of the realm through the traditional household officers to the lesser figures of knights, clerics, and chamberlains. As the young king sought to wrest the initiative from his great baronial counsellors, he was apparently too engrossed in the struggle to introduce radical changes in the composition of his court. Throughout the first decade he therefore accepted the pattern of personnel inherited from his father.

Although the great magnates had deserted the royal court in the early twelfth century, Louis VII had brought them back after the Second Crusade. From that point on, they were regularly in attendance at court, as demonstrated by the appointment of Thibaut, count of Blois, as the royal seneschal in 1154. In the second half of the twelfth century, these magnates at court constituted the embryonic origins of a royal *conseil*.[16] Barons and prelates of this rank remained at court throughout the first decade of Philip's reign. Philippe, count of Flanders, was the king's foremost counsellor at the coronation, but soon afterwards fell into opposition. By 1184, however, he was back in attendance and remained until he departed on the crusade.[17] Robert, count of Dreux and the king's paternal uncle, was also present on important occasions,[18] and Rotrou, count of Perche, served as Philip's envoy to England in 1189, coordinating preparations for the crusade.[19] But the magnates who were most visible at court throughout the decade were the three brothers from the house of Champagne: Thibaut, count of Blois; Etienne, count of Sancerre; and Guillaume, archbishop of Reims.[20] After his reconciliation with the king in 1182, Archbishop Guillaume became Philip's right-hand man and was in the king's presence at most recorded events throughout the 1180s and 1190s.[21] When the pope summoned the archbishop to Rome in 1184, Philip refused to allow him leave on the grounds that these were troubled times in which powerful men sought to take advantage of the king's youth. In Philip's words, Guillaume was the "vigilant eye of his counsels and the right hand of his affairs."[22] The chapter of Chartres, where Guillaume had previously been bishop, called him "the counsellor of the king and realm, as if a second king himself."[23] It was to be expected, therefore, that when Philip departed on crusade in 1190, he would confer the regency of the realm on his mother and her brother Guillaume.[24] Other than the archbishop of Reims, the only prelate who served the king with any regularity was Etienne, abbot of Sainte-Geneviève, who was Guillaume's substitute as royal envoy to the pope and composed letters for the king.[25]

Philip's court, like most medieval courts, also contained the five traditional household officers derived from a Carolingian prototype. These officers had originally been assigned domestic duties: the seneschal, for example, was responsible for provisions, the butler for drink, the chamberlain for the bedchamber, the constable for the horses, and the chancellor for the chapel. But these duties had long since been replaced by more political tasks. At the death of his father, Philip had inherited the following incumbents: Thibaut, count of Blois, as seneschal; Guy de Senlis as butler; Mathieu, count of Beaumont-sur-Oise, as grand chamberlain; Raoul, count of Clermont-en-Beauvaisis, as constable; and Hugues du Puiset as chancellor.[26] Although the names of these officers are fully accessible because they were appended at the end of all formal royal charters, it is more difficult to ascertain their governmental functions. The butlership had long been in the family of Senlis, and Gui and his son Gui, who succeeded him in 1186, profited from royal pensions but left no record of administrative service.[27] Similarly, the grand chamberlain, Mathieu, the count of nearby Beaumont-sur-Oise, benefited from royal service.[28] In the past, when Philip's grandfather and father had found their chancellors or seneschals troublesome, they had let the posts remain vacant on the incumbent's death so as to be free to choose a more amenable successor.[29] When the obscure Hugues du Puiset died in 1185, the king followed Capetian policy by keeping the position of chancellor vacant, but he never refilled it.[30] Although deprived of an official chancellor, the clerks of the chancery continued to produce royal charters and documentation without interruption. The only two household officers who actively performed political tasks during the first decade were the constable and the seneschal. The chroniclers remark that the former, Raoul, count of Clermont-en-Beauvaisis, corroborated the advice of the count of Flanders concerning the king's marriage, mediated between the count and the king, and finally urged the king to seek a divorce. In the eyes of Gislebert, he was "powerful in the royal counsel" and among the "special counsellors of the king."[31] The court activities of the seneschal, Thibaut de Blois, were due to his kinship with the Champagne party. He not only seconded his brother, the archbishop of Reims, in most important negotiations, but on one occasion was commissioned to arbitrate a dispute between the clergy of Mâcon and Girard, count of Vienne.[32] This was the closest a household official came to engaging in administrative tasks. Throughout the twelfth century the household officials, with the occasional exception of the seneschal, were recruited from the local castellans of the royal domain.[33] By the second half of the century the importance of these officials in royal government was obviously decreasing, as Philip Augustus followed his father's example in availing himself less and less of their services.

Since the magnates contributed mainly to important decisions, and the household officers' services had diminished, the routine tasks of the central court were naturally performed by lesser personages. Philip Augustus continued his grandfather's and father's practice of recruiting knights, clerics, and chamberlains for the royal court.[34] Since these figures were of little interest to contemporary chroniclers, their presence and activities were less often observed. Among those who may be ranked as knights were the Clément family, originating from Mez-le-Maréchal in the Gâtinais in the eleventh century. The brothers Robert Clément and Gilles de Tornella were present at the royal court at the end of the reign of Louis VII. The chronicler Robert d'Auxerre says that Robert Clément was tutor of the young Philip Augustus, and after his death in 1181 was succeeded by Gilles de Tornella as one of the influential counsellors at court. The family also produced a number of royal marshals of whom Alberic, the son of Robert Clément, was the most prominent.[35] Two other men of knightly rank at the French court were noticed by the English chronicler Ralph de Diceto because of peculiar circumstances. During the negotiations of 1186, King Henry sent a distinguished legation of prelates and barons to the French king at Noyon, but Philip virtually ignored them. He responded with an embassy of lesser men (*mediae manus homines*) from his household consisting of Gatho de Poissy and Gérard de Fournival, whom Henry received with respect despite their knightly station.[36]

As in the past, the chancery was the chief employer of clerics at the royal court. Despite the absence of a titular chancellor after 1185, the routine business of the chancery was nonetheless maintained by ordinary clerics. Their names have not been revealed, but at least seven different clerks working in the chancery until the king's departure in 1190 can be distinguished from their handwriting. One of these was inherited from the reign of Louis VII.[37] A handful of names of other royal clerics has survived in scattered royal charters,[38] but the chroniclers single out only Brother Bernard, who had been prior of Grandmont before he became head of a community of hermits at Vincennes. Rigord identifies Bernard as responsible for advising the king to despoil the Jews in 1180.[39]

Finally, Philip Augustus inherited from his father a group of lesser chamberlains, not to be confused with the grand chamberlain, Mathieu de Beaumont. Although their duties cannot be precisely ascertained, their names appear in the king's charters of the first decade because of the royal favor they enjoyed. They included a certain Adam, who died at Acre in 1191,[40] and especially his colleague known simply as Gautier the Chamberlain.[41] First appearing in the 1150s, Gautier had already performed long service in Louis VII's court. During Philip's reign he was present at the negotiations over Marguerite's dowry and at the settlement of Amiens in 1185. The following year he replaced Gérard as *prévôt* of Poissy.[42] A later chronicler remarks that Gautier was more noble in deeds than in ancestral origins, a trait confirmed by the fact that he did not adopt a toponymic.[43] Nevertheless, Louis VII married him to the heiress of the fief of Nemours, which formed the substance of the subsequent family patrimony. Philip Augustus provided him with an annual pension of 20 *livres* and issued numerous charters confirming his family transactions.[44] Gautier the Chamberlain had dealings within and without the royal court with the Clément family, Brother Bernard, and Adam the

Chamberlain. Before he died in 1205, he would see two sons succeed to his position as royal chamberlains and three others advance towards prelacies. (By 1188 his son Etienne had already obtained the bishopric of Noyon.)[45] Although of insignificant origins, Gautier founded an important administrative dynasty in the service of the royal chamber. He was buried in the abbey of Barbeaux at the foot of his royal master, Louis VII, as befitted a loyal chamberlain.

By noting only the magnates and ignoring routine affairs, the chroniclers obviously present a biased picture of the participants of Philip's court during its first decade. Nor can the picture be corrected by the royal charters, which omit all witnesses except the household officials. Yet one charter survives from the period that offers a brief glimpse into the court because it was composed according to English, and not Capetian, practice. At Gisors in her brother Philip's presence, Marguerite, the former queen of England, issued a charter concerning the settlement of her dowry in 1185. Among those recorded as present were the great magnates whom the chroniclers single out: the Champagne brothers, Archbishop Guillaume, Count Thibaut de Blois, and Count Etienne de Sancerre, the count of Flanders, and the count of Dreux. Also included were the constable, Count Raoul de Clermont, and Gautier the Chamberlain.[46] Although the lesser knights and clerics are neglected, this is the closest look we are permitted at the composition of the royal court. In respect to the kinds of people represented—magnates, household officers, and chamberlains—the gathering did not differ appreciably from comparable assemblies under Louis VII.[47] In personnel as well as in structure, Philip's court perpetuated that of his father.

The other traditional feature of government inherited from Louis VII was the local official called the *prévôt*, stationed in the royal domain. *Prévôts* had first appeared under Philip's great-grandfather, Philip I, at the turn of the eleventh century and were generally recruited from the castellans of the Ile-de-France, who also supplied the household officers.[48] Some posts fell to the hereditary claims of these families; others were more freely disposed of by the king, depending on his control in the individual locality. During the first decade of Philip Augustus's reign, the king employed about thirty-five (at most) stationed throughout the royal domain.[49] The surviving charters mention them frequently, but only by title: *prévôt* of Poissy, Sens, Bourges, and so forth.[50] The identities of a bare half dozen can be detected from individual circumstances, but these notices are insufficient to distinguish their social status.[51] For example, Gérard, the *prévôt* of Poissy, was present at Gisors in 1185 for the settlement of Marguerite's dowry. Rigord notes in a cryptic comment that the following year he brought 11,000 marks of silver to the royal treasury and was replaced by Gautier the Chamberlain.[52]

Since the *prévôts* were scattered throughout the domain and were usually uninvolved in the politics of the king's court, the chroniclers say little about them. They remain faceless to us. Beyond them were a host of lesser officials, lay and clerical, who served as sergeants and chaplains throughout the domain.[53] Their names, revealed in royal acts benefiting them, likewise yield little information about their activities.

Justice and Finance:
The Chief Business
of Government

Justice

Within the rudimentary framework inherited from Philip's father, the two underlying organs, the central court and the corps of local officials, were coordinated by making the local officials stationary at their posts and the central court moveable. Like all early medieval monarchs, Philip was constantly on the road surrounded by his entourage. This life of the tent and pack horse was motivated not only by the demands of warfare but also by the need to supervise his domain, to be seen by his subjects, and even to receive income from his lands. It was still easier to bring the court to the countryside than the reverse.[1] This collaboration between the central court and the local officials performed the essential tasks of government, consisting in the main of justice and finance. In elementary terms, justice was simply the providing of a forum or court in which disputes could be resolved. All medieval kings considered it their foremost duty to offer justice through their personal court, the *curia regis*.

The court of the early Capetian kings was virtually devoid of routine and specialization.[2] Following the king's incessant wanderings and occasioned by particular circumstances, it offered no fixed place or schedule of sessions where and when litigants were assured of finding it open for business. Nor could contesting parties expect permanent and specialized judges to hear their cases. Depending on the place and occasion, the court could be attended by different members: the king and his family, the household officers, great barons and prelates, lesser knights and clerics, and local officials through whose territory the court was passing. Only towards the end of Louis VII's reign did there appear men styled *viri prudentes* or *jurisperiti* who might suggest the formation of a corps of trained judges. The court rarely met unless the monarch was present, even at the end of his life when the king was debilitated by sickness. Though its decisions were occasionally formulated as judgments (*judicia*) or sometimes delegated to third parties for arbitration, most of its pronouncements were no more than agreements (*concordie*) between parties, confirmed by royal authority at the litigants' request. Lacking routine and regularity, the *curia regis* of the early Capetians was more an occasion than an institution. Perhaps most telling was its failure to keep records. No collection of decisions has survived and neither can there be found any indication that such records were attempted. In a perambulating, occasional institution with fluctuating personnel, such neglect impaired consistent and coherent judicial policy. The absence of systematic records also hinders any attempt to comprehend the scope of the *curia regis*'s competency. The decisions of the royal court survive largely in charters preserved by the benefiting parties. Since a significant proportion of these charters were collected by ecclesiastics, the Capetian court appears mainly as a defender of churches' rights. Bishops and abbots predominate among the litigants. Great barons appear only in suits against churches. Laymen of ordinary circumstances are virtually absent from the records. From other oblique sources we may suspect that lay litigants, whether magnates of the realm or lesser men of the royal domain, availed themselves of the *curia regis* in purely secular cases, but the full extent lies hidden.[3]

Throughout the reign of Philip Augustus, the nature of the documentation of the central *curia regis* changed little from that of his predecessors. As before, the overwhelming majority of surviving cases were recorded by beneficiaries, largely ecclesiastics. Seen from this perspective, the court appears to have been almost exclusively engaged in churchmen's suits. Of the thirty-one cases for which records exist that were heard before the king departed on crusade, all but two concerned ecclesiastical affairs.[4] The royal archives appeared after 1194 and the registers after 1204, but these new collections contribute only about 18 percent of the total surviving cases. Although these were secular compilations, ecclesiastical concerns still preponderate among the cases they list. It is perhaps not surprising that the thirty-one recorded cases of the *curia regis* in Philip Augustus's first decade markedly resemble those of Louis VII. But despite additional sources from the archives and registers, these characteristics are found to persist throughout the reign. Because the documentation and the essential operations of Philip's court remained basically unchanged, the workings of the *curia regis* throughout the reign may be viewed as a whole.

As Table 1 demonstrates, the *curia regis* followed Philip's displacements during the first decade, meeting at such centers of the royal domain as Lorris, Sens, Compiègne, and Senlis. This pattern continued throughout the reign. Often the court's business was prompted by its arrival in the vicinity. The abbot of Corbie, for example, raised a complaint against the bourgeoisie of the town when Philip visited in 1182.[5] As had been the case since the early twelfth century, the royal court increasingly held its sessions at Paris. In the first decade, 24 percent of royal *actes* were issued from Paris, a proportion that increased to 39 percent in the third decade after the great conquests. But this preponderance does not imply that Paris possessed a monopoly over important cases. The celebrated judgment over the succession of the county of Champagne in 1216, for example, was heard at Melun.[6] In the first decade, Fontainebleau, not far south of Paris, was also a popular place for conducting business, particularly in 1190 on the eve of Philip's departure for the Holy Land. During the last decade Paris shared the king's attention more equally with Saint-Germain-en-Laye (close by to the northwest), Melun (to the south), Compiègne (to the northeast), and Pont de l'Arche (on the confines of Normandy). Since most of the charters containing royal judgments cannot be dated precisely beyond the year, it is impossible to distinguish a fixed schedule among the court sessions.[7]

Nor are the charters helpful in identifying court members who participated in the decisions. For the most part, only prelates and barons are named, and no striking patterns emerge. During the first decade, Philip frequently stated that he judged "with the advice of his barons" (*baronum suorum consilio*).[8] As might be expected, when names are given, these included Thibaut, count of Blois; Robert, count of Dreux; and Guillaume, archbishop of Reims.[9] After 1190 only when the case was of great importance were the magnates associated with the judgment identified. In a de-

TABLE 1. Philip Augustus's Residency, 1179–1223

	Royal *actes* issued				
	1179 to 1190	1191 to 1203	1204 to 1214	1215 to 1223	Total
PARIS REGION					
Paris	73(24%)	110(32%)	189(39%)	111(28%)	483(31%)
Fontainebleau	82(26%)	14(4%)	12(2%)		108(7%)
Saint-Germain-en-Laye	7(2%)	8(2%)	28(6%)	69(17%)	112(7%)
SOUTHERN DOMAIN					
Lorris	14(4%)	10(3%)		1	25(2%)
Muret	3(1%)	11(3%)	3(1%)		17(1%)
Melun		3(1%)	26(6%)	59(15%)	88(6%)
Sens	7(2%)	4(1%)	9(2%)		20(1%)
Montargis	6(2%)	2(1%)	5(1%)	6(2%)	19(1%)
Bourges	6(2%)	4(1%)	2		12(1%)
NORTHEASTERN DOMAIN					
Compiègne	11(4%)	23(7%)	28(6%)	53(13%)	115(7%)
Senlis	15(5%)	3(1%)	5(1%)	2	25(2%)
Hesdin		10(3%)	2		12(1%)
Péronne		4(1%)	5(1%)	2	11(1%)
NORMANDY					
Vernon		13(4%)	3(1%)	7(2%)	23(2%)
Mantes	5(2%)	21(6%)	14(3%)	6(2%)	46(3%)
Anet		16(5%)	23(5%)	10(2%)	49(3%)
Pacy		6(2%)	7(1%)	19(5%)	32(2%)
Gisors	1	3(1%)	14(3%)	7(2%)	25(2%)
Evreux		5(1%)	5(1%)	1	11(1%)
Vaudreuil		1	7(1%)		8
Pont de l'Arche			16(3%)	33(8%)	49(3%)
OTHERS	79(26%)	75(21%)	84(17%)	14(4%)	252(16%)
Total	309(100%)	346(100%)	487(100%)	400(100%)	1,542(100%)

NOTE: Percentage figures are the percentage of total *actes* issued for each chronological period. Of 1,851 *actes*, 1,542 (83%) can be dated by place. Percentages are rounded off to the nearest percentage point and ignore figures under 1 percent.

SOURCE: *Actes* I–IV, supplemented and corrected by *Actes* V. See note to Table 13.

cision over regalian rights at Châlons-sur-Marne in 1202, for example, the counts of Beaumont and Ponthieu, Simon de Montfort, and three bishops were present. The great Champagne decision of 1216 involved one duke, seven counts, one archbishop, and eight bishops. The case between the king and the bishop of Paris over the Clos-Brunel in 1221 was adjudged by the royal heir, one archbishop, one bishop, and six counts.[10] Like his father's, Philip's charters occasionally note the presence of certain "learned experts" (*viris prudentibus, sapientibus*).[11] In 1189 these consisted of the bishop, dean, chanter, and chancellor of Paris.[12] In the Châlons-sur-Marne judgment of 1202, they included the bishops of Beauvais, Paris, and Meaux, and four lesser clerics.[13] Since none of these men turn up in other royal cases, it is difficult to see them as permanent learned counsellors; they were more likely advisors who were occasionally consulted. Evidence of a body of trained legal experts simply does not surface in the documentation.

Table 2 indicates that Philip Augustus's *curia regis* continued to formulate its decisions as judgments, arbitrations, and agreements. Examples of all three appear in the first decade and continue to do so in significant proportions until the end of the reign. Of the extant cases about a third (35 percent) may be classified as true judgments (*judicia*) in which the

TABLE 2. Judicial Decisions in the *Curia Regis*, 1179–1223

	1179 to 1190	1191 to 1203	1204 to 1214	1215 to 1223	Total
Agreements	14(45%)	21(50%)	46(70%)	30(45%)	111(54%)
Judgments	16(52%)	18(43%)	12(18%)	26(39%)	72(35%)
Arbitrations	2(6%)	6(14%)	10(15%)	14(21%)	32(16%)
Inquests	4(13%)	7(17%)	19(29%)	16(24%)	46(22%)
Total number of decisions	31	42	66	67	206

NOTE: Considerable overlap exists in the data. The categories of agreements, judgments, and arbitrations are normally mutually exclusive with only occasional exceptions when multiple procedures were employed. Since inquests usually supplemented judgments and arbitrations and occasionally agreements, this category overlaps with the other three. The total number of decisions, therefore, is always less than the sum of the categories. The percentages shown are the percentage of the categories to the total number of decisions in each chronological period.

Undoubtedly the total of 206 cases represents only a fraction of the business of the court. From 1207 to 1223 the extant record of the Norman exchequer contains 319 decisions (*Jugements* pp. 4–29). For the same period 118 have survived from Philip's *curia regis*.

SOURCES: *Actes* I–IV, supplemented and corrected by *Actes* V (179 decisions); Teulet I (8 decisions); miscellaneous (19 decisions).

sentence was rendered by the royal court itself. At times, as in 1186, the wording of the charter allows no doubt: *data fuit diffinitiva sententia nostreque juditio curie.*[14] Occasionally the sentence was phrased vaguely as a royal wish (*ad faciendum voluntatem nostram . . . didicimus . . . rex respondit et dicit*) and must be inferred from the context.[15] Or the sentence must be inferred from judicial acts such as annulment (*episcoporum et baronum nostrorum usi consilio . . . quassamus*) or quittance (*. . . coram nobis vendidit et quitavit*).[16] Most often the king and his court rendered the decision directly, but occasionally the sentence was delegated to subordinate officials. In a dispute between Notre-Dame d'Etampes and the cathedral of Orléans in 1190, the judgment was entrusted to certain Parisian clerics because the case was purely ecclesiastical.[17] In the second half of the reign, most of the important cases heard by the royal court—the regalia of Châlons-sur-Marne, the succession of the fiefs of Champagne and Beaumont—were resolved by the king's judgment.[18]

A second method for resolving disputes was arbitration (*compromisum, arbitrium*), by which both parties consented to one or several arbitrators, whose final decision was binding on the litigants.[19] These arbitrators differed from the delegated judges mentioned above because the arbitrators were chosen with the parties' consent, whereas the judges were imposed on the litigants by the court's choice. Occasionally, the parties chose the king as sole arbitrator, as the chapter and commune of Laon did in 1193,[20] or chose officials of the royal court.[21] Often third parties outside the court were appointed, as in 1186, when five members of the chapter of Paris were named arbitrators in the dispute between their church and Eudes d'Itteville.[22] In the course of Philip's reign, this method increased in popularity from 6 percent to 21 percent of extant cases, with an average of 16 percent. Since arbitration took place in the royal court, the king guaranteed the decision, often confirming it with a charter.

The most frequent procedure for resolving disputes, however, was simply an agreement (*concordia, pax, compositio, conventio, pactio*) between litigants in the *curia regis.* In 1185 the bishop of Laon and his men came to an agreement (*composuerunt*) over *tailles* and justice in the king's presence, and the Paris merchants and Gatho de Poissy resolved their disputes (*pax reformata*) over customs duties in the royal court in 1187.[23] Occasionally, the agreement was concluded "with the advice of wise men," or "through the offices of good and upright men,"[24] or assisted by royal officials.[25] Apparently the threat of royal intervention encouraged litigants to

arrive at their own settlements. The chapter of Tours, for example, negotiated independently with Dreu de Mello over customs and justice in
1216 before the king was able to render a judgment.[26] In all, more than
half (54 percent) of the disputes coming before the *curia regis* were resolved by such agreements. During the third decade, this procedure
increased to 70 percent, which explains in part why judgments by the
court dropped to 18 percent in the same period. We can only conclude
that the technique of allowing contending parties to arrive at their own
decisions, then to be confirmed by royal authority, was the preferred
method for resolving disputes in the royal courts. This practice was widespread throughout medieval Europe. Even in England, where royal justice was more effective, litigants frequently settled their differences by
final concord before the king's justices. The judges merely attested their
decision and provided a public record in rolls known as "feets of fines."[27]

Philip Augustus received these basic contours of the *curia regis* from
his father and transmitted them intact to his successor. The archaic character of his personal court was epitomized by its failure to collect its own
decisions. At the end of the reign, the royal scribe Etienne de Gallardon
introduced a new rubric into Register E: "The Records of Different Judgments" (*Scripta judiciorum diversorum*), but it was an abortive effort because only one case was inscribed and no others were added until 1255.[28]
No fundamental changes were introduced in the operations of the *curia
regis* until well into the reign of Louis IX, when the time and place of
sessions were finally scheduled, a permanent corps of judges was created,
and records appeared in the famous *Olim* of 1248. That the king's personal
court was the most resistant to change is not altogether unexpected. In
England the king's own court (*coram rege*) was the last to produce rolls of
its decisions.[29]

Under Philip Augustus, as under the early Capetians, the normal responsibility for justice throughout the royal domain fell upon the local
prévôt. This is illustrated by an exemption accorded to Jocius of London
in 1175. As a special privilege, Louis VII took all suits of this English
merchant under the *curia regis* and exempted him and his family from
the *prévôts'* jurisdiction throughout the royal lands.[30] We may assume that
this judicial system extended into the first decade of the reign of Philip
Augustus, although few details of the *prévôts'* judicial administration have
survived. Whenever the charters mention justice, it was performed by the
prévôts.[31] Closely related to the judicial sphere, the *prévôts* also executed
royal commands. As with most judicial cases, only those commands pro-

tecting churches have survived among the royal charters.[32] Because of the smallness of the royal domain, the ambulatory *curia regis* could adequately supervise the *prévôts'* justice. It required the extended absence of the king on crusade in 1190–1191 to prompt reforms in the system of local justice and to institute channels of appeal between the local courts and the central government.

Finance

In addition to justice, finance was the major concern of Philip Augustus's administration. The rudimentary fiscal system inherited from the early Capetians may be divided into ordinary and extraordinary revenues, and the former into regular and occasional revenues.[33] Regular revenues, those the king could normally count on each year, were drawn largely from the royal domain administered by *prévôts*. Philip inherited scattered lands in the Ile-de-France from his father, most densely located in the triangle formed by Mantes, Sens, and Orléans. In 1179 these lands were divided into about forty units called *prévôtés*, which were not strictly administrative districts with discrete boundaries but centers of concentration within the royal domain. They included sizable towns such as Paris, Orléans, Etampes, Compiègne, Senlis, Poissy, Laon, and Bourges, as well as small rural hamlets such as Fay-aux-Loges and Wacquemoulin. These forty *prévôtés* were overseen by about thirty to thirty-five *prévôts*. We can only be tentative about their number because the smaller *prévôtés* were occasionally combined under one official, and the larger ones, such as Paris, Orléans, and Bourges, were assigned two or three.[34] During the first decade, Philip Augustus himself added ten *prévôtés* from acquisitions in the Amiénois and Berry.[35] The *prévôts* were responsible for collecting and transmitting to the king the regular income on which his government depended.

From the time of the early Capetians, royal charters reveal the nature of the domanial revenues in a fragmentary way.[36] Philip Augustus's charters continue to furnish glimpses into this income, but between 1206 and 1210 a scribe in his chancery copied into Register A a series of accounts that afford a more systematic view. These comprise inventories of thirty-five *prévôtés* added to the royal domain from the beginning of the reign until the eve of the conquest of Normandy, plus the dowry lands of Queen Adèle, reintegrated into the domain after her death in 1206.[37] Although most of the *prévôtés* were acquired after 1190, at least three, Amiens, Roye, and Montdidier, entered the royal domain in 1185, and these accounts confirm the picture of the domanial finances found in contemporary charters. Register A attributes no name to the revenues, but the scribe of Register C, who recopied them without alteration, entitled them *Census et redditus statuti* (*Cens* and fixed revenues), to which Etienne de Gallardon added in Register E: *ad certum terminum et locum* (at fixed times and places). We shall call them the *Census* accounts. They therefore represent inventories of regular revenues that could be expected from the *prévôtés*.

Because they are mainly posterior, the *Census* accounts cannot be used to estimate the regular royal income during the first decade, but they nonetheless offer insight into the nature and variety of the revenues the *prévôts* collected from the royal domain. They included income from cultivated lands, woods, meadows, and fisheries, as well as from mills, ovens, presses, marketplaces, and commercial stalls. In addition, there were a great number of revenues derived from property: *cens* (fixed rents), *champart* (proportional rents), *tailles* (arbitrary payments), tithes, *terragium* (land taxes), *advocatio* (patronage fees), and many other *consuetudines* (customary dues). Some of the more lucrative sources of income were customs tolls, minting fees, exchange fees, and fees paid by Jews. Most of the items were small, amounting only to a few *livres*, but the customs tolls could produce as much as 1,400 *livres* annually. In general, the values were fixed, but occasionally it was noted that variations could be expected. The tolls at Roye, for example, were valued at 800 *livres*, but they could yield more or less in a given year. Revenue was expressed in the money of Paris and in kind: wheat, oats, wine, capons, hens, and eggs, quoted in the regional measures, for which Paris equivalents were often supplied. The scribes attempted to furnish total figures for only a fifth of the *prévôtés*, but sums were kept distinct for money, wheat, oats, and poultry.[38] No attempt was made to convert produce into monetary equivalents.

The *Census* accounts attempted to inventory domanial income in a way strikingly comparable to the surviving domanial accounts of the counts of Flanders, found in the *Gros Brief* of 1187, and to the *états* of the count-kings of Barcelona from 1178 to 1194.[39] These three sets of accounts depict a traditional method of domanial exploitation that was as old as the Capetian dynasty and persisted in the *prévôtés* to the end of Philip's reign, as revealed by a fragment of warehouse accounts surviving from 1227.[40] This consists of inventories of wheat, oats, and wine for about two dozen *prévôtés* scattered from Lens in the north to Bourges in the south. By accounting receipts, expenditures, and debits of produce, they underscore the agricultural basis of the domanial economy that nourished all medieval governments.

The *prévôts* were responsible not only for collecting the regular domanial revenues, but also for paying certain regular expenses from their *prévôtés*, chief among which were alms to churches and *fief-rentes* to knights. From early Capetian times, the French kings had been accustomed to make regular contributions to local churches drawn from *prévôtés*. From the outset Philip Augustus continued this practice of royal almsgiving.[41] By 1200–1205 the donations had become so numerous that a list was compiled of the obligations, which was copied into Register A shortly thereafter and then into the succeeding registers.[42] Although this inventory postdated the first decade, a large proportion of the recorded alms originated in the earlier period,[43] illustrating the extensive royal almsgiving that was a permanent feature of the reign. In addition to alms, the early Capetians provided regular incomes, called *stipendia* and later known as *fief-rentes*, to attach knights to their service. Probably modelled on ecclesiastical *prebende*, they supported lay familiars of the king.[44] Although appearing less frequently than alms in the records because of the scarcity of lay documentation, these *fief-rentes* were widely used by Philip Augustus. Before 1190, for example, Gautier the Chamberlain was supported by a revenue of fifty *sous* from the *prévôté* of Paris.[45] These obligations became numerous enough to warrant an inventory by *prévôté* that was copied into Register A between 1204 and 1212 and revised through subsequent copies in Registers C and E.[46]

Just how the *prévôts* transmitted the balance of the income to the king after expenses had been deducted eludes us.[47] Since revenue was in both agricultural products and money, we may assume that the procedure was informal and dependent on convenience. Richard fitz Nigel, the author of the *Dialogue of the Exchequer*, could remember the English sheriffs paying their revenues in produce (although they were accounted in money) during the reign of Henry I (1100–1135).[48] The French *prévôts* likewise could transport wheat and wine to the king's court, or they could sell them and transport the proceeds along with the other monies to the king or his treasury at Paris. Or the king might prefer to collect the goods and money directly while his court was itinerating through the domain. All these arrangements were possible and probably existed. One solution that facilitated transmission was "farming," or the commutation of regular revenues in money and kind into one fixed sum that could more easily be transferred. The farms were usually set low to allow the farmer a profit and to protect him against occasional unfavorable years. Although not an efficient method for exploiting the domain, the system ensured a fixed and calculable sum. This procedure depended on finding someone capable of assuming the responsibility of the farm. In 1179 Louis VII had conceded some of the revenues of the *prévôté* to the commune of Compiègne in exchange for a fixed annual payment. When Philip reissued Compiègne's charter in 1186, he adopted the procedure and increased the farm.[49] Two years later the newly created commune of Poissy assumed the income of the *prévôté* for a farm of 600 *livres*, and in the next year the commune of Sens took over its *prévôté* for the same amount.[50] The communes of the towns therefore pioneered in the procedure of farming that was extended to other *prévôtés* in the coming decade.

Another source of regular income available to a royal court constantly on the move was the right of hospitality, or *gîte* (*gistum, procuratio*). Like most medieval monarchs, the early Capetians were accustomed to visiting designated localities, where it was the obligation of the "host" to lodge and feed the royal entourage at his own expense, usually for one night.[51] Whereas the German emperor exacted this privilege from all bishops and most great barons, in France the *gîte* appears to have been based on the king's domanial possessions. Required of a few bishoprics and abbeys and none of the great baronage, it was regularly demanded from localities in the royal domain. Together with other royal resources, a chancery scribe copied a list of sixteen places owing hospitality into Register A between 1204 and 1212. Since it was obviously incomplete, the scribe Etienne de Gallardon added fifty-seven more names, bringing the total to seventy-three.[52] Even with these additions, the list is only a rough approximation, including places previously renounced[53] and omitting others still liable for the *gîte*.[54] As depicted by this list, the extreme geographic limits were the bishoprics of Arras to the north, Châlons-sur-Marne to the east, and Tours to the southwest, but the main concentration of places lay within an area inscribed by Laon, Sens, Orléans, Chartres, and Beauvais. Some of the localities undoubtedly reflect the late date of the list. Many others are close together in the triangle between Mantes, Orléans, and Sens, where the royal domain was focused during the first decade of the reign.

Since it was onerous, those who owed hospitality constantly pressed the king to renounce the right or exchange it for more tolerable terms. As early as 1185 Philip renounced his *gîte* at Amiens in return for recognition of his suzerainty over the county, and similar exchanges were negotiated in other places.[55] The obvious solution, however, was to commute the rights of hospitality for annual fixed sums, just as had been proposed for the farms of the *prévôté*. In 1186, for example, the king promised that the *gîte* of Beauvais would not exceed one hundred *livres* annually, and in 1189 he exchanged his rights to three annual visits at the commune of Laon for 200 *livres* a year.[56] These monetary commutations, however, formed an insignificant contribution to the royal income by 1202/03,[57] and the king continued to demand his *gîte* directly in his travels. At the end of the reign (1220–1223), a second *gîte* list was inserted into Register E, containing thirty-six names, which succeeding scribes increased to seventy. In scope this list was comparable to that of Register A, although it added a few places as far south as Saint-Pourçain and Clermont-Ferrand.[58] In the subsequent reigns of Philip's son and grandson, a new format for the *gîte* list was copied into Register E that furnished by year both the date and a monetary value for each visit, although we cannot be certain whether the hospitality was paid in money or in kind.[59] Nonetheless, it shows that the Capetian kings continued to exercise their traditional rights of hospitality well into the thirteenth century as they circulated throughout the royal domain.

The *prévôts* were also responsible for collecting ordinary income that materialized on an occasional basis. During the first decade of Philip's reign, these revenues consisted chiefly of regalian rights over churches, reliefs, feudal aids, and exploitation of the Jews. The early Capetians exercised rights over the regalia of certain bishoprics and abbeys throughout the kingdom that brought them economic profit in two ways: collection of the revenues of the church during its vacancy (from the death of the prelate to his replacement by a successor) and assignment of prebends and benefices during the vacancy that were normally at the disposal of the bishop. The first were known as the temporal regalia, the second as the spiritual.[60] On the eve of his departure on crusade (1190), Philip defined for the benefit of the regents the procedures that he and his predecessors followed. After outlining the process of electing bishops and abbots, he declared that the regents should hold the regalia in their hands until the new prelate was consecrated.[61] Then the regalia should be returned without obstacle. Furthermore, when prebends or ecclesiastical benefices fell vacant while the regalia were in royal hands, the regents should confer them on honorable and literate men with the advice of Brother Bernard of Vincennes, except for those which the king granted explicitly by patent letter.[62] These definitions of the regalia were traditional and not unlike King Henry II's formulation in the famous Constitutions of Clarendon in 1164.[63] Because of the fragmentary nature of the evidence and the fact that churches occasionally changed status, it is difficult to know precisely which churches were considered regalian, but we may estimate that when Philip came to the throne, he inherited about sixty-five regalian abbeys and at least twenty-five regalian bishoprics.[64] The evidence is too scattered to follow the pattern of vacancies among the abbeys, but during the first decade (1179–1190) about fifteen regalian bishoprics changed hands, enabling the king to profit from the temporal regalia.[65] How much the king profited, of course, depended on the length of the vacancy, which he was able to prolong by his influence over the election procedure. In 1139 the papacy had attempted to limit episcopal vacancies to three months, but this was often not possible in practice.[66] Because of the imprecision of the chronological data, we are able to measure only one vacancy in months between 1179 and 1190 (Auxerre: 12 months),[67] but there is little indication that any exceeded a year. To all appearances, therefore, Philip profited from his regalian income without abusing the royal prerogative by unduly extending vacancies.

The regalia were open to other abuses long practiced by the Capetians, however. Obviously, the king could profit from his spiritual rights by assigning prebends to his own agents, thus imposing unsuitable candidates on churches. On the temporal side, the *prévôts* could exercise what was called the right of despoiling while the church lands were in their hands. They could destroy productive capital by carrying off all the wood and iron fixtures, by cutting down the forests, and by consuming the grain, leaving nothing for seed. They could, moreover, occupy the prelate's houses and farms, despoiling moveables and livestock. They could interfere with the execution of testamentary bequests by confiscating personal property, and they could levy heavy *tailles* and other unusual exactions on the prelate's men. Responding to urgent complaints, Louis VII issued charters to specific churches curbing these despoliations. To the bishops of Orléans and Paris and the archbishop of Sens, for example, he limited *tailles* and unusual exactions to sixty *livres*.[68] As early as 1180, Philip Augustus issued a similar protection to the see of Mâcon, and he later renewed the charters to Sens and Paris and extended these privileges to other churches throughout his reign.[69] In 1190, for example, the move-

ables of the household of the bishop of Paris were exempted from despoiling, and *tailles* were limited to sixty *livres*. After 1204 many of his
father's charters were copied into the royal registers to remind his agents
of these restrictions.[70] But however much Philip supported his father's
policy against despoliation, it was difficult to curb the rapacity of royal
agents. Despite Louis's charter of 1159 protecting the archbishop of
Bourges's testamentary bequests, for example, Philip was obliged in
1199 to command his *bailli* to return all the moveables he had seized to
the executors of the late archbishop, Henri. In an inquest commissioned
in 1215, the king learned that even the personal property of the succeeding archbishop, Guillaume (d. 1209), had been confiscated by royal
agents.[71] Nor did Louis VII's charter of 1147 protect the bishopric of
Châlons-sur-Marne. When in 1202 Philip opened an inquest into the
rights of the *vidame* of Châlons over the regalia, it was discovered that at
the deaths of the preceding ten bishops, the bishopric had been despoiled
not only by the *vidame* but by many others, including royal agents.[72] In
1190 the king had acknowledged that the see of Paris would not be subject to more than 60 *livres* of *taille*, but in 1207 he admitted that at the
death of Bishop Maurice de Sully in 1196 he had taken more than 240
livres and promised—for what it was worth—that this would not set a
precedent.[73] The see of Auxerre was despoiled with unusual severity at
the death of Bishop Hugues de Noyers in 1206. Two local chronicles and
Pope Innocent III attest that the royal agents left little untouched.[74] Although the ravaged see of Auxerre stood in mute testimony to the excesses of the right of despoliation, such abuse did not negate the king's traditional claim to the normal revenues of vacant sees. The temporal regalia
of bishoprics and abbeys remained an important source of occasional income inherited from the early Capetians.

In addition, the French king claimed comparable revenues called reliefs
and aids from his lay vassals, devolving from his position as feudal lord.[75]
Since these incomes were traditional, the contemporary chroniclers seldom mention them, but we must presume that the king collected them,
although we are not able to estimate their value. We have little way of
knowing how many of Philip's direct vassals died during the first decade
of his reign, but we may suspect that the king's acquisition of Montargis
in 1184 was a relief when Pierre de Courtenay succeeded to the county
of Nevers, and that the annexation of Amiens, Montdidier, and other
places in 1185 was Aliénor de Vermandois's acknowledgement as heir of
the count of Flanders. When Richard promised Philip Augustus 24,000

marks sterling (43,476 *livres parisis*) at his accession to the fiefs of King Henry in 1189, this may also have been a relief. How much the French king actually received was, of course, another question. Beyond reliefs, feudal lords also required of their vassals personal military service and aid in the form of money in times of war. Again, we must presume that Philip exacted military service and aid throughout the wars of the first decade, but we cannot know how much. This presumption is confirmed by the ordinance-testament of 1190, which declared that if anyone waged war against the king's son (in the event of Philip's death) and the ordinary revenues (*reditus*) were not sufficient, the king's vassals would aid the son with their persons and goods and the churches would provide aid, just as all were accustomed to furnish these to Philip Augustus.[76]

Another major source of occasional income was the exploitation of the Jews. Like the English kings, the early Capetians considered the Jews to be their personal property. Whereas the English kings claimed all Jews in England and Normandy, the Capetians exercised jurisdiction only over the Jews of the royal domain, allowing the barons their own Jews. Within the royal domain, all Jews were "the king's Jews," whom he both protected with special privileges and profited from at will. Since commerce in general and money lending in particular were their chief activities, the king oversaw these transactions. In exchange for this special attention, the Jews recompensed their royal protector with gifts and arbitrary *tailles*. Whereas the king defended Jewish interests against all others, including churchmen, there was no one to protect the Jews against the king. Under Louis VII, who was unusually well disposed towards them, the Jews flourished in the royal domain, but their prosperity rested on the fragile foundation of the king's discretion.[77]

All of this suddenly changed upon the accession of Philip Augustus in November 1179. Beginning in February 1180, even before the ailing Louis VII was dead, and culminating in the spring of 1182, the young king precipitously and savagely turned against his Jews in three separate measures. He first captured them in their synagogues on the Sabbath and seized their gold, silver, and vestments. Then, on the advice of his ecclesiastical advisor, Bernard de Vincennes, he cancelled all Christian debts to the Jews, retaining a fifth of their value for himself. Finally, he expelled all Jews from the royal domain, allowing them to sell their moveables, but confiscating their landed property.

The royal chronicler, Rigord, who approvingly recounts these measures in detail, ascribes this sudden reversal to moral and religious motives. But many of the justifications were stereotyped anti-Jewish propaganda. Having prospered inordinately under Louis VII (they owned almost half of Paris, it was said), the royal Jews had insolently attempted to convert Christians in their domestic employ, oppressed townsmen, knights, and peasants with interest-laden loans, and committed sacrilege, including ritual murder.[78]

There is no doubt that the young king profited enormously from despoiling the Jews. The English chronicler Ralph de Diceto reports that the Jews paid 15,000 marks (31,500 *livres parisis*) to ransom the initial confiscations.[79] Although no figures survive for Jewish debts in the 1180s, the king's retention of 20 percent for their cancellation (his second measure) would have realized a very large sum.[80] Furthermore, Jewish property was converted into new sources of royal revenue. Though some of their holdings were donated to churches, others were rented to furriers, drapers, and goldsmiths.[81] Exploitation of the Jews that culminated in their expulsion could not, of course, be repeated, but it produced an enormous windfall for the king's finances.

Unlike the regalia, feudal reliefs, and taxation of the Jews, all of which derived from royal prerogatives, aids for the Holy Land were prompted by extraordinary circumstances outside the king's control.[82] Louis VII, advised by his financial counsellor, Abbot Suger, was the first on record to levy such a tax, which he did in 1146 before departing on the Second Crusade. Details of this tax have not survived, but it probably inspired a measure enacted by Henry II in 1166. In that year, urged on by Louis, the English king issued a radically innovative ordinance decreeing that all his continental subjects were to pay what amounted to one-fortieth of their moveable possessions and revenues over a period of five years. Whereas English taxes had hitherto been based on landholdings, this new levy tapped moveable wealth. Sophisticated techniques were devised to assess and collect these new sources of revenue. In 1185, two decades later, Henry II and Philip Augustus again imposed a crusading tax as they prepared for the forthcoming Third Crusade. The method of assessment and rates (one hundred-and-twentieth on moveables and one-hundredth on revenues) were different, but the tax base—moveable wealth—was the same.[83] Because of the confusion arising in connection with Henry's last years, it is not certain whether the levies of 1185 were ever collected. But after January 1188, when the two kings could no longer delay taking the cross, first Henry and then Philip decreed the famous Saladin tax. Although its sources (moveables and revenues) were no longer unusual, the rate was astronomic: one-tenth of moveables and income to be collected by crusaders from their vassals, both lay and clerical, who had not taken the cross.[84] This time there is little doubt about its collection. The pages of the chroniclers and contemporary observers resound with the outcries of the clergy, who protested that never were the poor and defenseless so oppressed as by this infamous tithe. Richard, who inherited his father's efficient government, persisted in the face of opposition and introduced the tax on moveables as a permanent feature of English finance. His agents later employed it in England to assemble his enormous ransom in 1194. John, in turn, confirmed its place in royal taxation when he imposed a levy of one-thirteenth part of moveables in 1207.

Philip Augustus, however, began to relent under pressure from churchmen who included his close adviser Etienne, abbot of Sainte-Geneviève. When he confirmed the count of Nevers's crusading tax on houses in 1188, he specifically promised that it would not become a precedent.[85] After a year had passed and the crusaders had not yet departed, though the taxes were collected, Philip finally capitulated to ecclesiastical opposition. In the summer of 1189 the king sent a letter to Guillaume, archbishop of Reims, and his province, which was undoubtedly duplicated for the other provinces, in which he renounced the tithe on moveables and returned to the situation forty days before he had taken the cross. Admitting the argument that God would not cause the crusade to prosper if it victimized the poor and defenseless, he promised that henceforth all moveables, domains, fiefs, and other rights would remain immune from such exactions.[86] When, in the ordinance of 1190, Philip prohibited his prelates and men from collecting any *tailles* or exactions (*talliam et toltam*) while he was in God's service he was, in all likelihood, prolonging this renunciation.[87] The only financial measure that remained in effect for the crusaders was an ordinance of March 1188 that instituted a moratorium on crusaders' debts.[88] Exactly how Philip, unlike Richard, anticipated undertaking the crusade without the aid of the Saladin tithe is unclear. We may suspect, however, that despite the renunciation of the tithe, not all of the money collected was returned. (In 1190 the king made provisions for restitution to those impoverished by his *tallia* in the event of his death.)[89] Henry's death in 1189 and Richard's subsequent promise of 24,000 marks sterling (43,476 *livres parisis*) as relief would have improved the French king's financial situation if it was paid. Of import for the future, however, was Philip's renunciation of the tax on moveables. Whereas Richard and his successors were able to establish the crusading impost as a permanent feature of royal taxation, Philip's hesitation was in all likelihood detrimental to Capetian finances. Not until the end of the thirteenth century was this important source of taxation utilized by the French monarchy.

The total income Philip Augustus realized from his ordinary and extraordinary revenues during the first decade of his reign is a matter of speculation because of the absence of direct contemporary evidence. Testimony has surfaced from the end of the reign, however, that has intrigued modern historians. A certain Conan, *prévôt* of the cathedral of Lausanne, resided in Paris and was present at the death of Philip in 1223. When he returned home he wrote a kind of chronicle, called *Note*, in which he reported a conversation about the king's finances among the royal officials at the funeral. Conan heard that Philip had received an income of no more than 19,000 *livres* from his father.[90] This figure is perplexing because it seems too low to represent Philip's entire income in 1179 if compared with his subsequent finances. If, however, it represents only the regular ordinary income from the king's *prévôtés*, it lies within a credible range.[91] If we add up the farms of the *prévôtés* in the royal domain in 1179 from the accounts of 1202/03, we arrive at the figure of 20,178 *livres*. This total was probably not too far from that of 1179 because the farms of the *prévôtés* changed slowly.[92] In any case, 19,000 *livres* may have been the traditionally accepted figure for fixed revenues under Philip Augustus. A century later, in 1302, Pope Boniface VIII, in a dispute over taxation with Philip the Fair, claimed that Philip Augustus had collected only 18,000 *livres* "in established revenues" (*de situatis redditibus*).[93] Since Philip Augustus's administration represented no significant advance over that of Louis VII, it is plausible that he could have managed on the modest (19,000 *livres*) fixed revenues of his father's domanial income. From 1179 to 1190, Philip added ten *prévôtés* to the domain. In terms of the receipts of 1202/03, this increased the regular domanial revenues by 4,429 *livres*, bringing them to a total of 24,607 *livres*, an increase of 22 percent.[94]

The crusade was an extraordinary expense that most medieval kings attempted to finance by extraordinary measures, carried out with ecclesiastical cooperation. But beyond the crusade, whose finances elude us, the king's own military campaigns against Champagne, Flanders, and Henry II and his sons also demanded unusual outlays of money, especially because Philip deployed notoriously costly mercenaries from Brabant.[95] He undoubtedly met these expenses through occasional revenues, including the regalia, and reliefs, but it is impossible to say how much these brought him. Philip's despoiling of the Jews at the opening of his reign was, however, an extraordinary measure that realized massive gains in ransoms (31,500 *livres*), expropriation of debts, and confiscation of property. In all likelihood, his Jewish policy was the expedient for financing the political program of the first decade.[96]

Whereas the local *prévôts* managed the king's properties and collected the revenues, the central court was responsible for supervising these activities, calling the *prévôts* to account and storing the monies as it travelled about. In early Capetian times the *prévôts* were most likely supervised by the seneschal since he was in charge of provisioning the royal household.[97] By the middle of Louis VII's reign, however, seneschals of baronial rank, such as Raoul, count of Vermandois, were probably no longer involved in these domestic matters. There is no evidence of the seneschal Thibaut, count of Blois, having performed these duties during the first decade of Philip Augustus's reign. It is likely that financial responsibilities had, by that time, been transferred to the royal chamber. There the major duties were discharged by lesser officials such as Adam and Gautier the Chamberlain, since the grand chamberlain, Mathieu, count of Beaumont, has also left no trace of activity in this department. Descended from the primitive Carolingian household, the royal bedchamber was traditionally the place where the king kept his valuables for safekeeping. The chamberlains were therefore responsible for the storage of money, clothing, jewels, and other precious items in the king's sleeping tents and for transporting them in wagons and on pack horses during displacements of the royal entourage.[98] That these domestic duties of the chamberlains persisted into the thirteenth century is revealed by a series of accounts transcribed into Register A. On 12 February 1206 the king handed over to Eudes the Chamberlain a large quantity of gold, several pieces of jewelry, and precious vessels in the shape of silver goblets, cups, and dishes, all of which were recorded in the royal register. To this nucleus Eudes added three successive accounts that inventoried the royal gems (emeralds, rubies, sapphires, diamonds, and so on) arranged according to receipts and expenditures.[99] In effect, this was an embryonic version of the jewel accounts that developed into the royal household accounts of the Argenterie in the fourteenth century.[100]

Since the chamberlains' domestic duties involved the royal treasure, it was a short step for them to extend their responsibilities to royal finances as well. Unfortunately, no contemporary evidence reveals their fiscal activities during the first decade of Philip's reign. In neighboring Flanders, Normandy, and England, however, the chamberlains had become the rulers' chief fiscal officers by the end of the eleventh century.[101] In England, where the operations of the chamber are best known, it supervised royal finances well into the thirteenth century, despite the existence of the treasury and the exchequer. As part of the household in constant attendance on the king throughout his travels, the chamber was where the king personally directed fiscal affairs. It could intercept revenues at royal convenience. It was active in disbursing monies, especially for military campaigns and fortifications in time of war. In short, it became the king's ad hoc fiscal agency for short-circuiting the regular channels of the treasury and the exchequer. Although the English chamber began producing its own records by the end of the twelfth century, these documents have left only faint traces because the ambulatory chamber seems to have been careless about preserving them. For this reason the chamber is the least known among the English financial organs despite its early importance, and its early activities can be deduced only from the existence of chamberlains.[102]

Later evidence suggests that the French chamber acted in ways comparable to those of England, Normandy, and Flanders during Philip's first decade. At the famous ambush of Fréteval in 1194, Philip lost his baggage to Richard, baggage that must have included the chamber because it consisted of household furnishings, treasure, and documents.[103] Recounting the incident, the royal chronicler Guillaume le Breton specifies that the king lost not only precious gold and silver plate, but also hoards of money (*nummis quibus arcta tumebant dolia, nec saccis quibus ornamenta latebant*) and fiscal records (*libellis computorum fisci . . . scripta tributorum fiscique cyrographia*). At the end of the reign, when Guillaume embellished the narrative in verse, he emphasized the fiscal nature of the documents.[104] In his opinion, therefore, the royal baggage carried not only treasure but also account books, fiscal charters, and inventories of census, tolls, and fiefs. As described, what Philip lost in 1194 seems remarkably to have resembled the contents of the English treasury listed by Richard fitz Nigel in his *Dialogue of the Exchequer*.[105] Although the English documents are more numerous and differentiated than the French, both collections of fiscal records appear to have been largely domanial in character. Moreover, although English treasure and records were normally kept at the treasury, they were also transported about by the treasurer and chamberlains. That Guillaume le Breton considered the lost

French records to belong to the chamber is suggested by the fact that the task of reconstitution was delegated to a chamberlain, Gautier the Young, son of Gautier the Chamberlain. Like the Old Testament prophet Ezra, who had restored the lost books of the Jewish Temple, Gautier repaired the losses of the king's records.[106] As depicted by Guillaume le Breton, the French royal chamber before Fréteval corresponded closely to the contemporary chambers of England, Normandy, and Flanders: beyond its domestic duties, it transported treasure, accounted for the domanial revenues, and in general supervised the royal finances. What became of its functions after 1190, when other fiscal organs were established, cannot be known from extant sources.

An itinerant chamber housed in tents and following the incessant movements of a prince by pack horse and wagon was not wholly satisfactory to safeguard governmental monies. By the mid–twelfth century the English, Normans, and Flemings had designated certain strongholds as permanent treasuries.[107] In France Louis VII kept treasure at the royal palace on the Ile-de-la-Cité in Paris in the early part of his reign, but before 1146 he moved it to the Temple, the castle of the Knights Templars, on the Right Bank. This selection of a crusading order as the royal treasury was undoubtedly made to facilitate preparations for the crusade.[108] Growing out of crusading activities, the Knights Templars had established a network of banks throughout Europe. The French kings, like the English (at the Temple in London) and the popes, made use of these facilities not only to safekeep treasure, but also to transfer funds, extend credit, and benefit from other banking services. Whether or not Louis retained the Temple as the royal treasury after his return is not known, and neither is there record of what happened to the treasury during the first decade of Philip's reign, but in the ordinance of 1190, acting also under the impulse of the crusade, Philip commanded his revenues to be brought to the Paris Temple three times a year and handed over to six Parisian townsmen and Peter the Marshal. Each was authorized to possess keys for the individual chests in which the money was stored and an additional key to the Temple.[109] From that time the Temple was the sole royal treasury until its suppression in the fourteenth century. In the accounts of 1202/03, the treasurer was a Templar, Brother Haimard, who received surplus revenues three times a year and paid out sums for the operations of government and the waging of war. He was still performing these functions in 1219 and most likely continued through the end of the reign.[110] The account of 1202/03 also recorded the movement of treasure (*denarii*). Except for the military operations in the Norman marches, most transport of treasure was centered on Paris. The *prévôt* of Paris, aided by other *prévôts*, regularly expended considerable sums for these purposes.[111] Unlike Henry II, who had five English treasuries and three in Normandy, Philip Augustus maintained a unitary treasury at Paris under the management of the Templars throughout his reign.[112]

From his father Philip had inherited a small domain whose regular income, when tax-farmed, probably did not exceed 20,000 *livres* a year. From his own territorial acquisitions, he could not have increased these revenues more than 20 percent. Such income was not substantial enough to carry out a vigorous royal policy against the great barons and against Henry II in particular. Undoubtedly, Philip was obliged to depend heavily on occasional revenues such as regalian rights, feudal aids and reliefs, and, especially, extraordinary measures such as despoiling the Jews. Richard's relief may have produced 43,000 *livres* and mulcting the Jews another 31,500 *livres*, both amounts that overshadowed regular annual income. Except for the extraordinary pillaging of the Jews, however, the basic nature of Philip's finances and fiscal administration remained unaltered throughout the first decade. Royal government relied on income drawn from domanial and feudal resources supervised by the chamberlains of the king's household.

Towns and
Churches: The Extension
of Royal Influence

Towns

The exercise of justice and management of finance through stationary *prévôts* and a travelling court brought the king's government into contact chiefly with the rural inhabitants of the royal domain, both free and servile. Apart from the magnates, such as the counts of Flanders and Blois, who served as court counsellors, the nobility outside the domain had little to do with the French royalty except in the rare instances when they brought their suits before the king's court. But the early Capetians had developed channels for reaching out to two other segments of the population, townsmen and churchmen. Their dealings with these social groups both intensified their hold over the royal domain and extended their influence far beyond.

The traditional Capetian policy towards towns was the creation of Louis VI and Louis VII.[1] Recognizing the importance of the growing urban communities produced by the upswing of commercial activity in the early twelfth century, these kings issued charters to towns throughout the northern half of France. The main purpose of these documents was to record and define the customs (*consuetudines*) that regulated a

59

broad range of diversified activities, including justice, finance, commercial dealings, and sometimes governance. On occasion these charters either acknowledged or created a commune (*communia*), which was simply a sworn association among the townsmen.[2] Like customs, communes were instituted for widely differing purposes: to secure existing customs, to seek new privileges, and occasionally to organize some form of self-government. So great was the diversity among communes that the only consistent element was the oath that held the townsmen together. Occasionally, the commune was not even limited to townsmen but encompassed loose confederations of rural communities. Although Louis VI and Louis VII were generally favorable to urban development, their attitude towards communes was fundamentally ambivalent. At times—and this was especially evident in episcopal towns when the bishopric was vacant—they encouraged the formation of communal associations. On other occasions they abolished them and were noticeably reluctant to allow them in the major towns of the royal domain. Paris, for example, was never permitted the privilege of a commune. Beneath the bewildering diversity of customs and communes was an underlying goal of establishing peace. Merchants and the noncombatants of the community needed protection; violence had to be suppressed; society and economy required regulation; sanctions had to be implemented. The particular circumstances and requirements varied for each community. Although the royal charters confirming these customs recorded this variety, they themselves expressed another constant—a growing concern for the well-being of towns. At the beginning urban customs and communes were acknowledged by ecclesiastics and lay lords as well, but as the century progressed the Capetians asserted interest in the urban movement. Louis VII began to consider the communes of northern France as worthy of his particular concern. By recognizing the growing urban phenomenon and issuing charters that dealt with its complexity, the Capetians extended their influence into new realms of the kingdom.

This traditional Capetian policy was perfected by Philip Augustus. From his accession to his departure on crusade, the king issued some twenty-eight charters to urban communities, many of which resulted from an understandable desire on the part of towns to receive reconfirmation of their customs from the new monarch.[3] These issuances naturally centered on those areas where Philip was especially active, notably the Vexin and northeastern France towards Flanders. In the Vexin, for example, he established a commune at Chaumont in 1182, and after

Mantes had stoutly resisted the incursion of Henry II in 1188, he accorded Mantes's privileges to the nearby towns of Pontoise and Poissy.[4] Since the northeast was France's most urbanized region, it was only natural that Philip issued his heaviest concentration of charters there while he was preoccupied with Flemish affairs. When in 1185 he acquired Amiens, the only significant town to be added to the royal domain during the first decade, he immediately issued a charter and granted a commune. But his concern for townsmen allowed him to go beyond the royal domain and also penetrate episcopal towns where he was not represented by *prévôts*, as, for example, at the important Champagne city of Reims (1182–1183), the seat of his uncle. In 1188 a dispute between the bishop and townsmen of Tournai provided Philip with an occasion to grant a commune there and to secure military support for the monarchy. Intervening on behalf of Burgundian churches, he used the conflict between Hugues, duke of Burgundy, and Hugues de Vergy to grant a commune to the inhabitants of Dijon, the duke's chief town, and to safeguard it in the future.[5] Through contacts with townsmen, therefore, the king was able to extend beyond the royal domain in the north and to the east.

Philip's charters detailing the customs of towns and rural communities ranged from short statements that former usages were to be observed to lengthy transcripts of specific regulations. The former are exemplified by Philip's grant of a commune to Saint-Riquier in 1189–1190; the latter by his charter to Tournai in 1188, which described with precision the mechanism of town government, its revenues, and the operation of justice. Many of the charters grew out of previous exemplars and can be assembled into family groupings that served as models. To rural communities such as Boiscommun, Voisines, Nonette, and Dixmont, the king granted the "customs of Lorris," established by his grandfather and reconfirmed by Philip in 1187.[6] These charters mainly dealt with personal liberties, taxation, and the abuses of royal and seigneurial agents. Among the towns, a particularly widespread family was that of Soissons, which was confirmed there in 1181 and extended to Beauvais, Vailly, Compiègne, Sens, and even to the Burgundian city of Dijon.[7] These were rather modest charters, concerned mainly with personal liberties and taxes, and had little to say about government and justice. Laon's charter, first granted by Louis VI in 1128, was reconfirmed in 1189–1190 and applied to the rural communes of Cerny, Crépy-en-Laonnois, and Bruyères.[8] Originating during a period of communal unrest, it was heavily oriented towards justice and jurisdiction. Mantes's customs, a brief ten articles first enumerated by Louis VII in 1150, became the basis for the Vexin group, as has been noted.[9] Yet even these family groupings were only approximations, which had customs in common but added different ones according to local circumstances. Nor did Philip's reissue of the charters introduce innovative regulations into town life during his reign. Derived from long-standing tradition and local conditions, his charters were preoccupied with the concerns of the individual locality. Since the options were few, his room for reform was necessarily limited.[10]

As to the establishment of communes—sworn associations—Philip Augustus retained his father's and grandfather's ambivalence during the first decade of his reign. Old established communes were reconfirmed.[11] New communes were set up in areas over which he struggled with the count of Flanders (Amiens, Tournai, Montreuil-sur-Mer, and Saint-Riquier) and with the king of England (Chaumont, Pontoise, and Poissy).[12] He even extended Laon's commune with its customs to the surrounding rural associations.[13] But like his forebears he also turned against particular communes when ecclesiastical pressure became strong. When the protests of the abbey of Saint-Martin finally moved the pope to dissolve the commune of Châteauneuf de Tours, Philip complied with the action.[14] The king was particularly sensitive to churchmen's objections while he was on crusade. While at Messina in 1190–1191, he bowed to the protests of the abbot of Corbie and the bishop of Laon by revoking the privileges he had granted to the commune of Corbie until he returned to the kingdom and by annulling altogether the rural commune in the Laonnois. During his reign no commune was permitted to the chief towns of the royal domain: Orléans, Bourges, and Paris.[15] The inhabitants of the capital had to remain content with improvements such as a new fair at the Champeaux, a new covered market, Les Halles, for the merchants, and paving of the major streets and squares.[16] Never did the Parisians receive from Philip the slightest hope of a commune, or even a statement of customs.

Philip's town policy, inherited from his predecessors and implemented during the first decade, was continued with little alteration until his death. The only discernible change was abandonment of his ambivalence over communes. In 1199–1200 he annulled the commune of Etampes— because of its injuries to churchmen and knights, as he said—but he was never to abolish a commune again.[17] From the time he returned from the crusade in 1191 until the conquest of Normandy in 1204, he drew up at least eleven charters for towns, all located in northeastern France, where he was preoccupied with consolidating territories inherited from the count of Flanders.[18] In the decade between the conquest of Normandy and the battle of Bouvines in 1214, he issued another twenty-eight charters, distributed among the major Norman towns, those in Poitou where the English had been expelled, and, finally, among northeastern towns in preparation for the showdown with the English, German, and Flemish coalition.[19] When Prince Louis was declared of age in 1209, he also issued new charters to Bapaume and Lens and confirmed grants to Arras and Aire in his Artois inheritance.[20] In the tranquil decade after Bouvines, Philip's interest in urban affairs subsided. Of the seven charters issued to towns in this period only those to Crépy-en-Valois, Beaumont-sur-Oise, and Chambly were of importance.[21]

This continual flow of urban charters stimulated the royal chancery to undertake the task of inventorying them. No sooner was the conquest of Normandy completed in 1204 than the scribe who initiated Register A copied a block of town charters under the running heading of *communie*, the only coherent section of the primitive register.[22] He and his colleagues added others until the clerk commissioned to transcribe Register C in 1212 gathered them all together in a single chapter.[23] In 1205 another clerk copied a list of twenty-nine communes into Register A to which a second hand added the names of Fillièvres (*Fererie*) and the eight Norman and Poitevin communes that adopted the customs of Rouen.[24] Through such copies and lists the chancery kept abreast of the royal grants. (See Map 1.)

Like the charters of the first decade, these later issues can be grouped in families of customs.[25] The Norman and Poitevin towns were accorded the "*Etablissements* of Rouen" formulated by the Angevin dukes in the last third of the twelfth century.[26] Later Rouen (1207) and Poitiers (1222) were granted new charters supplementing the *Etablissements*. Since the towns of Artois, Vermandois, and Normandy were located in the highly urbanized regions of northern France, their charters were long and minutely detailed, reflecting their advanced development. The later charters devoted more attention to municipal government, revenue, and justice. In particular, the *Etablissements* of Rouen, reflecting the vigorous government of the Angevin dukes, were preoccupied with mayors, councils, and courts. But beyond differences in emphasis, the customs of these later charters strongly resembled those of the first decade.

By and large, therefore, Philip's program towards the towns was well established by the time he left for the crusade. The advantages that he derived from towns were essentially threefold: revenues, defense, and the extension of royal influence. Those towns that belonged to the royal domain—and these included most of those we have considered—were naturally responsible for contributing to the king's domanial income. But because of their commercial assets, towns were in a better position to pay cash and thereby to commute their varied domanial revenues into fixed sums or farms. By 1190 Compiègne, Pontoise, Poissy, and Sens had already farmed their revenues and those of their *prévôtés*. This system, which offered the king the advantages of a fixed income, continued to spread among towns in the subsequent period.[27]

In the second place, the walls of towns offered defensive sites. Chaumont in the Vexin and Mantes, Pontoise, and Poissy in the Seine valley protected Paris from the Anglo-Normans in the early period. The towns of Artois, Vermandois, and Normandy provided strongholds in newly acquired lands. Throughout the reign, therefore, royal charters frequently specified the towns' obligation to keep their fortifications in repair.[28] During the first decade, however, military service, defined as host (*exercitus*—in an army) and *chevauchée* (*equitatio*—in a raiding party), was occasionally mentioned, but almost always limited to defensive purposes. The men of Chaumont, Pontoise, and Poissy, for example, could not be asked to fight beyond the Seine and Oise. Those of Bourges and Dun were confined to Berry, and the men of Lorris could advance no farther than they were able to return within the day.[29] Finally, an intangible, but no less important, benefit of the king's urban program was to expand the royal presence. By according communes and issuing charters of customs, he came directly into contact with townsmen. This enabled him not only to extend his influence into episcopal cities and to places such as Tournai and Dijon within the fiefs of his barons, but also to intensify his presence in his own lands by strengthening ties with these wealthy and influential members of society.

Churches

If Philip's contact with townsmen strengthened his hold on the royal domain, his relations with churchmen afforded him opportunity to extend his influence far beyond. As a consecrated king, he had sworn an oath to defend the church as its special protector and patron. Though this patronage may theoretically have applied to all the churches of the kingdom, in practice it was most effective in the case of those that were considered regalian. We have already seen how the king profited from the revenues of regalian bishoprics and abbeys during their vacancies. In a similar way his regalian rights enabled him to play a role in the choice of new prelates. By threatening to withhold temporal properties from any displeasing candidate, he could influence ecclesiastical elections. Defending the freedom of the church, the Gregorian reformers of the late eleventh and early twelfth centuries had opposed any threat of lay interference in ecclesiastical affairs. They defended the right of individual chapters and monasteries to choose their prelates freely. In the early twelfth century, however, a compromise was attained between the reformers and the French monarchy that permitted cooperation in selecting prelates without violating the outward forms of free elections. The king allowed the chapter the right to elect, and the churchmen allowed the king the right to confer the regalia, or temporal properties. The system required at least a modicum of consensus over the prospective candidate.[30]

The ordinance of 1190 prescribed for the regents the procedures Philip had followed. When a regalian bishopric fell vacant, the canons of the cathedral approached the royal authority to seek a free election, which was granted without opposition. In the interim the regalia were placed in royal hands. After the bishop had been elected and duly consecrated by church authority, the regalia were returned, again without opposition. Although this was the first time that a French king had published the electoral regulations in a general way, the particular procedures were those followed by Louis VII, and were comparable to Henry II's famous Constitutions of Clarendon of 1164, which defined the rules for England and Normandy.[31] From early Capetian times, the seeking of a license to elect—the *licentia eligendi*, as it was called—was standard practice. In 1182 Guillaume, bishop of the troubled see of Auxerre, urged his canons from his deathbed to seek it from the king without delay after he died.[32] By the end of the reign, requests for such licenses were occasionally collected in the royal archives.[33] The canons at Arras (1203), Langres (1203) "remote and on the confines of France and the Empire," and Mâcon (1209) were excused from requesting the license because of the distance, but these were clearly exceptional.[34] As under Louis VII, episcopal consecration that endowed an elected bishop with full sacramental powers was the sign that the vacancy was over and for the return of the regalia.[35]

Before the regalia were finally returned, however, the bishop was required to offer fealty to the king as a guarantee of the military service owed for the fiefs of the regalia. Not prescribed in the ordinance of 1190, this was demanded by Louis VII and was frequently mentioned in Philip's reign.[36] In 1203, for example, the bishop-elect of Arras offered fealty "just as all the bishops of the realm were accustomed to do."[37] Henry II had demanded it in the Constitutions of Clarendon, and when Philip acquired the Angevin's continental sees, he continued the practice. On the retirement of the bishop of Le Mans in 1214, Philip ordered an investigation into the bishop's obligation under Henry, Richard, and John, and thereafter continued to enforce it.[38] Because of the bishop's importance to both the church and the king, Philip emphasized in the ordinance of 1190 that the canons be admonished to choose a prelate "who was both pleasing to God and useful to the kingdom" (*qui Deo placeat et utilis sit regno*). Although this was traditional advice among the early Capetians, Philip kept repeating it whenever he issued licenses. Such cooperation was fundamental to his policy.[39]

With his hands on the regalia, the king was in a position to enforce his will upon the canons of a bishopric if he was not confident that a favorable candidate would be elected. In the opening years of his reign, Louis VII used these means to contest elections that displeased him in the sees of Reims, Poitiers, and Bourges. Upon his return from the crusade in 1149, particularly after the well-known scandal created by the Bourges dispute, Louis no longer intervened directly in episcopal elections.[40] How often Philip Augustus succumbed to this temptation can only be known from those cases that caught chroniclers' attention. In 1182 Philip appears to have threatened to withhold the regalia of Auxerre to persuade the canons, who were reluctant, to elect the brother of Gilles Clément, one of the king's leading counsellors. Although the royal candidate died soon afterwards on a trip to Rome, thus ending the dispute, the king had disposed of a number of vacant prebends in the interim.[41] A similar case occurred at Tournai in 1191 when Philip was absent on the crusade. The canons' election of Pierre, chanter of Paris, to their see was overturned by the archbishop of Reims, then acting as royal regent. The reasons for opposition escape us, but there is little doubt that the king's interests were behind the move, because the canons then proceeded to choose the king's cleric, Etienne, abbot of Sainte-Geneviève, who was certain to obtain royal approval.[42] Clouded with ambiguity though they are, these constitute the only two cases in which Philip Augustus can be accused of intervening directly either in behalf of or against an episcopal candidate. Like his father's similar actions, they occurred while he was still young.

As can be seen from the electoral results, Louis's renunciation of direct interference in episcopal elections did not mean that the chapters chose men who were unsatisfactory to the king. Whether or not a particular bishop was well disposed towards the king cannot be determined with certainty, but we may assume in general that men allied by blood or marriage ties to the king or his close entourage would have been considered desirable candidates. By the end of Louis's reign, the French sees had chosen over a score of bishops who were closely tied to the king. That most of these were elected after Louis's return from the crusade indicates that this informal policy of cooperation was more useful in promoting royal interests than direct intervention.[43]

The extent to which the policy of choosing bishops "pleasing to both God and the king" continued into the first decade of Philip Augustus's reign can be measured by comparing the bishops of regalian sees in office in November 1179 with those elected by the time of the king's departure in 1190. Of the twenty-five bishops presiding over regalian sees in 1179, only four (16 percent) had close ties to royalty.[44] They included Philippe, bishop of Beauvais, a member of the Capetian family of Dreux and the king's nephew; the celebrated Guillaume, archbishop of Reims, brother to the queen; Guy, archbishop of Sens, from the Noyers family, who was linked by marriage to the royal family; and Manassé, bishop of Orléans, a son of the royal butler and member of the Garlande family, which had dominated the royal entourage under Louis VI. In contrast to these "royal" candidates were thirteen (52 percent) "local" bishops who were either chosen directly from the chapter or had close ties with local barons. Although these categories were not mutually exclusive, because multiple influences could operate in the case of the same bishop, it is clear that those who possessed some bond with the king were in a distinct minority as compared with those whose election can only be explained in terms of local influence.[45]

In the decade preceding 1190, seventeen elections were held in the regalian sees, of which six successful candidates (35 percent) claimed connections with the monarch.[46] These included four related to the royal family, of whom Henri, bishop of Orléans, brother of Philippe de Dreux, and Henri, archbishop of Bourges, a royal cousin from the Sully family, were noteworthy. Renaud, bishop of Chartres (Bar and Moucon family), and Rotrou, bishop of Châlons-sur-Marne (Perche family), in addition to being royal cousins, had also both held the treasureship of the royal abbey of Saint-Martin of Tours, which was under royal patronage. Although Philip did not succeed in imposing his choice at Auxerre by direct intervention in 1182, the canons nonetheless proceeded to choose a "royal" candidate when they elected Hugues de Noyers, who was from a royal family with royal marriage ties. Finally, Noyon selected Etienne, the son of Gautier the royal chamberlain. These elections brought about a considerable increase in the number of "royal" bishops, and only five (29 percent) can be clearly attributed to local influence, a marked decline. In the opening decade of Philip's reign, therefore, the chapters of regalian sees were even more disposed to elect men pleasing to the king than under his father. Louis VII's policy of uncoerced cooperation worked still more advantageously for his son.

The twenty-five regalian sees, consisting of four archbishoprics (Reims, Sens, Bourges, and Tours) and twenty-one bishoprics, offered Philip Augustus not only occasional income but also extension of royal influence.[47] As in the case of towns receiving royal charters, some of these— Paris, Orléans, Sens, Senlis, and Laon—intensified the king's hold on the royal domain. Amiens, Thérouanne, Arras, and Tournai helped to prepare the way for Philip's intended acquisitions in Picardie and Artois. The regalian bishoprics were concentrated to the north and east of Paris in the ecclesiastical provinces of Reims, Sens, and Lyon (although the see of Lyon itself was outside the kingdom). They extended from Tournai in the north to Langres in the east to Clermont in the south and Tours in the west. At their peripheries they introduced the royal presence into neighboring fiefdoms: Tournai in Flanders; Reims, Troyes, and Chartres in the great Champagne complex; and Tours in the Touraine, a bastion of Angevin power.

In addition to the regalian bishoprics, Louis VII had accorded charters to distant sees that he placed under royal protection against the incursions of local barons. Since most of these sees lay to the south in the outlying province of Narbonne, far beyond the royal domain, the practical effect of this "protection" was minimal, but it did establish an intangible bond between the king and these bishoprics.[48] Philip continued his father's policy in the south in 1188 by confirming the regalia of the bishop of Lodève in perpetuity and forbidding local lords the right to despoil.[49] Although not a clear case, the see of Le Puy at the southeastern limits of the province of Bourges may also have enjoyed this "protected" status. In 1188 Philip appeared in the town, confirmed the concessions of his father, and placed it under royal jurisdiction.[50] Preoccupied with the Flemish and the English during the opening decade of his reign, however, Philip Augustus paid less attention to the southern sees than his father.

Given the importance of bishoprics, Philip was understandably sensitive to any proposed alterations in the ecclesiastical organization of the kingdom. By the twelfth century, France was composed of nine ecclesiastical provinces, each presided over by a metropolitan or archbishop.[51] Though the archbishop did not differ significantly from other bishops of his province, he provided nominal leadership within the province and was usually responsible for confirming the elections of his bishops and performing their consecration. The only province in which this organization was contested was Tours, where the bishops of Brittany claimed immunity from the jurisdiction of the archbishop. Since the ninth century, the Bretons had expressed their political independence from the Franks by elevating the bishop of Dol to metropolitan status and by seeking a Breton province separate from Tours. These schemes were encouraged by Henry II, who wished to isolate Brittany from the French influence of Tours.

Since the question of Dol's metropolitan status had not been settled by a papal decision, the church of Dol revived its claims during the first years of Philip's reign, undoubtedly testing the strength of the young king. When Pope Lucius III appointed ecclesiastical judges to hear the dispute in 1184–1185,[52] he elicited protests from both the archbishop of Tours and the king himself. In three letters composed in 1185 by Etienne, abbot of Sainte-Geneviève, the king defended Tours's metropolitan jurisdiction on political grounds. Since Tours, including the Breton bishoprics, had always belonged to the king and his ancestors, any attempt to separate them destroyed the integrity of the French kingdom and incited bloodshed between the king and the western princes. Succumbing to literary temptation, Etienne was unable to refrain from punning on the name of the pretender: Dol was the fraud (*dolus*) and grief (*dolor*) of France.[53] The king argued for tactical delays in the final decision. In 1185 he retained the archbishop of Tours by his side because of threats from the count of Flanders, the Breton princes, and the emperor. In 1186–1187 he requested another year's postponement, and in 1191 Queen Adèle, now regent, pleaded that no decision be taken until the king's return.[54] When the energetic Innocent III became pope in 1198, a final resolution of the controversy was attained.[55] A compromise that would, according to the chronicler Roger of Howden, have allowed Dol metropolitan status with two suffragans and would have permitted Tours primacy over Dol with authority to consecrate the archbishops of Dol, was flatly refused.[56] In the end, in 1199, the pope denied Dol archepiscopal rank and ordered its submission to Tours along with the other Breton bishoprics. In rehearsing the arguments of both sides, Innocent agreed with Tours's contention that since Brittany had always been subject to the authority of Tours, the Breton princes had merely advanced Dol's pretensions to contest the authority of the French king.[57] Writing directly to Philip Augustus, he requested the king to defend the now confirmed jurisdiction of Tours.[58] When the case was reopened in the 1180s, and in 1199 when it was finally adjudicated, the direct overlord of Brittany was not Philip Augustus but the English king. From the beginning, however, Philip defended the integrity of the province of Tours to buttress the unity of his kingdom.

Formulating traditional Capetian practice, Philip's ordinance of 1190 prescribed the same regulations for electing regalian abbots as for regalian bishops. When a regalian abbey fell vacant, the monks sought permission from the king to elect a new abbot, which was accorded without objection. After the monks had chosen a prelate pleasing to God and useful to the kingdom and he had been consecrated or blessed, the king returned the regalia without dispute.[59] Five years earlier, Philip reconfirmed to the bishop of Senlis another established procedure of his father that granted the bishop the exclusive right to install regalian abbots throughout the kingdom.[60] As with bishops, this procedure of seeking a royal license to elect (*licentia eligendi*) persisted throughout the reign. Towards its close, the chancery clerks began preserving such requests in the royal archives as they had episcopal requests.[61] In those that have survived, a slight variation appears. At times the monastery merely notified the king of the election and requested his approval, after which the regalia were returned.[62] Despite this occasional modification, it is nonetheless clear that regalian abbots were elected throughout the reign according to the general procedures formulated in 1190. What role the king played in monastic elections during the first decade cannot be determined because of lack of evidence. No report of his direct intervention has come to light, and neither is the documentation sufficient to evaluate the election results, as is possible for the bishops. It may be suspected that the king's interest and participation in the selection of regalian abbots was the same as for bishops.

Lack of documentation also hinders any effort to assess the proportion of regalian abbeys during the first decade. Whereas most English and Norman monasteries were considered regalian, this was not the case in Capetian France.[63] To distinguish specifically regalian monasteries from all others, Philip employed the term *abbatia regalis* in the ordinance of 1190.[64] It is unclear, however, what factors defined an abbey as regalian. Were they a royal foundation; control over the regalia and elections during vacancies; royal intervention in reforming the monastery, confirming privileges, and promising protection; or merely receipt of a royal charter? Faced with a variety of possibilities, modern historians have often resorted to the noncommittal term "royal" to convey a combination of factors. Even if we could agree on what precisely defined a regalian monastery, we are further hampered by the fragmentary nature of the sources. Whereas bishoprics were relatively few and are readily identified, monasteries were much more numerous and are identifiable only through the haphazard survival of charters that often offer only meagre information. For these reasons, historians of early Capetian France have compiled lists of royal abbeys that differ appreciably from one another. According to best estimates, Louis VII held no fewer than thirty, and in all likelihood more than sixty-five, "royal" abbeys. These were concentrated mainly in the royal domain, but they included houses as far north as Saint-Josse-sur-Mer and as far south as Tournus and Manglieu.[65] Although we may assume that Philip Augustus inherited most of them, it is difficult to confirm this.

Between 1204 and 1212 a cleric in the royal chancery compiled a list of nineteen churchmen in Register A whom he labelled *abbates regales*. When it was recopied into Register C in 1212, ten more names were added, but the adjective *regales* was omitted, perhaps in recognition of the difficulty of defining a regalian abbey.[66] When examined closely these two lists are found to consist exclusively of Benedictine houses of ancient foundation.[67] They were most likely incomplete even for the first decade because they omit celebrated Benedictine monasteries known to have been royal from charter evidence of Louis VII's reign.[68] Moreover, they could have included Benedictine houses for which charter evidence of their regalian status was lacking.[69] Though the chancery lists are not reliable in indicating the exact number of regalian abbeys during Philip's first decade, they do identify a representative core of ancient Benedictine foundations such as Saint-Denis and Saint Germain-des-Prés around Paris, Saint-Benoît and Saint-Mesmin in the Loire valley, and Saint-

Riquier and Saint-Josse-sur-Mer in the north.[70] In addition to these Bene-dictine houses, Philip claimed abbeys of regular canons (canons who lived under a monastic rule) among his regalian monasteries. In 1189 and 1190 he identified Notre-Dame and Sainte-Croix (both in Etampes), Saint-Vincent and Saint-Frambaud (both in Senlis), and Sainte-Geneviève of Paris as regalian houses.[71] Since these were already known as regalian under Louis VII, we may guess that other such houses also retained that status under Philip. It seems safe to presume, therefore, that the number of regalian monasteries during the first decade of Philip's rule was ap-proximately the same as under his father.

Philip continued to issue royal charters of protection both to distant bishoprics and to monasteries throughout the kingdom. The phrasing of these charters usually instructed the royal officers to take a specific house under their protection and custody and to defend its rights. Although our knowledge of such documents depends on the archives and cartu-laries of individual monasteries, enough (fifty-six) have survived to in-dicate some patterns.[72] Philip began issuing these charters at the outset and continued to the end of his reign. A significant proportion (eighteen out of fifty-six, or approximately 33 percent) were drawn up during the first decade, indicating eagerness to obtain support from the new king. Philip's preparations to depart on crusade also elicited renewed activity as churches sought written evidence of royal protection during the king's absence. Recipients included Benedictines, regular canons, and others, as well as regalian monasteries. When new lands entered the royal domain or were cleared of the English, celebrated houses, such as Bec, Saint-Wandrille, and Fécamp in Normandy, and Saint-Maixent in Poitou, re-ceived Capetian protection. Most noteworthy, however, were the Cister-cians, who during the course of the reign received more than half (thirty) of the extant charters. As early as 1181, Pontigny received a royal charter. In 1187 Philip commanded his *prévôts* and *baillis* to defend the property of all Cistercians in their territories. Then in 1190, on the eve of the crusade, he named thirteen Cistercian houses for royal safeguard, a list that was repeated in virtually identical terms in 1221. Louis VII had en-joyed cordial relations with the Cistercians, especially the influential Abbot Bernard de Clairvaux. Philip Augustus now also declared himself a solicitous protector of this new and influential monastic order.

Had Philip not returned alive from the crusade in 1191, his brief reign would scarcely be distinguishable from that of Louis VII. The young monarch had followed closely in his father's footsteps, not only in choosing officials and managing the royal domain, but also in dealing with townsmen and churchmen. Like both his father and grandfather before him, he issued a stream of charters to confirm the individual customs and privileges of townsmen. Although equivocal at first about encouraging communes, he had abandoned these hesitations by the end of the decade. In broad outline, royal policy towards towns remained constant throughout the reign. Adopting Louis VII's ecclesiastical reforms, Philip also granted regalian bishoprics and abbeys freedom to elect prelates in exchange for their choosing candidates favorable to the king, a policy of cooperation succinctly formulated in the ordinance of 1190. These ecclesiastical liberties became the fundamental policy on which Philip imposed further innovations during succeeding decades. The ordinance of 1190, as we shall see, did announce radical reforms for the period of the regency, which required the king's return for their full implementation and development, but by the eve of his departure Philip's actions had created no new patterns in government. The basic contours of government inherited from the early Capetians in fact persisted throughout the reign. The changes introduced in 1190 were not produced by abolishing the old, but by building on the existing foundations. Such was the nature of medieval change.

PART TWO

The Decisive Decade,

1190–1203

Narrative:
The Ill Fortunes of War

The Third Crusade

The Third Crusade summoned not only Philip Augustus and Richard but almost all of the major barons of France, including the duke of Burgundy and the counts of Flanders, Troyes, Blois, Sancerre, Dreux, Nevers, Clermont, Ponthieu, and Perche. In addition, Philip was accompanied by the bishops of Chartres and Langres and his influential cousin, Philippe de Dreux, bishop of Beauvais. The only baron of any consequence who remained behind was the distant count of Toulouse. The regency over the royal lands was confided to the king's mother, Adèle, and her brother Guillaume, archbishop of Reims. Although the departure of the kings and barons left France a moment of peace, the two monarchs carried their mutual competition off to the Holy Land. The crusade was a frustrating experience for Philip Augustus in particular. At every stage he arrived first, unobtrusively took command, and laid careful plans, only to be upstaged by the later appearance of Richard, whose greater wealth and flamboyant manner generated disturbances and raised rival objectives. In terms of posterior fame, however, Richard's greatest achievement was to have captured the imagination of the contemporary chroniclers. In all aspects of the crusade the major historians of the time were partial to the English king.[1]

After embarking in the late summer of 1190 from the ports of Genoa and Marseilles respectively, Philip and Richard were obliged to wait out the winter storms of the Mediterranean at the Sicilian town of Messina. The French king quietly appeared at Messina with one ship. His vassal the English king arrived a week later accompanied by the blare of trumpets and his entire fleet. Establishing himself at a wooden castle outside the city walls with a name provocative to the Greeks (Mategrifon: "Curb on the Greeks"), Richard prepared to settle his differences with the Sicilian king over the succession to the island kingdom. His soldiers and sailors inevitably quarrelled with the local inhabitants, and Richard sacked the town and extorted concessions from the king. Amidst these disturbances, Philip played the peacemaker, but he also had grievances against the English. The chief among these concerned Richard's marriage plans. Although Richard was still officially affianced to Philip's half-sister Alix, from whom he held Gisors as dowry, he had sent his mother Eleanor of Aquitaine to search for another bride. They decided on Berengaria of Navarre, whose father, King Sancho VI, was a potential ally in the southern provinces of Aquitaine. The imminent arrival of the prospective bride in the company of Eleanor and the count of Flanders required an urgent settlement of Alix's fate. Philip was ready to demand the return of Gisors and the Norman Vexin as the price for releasing Richard from his promise to Alix, but the count of Flanders, the first to arrive, persuaded him to modify his terms. In the end the kings agreed that Richard would be released from Alix in return for 10,000 marks of silver. This treaty of Messina of March 1191 contained other terms involving the Vexin, Berry, and Aquitaine, and attempted to define the feudal relations between the two monarchs. Since most of those provisions were abrogated by subsequent actions, they can be ignored. The only lasting result of the agreement was to free Alix.[2] In order to avoid a humiliating meeting with Richard's new bride and the dowager queen Eleanor, a woman the Capetians preferred to forget, Philip set sail for the Holy Land on 30 March 1191.[3]

The first objective of the Third Crusade was to expel the Moslems from Acre, a key seaport on the Palestinian coast and a vital link in the crusaders' supply lines. When Philip Augustus arrived at Acre on 20 April 1191, the crusaders had already laid siege to the city, which was situated on a peninsula. Although numerous, the crusaders were divided into competing groups. By asserting his superior rank, the French king was able to assume leadership over the westerners and to build rams, catapults, and towers, supervise miners, and direct plans for a systematic siege. In the meantime, Richard had diverted his journey from Messina to Cyprus, where he had other disputes to settle. In characteristic fashion, he did not leave the island until he had subdued it and carried off enormous booty. Although his final arrival at Acre in June offered welcome reinforcements, the two kings lost little time before they were quarrelling again. In accordance with a previous agreement, Philip demanded half of the plunder of Cyprus, which Richard naturally refused. Benefiting from the spoils of Sicily and Cyprus, the English king could outshine his French overlord by offering higher wages to his soldiers. In addition, a dispute between two western families over the kingship of Jerusalem further divided Philip and Richard. Philip supported Conrad of Montferrat, lord of Tyre, certainly the more capable and viable candidate, whereas Richard backed Guy de Lusignan, the ineffectual present king, whose claim had been weakened by the death of his wife, from whom he had inherited the crown. To aggravate the situation further, both Philip and Richard fell sick at Acre of a fever called *arnoldia*, which confined them to their tents and stripped them of their hair and nails.[4]

Despite these irritations the besiegers nonetheless made progress. Since the defenders were blockaded by sea, they faced land assaults with dwindling resources. In the main, the French commanded the siege engines while the English thwarted Saladin's attempts to relieve the town by land. The French opened the first breach in the walls on 3 July, but were repulsed with heavy losses, among them Alberic Clément, a royal marshal. An English attempt a week later was also unsuccessful. Cut off from the outside, the defenders recognized their position as hopeless, however, and they finally surrendered on 12 July. After the elation of victory, Philip Augustus announced a decision he had long contemplated: despite the fact that Acre was only the first of the crusaders' objectives, he would return immediately to France. This precipitous desertion of the crusading cause was undoubtedly motivated by several factors: the frustrating rivalry with Richard, which brought him no glory, recent news of the sickness of his infant heir at Paris, his own sickness, and, most important, the death of the count of Flanders at Acre on 1 June 1191. This reopened the delicate question of the Flemish succession, which Philip had prepared with great care. So important a matter required his immediate and personal attention.[5]

After assigning command of the French forces to the duke of Burgundy, resolving the Montferrat-Lusignan dispute over the crown of Jerusalem, and swearing to Richard to protect the latter's lands in France until forty days after the Angevin's return, Philip left Acre on 31 July 1191. Accompanied by the bishops of Chartres and Langres and the count of Nevers, he passed through Rome, where he complained to the pope with little effect of the injuries he had suffered from Richard. He reached Paris on 27 December, where he was given a festive welcome. Shortly thereafter he laid upon the altar of the abbey of Saint-Denis, his patron saint, a costly silk in thanksgiving for his safe return. His gratitude was well deserved because the rigors of the journey, the eastern sun, and the dangers of the siege at Acre had not failed to take their toll of the French baronage. Among the hundreds who died on the Third Crusade were the most important vassals of the French king, including not only Philippe, count of Flanders, but also the brothers Thibaut, count of Blois and royal seneschal; Henri, count of Troyes; and Etienne, count of Sancerre. Philip Augustus himself had survived, but he had left the major barons of his father's generation buried in the Syrian sands.[6]

The Flemish Inheritance

During the decade following his return, Philip was preoccupied with three major political issues: the Flemish inheritance; his plans to remarry to reinforce the royal dynasty; and his competition with the Angevins, his dominating concern. Whereas the first two were relatively discrete and can be treated separately, the last not only implicated the first two concerns but involved the pope and emperor as well.

Since it had been clear for some time that the count of Flanders would remain without children, his death at Acre merely set in motion the previously established arrangements for the Flemish succession.[7] The king could now take possession of Artois and parts of Vermandois to which the count was entitled only for his lifetime. Philip Augustus lost no time in dispatching a letter from Acre to the nobility of Péronne in the Vermandois region announcing the count's death and his own hereditary claims. Promising to respect their customs, he commanded them to offer fealty to the regent, Archbishop Guillaume, and to other lords commissioned to receive their submission.[8] In all likelihood the archbishop of Reims also took possession of Artois at the same time.

After inevitable maneuverings by all parties, a final settlement was achieved shortly after the king's return.[9] Three chief claimants sought to divide the count of Flanders's inheritance: Baudouin, count of Hainaut; Aliénor, countess of Beaumont; and the king. After payment to the king of a relief of 5,000 marks of silver, the count of Hainaut was designated heir to the county of Flanders by virtue of his marriage to Marguerite, Count Philippe's sister. Aliénor, now the wife of Mathieu, count of Beaumont-sur-Oise, claimed Valois and Vermandois as the sole surviving heir of the count of Vermandois in accordance with the terms of the treaty of 1185. In a royal charter enacted early in 1192, Philip Augustus reconfirmed her general claims to Valois and Vermandois and assigned her immediate possession of Saint-Quentin, formerly held by the count of Flanders. What had only been implicit in the treaty of 1185 was now made explicit: the king was to be her heir should she die without issue. His expectations could scarcely be concealed since the countess was still childless after four marriages. In exchange for reconfirming Aliénor's inheritance, the king received Péronne, formerly held by the count of Flanders, as well as confirmation of Montdidier and Roye, which he had possessed since 1185. For these concessions he paid the countess 13,000 *livres*.[10]

Beyond profiting from the Vermandois inheritance, Philip Augustus took possession of Artois, claimed in the name of his son, Louis, through Queen Isabelle's dowry. At this point Artois included Saint-Omer and Aire[11] and suzerainty over the counties of Lens, Guines, Saint-Pol, and, most important, Boulogne. The heiress of this last fief, located on the Channel between Flanders and Normandy, had been abducted and forcibly married by Renaud de Dammartin, one of the king's protégés. Now that Philip possessed the Artois, he could regularize this situation as Renaud's immediate lord. Early in 1192, he received the homage of Renaud and his wife, but exacted from them possession of Lens and 7,000 *livres* of Arras above the normal relief. These harsh terms were undoubtedly the price of overlooking Renaud's unorthodox methods.[12]

Philip's prompt attention to the Flemish inheritance had rewarded him well. He had reiterated his rights to the full succession of Vermandois, which required only the death of the countess for final realization. Of immediate importance, he took possession of lands to which he previously had had only theoretical claim. Péronne provided strategic access to the whole complex of Artois, which now included Lens, Saint-Omer, and Aire on the north. These lands were now added to the royal domain but, as in the past, they were only as secure as the king's strength to defend them. As appeared during the next decade, an independent count of Flanders supported by an energetic duke of Normandy would render their possession precarious.

Ingeborg of Denmark and Agnès de Méran

Philip's second major preoccupation upon his return from the crusade was the fragility of the Capetian dynastic succession. Queen Isabelle was dead, and the king's sole surviving heir was Louis, a child of four, who had only recently escaped death from serious illness. As a responsible monarch, Philip required a new wife to ensure further heirs. This was the clear and underlying principle of the royal matrimonial policy for the next decade, yet its means of execution defy rational explanation and can at best be explained by Philip's personal proclivities and neuroses.

The enigmatic story of the king's matrimonial plans begins with the person Philip chose as his next bride.[13] All that is known is that by 1193 the French king was negotiating with King Knud VI of Denmark for the hand of his eighteen-year-old sister, Ingeborg. Why a Danish princess was chosen among so many possible candidates is difficult to answer. During the twelfth century, exchanges took place between France and Denmark because the Danes, like many others in northern Europe, were attracted to the Paris schools. Conversely, a certain Guillaume, canon of Sainte-Geneviève in Paris, was called to Denmark to become abbot of Ebelholt. He was the chief advocate of the marriage at the Danish court, seconded at the French court by Brother Bernard de Vincennes, Philip's ecclesiastical advisor. The underlying political rationale, however, is less cogent. The English chroniclers, who were acutely sensitive to Philip's aggressions against Normandy during Richard's imprisonment, saw the marriage as preparation for invading England. According to William of Newburgh, Philip wanted to acquire the Danish claims to England and the Danish fleet and army to support them.[14] Even if this explanation was not purely a matter of English jitters, the project itself could have been little more than bluff. The validity of Danish claims to the English throne in the late twelfth century is dubious. The services of the Danish fleet and army—of whatever they may have consisted at the time—were categorically refused by King Knud. And surely, the conquest of England was hardly possible while Normandy remained faithful to Richard. Other political considerations, moreover, opposed the marriage. By this time the Danes were clearly allied to the Guelf party in the Empire and opposed to the Hohenstaufens, whom, as we shall see, Philip favored. The French king's only tangible benefit from this matrimonial alliance was a dowry gift of 10,000 marks of silver.[15]

Whatever the reasons for the Danish marriage, they were quickly overshadowed by a succession of even more puzzling events. After concluding an agreement with Knud, Etienne, bishop of Noyon, the head of the French envoys, brought the Danish princess to France. Philip met her for the first time at Amiens on 14 August 1193 and married her that very day. On the next, the feast of the Assumption of the Virgin, the bride and her husband were crowned by Archbishop Guillaume of Reims. During the ceremonies the king became pale, nervous, and restless, and could barely await their conclusion. Immediately thereafter, he separated from Ingeborg, dispatched her to the monastery of Saint-Maur-des-Fossés near Paris, and announced his intention of seeking an annulment. These precipitous and unexpected actions provoked immediate consternation among contemporary observers. Virtually all of the chroniclers and commentators of the two following decades defend the queen and protest that her beauty and virtue left Philip no grounds for complaint. His reasons must have been personal and sexual, however, because he steadfastly refused to see her for seven years. Even afterwards, when severe ecclesiastical pressure finally forced him to meet her again, he never consented to restore her conjugal rights despite the papacy's tireless efforts in her behalf. His official justification for seeking an annulment from Ingeborg at this time was close parentage within the church's prohibited degrees, an excuse commonly advanced in the twelfth century. (Philip had only to remember his father's separation from Eleanor of Aquitaine.)[16] On 5 November a council was convened at Compiègne under the presidency of Archbishop Guillaume of Reims at which fifteen bishops, counts, and knights declared under oath that Ingeborg was related to Philip's first wife Isabelle within the fourth degree of parentage. It was hardly a fair hearing for Ingeborg, because eight of the oathtakers were related to the king, and two others, Gautier the Chamberlain and his son, the bishop of Noyon, were loyal to the royal household. The council declared Philip legally separated from the queen because of the canonical defect of affinity as established by oath. But even the genealogy by which the parentage was computed was faulty, a fact the royal chancery later acknowledged.[17]

Sequestered in a royal monastery, unable to understand French, and deprived of all contact with her countrymen, the young queen refused to accept the council's decision and appealed her case to the pope, expressing her plight in vivid if crude Latin: *Mala Francia, Roma*! Despite the pleas from the Danish royal envoys, who pointed out the defects in the French case, the aged Pope Celestine III was slow to respond. Not until 1196 did he dispatch to France two cardinal legates who appointed a commission of French churchmen and convened a council of prelates at Paris in May to judge the affair. These actions had no effect on the king because, as Rigord phrases it, the churchmen were "like dogs fearing to bark for their hides."[18] For his part, Philip hastened to seek another bride, allowing no doubt about his resolve to marry again for the sake of producing additional heirs. After several futile attempts to attract new brides, who were doubtless frightened off by Philip's now unsavory reputation, he finally found a willing candidate from the Rhineland in Agnès, daughter of Bertold de Méran. Although this prospective marriage was also contaminated by consanguinity, the bride's family's politics were acceptable because Agnès's father had accompanied Frederick Barbarossa to the Holy Land and was a staunch supporter of the Hohenstaufen party in the Empire. In June 1196, only a month after the Paris council failed to dissuade the king, Philip married Agnès de Méran, who before her death in 1201 bore two of the desired children, a daughter, Marie, and a son, Philip. If only the technical difficulties with Ingeborg could be arranged, Philip Augustus had at last succeeded in reinforcing the royal lineage.[19]

Whereas in the past royalty and high nobility had been able to discard inconvenient wives by annulments based on close parentage, Philip Augustus was to discover that he could not expect the same results with Ingeborg. The chief reason for this difference was the appearance of Innocent III on the papal throne in 1198. Young, ambitious, and energetic, unlike his predecessor, he set as his highest goal the extension of papal influence through assertion of supreme authority to judge all matters within the church's competence. Greatly enlarged by the canonists of the twelfth century, these included the whole realm of matrimony, to which Philip's divorce and remarriage were an affront. In his very first letter to the French king, the pope admonished Philip to dismiss Agnès and restore Ingeborg to her rightful position as queen and wife.[20] Only then could Philip submit his plea for annulment to the judgment of papal authority. When, as in the past, Philip ignored these warnings, Innocent empowered his legate in France, Peter of Capua, to apply sanctions against the king, including the ultimate weapon of laying interdict upon the kingdom. The legate proceeded to call a council of French prelates at Dijon, and after the king failed to produce a satisfactory response, an interdict was announced for 13 January 1200.[21]

A general interdict, with its threat of closing churches and suspending religious services throughout the kingdom, created so many difficulties that Philip was obliged to take the papal demands seriously and to dispatch envoys to negotiate a speedy end to the sanctions. On his side, Innocent also desired a quick resolution because the French church was suffering the pillaging of the goods of prelates observing the interdict by royal officials. In the complex negotiations that followed, the pope repeated his conditions: if the king exiled Agnès beyond the borders of the realm and reconciled himself to Ingeborg, his plea for an annulment based on consanguinity could be submitted to the church's judgment. As before, Philip complained that he was being treated more harshly than his father, Louis VII, or Emperor Frederick Barbarossa, or even his contemporary John of England, all of whom had received separations with little trouble. Nonetheless, he was willing to make accommodations in his own way. He asked his uncle, the archbishop of Reims, who had presided over the divorce of 1193, whether the papal allegations that the former trial had been a farce were true. When his uncle acknowledged as much, Philip snapped back: "Then you are a fool for having pronounced such a judgment."[22] Having thus found a scapegoat and preserved his good faith, the king was able to tolerate a new trial, but he complained of the unsuitability of the legate, Peter of Capua. Innocent proposed a new legate, the cardinal Octavian, who was known and acceptable to the king. As to the preliminary conditions, Philip agreed to remove Agnès from his court, but since she was expecting her second child, he would not exile her from the kingdom. He also consented to a public meeting with Ingeborg before the legate and other churchmen, but this took place at the isolated manor of Saint-Léger-en-Yvelines, from which he then sent her directly to the royal castle at Etampes. The ceremonial reconciliation with Ingeborg at Saint-Léger, accompanied by an oath that Philip would not separate from her without the church's judgment, brought the interdict to an end in September 1200. A subsequent trial over the marriage was set for Soissons in the near future. By imposing the interdict, Innocent had won an important victory of principle. He had forced Philip Augustus to submit his marriage to the judgment of the church. But Philip had not sacrificed much of practical consequence to have the interdict lifted. Agnès remained close by, while Ingeborg was virtually imprisoned in Etampes, with her husband as inaccessible as ever. Meanwhile Philip nourished the hope of winning his case in a new trial.[23]

At the council of Soissons, held in March 1201 to pronounce upon the royal marriage, the king wagered his success on two conditions: first, that his case would be heard by judges favorable to him, and, second, that a judgment would be rendered quickly and without further appeal so as to settle once and for all the question of his annulment. On both accounts Philip was disappointed. Although Cardinal Octavian was well known to and considered well disposed toward the king, he was later joined by a second cardinal, John of Saint-Paul, a complete stranger to the royal party. When John refused gifts from the king, Philip began to fear his impartiality. Moreover, there began to be delays in the proceedings. Before the second judge's arrival the Danes presented their arguments, and when a decision was not reached, they registered an appeal and departed, leaving Ingeborg alone without counsel to face the king and his advisors. In the presence of Octavian, now joined by John, Ingeborg's defense was conducted by local clerics, who introduced delaying tactics. After two weeks, when no decision had been reached and the second judge appeared little disposed to the royal cause, Philip suddenly left the assembly, taking Ingeborg with him. In justifying his actions to the pope later, Philip claimed that he had hoped for a clear and decisive resolution, but the judges and the queen had obstructed the affair by multiplying appeals and delays. Since it had become clear that he could not be assured of a favorable decision, he preferred to leave his case unresolved.[24]

This time, however, other events came to the king's aid. In July 1201, not long after Philip's departure from Soissons, Agnès died at Poissy after having been delivered of a son, Philip. The king buried her with great honor in the church of Saint-Corentin at Mantes, to which he made generous bequests. Agnès had served Philip well by producing a second male heir. By dying at this crucial moment, she moreover released him from his irregular marital status. No longer bigamous, the king had a further goal—to legitimize his new offspring. Once again, Philip acceded to the pope's authority and requested Innocent to declare young Marie and Philip his legitimate children. Reminding the pope that he had no heir besides Louis, Philip argued that he had believed the annulment of his marriage to Ingeborg to be valid, and that therefore his marriage to Agnès had been in good faith. Here also politics assisted the royal cause. For some time Innocent had attempted to enlist the French king's support of his candidate in the forthcoming election of a German emperor. The pope was then backing Otto of Brunswick, the leader of the Guelf party and nephew of King Richard of England, a candidate the French opposed for many reasons. Innocent nonetheless hoped to be able to persuade Philip Augustus, and undoubtedly he saw the king's request as an opportunity to win favor. In November 1201, therefore, recognizing the utility of such action to the Capetian kingdom, the pope declared Philip's children by Agnès to be legitimate heirs, but without prejudice to the dispute with Ingeborg.[25]

The quarrel between Ingeborg and Philip was by no means over, and for all his trouble Innocent received no French help in the imperial election. The papal bull of November 1201 did, however, bring the first phase of Philip's marital difficulties to a conclusion that was satisfactory to both the pope and the king. For the second time in a little more than a year, Innocent had obtained acknowledgment of his final authority in matrimonial matters. For his part, Philip had attained his goal of procuring a second legitimate son to ensure the survival of the Capetian dynasty. To be sure, Ingeborg's unresolved claims as queen and wife remained to trouble Philip for another dozen years, but they persisted as an irritation, not as an urgent and fundamental problem.

John Against Richard

Philip Augustus's supreme task upon his return from the crusade was to dislodge the Angevins from their continental possessions. King Richard's and King John's determined resistance to this attack resulted in a long and confusing decade of warfare between 1191 and 1203. Since no decisive battles were risked, most of the fighting centered on sieges of castles, followed by fragile truces. Though some of these truces were transformed into signed peaces, they were all abrogated soon afterwards. The ravages of war were accompanied by hailstorms, inclement weather, and crop failures that in turn produced famines and rises in the price of foodstuffs. Contemporaries believed that the days of Pharaoh had returned and that God himself was punishing the country for the wickedness of the kings.[26] As in the past, military operations were centered on the Vexin, extending towards Normandy, and on Berry, extending towards the south, but they also penetrated as far to the southwest as Limousin in Aquitaine. The count of Flanders and his neighboring vassals were increasingly embroiled in the hostilities, and as the intensity of the fighting increased, the pope, the German emperor, and even the hapless Ingeborg were also involved. Philip's persistent efforts were frustrated by failures and misfortunes, alleviated only by occasional strokes of luck. Informing all of his tactics, however, was the traditional Capetian policy of playing one Angevin against another, a technique Philip had perfected during the first decade of his reign. The French campaign against the Angevins can therefore be divided into two phases: the deployment of John against King Richard and, when John became king, the deployment of his nephew Arthur against John.

After the victory at Acre, Richard maintained the crusading momentum by retaking the major seaports down the Palestinian coast to Jaffa. Although he thereby succeeded in reestablishing the Latin kingdom of Jerusalem, he was not able to recapture the Holy City itself. Beset by illness and troubled by bickering among the French contingents, he finally decided to negotiate a five-year truce with Saladin that permitted access by Christian pilgrims to Jerusalem (but not to the French crusaders). In October 1192 he set sail for home in hopes of escaping the Mediterranean winter storms. Bad weather, however, forced him ashore at Corfu. Fearing capture by Isaac II, the Greek emperor, Leopold, duke of Austria, and Henry VI, the German emperor, all of whom he had recently antagonized, he tried to elude his enemies by proceeding overland in disguise. But in December he was discovered near Vienna and made prisoner by Leopold, who turned him over to Henry VI. Elated by his prize, the emperor at once informed Philip Augustus and began to treat with Richard for a ransom worthy of his position.[27]

The French king responded to this stroke of fortune with two diplomatic initiatives. He attempted by all means to persuade the emperor to keep Richard in confinement as long as possible. His cousin the bishop of Beauvais, who had returned from the crusade spreading reports that Richard had plotted to assassinate Philip, was dispatched to the imperial court. When his ability to convince lagged, he was followed by the archbishop of Reims, the king's uncle, who was empowered to offer monetary inducements—matching even the amount of the ransom—to have Richard transferred into French hands or further detained in Germany.[28] Closer to home, Philip began negotiating with Richard's younger brother John, count of Mortain, for disposition of the Angevin fiefs. In the early months of 1193, John came to Paris, where he did homage to Philip for Normandy and other Angevin lands. In exchange Philip offered him

6,000 marks in loan and the hand of his sister Alix, along with the recently acquired Artois as dowry.[29] John's overt betrayal of his brother culminated in January 1194 when he sealed a written agreement at Paris consigning to Philip all of Normandy east of the Seine (except for Rouen), Le Vaudreuil, Verneuil, and Evreux. This charter, by which John surrendered the borders of Normandy to the French king, as well as Tours and Loire fiefs, was carefully preserved in the royal archives.[30]

Philip lost no time in following these diplomatic thrusts with military action. In 1192, when Richard was still in the Holy Land, the French king had restrained himself, for the most part, from overtly attacking the lands of a crusader.[31] But as soon as Richard was in a German prison, Philip was no longer hindered by such scruples. In the spring of 1193 he invaded Normandy, taking Gisors, Neaufles, and Châteauneuf, the major castles along the frontier of the Epte, as well as Gournay, Aumale, and Eu. The great fortress of Gisors was surrendered through the treachery of its castellan. Accompanied by Baudouin of Flanders, Philip proceeded down the Seine to Rouen, but when he met with resistance from the city's defenders, he withdrew.[32] Whether Philip seriously intended to invade England at this point, as the English chroniclers feared, is doubtful, but he was allowed one more season against Normandy in the spring of 1194 because Richard's captors did not release him until February. This time Philip attempted to take possession of the remaining castles John had promised him in January. He took Neuburg, Le Vaudreuil, and Evreux. Confiding Evreux to John's care, he laid siege to the important castle of Verneuil.[33] Philip worked quickly to profit from Richard's captivity, but Gisors, the key to the Vexin, was the only important and lasting conquest of the 1190s.

Having purchased his freedom with a regal ransom of 100,000 marks of silver, Richard returned to England and quickly appeared in Normandy in May 1194 with an army, prepared to redress the balance. The first result of his appearance was John's immediate defection from the French side. Prostrating himself at his brother's feet, John received Richard's forgiveness. This magnanimity he rewarded by betraying the French garrison at Evreux to Richard's forces. Richard himself sped to the rescue of Verneuil and forced Philip to beat a retreat and to abandon costly materials and booty at the siege. The Angevin then turned to the south to attack Tours and once again caught Philip at Fréteval near Vendôme, causing him to leave behind his baggage train loaded with treasure and documents.[34] Amidst these defeats, French successes were limited to retaliating against Evreux and Richard's churches around Tours and to capturing Robert, count of Leicester. A truce negotiated by papal legates in July 1194 did not prevent hostilities from breaking out around Gisors and in Berry the following summer.[35] By January 1196 Richard had regained sufficient ground to encourage Philip to agree to a peace, signed between Gaillon and Le Vaudreuil. In a long and detailed document, Richard allowed Philip to retain the castles of Gisors and Neaufles that he had taken along the Epte, as well as Pacy and other castles along the Norman border belonging to Robert of Leicester. But Philip was obliged to abandon Le Vaudreuil, Evreux, and all of his conquests east of the Seine (except for the Vexin), as well as Issoudun and Graçay in Berry. In the end, therefore, Philip resigned to Richard all the principal conquests (except for Gisors) gained during the latter's captivity.[36]

The peace of Gaillon did not, however, prevent the outbreak of hostilities both following summers. In 1196 and 1197 Philip campaigned against Aumale and Nonancourt to the east and south of Normandy, and Richard made incursions into Brittany, Berry, and the Beauvaisis. On the last expedition his troops captured the Capetian king's cousin Philippe de Dreux, bishop of Beauvais, Richard's old antagonist in Germany. An energetic military captain despite his ecclesiastical dignity, the bishop used his see as a base of operations against Normandy. In defiance of church sanctions, Richard kept the bellicose bishop securely imprisoned at Rouen and later at Chinon.[37] During this period the English king's most important activity was the construction of the great Château Gaillard. Perched high upon a rock above the Seine at a strategic bend in the river, this castle was designed to replace Gisors as the key to the Norman defenses in the Seine valley. Learning from his experiences in the Holy Land, Richard built the most spectacular castle in western Europe. To protect its approaches, he constructed a smaller fortification called Boutavant on a nearby island in the Seine. The chief hindrance to building Gaillard was that its site, named Les Andelys, belonged to Walter, the archbishop of Rouen. In the treaty of January 1196, Richard had promised not to fortify the area. The archbishop opposed Richard's plans by imposing an interdict on the duchy, but the king countered by impressing on the pope the importance of the project for the peace of Normandy. A compromise was finally arranged whereby Andelys was exchanged for the prosperous seaport of Dieppe with all of its revenues. From gallant Château Gaillard, Richard could challenge the French king to threaten Rouen and the heart of Normandy.[38]

By 1196 the contest between the two kings broadened into a search for allies among the great barons. Richard's aggressions against Brittany provoked a contrary reaction among the local nobility, who looked to the French court for help. When Richard demanded custody of his brother Geoffrey's nine-year-old son, who bore the proud Celtic name of Arthur, the Breton clergy confided him to Philip Augustus for safekeeping.[39] The French king also turned his attention to Flanders and the northern barons. Baudouin, count of Hainaut and Flanders, and Philip's former father-in-law, had remained faithful to the royal cause in his later years. At his death towards the end of 1195, he was succeeded by a son of the same name, who had been raised in the German court and was therefore inclined to be more independent. The king attempted to attach the young Baudouin more closely to the Capetian cause by marrying Baudouin's brother, Philippe, marquis of Namur, into the family of Courtenay-Nevers, who were royal cousins, and by insisting on the count's liege homage, except for his obligations to the emperor and the bishop of Liège. Recognizing the concession of Artois, Baudouin likewise conceded the overlordships to the important counties of Boulogne and Guines.[40] In 1195 Philip married his half-sister Alix, Richard's long suffering fiancée, to Guillaume, count of Ponthieu, whose territory also neighbored that of Flanders. The king embellished this wedding with Eu and Arques as dowry and with a loan of 5,000 marks to the bridegroom.[41] All of these measures were designed to draw the Flemish region more securely into the royal orbit. Forced to acquiesce, Baudouin accompanied the king at the siege of Aumale in 1196. Finally, Philip Augustus involved himself in the Limousin, deep within the duchy of Aquitaine, where Richard was constantly at odds with the *vicomte*. In April 1198 Philip promised to aid Adémar, *vicomte* of Limoges, who in turn broke his ties with Richard and allied himself with the French king.[42]

In the competition for allies, however, Philip was outdone by his English rival. Richard benefited both from his deserved renown for open-handed generosity and from Philip's unsavory reputation as a violator of the property of crusaders and a tyrannical husband to spin a web of alliances around the French king. To the south Richard's marriage to Berengaria of Navarre protected his flank. Her brother Sancho had come to Richard's aid in Aquitaine as early as 1192 and had participated in his campaign against Tours in 1194.[43] To strengthen his southern position, Richard resolved his differences with the count of Toulouse and sealed this new alliance in 1196 by giving the latter his sister Joan in marriage.[44] To the west Richard made peace with the count of Blois and the Bretons, thus detaching Arthur from the French king.[45] His greatest successes were, however, in the north, where, offering lavish gifts, Richard made agreements with the counts of Boulogne, Saint-Pol, and Guines. Renaud, count of Boulogne, was an especially noteworthy prize because he owed his entire position to the French king's patronage. Of the northern magnates only the advocate of Béthune and the castellan of Saint-Omer resisted Richard's blandishments and remained faithful to Philip Augustus. The capstone of Richard's alliances was a treaty with Baudouin, count of Hainaut and Flanders, which was formally signed in September 1197. Under threat of economic reprisal as well as promises of gifts, the Flemish count acknowledged that neither he nor Richard would make peace with the king of France without the other's consent. As the French royal historiographer Rigord judged the situation, these English alliances with the counts of Flanders and Boulogne brought great misfortune to the kingdom.[46]

The result of these alliances was to increase military activity in the north. During the summer of 1197, even before the treaty with Richard, Baudouin invaded the Tournaisis, whose episcopal see belonged to the French crown. The subsequent taking of Douai and the siege of Arras finally provoked a response from the French king. Totally unprepared for the campaign, Philip pursued Baudouin deep into Flanders, only to find his supply lines cut by the Flemings, who broke down the bridges. Thus entrapped, Philip had to sue for an embarrassing peace, which he was lucky to obtain. Baudouin's attacks were supported by Renaud de Boulogne, who ravaged French lands. The following year the count of Flanders, accompanied by the counts of Boulogne and Guines, captured Aire and Saint-Omer, comprising the northern borders of Artois.[47] Philip's humiliation in the Flemish campaign of 1197 was matched in 1198 by another in the Vexin at the hands of Richard. While Baudouin was threatening the north, Richard invaded the Vexin and menaced the castles surrounding Gisors. When Philip came to the rescue, Richard caught his army unawares in marching formation and sent him fleeing in disarray for the safety of Gisors. The bridge over the Epte before the gate of Gisors broke under the weight of the heavily armored French knights. At least twenty drowned, and Philip himself was fished from the river. But more important than the personal indignity, hundreds of knights and much equipment fell into the hands of the English.[48]

As the tempo of the war quickened in 1197–1198, two external events contributed to expand the scope of conflict to include parties outside the kingdom. The first was the unforeseen death in September 1197 of the emperor Henry VI, who left only a three-year-old son, Frederick, to succeed him. Despite Henry's attempts to secure an orderly succession, Hohenstaufen hopes for controlling the imperial throne were thus dealt a serious blow. In the ensuing confusion a contending candidate from the Guelf party appeared in the person of Otto of Brunswick, who was supported by Richard of England and seconded by Baudouin of Hainaut and Flanders. Born in Normandy, Otto was the youngest son of Mathilda of England and Henry the Lion, duke of Saxony, and hence Richard's nephew. His position was due entirely to his uncle, who made him earl of York, count of La Marche, and finally count of Poitou. With the aid of Richard's money and influence, Otto was crowned king of the Romans by Adolph, archbishop of Cologne. Faced with such Guelf, English, and Flemish support for Otto, Philip Augustus had no other recourse than to support the candidacy of Philip of Swabia, Henry's brother, to whom the defense of the Hohenstaufen cause had fallen. In June 1198, shortly after Philip of Swabia was elected king of the Romans by his adherents, the French king signed an alliance of mutual assistance with the Hohenstaufen candidate.[49] The fate of this contested imperial election awaited the decision of the new pope, Innocent, whose accession in February 1198 was the second major event of the period. We have seen that Innocent's goal was to make the papacy the supreme judge over matters subject to its authority. In Innocent's view these included not only the French king's marriage but the imperial election. Though at this point the pope remained officially neutral between the two parties, the long papal enmity with the Hohenstaufens inclined him to favor Otto and the Guelfs. In addition, Innocent set as one of his immediate objectives the calling of a new crusade to rescue the Holy Land. Like the former crusade, the new expedition required peace between the kings of France and England.[50]

When Innocent dispatched his legate, Peter of Capua, to France, late in 1198, he commissioned him to deal expressly with three issues: the crusade, peace between the kings, and Philip's treatment of Ingeborg. In the background, however, the German election could not be ignored, since both kings had already taken sides. Despite the mediation of the legate, it became clear that a permanent peace was impossible. Even arrangements for a five-year truce dissolved before Richard's wrath at the suggestion that the bishop of Beauvais be released from prison.[51] When further negotiations reached a stalemate over impossible conditions (the French, for example, were asked to support Otto), Richard left to defend himself against Philip's allies in the south and in particular to punish the *vicomte* of Limoges and the count of Angoulême for switching to the French king. While engaging in these operations, Richard besieged the castle of Châlus-Chabrol, belonging to the *vicomte* of Limoges, on the pretext that a knight who had found a treasure rightfully belonging to Richard had taken refuge there. By chance a crossbowman caught the king with a random shot, and a few days later, on 6 April 1199, Richard died from the wound. Since at forty-one the English king was in the prime of his energy and ambition, nothing could have come as a greater surprise. Like Richard's captivity, his death was a magnificent stroke of fortune for Philip Augustus.[52]

Arthur Against John

Richard's sudden death did little to alter the underlying strategies of the Capetian and Angevin parties. Philip and John continued in directions that had been established for decades. But Richard's death favored the French king because it brought to the fore an antagonist of decidedly different character. Richard had been a soldier without peer and, in terms of his continental interests, a resolute and effective politician. John's military skills had not yet been seriously tested, but his political mettle was already apparent. He was given to vacillation to the point of fickleness, as amply demonstrated by the ease with which he was recruited against his brother and the readiness with which he capitulated when Richard returned. Philip was furthermore fortunate because Richard had no sons, thus leaving John to a doubtful succession. English, Norman, and Angevin customs were not clear as to who had the better claim: the younger brother, in this case John, or the son of the older brother, Geoffrey, in this case Arthur of Brittany. As it worked out, John was supported largely by the English and Norman barons. His mother Eleanor rallied the Poitevins to his cause and did homage to the French king in his name. Arthur found numerous adherents among the Breton and Angevin barons. Nearly all the Bretons accepted him as heir to Brittany, and the Angevin nobility were strongly influenced by the example of one of their prominent members, Guillaume des Roches. Although of poor origins, Guillaume had married the heiress of the Sablé family, who in turn had close ties with the houses of Mayenne, Laval, and Craon, the leading barons of Anjou and Maine. These Angevins for the most part followed the lead of Guillaume des Roches, who supported Arthur by bargaining between Philip and John.[53]

The dispute between John and Arthur offered Philip Augustus a classic opportunity to align himself with the younger and weaker against the older and stronger, a technique of which he had already demonstrated mastery. He chose the twelve-year-old Arthur over his uncle. In the spring of 1199 he received the count of Brittany's homage and confirmed the count's gifts to his supporters, including the granting of the seneschalship of Anjou to Guillaume des Roches.[54] Later the lord of Châteauroux and the *vicomte* of Thouars, important barons in Berry and Poitou, also allied themselves to Arthur. (Guy de Thouars, brother of the *vicomte*, married Arthur's mother, Constance, countess of Brittany.)[55] Once again, Arthur was delivered to Paris for safekeeping. Encouraged by this Angevin support, Philip Augustus made an incursion into Maine and took a place called Ballon to the north of Le Mans. Guillaume des Roches, who accompanied the expedition on Arthur's behalf, argued that Ballon be turned over to the count of Brittany, but the king refused. Desiring Arthur to be as independent of the Capetians as of the Anglo-Normans, Guillaume, followed by the Angevins and some Bretons, immediately deserted Philip and offered to negotiate between John and Arthur. For this service John rewarded Guillaume with the town of Le Mans and his own grant of the seneschalship of Anjou.[56]

Whereas John labored under the burden of a disputed succession, Philip suffered from an impending interdict upon his lands because of the rupture with the queen. The threat of these sanctions, which were officially promulgated in January 1200, affected his relations both with the Flemish barons and with John himself.[57] Inheriting Richard's strong position in northern France, John naturally renewed his brother's ties with Flanders, Boulogne, Guines, and other Flemish lords, and offered hopes of continued English generosity. As early as May 1199, Baudouin of Flanders had made incursions into Artois, although Philip parried them with the capture of prominent members of the Flemish nobility, including Philippe of Namur, Baudouin's brother.[58] Nonetheless, the imminent interdict induced the king to treat with the count of Flanders, and a treaty was signed at Péronne in January 1200. Fearing for the safety of his brother and that John's promises were not worth those of his brother, Baudouin gave up his alliance with the king of England. In exchange, Philip conceded Saint-Omer and Aire in Artois and the lordship over

Guines and other adjacent fiefs to Baudouin. All the rest of Artois, however, was confirmed to Philip as the inheritance of Prince Louis. If Louis died without heir, Artois would return to Flanders. Compared to the agreements of 1192, those of Péronne were a backward step for the French king, since he conceded to Flanders the fruits of Baudouin's aggressions in 1197. But the treaty of Péronne did stabilize the northern region.[59] The following year Renaud, count of Boulogne, made peace with his sovereign and reentered Capetian counsels. To seal this reconciliation the king gave his son Philip, newly born of Agnès, in marriage to Renaud's daughter, heiress to Boulogne.[60] Of equal import, the peace of Péronne disposed Baudouin to accept the cross that Innocent was urging upon the French nobility. The departure of the count of Flanders on the Fourth Crusade in 1202, in the company of the counts of Troyes, Blois, and others, removed numerous unruly barons from France at this crucial juncture, among them former allies of the English king.[61] Philip Augustus, needless to say, well remembering his experiences of the previous crusade, resisted the papal summons with little difficulty.[62]

The same interdict also prompted Philip to treat directly with John. In the spring of 1199, immediately after John's accession, Philip invaded Evreux, on which he had had designs since his treaty with John in 1194. A subsequent meeting between Philip and John in the Seine valley in August revealed the same conflicting issues as with Richard.[63] But the papal legate's continued persistence induced John to release the bishop of Beauvais at the price of 2,000 marks of silver and the good bishop's oath never to shed Christian blood again (such was John's sense of humor)[64] and obliged Philip to sign a formal peace with John at Le Goulet in May 1200.

Although the terms were modelled on those of 1196 between Philip and Richard, both sides made new concessions. Philip Augustus recognized John as Richard's lawful successor inheriting the titles to Normandy, Anjou, and Aquitaine, for which he accepted homage. More important, the French king abandoned Arthur, compelling him to do homage directly to his uncle for Brittany. Although John agreed to respect Arthur's rights, they were only protected in John's court. Thus John received recognition of his succession and the submission of his rival, but he also paid a price. For his part, he recognized the validity of the treaty of Péronne by conceding the liege homage of the count of Flanders to the French king and promising not to aid the Flemings against Philip. Moreover, John abandoned his alliances with Otto of Brunswick and agreed to restore the count of Angoulême and the *vicomte* of Limoges to their former positions as vassals. Among the more tangible concessions, he handed over to Philip the Norman border regions of the Evrecin (including the episcopal city of Evreux) and the Vexin (with the exception of Les Andelys, containing Château Gaillard), as well as the fiefs of Issoudun and Graçay in Berry.[65] Finally, in recognition of Capetian lordship over all his continental fiefs, John paid the considerable sum of 20,000 marks sterling both as a relief and a release of Brittany. Characteristically of such affairs, the transaction was sealed by a marriage uniting Prince Louis of France with Blanche of Castile, John's niece.[66] By giving up Arthur, at least for a time, Philip had exacted from John the major military objectives he had been unable to win from Richard. During the brief euphoria following the peace of Le Goulet, John paid a visit the following summer to Paris, where Philip spared no expense in food, drink, and presents to entertain the English king.[67]

Having achieved a moment of peace in Normandy, John turned his attention to Aquitaine, whose problems had absorbed Richard at the time of his death. Upon the latter's demise, Philip had renewed his alliances with Adémar, *vicomte* of Limoges, and his half-brother Adémar, count of Angoulême,[68] and in the treaty of Le Goulet had forced John to take these two troublesome barons back into favor. John now continued his brother's alliances in the south. When his sister Joan died in 1199, he renewed Richard's agreements with the count of Toulouse, and he did likewise with Sancho of Navarre in 1202.[69] But a serious problem appeared in central Aquitaine when Isabelle, the only daughter and heiress of Adémar, count of Angoulême, was affianced to Hugues de Lusignan, count of La Marche. The uniting of these two important families would not only be an obstacle to John's communications between Poitiers and Bordeaux but would strengthen the independence of the troublesome Angoulême lords and their neighbors, the *vicomtes* of Limoges. John's solution to this new problem was ingenious. Having recently shed his first wife, Isabella of Gloucester, on the grounds of consanguinity, he swooped into Aquitaine, carried off the heiress of Angoulême, and married her forthwith. Whether or not he was seized by a passion for the beauty of the twelve-year-old Isabelle, as contemporary chroniclers declare (confirmed, in fact, by his later behavior), the marriage was a potentially astute political move, because it won him the loyalty of an influential and troublesome barony. The honor of the Lusignan family was outraged, of course, but under normal circumstances it could have been appeased by due satisfaction. None was forthcoming, however. Having executed a brilliant diplomatic stroke, John was incapable of attending to its consequences. Not only did he refuse restitution, he brazenly insulted the Lusignans by challenging them to a single combat by champions, and then in the spring of 1201 invaded the county of La Marche and besieged the Norman county of Eu, belonging to Raoul de Lusignan, Hugues's brother. Although the Lusignans complained bitterly to the French king of John's aggressions, Philip, who was then entertaining the English king at Paris, was not yet ready to break the peace.[70]

The peace of Le Goulet was, however, as fragile as all the preceding truces had proven to be. Not only did John continue to harass the Lusignan castles in Aquitaine and to dispossess the count of Eu well into the autumn of 1201, he also began to ravage French possessions around Tours.[71] When John resumed his support for Otto of Brunswick, Philip renewed his ties with Arthur of Brittany by engaging him to his daughter by Agnès de Méran, Marie.[72] Both actions violated the agreements of Le Goulet. When the Lusignans persisted in their complaints about John's aggressions, Philip, the mutual overlord as established by the treaty of Le Goulet, summoned John to appear in Paris in April 1202 to answer for injuries to the Aquitainian barons and the church of Tours. John pledged his castles of Boutavant and Tillières for his appearance,[73] but he began to argue that as duke of Normandy he was required by custom to present himself only on the Norman borders. What he refused to recognize was that he was being summoned as duke of Aquitaine. In all events, he failed to appear on the appointed day. As the English chronicler Ralph of Coggeshall phrases it, on 28 April 1202 "the court of France, being assembled, adjudged the king of England to have forfeited all the lands which he and his ancestors had before that time held of the king of France for the reason that he and they had long neglected to render all the services due from the lands and had nearly always disobeyed the summonses of their lord the king."[74] After the royal court had decided that John had defaulted on his possessions through non-appearance, Philip took immediate steps to seize Boutavant and the other castles John had pledged. At last Philip Augustus had a judgment against John that would clothe all further actions against his antagonist with legality. The question of whether he could enforce the decision remained. He had been unsuccessful against Richard in the past, and his future depended on his now garnering sufficient resources for the task.

If Philip Augustus had drawn up a balance sheet of gains and losses over the decade since his return from the crusade, he would have had to admit that negotiations had profited him more than fighting. His constant warfare against Richard had brought him only Gisors and the neighboring castles along the Epte.[75] Totalled up, these were small rewards for the relentless campaigns of the 1190s. Conversely, the death of Philippe of Flanders in 1191 delivered the fruits of careful preparations during the preceding decade. The king took possession of parts of Vermandois, including Péronne, and all of Artois, the inheritance of his son. (By 1200, however, Artois was reduced in extent because the military feats of the count of Flanders had cost Philip Saint-Omer and Aire.) Moreover, Richard's sudden death and John's disputed succession enabled Philip to add the important territories of the Vexin and Evreux on the Norman borders to these northern acquisitions and to regain Issoudun and Graçay in Berry. Also in the south were gains in the Gâtinais resulting from marriage negotiations. When Philip proposed a marriage between Philippe, marquis of Namur, and Mathilde, heiress to his cousin Pierre de Courtenay, count of Nevers, as we have seen, the king was reconfirmed in his possession of Montargis, acquired in 1184.[76] But the marquis of Namur's military collaboration with his brother, the count of Flanders, and his subsequent capture by the king brought royal disfavor and opposition to his marriage. The count of Nevers, on his side, encountered rivalry from one of his major vassals, Hervé, the lord of Donzy. When Hervé roundly defeated the count, the king took the opportunity to alter the marriage arrangements. Mathilde, the heiress to Nevers, was married to Hervé de Donzy in 1199, and Philip Augustus took as his price the fief of Gien and 3,000 marks of silver.[77] Added to Montargis, Gien strengthened the royal grasp on the Gâtinais, which linked Bourges with Paris.

Unfortunate in battle, Philip Augustus nonetheless slowly but steadily added to the royal domain through negotiations with Flanders, the Angevins, and Nevers. These accretions of the 1190s, although eclipsed by the spectacular conquests of the following decade, represented significant expansion of the territorial base of the Capetians. The financial accounts of 1202/03 furnish one standard by which to gauge this growth. In 1179 the royal domain contained forty-one *prévôtés*, which in terms of domanial revenues collected in 1202/03 were worth 20,178 *livres* annual income. By 1190 it had increased to fifty-two *prévôtés*, producing 24,607 *livres* of revenue (again in 1202/03 prices). The gains of the final decade brought the number of *prévôtés* to only sixty-two in 1202/03, but they were yielding 34,719 *livres* of domanial revenue.[78] The importance of these figures is not absolute but comparative, because they do not represent the entire royal income. They do show, however, that the yield of Philip's domain had increased 72 percent since the beginning of the reign, 22 percent from 1179 to 1190, and 50 percent from 1190 to 1203. These increases demonstrate that Philip was, in fact, beginning to amass sufficient resources for a great offensive against John.

The glamorous crusade, the protracted sieges of castles, the intermittent skirmishing, the shifting baronial alliances, and the provisional declarations of treaties all naturally attracted the attention of the chroniclers of the 1190s. The English historians, in particular, recount in vivid detail the victories of Richard's arms and the success of the Angevin coalitions. Though the Capetian historiographers could not ignore the defeats sustained by Philip, they preferred to skip over the worst aspects. Rigord, for example, deals with the rout of Fréteval in one sentence and depicts the French king fighting against overwhelming odds at Courcelles-lès-Gisors. Not until after Bouvines, when Capetian confidence was finally secure, could Guillaume le Breton acknowledge the losses of treasure and documents at Fréteval and admit that the bridge over the Epte at Gisors had collapsed under the weight of retreating French knights, among them the king himself.

Preoccupied with castles, the clash of arms, and the terms of fragile treaties, contemporary chroniclers, both French and English, viewed the 1190s as dark days for Capetian fortunes. Unacquainted with government documents now available to modern historians, they failed to recognize the fundamental changes that the king was preparing amidst these military and political disasters. Attracted to the great baronial figures, they were unaware that Philip's government was increasingly confided to a new entourage composed of lesser men. The reorganization of justice throughout the royal domain, the regular institution of new officials called *baillis*, and the establishment of a finance bureau at Paris with new accounting techniques to manage the royal revenues and war expenditures escaped their attention. Most important, the chroniclers did not see the significance of the new territories added to the domain through negotiation. These fundamental transformations of personnel, justice, and finance, which were gestated during the 1190s unobserved by the contemporary chroniclers, made possible Philip's spectacular victories of 1204 over the Angevins.

The King's New Men

The period from the eve of the crusade (1190) to the eve of the conquest of Normandy (1203) was one of extraordinary innovation in Capetian government. The Third Crusade, more than any other event, constituted a great divide between the government bequeathed by the early Capetians and that crafted for the future by Philip Augustus. The following decade witnessed transformations in both personnel and institutions that rendered it the decisive *tournant* of Philip's reign, indeed of early Capetian history. These far-reaching changes were embodied in, and are revealed by, new sources of documentation that emerged throughout the decade. An ordinance-testament outlining the operation of government was drafted in 1190 as the king prepared to depart. A permanent archive that carefully stored official documents received by the royal court was established after 1194 when Philip lost his baggage to Richard at Fréteval. And the fiscal accounts that were commanded in 1190 produced a series of financial records, of which one has survived from the fiscal year 1202/03. These sources furnish a direct view of the men and operations of Philip's government that lay hidden to contemporary chroniclers preoccupied with the misfortunes of war. Even an embryonic jewel account from 1206 buried in Register A and unnoticed until now affords us a

101

detailed catalogue of those who enjoyed royal favor.[1] But the brilliant, if momentary, beam of light cast by the fiscal accounts illuminates 1202/03 as the most clearly revealed year of Philip's reign. This chapter approaches this decisive decade of the 1190s, framed by the ordinance-testament and the financial accounts, by identifying those who participated in royal government. Their judicial and financial functions will be investigated in greater detail in chapter 7.[2]

The Regency (June 1190–December 1191)

The departure of Philip Augustus in 1190 generated what might be called the first constitution of Capetian history—an official description of royal government. Rigord, who preserved its text, informs us that the king convoked his friends and familiars at Paris in June to draw up his *testamentum* and to make an *ordinationem* for the whole realm.[3] Rigord's terminology accurately describes the document because the king expressly decreed how the affairs of the kingdom should be handled during his absence and how his legacies should be distributed in the event of his death. This ordinance, to which we shall refer on many occasions, was preoccupied with the subjects of justice, finance, and regalian rights over churches. Looking both backward and forward, it confirmed old customs such as those governing regalian bishoprics and abbeys. Since it was to be in effect only during the king's absence, some of its features were naturally temporary, but a number of its provisions introduced innovations that became permanent in royal government.

As to personnel, the ordinance officially confided the regency during the king's absence to the queen mother, Adèle de Champagne, and her brother, Guillaume, archbishop of Reims. By July 1190 Philip had obtained his barons' agreement to the regency.[4] Although the old Champagne party was once again in power, the ordinance placed express limits on their authority and assigned the collaboration of lesser personages. The affairs of the capital were to be handled with the concurrence of six Parisian bourgeois, designated only by their initials T, A, E, R, B, and N. It was not the regents, but they, along with Pierre the Marshal, who supervised the financial accounts three times a year at the Temple. (If one of the seven should die, Guillaume de Garlande was responsible for finding his replacement.) A royal clerk, Adam, was assigned to write down the accounts as they were rendered. When distributing prebends and church positions in the king's gift, the regents were to act with the advice of Brother Bernard de Vincennes.

One charter from the queen and archbishop and ten from the Parisian bourgeois are all that survive from the regents' operations during the eighteen months of the king's absence.[5] But this random evidence none-theless preserves the name of every figure mentioned in the ordinance, thus confirming that all were active during the period. The Parisian bour-geois operated in groups ranging from three to eight persons, and there-fore included a wider circle of personnel than the six originally desig-nated.[6] Their chief duty was to execute gracious jurisdiction—that is, to attest and confirm in the king's name transactions performed in their presence, for which they possessed a special seal.[7] Since in one case they attested a *concordia* between two litigants, they were involved in judg-ments as well.[8] The most striking feature, however, was that at least half of their charters involved transactions outside the Paris region. (The Nor-man abbey of Saint-Ouen at Rouen, for example, received three char-ters.)[9] The bourgeois of Paris, therefore, exercised broader jurisdiction than simply serving as a council for the *prévôts* of Paris. In all likelihood, they acted directly for the king, in whose name they attested.

Those named in the ordinance of 1190 were all previously known in royal circles. In addition to the regents from Champagne, Guillaume de Garlande was descended from a family that had been prominent at the royal court in the early twelfth century. (His grandfather had been royal seneschal.)[10] Brother Bernard, leader of the hermits of Vincennes, had been consulted by the king on his Jewish policy since the beginning of the reign.[11] Adam the clerk was most probably the canon of Noyon for whom the king provided a house in 1189.[12] Even the enigmatic Pierre the Marshal was associated with royal familiars as early as 1179.[13] Four of the six bourgeois whose initials are furnished by the ordinance can be identified with some assurance from subsequent charters: Thibaut le Riche, Athon de la Grève, Ebrouin le Changeur, and Robert de Chartres.[14] They undoubtedly originated from Paris, as is suggested by Athon's sur-name, which was taken from Place de la Grève, one of the principal mar-ket squares on the right bank. Surnames like "le Changeur" (Money-changer) confirm their commercial interests. Thibaut the Rich may have originated from the "Le Riche" family, a dynasty of knights prominent in the Parisian region since the early twelfth century, but by Philip's reign he was designated as bourgeois and was a notorious usurer.[15] Whatever their origins, these men of the regency were united by property and family ties with one particularly important figure of the royal household, Gautier the Chamberlain, also a prominent landholder of Paris.[16] Although it may be surprising that the name of the king's faithful chamberlain did not appear in the ordinance of 1190, Gautier was nonetheless closely associated with the men responsible for operating the central government during the king's absence.

The men of 1190 were chosen from a generation reaching back to the time of Louis VII. Some of them remained at the royal court for another decade. We shall see that the archbishop of Reims retained his prominence until the interdict of 1200. Gautier the Chamberlain remained with the king until his death in 1205, but his functions were increasingly assumed by his sons. Guillaume de Garlande was also succeeded by a son.[17] Brother Bernard played an active role in the king's marriage and subsequent relations with Ingeborg until 1200.[18] Others, like Adam[19] and Pierre the Marshal, dropped out of sight. The queen mother Adèle went into retirement after the king's return. Obviously a temporary expedient, the Parisian bourgeois never reappear in royal documentation. The figures to whom the king confided the regency were either provisional or of an older generation who did not outlast the 1190s. It was not a time to try new men.

The Withdrawal of the Magnates

Having left the baronial counsellors of the first decade of his reign behind in the sands of the Holy Land, Philip Augustus made no effort to replace them with their peers after his return to France. Following established Capetian policy, he left vacant the important post of royal seneschal, open since the death of Thibaut de Blois, just as he had left the chancellorship vacant in 1185. Thereafter the formulae of royal charters intoned *dapifero nullo* and *vacante cancellaria* to emphasize the king's liberation from these two powerful household officers. When the constable, Raoul, count of Clermont, also died at Acre in 1191, his office was filled in 1193 by Dreu de Mello.[20] Drawn from a family of castellans related to the Garlandes near Senlis, Dreu was frequently present in the royal entourage until his death in 1218. Unlike his colleagues the butler and the chamberlain, however, the constable continued to play a moderately active role in royal affairs. He served as one of Philip's envoys in the truce of 1194 with Richard and supervised the fortifications of Châteauneuf at

Tours according to the terms of the peace of Gaillon in 1196.[21] Around 1198 he was named a royal judge in a dispute between the lord of Corbeil and the church of Saint-Victor.[22] Most of his activities were oriented south of Paris, where he was closely associated with Pierre, count of Nevers and Auxerre. After the conquest of the Loire valley, Philip rewarded Dreu with the seigneury of Loches.[23] Although Dreu was classified among the second lowest category of castellans in an inventory compiled in Register A that listed the feudal nobility according to rank, he was nonetheless the most important feudal lord active in the royal entourage.[24]

The great barons, though naturally present on important occasions, rarely provided the king with administrative service. The annulment proceedings at Compiègne in 1193 included the counts of Blois, Troyes, Dreux, and Nevers (all related to the king), who swore to the alleged kinship between Ingeborg and Isabelle de Hainaut.[25] The treaty of Le Goulet in 1200 brought forth the counts of Blois, Troyes, Dreux, Flanders, and Perche.[26] Appearing only on such formal occasions, these barons did not undertake the active role that Philippe of Flanders and Thibaut de Blois had exercised in the decade before the crusade. Similarly, the royal bishops, taken as a group, provided the king with little regular service in the 1190s. To be sure, seven bishops participated in the annulment at Compiègne, five being related to the king and one, Etienne of Noyon, being the son of Gautier the Chamberlain.[27] Three bishops (Beauvais, Paris, and Meaux) were also instructed to conduct an inquest into regalian rights over the bishopric of Châlons-sur-Marne in 1202.[28] Individual bishops were assigned particular missions. The bishop of Arras naturally assisted in taking possession of Artois in 1192.[29] Others served the king in the celebration and annulment of his marriage to Ingeborg. Etienne of Noyon was Philip's official envoy to Denmark to negotiate the marriage agreement in 1193 and was also dispatched to the pope in 1196 to demand the separation, along with the bishop of Soissons. (The latter was also sent on a mission to Philip of Swabia in 1198.)[30] Pierre de Corbeil, newly transferred to the archbishopric of Sens, was sent to Rome in 1200 to persuade the pope to lift the interdict, because he had been Pope Innocent's teacher of theology during the pope's student days at Paris.[31]

The two notable exceptions to this minimal participation in royal government were, of course, the king's two close relatives, Philippe de Dreux, bishop of Beauvais, and Guillaume de Champagne, archbishop of Reims. Philippe of Beauvais vigorously supported his royal cousin by spreading malicious rumors about Richard on his journey back from the crusade, by negotiating with the emperor to prolong the English king's imprisonment, and by harassing the Vexin from his base in the Beauvaisis, until 1197, when Richard captured him and held him prisoner for three years. Released by John, he showed up for the peace of Le Goulet.[32] The archbishop of Reims's prominence, attained during the first decade, naturally survived the crusade. Not only was he official regent, he continued to perform important services. He was charged with taking possession of Artois; travelled to Germany during Richard's captivity and later returned there on a mission of imperial diplomacy; was involved at every point in Philip's dealings with Ingeborg, including her coronation at Amiens (which he claimed as his prerogative) and the annulment at Compiègne; and was present at every important transaction between the king and his barons until 1200. After that date, however, when he was forced to accept responsibility for the fraudulent oath at Compiègne, he drops out of sight.[33] His name is not mentioned among those of the numerous bishops and barons at Le Goulet in 1200. The last of Louis VII's generation, he was by this time an expendable old man. He died soon afterwards, in 1202.

The King's New Men

As the surviving baronial counsellors wound down their careers in the 1190s, Philip's return from the crusade permitted him to begin afresh in assembling a new entourage of familiars. This time "afresh" meant young men of lesser station. Being dependent on royal favor for their positions, these new men were more congenial, reliable, and effective than the former barons. The emergence of the royal archives by mid-decade permits glimpses of men in constant attendance on the king who were unnoticed by the chroniclers because of their youth and modest status. Moreover, the piercing beam of the fiscal accounts of 1202/03 allows a close examination of their activities for a brief moment. As a group, these men cannot be distinguished by their functions because, resisting specialization, they performed many and varied duties. They do, however, fit into social categories inherited from the earlier Capetian court, being lesser chamberlains, knights of the king, and clerks of the king. After years of service, certain individuals stood out among the rest in each of these groups. When these new men finally did come to the chroniclers' attention during the second decade of the thirteenth century, four in particular were singled out: the chamberlain Gautier the Young, the knights Barthélemy de Roye and Henri Clément, and the cleric Brother Guérin.[34] Each was very likely typical of his group.

CHAMBERLAINS: THE SONS OF GAUTIER

Since Mathieu, count of Beaumont, was virtually inactive throughout his entire tenure as grand chamberlain of the royal household (1180–1208), the chief responsibilities of the chamber were assumed by Gautier the Chamberlain and his family.[35] Gautier was a significant link between the courts of Louis VII and Philip Augustus. Having entered royal service in the 1150s, he was an old man in the 1190s. In 1198 he drew up his testament, and he died in October 1205, although he was still well enough to be present at the surrender of Rouen in June that year.[36] Active until the last, he was called upon by the king in 1200 to undertake the delicate affair of punishing the royal *prévôt* Thomas, who had outraged the scholars of Paris.[37] Since Gautier was a venerable fixture of the royal court, the successful careers of his numerous sons, despite their low social station, did not entirely escape the chroniclers' notice. Later in the reign, contemporary historians note three of them achieved high promotion in the church.[38] As we have seen, Etienne became bishop of Noyon in 1188 and aided the king in his marital negotiations with Ingeborg. Pierre was canon at Paris and treasurer at Tours before attaining the bishopric of Paris in 1208. And Guillaume became successively canon of Chartres, chanter and archdeacon of Paris, and, finally, in 1213, bishop of Meaux.[39] Three other sons, Philippe, Ours, and Gautier the Young, followed their father into the royal court. The career of Philippe, the eldest, was cut short when, like so many, he met death at Acre in 1191.[40]

Ours, Gautier's second son designated for a lay career, served as a royal guarantor in the truce with Richard in 1194. Entitled "chamberlain of the king" like his father, he participated in the royal entourage throughout the reign.[41] In 1196 he was an envoy to the archbishop of Rouen over Richard's fortifications at Andelys.[42] In the accounts of 1202/03 he received money with Barthélemy de Roye for military actions in the Vexin. At that time his daily wage was one *livre*, the highest rate paid to a *bailli*.[43] By 1206 he was entrusted with royal jewels and rewarded with fiefs near Bourges.[44] In the second half of the reign, however, Ours left Philip's direct service to become increasingly attached to Prince Louis.[45] In the climactic military campaigns of 1214, he was not with the king at Bouvines but with Louis at his resounding victory over John at Roche-au-Moine in the south. Two years later he accompanied the prince on his ill-fated expedition to England.[46] Starting in the steps of his father as a close royal familiar, Ours gradually ceded his place to another brother.

Gautier the Chamberlain's true successor in the royal court was a third son, Gautier the Young. Soon after the latter appeared in the king's entourage in 1197, the old chamberlain was referred to as Gautier the Father to distinguish him from his namesake.[47] As we shall see, writing at the end of the reign, the chronicler Guillaume le Breton attributed the reconstitution of the royal archives after the losses at Fréteval in 1194 to Gautier the Young. Since the documents the chronicler mentions were of a fiscal and domanial character, appropriate to the chamber, we may assume that Gautier the Young, like his father, functioned as a chamberlain.[48]

Before he left royal service in 1218, departing on the Fifth Crusade, an expedition that cost him his life, Gautier the Young frequently attended the king and performed a wide range of duties.[49] The fiscal accounts of 1202/03 reveal his receiving monies for unspecified tasks.[50] In the military preparations on the Norman marches, he was even more active than his brother in disbursing funds at Gaillefontaine, Gisors, and Lyons-la-Forêt; and he was entrusted with both receiving and distributing jewels in 1206.[51] In 1201 he served as oath helper in the marriage agreement with Renaud, count of Boulogne.[52] The following year he acted as Philip's agent to punish the *vidame* of Châlons-sur-Marne for his abuse of regalian rights over the bishopric, and he may have been sent to Rome over the king's matrimonial difficulties.[53] About a decade later he participated in a royal inquest into the forest rights of the count of Soissons.[54] The military campaign of 1214 saw Gautier at the king's side at Bouvines while his brother Ours was with Prince Louis.[55] After Gautier's death in 1218, Ours probably replaced him at the royal court.

Gautier's activities were centered on Normandy after the conquest of the duchy. When the sessions of the Norman exchequer were reestablished in the spring of 1207, he presided regularly over the court at Falaise until his departure on the crusade in 1218.[56] He also served in the exchequer at Rouen, on one occasion transferring a case from that court to the sessions at Falaise.[57] The king confided to him the custody of the castle of Fontaine-Gérard in the Seine valley and later granted him the surrounding lands.[58] Gautier's son Adam married the daughter of an important Norman baron, undoubtedly a royal gift.[59]

Aside from Gautier's sons, no other chamberlain comes into clear focus. The financial account of 1202/03 attests the activities of four other chamberlains. Three of them seem to have performed only domestic duties,[60] but the fourth, named Eudes, accounted for various sums and disbursed military funds on the Norman marches like Gautier the Young.[61] This Eudes was probably the same chamberlain who drew up the account of the royal jewels in February 1206 that was copied into Register A,[62] and may have been the brother of a certain Phillippe who originated from Béthisy and was chamberlain for Prince Louis.[63] That these chamberlain services were often concentrated in families is further suggested by the case of the Tristan family.[64] Pierre, Gervais, and Jean Tristan, sons of a certain Arnoul from the Soissonais, appear as chamberlains between 1207 and 1222. Although the king attested many of their land transactions, virtually nothing is revealed of the nature of their service. Pierre Tristan was probably the *Petrus Tristanides* who saved Philip Augustus from danger at Bouvines. Although he was present when the count of Soissons abandoned his rights over the bishop of Senlis in 1215, the lack of further information about the Tristans' duties suggests that they were limited to the domestic sphere.[65] Other men designated as chamberlains remain only names.[66]

The routine of the royal household required great swarms of servants, designated variously as cupbearers (*scantiones*), squires (*scutiferi*), pantlers (*panetarii*), cooks, and falconers, all of lesser importance than the chamberlains. Since they are identified only through royal charters that bestowed favors on them, they appear primarily in performance of their domestic duties, but a few were assigned administrative tasks. Renaud l'Archer, who was both a cupbearer and royal sergeant, acted as judge.[67] A certain Thibaut, a pantler, conducted an inquest into the forest at Breteuil with the royal *bailli*,[68] and Simon "our pantler" was sent as a messenger to the duke of Burgundy.[69] Lowly service could also lead to higher rank. The Norman *bailli* Guillaume Poucin and the great counsellor Barthélemy de Roye began their careers among these domestic servants.[70]

KNIGHTS OF THE KING:
BARTHÉLEMY DE ROYE AND HENRI CLÉMENT

Two groups, epitomized by two figures, may be discerned among the king's knights who frequented Philip's court. Barthélemy de Roye stands out among those whose principal duties were administrative, and the marshal Henri Clément may be taken to represent those who, although present at court, served primarily in a military capacity, as might be expected of knights.

In the treaty of 1194 between Philip Augustus and Count John (King Richard's brother), the first document to be preserved in the newly established archives, the king declared that a certain Barthélemy de Roye, "his knight," would swear an oath to guarantee the agreement.[71] Two years later Philip addressed him as "the first pantler of our household."[72] Although this title suggests that Barthélemy's royal service originated in the domestic sphere, he was normally designated as a "knight of the king" until 1208, when he was created grand chamberlain upon the death of Mathieu, count of Beaumont.[73] Since the office of grand chamberlain had become purely honorific, it contributed to Barthélemy's dignity without altering his functions. None of the king's new men appeared on the scene as early, was more constant in attendance, or lasted longer than he.[74] Thus emerged a new figure, who, together with the cleric Brother Guérin, was preeminent in the royal entourage.

Before appearing in the king's company, Barthélemy had been associated with the old seneschal Thibaut, count of Blois, whom he had accompanied on the crusade.[75] He was a younger son of the family of Roye in Vermandois, whose lands had entered the royal domain in 1185. The Royes were only minor lords, but with the king's consent Barthélemy married Perronelle de Montfort, daughter of the Norman count of Evreux and the countess of Leicester. Having no sons himself, Barthélemy found illustrious husbands for his own daughters, including the eldest son of the count of Alençon, the brother of Jean de Nesles, castellan of Bruges, and Guillaume Crespin, an important Norman lord. Since each alliance was confirmed by a royal charter, these successful marriages were undoubtedly the result of royal patronage.[76] The royal charters also contain numerous benefactions to the faithful knight. As early as 1196 Philip gave Barthélemy the house of Gautier the Helmet-maker at Paris.[77] In the accounts of 1202/03 Barthélemy was more favored than the other royal agents, receiving rich gifts of clothing and the large payment of 100 *livres*. In the jewel account of 1206 he was confided with an abundance of rubies, emeralds, sapphires, diamonds, and a silver chest.[78] By the time of Bouvines (1214), and at the height of his career, the royal chamberlain had accumulated impressive landed holdings, a large part of which were the king's gift. In Vermandois he held ancestral lands at Roye and Montdidier,[79] and in addition to the house mentioned above, he acquired other houses in and around the capital.[80] By the completion of the conquest of Normandy, the king had granted him fiefs at Mantes, Montchauvet, and Acquiny.[81] Except for bestowing on him a great barony, the king could not have rewarded his faithful knight and grand chamberlain more handsomely. Yet Barthélemy's services were also sought by King John and the count of Champagne, both of whom were paying him *fief-rentes*.[82]

In the account of 1202/03 Barthélemy de Roye received and disbursed funds with the chamberlain Ours for the military preparations on the Norman marches.[83] He was present at Rouen's surrender in June 1204 and was active in the campaigns of northeastern France preparatory to the great showdown at Bouvines.[84] On the field of Bouvines, he fought with the king, and after the battle was entrusted with Ferrand, the count of Flanders, one of the prize captives.[85]

Barthélemy's major service, however, was not military but political and judicial. Not only was he present, as we have seen, at most important events, but he also stood security for many of Philip's agreements.[86] He performed missions for the king such as that to Courtrai in 1206 to execute a marriage settlement between the counts of Namur and Flanders.[87] He first appeared in a judicial capacity in 1202 at the inquest and decision over regalian rights at Châlons-sur-Marne.[88] After the conquest of Normandy, Philip sent him with Brother Guérin and a Norman baron to mediate between the chapter and commune of Rouen.[89] Perhaps because of his landed interests in the duchy, he became increasingly involved in Norman justice. He participated in the celebrated judgment concerning the inheritance of Guillaume Painel at Rouen in 1214.[90] Four years later he succeeded Gautier the Young as the chief lay judge at the biannual sessions of the Norman exchequer at Falaise and later at Caen, a position he held for the remaining years of the reign.[91] What evidence survives of decisions elsewhere in the realm shows that Barthélemy was also active as a royal judge outside of Normandy. For example, in 1215 he headed the royal officials at Compiègne who attested the count of Soissons's renunciation of forest rights over the bishop of Senlis.[92] Closely connected with these judicial duties were his inquests into the fiefs of Hersin and the tolls of Bapaume in his native Vermandois before 1205.[93] With Brother Guérin he investigated regalian rights at Bourges in 1215 and in 1219 assessed the limits of royal land around the city of Melun.[94] Without doubt Barthélemy de Roye was the most wide-ranging and active layman among Philip Augustus's new *familiares*.

A representative of an older generation among the "knights of the

king" was Phillippe de Lévis, who originated from Toucy (Yonne) and
held fiefs in the castellany of Montlhéry.[95] After returning with the king
from the crusade, he first appeared in royal service in 1192 as a royal *assessor* in the company of the *bailli* of Etampes.[96] In February 1200 the
king confirmed a judicial decision made by his court and by "his faithful
knight Philippe de Lévis."[97] A few months later, with the elder Gautier
the Chamberlain, he was assigned the delicate task of punishing Thomas,
the *prévôt* of Paris, for his outrages against the scholars of Paris.[98] In 1202
he participated in the judgment over the regalia of Châlons-sur-Marne,
but he had died by May 1203.[99] He was survived by at least five sons, of
whom the eldest, Miles de Lévis, followed his father into royal service as
the distinguished *bailli* of the Cotentin in Normandy.[100]

Another knight active in administrative service was Aubert de Hangest, who, like Barthélemy de Roye, came from Vermandois. With fiefs
concentrated around Montdidier and Chauny, Aubert was listed as a
simple *vavassor* in the royal feudal inventories.[101] His relationship to the
castellans of Hangest, who dominated the region, is unclear.[102] Aubert
was at the surrender of Rouen in June 1204, after which the king rewarded "his friend and *fidelis*" with the village of Pont-Saint-Pierre in
Normandy, and he also participated in the campaign of 1214.[103] His chief
royal service, however, was political and judicial, particularly in the Vermandois region. In 1203 he was dispatched with a Master Guillaume and
the *prévôt* of Amiens on a mission to Flanders for which he was reimbursed from the *prévôté* of Amiens. In the jewel account of 1206 he
was confided a sapphire.[104] He participated in at least half a dozen judgments, beginning in 1213 with a case at Paris between the chapter and
commune of Saint-Quentin.[105] Even more frequently he served as an administrator and a local juror in numerous inquests. Dealing with such
matters as the tolls of Bapaume, the fiefs of Hersin (both before 1205),
and with forest rights, most of these inquests concerned Vermandois.[106]
Though some of his royal service took place at Paris and in the king's entourage, much was localized in the northeast of France. For this reason it
is difficult to determine whether Aubert de Hangest was a knight in the
royal entourage like Barthélemy de Roye or a local agent for Vermandois.

Beyond the three figures considered above, other knights performed
political and administrative tasks for the king in individual cases. Men
like Philippe de Nanteuil and Pierre du Mesnil delivered judicial decisions and served on missions, but since their names appear with little
regularity in the royal records, we must assume that their service was ei-

ther occasional or local.[107] In effect, therefore, Philip relied on only a small number of lay counsellors from his immediate entourage to perform the constant and necessary duties of the central administration.

Since a knight's express function was to fight, it might be expected that his responsibilities in the king's entourage would be more military than administrative. Though the royal constable may be presumed to have supervised the armies, lesser figures called marshals actually led the troops. Of these the outstanding representative was Henri Clément, the son of the marshal Robert Clément (who, it will be remembered, was the young king's guardian before 1181) and the brother of Alberic Clément, who died in the breach of the walls of Acre in 1191.[108] Henri's military activities on the Norman marches are recorded in the account of 1202/03, and he was present at the capitulation of Rouen in June 1204, at which time the king presented him with the castle and forest of Argentan.[109] He accompanied the seneschal of Anjou on the expedition into the Loire valley in 1207–1208 and was further rewarded with the castle of Parthenay.[110] In the great campaign of 1214 Henri served with Prince Louis in Anjou. He died shortly after the victory of Roche-au-Moine, probably from wounds received in the battle. The royal chronicler Guillaume le Breton specially notes that his death was mourned by many because of his great popularity throughout France. Although the marshalship had not yet been made hereditary, the king conferred the office on Henri's infant son in recognition of his father's services.[111] Shortly before his death, Henri joined Barthélemy de Roye and Brother Guérin in the inquest at Compiègne into the forest rights of the count of Soissons,[112] the only administrative duty performed by him of which record survives. It is evident that his great service to the king was on the battlefield.

Two other families, the Garlandes and the Barres, long associated with the royal court, also excelled in military service. Descended from a royal seneschal, Guillaume de Garlande fought loyally at Gisors and Mantes in the campaigns of 1188, and in 1190 he participated in the regency at Paris.[113] His son with the same name—and therefore difficult to distinguish—accompanied Philip Augustus on the crusade.[114] On the eve of the conquest of Normandy, Guillaume (probably the son) commanded a contingent of troops (*ballia*) on the frontier and later took part in the victory at Bouvines.[115] Although often present in the royal entourage at the turn of the century, his administrative contributions were limited to the judgment over the regalia of Châlons in 1202 and the count of

Soissons's forest rights in 1215.[116] His services as a warrior, however, were amply rewarded by the king. Gifts of livery were noted in the accounts of 1202/03 and donations of lands were recorded in royal charters, in which the king characteristically called him "our friend and *fidelis*" and "our knight."[117] Undoubtedly at the king's instigation, he married the sister of Gaucher de Châtillon, a royal cousin, and his three daughters were given the count of Beaumont, the count of Grandpré, and the royal butler as husbands.[118] So many transactions involving the Garlande family were confirmed by royal charters that a chancery scribe compiled a special dossier of *Carte Guillelmi de Gallanda* in Register C soon after the death of Guillaume (the son) in 1216, when his inheritance was adjudicated by the royal court.[119]

Notable among the knights from the Vexin listed in the feudal inventory of Register A were five members of the family of Barres, two of whom, father and son, both called Guillaume, excelled in royal service.[120] Like the Garlandes, the two Guillaume des Barres are not easily distinguished from each other in the records. Guillaume des Barres had married his daughter to Raoul du Sart by 1201, and another Guillaume took as wife Amicie, countess of Leicester and widow of Simon de Montfort.[121] Before the former marriage, the Guillaume in question was already the beneficiary of a royal *fief-rente* amounting to forty *livres* annually from the *prévôté* of Bapaume.[122] Few names are more prominent in the pages of the royal historiographers, especially in the *Philippidos* of Guillaume le Breton.[123] Beginning in 1186, a Guillaume des Barres participated in every important military campaign throughout the reign.[124] One of them, probably the elder, accompanied Philip on the crusade and especially antagonized Richard. The English chronicler who recounts their quarrel describes him as "a vigorous knight of the *familia* of the French king."[125] Yet Richard respected Guillaume's military prowess enough to attempt to purchase his services in 1197. Active in the operations of 1214, Guillaume distinguished himself at Bouvines, where he came to the king's rescue when Philip was unhorsed and almost succeeded in capturing Emperor Otto before he fled the field. Yet beyond their military exploits and their frequent appearances at the royal court, the Guillaume des Barres only occasionally participated in administrative business.[126] One of them was at the judgment of the regalia of Châlons in 1202. Another took part in an inquest into the fiefs of his son-in-law (or brother-in-law) Raoul du Sart.[127] Like the Cléments and the Garlandes, it was not by these duties but by their swords that the Barres best served the king.

CLERICS OF THE KING: BROTHER GUÉRIN

At the turn of the year 1201–1202 the royal charters, which since 1185 had ended with the formula "the chancery being vacant," abruptly began to add a new phrase: "given by the hand of Brother Guérin."[128] This chancery phrase announced the name of a personage who dominated the king's central administration throughout the second half of the reign.[129] With the appearance of each new series of royal documents, Brother Guérin's role emerges more clearly. The fiscal account of 1202/03 reveals him as second to none in receiving and disbursing monies. After the conquest of the duchy, the Norman judicial rolls designate him as presiding over the regular sessions of the exchequer. The scattered documentation collected in the royal archives, the registers, and elsewhere shows him judging, holding inquests, issuing commands, and serving on missions more frequently than any other, with the possible exception of Barthélemy de Roye. From 1209 to the end of the reign, he was present at virtually all important recorded sessions of the king's court.[130] Appearing shortly before the death of the archbishop of Reims, Brother Guérin became, in effect, his replacement in Philip's government.[131]

Guérin's title of "Brother" stemmed from membership in the crusading order of the Knights Hospitalers of Jerusalem, which suggests the channel through which Philip discovered this cleric. He was elected bishop of Senlis, close by to Paris, in 1213–1214, doubtlessly with the king's approval but also perhaps as a result of the pope's intervention. The preceding bishop, Geoffroi, had requested papal permission to resign because of age and obesity, which could have placed the see of Senlis in papal hands. Pope Innocent III had promised to favor Brother Guérin if he would exercise a favorable influence on Philip during the king's matrimonial difficulties. When Philip finally announced his reconciliation with the queen in 1213, the pope may have rewarded Guérin with Senlis.[132] However Guérin came by his new dignity, he nonetheless remained faithful to his former order by continuing to wear his Hospitaler habit.[133] A contemporary chronicler asserts that he rose from humble origins. Since this testimony is not contradicted by other contemporary evidence, we may assume him to have been of low extraction. All that is known of his family are the names of the usual nephews and nieces who clustered around great prelates.[134] He was well endowed with property, principally to the south of Paris, persuasive evidence of royal favor. Already in 1202/03 he possessed houses at Saint-Léger-en-Yvelines, Orléans, and

Lorris, and later he acquired another at Montreuil-Bellay (Maine-et-Loire).[135] In the account of 1203 he was remunerated by the *bailli* of Paris.[136] After his election to the see of Senlis, both he and his church received important benefactions from the king, as was to be expected.[137]

Guérin's first and most lasting functions were performed in the chancery. From 1201 to 1210, with only occasional omissions, the royal diplomas concluded with *data vacante cancellaria per manum fratris Garini*,[138] and although the *per manum* is not conclusive, it suggests that Guérin managed the operations of the chancery while the chancellorship was vacant.[139] In 1207 a Norman chronicler called him vice-chancellor (*vices cancellarii agens*), but this term, reflective of Anglo-Norman usage, is not sufficient evidence for Guérin's official position.[140] Moreover, when the *per manum* was discontinued in 1210, it did not signify the end of Guérin's association with the chancery. His presence can be detected in successive chancery records.[141] As late as 1220 it was he who commissioned his clerk, Etienne de Gallardon, to compile Register E, the last of the series, and Etienne's handwriting can be found on the earliest Register A, begun in 1204.[142] After Philip's death, Louis VIII briefly revived the chancellorship and bestowed it on Guérin, who held it until his death in 1227.[143]

A second sphere of Guérin's activity was judicial. From 1207 to the end of the reign, he presided regularly over the biannual sessions of the Norman exchequer at Falaise (after 1220 transferred to Caen) with only two exceptions: the sessions of 1213–1214, when he was elected bishop and fought at Bouvines, and one session in 1216. His name followed that of his co-judge, Gautier the Young, until 1216, after which Guérin received the place of honor because of his episcopal dignity. For all practical purposes he was the sole clerical judge at the Norman exchequer after the conquest of the duchy.[144] Except for his journey to Falaise twice a year, however, he left little evidence of other judicial activities in Normandy.[145] The scattered records of judgments and inquests reveal that the great majority of his judicial duties were elsewhere. He judged, for example, between the church of Saint-Nicolas d'Acy and the commune of Senlis in 1215 and participated in most of the important decisions at the royal court.[146] He was chosen arbitrator in numerous disputes ranging from Chartres, to the southwest of Paris, to Amiens in the north, and he conducted inquests into such diverse matters as forest rights at Retz, the regalia of Bourges and Reims, and justice at Laon.[147] Although the fragmentary documentation offers only samples of Guérin's judicial activities, there is no doubt that no judges in the central court were more active than he and Barthélemy de Roye, with whom he frequently collaborated.

The accounts of 1202/03 reveal the diversity of Guérin's other services to the king. Except for the treasurer, no one else performed as frequently and in such different capacities. Whereas the chamberlain Gautier the Young appeared in six different transactions, and Barthélemy de Roye in four, Guérin was recorded at least fifty times. Geographically his activities extended from the Norman marches to Bourges and Soissons. He dealt with sums of money ranging from 45 *sous* to 2,360 *livres* in the currencies of Paris, Anjou, and Gien. Though local agents occasionally acknowledged transfer of funds from Guérin, the overwhelming majority of his transactions were assignments of sums for expenditure. The accounts rarely illuminate the precise reasons for these expenditures, but he may be found making payments to the chapter of Soissons, to Mathieu, count of Beaumont, for cloaks, and to the count of Auxerre for the military build-up on the Norman marches.[148] On three occasions he had dealings with the Jews.[149] Two clerks assisted him in these activities and perhaps in the chancery.[150]

This picture of Guérin as a wide-ranging, omnicompetent administrator persists through the second half of the reign. In 1206, when the chamberlain drew up the inventory of jewels, he did it in the presence of Brother Guérin, who himself parcelled out individual gems.[151] In 1207 Guérin joined Barthélemy de Roye to intervene in the dispute between the commune and chapter of Rouen.[152] Pope Innocent III wrote him in 1212 as one who had special influence over the king in the interminable quarrel over the annulment of the royal marriage, and Guérin was probably responsible for bringing the dispute to its final resolution.[153] But Guérin enjoyed the confidence of Ingeborg as well, because she appointed him as executor of her will.[154] He assumed responsibilities in the military operations leading up to Bouvines.[155] On the eve of the battle, the bishop-elect opposed the advice of the barons and pressed for immediate engagement of the enemy. According to Guillaume le Breton, he harangued the troops before the battle and received the surrender of the arch-traitor Renaud, count of Boulogne, for which Philip rewarded him with Argenteuil, confiscated from the count.[156] Five years later he accompanied Prince Louis on his expedition into the south against the Albigensian heretics.[157] As a cleric and later a bishop, Guérin naturally attended to purely ecclesiastical affairs, involving, for example, the investigation of heresy at Paris in 1209 and the adjudication of numerous disputes between churches.[158] As bishop of Senlis, he had the exclusive right to install royal abbots.[159] As the king's grip on affairs failed towards the end of the reign, private persons and even royal *baillis* addressed royal business directly to the bishop of Senlis.[160]

Writing of Guérin's election to the see of Senlis in 1213–1214, the royal chronicler Guillaume le Breton emphasizes the cleric's role in the king's government. Brother Guérin, he declares, was "the special counsellor of King Philip because of his wisdom in the royal hall and his incomparable gift of counsel . . . so that he handled the affairs of the kingdom and the needs of the churches as if he was second to the king." In the poetic version of the *Philippidos* this passage was rendered: "The special friend of the king who with the king handled the difficult business of the kingdom." At the same time a northern chronicler identifies him as "master of the royal *conseil*."[161] *Secundus a rege* was a common expression for designating chief royal ministers, but it was indeed apt for Guérin. Having served Philip in the chancery, the judiciary, and as his right-hand agent, he was the true successor to Guillaume, archbishop of Reims.

Only one name occurs with greater frequency than Brother Guérin's in the fiscal accounts of 1202/03. After the *prévôts* and *baillis* rendered their individual accounts, they turned over the balance of funds to a certain Brother Haimard. Since this figure is also known from other sources as the treasurer of the Knights Templars at Paris,[162] it is apparent that he acted in the same capacity as the six Parisian bourgeois of the ordinance of 1190. Whether he was responsible for transcribing the financial roll like Adam the royal clerk of 1190 is not clear. Philip may have found him on the crusade, or more likely, at the Temple of Paris. In all events, he was still functioning in this capacity in the now lost account of 1219,[163] and was active until 1227. Unlike Guérin, who performed a great variety of tasks, Brother Haimard specialized in finance. Though he was occasionally present on noteworthy occasions and substituted for Guérin as the clerical president of the Norman exchequer in 1213 and 1214,[164] most of his recorded activities dealt with money. His advice was sought, for example, in setting the exchange rates for Norman currency shortly after the conquest of the duchy.[165] He was naturally involved in transferring payments, transactions that have been brought to light by chance evidence.[166] Along with a *bailli* he evaluated landed revenues in an exchange of fiefs between the king and the count of Blois.[167] Like Guérin he was one of the executors of both the king's and Queen Ingeborg's wills, and served Gautier the Young in the same capacity.[168] Since the Templars had other accounts than the king's, he was also busy collecting crusading taxes for the popes and handling the finances of the countess of Champagne. Brother Haimard was obviously a banker with widespread connections throughout northern France and one with other clients than the king.[169]

Aside from the commanding figures of Brothers Guérin and Haimard at the central court, a score of other "clerks of the king" may be identified from repeated acts of service, from enjoyment of the king's patronage, or from the simple designation *clericus regis*. One of these of sufficient importance to be noticed by the chroniclers was Master Anselme, dean of Saint-Martin de Tours. A large collegiate church of ancient foundation, Saint-Martin was the object of rivalry between the French and English kings. Though traditionally under the patronage of the Capetians, it lay in territory dominated by the Angevins. Enjoying the favor of Philip Augustus, Anselme was elected dean in 1192 during Richard's absence on the crusade. On his return to France in 1194, Richard demanded fealty from the dean. When Anselme refused, the Angevin dispersed the canons of the church and drove the dean into exile, where he sought the French king's protection.[170] Throughout the summer of 1194, Philip used Anselme as his agent in the negotiations with Richard. He was one of the four French representatives at the conference at Vaudreuil, and with the constable Dreu de Mello and the chamberlain Ours he later issued a proclamation of truce.[171] In 1196 he also accompanied Ours as Philip's envoy to Walter, archbishop of Rouen, to arrange a settlement over the Vexin. He was most likely the Master Anselme who was elected bishop of Meaux in 1197.[172]

Anselme was representative of a frequently encountered pattern at Saint-Martin.[173] His successor was Eudes Clément, who before his election had a long record of royal duties. Brother of Alberic and Henri Clément, of a family that supplied the king with many familiars, Eudes advanced from vicar of Saint-Spire de Corbeil to archdeacon of Paris, and finally to dean of Saint-Martin (1211–1216).[174] As archdeacon and royal clerk he administered the regalia of the bishopric of Mâcon in 1198–1199.[175] In the account of 1202/03 he received fifty *sous* from the *prévôté* of Paris for an undesignated service.[176] In 1208 he collaborated with Gautier the Young and Brother Guérin at the exchequer of Rouen.[177] His Norman experience was probably considerable, because as dean of Saint-Martin he was recalled in 1213 to preside over the exchequer at Falaise in Brother Guérin's place.[178] In addition to these royal clerks, Saint-Martin also harbored close relatives of the king's. Louis VII's brothers had been both dean and treasurer of the church. Philip Augustus himself gave the latter office, which was in his patronage, to his illegitimate son Pierre Charlot.[179]

Because of the nature of the sources, royal clerks are more readily perceived when performing missions for the king. When they were at home, their routine duties may have escaped notice, but when they travelled, they attracted attention. The account of 1202/03, for example, records the expenses of two clerks: Guy, who travelled to Germany, and a Master Guillaume, who went to Flanders accompanied by two laymen.[180] This Guy was probably Guy d'Athée, "the faithful and familiar clerk of the king" whom Philip sent to the pope in 1208–1209 to request the annulment of his marriage.[181] In any case the king commanded Guy d'Athée and the seneschal of Anjou in 1214 to hand over the regalia to Hamelin, bishop-elect of Le Mans.[182] In subsequent years Guy was transferred to the service of Prince Louis.[183] Master Guillaume may have been the "Master W," treasurer of Saint-Frambaud de Senlis, who was an envoy to the pope in the summer of 1202, also to negotiate the annulment of the king's marriage.[184] He is less likely to have been Master Guillaume de Saint-Lazare, who defended Philip against Richard before the pope in 1198.[185] With Gautier the Young, this Master Guillaume was sent by the king in 1202 to punish the *vidame* of Châlons-sur-Marne for unlawful seizure of the regalia.[186] That same year Guillaume de Saint-Lazare was elected bishop of Nevers. Both Master Guillaumes were accompanied by a colleague, Master Folques, dean of the chapter of Orléans and the king's agent in Rome in the unsuccessful effort to transfer Philippe, bishop of Beauvais, to the vacant archbishopric of Reims in 1203.[187] Missions to Rome were then normal employment for royal clerks, but Philip's protracted negotiations with Innocent III over his marriage probably increased the number beyond the usual. In addition to the above, he sent his chaplain, Master Guillaume le Breton, in 1200, and the abbot of La Trappe and the king's clerk J in 1212.[188]

Though papal missions drew heavily upon the king's clerks, there were other assignments as well. In 1212 Philip sent a certain Master B along with a knight to represent him at the election and coronation of Emperor Frederick II.[189] The clerk may also have been the royal messenger dispatched in 1217 to negotiate with Pope Honorius III concerning Prince Louis's abortive expedition to England.[190] Similarly, in 1220 Master Simon de Maisons, a cleric, and Guillaume *de Valle Gloris*, a knight, were the king's envoys to London to receive oaths to respect the truce between Philip Augustus and Henry III.[191]

Other royal clerks performed duties in fixed regions. For example, in 1206 the dean of Saint-Aignan d'Orléans requested that the king appoint two proctors, Yves, "canon of Meaux and clerk of the royal court," and Master Gautier, "royal clerk at Orléans," in a settlement over manumission of serfs.[192] Though the former is merely a name to us, the latter is found as early as 1202 in the fiscal account receiving and disbursing funds from the vineyards of Orléans.[193] He was most likely identical with the better-known Master Gautier Cornut, "beloved and faithful clerk of the king," whose bequest Philip attested in 1215.[194] This Gautier Cornut, whose mother was the sister of Alberic, Henri, and Eudes Clément, became successively canon and dean of the chapter of Paris. His election to the bishopric of Paris in 1220 was opposed by the papacy, but in the last year of the king's life, he was rewarded with the archbishopric of Sens.[195] In another example from northeastern France, Master *Boso* (or Bons), clerk of the king, received the fealty of the *bourg* Saint-Remi de Reims in 1218.[196] He was most likely identical with Master *Bovo*, clerk of the king, who was custodian of the regalia of Beauvais in 1220 and of the church of Saint-Quentin in 1221.[197]

Some royal clerks come to light only because of the king's efforts to secure them prebends. For example, Philip requested the abbot of Saint-Denis in 1209 to present Master Etienne de Pithiviers with a church in the patronage of the abbey.[198] In 1210 the king, exercising his regalian rights over the vacant bishopric of Laon, conferred a prebend on his clerk Master Thomas d'Argenteuil, which was contested by another person, who appealed to the pope.[199] This Master Thomas was particularly noteworthy because he was patronized by the kings of both England and France. In 1200 King John, calling him "our clerk," provided him with an annual salary from the exchequer at Caen until a regular living could be found.[200] Again in 1214 the English king, now calling him the clerk of the king of France, assigned him the church of Salekil in England.[201] He may also be the Master Thomas who represented Philip Augustus at Rome in 1215.[202]

We must assume that this handful of royal clerks represents only a small fraction of the total because their names emerge under unusual circumstances. Despite the fortuitous character of this sample group of *clerici regis*, recognizable characteristics emerge from it. Not surprisingly, Philip Augustus drew his clerks from long-established sources of a kind available to most medieval monarchs. Certain clerks, like Eudes Clément and Gautier Cornut, came from families fertile in producing men for the royal service. Philip's court, like that of the English kings, relied on families whose loyalty to their sovereigns had long been tested. Also like the Anglo-Norman administration, royal churches, such as Saint-Martin de Tours and Saint-Frambaud de Senlis, and regalian bishoprics, such as Amiens and Laon, had long supplied livings for royal clerks. The prebends of the treasurers of Saint-Martin and of Saint-Frambaud, for example, were reserved for the king's nominees.[203] When Guérin became bishop of Senlis, a prebend in the chapter was set aside for the nephew of Barthélemy de Roye and then for the royal chronicler Guillaume le Breton.[204]

Furthermore, over half of these clerks boasted the academic title of "master," indicating formal education. Philip was recruiting his administration from the numerous schools of France, of which the most celebrated were at Paris. This indication of reliance on the educational resources of the kingdom is probably exaggerated, however, because our sample is heavily weighted by those sent to Rome to negotiate with the pope over the king's marriage. In all likelihood more education was required of these men than of regular *familiares* such as Brother Guérin and Eudes Clément. Other evidence suggests that Henry II, Richard, and John actually employed masters in greater numbers than did Philip Augustus. Though French schools led western Europe in producing educated men, the Anglo-Norman government offered them more jobs.[205] The careers of Brother Guérin, Guillaume de Saint-Lazare, and Gautier Cornut also suggest that royal clerks were rewarded by promotion to episcopal rank. However, five (at the most) king's clerks elevated to episcopal rank out of eighty-four elections during the reign is not a high proportion.[206] By comparison to the Anglo-Norman realm, where episcopal sees were most often filled by clerks from the royal court, the number under the Capetians was strikingly low. In Philip Augustus's France freedom of church elections was taken seriously, and the chapters were not under pressure to elect royal clerks. A French royal clerk, unlike his English counterpart, could not ordinarily expect to end up as a bishop.

Visible to us because of the new governmental documentation of the 1190s, Philip Augustus's new men did not attract the attention of contemporary chroniclers for decades. To be sure, individuals were noticed in fleeting glimpses. An English chronicler witnessed the chamberlain

Ours negotiating for Philip in 1194, and in 1209 Guillaume le Breton identified Brother Guérin as "a counsellor of the king" who joined an investigation into heresy at Paris.[207] Only in 1207 did a Norman chronicler notice that Barthélemy de Roye and Brother Guérin, both "noble and important in the royal counsel," had been dispatched to Rouen to mediate between the commune and the chapter.[208]

It was not until 1213, however, that contemporary historians took notice of Philip's intimate counsellors as a group. In that year, when Guillaume le Breton recognized Guérin's importance on his elevation to the episcopacy, the anonymous chronicler of Béthune speaks of the inner *conseil* of Philip Augustus. In both versions of the chronicle, he relates that when the king deliberated on a project for invading England, he called together his trusted counsellors, Brother Guérin, Barthélemy de Roye, and Henri Clément. These three summoned a fourth, the chamberlain, who was unnamed. Since the grand chamberlain Barthélemy de Roye was already present, this chamberlain was undoubtedly one of the sons of Gautier, most likely Gautier the Young. In the chronicler's brief portraits of the three who were named one can sense a tinge of hostility on the part of a vernacular writer articulating the high aristocracy's disdain for the inner circle of lesser men. Brother Guérin, the Anonymous declares, was a Hospitaler who spoke well but was too clever and dominant over the king. Although he had become bishop of Senlis, he was of low birth (*de basses gens*). Henri the Marshal was a small knight (*petit chevalier*), but because he had served the king well in war, he had been rewarded with the great fief of Argentan in Normandy. Barthélemy de Roye, a "great knight" (*gras chevalier*), was also much favored in the king's *conseil*. Avoiding the term *prud'homme*, which normally denoted aristocratic approval, the chronicler makes pointed reference to Guérin's low birth and to Henri's lesser station, which rendered their promotions and rewards all the more remarkable.[209]

Actually this inner circle had been working together as early as 1195. In that year Ours, chamberlain of the king of France, Gautier his brother, Henri the Marshal, and Barthélemy de Roye witnessed a transaction conducted in the presence of the mayor of Amiens.[210] Scattered charters offer further glimpses of their collaboration in 1206, 1208, and 1216 in Paris and Normandy.[211] When Philip made his painful decision to burn his fleet at Damme in 1213, he did it on the advice of Gautier, Barthélemy, and Guérin. "These were the only people," in the words of Guillaume le Breton, "to whom the king was accustomed on all occasions to open his soul and reveal his secret thoughts." As was to be expected, this inner circle remained at Philip's side during the hours of his great triumph at Bouvines. Here Guillaume again notes that Gautier, Barthélemy, and Guillaume de Garlande dwelt with the king both at home and in war, because, as everyone knew, he rarely proceeded without their counsel, for which he reimbursed their expenses.[212]

When Philip drew up his testament in 1222, Gautier the Young and Henri Clément were dead, but Guérin and Barthélemy were appointed executors of his will, along with the treasurer, Brother Haimard.[213] Outliving the king and furnishing up to thirty years of service, Barthélemy and Guérin must have been young men when they entered the royal court. This new generation of royal *familiares* gave the central administration remarkable continuity. Lacking great wealth and position of their own, they were completely dependent on the king for their substance and status. Although well rewarded, neither they nor their descendants were able to profit from their royal service to rise to baronial rank, unlike so many *familiares* at the English court.[214] Among the inner group, only Guérin became a magnate by virtue of his election to episcopal dignity, a reward that was a normal expectation for English royal clerks. Yet the loyalty and effectiveness of Philip's new men were apparently beyond reproach because no dismissals have come to light among these intimates of the king.

The royal historiographer Rigord maintains that Philip Augustus from the outset rendered his important decisions with *consilium*.[215] In contemporary parlance the term bore a twofold and overlapping connotation well articulated in its English equivalents: *counsel* as in advice and *council* as in a group of people. Similarly, *consiliarii* could mean either counsellors (advisors) or councillors (members of the council). We have seen that in the second half of the twelfth century, Philip's father created a specifically royal *conseil* (the French word preserves the double meaning) out of the preceding and ubiquitous feudal *conseil* owed by vassals to their lord.[216] Although this royal *consilium* was by no means fully developed, it increasingly became a permanent institution in which the king consulted his *consiliarii*, even if their consent was not overtly and regularly required. After the Second Crusade, the men who comprised the *consilium* included not only the lowly chamberlains, knights, and clerks of the king's household, but also the *proceres*, *optimates*, and magnates of the realm. This situation was inherited by the young Philip Augustus and remained in force until his departure on crusade. After his return in 1191, however, the numbers of his *consiliarii* began to contract and their character to change. The terms *consilium* and *consiliarii* were applied to his new men. In Guillaume le Breton's language, Brother Guérin was *regis consiliarius*, even *specialis consiliarius*, exercising the *incomparabilem consilii virtutem*. The Norman chronicler saw both Guérin and Barthélemy de Roye as *nobiles et majores in consilio regis*. By 1213 the northern chroniclers narrow the inner circle of Philip's court to four *conseillieres*, of whom Guérin was *maistres de son consel* and Barthélemy was *bien de son conseil*.[217] Most of the important duties of central administration were in fact borne by this small group.

The emergence of a restrictive nucleus of lesser *consiliarii* not only deviated from Capetian practice before 1190, but also distinguished it from Anglo-Norman government. From at least Henry I's time (1100–1135), the courts of the English kings were large affairs, comprising not only cliques of lesser *curiales* raised to prominence by royal patronage, but also the wealthiest landholders and tenants-in-chief, who were equally drawn into the royal entourage by the king's munificence.[218] By contrast Philip Augustus's working *curia* was limited to a handful of his new men. In 1200 the poet Gilles de Paris complained that the king rarely took counsel from anyone except the few whom he tolerated at court. Among Philip's numerous traits observed by the chronicler of Tours was a propensity to avail himself of the counsel of lesser men.[219] By the end of the reign this disparity between English and Capetian practice became fully evident. In 1227 a citizen of Caen sent an intelligence report to Henry III of England of a conversation he had overheard between the castellan of Caen and Master Nicolas, the clerk of Brother Guérin. The two Frenchmen contended that the English kings did not have the good sense of the French in taking counsel. Whereas King Philip consulted Brother Guérin and Barthélemy de Roye, and only these two, the English kings took counsel from a great number. When the English kings wished to declare war, therefore, their intentions were publicized even before the decision was taken.[220] Behind this practical advantage lay a significant difference in the sizes of the French and English *conseils*.

BAILLIS

The ordinance-testament of 1190 entrusted local affairs to two groups of royal agents, *prévôts* and *baillis*. Already well established in Capetian administration, the *prévôts'* financial and judicial functions were tacitly assumed in the constitution of 1190.[221] By 1202/03 their number had increased to about forty-five *prévôts*, with jurisdiction over sixty-two *prévôtés* (an addition of ten since 1190).[222] As in the past, these men were identified only by the location of their posts and therefore remained nameless, for the most part, as individuals. The ordinance of 1190 further specified that the *baillis* were to appoint four local men in each *prévôté* with whose advice (or, at least, that of two of them) the *prévôt* must conduct his business. Like the six bourgeois of Paris, these advisors were an expedient to circumscribe the *prévôts'* authority and was probably limited to the duration of the regency, because no subsequent trace has been found of its operation. In addition, the ordinance commissioned the *baillis* to report crimes or injustices committed by the *prévôts* to the regents three times a year. This second device for supervising the *prévôts* probably lasted through the reign.[223] These provisions announced an important innovation in local administration, the creation of a new royal agent, the *bailli*.

Prior to 1190 the royal charters divulge little precise information about the *baillis'* functions. In the ordinance of that year, in which the *baillis* play a dominant role, they appear chiefly as judicial officers, for whom supervision of *prévôts* was just one of their duties. More important, they were instructed to hold monthly assizes in their regions, where they heard pleas and recorded fines. When the regents heard pleas three times a year at Paris, the *baillis* were required to attend and to give account of the affairs of the realm. In the accounts of 1202/03 they not only reported the profits of justice, but were responsible for collecting occasional revenues such as regalian rights, forest income, *tailles*, and so on. Beyond these judicial and financial responsibilities the *baillis* were recipients of royal commands to protect churches, make payments of royal alms, and hold inquests to inform the king about his rights and resources throughout the domain. We shall have occasion to examine these duties in greater detail when we turn to royal justice and finance.

As active officials, *baillis* were virtually unknown in Capetian charters before the reign of Philip Augustus.[224] In March 1184, however, when the king conceded to the lepers of Survilliers dead wood from his forest of Montméliant, he ordered not only his *prévôts* but also his *baillis* not to interfere.[225] Thereafter, the royal charters increasingly associated the *baillis* with *prévôts* as recipients of royal commands.[226] On the eve of Philip's departure for the crusade, and simultaneously with the ordinance of 1190, the king issued a stream of charters in which *prévôts* and *baillis* were instructed to protect churches during his absence.[227] Whereas before the ordinance the *baillis* almost invariably followed the *prévôts* as recipients of royal commands, during the king's absence the regents began addressing the *baillis* first, followed by the *prévôts*.[228] After Philip's return in 1191 royal instructions were increasingly dispatched to *baillis* alone.[229] If *prévôts* were included, they almost invariably followed the *baillis*.[230] The ordinance was therefore a turning point in the evolution of the *bailli*'s office and signalled their eventual supremacy over the *prévôts* as the most active officers of the royal domain.

For the most part, Philip Augustus effected this transition by merely appointing new *baillis* and assigning them new duties, while allowing the older *prévôts* to continue their accustomed tasks. In one unusual case, however, the king transformed a *prévôt* into a *bailli*, and his career illustrates the differing responsibilities exercised by these royal officials. In 1186, immediately following the treaty of Boves, Pierre de Béthisy appeared as *prévôt* of Amiens working in concert with Bernard de la Croix, mayor of the city.[231] After the king decreed in 1190 that general pleas should be heard at Amiens three times a year, corresponding to the *baillis'* monthly assizes, Pierre and Bernard presided over such pleas in January 1192.[232] Five years later Pierre began collaborating with northern *baillis* such as Pierre de Villevoudée, Guillaume Pastez, and Pierre's brother, Renaud de Béthisy, in hearing pleas, issuing commands, attesting charters, and holding inquests.[233] The accounts of February 1203 indicate that he went on a mission with Master Guillaume and Aubert de Hangest.[234] In the *prévôts'* accounts of that fiscal year he acknowledged his farm and deducted his expenses like ordinary *prévôts*,[235] but in the *baillis'* accounts he collected large sums from justice (*expleta*), forests, and feudal service—all of which were the *baillis'* responsibility.[236] Although still entitled a *prévôt*, Pierre de Béthisy had, in fact, also become a *bailli* like his brother Renaud.[237]

In the decade following the ordinance of 1190, these new royal agents were identified by varied terminology, characteristic of a formative period.[238] In addition to the title of *ballivi*, they were also called *assessores* to the south of Paris, thus indicating their role in the local assizes. For example, Hugues de Gravelle was "assessor of the king" at Etampes in 1192, and in 1204 Guillaume Menier, Adam Héron, and Barthélemy Droon were all designated "assessors of Etampes."[239] On the other hand, Guillaume de la Chapelle called himself *officialis domini regis* at Lorris in 1201. When in that year the king referred to the same incident, he designated Guillaume as *bailli*.[240] At the assizes of Gisors in 1196 Pierre de Neuilly and Eustache *de Hadencost* styled themselves as "knights and *justicii* of the Vexin."[241] *Justicii* and *justiciarii* were standard Norman terminology and persisted after the conquest of the duchy.[242] Yet in 1196 Pierre and Renaud de Béthisy were called "*baillis* of Philip king of the French in the land of Pierrefonds," a title that was shared by Pierre de Villevoudée the following year.[243] By the year 1200, however, most of the identifiable *baillis* were entitled either *ballivi domini regis* or simply *ballivi* at some point in their careers.[244] This emergence of standardized terminology indicates that the *baillis* were becoming a regularized institution.

Whereas *prévôts* were identified simply by the location of their *prévôtés*, the *baillis*, at least in the beginning, were not as closely linked with a geographic jurisdiction. In the ordinance of 1190 Philip Augustus declared "that he was placing *baillis* in lands that were distinguished by their own names" (*que propriis nominibus distincte sunt*.)[245] Although the phrase is ambiguous he must have meant that the various parts of the royal domain were to take their names from the *baillis* rather than vice versa. This was, in fact, the practice in the fiscal accounts of 1202/03, in which the *baillis*, in contrast to the *prévôts*, were listed by name without territorial designations. Yet *baillis* also, in fact, operated in local areas with which they became associated. As early as 1191 and 1192 royal charters referred to the "*bailliages*" of Etampes and Paris. In 1194 the king issued an order to the *bailli* of Sens.[246] The northernmost *bailli*, Nevelon the Marshal, styled himself "*bailli* of Arras" throughout his long career from 1201 to 1222, and his example was followed by the adjacent *baillis* of Saint-Omer, Aire, and Hesdin.[247] How these two opposing tendencies coexisted can be seen in the accounts of 1202/03. Although the *baillis* bore no geographic titles, they actually worked in different directions out of Paris—directions that were not discrete because each *bailli*'s sphere of operations overlapped and interlaced with those of his neighbors. Thus emerged territorial jurisdictions (later called *bailliages*) that were not yet clearly and fully delimited.

In the accounts of 1202/03, which provide the most comprehensive picture available, twelve *baillis* were active in the royal domain.[248] (See Map 2.) At the center, based on Paris, was Robert de Meulan, whose dealings extended to the west as far as Vernon and Evreux, to the north to Chaumont and Senlis, southward to Etampes, and up the Seine to Corbeil, Melun, and Moret-sur-Loing. To the west he was bordered by two minor figures: Aleaume Hescelin, who concentrated on Meulan but extended to Chaumont in the north and to Saint-Germain-en-Laye in the southeast, and Mathieu Pisdoë, who was active in Mantes and Vernon.

Three principal *baillis* worked to the south of Paris. The closest was Hugues de Gravelle, whose activities were concentrated at Dourdan and

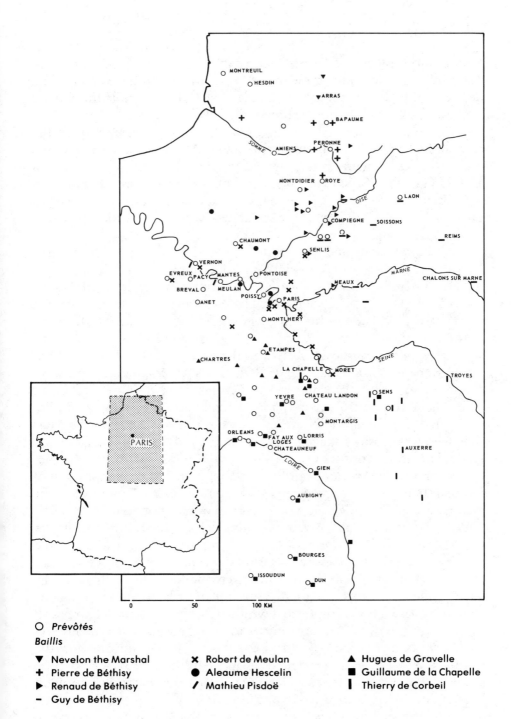

MONTREUIL
HESDIN
ARRAS
BAPAUME
SOMME
AMIENS
PERONNE
MONTDIDIER ROYE
OISE
LAON
COMPIEGNE
SOISSONS
REIMS
CHAUMONT
SENLIS
VERNON
EVREUX
PACY
MANTES
PONTOISE
MARNE
CHALONS SUR MARNE
BREVAL
MEULAN
MEAUX
POISSY
PARIS
ANET
MONTLHERY
ETAMPES
CHARTRES
LA CHAPELLE
MORET
SEINE
YEVRE
CHATEAU LANDON
SENS
TROYES
MONTARGIS
ORLEANS
FAY AUX
LOGES
LORRIS
CHATEAUNEUF
AUXERRE
LOIRE
GIEN
AUBIGNY
BOURGES
ISSOUDUN
DUN

PARIS

| 0 | 50 | 100 KM |

O *Prévôtés*

Baillis

▼ Nevelon the Marshal   ✕ Robert de Meulan   ▲ Hugues de Gravelle
✚ Pierre de Béthisy   ● Aleaume Hescelin   ■ Guillaume de la Chapelle
▶ Renaud de Béthisy   ╱ Mathieu Pisdoë   ▮ Thierry de Corbeil
━ Guy de Béthisy

Map 2. Prévôtés and Baillis of the Royal Domain in 1202/03

Etampes, but ranged as far as Chartres in the west, Vitry-aux-Loges in the south, and Nemours in the east. Further to the south was Guillaume de la Chapelle, whose affairs were centered on Orléans. Guillaume ranged farthest of all the *baillis*, extending to Janville in the north, Chartres in the northwest, Bourges, Issoudun, and Dun in the south, Sens in the east, and Chapelle-la-Reine in the northeast. He was also aided by two minor figures: Abelin around Issoudun and Dun, and Guy Bernovin around Châtillon-Coligny. Finally, working in a southwesterly direction was Thierry de Corbeil, whose main operations extended from Sens to Dixmont to Auxerre, but who also ranged to Vézelay in the south and Troyes in the east.

Four *baillis* dominated Vermandois and Artois to the north of Paris. Renaud de Béthisy worked principally at Compiègne and Montdidier, but also covered Péronne to the north, Beauvais to the west, Senlis to the south, and Meaux to the southeast. His relative Guy de Béthisy worked to the east, with Laon as his center. He extended to Noyon in the west, Verberie in the southwest, Rebais in the south, and Reims and Châlons-sur-Marne in the southeast. Farther to the north lay the sphere of activities of Renaud's brother, Pierre de Béthisy. As *prévôt-bailli* of Amiens he was most active in that city and in Péronne, but he also reached to Abbeville in the west, Roye in the south, and Bapaume in the north. Beyond Pierre de Béthisy and farthest to the north was Nevelon the Marshal, who was mostly engaged at Arras and Lens. We owe this map of the *baillis'* operations to the fortuitous survival of the accounts of 1202/03, the eve of the military campaign against King John. After the conquest of Normandy in the west and Anjou and Touraine in the Loire valley, the process of territorial delimitation became more pronounced.

Paris was naturally at the center of this emerging distribution of *baillis*, but its local officials remain obscure. As the developing capital of the kingdom, Paris had possessed at least two *prévôts* working together since early Capetian times, but their names were rarely recorded. It was only when Philip Augustus punished the *prévôt* of Paris for mistreating the scholars in 1200, for example, that we learn that he was called Thomas.[249] Moreover, the older *prévôts* are difficult to distinguish from the newly created *baillis* of the region.[250] In the accounts of 1202/03, for example, the unnamed *prévôt* of Paris accounted separately from the *bailli*, Robert de Meulan. Although Robert received sums from the *prévôt's* accounts in May 1203, three years earlier he had himself been designated one of the *prévôts*.[251] It is possible therefore that Robert de Meulan was also one of the *prévôts* in 1202/03. By 1217 the accounts both of the *prévôté* and of the *baillis* were confided to Nicolas Arrode and Philippe Hamelin, and they were consolidated into one account in 1219.[252] From that point on, if not earlier, it became proper to speak of a *prévôt-bailli* of Paris. Yet even this important royal official has left fewer traces of his identity than the other *baillis*.[253]

The meager sources divulge one consistent trait about the *prévôt-baillis* of Paris—that they usually worked in pairs. Robert de Meulan and Pierre du Thillai in 1200, Eudes Popin and Eudes Arrode in 1205, and Nicolas Arrode and Philippe Hamelin in 1217 were associated probably to share the burdens of the large farms assessed to the *prévôté* of Paris.[254] Yet such collaboration was also characteristic of *baillis*, where responsibility for *prévôtal* farms was not in question. For example, Guillaume Menier, a *bailli* most active around Etampes, worked frequently with at least five other *baillis* in the southern region. At the assizes of Etampes in 1204 he executed a judgment with Adam Héron and Barthélemy Droon. In the company of Guillaume de la Chapelle he imposed a fine upon the *prévôts* of Orléans in 1210.[255] With Guillaume de Azaio, *bailli* of Touraine, he conducted an inquest into a dispute between Saint-Martin of Tours and Dreu de Mello. At the end of the reign he collaborated with Etienne de Hautvilliers.[256] In his long career (1203–1235) Guillaume Menier was in contact with every important *bailli* in the southern domain from Etampes to Tours.

This pattern of collaboration is best seen in the northeastern region, where the *baillis* developed a system of teamwork. By 1203 Guillaume Pastez was working either with Renaud or Pierre de Béthisy or both. Pierre de Béthisy dropped out in 1205, and he had been replaced by Gilles de Versailles by 1207. Guillaume, Renaud, and Gilles worked in close concert until 1215, when Guillaume Pastez dropped out, to be replaced by Soibert de Laon in 1216. The new team continued until 1221, when Renaud de Béthisy disappeared from the scene. Guillaume de Châtelliers joined the group in 1216, becoming increasingly active after 1220.[257] These teams of two to three *baillis* ranged widely over an area bounded by Senlis, Beauvais, Amiens, Bapaume and Laon, holding assizes, making judgments, conducting inquests, attesting agreements, and executing the king's commands. Moreover, none of these southern or northeastern *baillis* who worked in teams designated himself geographically. Their titles were "*bailli* of the king" or simply "*bailli*." This collaboration was therefore apparently designed for the southern and northeastern domain, where geographic divisions were not yet fully developed. By contrast, Artois seems to have been more clearly defined. Its *bailli*, Nevelon the Marshal, for example, worked with two colleagues early in his career,[258] but carried out his duties alone during the remainder of the reign.

In the second half of the reign, when the evidence becomes more plentiful, this teamwork among neighboring *baillis* was expanded to collaboration with colleagues far from the normal sphere of operations. Thibaut le Maigre, for example, who usually worked in the Vexin, was associated in 1210 with two southern *baillis*, Guillaume de la Chapelle and Adam Héron, in a decision involving the commune of Jard to the south of Paris.[259] In the opposite direction, Guillaume Menier, who normally worked around Etampes, participated in decisions taken at Compiègne and Dampierre in 1215 and 1218.[260] As was to be expected, *baillis* from all directions worked closely together during their scheduled visits to Paris three times a year. For example, Guillaume Pastez and Gilles de Versailles from the north, Guillaume Menier from the south, and Hugues de Bastons from the Paris region judged between the abbey of Saint-Denis and the lords of Mello in the king's court at Paris in 1207. Gilles de Versailles from the north, Thibaut le Maigre from the Vexin, and Guillaume de la Chapelle from the south attested a property recognition in the royal court at Paris on 8 February 1212. Since this coincided with the Purification convocation of the *baillis*, it was obviously part of their triannual meeting.[261]

Some of this movement suggests, however, that individual *baillis* were transferred from region to region. Pierre du Thillai, for example, first appeared in 1200 as *prévôt* of Paris. In the fiscal account of 1202/03 he collaborated with Guillaume de la Chapelle in the south, where Pierre was entitled *bailli* and assessor of Orléans. From 1205 and until the end of his career (1224) he was the active *bailli* of Caen in Normandy.[262] Similarly, Barthélemy Droon was assessor of Etampes in 1204 before his long service as *bailli* of Verneuil in Normandy (1209–1227).[263] Renaud de Cornillon was *prévôt* of Paris in 1202 before he became *bailli* of the Contentin.[264] In the steps of Renaud's career, Miles de Lévis collaborated with the *prévôt* of Paris in 1202, guarded royal castles in the Auvergne, and finally also became *bailli* of the Contentin from 1215 to 1223.[265] The most striking example of frequent transfer, however, was Guillaume de la Chapelle. First appearing in 1200 as one of the team who adjudicated the borders of Evreux, he was active around Orléans in the following year.[266]

He later returned to Normandy at the exchequer in 1209 and 1214 and substituted as president for Gautier the Young in 1213 and for Brother Guérin in 1216.[267] On another occasion he was designated castellan of Arques.[268] Yet in 1215 he actively participated in judgments and inquests around Compiègne.[269] By 1216 or 1217 he had returned to the southern region, where he ended his career. These examples suggest that some *baillis* were discouraged from putting down roots that permitted them independent authority in any one place and were frequently moved around the domain to keep them dependent on their royal master.

Remuneration was, of course, the most effective means for controlling royal officials. In the later thirteenth century Norman *baillis* were paid handsome salaries.[270] In 1202/03 the daily wages of three *baillis* were recorded: Robert de Meulan received one *livre*, Mathieu Pisdoë 15 *sous*, and Hugues de Gravelle 10 *sous*.[271] Since 10 *sous* equalled the highest rate for mercenary knights and was almost three times the wage of the highest-paid artisan,[272] these *baillis* were earning attractive salaries. In addition to his salary Hugues de Gravelle received gifts of clothing from the master of the royal wardrobe, as did Guillaume Pastez.[273] Among those granted precious stones in the jewel account were four *baillis*.[274] For reasons that are not clear, however, wages for the other *baillis* were not reported in 1202/03. We shall see that the conquest of Normandy provided confiscated fiefs and other lands for enriching the *baillis* of the duchy, but this remuneration seems not to have been employed during the first decade.

On the eve of the conquest of Normandy, the social composition of the corps of *baillis* was already distinct, and the pattern persisted through the remainder of the reign. Like the lay members of the royal court, the overwhelming majority of *baillis* were knights.[275] The exceptions were few and usually singled out. Guillaume de la Chapelle, Renaud de Cornillon, Aleaume Hescelin, and Renaud the Archer were designated as the king's sergeants.[276] The *bailli* Soibert was always carefully distinguished as a bourgeois (*civis*) of Laon.[277] Guillaume Poucin entered royal employment as a pantler (*panetarius*).[278] And we have seen that the office of *prévôt* was an occasional source for recruiting *baillis*. Pierre de Béthisy served a long tenure (1186–1211) as *prévôt* and then *bailli* at Amiens,[279] and Guy de Béthisy was also simultaneously *bailli* and *prévôt* of Laon.[280] The *prévôts* and *baillis* of Paris had become amalgamated by 1219.

The repetition of surnames also suggests family connections among the royal *baillis*. The double occurrence of such names as Meulan (Hugues

and Robert at Paris), Arrode (Eudes and Nicolas at Paris), Hautvilliers (Etienne and Nicolas in the southern domain), and Ville-Thierri
(Guillaume at Gisors and Renaud at Bayeux-Avranches) leads us to suspect kinship, though blood relationships cannot be demonstrated as yet
for lack of evidence. The surname La Chapelle, borne by at least five *baillis*, was a common one. Though the parentage of Hugues and Colin de la
Chapelle (both from Bourges) is unknown, Guillaume de la Chapelle was
clearly the father of Geoffroi and Thibaut, and all three were *baillis* in the
Norman Caux.[281] Miles de Lévis, *bailli* of the Contentin, was the eldest
son of Philippe de Lévis, one of the king's early and trusted familiars.[282]
Guillaume Escaucol, *bailli* at Rouen, was the brother of Jean *Palae*, another royal agent.[283] The Béthisy family produced two northeastern *baillis*,
Pierre and Renaud, who were brothers, but it is unlikely that Guy of the
same surname was as closely related.[284] Guillaume Pastez most probably
came from the family that had previously supplied Baudouin Pastez as
prévôt of Bapaume for Philippe, count of Flanders.[285] Out of ninety
baillis, this paucity of examples of known or suspected parentage in the
profession indicates that family connections played a relatively minor role
in recruitment. The family who came closest to establishing an administrative dynasty were the La Chapelles, of whom Guillaume, Geoffroi,
and Thibaut succeeded to, and collaborated with, one another as *baillis*
of Caux.

The old royal domain produced most of the *baillis* whose origins are
known. In the Paris region, Aleaume Hescelin came from the city itself,
Pierre du Thillai from Gonesse (as did his colleague and son-in-law,
Eudes de Trembley), and Jean de Rouvrai from Rambouillet.[286] Many
baillis were also recruited from the southern domain. Guillaume de la
Chapelle's family originated from the Orléanais, and Renaud de Ville-
Thierri from the diocese of Sens.[287] The Lévis family held their most important lands around Montlhéry.[288] Barthélemy Droon began his career
in royal service at Etampes. As was to be expected, the king's ancestral
lands, whose families were well known and whose loyalties were long
tested, supplied the most active officials.

Like the close *familiares* at court, Philip Augustus's *baillis* gave the king
many years of service. Although the span of their activities is only known
through the chance survival of charters, it can nonetheless be determined
that twenty-three *baillis* were in royal employ for at least ten years, fifteen
for at least fifteen years, and nine gave twenty or more years of service.
Guillaume Menier was active for a record thirty-two years (1203–1235),

mainly in the southern domain. With a life expectancy of fifty-five and with allowance for old age and retirement, these figures suggest that many of Philip's *baillis* entered royal service as comparatively young men. The length of service, together with the fact that no dismissals (with one exception, a Norman case)[289] of *baillis* have come to light, also suggests that Philip's *baillis* were both loyal and effective agents.

Newly created by the king, the *bailli* under Philip Augustus possessed untried and not fully defined powers. As a novel exponent of royal authority in the provinces, he provoked feelings of fear and mistrust among his subjects. Nevelon the Marshal, royal *bailli* of Artois since 1201, for example, established a reputation for rapacious exactions. The Anonymous of Béthune claims that after the king had restored lasting peace to the realm following the battle of Bouvines, it was disturbed only by Nevelon. So greatly did he enslave the land that people wondered how long their sufferings could endure. Gerald of Wales, who was also well informed on French affairs, calls him "that most wicked custodian of Arras." Later investigations under Louis IX amply confirmed these charges.[290] A similar mistrust of *baillis* later inspired an *exemplum* that became attached to Philip Augustus's name. Its fullest version, reported by the historian Richer de Senones, depicts a royal *bailli* of Paris (a royal *prévôt* in another version) who employs ruses to defraud the widow of a royal knight of her inheritance of a vineyard. Only through Philip's astuteness is the fraud discovered and the *bailli* punished.[291] Whether or not the actual story can be authenticated, the *exemplum* surely reflects the fear *baillis* like Nevelon the Marshal inspired among contemporaries.

By instituting *baillis* Philip superimposed on the older *prévôts* new officials to hear pleas of justice, to collect occasional revenues, and to execute royal commands. Circulating in teams throughout the royal domain, the *baillis* were more mobile than the *prévôts*. Required from the beginning to report three times a year to the central court, they were more responsive to royal wishes. Other rulers of northwestern Europe were similarly creating new agents more effective at local administration. Almost a century earlier the Anglo-Normans had experimented with new officials to operate alongside the sheriffs who had traditionally presided over the local shires in England. From these experiments emerged travelling justices (*justiciarii itinerantes*), who by the reign of Henry II were organized into circuits of three each to hear pleas throughout the realm.[292] Among the counts of Flanders, Philippe of Alsace (1163–1191) also introduced new local officials to provide justice, collect revenues, and defend the

counts' rights beyond those duties traditionally performed by the domanial agents. Appearing first in the Vermandois region by 1167, they
were known under various titles: *ballivi, justiciarii, ministeriales, nuntii*,
and so on, indicative of their experimental character. During the thirteenth century they were uniformly called *baillis*, their functions standardized, and their jurisdictions defined as *bailliages*.[293] It is difficult to
assess to what extent Philip Augustus's *baillis* were inspired by the Anglo-
Norman and Flemish experiments, but it is clear that the French king was
responding to similar needs to extend central authority into the localities
of the domain. At all events, Philip considered his *baillis* to be the equivalent of the English kings' travelling justices. When Richard and Philip
drafted a treaty in December 1189 for the mutual protection of their
lands during the crusade, they appointed their respective *justitiarii et bai-
livi* to safeguard its provisions.[294] As we consider the judicial and financial functions of these agents more closely, we shall see how similar their
duties were.

The Reorganization of Justice and Finance

The Expansion of Justice

In the ordinance of 1190 Philip Augustus addressed three principal concerns: justice, finance, and the regalian churches. As to the first, his intention was to expand the machinery of the royal court for settling disputes. He instructed the *baillis* throughout the domain to set aside one day each month to hold assizes at which they were to receive appeals, do justice without delay, defend royal rights, and record in writing fines due to the king. The *baillis* were undoubtedly assisted in these tasks by the four local men appointed to each *prévôté*.[1] Since no evidence of assizes before 1190 has surfaced in the Capetian domain, we are led to conclude that Philip created the system of assizes when he regularized the *baillis*.[2] The assizes were one of two judicial innovations of 1190 to become permanent fixtures of royal justice. In 1192 five assizors (*assessores*) operated at Etampes, one of whom, Hugues de Gravelle, was a *bailli*. The royal *bailli* Pierre du Thillai was also designated by the title of assizor when he attended the assizes of Orléans in 1203. In the following year the *baillis* Adam Héron and Barthélemy Droon participated in the assizes of Etampes.[3] In the northern domain three *baillis*, Guillaume Pastez, Pierre de Béthisy, and

Renaud de Béthisy, held a day of assizes (*die sessionis*) in the bishop of
Noyon's house at Péronne in 1205.[4] By the end of the reign, full assizes
(*assisia plena*) were held at Chauny, Compiègne, Senlis, Montdidier,
Clermont-sur-Oise, Péronne, Laon, and Amiens.[5] Since their existence is
attested only by scattered charters, we cannot determine whether or not
these sessions maintained the monthly schedule decreed by the ordinance
of 1190. Although the term *assize* apparently echoed preceding Anglo-
Norman practices, the institution was established in the French royal domain before the acquisition of Norman territories. When Philip took
over Gisors, Evreux, and the rest of Normandy, his previous experience in
the royal domain facilitated assimilation of the Norman assizes.[6] Through
the *baillis* and their assizes, the French king permanently extended the
services of his court to the local inhabitants of the domain.

Philip's ordinance of 1190 also envisaged reforms in the central *curia
regis* during his absence. The regents were instructed to hold court at
Paris three times a year to hear appeals (*clamores*) from the men of the
realm and to decide them for the honor of God and the utility of the
kingdom.[7] Though the exact dates were not specified, these sessions most
likely coincided with the triannual accountings of the *prévôts* and *baillis*.
At the same time the *baillis* were to report on the affairs of the realm and
the conduct of the *prévôts*. If anyone, moreover, had a complaint against
the *baillis*, he was to present it to the regents during these sessions. (The
regents were not, however, empowered to remove *baillis* except for such
gross offenses as murder, rape, or treason.) From all this information,
gathered three times a year, the regents were to report to Philip on the
state of the kingdom.[8] The one surviving charter from the regents is not
sufficient to indicate how the reforms of 1190 were put into effect during
the king's absence.[9] We have seen that other charters suggest that the regents shared their judicial functions with the Parisian bourgeois who supervised royal finances.[10]

In effect, the ordinance of 1190 instituted triannual sessions of the
curia regis to be held at Paris for three distinct purposes: to report to the
absent king on the affairs of the kingdom, to review and correct the conduct of local officials, and to set up judicial channels by which inhabitants
of the royal domain could appeal the decisions of the *baillis'* monthly assizes. The first was an explicitly temporary expedient that came to an end
with the regency. Some evidence suggests that the correction of *prévôts* by
the *baillis* continued after Philip's return,[11] but no extant information allows us to determine whether or not the procedure for correcting *baillis*

remained in effect. The system of regular sessions did not, however, survive the king's return. Paris no longer remained the exclusive locus for the royal court's sessions, and the surviving charters do not reveal continuation of a triannual schedule. In all likelihood the *curia regis*, now dependent on the king's personal participation, reverted to its former habits of following the royal peregrinations and of holding irregular sessions according to the demands of circumstances.

Although the royal court no longer held stated periodic sessions, it nonetheless pursued a policy of setting fixed times for specific cases. In 1202, for example, Philip assigned a day at Paris to which he convoked his counsellors to render a judgment over the noteworthy case of the regalia of Châlons-sur-Marne.[12] The clearest example for scheduling a case comes from the dispute between the bishop of Clermont and Ponce de Chapteuil over the castle of Vertaizon. After receiving a complaint from the bishop, the king summoned Ponce to Souvigny and assigned a day. When the latter neglected to appear, the hearing was rescheduled for Châteauroux. This time only Ponce's wife appeared, and a third day was assigned before the *bailli* Hugues de la Chapelle. When once again Ponce failed to respond, Philip's court adjudged the castle to the bishop in January 1205, because the prelate had personally appeared at all three hearings prepared to prove his case.[13] This example illustrates not only the procedure for scheduling a case, but also the difficulty of citing litigants before a wandering *curia regis*.[14]

Although the triannual sessions of the *curia regis* did not outlast Philip's return to France, it is nonetheless likely that the king's court continued to receive appeals on an irregular basis. At Péronne and Orléans the king's agents shared justice with the communes and other lords, but this was not a system of appeal.[15] An ancient and traditional device did, however, facilitate the transfer of a case from one court to another. By "default [*defectus*] of justice" a party could declare that a judge had refused to hear his case, was unable to come to a decision, or had not treated it with due seriousness. Although this was not in the strict sense an appeal (since an original judgment had not been rendered), it functioned like one in effecting the transfer of a case from one court to another.[16] For example, in 1200 Mathieu, lord of Montmorency, and Hugues, abbot of Saint-Denis, set up a procedure to solve their disputes. They appointed two men from each party who would meet at a designated elm, conduct inquests into the matters, and come to agreement. If three of the men could not agree, however, they could refer the dispute to the king's court, where it would be resolved on the men's advice.[17] And in 1211, when the king conceded the "pleas of the sword" (those pleas reserved for the duke) to the abbey of Fécamp in Normandy, he specified that cases could be heard in the French court (*curia gallicana*) in default of justice.[18] Similarly at Reims, if the citizens and *échevins* considered the archbishop's bans to be unreasonable, they could seek the king's arbitration if the archbishop refused to hear their complaint.[19] These examples, to which others could be added, merely reflect occasional remedies and constituted no regular system of appeal.[20] Moreover, they were limited to the royal domain and did not extend to the courts of thousands of lords both great and small throughout the kingdom. It would appear, then, that the king's or *baillis'* courts made no effort to encroach on this vast field of private jurisdiction to transfer cases from seigneurial to royal justice.

One curious exception to this general rule appeared in 1185, however, when the king arbitrated a dispute between the bishop of Laon and his men over *tailles*. Although Philip confirmed the bishop's traditional right to settle disputes among the bishop's men or between the bishop and his men, the king established a separate court of twelve *échevins*. If the *échevins* were unable to arrive at a judgment, they were to seek a decision in the bishop's court. If this failed, they were to come to the royal court, where all disputes were to be terminated within three months.[21] At the bishopric of Laon a procedure was therefore established for transferring cases from the *échevins* to the bishop to the king.

No other information about this practice is available until the end of the reign (1221), when the king ordered Guérin, bishop of Senlis, to conduct an inquest into royal rights in the episcopal city, county, and duchy of Laon. Although the bishop of Laon, Anselme, refused to participate, the inquest proceeded without him and was recorded. The report made by the fourteen jurors indicates that the system of appeals to the royal court continued to operate, but with modifications. If a dispute arose that did not pertain to the church's spiritual jurisdiction, an appeal (*appellatio*) could be made to the king as in the past. When the appeal came to the royal court, the king's *prévôt* or *bailli* commanded the *échevins* to decide whether there was default (*defectus*). If so, the case remained in the royal court. If not, it was returned to the original seigneurial court to be decided by the appropriate judges, but without additional expense or fine. Gautier, the bishop's chamberlain, who was among the jurors, attested to the operation of the bishop's secular court, which also handled appeals involving fiefs, domains, immovables, and chattels. As judge of this court, he first determined whether appeals pertained to spiritual matters, such as usury, marriage, and oaths. In that case they were immediately transferred to the court of the bishop's *officialis*. Secular cases remained in the chamberlain's court. If, however, an appeal was made from the chamberlain's court to the king's, the plea was transferred when default of justice could be proved. This inquest shows that, at the end of Philip's reign, cases at Laon continued to be appealed to the bishop's secular court and thence to the royal court in default of justice. Only the role of the *échevins* had changed. Though earlier they had held their own court, they were now incorporated into the royal court to judge whether a default of justice had occurred. As the inquest specified, they were the free men of the king (*francos homines*) who could judge knights and other free men of the region.[22]

The unusual feature at Laon was not the operation of an assize, but the system of appeals established between it and a seigneurial court, in this case that of the bishop. By mid–thirteenth century any defendant could refuse the jurisdiction of a seigneurial judge and transfer his case to the royal judges of the *bailliage* of Vermandois, seated at Laon. This procedure, known as the *appels volages du Laonnois*, was considered to be of ancient origin. It was widely opposed, not only by the bishop and other lords of the region, but also by outlying inhabitants of the Laonnois, who were obliged to travel considerable distances to the royal court. Although its origins and functions are obscure, a system of appeals undoubtedly functioned at Laon during the reign of Philip Augustus, which distinguishes this region from the rest of the kingdom.[23]

In addition to the *baillis'* assizes, one final judicial device became a permanent feature after 1190. This was the sworn inquest (*inquisitio*), which consisted of the court gathering a number of persons who had knowledge of a case, placing them under oath to tell the truth, and requiring an answer to questions put to them. These jurors (*jurati*) of the inquest were empowered to arrive at their decision in cases decided by agreement, arbitration, or judgment of the court. They differed from older, customary oath helpers or mere witnesses because they were not selected to support one of the contending parties, but were produced by the judge or the court to tell the truth, regardless of its consequences. Originating in early Frankish times, the inquest was widely employed by the Carolingians. In the late eleventh and twelfth centuries it survived notably in Normandy and Anjou. Though Louis VII may have made occasional use of it and Philip availed himself of the device during the first decade, it did not become a standard feature of French royal justice until 1190.[24] After that date about 22 percent of the decisions in Philip Augustus's *curia* made use of an inquest.[25] (See Table 2.)

With some variations, the French court employed two prevailing kinds of inquests, distinguished by those who chose the jurors. In one type, which may be called Norman because of its popularity in the Anglo-Norman realm, the judge selected the jurors from the vicinity and they arrived at their verdict collectively. Since the jurors' proceedings were mainly oral, only their final opinion was recorded in writing. In the other kind of inquest, inspired by canon law, the jurors were named by the contending parties but were nonetheless obligated to tell the truth under oath whatever the consequences for their respective litigants. Since the jurors were asked to furnish credentials and to answer a specific schedule of questions, they usually responded individually, and their replies were often recorded separately. Both kinds of inquests were deployed in varying ways in the court. At times the testimony of the jurors was merely taken into consideration when the court itself rendered a decision; at other times, the litigants agreed beforehand to accept the decision rendered by the inquest jurors. Royal charters and other documents that record the inquests are usually vague and imprecise. The verb *inquirere*, from which *inquisitio* derived, could designate any kind of investigation and was not necessarily limited to inquests. Though the formula *de inquisitione facienda . . . per legitimos homines terre*[26] leaves no doubt that the inquest was of the Norman variety, the phrase *facta diligenti inquisitione*[27] might suggest an inquest, but does not specify its kind. Often, however, the type of inquest is suggested by the phrasing of the royal charter. We might expect the canonical type, requiring more documentation, to be easier to identify, and the Norman variety, relying on oral decisions, to be reported more summarily. Almost never was the number of jurors specified in the decision, but twelve was a common figure in Normandy. The one designated figure of twenty in 1211 was perhaps mentioned because it was exceptional.[28]

Both Norman and canonical inquests appear in the decisions of the *curia regis* of 1190 and thereafter. Even before the acquisition of Norman territory, Philip Augustus began to apply the Norman type of inquest to his decisions. In July 1190 in a dispute between the church of Saint-Martin of Tours and King Richard of England over mutual rights in the town of Tours, he and Richard convoked a group of aged clerics and bourgeois, among whom the more honorable were put under oath to tell the truth about the former customs.[29] Lest it be thought that Richard's presence determined the choice of a Norman inquest at Tours, Philip also employed this type at Compiègne in 1200 in a case involving parties from Vermandois, and at Paris in 1201 in a case involving Saint-Denis.[30] After the conquest of Normandy in 1204, all inquests pertaining to the duchy naturally followed Norman precedents.[31]

At Tours in 1190, however, another dispute between King Richard and the archbishop of Tours was resolved through an inquest of the canonical type, and the decision was confirmed by Philip Augustus.[32] During the king's absence, moreover, the regents decided between the bishop of Autun and the abbot of Flavigny by conducting an inquest using the testimony of the bishops of Mâcon and Chalon-sur-Saône, called by the former litigant, and the abbots of Cluny and Saint-Pierre de Chalon, chosen by the latter.[33] But the most explicit case of a canonical inquest, and also the most informative example of a judgment by the *curia regis*, occurred in 1202, when the king contested the *vidame* of Châlons-sur-Marne's right to the regalia of the bishopric.[34] Answering the *vidame*'s request for a judgment by inquest, Philip assigned a day for the purpose at Paris, where he convoked, as we have seen, seven *sapientes* (three bishops and four learned clergymen) and nine barons (including a number of the king's familiars). After the inquest was complete and counsel had been pondered for a long time, the court decided against the *vidame* for four reasons: (1) that the common law of the realm permitted the regalia of other churches only to the king, (2) that a privilege of Louis VII assigned these regalia specifically to the king, (3) that Roman law (*jus scriptum*) prevented prescription of fiscal matters,[35] and (4) that the sworn jurors whom the *vidame* had summoned did not prove his right, but, on the contrary, much of their testimony supported the king. At this point, the royal charter appended a record of the inquest, which broke off after the eighth juror. Elsewhere, in a collection of administrative inquests found in Register A, the testimony was continued by nine more jurors.[36] These seventeen jurors offered ample evidence in the king's favor. Although the regalia had often been despoiled by many people, including the *vidame*, none of the jurors could swear that the *vidame* had a right to the regalia. The jurors (*jurati*) were listed by their names, positions, age in the case of those over fifty (one juror claimed to be a hundred), and their sworn testimony as to past practice. Since many of the jurors were designated *ex parte* of the *vidame*, and their evidence was listed separately, this inquest was clearly of the canonical type, which by the mid–thirteenth century had become the exclusive procedure of the Capetian court.[37]

Whether Norman or canonical, the inquest was a valuable instrument and one widely employed for resolving conflicts in the *curia regis*. For example, when a certain knight offered pledges for good conduct in 1216, he was warned that his future actions would be investigated by an inquest conducted by two knights from the king's household and judged by the royal court.[38] Increasingly, inquests were administered by *prévôts*, *baillis*, and seneschals, who were better situated to select competent jurors from the locality of the dispute.[39] As might be expected, inquests were frequently employed in the assizes of the *baillis*, not only in Normandy but throughout the royal domain. When the king himself was a party to the dispute, an inquest was also held because the information served administrative as well as judicial purposes by furnishing inventories of the royal rights and resources in the domain.[40]

With the ordinance of 1190, Philip Augustus imposed the first semblance of organization upon the informal administration of justice exercised through stationary *prévôts* and an ambulatory court inherited from his father. The *baillis* superseded the *prévôts* as local judicial officers, held monthly assizes throughout the royal domain, and regularly transmitted appeals to the regents' court at Paris three times a year. After his return in 1191, Philip retained the first two features, but attenuated the third. Although the *curia regis* continued to receive appeals from the *baillis*' assizes, its reversion to previous informal habits eliminated the triannual schedule. Despite this procedural regression, Philip continued to encourage appeals from the seigneurial courts based on "defect of justice" and on the special remedy of the *appels volages de Laonnois*. He moreover continued to improve the quality of royal justice by more frequent use of inquests. Although the differing procedures of the Norman and canonical inquests were not yet standardized in the royal courts, the judicial inquest became a permanent feature of royal justice after 1190, and with the creation of the *baillis*' assizes constituted one of the two major judicial reforms of the second decade.

Fiscal Accounts

The years 1190 to 1203 likewise mark a *tournant* in royal finances. The first indications of a central accounting bureau and the first extant accounts themselves date from this period.[41] When Philip confirmed privileges to Compiègne in 1186, for example, he conceded that the commune's men need not leave town to render account of their revenues—

implying that the king's court performed its audits during its wanderings.[42] Whatever records the chamber had kept of the king's revenues prior to that time were most likely limited to particular domanial accounts or *états* and were apparently lost in the ambush at Fréteval in 1194.[43] In the ordinance of 1190, however, Philip Augustus commanded his revenues to be brought three times a year to the six bourgeois and Pierre the marshal at Paris, where Adam, the royal clerk, recorded them.[44] The first surviving such exercise dates from 1202/03, twelve years later, transcribed on rolls of parchment and designated simply as the "accounts" (*compoti*). These and fragments from 1217, 1219, and 1221 were all that remained from the reign of Philip Augustus after the fire of 1737 obliterated the Chambre des Comptes.[45] They reveal the orderly procedures of a bureau of audit extending back to 1190. Like the accounts themselves, this bureau was designated simply *in compotis*, only later in the thirteenth century to be called the *curia in compotis*, and finally the Chambre des Comptes.

Following the instructions of 1190, the accounts for the year 1202/03 were divided into three terms, All Saints' (1 November), Purification of the Virgin (2 February), and Ascension (variably in May and June).[46] From scattered indications it is evident that this triannual system had been superimposed on other biannual and annual schedules that were customary in certain parts of the domain.[47] Each term was further divided into three chapters for *prévôts*, *baillis*, and marches.[48] The November term included a fourth chapter for sergeants.[49] The marches' accounts recorded the finances on the Norman frontiers in preparation for the invasion of Normandy. A wartime expedient in 1202/03, this chapter did not reappear in subsequent accounts throughout the thirteenth century. The sergeants' account similarly recorded a war levy, the *prisée des sergents*, which was not included again in a general account. Since the latter two chapters dealt primarily with military finances, we shall defer them to later discussion.[50] But the chapters devoted to *prévôts* and *baillis* became the permanent feature of the Capetian triannual accounting system.[51] These two principal chapters within each term contained a series of smaller accounts of individual *prévôts* and *baillis*. Since no overarching organization or precedence are apparent within these individual units, the accounts of the *prévôts* and *baillis* were most likely recorded in the order in which these royal officials presented themselves at Paris.

In the *prévôts*' chapter, each *prévôt* accounted for his farm, deducted expenses, and turned over the balance to Brother Haimard, the treasurer.

For example, the *prévôt* of Paris accounted for 1,233 *livres*, 6 *sous*, 8 *deniers* each term, exactly one-third of 3,700 *livres*, the annual farm of Paris.[52] To this were added the revenues from the *taille* of bread and wine (1,000 *livres*) and a few minor sources. From this income the *prévôt* deducted the fixed alms owed to ten churches and clergymen (including the Knights Templars, the lepers of Saint-Lazare, and the abbeys of Saint-Martin-des-Champs and Montmartre) and the fixed *fief-rentes* owed to four noblemen (including Gautier the Chamberlain and Guy de Senlis, the royal butler). These were the standing expenses of alms and *fief-rentes* for which separate accounts were kept in Register A.[53] Aside from these fixed obligations, the *prévôt* paid the occasional expenses of Prince Louis and his wife Blanche; daily wages to over a dozen artisans (such as Master Bernard de Limoges, Renaud the Smith, Hugues the Hat-maker, and Gautier the Helmet-maker); for supplies such as coal, hides, wax, and cord; and for the maintenance of the towers, the upkeep of the prisons, and the transport of treasure. Since the *prévôté* of Paris bore the costs of the capital, its expenses were larger and its accounting more complicated than those of the others. The *prévôt* was allowed to keep the balance between revenues and expenses, and only in the final term did he transfer the insignificant sum of 200 *livres* to Brother Haimard.

Whereas the *prévôts'* chapters were limited to the *prévôts'* accounts, the *baillis'* chapters were not restricted to the twelve active *baillis*, but were actually potpourris of many accounts. They also included half of the *prévôts* who regularly appeared in their own chapter[54] and over a score of miscellaneous individuals, some of whom had specialized responsibilities that can be identified. Jean de Betefort, for example, was keeper of the wardrobe. Jean de Paalé and Guy de Béthisy accounted separately for the regalia of the vacant bishoprics of Châlons-sur-Marne and Reims. Jean Cherchelarron was charged with the Jews, and a certain Godard with the forests. Between twenty-three and thirty-eight individuals rendered accounts in their own names, and unlike the *prévôts'*, both their revenues and their expenses were clearly of an occasional nature.[55] Robert de Meulan, the *bailli* of the Paris region, for example, accounted for over fifty different sources of income in his three separate accounts.[56] These included revenues from the Jews, debts (at Senlis and in Champagne), scutage (from Melun and Corbeil, Châteaufort, and Senlis), sale of grain (from Gonesse), the *taille* of Paris, forests (Yvelines), and scores of other sources identified only by the name of a layman, an ecclesiastic, or a church. The expenditures charged to Robert de Meulan's account were so diverse that it is difficult to make generalizations. Although fixed alms and *fief-rentes*, which were usually charged to the *prévôts*, do not appear in Robert's account, they may be found occasionally in other *baillis'* accounts.[57] But like the Paris *prévôt*, Robert expended money on the royal stables, the jail, palace, and towers at Paris and paid wages and furnished supplies to many of the artisans listed in the *prévôt's* account. Many of the sums in the receipts and expenses were, however, merely transfers of money to and from other *baillis* or royal agents such as Brother Guérin and Jean Cherchelarron.[58] These *baillis'* chapters were therefore the appropriate place for recording irregular and occasional revenues as well as widely diverse expenditures.

By dividing each term between the *prévôts'* and *baillis'* chapters, the accounting bureau was in effect recognizing the distinction between the regular and occasional categories of ordinary finance. Exceptions and anomalies can be found, to be sure, but in general the *prévôts* recorded in their chapters the farms and fixed customary expenses that were roughly the same each year. The *baillis'* chapters, however, included not only the twelve active *baillis*, but *prévôts* and other specialized agents whose income and expenditures included the profits of justice, the regalia, forests, and many miscellaneous items, all clearly of an occasional nature.

When the Capetians established a bureau of audit at Paris in 1190, whose first surviving records appeared in 1202, they were at least a half-century behind the fiscal institutions of their more precocious neighbors. The Anglo-Normans had created an exchequer in England by the first decade of the twelfth century, and the first extant Pipe Roll appeared in 1130. A comparable exchequer was established at Caen in Normandy not long after, of which the first roll survives from 1180. The counts of Flanders had developed a central fiscal system as early as 1089, and one account of Flemish auditing sessions during the second half of the twelfth century, the *Gros Brief*, has survived from the year 1187. Farther away, the count-kings of Barcelona had assembled *états* for their domains since the 1150s.[59] Before the appearance of the first royal French account of 1202, Philip Augustus had acquired Artois (1191), and Evreux (1200), where the Flemish and Norman fiscal institutions were functioning well. This raises two related questions. To what extent did the precocious fiscal institutions of Flanders and Normandy influence the Capetians before or after the annexation of these territories? And if the influence was slight, how were the well-established practices of Artois and Evreux accommodated to the French system?

Fortunately, specific fiscal records survive for both these territories that permit comparison. In the *Gros Brief* of 1187 there is a section devoted to the Artesian lands of Bapaume,[60] and the extant Norman roll of 1198 contains the records of the county of Evreux.[61] Both reappear in the French accounts of 1202/03. By comparing the accounts of these two territories before and after they were acquired, we may respond to our questions.

As might be expected of early fiscal systems, the incipient accounts of the Flemings, Normans, and Capetians shared common features. Their chief purpose was to supervise local officials. Baudouin Pastez was the local receiver who rendered account of Bapaume in 1187. Although the *prévôt* who succeeded him in 1202/03 was unnamed in accordance with Capetian practice, he was probably Pierre de Béthisy or Guillaume Pastez, doubtless from the same family as Baudouin.[62] Richard d'Argences was the Norman agent who accounted for Evreux in 1198. Although still mentioned in the French accounts of 1202/03, he had been succeeded by Nicolas Harchepin.[63] These local agents all rendered accounts for the domanial revenues for which they were responsible. In the Flemish *Gros Brief* this income was listed according to money and to kind, but in both the Norman and French records the domanial income had been converted into farms expressed in round sums of money.[64] The Norman and French agents also included judicial fines and revenues not found in the Flemish accounts. From this revenue the Flemish receivers, the Norman *vicomtes*, and the French *prévôts* deducted customary fixed expenses. All three note alms owed to specified churches. For example, seven churches receiving alms from Baudouin Pastez at Bapaume in 1187 were paid the exact amounts by the royal *prévôt* in 1202.[65] Most of the churches and ecclesiastics benefiting from alms at Evreux in 1198 were also included in the French accounts of 1203.[66] Both the Norman *vicomtes* and the Capetian *prévôts* paid out *fief-rentes* to knights, although the recipients were no longer the same. Other fixed expenses differed according to locality, but the Norman and French accounts note similar expenditures for building repairs and improvements.

Although the principal sources of revenue and some of the outstanding expenses were similar, as would be expected from shared domanial economies, the differences between the three accounts are striking, particularly in regard to accounting procedures. Whereas the Bapaume account of 1187 separates both revenues and expenses into strictly delimited categories of money and produce (wheat, oats, peas, money, chickens, lambs, and so forth), the Capetian version of 1202/03 converts all income and expenses into money and computes an all-embracing farm. The *Gros Brief* therefore more closely resembles domanial *états*, such as those found in the Capetian *census* of Register A, than the Norman and French audit-bureau accounts that were expressed entirely in monetary terms.[67] The Capetian Evreux accounts were computed in both *livres parisis* and *livres angevins*, with the final totals converted into Paris currency. Moreover, both Norman and Capetian agents included occasional revenues, such as justice, which exceeded the more strictly domanial resources collected by the Flemish receivers.

If the French version of 1202/03 resembles the Evreux account of 1198 in that it converts all figures into money, computes farms, and includes similar revenues and expenses, there are noticeable differences as well. Following English practice, the Norman exchequer rolls provide lengthy descriptions of each item, whereas the French accounts record only the source or the recipient along with the sum, rendering them more difficult to interpret.[68] The more expansive character of the Norman rolls permitted the notation of royal writs. At the end of the Evreux account, for example, Richard d'Argences lists the king's writs commanding repairs, transportation, provisioning, and payment of the troops at the castle.[69] In contrast, the laconic style of the French records omits virtually all mention of these letters. Since such royal letters were frequently issued by Philip and have survived in other contexts, their omission in the fiscal records can only be explained by deliberate accounting policy that departed from Norman practice.[70]

The most important differences between the Flemish *Gros Brief* and the Norman exchequer accounts on the one hand and the subsequent Capetian accounts on the other consist of the overall framework imposed on the accounting procedures. Whereas the Flemish receivers, like the French *prévôts*, delivered their revenues three times a year, in their case on St. Martin's Day (11 November), Purification (2 February), and Ascension (variable in May and June), they made an accounting only once a year.[71] After collecting the Ascension payment, they rendered their accounts in June in order of appearance. Following English precedent, the Norman exchequer met at Caen twice a year—at Easter and Michaelmas (29 September). The Easter session was merely preparatory. At it the *vicomte* submitted a preliminary account (view) and paid half the sum due (proffer). The important reckoning took place at Michaelmas, when the balance was delivered, and a final record was inscribed on the roll.

When Philip took over Bapaume and Evreux, the royal accounting bureau converted these annual and biannual systems into a triannual schedule.[72] Not only were revenues collected three times a year, but separate accounts were drawn up for each term.

Within each term, moreover, the Capetian bureau imposed a characteristic division between the *prévôts'* and the *baillis'* accounts. Since most of the revenues and expenses recorded by Baudouin Pastez in 1187 were of a domanial nature, they were reported by his royal successors in 1202/03 in the appropriate format of the *prévôts'* accounts, where regular finances were normally included.[73] At Evreux, however, the farm and its fixed customary expenses—what Richard fitz Nigel called "the body of the county" (*corpus comitatus*)[74] at the English exchequer—were placed by Richard d'Argences at the head of his account in 1198. In 1202/03 these items were relegated to the *prévôts'* chapters as domanial revenues and expenses. In 1198 Richard d'Argences followed the "body" with a long series of smaller individual accounts, each computed separately, including revenues drawn from justice, loans, *tailles*, other occasional income, and expenses for provisioning or repairing the castle. As occasional income and expenditures, these individual items were grouped together in the *baillis'* chapter by the accounting clerks of 1202/03. The Capetian distinction between regular and occasional finances, reflected in the division between the *prévôts'* and *baillis'* chapters, was therefore superimposed upon the English-Norman serial format in which the "body" of the county (farm and customary payments) was followed by a listing of occasional revenues and expenses.

Such comparisons help to answer the two questions raised about the relationship between the earlier Flemish and Norman fiscal systems and the subsequent Capetian version. Although all three were rooted in the same domanial economy, the differences among them are too great to postulate a simple and direct borrowing by Philip Augustus. Whatever indirect and undefined influence the Flemings and Normans may have exerted previously—and this can never be excluded—it is clear that the Capetians did not take over intact the Flemish and Norman fiscal systems after acquiring Bapaume and Evreux. Chronology prevents this assumption. Philip had created the two characteristic features of Capetian fiscality before he annexed these territories. The triannual schedule and the division between the functions of *prévôts* and *baillis* were already formulated in the ordinance of 1190. Not only was Flemish and Norman influence slight, but Philip consciously imposed the characteristic Capetian fiscal system upon the newly acquired territories. The rapprochement was facilitated by the goals of managing the domain and supervising local officials, which were shared by all three systems.

Since the French, Norman, English, and Flemish fiscal rolls were principally the accounts of local officials, they disclose most readily the activities of the latter. They reveal less clearly the operations and personnel of the central bureaus. Richard fitz Nigel's *Dialogue of the Exchequer* provides an intimate picture of the English exchequer, however, offering details as to who attended the sessions, even where they sat, and what their precise duties were.[75] Each session took place in a room around a table spread with a cloth marked with columns like a chess board (*scaccarium*). Since each column was assigned a unit of money (penny, shilling, pound, twenty pounds, a hundred pounds, a thousand pounds, and so forth), the table could be employed as an abacus to compute the accounts. Because the Norman bureau was called an exchequer and its rolls followed the pattern of the Pipe Rolls, there is no doubt that it also employed the abacus system. The term *scaccarium* also appeared in the Flemish *redeninge* (reckonings) in the early thirteenth century.[76] The lack of any description like Richard fitz Nigel's and the survival of only the general account make it difficult to envisage the precise operations of the French bureau. Its units of computation were nonetheless those of the English and Norman exchequers, and its arithmetic was performed in Roman numerals, to which the abacus was adapted. Although the term *scaccarium* was not applied to the French bureau of audit, it is difficult to visualize its operations without the abacus.

Richard fitz Nigel depicts the English exchequer as a court the sheriff entered as a defendant to face his judges across the chequered table. The latter were the barons of the exchequer, composed of the justiciar, chancellor, and treasurer, accompanied by their clerks, whose duties Richard describes in minute detail. It is possible to imagine the *prévôts* and *baillis* at the French bureau in the same position as the sheriffs, but more difficult to identify the judges. During the regency of 1190–1191 the accounts were presided over by the six bourgeois and Pierre the Marshal,[77] but we do not know who took their places after their disappearance. Brother Haimard acted as treasurer in 1202/03 and received the balance of revenues, but his specific role in the accounting procedure cannot be determined. Although Brother Guérin was an active fiscal agent, widely receiving and disbursing money, those activities do not place him at the Temple presiding over the audit sessions.[78] The personnel and routine of Philip Augustus's bureau of accounts therefore remain obscure for lack of sources.

The Royal Income, 1202/03

The only fiscal records to survive intact from the reign of Philip Augustus are the accounts of 1202/03.[79] (Those from 1217, 1219, and 1221 are fragmentary, and those contained in the Registers are too specialized to be of general use.) If we aspire to a quantitative assessment of Philip's finances we are therefore limited to the three terms from November 1202 to May 1203. To make a virtue of this necessity, we should recognize both the advantages and limitations of the existing record. The fiscal year 1202/03 is fortunately situated in time. Standing on the eve of Philip's great war against the English king in Normandy and the Loire valley, it records military revenues and expenses in the sergeants' and marches' chapters. Yet we may surmise that the war had not yet advanced so far as to engulf Capetian finances. A more normal picture of the royal finances probably survives in the *prévôts'* and *baillis'* chapters. Although no year can fully qualify as a "normal" year, it was a felicitous accident that the year that survived was 1202/03.

The limitations of French accounting practices must be made explicit, however, if this isolated account is to be of value. In all likelihood the Capetians' records are not complete in reporting either revenues or expenditures. As we have seen, the *Gros Brief* excluded the more important occasional revenues of the Flemish counts, such as justice. Students of Anglo-Norman finances repeatedly assert that the Pipe Rolls and Norman exchequer rolls were incomplete despite their fullness of detail because they did not include the extraordinary revenues handled by the chamber and treasury.[80] Like the Flemish and Anglo-Norman records, the Capetian rolls of 1202/03 were actually a series of individual accounts for recording and controlling the finances of local officials.[81] Though the central bureaus of audit possessed in the abacus the technical means for computing total receipts and expenditures, in fact they did not do so. Nor, as we shall see, did they organize their records to facilitate arriving at global sums. Their immediate intention was to supervise the local officials, not to devise a total budget. Although their records did not include all of the royal income, they may nonetheless accurately reflect "ordinary" revenues, particularly those derived directly from the domain.[82] If careful and critical attention is paid to the accounting methods of the central bureau, these "ordinary" finances may be profitably investigated.

At first glance the French accounts of 1202/03 show each *prévôt* and *bailli* providing totals for his receipts and expenses and computing a balance. To arrive at the total revenues for the year, one is tempted to add up all of the receipts, an operation that can be easily accomplished.[83] But these brute figures do not represent total income. Closer inspection reveals that many of the receipts and expenditures were merely transfers of money among the *prévôts*, *baillis*, and war treasurers. Brothers Haimard and Guérin were particularly active in effecting these movements of funds. Often the same sum was listed among the receipts and expenses of several agents. In addition, when many *prévôts* and *baillis* closed their accounts, they did not return all of the balance to the treasury, but kept part as a *debit*, which was credited to their receipts at the next term as *de compoto* or *de veteri*. At times the balance carried over was the same; at other times it was less because part had been transferred to other accounts in the meantime. By careful auditing many transfers or duplications can be eliminated. By comparing preceding *debit*'s with succeeding *de compoto*'s, discrepancies in balances can be explained. These audits can be carried out for the terms of February and May 1203, but not for November 1202 because the preceding May account is lacking. With estimations from the May 1203 figures, however, the November 1202 account may be corrected approximately.[84] Finally, it should be recognized that the brute receipts of the marches' accounts did not represent new income or revenue. The great proportion of the monies received by the march treasurers came from the treasury through Brother Haimard, or Brother Guérin, or directly from *prévôts* and *baillis*. Only 8,671 *livres* drawn by the treasurers from local revenues can be counted with the annual income.[85]

Subjected to careful auditing, the accounts of 1202/03 can yield different estimates of annual income for differing purposes. For example, by eliminating duplications and the discrepancies in the balances carried forward, we can arrive at figures for revenue "that has been utilized." These are minimal estimates and err by being too low.[86] Of more use for our purposes are estimates of annual income obtained by simply deducting "the balances carried forward" (*de compoto*) from each term. By ignoring how much of this money was actually spent, this computation yields esti-

TABLE 3. Annual Income for the Three Terms
of 1202/03 (in *livres parisis*)

	November	February	May	Totals	
Prévôts' chapters	10,554	9,983	11,244	31,781	
Baillis' chapters	15,102	26,460	33,122	74,684	115,136
Marches' chapters				8,671[a]	
Total ordinary income	25,656	36,443	53,037		141,589
Sergeants' chapter	26,453			26,453	
Total annual income accounted	52,109	36,443	53,037		

SOURCE: *Budget* pp. 49–51.

[a]The annual income from the Marches has been placed in the totals column.

mates in *livres* of the annual income of Philip Augustus's government as accounted in 1202/03 (Table 3).[87]

The division between *prévôts'* and *baillis'* chapters, which distinguished the Capetian accounts from the Anglo-Norman, was basically an auditing decision. Yet we have seen that it also represented a rough distinction between ordinary regular income, found in the *prévôts'* chapters, and ordinary occasional income, assigned to the *baillis'* chapters. The *prévôts'* farms comprised 92 percent of the receipts in their chapters. Since this income was divided into three equal portions, the *prévôts'* income did not vary much from term to term.[88] On the other hand, the income in the *baillis'* chapters, judged by the receipts, fluctuated considerably. Yet the distinction between fixed and occasional was not absolute. The *prévôts'* chapters contained a small proportion (8 percent) of revenues normally assigned to the *baillis*, and as we have seen, the *baillis'* chapters contained the farm of Péronne-Bapaume, second in importance to that of Paris.[89]

Despite its imperfections, we shall use the figure of 115,000 *livres parisis* to represent the total "ordinary" royal income of the French monarchy in 1202/03. "Ordinary" is defined to include the normal revenues of the royal domain, both regular and occasional, but to exclude "extraordinary" revenues such as the wartime *prisée des sergents* (26,453 *livres*) and King John's relief of 20,000 marks sterling from the treaty of Le Goulet in 1200.[90] Since the latter does not appear in the 1202/03 record, it is possible that John paid up his relief by November 1202, but there is no indication in the royal accounts of other feudal reliefs or of other unusual sums received that year.[91] In all likelihood such feudal windfalls were collected and accounted for outside the central accounting bureau, probably by the chamber. We have included in our sum of "ordinary" income the 8,671 *livres* collected by the war treasurers on the Norman marches. In the summer of 1202, following John's condemnation at Paris, Philip took the castellanies of Gournay, Gaillefontaine, Ferté, and Lyons-la-Forêt, from which the war treasurers collected both domanial income and proceeds from justice, revenue that would have been handled by *prévôts* and *baillis* under normal circumstances.[92]

Although such distinctions are only approximate, we have seen that the central accounting bureau made a fundamental distinction between regular and occasional income when it placed the farms in the *prévôts'* chapters and most other income in those of the *baillis*. By assigning a wartime tax to another chapter and by omitting feudal reliefs and other large sources of income, the bureau may also have had in mind a further division between "ordinary" and "extraordinary." The Paris audit, therefore, was only concerned with the regular and occasional revenues that comprised the "ordinary" income of the royal domain. As any close inspection of governmental finances reveals, the distinctions regular-occasional and ordinary-extraordinary are artificial, but they are nonetheless a useful convenience. In all events, it appears that Philip's "regular" revenues collected by the *prévôts* had increased 72 percent since the beginning of the reign and 50 percent since 1190.[93]

Philip Augustus's revenues may also be classified by categories of income summarizing the long and variegated series of individual revenues the Capetians traditionally collected as kings and lords. Although collected for centuries, these revenues can be quantified for the first time for 1202/03 and their relative importance assessed. They are set forth in Table 4, and discussion follows.

THE AGRICULTURAL DOMAIN

The acquisition of territory in Artois, Vermandois, and Normandy after 1190 increased the number of *prévôtés* from fifty-two to sixty-two by 1202/03. A little more than forty-five *prévôts* accounted for farms that yielded 33,164 *livres*, or 32 percent of the ordinary annual income.[94] These farms ranged in annual value from 35 *livres* (Vitry-aux-Loges) to 3,700 *livres* (Paris) and were paid in three equal installments.

As we have seen, the *Census* accounts (1206–1210) list the domanial

TABLE 4. Sources of Ordinary Income in 1202/03

	Income (in *livres parisis*)		Percentage of Total Income
AGRICULTURAL DOMAIN			
Prévôts' farms	33,164		32%
Produce outside the farms	10,353		10%
Gîte	1,215		1%
Forests	7,432		7%
Total		52,164 =	50%
TOWNS AND COMMERCE			
Tailles	6,848		7%
Other urban revenues	4,186		4%
Exchange and minting	256		
Money taxes	8,150		8%
Jews	1,250		1%
Total		20,690	20%
CHURCHES' REGALIA		4,747	5%
JUSTICE		6,807	7%
MILITARY			
Vavassores	770		1%
Sergeants	1,037		1%
Total		1,807	2%
UNDIFFERENTIATED NAMES		11,633	11%
MISCELLANEOUS		4,986	5%
Grand Total		102,834	100%

NOTE: 102,834 = 89% of 115,000
SOURCE: *Budget* pp. 1–205.

produce that constituted the *prévôts'* farms. Fortunately, sufficient information is provided by the general accounts of 1202/03 and the *Census* to allow us to see the domanial revenues that lay behind the round figure for the farm of Péronne-Bapaume. In 1202/03 the *prévôt* included in his annual farm of 3,636 *livres* not only the major *prévôtés* of Péronne and Bapaume but also the minor localities of Athies, Boucly, Clary, and Cappy.[95] Since all of these places were entered into the *Census* accounts, we can calculate what they produced in terms of money, wheat, oats, and chickens. Bapaume, for example, yielded 1,400 *livres* from its famous tolls, 80 *livres* from its lesser revenues, 25 *muids* of wheat, and 48 chickens. Péronne yielded 17 *livres* from its tolls, 141 *muids* of wheat, and 160 chickens. We are able to estimate the price of wheat and oats at Bapaume from sales of surplus produce in May 1203, and we can therefore arrive at approximate totals for the major items of produce these localities provided. The *prévôt* of Péronne-Bapaume, who owed a farm of 3,636 *livres*, realized at least 3,782 *livres* of income in 1206.[96] This figure is low because it does not include the yield of chickens and uncultivated land, the value of which cannot be estimated. In May 1210 Philip Augustus alienated the village of Boucly, included the *prévôté* of Péronne-Bapaume, to Gautier, the castellan of Péronne, for an annual rent of 124 *livres*. According to the *Census* accounts, Boucly had been producing an annual yield of at least 439 *livres* four years earlier. The king may have submitted to these apparently disadvantageous terms because he retained the tolls and woods and because this transaction was joined to a more important sale of other properties.[97]

The *Census* account also suggests that when Philip Augustus acquired Artois he was able to realize less domanial income than the count of Flanders had. Two localities inventoried in the *Census* accounts, Bapaume and Hesdin, were also included in the *Gros Brief* of 1187. Although the two accounts are not entirely comparable, Bapaume and Hesdin yielded more in the major categories of money, wheat, and oats to the count than to the Capetian king. For example, the *prévôté* of Hesdin and Auchy was worth 520 *livres* to the count and only 300 *livres* to the king. The disparity might be explained for money rents by the strength of royal currency as against the local money, but it also existed in produce, where the same measures were retained. For example, Bapaume produced 670 chickens in 1187, but 48 annually in the thirteenth century. The *cens* yielded 89 *muids* of wheat in the *Gros Brief*, but only 27 *muids* in the *Census*.[98] Despite the possible superiority of royal money over local currency, Philip Augustus continued to maintain the alms that the count of Flanders had been accustomed to pay to the local churches.[99] By this policy he doubtless won the favor of the Artesian clergy, but it also suggests an explanation for the decline in revenues from Bapaume and Hesdin. By reducing rents from his newly acquired domain, he may have sought the good will of his new subjects.

In addition to the fixed farms, the domain yielded produce such as wheat, oats, wine, and chickens that was sold separately by the *baillis* and, to a lesser extent, by the *prévôts*. The treasurers on the marches also collected domanial produce, not all of which was accounted in money.[100] In sum, the domain produced at least 10,353 *livres* (10 percent of total income) in revenues beyond the farms.[101] We have seen that the right of hospitality, called the *gîte*, was another domanial revenue traditionally exacted by the Capetians. In 1202/03, however, its commutation into money produced only the insignificant sum of 1,215 *livres*.[102] Apparently, Philip's major benefit from the *gîte* was the enjoyment of it during his annual tourneys.

Closely related to domanial revenues was income from the royal forests, which in 1202/03 amounted to 7,432 *livres*, or 7 percent of normal revenue.[103] Most of this sum (5,325 *livres*) was collected by a certain Godard, clearly a royal agent for the forests around Paris. Etienne de Bransles and Jean Minctoire were responsible for the forests of Orléans. Most of the forest revenues consisted of relatively small sums, but Vincennes and Saint-Germain-en-Laye under the management of Godard produced 3,200 and 1,300 *livres* respectively.[104] In the English exchequer the forest revenues were termed a *census*, because, according to Richard fitz Nigel's playful pun, they could not be fixed but as*cended* and des*cended* over the years.[105] They included the sale of wood and other forest products, rents, customary dues, and judicial fines.

TOWNS AND COMMERCE

Though Philip undoubtedly considered townsmen part of his domain, they may be separated from the agricultural sectors by their predominantly commercial interests. Their main contribution to the royal income was in the form of *tailles*. An arbitrary and burdensome tax, the *taille* had been exacted from all inhabitants of the domain from the time of the early Middle Ages.[106] By 1202/03, however, it was collected by the royal *baillis* chiefly from towns such as Paris (2,995 *livres*), Etampes (1,500), Orléans (1,500), Montargis (300), and Château-Landon (200), and produced a total of 6,848 *livres*.[107] The *tailles* of Paris appear to have fluctuated arbitrarily: the *bailli* received only 1,500 *livres* in 1217.[108]

Hardest hit by the *taille* were Paris, Orléans, and Etampes, towns in the old Capetian domain. With the exception of Bapaume, the prosperous cities of Vermandois and Artois acquired after 1185 were permitted to retain the exemption from these arbitrary taxes granted them by the counts of Flanders and other lords,[109] and the Norman towns asserted similar privileges when Philip confirmed their charters after 1204. Encouraged by these examples, the men of Etampes and Orléans also contested their *tailles* in 1210 and 1216, but they nonetheless remained liable, although the occasions on which the king could request *tailles* were more clearly limited and defined.[110] Despite his liberality to newly annexed towns, Philip maintained his traditional seigneurial prerogatives over those of the ancient domain.

In addition to revenues specifically designated as *tailles* or their equivalent, Philip collected sums identified only in general terms. Most of these were small, 100 *livres* or less. For example, the *bailli* Thierry de Corbeil received 100 *livres* from Auxerre *pro consilio*, which may have implied a *taille*.[111] Most likely the undesignated 530 *livres* that Thierry de Corbeil later received from Auxerre and the 500 *livres* accounted by the mayor of Sens also concealed *tailles*.[112] The total of these miscellaneous unidentified payments received from towns amounted to 4,186 *livres*.[113]

A long-established source of royal income deriving from commercial activities was charging fees for exchange and minting. For example, in 1200 Philip regulated the conditions under which money was exchanged at Orléans, for which he demanded an annual payment of 10 *livres* at All Saints' and 5 at Easter. When Geoffroi Gammard gave the *bailli* of Orléans 10 *livres* in November 1202 for the exchange of 100 marks, he was most likely a money changer fulfilling this obligation.[114] In all events, the *bailli* Robert de Meulan received 125 *livres* for the exchange of large sums (1,000 and 500 marks) from the Jews at Paris. At best, however, the king received only 256 *livres* from money exchange in 1202/03, a negligible sum.[115] Furthermore, *seigneuriage*, or profits from minting coins, yielded Philip almost nothing in 1202/03. Whereas Louis VII had charged for minting coins at Paris, Senlis, and Laon, Philip realized only a bare 10 *livres* from his mint at Laon. In all likelihood he had alienated most of these revenues as he did at Tournai in 1202.[116]

In place of direct *seigneuriage*, Philip relied on another traditional profit from his coinage, the money tax. As early as the reign of Louis VI, the Capetians had collected taxes from their towns in exchange for a promise that they would maintain their currency without debasement. These money taxes were imposed on hearths (*fumagium*) at Compiègne, but were more often levied on bread and wine (*tallia panis et vini*), as at Etampes, Orléans, and Paris. Collected every three years, they reimbursed the king for his coinage services. Although this *taille* might have resembled the other urban *tailles*, it was nonetheless kept distinct in the accounts of 1202/03 and yielded 1,000 *livres* from Paris and 450 from Orléans.[117] The dukes of Normandy had exercised a long-established money tax called the *fouage* (*de faogio*), which triennially imposed one *sou* on every hearth, and Philip Augustus retained this revenue with great profit after the conquest of the duchy. It is also likely that he began to collect it when he acquired the Norman border territories in the 1190s. In May 1203 the *bailli* Guillaume Poucin received 6,600 *livres de fraagio et tessamentis de Tooni et aliunde.* The reference is far from clear, but the amount is significant, comparable to the later Norman *fouage.* If *fraagium* is a misspelling of *foagium* and *Tooni* refers to Tosny (Eure, *arr.* Louvier *cne.* Gaillon) on the borders of the duchy, this was an early realization of the Norman money tax. At the same time, Aleaume Hescelin, also a *bailli* on the frontier, received 100 *livres de freagio.*[118] If these conjectures hold, Philip received the significant sum of 8,150 *livres* from his money taxes.

The Jews, who lived in towns and were commercially active, particularly in lending, were a potential source of important revenues. Philip Augustus had, however, exhausted this opportunity in one sweeping stroke at the beginning of his reign when he confiscated the Jews' property and expelled them from the domain. Though these measures may have financed his military ventures of the 1180s, the king had deprived himself of significant income in the decade after the crusade. The Jews settled in neighboring territories, particularly in Champagne, which surrounded the royal domain to the east and south, where they continued to supply commercial services and credit to the inhabitants of the royal domain without the king's control or profit. In 1198, therefore, a wiser Philip returned to the policy of his father and allowed them to reenter the royal domain—"much against the opinion of everyone and his own decree," grumbled the historiographer Rigord.[119]

Reviving the policy of stabilization in 1198, Philip concluded an agreement with Thibaut, count of Champagne, that separated the Jews of the two domains and guaranteed to each group exclusive rights over money lending in their respective lands. In exchange for reciprocal promises, Thibaut promised not to retain the king's Jews or permit his own Jews to lend in the royal domain. At the same time the king ordered his *baillis* and *prévôts* to enforce payment of legitimate debts owed to Champenois Jews to compensate prior obligations.[120]

The policy of stabilization was accompanied by supervision by the king's officials, the keeping of records of Jewish loans, and royal exploitation. As early as 1179, Louis VII had installed a *"prévôt* of the Jews" at Etampes to aid them in collecting debts. The accounts of 1202/03 indicate that Philip Augustus had reinstituted such officials in his own domain since 1198. Jean Cherchelarron emerged as a keeper of the Jews and transmitted taxes paid by them from Senlis. References to letters and seals of the Jews at Senlis, Pontoise, Béthisy, Poissy, and Mantes demonstrate that Jewish debts were certified and recorded at those localities. (The seal of the official at Pontoise has even survived.)[121] The underlying features of Philip's administration of the Jews were therefore already in place before the conquest of Normandy. But the machinery was as yet too new to produce significant income in 1202/03. In that year the Jews brought to the king a modest 1,250 *livres* at most, barely 1 percent of ordinary income.[122]

REGALIAN CHURCHES

The ordinary revenues drawn from churches were based on the king's regalian rights. Although it would be difficult to estimate the income from the royal abbeys,[123] we know that from 1191 to 1203 about eighteen bishoprics became vacant and their revenues went into the royal treasury. Since at least three of these—Châlons-sur-Marne, Reims, and Laon— were vacant from November 1202 to May 1203, we are able to assess what the regalian rights were worth that year.[124]

When Rotrou, bishop of Châlons, died in 1201, the chapter was unable to decide on a successor. Two candidates appealed to the pope for support the following April, but a third, Master Gérard de Douai, canon of Paris, was, in fact, elected bishop in 1203.[125] Meanwhile the king contended with the *vidame* of Châlons over the regalia of the bishopric. Conducting an extensive inquest into the matter at Paris, Philip decided that the regalian rights over Châlons belonged exclusively to the king. The royal agent, Jean Paalé, accordingly received 1,527 *livres* (2,047 *livres* Provins) from the bishopric in November 1202.[126]

With the death on 7 September 1202 of Philip's uncle Guillaume de Champagne, the great archbishopric of Reims also lay vacant until July 1204, when Guy Paré, a Cistercian abbot and papal legate, finally succeeded to it. After a quarter of a century under an influential prelate, the canons of Reims also found it difficult to agree upon a successor. This prolonged vacancy enabled the king to profit from the income of the rich see. The *bailli* Guy de Béthisy entered a detailed record of the regalian revenues in the account of February 1203, which included rents, the collection of *tailles*, profits of justice, and the sale of produce (wood, grain, wine, livestock, and so on). After the expenses of managing the properties and the archbishop's obligations had been deducted, the regalian rights of Reims produced 2,620 *livres* for the first twenty weeks.[127] Guy de Béthisy was also responsible for the regalia of Laon, which had been in the king's hands since the resignation of Bishop Roger in 1201. In February 1203 the *bailli* acknowledged a lump sum of 500 *livres* but provided no detailed accounting.[128] At the same time the *bailli* Thierry de Corbeil received 100 *livres* from the regalia of Troyes. Although that see was not vacant, Bishop Garnier was absent in the east on a crusade. The county of Champagne had been under royal wardship since the death of Count Thibaut in 1201, and the king was evidently enjoying the regalia of Troyes as a result.[129]

Because of the fortuitous nature of regalian income, its annual yield was unpredictable, yet in 1202/03 Philip Augustus realized 4,747 *livres* (or 5 percent of the total income) from this source. Even though three of these vacancies were lengthy (Châlons was vacant for over a year, Reims for a year and ten months, and Laon for six years) and therefore profitable to the king, the delays were not due to Philip, but to internal disputes in the two cases (Châlons and Reims) about which we have information. At all events, these revenues were a significant factor in royal income. By the date of the election of Archbishop Guy, the bishopric of Reims had perhaps netted the king as much as 12,000 *livres*.[130] Regalian revenues were legitimate ordinary income and did not include the more dubious despoliations Philip was tempted to engage in from time to time or the punitive measures he took against the churches during the interdict of 1200.[131] Irregular profits such as these were not recorded in 1202/03.

JUSTICE

The ordinance of 1190 commanded the *baillis* to record the judicial fines (*forefacta*) that they received in their monthly assizes. Accordingly, Guillaume de la Chapelle and Pierre du Thillai accounted for 346 *livres* from Orléans, and the four *baillis* working in the northeast reported 256 *livres* in 1202/03.[132] Totalling 5,142 *livres*, these judicial fines (*expleta*) varied widely (39 *livres* from Péronne and 2,318 from Arras) and exhibited little regularity. When miscellaneous fines, forfeitures, and similar amounts collected by the *prévôts* and treasurers of the marches were added, judicial income totalled 6,807 *livres*, or only 7 percent of ordinary income.[133]

This figure cannot, therefore, represent the total revenue from the administration of justice. It will be remembered that the *baillis'* accounts also contain hundreds of receipts identified only by the name of a layman, cleric, or church. Some of these items conceal sums given for charters or for "offers"—to use English parlance—to facilitate judicial proceedings. For example, from 1200 through 1204 Mathieu de Montmorency was engaged in litigation with the abbey of Saint-Denis in which the king's court was assigned the final resort. When Mathieu paid 50 *livres* to the *bailli* Robert de Meulan in November 1202, this may have been related to his trial.[134] In November 1202, too, the monks of Saint-Denis paid Robert de Meulan 20 *livres* "for a certain charter," perhaps an offer for the royal charter dated 1202 in which the king confirmed the church's judicial authority over Boissy-Laillerie.[135] In another instance, in 1203 the king decided a lengthy dispute between the canons of Saint-Aignan of Orléans and Aubert and Jean de Santilly over the manumission of the latter's serfs. When the canons paid 200 *livres* to the royal agent Pierre de Gonesse in February 1202 and at the same time Jean de Santilly also contributed a sum, these may have been payments for the settlement of the case.[136] Since no judicial records were systematically kept either at the central court or in the *bailliages* before the acquisition of Normandy, whatever royal decisions have survived are due to the care of the litigants. Only by chance, therefore, can an item in the accounts be identified with a judicial proceeding. The financial accounts of 1202/03 list about 11,633 *livres* of receipts identified only by a proper name.[137] Some proportion of this figure, impossible to estimate, may be assigned to judicial income.

MILITARY REVENUES

Since the fiscal year 1202/03 stood on the eve of the great campaign against the Angevin kings, the ordinary receipts of the *prévôts* and *baillis* contain a few amounts specifically designated for military purposes. In the November term, for example, the *baillis* acknowledged small sums identified as *de* (or *pro*) *vavassoribus*. The term *vavassor* covered the lowest category of knights in the hierarchical ranking of feudal personages in Register A. These sums therefore appear to indicate the redemption of liability for military service by members of the bottom echelon. This French form of scutage (to use the English term) produced only a meagre 770 *livres*.[138] In addition to the separate chapter devoted to sergeants (discussed below), the *prévôts* and *baillis* reported another small sum (1,037 *livres*) for these combatants.[139] Also, among the hundreds of undifferentiated contributions, which totalled 11,633 *livres*, there were probably payments in lieu of military service by churches and lords. When the royal abbey of Saint-Riquier paid 40 *livres* to the *prévôt-bailli* of Amiens, for example, the item was designated "for annual *servitium* to the king."[140] The count of Sancerre's contribution of 100 marks and 100 *livres* was earmarked "for the army," as was Manessier de Mello's of 120 *livres*. It is not impossible that the six payments listed after Manessier's also fell under this heading.[141] We may conclude, therefore, that many churches and lords found in the group whose purposes are undifferentiated were contributing to military service, but, as in the case of judicial revenue, it is difficult to estimate the proportion.[142]

In classifying the receipts of the *prévôts'* and *baillis'* chapters in the account of 1202/03, the editors Ferdinand Lot and Robert Fawtier identify 4,986 *livres* of miscellaneous items that are either obscure or awkward to associate with the major categories of income.[143] The principal items include 1,767 *livres* from debts and loans,[144] 1,041 *livres* from unidentified *preda*,[145] and 720 *livres* from the enigmatic *de sario Remis* and *de seerio de Gant*. By making use of Lot and Fawtier's calculations and by adding the major receipts, it is possible to account for 102,834 *livres* of ordinary revenues reported in the *prévôts'*, *baillis'*, and marches' chapters. This amounts to 89 percent of the adjusted receipts arrived at by subtracting the balances carried forward from the gross receipts. The difference between these two procedures of subtracting and adding (amounting to 12,302 *livres*) consists of advances from the Temple and other transfers difficult to trace with certainty.

Expenses

The ordinary expenses of the *prévôts* and *baillis* in 1202/03 were discussed above in connection with accounting procedures. The *prévôts* of Paris, Péronne-Bapaume, and Evreux, for example, deducted expenditures for local repairs, maintenance, wages, services, and supplies from their farms, as well as fixed obligations for alms and *fief-rentes*, for which inventories were kept in the royal registers. Although the *baillis'* expenses were more diversified, those of Robert de Meulan, for example, included similar expenditures. We have seen, however, that most of the items attributed to the *baillis'* expenses were not actually expenditures but transfers of money involving justice and military service. Ferdinand Lot and Robert Fawtier in their edition of the accounts have attempted to classify these various expenses and add them up. Because of the difficulty in interpreting the *baillis'* accounts, their calculations can give only rough approximations.[146] In addition to ordinary expenses, they discovered, the *baillis* paid out 13,500 *livres* for items that might be considered as military costs, and the *prévôts* accounted for 3,600 *livres* for similar purposes.[147] Military expenditures are often difficult to distinguish from ordinary outlays, but the *prévôts* of Chaumont and Amiens occasionally reported items comparable to those of the war treasurers who accounted for troop wages on the marches.[148]

Because of the scope of the *prévôts'* and *baillis'* accounts, most ordinary expenditures listed in them were for local needs. These accounts omit the expenses of the central court with the exception only of three accountings by Jean de Betefort in the *baillis'* chapters with respect to the wardrobe. Over the year 1202/03, Jean received 500 *livres* from the Temple and 100 *livres* in loan, from which he deducted clothing expenses for the king, queen, Prince Louis, his wife Blanche, and the "children of Poissy" (Marie and Philip, the infants of the recently deceased Agnès de Méran). Also debited were gifts of robes to royal counsellors, chamberlains, *baillis*, and other court personnel. But the total paid out (558 *livres*) involved only clothing and was scarcely sufficient to comprise the whole account of the royal court, later known as the *hôtel*.[149] The earliest extant figures for the expenses of the Capetian *hôtel* are those for the February term of 1227, which amounted to 21,698 *livres* for ninety-three days, or 85,168 *livres* annually. By comparison to accounts later in the thirteenth century, these *hôtel* figures for 1227 were high, but they indicate that the central court expended large sums. Whatever the costs of Philip Augustus's central court were, they were not accounted for among the ordinary expenses of 1202/03.[150]

According to Lot and Fawtier's calculations, in 1202/03, Philip's *prévôts* and *baillis* accounted for the expenses and deposits shown in Table 5.[151] In effect, therefore, the total expenses (both ordinary and military) reported by the *prévôts* and *baillis* amounted only to 29,500 *livres*, or a mere 28 percent of the total revenues collected. Local government, moreover, consumed only 12,400 *livres*, or 12 percent of royal income. The king therefore enjoyed a balance of perhaps 77,000 *livres* (total revenues minus total expenses)[152] or at least 60,000 *livres*, which was explicitly deposited at the Temple with the treasurer, Brother Haimard, or with Brother Guérin, the chief counsellor. These extraordinarily large surpluses (72 to 57 percent of total receipts) suggest that the main expenses of Philip's government were warfare and the *hôtel*. These were disbursed

TABLE 5. Ordinary and War Expenses and Deposits
in 1202/03 (in *livres parisis*)

	Prévôts	*Baillis*	Total
EXPENSES			
Ordinary	6,400	6,000	
War	3,600	13,500	
Total expenses	10,000	19,500	29,500
DEPOSITS			
To Brother Haimard at the Temple	18,000	37,000	
To Brother Guérin		5,000	
Total deposits	1,800	42,000	60,000

SOURCE: *Budget* pp. 111, 128, 129, with Appendix A.

by the military treasurers and the chamberlains, and only the accounts of the military treasurers on the Norman marches have survived.

War and Finances

During the fiscal year of 1202/03, Philip Augustus's overwhelming expense was, of course, the military operations against the Angevin king. Having obtained a judicial condemnation of John in April 1202, Philip seized Boutavant near Andelys and destroyed it. Turning his attention to the eastern borders of Normandy, he took the castles of Longchamps, Lyons-la-Forêt, Gournai, Ferté, Gaillefontaine, and Driencourt in rapid succession, and assembled siege engines to invest Arques, an important fortress that served as the administrative center and stronghold of eastern Normandy. When he heard the news of Arthur's capture at Mirebeau in August, however, Philip hastily abandoned the siege and turned south. The consequences of this fateful event in Poitou will be examined in chapter 9. Its immediate effect, however, was to divert the Capetian's attention from Normandy to the Loire valley. From the fall of 1202 to the spring of 1203, Philip was, as a result, personally absent from the Norman campaign.[153]

The extant accounts shed light on the organization of warfare and its finances on the Norman borders during that period. As we have seen, the accounts of 1202/03 devoted separate chapters to the war treasurers serving in this theater of operations.[154] Though the four to six treasurers reporting each term changed frequently, the groupings of castles under their charge remained constant. Protecting the Norman border from northeast to southwest, they consisted of five units, each clustered around a major fortress:

1. Gournay, with Ferté, Gaillefontaine, and Driencourt, under the supervision of Guillaume Borgonel and Renaud de Cornillon
2. Lyons-la-Forêt, supervised by Eudes the Chamberlain and the castellan of Lyons (probably Pierre Mauvoisin)
3. Gisors, with Neufmarché, Longchamps, Talmontiers, Châteauneuf-de-Saint-Denis, and Neaufles, under the supervision of the *prévôt* of Chaumont
4. Vernon and Evreux, with Pacy, Grossoeuvre, Le Goulet, and Gaillon, under the supervision of the *prévôt* of Vernon and Eudes Plastrart, the castellan of Vernon
5. Anet, Nonancourt, and Avrilly, under Nicolas Bocel

In addition, Thibaut de Chartres accounted once in May 1203 for disbursements to prominent military captains.

The French treasurers rendered detailed accounts of soldiers' wages, which provide a record of the deployment of troops on the Norman frontiers. Most of the payments went directly to contingents of knights, crossbowmen, and sergeants, but Eudes the Chamberlain designated some five figures who were undoubtedly captains of companies of foot-sergeants.[155] Operating west of the Seine, Henri Clément, the royal marshal, received payments for contingents of knights from the *prévôt* of Vernon and Nicolas Bocel.[156] Guillaume de Garlande, to whom Philip had confided the castle of Neufmarché in 1195, was a commander in the region of Gisors and designated his troops as his *ballia*.[157] Cadoc, who commanded a celebrated band of *routiers*, received his disbursements from Thibaut de Chartres in one lump sum without further accounting, as did Count Robert de Dreux and his brother Guillaume, lord of Bray, Torcy, and Chailly.[158] Although there were continual movements of troops among the castles,[159] the financial accounts indicate that throughout that year Philip concentrated his troops west of the Seine. The castles around Vernon and Evreux sheltered about twice as many knights and foot-sergeants as the important Vexin fortresses around Gisors and Lyons-la-Forêt.[160] The fact that Prince Louis and his companies resided at Le Goulet from November through February also supports the view that the

French intended to push down the Seine valley from the west bank, and would have done so had not the disaster at Mirebeau diverted Philip's attention.[161]

No clear and overall pattern appears for the foot-sergeants. The garrison at Vernon dropped from 500 to 20 between December and June, but that at Evreux remained constant at 300. Gisors and Neufmarché dropped from 172 to 50 between June and November, but Gournay rose from 120 to 230 in the same period and Ferté from 50 to 140 between August and June.[162] Apparently, foot-sergeants were merely shifted from castle to castle. By contrast, a striking drop occurred among the garrisons of knights throughout the period. All the castles experienced a decrease in this category, with the most telling examples furnished by the more important fortresses: Evreux (50 to 16), Vernon (20 to 12), Grossoeuvre (100 to 20), Gisors (30 to 20), and Lyons (58 to 19).[163] Evidently, Philip Augustus drew heavily on his Norman garrisons for knights who could follow him quickly into the Loire valley.[164] By February 1203 the names of major commanders such as Henri Clément and trusted agents such as Barthélemy de Roye had disappeared from the marches' accounts.

The constant shifting of troops from castle to castle and the removal of contingents of knights to the Loire valley make it difficult to provide exact figures for the troops Philip Augustus stationed on the Norman borders in 1202/03, but estimates can be offered: knights, 257; mounted sergeants, 245; mounted crossbowmen, 71; crossbowmen on foot, 101; foot-sergeants, 1,608; total, 2,282.[165] These figures do not include the few miners, engineers, and artisans who accompanied the troops[166] or the band of *routiers* for whom Cadoc received 3,290 *livres* (4,400 *livres angevins*) from Thibaut de Chartres. At the known rate for foot-sergeants, this sum could have produced no more than 300 additional foot soldiers, but these troops were subcontracted by their leader and were not the responsibility of the military treasurers.[167]

Even by the standards of the day, 2,300–2,600 troops, of whom only some 250 were knights, do not appear to be an impressive army, but it was permanent in the sense that it was not dependent on feudal service and was fully paid for a year from the royal treasury. In 1197 King Richard had attempted to convert the feudal service owed from England into a permanent force of 300 knights to defend his continental holdings throughout the year, but he failed to secure baronial support for this project.[168] Philip Augustus was, however, able to pay a comparable force from his treasury, and it undoubtedly served as the nucleus of the army that eventually succeeded in expelling the Angevins from northern France.

Though the treasurers' accounts provide only rough estimates of the numbers of troops, they furnish precise figures for the costs of warfare because they were computed, for the most part, in money. They included expenditures for fortifications, provisioning, and indemnification. Since Gournay, Ferté, Gaillefontaine, and Driencourt had only recently been taken, Guillaume Borgonel and Renaud de Cornillon made important outlays for their repair.[169] These castles were also in need of new supplies, and the two treasurers were therefore busy procuring grain, bacon, and wine.[170] Apparently, the garrisons on the west bank of the Seine at Vernon and Evreux had recently been engaged in military action, because the *prévôt* of Vernon made considerable disbursements (*perdira*) to knights to compensate for losses of horses.[171] The treasurers' accounts list no purchases of armaments, although such items may be found scattered throughout the *prévôts'* and *baillis'* chapters.[172] Evidently the procurement of the necessary arms was not, in principle, the treasurers' responsibility. Register A does nonetheless contain an inventory of armaments stored in the border castles in French hands between 1200 and 1202. Gisors on the east bank and Pacy and Evreux on the west were, as would be expected of the principal castles, depots for heavy crossbows and coats of mail.[173]

Judging by the accounts, the chief duty of the war treasurers was to pay daily wages to the troops, for which the treasurers furnished detailed reports. From this information the normal daily wage scales can be determined for five major categories of combatants: knights (72 *deniers parisis*), mounted sergeants (36 *d.*), mounted crossbowmen (48 or 54 *d.*), crossbowmen on foot (12 or 18 *d.*), and foot-sergeants (8 *d.*).[174] Contemporary Norman accounts indicate that King John's wages were 30 percent less than those of Philip Augustus.[175] More significant are the total sums of money that Philip's treasurers disbursed to French troops on the Norman marches in 1202/03, as seen in Table 6.[176] The total of 27,370 *livres parisis* did not include the 3,290 *livres* paid to Cadoc for his *routiers* or the numerous sums designated for individual knights and military commanders that were undoubtedly reimbursement for military service. Often these were designated as gifts (*dona*). Out of a total expenditure of 65,931 *livres* for the war on the Norman marches,[177] therefore, not quite half consisted of military wages.

Aside from the 65,931 *livres* accounted for by the treasurers of the marches, there were an estimated 17,100 *livres* paid out by *prévôts* and *baillis* for wartime expenses.[178] But even this sum of 83,000 *livres* did not comprise the total cost of the war in 1202/03. During that year Philip

TABLE 6. Wages Paid to French Troops
on the Norman Marches, 1202/03 (in *livres parisis*)

Knights	9,512
Mounted sergeants	4,014
Mounted crossbowmen	2,196
Crossbowmen on foot	1,556
Foot-sergeants	10,092
Total for troops paid daily wages	27,370

SOURCE: Audouin, *Essai sur l'armée* 118.

personally fought in the Touraine and Anjou. Since none of the expenses of that campaign appear in the marches' chapters or elsewhere in the accounts, they were undoubtedly the responsibility of the royal chamber accompanying the king. Unlike John's chamber, Philip's left no traces in the accounting system, yet it must have disbursed considerable sums in the Loire fighting. Moreover, besides repair of the recently taken Norman castles, Philip Augustus was engaged in a widespread program of fortifying the major towns of the royal domain, another significant cost of war. Rigord reports that in 1190, on the eve of the crusade, the king commanded the bourgeoisie of Paris to enclose the right bank of the royal capital with walls fitted with gates and turrets, and he subsequently extended this order to the other cities and strongholds of the kingdom. Since these fortifications, together with the tower of the Louvre, the key to Paris's defense, were completed before the accounts of 1202, their cost is not known.[179] But in November 1202 Abelin, the *bailli* of Bourges, was still occupied with the construction of the tower and bailey of Dun, which were erected according to the same measurements as the Louvre and cost 2,170 *livres*.[180] Philip's total outlay for defensive works around his cities during this decade cannot be calculated, but it was undoubtedly considerable.

The 66,000 *livres* spent by the military treasurers on the Norman borders in 1202/03 was provided largely by the royal treasury. Only 8,671 *livres* came from domanial revenues and justice in the newly conquered castellanies around Gournay and Lyons-la-Forêt.[181] Occasionally Nicolas Harchepin, the *prévôt-bailli* of Evreux, and the *prévôt* of Chaumont, who were active on the marches, drew small sums from their *prévôtés* to contribute to military expenses.[182] The remainder of the funds (no more than 57,000 *livres*) came indirectly or directly from the Temple. The *prévôts* of

Chaumont and Vernon and Brother Guérin transmitted large sums whose origins were not specified. Guérin, who collected close to 5,000 *livres* in the *baillis'* chapters, was the most active in dispensing funds (reaching on one occasion to 2,300 *livres*) throughout the marches.[183] Most of the military treasurers' receipts originated directly from the Temple, however, sometimes transmitted by the *prévôt* of Chaumont, Gautier the Young, or Robert de Meulan, *bailli* of Paris.[184] If we are correct that the Temple accumulated a balance of 60,000 to 77,000 *livres* from the *prévôts* and *baillis* during the fiscal year 1202/03, it had ample reserves to cover the expenses of war on the Norman marches for that year.[185]

It is not possible to assess the costs of the military campaign in the Loire valley and of the royal "hotel," which do not appear in the accounts of 1202/03. Nor can the extraordinary receipts that undoubtedly accumulated in the treasury from preceding years be estimated. These consisted chiefly of large feudal reliefs and the spoils of mulcting the church. In 1191 Count Baudouin paid 5,000 marks (10,500 *livres*) for the relief of Flanders; in 1192 Count Renaud paid 7,000 *livres* for Boulogne; in 1199 Count Hervé paid 3,000 marks (6,300 *livres*) for Nevers; and in May 1200 King John delivered the spectacular sum of 20,000 marks sterling (36,230 *livres*) for the recognition of his continental inheritance. In addition, Ingeborg's dowry brought 10,000 marks (21,000 *livres*) in 1193. These large sums, which were revealed only by chroniclers' reports and in occasional charters, were probably not accounted through the ordinary procedures of *prévôts* and *baillis*, but were collected directly by the royal chamber.[186] Moreover, when the papacy levied an interdict in 1200, Philip increased the royal revenue by confiscating properties of the observing bishops.[187] Undoubtedly such extraordinary measures, combined with the large feudal reliefs, produced a surplus in the treasury beyond the normal balance that helped to finance Philip's war efforts after 1202.

Although we can only speculate about the total amount of these extraordinary revenues, there was one special war tax for which careful accounts were kept, the *prisée des sergents*. The towns of the old royal domain owed the king military service, but when Philip issued new charters to communes in the first decade of the reign, he usually limited this service to local defense in an effort to gain favor with the town populations. In the 1190s, however, Philip began to rescind this limitation. Crandelin and its surrounding villages in 1196 and Crépy-en-Valois in 1215— to cite two examples—were required to furnish "host and expedition" throughout the realm like the other royal communes.[188] By 1194 not only the towns of the king's domain but also the royal abbeys owed Philip specified contingents of foot-sergeants. In 1194–1195 Philip Augustus drew up an inventory called the *Prisia servientum* that declared the number of sergeants and wagons owed by each town and abbey.[189] In certain cases a monetary equivalent was substituted for the men and equipment. In 1204 a scribe copied this inventory into Register A, which preserves the earliest surviving version. While recopying, he attempted to separate the communes from the other towns and abbeys in the royal domain (not always successfully), but he neglected to correct the totals, which were at variance with the numbers he supplied because of previous changes and additions. With these discrepancies, the recopied *Prisia* accounted for eighty-three towns and abbeys, of which seventy supplied a maximum of 7,695 sergeants and 138 wagons. (The wagons were apportioned at the rate of 1 for every 50 sergeants or fraction thereof.) In addition, fifteen towns commuted their service for a maximum of 16,463 *livres*. As Philip mounted his attacks against Richard in the 1190s, he therefore not only increased the military service owed by communes, but also assessed the royal domain for an army of foot-sergeants with the possibility of converting that army into a war tax. The royal chronicler Rigord complains that such heavy and uncustomary exactions oppressed the churches. Philip contended (Rigord continues) that his sole intention in amassing such wealth was to defend the Holy Land from the Saracens and his realm from its enemies. In the past the French kings had been so poor that they could not hire mercenary troops, and the kingdom had as a result suffered greatly.[190]

By the time the *Prisia* of 1194 was recopied into Register A, it was already out of date, because the accounts of 1202 indicate that by then Philip had realized the possibility of commuting all men and equipment into a money tax. In the account of November 1202 a special section entitled *servientes* was inserted between the *prévôts'* and *baillis'* chapters. Grouped under the four chief *baillis*, Guillaume de la Chapelle, Hugues de Gravelle, Renaud de Béthisy, and Robert de Meulan, sixty-four towns and abbeys were assigned sums of money owed for their sergeants, producing a grand total of 26,453 *livres*. In a little more than a third of these cases (twenty-five) the number of sergeants on which the money contribution was based is given, and the first item specifies that the length of service was three months. Scrutiny of these statistics shows that the sergeants were assessed at the rate of 8 *deniers* a day (the normal rate on the Norman marches) or 3 *livres* for three months, and the wagons at 13 *livres* 10 *sous* for three months.[191]

It is somewhat awkward to compare the two versions of the *prisée* because that of 1194 was computed in men, equipment, and money and that of 1202 in money alone.[192] Though the 1194 inventory contains nineteen more towns and abbeys than the 1202 account, some of these missing items appear in subsequent *prévôts'* and *baillis'* chapters. These arrears, however, amounted to only an insignificant sum (1,037 *livres*).[193] The *prisée* of 1202, however, was clearly assessed on a different basis than that of 1194. When some twenty items that are common to both dates are compared, we discover that the individual assessments in terms of sergeants and wagons never remained the same. Most (fourteen) were increased in 1202, but a few (six) decreased.[194]

The discrepancies between the totals and, most important, between the individual assessments of sergeants from 1194 to 1202 strongly suggest that the *prisée des sergents* was a war tax that could be assessed according to need. This suspicion receives further support when the total reported in the sergeants' chapter (26,453 *livres*) or the total that included the explicit arrears (27,490 *livres*) is compared with the actual wages (27,370 *livres*) paid out to troops on the Norman marches in 1202/03.[195] Whether intended or not, the *prisée des sergents* in fact paid the wages of the army on the Norman borders for that year. In England the treasurer Richard fitz Nigel formulated the classic definition of scutage as a payment (say a mark or pound) from every knight's fee to hire soldiers because the prince prefers to expose mercenaries (*stipendarios*) rather than his own knights (*domesticos*) to the hazards of war.[196] In a similar way Philip Augustus assessed a kind of scutage on his towns and abbeys to support a paid army. Whereas the English adjusted the fee to the unit (knights) to meet their needs, the French adjusted the unit (sergeants). Admittedly, the chief evidence for rationalized war finance rests on the coincidence of the receipts of the sergeants' chapter with the expenditures in wages in the marches' chapter; nonetheless, the careful and detailed accounting practiced by the *baillis* and the war treasurers in 1202 made such a "military budget" feasible. Naturally, wages for the army facing Normandy did not constitute the total costs of warfare, but there was a certain logic in assessing the wages of a paid army consisting largely of sergeants to towns and abbeys whose contributions were similarly based on sergeants. Whatever the underlying rationale, Philip Augustus enjoyed a war tax of at least 27,000 *livres*. Added to the current balance of 60,000–77,000 *livres*, this permitted him at least 90,000 *livres*, not counting previous surpluses, to sustain his war effort in the invasion of the Norman and Angevin territories.

The fiscal accounts of 1202/03 furnished by the bureau of audit in operation since 1190 provide the first assessment of Capetian finances based on figures provided by the royal administration itself. They do not give the total receipts, because extraordinary revenues, except for the *prisée des sergents*, were excluded. Doubtless collected by the royal chamber, this extraordinary income would have increased ordinary revenue by 36,000 *livres* when John paid his relief in 1200 or by 10,500 *livres* when Baudouin of Flanders paid his relief in 1192. Nor do the accounts reflect total expenditures. Except for the expenses of the marches and some minor items reported by the *prévôts* and *baillis*, the great costs of warfare were excluded. Apart from a minimal budget for the wardrobe, the expenses of the king's "hotel," and therefore his central government, were also excluded.

Despite these omissions, the accounts of 1202/03 furnish a sufficiently large picture of royal finances in that year to permit plausible conclusions. Philip's government realized an ordinary annual income of 115,000 *livres*. Not quite 30 percent was furnished by sources such as the *prévôts'* farms that could be relied on each year. A little more than 70 percent came from occasional sources such as justice, forests, and the regalia. Of this ordinary income, more than half was supplied by the agricultural domain and another 20 percent by townsmen, Jews, and commerce. The profits from justice and military obligations, difficult to separate in the accounts, brought in another 20 percent. In 1202/03 the regalian churches provided only 5 percent. All of these sources were more than sufficient to cover the expenses of local administration, which consumed no more than 12 percent of ordinary revenue. An overwhelming surplus was therefore available for the costs of the "hotel" and the military campaign against John. Aside from the 60,000–77,000 *livres* of ordinary income, there were the extraordinary levy of 26,000 *livres* from the *prisée des sergents* and other unspecified revenues collected by the chamber. More than sufficient to cover the 83,000 *livres* of war expenses accounted for by the *prévôts*, *baillis*, and treasurers on the Norman marches, they even provided surpluses for the chamber to carry on the fighting against John. The accounts of 1202/03 therefore convey the distinct impression that Philip's finances were indeed in order and adequate to his political designs against the Angevin lands on the Continent.

The overall purpose behind the accounts of 1202/03 was, however, to supervise and control the operations of local agents, not to budget for a war. But the fiscal reports of the military treasurers on the Norman marches suggest that one of the purposes behind their detailed accounts may have been to assess a war tax, the *prisée des sergents*. Whether or not such budgeting can be fully demonstrated, the marches' chapters of 1202/03 do show that accounting techniques were now extended to war as well as to government. Such fiscal records, along with their suggestions of financial budgeting, illustrate the penetration of rational processes into Capetian government, which was already well under way before the conquest of Normandy.

The Blessings
of Ecclesiastical
Liberties

Although royal churches contributed only 5 percent to the total ordinary income accounted in 1202/03, the regalia, depending on circumstances, could provide more. Aside from this financial support, however, royal prelates extended the king's influence far beyond the immediate royal domain. From his father Philip had inherited a policy of cooperation with churchmen that had served the Capetians well. These amicable relations between the monarchy and the prelates were to receive severe testing in the 1190s, chiefly because of the king's personal matrimonial difficulties. As Philip laid plans for the great offensive against the Angevins, therefore, he needed the concurrence of churchmen more than ever and was prepared to exceed even his father's policies in making concessions to his prelates.

Throughout the 1190s Philip Augustus's dealings with his churches proceeded along the lines established a half-century earlier. In the ordinance-testament the king promised royal bishoprics and abbeys freedom to elect their leaders as long as the canons and monks chose men who were both "pleasing to God" and "useful to the kingdom." Cooperation, with both parties respecting mutual interests, was Philip's guiding principle.[1] With the possible exception of Tournai, no disputed elections caused by royal interference have come to light among the royal bishoprics from 1191 to 1200.[2] Although the evidence is less abundant, similar conditions seem to have prevailed among the abbeys. In 1193, for example, when Nicolas, abbot of the royal monastery of Corbie, resigned his post, he granted to the king the power of choosing his successor. Philip designated his *familiaris* Gérard, formerly abbot of the royal monastery of Compiègne, but he was careful to obtain the monks' consent and promised that this case would not serve as precedent. Since the incident was exceptional, the monks carefully preserved the royal letters in their cartulary.[3]

Among the bishoprics, where the effects of Philip's policy of cooperation can be measured, the results were doubtless gratifying to the king. Of the fourteen bishops elected to royal sees from 1191 to 1200, at least six (46 percent) had discernible connections with Philip.[4] Two, Robert d'Auvergne (Clermont, 1195) and Eudes de Sully (Paris, 1197), were royal cousins. In 1198 the chapter of Orléans elected Hugues de Garlande, a member of a castellan family prominent at the Capetian court for almost a century. The chapters of Tournai and Meaux chose two royal clerics, Master Etienne and Master Anselme respectively, in 1193 and 1197. The former had served the king while abbot of Sainte-Geneviève and the latter as dean of Saint-Martin of Tours.[5] Finally, the king's cousin Eudes de Sully, bishop of Paris, became the liaison with the regalian sees, a role comparable to that of Brother Bernard de Vincennes. Two contemporary chroniclers note that five regalian bishops were elected at Eudes's suggestion. The first of these, Guillaume, archbishop of Bourges (elected in 1200), had previously been abbot of Chaalis, but he had been canon of Paris as well. In fact, all of the candidates proposed by Eudes de Sully had had careers at Paris, which explains how Eudes came to know them and how they may have come under royal influence.[6] Although a small sample, the six candidates who exhibit royal connections suggest that the chapters were even more concerned to find bishops "useful to the king" than they had been in the previous decade.

Philip continued to employ his regalian churchmen for the important affairs of the realm after his return from the crusade. Five of the sixteen members of his court who swore the oath at Compiègne in November 1193 enabling him to separate from Queen Ingeborg were bishops, and all of them, including the great archbishop of Reims, were connected by

family ties to the royal house or to the king's *familiares*.[7] In 1196, as
Philip searched for allies to oppose Richard's mounting offensive, the
archbishop of Reims and the bishops of Arras, Tournai, and Thérouanne
enforced with ecclesiastical sanctions the oaths of liege fealty to the king
of the young Count Baudouin of Flanders and Count Renaud of Boulogne.[8] Four abbeys, two of them regalian (Marmoutier and Saint-
Denis), and one with close French ties (Charité-sur-Loire), stood as sure-
ties for Philip Augustus in the treaty of Gaillon of 1196.[9] Additionally,
abbeys were listed along with communes as contributors to the *prisée des
sergents*. In 1194 some twenty monasteries furnished 1,485 sergeants, or
19 percent of the total, to this military levy.[10]

Philip Augustus's policy of cooperation underwent a severe test during
the great interdict of 1200 after the king stubbornly refused to dismiss
Agnès de Méran and return Ingeborg to her rightful position as his wife
and queen. It is difficult to determine the full extent of the sanctions in
effect from January to September 1200. Innocent III urged the archbishop of Rouen to promulgate the sentence, but whether it included
Normandy or just the French Vexin cannot be known. The pope later
commiserated with the sufferings of the archbishop of Lyon for observing the measure, although the archbishopric was technically outside the
French kingdom.[11] Most contemporary chroniclers assume that it affected the entire kingdom, but Innocent later wrote that the cardinal-
legate applied it only to the lands then adhering to the king (*in terram
illam . . . que regi tunc temporis adherebat*).[12]

No evidence has survived as to the stand taken by six regalian bishoprics located on the eastern and southern perimeters of the royal domain.[13]
The awesome sanctions nonetheless compelled the great majority of the
twenty-five royal bishops to declare a choice between their two superiors,
the pope and the king. The responses of nineteen French bishops are
known from papal sources.[14] At the moment of promulgation, the archbishopric of Sens was vacant, but the canons sided with the pope. Five
other bishops also defied the king, including Senlis, Soissons, Amiens,
Arras, and Paris. All were recruited from local families, except for the last,
Eudes de Sully, the newly elected bishop of Paris, who as a royal cousin
subsequently suffered the full force of Philip's wrath.[15]

In sharp contrast to these six were the thirteen remaining bishops who
braved suspension to remain loyal to the king. The archbishopric of
Bourges was also vacant at the time, but the newly elected incumbent, the
saintly Guillaume de Donjon, was nonetheless suspended for accepting
consecration during the interdict. (He was later excused on the grounds

of ignorance.)[16] The other dozen bishops who refused to obey the interdict were those who had the closest ties to the monarchy and those who occupied the regalian sees. They included the king's relations (the archbishop of Reims and the bishops of Auxerre, Beauvais, and Chartres), those related to royal *familiares* (such as Noyon and Orléans), and the two royal clerks (Meaux and Tournai). Only four (Thérouanne, Troyes, Nevers, and Laon) cannot be directly associated with the royal circle. In addition, two royal abbeys, Saint-Denis and Saint-Germain-des-Prés, defied the pope.[17] In this crucial test of strength, therefore, Philip's policy of cooperation had secured the loyalty of the majority of the French regalian bishops.

The king's immediate response to the interdict was to harass the bishops who obeyed the sentence. The nearby bishop of Senlis was forced to flee his see. Adept at despoiling churches when provoked, Philip seized the lands and expropriated the goods of the observing clergy. The royal cousin at Paris, Eudes de Sully, was a special victim.[18] So violently did he suffer from the royal sergeants that Philip was later obliged to grant the bishop special privileges to compensate for damages.[19] After this initial reaction, however, the interdict encouraged the king to reevaluate his ecclesiastical policy. Just as the papal measure prompted accommodation with the count of Flanders and King John, so it also induced important concessions that liberated the French churches even more than Philip's father had envisaged.

In June 1200, just one month after Philip acquired Evreux by the treaty of Le Goulet, he published the results of an inquest into electoral procedures in the Norman see. Declaring that neither King Henry nor King Richard had ever exercised the right to oppose an elected candidate, he granted the chapter free power to choose a bishop whenever the see fell vacant, "just as the other canons of French churches have the power to choose their bishops." So precious was this privilege that the chapter copied it into the cartulary and had it quickly confirmed by the pope.[20] As history, the findings of the inquest were dubious. The two preceding bishops of Evreux had both been king's men: John fitz Luke (1180–1192) had been clerk to King Henry II, and Guarin de Cierry (1193–1201), a former archdeacon, was King Richard's close collaborator. Evreux had fitted the general Norman pattern according to which the English kings, although inclined to respect the formalities of canonical election, saw to it that the sees were filled by candidates drawn from prominent Anglo-Norman families or from among the royal clerks, all loyal to the crown.[21]

By contrast, Philip Augustus permitted the chapter of Evreux freedom of election as guaranteed to all French regalian bishoprics by the ordinance of 1190. Since Evreux was not then vacant,[22] the royal charter of 1200 was a gratuitous proclamation, intended to alert the other Norman sees to French policy. Its significance became fully apparent by 1202, when King John revealed his own intentions not to lessen his grip on the Norman church. In that year three new bishops were appointed in Normandy. Virtually nothing is known about the background or manner of selection of Vivian, bishop of Coutances, but the see of Lisieux was filled by Jordan du Hommet, son of the constable of Normandy. The crucial case was Sées, where the Angevin kings were accustomed to impose their candidates. This time John's candidate was the dean of Lisieux, an outsider from a family the chapter considered unfriendly. Because the church of Sées had previously suffered from the depredations of outside bishops, the canons swore an oath to choose only from the chapter. Whether or not they were encouraged by Philip Augustus's charter to neighboring Evreux, they nonetheless opposed royal demands to elect the dean of Lisieux, offering instead a series of rival candidates, including Sylvestre, the archdeacon of Sées. During the stormy dispute that followed, the chapter withstood John's wrath as he confiscated the treasury, quartered soldiers in the chapter house, and attempted to starve the canons into submission. In 1203 the conflict was finally appealed to Pope Innocent, who decided for Sylvestre. Under threat of the imminent French invasion, John finally consented to Sylvestre's election, but he protested that this decision in no way compromised his rights over Norman elections.[23]

In Guillaume le Breton's account of the conquest of Normandy at the end of the reign, the royal chronicler repeats that Philip had of his own accord introduced free elections into Normandy. In comparing Philip's liberal policies with the arbitrary practices of the English kings, Guillaume was undoubtedly underscoring the contrast between Philip's concessions to Evreux and John's harsh treatment of Sées.[24] Evreux was Philip's channel for announcing his policy and for enlisting the support of the Norman bishops in the forthcoming invasion. The crisis of the interdict had taught him that his best hope for retaining his bishops' loyalties was to reconfirm their electoral liberty and to offer it to the Norman bishops as well.

The four bishops chosen by regalian sees after the proclamation to Evreux in June 1200 and before the invasion of Normandy in 1203 probably constitute too small a sample to provide a clear assessment of the effect on his bishoprics of Philip's renewal of electoral freedom. But two, perhaps three, of the chapters went on to elect bishops considered favorably disposed towards the king. Nevers chose Master Guillaume de Saint-Lazare, a royal cleric, in 1202, and in 1203 Châlons-sur-Marne elected Gérard de Douai, a former canon of Paris. The most interesting case was Evreux, which one year after Philip's charter of liberties chose Robert de Roye, who was related to the king's most prominent *familiaris*, Barthélemy de Roye. Two years later, in 1203, however, the canons turned to a local candidate, Luc, formerly archdeacon and dean of the chapter.[25] Measured in terms of its overall effect, Philip's renewal of free elections did not lessen, and perhaps even strengthened, his influence over the royal bishops.

More light is shed on elections to regalian sees by the appearance in 1198 of papal registers recording disputes appealed to Rome. From 1198 to the end of the reign, fifteen elections in French regalian sees were contested and appealed to the pope. Of these, only four indicate royal involvement, three of which occurred shortly after the proclamation of 1200.[26] When the archbishopric of Sens fell vacant in 1199, the chapter, with the king's explicit consent, elected the bishop of Auxerre, Hugues de Noyers, whose family had marriage ties with the royal house. Innocent III, however, denied permission to translate Hugues, who had refused to obey the interdict, to a church that had sided with the pope. When Innocent succeeded in obtaining the election of Master Pierre de Corbeil, bishop of Cambrai, and the pope's former teacher of theology at Paris, Philip acquiesced in the choice. In the end, the king found Master Pierre a congenial prelate and, as we have seen, called on his services to negotiate with the pope over his marriage.[27]

In addition to Sens, the royal archbishopric of Reims was naturally of particular concern to the king. When Philip's uncle, the influential Archbishop Guillaume, finally died in 1202 in disgrace after the debacle over Ingeborg, the king strongly supported the candidacy of his cousin Philippe de Dreux, bishop of Beauvais. But the election was thwarted in the chapter by the obstinate opposition of the archdeacon, Thibaut du Perche. A second candidate appeared in the youthful Miles de Nanteuil, who was also related to the Capetian family of Dreux and who attempted to improve his prospects by offering the chapter 3,000 marks. His election also met with the determined opposition of the archdeacon. After almost two years of bickering, Innocent imposed his own choice on the chapter, Guy Paré, a Cistercian abbot and papal legate. As far as the sources reveal, Philippe de Dreux and Miles de Nanteuil failed for no other reason than the archdeacon's hostility.[28] When the archbishopric fell vacant four years later, the chapter chose Master Alberic de Humbert, archdeacon of Paris, on the suggestion of Eudes de Sully. His election, too, was opposed by the obstructionist archdeacon, but this time the pope sided with the king and chapter, confirmed the choice, and disciplined the unruly archdeacon.[29] These three cases, for which the papal registers furnish details, indicate that the chapters continued to choose royalist candidates like Hugues de Noyers and Philippe de Dreux under the regime of free elections, which was reaffirmed during the interdict. When opposition to these men arose from the pope or from within the chapter, the king did not attempt to impose his will like King John. In return for the chapter's consideration of royal candidates, Philip allowed the canons the final decision. He was therefore as good as his word when he claimed that the free elections granted to Evreux were, in fact, enjoyed by all chapters throughout France. This policy was fruitful in supplying Philip with congenial prelates such as Pierre of Sens and Alberic of Reims.

Though the Evreux proclamation confirmed and extended the principle of free elections formulated in 1190, it did not alter the underlying status of the twenty-five bishoprics of which the king enjoyed the regalia during vacancies. We have seen that Philip's judgment over the regalia of Châlons-sur-Marne in 1202 abolished the rights of the *vidame* and reconfirmed the king's rights over the church's temporalities.[30] At about the same time, the chapter of Mâcon was fined for resisting royal agents who had arrived to collect the regalia, and Ponce, the newly elected bishop, was required to recognize the royal prerogatives over his see in writing.[31] In 1203, however, on the eve of the hostilities against King John, Philip instituted a new policy of renouncing regalian rights.[32] At Langres, "remote and on the confines of France and the Empire," the king not only excused the chapter from seeking a license to elect, but also conceded to the canons the administration of the regalia, the proceeds of which were reserved for the future bishop. Simultaneously, the same privileges were conferred on Arras on the northern borders.[33] During the next six years this movement to remove sees from regalian status was extended in rapid succession to Auxerre (1207), Nevers (1208), and Mâcon (1209).[34] The grants to Arras and Auxerre included the specific renunciation of the spiritual regalia as well, a privilege extended to Troyes in 1207.[35] In such instances the chapters were instructed to reserve the vacant prebends for assignment by the succeeding bishop. As might be anticipated, the chapters paid the king handsomely for these liberties. Local chroniclers note that Guillaume de Seignelay, the newly elected bishop of Auxerre, paid great sums, but extant charters specify that these privileges cost the chapters of Arras and Nevers 1,000 *livres* apiece.[36]

Simultaneously with renouncing his rights to the regalia of certain bishoprics altogether, Philip permitted an innovation that shortened the length of vacancy. In accordance with traditional Capetian practice, the ordinance of 1190 stipulated that the consecration of a bishop-elect by the archbishop and his suffragans ended a vacancy and obliged the king to return the regalia. Perhaps as early as 1200 in the case of Langres, and certainly by 1203 in the case of Arras, the act of confirmation now replaced consecration as the end of the vacancy.[37] Consecration, the solemn ceremony that bestowed on bishops their apostolic and divine powers, took longer to prepare, whereas confirmation merely certified the regularity and authenticity of the election and could be performed with dispatch by the archbishop or another duly authorized prelate. The practical effect of this innovation was to permit bishops their regalia with less delay. As indicated by letters from Evreux and Orléans preserved in the royal archives, confirmation had become the accepted conclusion of a vacancy by the end of the reign.[38]

Whereas the shortening of the vacancy was a minor adjustment, the renunciation of the regalia was a radical innovation. Both changes had been introduced by 1203. Whether they were directly inspired by Philip's experiences during the interdict is difficult to say, but like freedom of elections they were designed to court favor with the French episcopacy and to ensure its support at a crucial moment.

Another area where Philip Augustus made important concessions to churchmen during the interdict was that of criminal jurisdiction. In July 1200 the king issued a solemn charter to the scholars of Paris that clarified their legal status.[39] Since the days of Abelard early in the century, the celebrated schools of Paris had drawn increasing numbers of masters and students. Constituting a substantial segment of the city's population by the end of the century, these scholars enjoyed clerical privileges that exempted them from normal police jurisdiction and posed a threat to order at Paris.

Philip's charter of 1200 was based on practices reaching back into the twelfth century, when the ecclesiastical courts had formulated two sets of privileges to protect the clergy. The first was termed the *privilegium canonis*, under which the clergy were considered sacred personages. Any physical violence against them was therefore sacrilege and punishable by immediate excommunication, for which absolution could be obtained only by arduous penance. Under the second, the *privilegium fori*, the clergy were exempt from the secular courts and subject exclusively to ecclesiastical jurisdiction. Since clerics enjoyed the *privilegium canonis* at all times, the church courts could not corporally punish them, but were restricted to spiritual sanctions. The formulation of the *privilegium canonis* received little opposition, but the *privilegium fori* posed evident problems for the secular authorities. Under its regime murder, rape, robbery, and the most heinous crimes went unpunished among the clergy.[40]

In an effort to repress the endemic violence that had proliferated in England during the anarchy of King Stephen's reign, King Henry II attempted to define the clergy's status in a way that discouraged clerical crime but respected clerical privileges. In the famous article 3 of the Constitutions of Clarendon of 1164, he decreed that any cleric accused of serious offense against the king's peace be summoned before the royal court and then be transferred to an ecclesiastical court to be tried under canon law, but in the presence of a royal officer. If found guilty, the cleric was to be degraded, that is stripped of his clerical status, and returned to the king's court, where as a laymen he could receive corporal punishment.[41] Thomas Becket, the archbishop of Canterbury, opposed this cooperation between royal and ecclesiastical justice, however, and in particular, the final punishment by secular authority. Asserting that God does not punish the same crime twice, Becket insisted that degradation was sufficient punishment. Only if the degraded cleric committed a second crime could he be punished by secular justice. The archbishop defended this principle with his life in the most famous martyrdom of the century. The king was forced to abandon his proposal, and Pope Alexander III had adopted Becket's position by 1178, forbidding the handing over to secular justice of any cleric degraded for a serious crime.[42]

Becket's principle had been introduced into Normandy by 1190. With King Richard and the archbishop of Rouen absent on crusade, the seneschal Guillaume fitz Ralph and Jean de Coutances, dean of Rouen, concurred that secular authorities were not to apprehend clerics except for the serious crimes of murder, theft, and arson, cases that pertained to ducal jurisdiction. If requested by the church authorities, the accused cleric was to be handed over to ecclesiastical justice. Since no further mention was made of secular involvement, the penalties of the church court were deemed sufficient.[43] In 1198 Richard confirmed the essentials of this agreement at La Roche d'Orival in the presence of his seneschal and the archbishop of Rouen. Arrested clergymen were to be turned over immediately to the church authorities on the request of the bishop, and the hanging of priests was specifically condemned as sacrilege.[44]

At Paris, where scholars formed an important part of the population, the problem of repressing clerical crime was even more acute than in England and Normandy. Youthful students and masters enjoying the *privilegia canonis* and *fori* as members of the clergy were known for their brawling and rioting, as well as for committing more violent crimes. Their protected status encouraged aggressive behavior. Philip Augustus himself was reported to have observed that clerics exhibited greater rashness than knights. Whereas knights fought only in armor, clerics sprang into the fray brandishing knives and without helmets to protect their clean-shaven pates. In fact, the tonsure, the unmistakable sign of clerical status, afforded better protection than a helmet.[45] Undoubtedly the king well remembered the famous student riot at Paris of 1200 and its fateful resolution, which had defined the legal status of scholars.

As narrated by the English chronicler Roger of Howden, the affair unfolded in a pattern that became classic in the thirteenth century. A number of German students were involved in a pre-Lenten tavern brawl in which they wrecked the tavern and severely beat the owner. In retaliation, Thomas, the royal *prévôt* of Paris, attacked the German hostel with a band of urban militia, killing some students in the melee. Outraged by this incident, the masters joined the students to demand redress of their injuries. Fearing that the scholars might boycott the city, according to the chronicler, Philip came to terms with them and issued a charter in July 1200 that addressed three major issues.[46] The immediate object was to punish the *prévôt* and his accomplices. The scholars proposed that the malefactors be whipped like schoolboys, but the king settled on his own punishment. Thomas was to be imprisoned for life unless he chose to submit to the ordeal by water. If he failed it, he was to be executed; if he passed it, he was nonetheless forever prohibited from holding the office of *prévôt* or *bailli* and from returning to Paris. Similar measures were taken against his accomplices, who were subject to an inquest conducted by Gautier the Chamberlain and Philippe de Lévis. If they fled the city, they were adjudged guilty and condemned.

In the second place, after avenging the scholars' honor, the king promised to reinforce the *privilegium canonis* by commissioning the agents of royal justice to protect clerics from assaults by laymen. If the townsmen saw any layman assaulting a student at Paris, except in self-defense, they were obliged to apprehend the offender, to hand him over to royal justice, and to give testimony against him. The *prévôt* was empowered to conduct inquests and to bring to justice those suspected of clerical assaults, notwithstanding their denial or their offer to purge themselves by duel or the ordeal by water. In the third place, Philip commanded his officers neither to arrest clerics accused of crimes nor to seize their chattels (*capitale*) without serious cause. If arrest was deemed necessary, the cleric was to be delivered immediately to an ecclesiastical court, which would attempt to satisfy the king and the injured party. If the arrest occurred at night, when the church courts were inaccessible, the *prévôt* should not imprison the cleric with common criminals, but detain him at his hostel until the ecclesiastical authorities could take charge. To respect the *privilegium canonis*, particular care was to be exercised to avoid physical injury to the cleric unless he resisted arrest. All complaints of violence were to be investigated by inquest. Both the *prévôt* and the people of Paris were required to observe these measures under oath. The *prévôt* took his oath before the scholars in a church on the first or second Sunday after assuming office. What is noteworthy about these regulations governing criminous clerics is what they omitted. The function of royal justice was limited simply to apprehending accused clerics. There is no mention of further royal involvement after the offender was turned over to the ecclesiastical authorities. In accordance with Becket's principles and English and Norman practice, ecclesiastical sanctions were deemed sufficient punishment for clerical crime.[47]

This interpretation, which allowed clerics complete immunity from royal justice, increased the *prévôt*'s difficulties in maintaining order at Paris. Undoubtedly, Philip Augustus was under pressure from several quarters to accede to a situation disadvantageous to royal authority. The scholars' threat to migrate, reported by the English chronicler, was most likely a real danger to the city. The memory of Thomas Becket's martyrdom was still strong after thirty years. His position on clerical crime was vigorously defended by a reform party of masters and clerics at Paris in the last decades of the century. One of their leaders, Master Pierre the Chanter, had argued Becket's case in public debate with a Master Roger the Norman, who supported the royal cause.[48] In July 1200 Philip Augustus also had another reason for granting this unusual privilege. His lands were still under interdict and he was competing with the pope for the allegiance of French churchmen. This charter, like the Evreux proclamation of free elections, helped him win their loyalty.

Whatever concessions Philip offered the clergy between 1200 and the eve of the Norman invasion, his most tangible means of courting their favor was to make donations directly to individual churches. Throughout the second decade of his reign, as in the past, Philip continued to give regularly apportioned alms to the churches of his domain, which were duly recorded in the fiscal accounts of 1202/03 and in the alms accounts of the Registers. There is little indication that he made significant changes in this traditional pattern.

Of greater interest are Philip's gifts to the churches of Artois and Evreux, where he found opportunity to display generosity in the newly acquired provinces. No sooner had the king taken possession of Artois after Count Philippe's death in 1191 than he began reconfirming to churches the alms they had formerly enjoyed.[49] Since Philip Augustus became heir to Aliénor, countess of the adjacent Vermandois and Valois, at the same time, he also confirmed her alms, but only up to the limit of 100 *livres parisis*.[50] The extent of the royal liberality may be sampled by comparing the Flemish accounts at Bapaume in 1187 with those of the king in 1202. Seven individual churches appear in both accounts and in each instance the amount of donation was identical. Because of alterations in jurisdiction, it is impossible to compare the total funds expended in alms in 1187 and 1202; nonetheless, the sample items suggest that Philip Augustus maintained the traditional beneficences. The only new advantage the churches enjoyed under the king, therefore, was that they received their donations in *livres parisis*, which were in most cases worth more than the local currencies paid by the count.[51]

In Normandy the Capetians had long-established relations with individual monasteries. Louis VII had, for example, issued charters in favor of Bec, Jumièges, Fécamp, and Valasse.[52] Philip Augustus continued this tradition by placing these and other abbeys under royal protection during the opening decade of his reign. The major benefit derived from such status was exemption from tolls whenever the goods of these abbeys passed through the royal lands.[53] When Philip acquired the Norman *prévôté* of Pacy in 1196, he assured the monks of Bec and Lyre that they would continue to receive their accustomed revenues from that region.[54] His great moment to prove his liberality to the Norman churches (as well as being a liberator of elections) came, however, with the acquisition of Evreux in 1200. His value as patron can be measured by comparing the Norman exchequer roll of 1198 with the French accounts of 1202 and the alms inventory in the Registers.

From an annual farm of 540 *livres angevins* under King Richard, Richard d'Argences paid 154.47 *livres angevins* (equivalent to 105.78 *livres parisis*) in fixed alms to the churches of Evreux.[55] Norman accounting procedure grouped the individual gifts together under the sources that generated them, such as the *vicomté* and various mills and domains. In February 1203 the French *prévôt* Nicolas Harchepin paid 64.7 *livres angevins* and 78.61 *livres parisis* (or the total equivalent of 122.9 *livres parisis*) to the churches from an annual farm of 900 *livres parisis*. In the alms accounts of the Registers, these donations were valued at 104.02 *livres parisis*. Not only were the French accounts computed in mixed currencies, but they were organized according to the beneficiary rather than the source. When the Norman account is rearranged according to the French system and all of the *livres angevins* converted into *livres parisis*, however, the Norman and French accounts are, in fact, seen to have included the same beneficiaries, six churches and two chaplains. A number of the individual gifts remained exactly identical; for example: 40 *livres angevins* to the Hôtel-Dieu of Evreux and one *livre angevin* for candles to the nuns of Saint-Sauveur. Some beneficiaries, however, received significantly greater alms in 1203 than in 1198—for example, the cathedral of Notre-Dame and the chaplain of the local castle. The king gave to the monks of Saint-Taurin an annual rent of eleven *setiers* of grain taken from his mill below the tower of Evreux in exchange for nine and a half *setiers* from the mill at the gate Aux Fèvres, but unfortunately for the monks the price of grain dropped so much that the rent, which had produced 5.21 *livres parisis* (7.6 *livres angevins*) in 1198, only realized 3.55 *livres parisis* in 1203.[56] Only one party of beneficiaries, the nuns of Chaise-Dieu du Theil, suffered an inexplicable loss. Philip Augustus paid a total of 122.9 *livres parisis* to the churches of Evreux in 1203 as compared to 105.78 *livres parisis* paid by King Richard in 1198, an increase of 16 percent. When the donation to the chaplain of the castle was omitted in the alms account of the Register, the total dropped to 104.03 *livres parisis*, approximating that of 1198.

As a patron of churches in newly acquired territories, Philip was thus not extravagantly generous. The Artesian churches benefited only from an improved royal coinage. Certain churches profited dramatically at Evreux, but the total cost the king only a modest increase. If the alms accounts in the Registers represent his long-term goals, he was prepared to pay little or no more than his predecessors. If Evreux's example could be trusted, the Norman churches could look forward only to modest gains on the eve of the great invasion. Philip was a king who was more careful with his purse than with his promises of liberties. In addition to reaffirming free elections, his chief means for securing the loyalty of prelates were the renunciation of regalia in selected churches and the confirmation of clerical immunities from the police.

PART THREE

Conquest
and
Consolidation,

1203–1214

Narrative: The Great Conquests and the Victory at Bouvines

The Invasion of Normandy and the Loire Valley
(1203–1206)

After the French court formally condemned John on 28 April 1202, Philip Augustus went into immediate action against the Norman castles east of the Seine.[1] His plan was to accompany this attack on the duchy with a campaign in the Loire valley led by Arthur of Brittany. When Gournay fell in July, Philip knighted the young prince and received his homage for Brittany, Anjou, Maine, Touraine, and Poitou, to be bestowed on him if and when they were captured.[2] Provided with money and two hundred knights, Arthur was dispatched to Poitou, where he was joined by the Lusignans, Savery de Mauléon, and other barons. Learning that his grandmother, the old dowager queen, Eleanor of Aquitaine, was at Mirebeau between Angers and Poitiers, Arthur was unable to resist the temptation to capture her, despite Philip's warning to proceed cautiously. The castle did not yield easily, thus allowing John time to catch up with his nephew. On the urging of his seneschal, Guillaume des Roches, John rushed from Le Mans to Mirebeau, surprised the besiegers on 1 August, and took them all captive. In one sweeping stroke John thus laid hands on his major enemies in the Loire region: Arthur of Brittany, his archrival, along with Arthur's sister Aliénor; Hugues and Geoffroi de Lusignan, his outraged vassals in Poitou; and Savery de Mauléon, André de Chauvigny, Hugues de Châtellerault, and many other important lords. When the news of the disaster reached Philip Augustus at Arques, he abandoned the siege there with bitter disappointment and turned his attention to the Loire valley for the remainder of the season of 1202/03.[3]

The military campaign of 1202 therefore opened at Mirebeau with a stunning victory for John. True to character, however, the king was incapable of preserving the fruits of good fortune. Obsessed with a desire for revenge, he treated the prisoners with complete caprice. André de Chauvigny was released on his word, but the resentful Lusignans were bound in chains and later ransomed. Arthur disappeared into prison at Falaise, and his sister was sent to England for safekeeping. Not only did John neglect to reward Guillaume des Roches for his services, he refused to listen to further advice. Guillaume judged the king to be beyond the reach of reason and fled the English court, accompanied by the Poitevin baron Aimery de Thouars. John reacted by promptly assigning the seneschalships of Anjou and Touraine to two court familiars.[4] The action of Guillaume des Roches and Aimery de Thouars provoked a wave of defections among the most important barons of the Loire valley and the Norman borders. A spectacular example was Robert, count of Alençon. After entertaining John for five days in January 1203, Count Robert offered Philip homage for his lands on the Norman frontier on the very day of the English king's departure (John was even served breakfast that morning).[5] Among the Breton and Angevin baronage such desertions were particularly motivated by mounting anxiety over Arthur's fate. When the young prince failed to reappear after months of imprisonment, ugly rumors began to circulate that he had been hideously murdered. How or when the deed was executed may never be known (in all likelihood Arthur was dead by April 1203), but the circumstances point conclusively to John, since the Breton prince was never seen again.[6] In March 1203, when his fate was still in doubt, Guillaume des Roches, Juhel de Mayenne, and Maurice de Craon, in the company of ten important lords from Anjou, Maine, Touraine, and Poitou, proffered their liege-homage in writing to the French king at Paris, at a time when Arthur was presumed to be in prison. Should he be released, they would remain his vassals, on the condition that he respect their homage and agreements with Philip. Should he be dead, they would accept as heir only a husband married to his sister with the French king's consent. In exchange for this liege-homage, which superseded Arthur's own claims, Philip promised not to make peace with John without their concurrence.[7] In the end, John lost more because of his barbaric treatment of Arthur than he had won at Mirebeau.

Defended by Arthur's vassals in Brittany and the Loire valley, Philip Augustus returned in May 1203 to his chief objective, Normandy. His major obstacle was Richard's formidable Château-Gaillard, which obstructed the Seine valley between Paris and Rouen. Before it could be directly assaulted, its system of supporting castles had to be reduced. Philip's operations proceeded from the west bank, where he had concentrated his troops.[8] The count of Alençon's example prompted new defections in Normandy. Pierre de Meulan conceded Montfort-sur-Risle, and Hugues de Gournay handed over Beaumont-le-Roger. Château-Gaillard's principal support on the west bank was Le Vaudreuil, which had been strengthened by Richard. Philip prepared for a stubborn siege, but its English defenders, led by Robert fitz Walter and Sauer de Quincy, suddenly surrendered without a fight, much to everyone's astonishment. Philip further isolated the great fortress by capturing the Ile d'Andely at the foot of Gaillard and by reducing Radpont on the east bank. He began the siege proper in September 1203. The French strategy was to draw up a circumvallation and starve out the garrison. In the meantime, John, keeping mainly to the western portions of Normandy, had barely exerted himself to defend the duchy. One English chronicler attributed this strange behavior to John's youthful queen, Isabelle d'Angoulême, whose presence, he averred, kept the king in bed each day until noon.[9] Whatever the excuses, John refused to come personally to Gaillard and sent only a letter of encouragement. When it was ascertained that he had left for England in December 1203, taking his wife with him, all prospects of rescue were extinguished. The garrison, bravely commanded by Roger de Lacy, constable of Chester, nonetheless resisted until 6 March 1204, when, virtually exhausted, it finally succumbed to Philip's direct assaults.[10]

With Gaillard's fall and John's absence, the duchy was vulnerable, but it could still have been defended. Resistance was only spotty, however. Important castles at Falaise, Caen, Bayeux, Pont-Audemer, and Bonneville-sur-Touques gave up quickly. Guy de Thouars, widower of Constance of Brittany, who had recently defected to Philip, attacked the duchy from the west, taking Le Mont-Saint-Michel and Avranches. Only Verneuil, Arques, and, most important, Rouen put up a defense. Under the leadership of Pierre de Préaux, the Rouennais finally agreed to a truce whereby they promised to surrender if John did not send aid within thirty days.

When it became clear that such hope was vain, the city capitulated on 24 June 1204, even before the time had expired. Verneuil and Arques immediately followed suit.[11]

In two military campaigns between the spring of 1203 and the summer of 1204, Philip Augustus had succeeded in conquering the entire duchy of Normandy. Undoubtedly, John's unwillingness to come personally to its defense contributed much to the French victory. Refusing to fight, the English king relied heavily on papal intervention in his behalf. As early as May 1202, Pope Innocent ordered the archbishops of Rouen and Canterbury to excommunicate those vassals rebelling against King John, but with little effect.[12] The following year the pope commissioned a papal legate, Gerard, abbot of Casamari, to negotiate a peace between the kings, whose hostilities were harming the church and obstructing a new crusade. Since by this time Philip Augustus was the obvious aggressor, the papal efforts, enunciated in letters of May and October 1203 and June 1204, had the effect of favoring John.[13] When Philip protested that his dispute with John was merely over a fief—over which the pope had no jurisdiction—Innocent granted Philip's premise but justified intervention on the grounds of general authority to judge sin. In fact, the pope insisted that he defended John in the interests of peace just as he had sided with Philip against Richard in 1199. With military victory within grasp, neither the Capetian nor his barons allowed the papal actions to deter them. The overtures of May 1203 provoked Renaud, count of Boulogne; Eudes, duke of Burgundy; Blanche, countess of Troyes; Hervé, count of Nevers; and other great barons (fifteen in all) to write to the king urging him to resist all papal efforts to impose a peace. (Their sealed letters were carefully preserved in the royal archives.)[14] When Philip called together his barons at Mantes in August 1203, he was further advised to inform the papal legate of his rejection of Innocent's demands. The legate then turned to the French prelates and called them to a council at Meaux in June 1204, but they also opposed the legate's decision and appealed it to the pope.[15] Since the conquest had become an accomplished fact, neither barons nor churchmen wished to disturb the Capetian victory.

After Normandy's submission, the great Loire fiefs were Philip's next objective. While the French king was occupied with Normandy, a coalition of Angevin barons under the leadership of Guillaume des Roches had wrested Angers, Beaufort, Saumur, Châteauneuf-sur-Sarthe, Le Mans, and Tours, all to the north of the Loire, from John. Everything to the south, including the key fortresses of Chinon and Loches, remained faithful to the English. Philip's one incursion into Poitou established friendly relations with the family of the *vicomtes* of Thouars, who were promised title to Brittany should Arthur's death be confirmed. After the fall of Rouen, Philip appeared in Poitou in August 1204 with a strong army and took the city of Poitiers. Approaching the Loire from the south, he invested the two great fortresses, assigning Loches to Dreu de Mello, son of the royal constable, and Chinon to Guillaume des Roches. At the same time, the latter and Aimery de Thouars were appointed seneschals of Anjou and Poitou respectively. Since, as in Normandy, John neglected to come to the aid of his beleaguered castles, it was only a matter of time before Loches and Chinon surrendered, despite their faithful English captains. Finally, Philip returned with another army in the spring of 1205, when Loches and Chinon capitulated. Although the fiefs south of the river were now exposed, Philip was unable to make permanent headway. Further incursions into Poitou were prevented by the Thouars family, who had returned to John's side. Renewed fighting took place during the summer of 1206, when Philip harassed the Thouars and John attempted to penetrate north of the Loire by taking Angers. By the end of the season, however, Philip had retaken John's gains north of the river, although he was himself unable to proceed further south.[16]

Given this state of affairs, Philip and John finally agreed to a truce at Thouars to last for two years from 13 October. Both kings retained the fealty of those who fought openly for them at the time, but the treaty stipulated that the lords of Normandy, Maine, Brittany, Touraine, and Anjou north of the Loire could only choose Philip. This left John with the barons of Poitou and Anjou south of the Loire. Among those proffering pledges to Philip were the counts of Brittany (Guy de Thouars), La Marche, and Eu; the *vicomtes* of Limoges and Châtellerault; Geoffroi de Lusignan; and others. John's pledges were limited to those of the *vicomte* of Thouars; Savery de Mauléon; and other lesser lords. Since John was particularly vulnerable to reprisals and hostility from the Angevins and Bretons, he insisted that the two most prominent Angevins, Guillaume des Roches and Maurice de Craon, and two minor Breton lords specifically swear to keep the truce. To prevent further conspiracies and political realignments, all men of one king were forbidden to attend the court of the other without explicit permission, although free travel was otherwise permitted. In effect, therefore, the truce of Thouars sought to stabilize Philip Augustus's conquests roughly down to the Loire for two years. Although the victorious Capetian had attracted a significant following from the baronage,[17] how long he could keep their loyalty naturally depended on his future strength.

The Intervening Lull (1206–1212): The Realignment of the Great Fiefs

Philip's rapid conquest of Normandy and the fiefs north of the Loire in one stroke dismantled the political structure of France established by Henry of Anjou in 1154. Although John's resistance to Philip's thrusts lacked determination and constancy, he had not fully resigned himself to the loss of his father's lands. English chroniclers quote him as excusing his inaction by promising to return to retrieve his continental holdings.[18] Such recourse, however, required careful preparations, which in turn produced a lull in military activities. The period between 1206 and 1212 lacks a succession of events that can be recounted as a narrative, unlike the preceding and following years when Philip and John were locked in direct conflict. The fundamental dislocations brought about by the conquest of Normandy, however, stimulated further realignments among the great French fiefs. Some, like Champagne, Brittany, and Auvergne, acquiesced in Capetian dominance. Others, like Boulogne and Flanders, resisted the change and eventually joined forces with the English. Since John's nephew, Otto of Brunswick, was the leading contender for the German imperial throne, neither the emperor nor the pope could be indifferent to France, and they, too, sought to make their influence felt. These readjustments among the great fiefs preparatory to the final conflict produced a lull in hostilities between 1206 and 1212.

Through the queen mother, the counts of Blois and Sancerre, and the archbishop of Reims, the house of Champagne had played a leading role during the first decade of Philip Augustus's reign. Thereafter, however, the family suffered severe misfortunes resulting from their crusading ambitions and dynastic accidents.[19] The counts of Blois and Sancerre died at Acre in 1191, and their nephew Henri II, count of Troyes, the foremost figure in the family, remained in the Holy Land, where he married the widowed Isabelle, queen of the Latin kingdom of Jerusalem. When he died in 1198 (after falling out of a window), his fiefs in France were inherited by his brother Thibaut III, whose succession and homage the king immediately accepted.[20] Unable to resist the crusading appeal, Count

Thibaut also took the cross, but fell sick and died at the age of twenty-two in May 1201, leaving a young daughter and an unborn son, the future Thibaut IV. Philip Augustus brought the great fief under his guardianship with remarkable alacrity. In the week between the death of the count and the birth of his son, the king received the homage of Blanche de Navarre, Thibaut's widow, on condition that she agreed neither to remarry without the king's consent nor to allow her daughter to marry without the approval of the king and the Champenois baronage. If the unborn child were a boy, Blanche promised to concede the castles of Bray-sur-Seine and Montereau-faut-Yonne (and 500 *livres provins* annually for their maintenance) to Philip as securities for her son and presumptive heir. To insure the countess's conformity to these severe conditions, important Champenois barons stood as her guarantors.[21]

Blanche undoubtedly submitted to this heavy tutelage not only because she was a widow and her son a minor but also because the infant Thibaut's succession was contested. Count Henri II's marriage to Isabelle of Jerusalem had produced three daughters, one of whom, Philippa, married Erard de Brienne, a younger son of the Champenois family of Ramerupt. Although Henri's daughters were considered illegitimate by the papacy, Philippa and Erard raised a claim to the succession and attracted support from the Champenois nobility who opposed Blanche and Thibaut IV. As the opposing party gained strength, Philip Augustus required more concessions in a new agreement concluded in July 1209. According to French custom, the king promised that Thibaut would not be required to answer pleas in the royal court against his succession until he reached the age of twenty-one, and that at that time (1222) Philip would receive Thibaut's homage for all fiefs held by his father. For this protection the king further demanded personal custody over the young count for four years (until February 1214), the continued possession of the castles of Bray and Montereau until 1222, and an additional payment of 15,000 *livres*.[22] When the time neared for the young Thibaut to be returned to his mother, Philip once again profited from the countess's discomfiture and demanded new concessions in November 1213. As the king prepared for the great conflict with John and his allies, he wished to tighten the bonds of wardship over Champagne. The former promises and agreements were renewed, but this time Philip specified that Thibaut was not to give or receive homages beyond those specifically allowed until he came of age; nor was the king required to receive Thibaut's homage until that time. In addition, Blanche and Thibaut promised not to fortify

Meaux, Lagny, Provins, and Coulommiers until 1222. Like the former agreements, the new terms were guaranteed by the major Champenois vassals, and Blanche obligated herself to a fine of 20,000 *livres* should she fail to execute the conditions.[23] Profiting from Blanche's vulnerability as a widow and Thibaut's as a minor and contested heir, Philip Augustus thus both kept the great fiefs of Champagne under close control and made his wards pay dearly for protection.

Brittany also faced a dynastic crisis, in this case created by John's brutal treatment of Arthur.[24] When the young count disappeared into a Norman prison in 1201, never to be seen again, his sister Aliénor was removed to England, where she passed most of her remaining years. Although Arthur had probably been killed by April 1203, Philip Augustus still considered his survival possible in October 1203.[25] Soon, however, it became apparent that the question of the Breton succession had to be faced. In the meantime, Arthur's mother, Constance, had taken as her third husband the Poitevin noble Guy de Thouars, with whom she had two daughters, the eldest being named Alix. As the countess's husband and the potential heiress's father, Guy acted as nominal count of Brittany. In attempting to win over the Thouars family in Poitou, Philip treated with Guy in Brittany.[26] Guy's brother Aimery, *vicomte* of Thouars, was too unstable to be trusted, however, and Guy's own influence in Brittany too negligible. With Arthur presumed dead by 1209 and with Aliénor inaccessible, Philip Augustus therefore turned to Alix to solve the Breton succession. In the king's presence a marriage agreement was drawn up by which Guy affianced Alix to Henri, son of Alain de Tréguier, a Breton noble favorable to the Capetians. Since Alix was only ten and Henri four, the king demanded the children's custody until the marriage could be consummated. As in the case of Champagne, he could look forward to a long wardship. The treaty moreover explicitly recognized the close kinship between the pair (actually four and three degrees) and anticipated potential objections from churchmen.[27]

Ecclesiastical opposition probably did materialize, because three years later Philip found another husband for Alix, Pierre de Dreux, the second son of a royal cousin, Robert II, count of Dreux. In November 1212 Pierre promised to respect all former agreements between the king and Guy de Thouars and not to attack his Breton vassals without a decision in the kings's court. His father, his uncle Philippe, bishop of Beauvais, and his brother Robert served as pledges and promised to restrain him if he went against the king. Reaffirming these conditions the following January, Pierre offered the king liege-homage for Brittany and swore that the homages and fealties of all his vassals would be invalid if he broke his agreement with the king.[28] When Guy de Thouars died in April 1213, Pierre became fully the lord of Brittany by right of marriage. Philip Augustus thus finally found a replacement for Arthur. The prospect of a minor heir and a long wardship on the pattern of Champagne envisaged for Henri de Tréguier was replaced by a policy of securing loyalty through kinship. The success of this policy naturally depended on Pierre de Dreux's dependability, and Philip attempted to bind him closely to the Capetian interest by formal agreements.

Except for Auvergne, no major realignments occurred between 1206 and 1212 among the great baronies south of the Loire. When the truce in Poitou expired in 1208, Philip Augustus renewed attacks on the house of Thouars, but sickness forced him to return to Paris. Henri Clément and Guillaume des Roches continued the royal offensive against Thouars and Savery de Mauléon. Although they succeeded in capturing local lords, among them the son of Aimery de Thouars, no lasting gains resulted.[29] Southern France was further unsettled by the inability of the clergy to contain the growing heresy of the Albigensians in the region of Toulouse. When the shocking news of the assassination of the papal legate Pierre de Castelnau reached Innocent III in March 1208, he called upon the French king to lead a military crusade against the heretics. Although Philip allowed his vassals to support the cause, he refused to intervene, one of his excuses being that he could not risk doing so without a truce with John.[30]

Further gains in Poitou appeared unlikely, but the mountainous and inaccessible lands of Auvergne attracted Philip's attention. In the twelfth century the fiefs of Auvergne were divided between two branches of counts: the major, whose principal center lay at Riom, and the minor, sometimes entitling themselves counts of Clermont as well, who possessed Montferrand. Both branches strove for independence by alternating their allegiance between the kings of France and the dukes of Aquitaine as direct suzerains.[31] Under the difficult circumstances attending his death in 1189, Henry II had renounced his overlordship of Auvergne in favor of the Capetians,[32] but it remained for Philip to enforce his feudal authority by arms. Having received little support from King Richard, Dauphin, the head of the minor branch, offered the Capetian homage in 1199. His son Guillaume also remained on good terms with Philip.[33]

Guy II, count of the major branch, however, persisted in the inveterate family habit of fighting with his relatives, the bishops of Clermont. (In 1208 Guy had actually imprisoned his brother, Bishop Robert.) When Aimery, the royal constable in the region, was unable to prevent these outrages, and Guy went on to plunder the royal abbey of Mozac, Philip Augustus decided to intervene. Asserting the long-established Capetian policy of defending the Auvergnat churches, Philip entered into agreements with the bishop of Clermont and the neighboring bishop of Le Puy. On his side, Guy turned to John for financial support. By 1213 Philip was unable to attend personally to this campaign because of the mounting crisis in the north, but he dispatched the mercenary captain Cadoc and Guy de Dampierre, lord of Bourbon and formerly seneschal of the counts of Champagne, to conduct it. In quick succession the royal forces took the strongholds of Riom, Nonette, and Tournoël and recovered much that had been plundered from churches.[34] Count Guy II was dispossessed of his lands, which were then handed over to Guy de Dampierre and his son Archembaud, who, styling themselves constables of Auvergne, acted as the king's agents.[35] By reviving the traditional Capetian policy of defending southern churches against the depredations of local lords, a theme that Guillaume le Breton emphasizes in his account of the campaign, Philip thus found a pretext to acquire a major barony and to place it directly under his rule.

At the same time that Philip Augustus completed the military conquest of Auvergne, he resolved the succession to Vermandois. Aliénor, countess of Valois and Vermandois, died in June 1213 without children, as had been long foreseen. In accordance with the agreement of 1182, her cousin the king inherited her lands, which by then consisted of Valois (principally Crépy) and the remainder of Vermandois (chiefly Chauny, Saint-Quentin, and Ribemont). This completed the Capetian acquisition of northeastern territories that had been in progress for a half-century.[36]

The ease of Philip's final assimilation of the lands of Vermandois-Valois was not matched, however, in his dealings with the other northern barons of the kingdom. The conquest of Normandy was particularly unsettling to the counts of Boulogne and Flanders, because it inhibited their traditional means of ensuring independence by playing the Anglo-Normans against the Capetians. With Normandy in his hands, Philip Augustus now sought to curb their freedom of action, even as the northern counts sought to preserve it. Of particular concern was the county of Boulogne, which lay on the Channel coast between Normandy and Flanders. Boulogne had been acquired in 1191 by Renaud, the son of the count of Dammartin, who had abducted and married the heiress. Philip Augustus had acquiesced in this unconventional procedure and confirmed the marriage in 1192, but Renaud rewarded the king's complaisance, and revealed his characteristic unruliness, by joining Richard's alliance in 1197 and renewing it with John in 1199. With the settlement between Philip and John at Le Goulet in 1200, however, Renaud's position once again became tenuous. He now no longer had John's protection.[37]

In the face of Renaud's evident instability Philip set about regaining the count's loyalty by two traditional bonds, marriage and gifts of land. In August 1201 the king affianced his infant son Philippe Hurepel (by Agnès de Méran) to Mathilde, daughter and heiress of Renaud. In addition, Philip granted the county of Dammartin to Renaud upon the payment of a relief of 3,000 marks of silver, since Renaud's father had recently died.[38] Already count of Boulogne and Dammartin, Renaud was further rewarded with three additional Norman counties acquired by conquest—Varenne, Aumale, and Mortain—and by other lands in exchange for the castle of Mortemer, which Philip wanted for its strategic position between Normandy and Ponthieu.[39] To strengthen the count's position in the neighboring fiefs, the king also arranged a marriage between the daughter of the count of Ponthieu and Renaud's brother in 1208, and supported Renaud's military actions against the count of Guines in 1209.[40] While enjoying this royal beneficence and backing, Renaud remained a loyal counsellor, urging the king to resist papal intervention in 1203 and advocating the expedition against the heretics in 1208.[41]

The count of Boulogne's inveterate ambition and familiarity with the Anglo-Norman party, however, made him susceptible to new intrigues on the part of King John. As early as 1209 Renaud may have been in contact with Eustache le Moine, a renegade monk and former seneschal of Boulogne, who was then receiving favors from John. In all events, at an unspecified date—but probably in 1210—the king was sufficiently suspicious of these dealings to demand from the counts of Boulogne and Ponthieu and other northern lords an oath to abjure contact with Eustache le Moine, Hugues de Boves, and other known English agents.[42] Anticipating treachery, Philip Augustus undoubtedly decided to proceed with the marriage between his son and Renaud's daughter in order to limit the count more strictly by the detailed terms of the agreement foreseeing all eventualities. In November 1209, to forestall attempts to avoid the marriage, Philip forced the count to reconfirm his former promises under penalty of forfeiting his fiefs.[43] The child couple were married in May 1210, which required Renaud to begin assigning lands to the royal prince. The count was now apparently less willing to part with his possessions than he had been in 1201 when he had sought to regain royal favor. New negotiations intervened, and a third agreement was signed at the marriage, specifying that Renaud was to make over his Norman lands in Caux and the county of Aumale to his son-in-law.[44]

This mounting tension between the count of Boulogne and the king needed only a pretext to provoke an open rupture. Philippe de Dreux, the bellicose bishop of Beauvais, provided the excuse by engaging the countess of Clermont in open conflict over border castles. Championed by her kinsman Renaud, the countess was in turn opposed by the powerful Dreux family of royal cousins. When Renaud's complaints to the king went unheeded, he began fortifying his stronghold of Mortain in western Normandy. Responding to an act that bordered on rebellion, Philip demanded that Mortain be handed over as security for Renaud's fidelity by 8 September 1211; otherwise the king threatened to judge him in default. Renaud wanted no court decision and needed more time to enlist allies. When he proposed to render the fortress to the king personally at a later date, Philip Augustus refused the offer, adjudged the count in default, and took Mortain after a siege of four days. He then proceeded to seize Aumale and Dammartin. Finding no help within the kingdom, Renaud resigned the county of Boulogne to Prince Louis, who, as lord of Artois, was his immediate suzerain, and sought refuge with the count of Bar-le-Duc on the eastern borders.[45] Philip immediately demanded guarantees from two other northern lords and the commune of Airaines that they would offer no aid to the count of Boulogne, Otto of Brunswick, or King John.[46] This shows that Philip Augustus had by this time realized that Renaud was negotiating with his enemies in Germany and England. His attempts to secure the count of Boulogne's loyalty through gifts had failed, but through his young son, Philip Hurepel, the king at least had the means to bring the county of Boulogne under control.

Like Champagne, Flanders also fell victim to the ineluctable summons of the crusade. Not long after the counts of Troyes and Blois, Baudouin, count of Flanders and Hainaut, took the cross in February 1200 and left his fiefs in the summer of 1202. When the expedition was diverted and terminated with the capture of Constantinople, Baudouin was elected emperor of the newly founded Latin empire in May 1204. He was taken prisoner at Adrianople the following year in fighting against the Bulgarians and was killed shortly thereafter. Marie, his wife, had died of the plague at Acre in 1204, leaving two young girls as heiresses to the counties of Flanders and Hainaut. The crusade thus removed another potential Anglo-Norman ally at a time when Philip was intent on conquering Normandy, and, as in Champagne, provided the king with the opportunity to dispose of an important barony.[47]

During Baudouin's absence in the east the regency was confided to his brother Philippe, marquis of Namur. When Philip Augustus learned of Baudouin's imprisonment in June 1206, he immediately dispatched Barthélemy de Roye to Courtrai to negotiate with Philippe de Namur. Philippe swore fealty to the king against all except his brother (should he return safely) and promised not to give Baudouin's daughters in marriage without the king's consent. Barthélemy was further instructed to secure the oaths of the barons, communes, and knights of Flanders and Hainaut to support these conditions. And, to reinforce Philippe de Namur's loyalty, the king promised to give his daughter Marie, born of Agnès de Méran, to the marquis in marriage.[48] By matrimonial ties with the regent and by wardship over the young and apparently orphaned heiresses, Philip Augustus intended to extend his grasp to the county of Flanders.

The king's dealings with the marquis of Namur were merely preparatory to more important business, the marriage of Jeanne of Flanders, the elder of the two heiresses (she was born in 1200). Taking custody of the Flemish sisters in September 1208, Philip Augustus promised not to marry them without the marquis's permission before they came of age. In return the marquis promised not to oppose the king's choice at that time.[49] Guardianship over the heiresses not only brought royal control over Flanders but also the opportunity to make a profit. In 1211 Enguerran, lord of Coucy, offered the king a relief of 30,000 *livres* for the hand of Jeanne for himself and that of her sister for his brother, Thomas. In an undated charter, Enguerran later raised his offer to 50,000 *livres*.[50] Probably because of hostility of the count of Boulogne,[51] and of the Flemish nobility, who were alienated by Enguerran's troublesome reputation, the lord of Coucy's offer was not accepted. The next candidate to appear was Ferrand, son of King Sancho of Portugal and nephew of Mathilde, the dowager widow of the long-deceased Count Philippe of Flanders. When Mathilde matched Enguerran's relief of 50,000 *livres*, the couple were married in January 1212 at the royal chapel in Paris. The king knighted the twenty-four-year-old count, who performed homage secured by pledges.[52] Whether at the king's explicit command or on his own initiative, Prince Louis's reaction was to hasten to Ponthieu and from there to attack the northern Artesian towns of Aire and Saint-Omer, aided by the sons of the count of Dreux. Taking the two towns within a week, he strengthened his hold on Saint-Omer by erecting a tower. With this bold stroke he nullified Count Baudouin's gains in 1197, confirmed by the treaty of Péronne in 1200, which had deprived Louis of part of his mother's dowry in Artois. Powerless against this swift action, Ferrand and Jeanne were forced to renounce their rights over the two cities. Although Philip Augustus had carefully managed the Flemish succession and had handsomely profited from it, he nonetheless created an embittered count, who deeply resented the Capetians' brutal opportunism.[53]

Equally a vassal of the German emperor and of the French king, the count of Flanders and Hainaut was susceptible to the shifting fortunes of imperial politics. Philip Augustus was likewise obliged to take German affairs into account, both because of his extensive eastern borders and, more especially, because one of the major contenders for the imperial crown was the Guelf candidate, Otto of Brunswick, nephew and protégé of King John. The papacy, also, since the accession of Innocent III in 1198, had taken an active interest in imperial matters and claimed the right to judge the fitness of candidates seeking the emperorship. After the death of the Hohenstaufen emperor Henry VI in 1197, two principal candidates emerged in Otto of Brunswick and Philip of Swabia, the brother of the deceased Hohenstaufen. Within the Empire Otto was supported chiefly by the principalities of the lower Rhine. He was allied, for example, with the bishop of Cambrai and attempted to gain support from the duke of Brabant through a marriage alliance.[54] Outside the Empire, he enjoyed generous financial backing from his uncle, the king of England, and could count on sympathetic treatment, if not direct intervention, from Pope Innocent, who preferred a Guelf candidate to the traditionally antipapal Hohenstaufens. Because of Otto's close connections with John, Philip Augustus's only tenable position was to oppose Otto with all the means at his disposal. In fact, the Capetian was the one consistent participant in imperial politics throughout the period. The French king first allied himself with Philip of Swabia, who was crowned at Aachen in January 1205.[55] By 1207 Philip Augustus's victories in France had been matched by Philip of Swabia's similar achievements in Germany. These successes engendered a short period of rivalry between the two allies, and when Philip of Swabia sought a personal meeting with the French king to resolve their differences, Philip Augustus refused.[56]

Philip of Swabia's assassination in June 1208, however, removed the last serious obstacle to Otto of Brunswick's supremacy in Germany. With Innocent's approval and John's money, Otto was recrowned emperor in October 1209. Once secure, Otto proceeded to seek revenge against Philip Augustus for opposing him in Germany and despoiling his uncle in France. At the same time he began reviving the former Hohenstaufen imperial policies in Italy and towards the churches. This latter move produced papal consternation, forcing the pope to seek help from the French against his former favorite. In a letter to Philip Augustus of February 1210, Innocent complained bitterly of Otto's new policies and admitted that he had misjudged Otto's character. When the pope asked for 200 knights to fight directly against the emperor in Italy, the French king raised objections, but he did consent to papal taxes in France, provided that they were raised only from churchmen and that France itself was not in danger of invasion.[57]

Philip nonetheless remained concerned with the imperial election. As early as August 1208, two months after the assassination of Philip of Swabia, Philip Augustus proposed the candidacy of Henri, duke of Brabant. The duke had performed homage to the French king in 1205 and had received a regular *fief-rente*. Now in 1208, in exchange for a loan of 3,000 marks, which he could retain if he were elected king, Henri swore to aid neither John nor Otto.[58] This early wager on the imperial election was hardly serious because it entailed neither great sums nor risks. Taking advantage of Otto's shift in policy following his coronation, Philip urged the pope to exercise spiritual and temporal authority over the emperor. When Innocent excommunicated Otto and released his subjects from their oaths of fealty, Philip took additional steps to intervene in imperial politics.[59] His new candidate was Frederick Hohenstaufen, the young son of Henry VI, who lacked funds in contrast to Otto's ample subsidies from John. A meeting was arranged between Frederick and Philip on the border between Toul and Vaucouleurs, the place where Louis VII had parleyed with Frederick Barbarossa in 1171. When the appointed time arrived in November 1212, however, for some unexplained reason, Prince Louis attended in place of his father. The results were nonetheless satisfactory to the young Hohenstaufen. In exchange for an agreement not to conclude peace with Otto or John without each other's concurrence, Frederick received a loan of 20,000 marks from the French king. A month later the young Hohenstaufen was elected in the presence of French envoys at Frankfurt and crowned king at Mainz.[60] At last Philip Augustus had found a German rival to set against Otto of Brunswick.

The papal legates who travelled between Rome and France seeking to influence imperial affairs, negotiating peace between the French and English kings, and preaching the crusade against the Albigensian heretics were invariably instructed to treat one other unresolved issue: Philip Augustus's unsatisfactory marriage to Ingeborg. As to their personal lives, the situation had most likely improved. In December 1204 the queen had been confided to the care of the *bailli* Guillaume Menier, who saw to it that her living conditions became more tolerable.[61] The king, for his part, apparently consoled himself elsewhere, because during this period a royal bastard, Pierre Charlot, was born to a "certain lady of Arras."[62] Still, the underlying conflict between Philip and Ingeborg remained unresolved. Between 1201 and 1212, however, the focus of contention shifted from consanguinity to new grounds—non-consummation. In canon law marriages could be annulled for lack of consummation caused by impotence, frigidity, sickness, and so on, if the parties had cohabited for three years. This legal stratagem had been suggested as early as 1202 by the pope himself in a letter to the archbishop of Reims.[63] The king did not avail himself of the argument until 1205, when he claimed that he had been unable to consummate the marriage because the queen had bewitched him.[64] Thereafter, non-consummation because of sorcery became the chief argument of the royal messengers, although the charges were persistently denied by Ingeborg. At this point, Philip clearly had abandoned prosecution on the basis of consanguinity probably because of the inadequacy of the evidence relating him to Ingeborg within the prohibited degrees. If the genealogical tables newly compiled in the royal registers proved anything, it was not the desired impediment between Philip and Ingeborg, but a more significant consanguinity between Philip and Isabelle de Hainaut, which threatened the legitimacy of Prince Louis.[65] The king even attempted to persuade the queen to take the vows of a nun, but this ploy, like the others, was unsuccessful.[66]

As in the past, the marriage negotiations continued to be heavily influenced by imperial politics. In the light of Philip of Swabia's victories against Otto of Brunswick in 1207, and given the pope's persistent need for a crusading force against the southern heretics, Innocent, on his own account, revived prospects of an annulment and even suggested that if non-consummation through sorcery could be proved, the three-year cohabitation requirement might be dispensed with.[67] When Philip of Swabia's assassination assured Otto's supremacy, however, Innocent returned to a stricter policy concerning Philip's marriage. The papal legate Guala was instructed in 1208 to investigate three possible grounds for annulment: consanguinity, non-consummation through sorcery, and the queen's entry into a nunnery. When the pope insisted that Ingeborg's free choice be respected, and it became apparent that the legate intended to conduct the process according to strict legal forms, with full recourse to appeals, Philip realized that he faced the prospect of another interminable trial. As in 1201, he abruptly put an end to the proceedings, this time by dismissing the legate.[68] The king also used imperial politics to further his marital objectives. In 1210 he proposed to marry the daughter of the margrave of Thuringia, who had vacillated between the imperial candidates but had finally opposed Otto. Philip's prime condition for thus honoring the German prince was that the margrave obtain a papal annulment of the marriage between Philip and Ingeborg.[69] But Innocent could hardly be expected to pay this price for the margrave's support. Although political alignments and legal arguments shifted, the long stalemate between the king and queen persisted.

The Climax of Bouvines (1212–1214)

By 1212 Philip Augustus's conquests in Normandy and the Loire valley, and the subsequent realignment of the great feudatories, had produced a group of figures who had deep-seated reasons for opposing the Capetian advance. First and foremost was King John, who was resolved to regain his lost continental possessions. Second was John's nephew, Otto of Brunswick, who keenly resented Philip's opposition to his election to the imperial throne and support of his rival, Frederick of Hohenstaufen. Equally hostile was Renaud, the unstable count of Boulogne, whom the French king had recently dispossessed of his fiefs. A potential fourth opponent was Ferrand, newly acceded to the county of Flanders and Hainaut, who was angered by the highhanded manner in which the Capetians had deprived him of Saint-Omer and Aire. Because of his recent arrival on the scene and his dependence on his French suzerain, however, Ferrand was obliged to be more circumspect than the first three in showing his discontent. Finally, there were many others, ranging from the duke of Brabant to the mercenary captain Eustache le Moine, who might be persuaded to join any alliance against the Capetians if they could be convinced of its probable success. Because of this common hatred, little magic was required to assemble a formidable coalition against the French king.

The natural catalyst for this coalition was the count of Boulogne, who had long experience in plotting against Philip. When Renaud sought to regain his fiefs, the king offered to hear the count's plea in the royal court, the proposal he had made to John a decade earlier.[70] Since Renaud expected to gain little from this recourse, he sought aid from Otto. The emperor was at Frankfurt in March 1212, attended by partisans from the lower Rhine, among them Henri, duke of Brabant, who looked for help in his quarrel with the bishop of Liège. Otto offered to intercede with John to receive Renaud back into the favor he had enjoyed under Richard. Accredited with imperial letters, Renaud travelled to England, where, in the company of Hugues de Boves and Eustache le Moine, he did homage to John and signed an agreement of mutual assistance against Philip Augustus in May 1212. Renaud was restored to his English possessions and received a yearly payment of 1,000 pounds sterling. John followed this alliance with a series of messages and gifts of money to the dowager countess Mathilde, the duke of Brabant, and other lords in the Low Countries. The English king then proceeded to summon a feudal levy in June 1212, and Philip countered by seizing all English ships in his ports, to which John responded in kind.[71] Thus opened the hostilities that led to the climactic battle on the fields of Bouvines.

As Philip Augustus prepared to meet the threat of John and his emerging coalition, two other developments came into play in the opening months of 1213 that worked in Philip's favor, or at least complicated the situation. The most urgent grew out of an internal ecclesiastical dispute in England and John's personal character. When Innocent III sought to impose his candidate, Master Stephen Langton, in a disputed election to the archbishopric of Canterbury in 1206, John resisted this papal interference. Relentlessly refusing to accept Langton, he suffered papal interdict against his lands in 1207 and personal excommunication in 1209. The severity of the quarrel had, in the meantime, virtually cleared England of all high-ranking prelates and had begun to unsettle the loyalty of the lay barons.[72] Finally, at the beginning of 1213, Pope Innocent threatened John with deposition and called upon the French king to lead a crusade against this opponent of the church's freedom.[73] At the very time when John was organizing a coalition against Philip, he was therefore threatened with a counterattack from the French king sponsored by the papacy.

The second development grew out of the crusade against the Albigensians in southern France, which gave rise to a contest between the count of Toulouse and Simon de Montfort, who headed the northern French barons. Recently, the count had found support from King Peter of Aragon, who had won a decisive victory against the Moslems at Las Navas de Tolosa in July 1212. As friction increased between the competitors, both sought aid from the French king. The king of Aragon contemplated a marriage alliance, seeking the hand of Philip's daughter, Marie, recently widowed from the marquis of Namur. To counter the growing influence of Toulouse and Aragon, Simon de Montfort's party implored Prince Louis's intervention, and in a burst of enthusiasm the latter took the cross against the heretics. At an assembly of barons at Paris in March 1213 plans were accordingly laid for the prince's imminent departure for the south.[74]

Confronted with challenges from England and the south within the space of a few months, Philip Augustus was faced with a choice, since simultaneous responses in both directions were out of the question. Yet there could be little doubt as to the decision, because King John's plans in the north represented the greatest danger. Philip summoned his barons to Soissons on 8 April 1213 and there commissioned his son Louis to lead an expedition against England, despite the latter's recent crusading vow against the heretics. In undertaking the new venture, however, Louis signed a formal agreement with his father that strictly monitored his future actions.[75] If Louis succeeded in capturing John, he promised Philip not to make any distribution of English fiefs, lands, or goods without his father's consent. If Louis were crowned king of England, the homages of all the English barons, knights, and men would first be received by the king of France. And, finally, Louis promised that as long as his father lived he would not make any claim to lands in France except for holdings inherited from his mother. Whatever Louis's future success, Philip was determined to remain in full control.

The great barons who attended the assembly gave assent to the enterprise, except the count of Flanders, who, smarting from his recent treatment, demanded that Louis return Saint-Omer and Aire as the price of his participation. In the above agreement Philip had already extracted from Louis consent to any land that the king wished to give Ferrand as inducement to join the venture, but apparently the king had no intention of restoring Saint-Omer and Aire. When Philip offered him other compensation instead, Count Ferrand refused and left the assembly. As

Ferrand's disaffection increased, Philip sought other allies in Flanders. Once again he turned to Henri, duke of Brabant, to whom he now offered both his daughter Marie in marriage and his offices as mediator with the bishop of Liège. For these benefits Henri promised to take part in the expedition against the English and to support Frederick of Hohenstaufen or any other French candidate in the imperial election.[76]

While Philip laid plans for the English invasion, he took one further step that may have come as a surprise to many. Less than a year after he had abruptly broken off negotiations for separating himself from Ingeborg, he suddenly announced his reconciliation with the queen. We can only guess at the motives behind this dramatic gesture. It is unlikely that the Danish princess's claims to the English throne, discussed by the English chroniclers in 1193, were considered any more seriously twenty years later. Besides, the projected expedition had been entrusted to Louis, who was unrelated by blood or marriage to Ingeborg. The coincidence of the king's decision with the assembly of Soissons suggests the most telling reason behind Philip's reversal. At this crucial moment in the history of his reign, Philip's estrangement from his wife was the one serious obstacle between the king and the church. Almost forty-eight years of age, blessed with two healthy legitimate sons, and no longer feeling the urge to remarry, Philip finally set aside his personal preferences to make peace with the church. The news was received with popular rejoicing, which Philip undoubtedly interpreted as an omen that God would bless him at this crucial hour.[77]

As the hour of conflict neared, John, too, was moved to reconcile himself with God and the church. Confronted with three opponents, the restive barons, the French king, and the pope, John calculated that submission to the last would cost least. He met the papal legate Pandulf on 13 May 1213, swallowed his royal prerogatives and personal feelings, and promised to accept Stephen Langton as archbishop of Canterbury, for which concession the legate lifted the interdict. Then, on 15 May, John offered England and Ireland as fiefs to the pope and agreed to pay an annual tribute of 1,000 pounds sterling. This act, for which King Peter of Aragon had set a precedent when he submitted his kingdom as a fief to the papacy in 1204, was a brilliant diplomatic stroke. Not only had John nullified papal opposition by accepting Langton, he had now won over the pope as special protector of England, for which he paid very little. The fruits of this diplomacy were realized immediately. Crossing the Channel, Pandulf met the French king at Gravelines a week later and forbade the invasion under pain of papal excommunication.[78]

During May Philip had been occupied with assembling an invasion fleet along the Flemish coast. Boulogne, Gravelines, and finally Damme, the commercial harbor for Bruges, were successively selected as points of assembly for the ships. When the papal legate arrived at Gravelines on 22 May, it was obviously too late to renounce the ships, men, and money committed to the enterprise. The most serious question now was the co-operation of the count of Flanders, which required clarification before the invasion could proceed. Professing neutrality, Ferrand temporized in fulfilling his service. Philip finally confronted his reluctant vassal at Ypres on 24 May and demanded participation in the expedition. Ferrand re-fused, alleging that his liege homage to the French king did not extend outside of the kingdom—and certainly not to dispossess another king—and renewed his complaint over Saint-Omer and Aire. In the face of this defiance, Philip dismissed the count from the court.

After the rupture, Philip sought to protect his embarkation by de-manding the submission of Ypres and Bruges and preparing to besiege Ghent, which still offered resistance. Meanwhile, the security of the fleet at Damme was entrusted to the count of Soissons and Aubert de Hangest, who joined the Poitevin Savery de Mauléon and the mercenary captain Cadoc. After dismissal, Ferrand's only recourse was to follow the count of Boulogne and seek direct help from the English king. John lost no time in dispatching Renaud de Boulogne, Hugues de Boves, other Flemish lords, and his half-brother William of Salisbury with ships, troops, and money to the Continent. With remarkable speed the allied force arrived at Muiden, not far from Damme, on 28 May. Unaware of the presence of the allies, Savery de Mauléon and Cadoc were busy plun-dering the inhabitants of Damme. Only part of the French fleet could be accommodated in the harbor; the rest was anchored outside in the river Swin. On 30 May the allies swooped down on the unguarded ships, plundered and burned those in the harbor, and cut loose those in the river. Hearing of the assault, Philip reacted immediately with a counter-attack. This time it was the allies who were caught by surprise, but the main leaders escaped, although the count of Boulogne barely avoided capture. When the French king surveyed the damage at Damme, he reluc-tantly conceded that an invasion of England was no longer possible. On the advice of his intimates Guérin, Barthélemy de Roye, and Gautier the Young, he put the remnants of the fleet to the torch to prevent the ships from falling into his enemies' hands.[79]

Although Innocent III's reversal and Ferrand's defection presented obstacles that might have been overcome, the debacle at Damme effectively annulled all possibility of invading England at this time. Since Philip had now lost the initiative, his only recourse was to prepare himself for the onslaught of John and his allies. With the pope as defender and a French landing no longer imminent, John now had time to complete his preparations at leisure. From the spring of 1213 to the summer of 1214 he concentrated on two major objectives that would encircle the Capetians and threaten them on two broad fronts. He arranged a formal alliance with Ferrand of Flanders in July 1213, which was sealed personally by the count's journey to England in January 1214 and by his performance of homage for his English possessions.[80] Amply supported by John's treasure, Ferrand's task was to keep Philip engaged in northern France while the English king organized an expedition in Poitou that would approach from the south. The bishop of Norwich and William, count of Salisbury, were dispatched to Otto to apprise him of the plans and to coordinate the final assault.[81]

From the spring of 1213 to the summer of 1214, therefore, Flanders bore the brunt of John's strategy. While John sustained his Flemish allies with money, Philip Augustus and Prince Louis attempted to punish Ferrand, Renaud, and their adherents. In the process the county was devastated by an extended series of attacks and counterattacks. Though all on a local scale, these nonetheless reduced the towns to ashes and the population to desolation. Immediately after the debacle of Damme, Philip returned to Ghent, took the city, and demanded hostages. Other major cities, such as Bruges, Ypres, and Douai, also yielded hostages, who were entrusted to the Artesian communes of Arras, Hesdin, and Saint-Omer. Lille, on the border of Artois and Flanders, was chosen as the center for supervising operations in the region.[82] But the hostages were not sufficient to guarantee the fidelity of Bruges, Ghent, and Ypres. When they defected along with Courtrai, Louis burned the latter town in July in retaliation.[83] Nor were the Capetian forces strong enough to protect Lille and their own episcopal city of Tournai. Both cities were taken and severely damaged by the count of Flanders in September before the French could return. Only Douai remained securely in French hands.[84] After Cassel had been attacked by Renaud de Boulogne in January 1214, Louis counterattacked and burned the city along with the neighboring Steenvoorde. The latter, called Estanfort in French, was renowned for the cloth to which it gave its name. When the flames could be seen high above the roofs, Brother Guérin uttered his infamous pun on this grisly occasion: "My lords," he exulted, calling his knights together, "have you ever seen an *estanfort* better dyed in scarlet?"[85]

While the Capetians and English allies were wreaking havoc in Flanders, local lords took the opportunity to vent lesser quarrels. Throughout the period the duke of Brabant skirmished with his inveterate enemy, the bishop of Liège. By intervening in this struggle, Otto was able to win the duke over to the allies' cause, confirmed by the emperor's marriage to the duke's daughter in May 1214.[86] During the spring the emperor himself was involved in a campaign in the lower Rhine valley,[87] and the counts of Boulogne and Flanders ravaged the lands of the count of Guines, an old rival of Boulogne and a Capetian ally.[88] As late as June 1214 Ferrand besieged Aire and thereby threatened the province of Artois.[89]

With his allies diverting the Capetians' attention in Flanders, John prepared his offensive from the south, but when his barons balked at accompanying him overseas without special remuneration, he postponed the expedition to the opening months of 1214. On 15 February he finally appeared at La Rochelle, accompanied, according to the chroniclers, by numerous knights but few barons. His major strategy, apparently, was to compensate for this deficiency by regaining support from the southwestern baronage. To make his presence felt, he made incursions around La Rochelle and into the Angoumois, Limousin, and Saintonge. Although this policy took time, it eventually won him adherents, including the *vicomte* of Limoges and, finally, his old archenemies, the Lusignans. To compensate these Poitevin barons for the earlier loss of their bride, John now offered the hand of his own daughter Johanna to the son of Hugues, count of La Marche, with dowry lands in Poitou, Anjou, and Touraine. Strengthened by these allies, he finally ventured north into the Loire valley in May 1214. When he met stiff resistance at Nantes, he turned east to Angers, which he entered on 17 June. Guillaume des Roches, the French seneschal of Anjou, had chosen not to defend Angers, because its walls were still ruined from the previous campaigns, but he had strengthened the surrounding castles. Feeling insecure in Angers itself, therefore, John set about reducing the countryside. Two of the castles succumbed quickly, but the garrison of a third, La Roche-au-Moine, took a heavy toll from its attackers and refused to surrender.[90]

Although involved in Flanders, Philip Augustus could not ignore John's expedition in the southwest. Lack of documentation, however, prevents us from following his countermovements in detail. The chief evidence for his activities stems from Register C, where pledges for the fealty of western barons such as Hervé de Bello Mortario, Guillaume de la Guierche, Jocelin de Blou, and Guy Sénébaud were recorded in February and April 1214.[91] How far south Philip proceeded to meet John's advances cannot be told, but he did reach Châteauroux on the borders of Berry and Poitou in the company of his son. There, according to Guillaume le Breton, he entrusted the defense of the south to Louis and turned north again to meet renewed Flemish incursions. Louis took up position at the Loire castle of Chinon, where he learned of John's activity around Angers and the siege of La Roche-au-Moine. It was now clear to the Capetians that they must either make a stand against the English advances or risk increasing desertions from the Loire baronage. Receiving instructions from his father, Louis proceeded immediately to the relief of La Roche-au-Moine, accompanied by Guillaume des Roches, Aimery de Craon, the marshal Henri Clément, and 800 knights assigned to the prince. When the English camp heard of the approach of this strong force, the Poitevin barons, who included the counts of La Marche and Eu and Aimery de Thouars, refused to join battle, citing their unpreparedness or their unwillingness to fight against their suzerain.[92] At that critical moment on 2 July, as often throughout his military career, John was struck with panic. Believing himself to be hopelessly outnumbered, whether rightly or wrongly, he fled the scene with amazing alacrity. Two days later he reached the abbey of Saint-Maixent, a crow's flight of 115 kilometers. When he arrived at La Rochelle the next week, he wrote a letter to his followers announcing his safe arrival and thanking them for their aid. Although his thrust from the south had failed to destroy Louis's army, he had nonetheless separated the Capetian forces at a crucial moment as Otto prepared to invade from the north. The war was not yet lost if the allies could defeat the French army in the north under Philip Augustus. Undoubtedly, John sent messages to the emperor and his allies to commence the northern offensive.[93] Then, moving to Le Blanc on the borders of Poitou, he awaited news of the outcome.

The fate of John's dual strategy was decided at the end of July on the borders of France and the Empire between the armies of Philip Augustus and John's coalition led by Otto. Unlike normal warfare (designated *guerra*), which was usually fought around castles, for immediate goals, and with inconclusive results, Philip and Otto were determined to fight a true battle (*prelium, bellum*). It was the first battle that the Capetians had risked since 1119, when Louis VI had been defeated decisively by Henry I at Brémule. Preparation for the conflict recalled the great summons of 1124, when Louis VI had assembled the barons of the realm to withstand a threatened invasion from the east by Emperor Henry V, an invasion that never materialized. In contrast to *guerra*, a *bellum* sought to

obtain a definitive decision over important objectives. As a wager of total victory or loss, it was considered, in the final analysis, a judgment
of God.[94]

The Capetians' victory inspired the composition of the principal accounts of the battle, and the fullest and most accurate of these were composed by the royal historiographer Guillaume le Breton, who, stationed
directly behind the king, was an eyewitness to events as they unfolded.
Writing after the victory, Guillaume depicts the course of the struggle in
symmetrical patterns, pairing opponent against opponent and action
with reaction, seeking parallel movements; from his perspective the conflict appears as a vast ritual choreography. Having already announced
the outcome to his readers, the royal historian begins: "And now we proceed to describe the aforesaid victory, as much as we can with the help
of God."[95]

The first task of the two armies was to find each other by feints at plausible objectives. Otto assembled his allies, including the counts of Boulogne and Flanders, the earl of Salisbury, the duke of Brabant, and numerous German barons, at Valenciennes, whence he dispatched Hugues de
Boves against the Cambrèsis. According to later reports, their final goal
was Paris and the royal domain, which they had already divided among
themselves.[96] Then the allies moved north to the castle of Mortagne. In
the meantime, Philip rallied his forces at Péronne and continued to Tournai, which was the usual Capetian base of operations against Flanders.
With the French at Tournai and the allies at Mortagne, the armies had
unknowingly passed each other, and neither dared proceed farther for
fear of being cut off. When Philip learned that Otto was at Mortagne, he
felt exposed at Tournai and decided to return to Lille along the road that
crossed the river Marcq at the bridge of Bouvines. Otto, hearing of
Philip's retreat, thereupon moved northwest to intercept the French army.
The only question remaining was at what moment the battle was to take
place, because it was then 27 July, a Sunday, on which Christians were
forbidden to fight. As recounted by Guillaume le Breton, both kings
took counsel with their barons to resolve this problem. During Otto's
deliberations, Count Renaud advised waiting until the holy day had
passed and the allies could carefully prepare their attack, but Hugues
de Boves urged immediate pursuit to catch the French divided as they
crossed the bridge. The latter course was chosen.[97]

When the French rear guard spied the allies in full battle array, Brother
Guérin, now bishop-elect of Senlis, proposed that Philip draw up his

lines to meet the enemy, but he was outvoted by the rest of the counsellors, who thought that the allies were moving on to Tournai and would not fight on Sunday in any event. The duke of Burgundy, in command of the rear guard, reported fierce attacks from the allies, however, and Guérin's judgment was confirmed. The king ordered immediate preparations for combat. The counsel of Hugues de Boves and Guérin had prevailed: the great battle was to be fought on Sunday.

This crucial decision was taken at noon near the bridge of Bouvines, where Philip was resting in the shade of an ash tree. In rapid succession the king performed the requisite rituals to consecrate the forthcoming encounter as a true *bellum* in which God's judgment would be revealed. He entered a nearby chapel to pray briefly, armed himself quickly, and mounted his horse "as if summoned to a wedding feast." Trumpets recalled the contingents of foot-sergeants who had already crossed the bridge, and they brought with them the Oriflamme, the banner of Saint Denis and of France. Philip harangued his troops in a brief speech, reminding them that they were fighting for God and his church against enemies who had been excommunicated by the pope. While the historian Guillaume le Breton and another royal chaplain chanted psalms of victory, the king then blessed his troops with outstretched hands. To the blare of trumpets the battle formations were drawn up in three groups facing the field and extending across the road. In the center was the king, surrounded by his trusted familiars, Gautier the Young, Barthélemy de Roye, Guillaume de Garlande, and Guillaume des Barres. The right wing was commanded by Guérin and the duke of Burgundy, newly arrived with the rear guard. The left wing was entrusted chiefly to Count Robert and Bishop Philippe of Beauvais, both of the house of Dreux and royal cousins. Contingents of sergeants from the communes were stationed at the center and on the left. Thanks to the resistance of their rear guard, the French lines were well formed on the arrival of the allies. Strung out in a long line, the latter were forced to regroup quickly before those in the rear had come up. Although they occupied higher ground, they faced west and the blinding sun of the hot afternoon.

As narrated by Guillaume le Breton from his central vantage point, the action of the battle unfolded in three scenes. The French right wing was first to engage, then the center, and finally the left. On the right, Guérin, Eudes, duke of Burgundy, and their French knights faced the Flemish knights led by Count Ferrand. Following an initial strategy of acting quickly to prevent the enemy from taking formation, Guérin ordered a contingent of lightly armored cavalry from the Val-de-Soissons to attack immediately. This thrust was ineffective against the heavily armored Flemings, but it nonetheless precipitated hostilities before the Flemish and French foot-sergeants had had time to form ranks. On the right wing, therefore, the fighting was limited to a long series of cavalry engagements in which individuals on both sides distinguished themselves by heroic exploits. The count of Saint-Pol, for example, who had withdrawn from the press to rest, returned immediately to the fray to rescue one of his men who had been completely surrounded. During the three hours in which the French and Flemish knights exchanged blows, the corpulent duke of Burgundy was unhorsed, but saved by his men, he returned to battle vowing vengeance. In the end, the Flemish ranks were thinned, and the badly wounded and unhorsed Count Ferrand was forced to yield.

On the central, royal stage, Philip Augustus and his banner, the Oriflamme, confronted Emperor Otto with his terrifying insignia of an eagle mounted above a dragon, transported on a four-wheeled chariot. Since it was reported that Otto, Ferrand, and Renaud had all sworn to fight until the French king was dead, this theater of action saw the fiercest struggle.[98] By now contingents of foot-sergeants from Corbie, Amiens, Arras, Beauvais, and Compiègne had been able to recross the bridge and draw up in formation in front of the king's knights. The attack in this sector was opened by the imperial knights. During the cavalry melee, which fully occupied the French knights, the imperial sergeants were able to break through the lines of French footmen and to unhorse Philip with long hooks. Heavy armor and a quick response from his household knights saved the king's life. Surrounding Philip, they offered him a fresh horse and conducted him to safety. The fighting may have been fiercer in the center than elsewhere, because the only French casualty reported by Guillaume le Breton, the Norman Etienne de Longchamps, was killed at this point. The imperial attack was matched by a French counterattack that equally imperiled Otto's life. Two French knights and the valiant Guillaume des Barres got close enough to unhorse him, but Otto's life was also saved by his armor and his household knights. In the end, four imperial knights succeeded in conveying the emperor to safety, although they themselves were captured. When it was clear that Otto had fled, Philip gleefully exclaimed: "You will not see his face anymore today!" The battered imperial insignia were triumphantly presented to the king.

The final act focused on the left wing, where Count Robert and Bishop Philippe de Dreux faced their former rival Renaud, count of Boulogne, supported by William, earl of Salisbury. By that time the allies had suffered severe losses on the right and center, further aggravated by the flight of the dukes of Brabant and Limbourg and Hugues de Boves. But the archtraitor Renaud held out to the last by devising an unusual tactic. Forming a defensive circle of foot-sergeants armed with pikes, he fashioned an island of refuge from which he and a half-dozen knights sortied out and returned for respite. Eventually, however, a French sergeant brought down Renaud's horse, which pinned the count to the ground. A lively dispute ensued among the French knights as to who would have the honor of capturing the traitor, but Renaud surrendered to Guérin, whose victories on the right wing had enabled him to pass to the left. Although Renaud made one further effort to escape, he was finally delivered to the king. The earl of Salisbury was captured by the bishop of Beauvais, who, despite his former oath to avoid bloodshed, could still not resist a lively melee.[99] As night approached, Philip limited the search for fugitives to one mile, fearing that he might lose the rich prizes already taken. Finally, at the call of trumpets the French troops returned to their camp with great rejoicing.

Beneath Guillaume le Breton's elegantly choreographed tableau, balancing champion with champion and action with reaction, of course, lay the bewildering confusion of the actual battleground, obscured to observers by the dust raised by thousands of horses and men. Guillaume's attention was naturally drawn to the contests between brilliant adversaries on both sides, who best exemplified knightly glory and renown, but he also divulges evidence suggesting that the battle was not limited to chivalric prowess. On the allied side, in particular, knights cooperated with foot-sergeants in tactical units that seriously endangered Philip Augustus's center and prolonged Renaud de Boulogne's resistance on the left.

In the final analysis, victory went to the side able to deploy the largest number of troops. Guillaume does not state the size of Philip Augustus's army, but there is sufficient corroborating evidence to estimate that the French fought with about 1,300 knights and 4,000–6,000 foot-sergeants, drawn up in careful array. Guillaume's claim that the allied armies outnumbered the French three to one may be suspected as conventional hyperbole to magnify the victory. More probable estimates give the allies 1,300–1,500 knights and 7,500 foot-sergeants. But whatever the numbers, it is evident that the allies were unable to bring all their units into play. The Flemish sergeants from Bruges and Ghent did not figure in the battle, for example, and the early flight of the duke of Brabant and Hugues de Boves deprived Otto of combatants. Moreover, arriving late on the field and being forced to give battle before they had had time to organize fully must have hindered the allies from acting as tactical units. Ultimately, therefore, Guérin's strategy of precipitating an early battle against an unorganized enemy won the day.[100] Had Otto listened to Renaud de Boulogne's advice to delay, the outcome might have been different.

Philip Augustus's victory at Bouvines was spectacular. Otto had fled, abandoning his choice knights and his awesome standard. Those captured were both numerous and renowned. One hundred and thirty were assigned to prisons and custodians and their names carefully recorded in Register C. Among them were twenty-five bannerets and five counts, three of them leaders of the coalition. The count of Boulogne was assigned to Jean de Nesles, the count of Flanders to Barthélemy de Roye, and the earl of Salisbury to Robert, count of Dreux.[101] With its leadership incarcerated at the Louvre and Péronne, John's coalition dissolved, leaving no tangible results for all of his expense. Philip's remaining task was to deal with John himself, who continued to circulate south of the Loire. By mid-August the English king had certainly heard of the fate of his northern allies, but when Philip appeared with an army of 2,000 knights at Loudun, this Capetian show of force did little to intimidate John's Poitevin friends. Renouncing further military campaigns for the moment, Philip therefore agreed to a five-year truce at Chinon in September 1214. Its terms did little more than perpetuate the 1206 truce of Thouars. But in contrast to that of 1206, the truce of 1214 revealed Philip's weaknesses south of the Loire. Except for the faithful Angevins Juhel de Mayenne and Aimery de Craon, Philip's document was subscribed by no important baron of the Loire region. Unlike in 1206, John's copy was signed by the major Poitevins, including the counts of Eu and La Marche and the families of Lusignan, Thouars, and Larchevêque.[102] Faithful to their reputation, the Poitevins preferred to stand with a distant and weaker suzerain.

Despite the stalemate in the south, Bouvines was nonetheless a true battle (*bellum*) and rendered a conclusive decision. Nullifying John's twofold strategy to regain his lost territories, it confirmed Philip's conquests of 1204–1206. Deprived of further recourse, John returned to England on 13 October 1214, never to leave the island again. For the remainder of his reign Philip Augustus was free of the unsettling presence of the Angevin kings of England.

Baillis and Seneschals: Justice and Finance in the New Domain

The acquisition of Normandy and the Loire fiefs naturally required new adjustments to the administrative machinery created in the 1190s. When Philip Augustus knighted Arthur of Brittany at Gournay in July 1202, he received homage for Anjou, Maine, Touraine, and Poitou, whenever they might be taken, but Normandy was to be retained at the king's exclusive disposition (*ad opus nostrum retinebimus quantum nobis placuerit*).[1] Even before the great military campaigns were launched, therefore, it was decided that Normandy was to be separated from the other Angevin territories and added directly to the Capetian domain. After the conquests were achieved, Philip retained this distinction between the new provinces. Normandy was administered through *baillis*, whereas his other new fiefs were governed through seneschals.

The Norman Baillis

For its time the Normandy acquired from the Angevin duke-kings possessed an unusually efficient administration to handle routine matters of finance and justice. In traditional fashion all government theoretically

220

pertained to the duke's court, whether he was present or not, but in practice jurisdiction was distributed through multiple levels, particularly after the reforms introduced in 1176 by Richard of Ilchester, bishop of Winchester. If present, the duke presided over his personal court, which took precedence over all other jurisdictions. When absent—which was frequently the case—he was represented by his seneschal, who sat at the head of the court of the exchequer. Twice a year at Caen (Easter and Michaelmas), this court audited the financial accounts of the *vicomtes* and other local officials. At other times and places it heard judicial business, aided by justices, who were also periodically sent out in eyre to hold local assizes throughout the duchy, thus extending the scope of the duke's justice. Since Angevin times, local officials called *baillis* had also held court in their jurisdictions (*bailliages*), as did the older domanial officers, the *vicomtes*. But the operation of these courts and their relationship to the periodic assizes of the travelling justices are not entirely clear. Nonetheless, the functioning of this administrative machinery produced documents that correspond to those generated by their English counterparts. The Norman exchequer drew up an annual financial account and recorded its judicial decisions on rolls. And, most important, the Norman justices followed a customary law that closely paralleled the common law of England. Working in close symbiosis for over a century, the duchy and the island kingdom developed comparable governmental institutions.[2]

Both in recognition of this efficiency and in an effort to win the Normans' loyalty, Philip Augustus was disposed to perpetuate the administrative machinery intact, especially because its officials corresponded to those created for the Capetian domain. Roughly speaking, the Norman *vicomtes* performed functions similar to the Capetian *prévôts*, and the Norman justices in eyre resembled the Capetian *baillis*. Despite the identical title, only the Norman *bailli* was without a direct Capetian counterpart. After a moment of hesitation, Philip's first major change in the Norman administration was to abolish the post of seneschal, as he had done in 1191 at the royal court. Before the fall of Rouen in June 1204, Philip designated Guérin de Glapion, John's former seneschal, as "his seneschal of Normandy," but this office never reappeared thereafter.[3] His place in the judicial sessions of the exchequer was assumed by a team of *familiares*, a cleric and a layman, detached from the French court. From 1207, when the judicial exchequer records appeared, to the end of the reign, the clerical position was filled by Brother Guérin. He was accompanied by the chamberlain Gautier the Young until Gautier's death in 1218, and thereafter by Bartnélemy de Roye. During the tumultuous years 1213 and 1214, Brother Haimard (Easter 1213 and Easter 1214) and Eudes Clément (Michaelmas 1213) substituted for Guérin, and the *bailli* Guillaume de la Chapelle for Gautier the Young (Easter 1213) and, later on, for Guérin (Easter 1216). Because the presidents were borrowed from the royal court, the Norman judicial sessions were now held at Falaise, which was closer to Paris, but in 1220 they returned to Caen.[4] Less evidence survives of the exchequer's financial sessions. All indications are that the Angevin biannual schedule of Easter and Michaelmas was maintained, but the meetingplace is unknown.[5] After the reestablishment of order in 1207, other modifications of the Angevin system were applied to local officials. The old domanial officers, the *vicomtes*, began to disappear from the record.[6] More important, the justices travelling in teams and holding assizes lost their former prominence. As the terms *justicii* and *justiciarii* began to disappear, the holding of assizes and collection of revenues were increasingly assumed by men designated *baillis*.[7] The *bailli* became the chief local officer of the duchy during the first decade after the Capetian conquest.

The names of about two dozen *baillis* who served Philip Augustus after the conquest can be identified from the records. As might be expected, those on whom the king relied most had already demonstrated loyal service in the Capetian domain. Pierre du Thillai, for example, after having served around Paris and Orléans, was recruited for Caen and Falaise, where he remained from 1205 to 1224. Guillaume de la Chapelle, also from Orléans, was made *bailli* in the Caux from 1209 to 1214, where he was succeeded by another member of his family, Geoffroi de la Chapelle (1212–1238). Barthélemy Droon worked at Etampes before he became *bailli* of Verneuil (1209–1227). Renaud de Cornillon was *prévôt-bailli* of Paris before his appointment to the Cotentin (1202–1214), at which post he was succeeded by Miles de Lévis (1215–1223), recruited from another loyal family of *familiares*. Like the other Capetian *baillis*, they were predominantly laymen. The only surviving example of the Anglo-Norman custom of employing clerics as *justiciarii* appears briefly in 1211–1212 when Robert *de Waceo*, a priest, served with Eudes de Tremblay, the son-in-law of Pierre du Thillai.[8]

Although Norman *baillis* were well-paid during the reign of Louis IX, no salary figures have survived for that of Philip Augustus.[9] The newly conquered territory nonetheless provided the king with opportunities to reward his officials with lands and fiefs. The royal registers contain frequent notices of grants of fiefs to favored *baillis*. Cadoc, the *bailli* of Pont-Audemer, for example, was given the fief of Tosny and the castle of Gaillon with its lands. In 1216 Cadoc, the *bailli* Guillaume Escuacol, and Jean Luc, formerly major of Rouen, received the square before the old castle of Rouen. Most of these grants specified an annual income from the lands. After the encumbrances had been deducted, they afforded Philip's *baillis* yearly revenues ranging from 50 to 140 *livres*.[10] Apparently these sums were considered fixed remuneration because Jean de Rouvrai was instructed to return anything over his allotted amount. In all likelihood they did not exclude other emoluments because the highest figure barely equalled the lowest annual salary paid to *baillis* in the Capetian domain in 1202/03.

These fiefs allowed favored *baillis* to establish themselves as important lords in Normandy. To provide 70 *livres* of income, for example, Philip Augustus gave Pierre du Thillai the fiefs of Fribois, Mesnil-Mauger, and Barneville. As a royal official, the *bailli* also acquired fiefs at Saint-Contest, Percy, Falaise, and Giberville. So extensive were his Norman holdings that in 1220 Pierre, after completing a survey of fiefs in his *bailliage* for the king, drew up an inventory of his own lands and revenues. This register survives today as testimony to the success of an enterprising *bailli*.[11]

The king was apparently as satisfied with his Norman *baillis* as with those of the old domain, because their employment was comparably long and free from scandal. The notable exception was Cadoc, but his credentials were unusual. As a captain of Philip's mercenary *routiers* and a participant in most of the king's important campaigns, Cadoc's qualifications were primarily military. During the conquest he was granted the castle of Gaillon and jurisdiction over the small *bailliage* of Pont-Audemer. Although his activities do not differ from those of his colleagues in the contemporary records, later inquests reveal that he profited from the unsettled conditions by extortion of victims who did not dare protest. In 1219–1220, under circumstances that now elude us, he was suddenly imprisoned and his goods confiscated, and he disappears from sight until his release in 1227. His singular failure highlights, by contrast, the success of Philip's other Norman *baillis*.[12]

As the Norman *baillis* increasingly replaced the *vicomtes* and travelling justices, their mode of operation was transformed in ways that distinguished them from their namesakes in the Capetian domain. These transformations had undoubtedly begun during the reigns of Richard and

John, but become better documented after the French conquest. In contrast to the Capetian domain, the Norman *baillis* were more frequently identified geographically. Although occasionally entitled by the unspecific *ballivus domini regis*, Pierre du Thillai was identified as "*bailli* of Caen" as early as 1205. Within the first decade after the conquest, virtually all of the active Norman *baillis* were identified by geographic location, terminology that suggests delimitation of jurisdictions.[13]

Closely related to this trend was the corollary that the Norman *bailli* increasingly worked alone. When designated *justiciarii*, they worked in pairs: for example, Pierre de Neuilly and Eustace de Hadencourt at the assizes of Gisors in 1196, Renaud de Ville-Thierri and Garin Tirel at Falaise in 1206, and Eudes de Tremblay and Robert *de Waceo* at Mortain in 1211.[14] Nothing prevented the king, of course, from addressing commands to multiple *baillis* at once, as he did in 1220 to Renaud de Ville-Thierri, Barthélemy Droon, and Jean de la Porte.[15] The brothers Geoffroi and Thibaut de la Chapelle, *baillis* of Caux, occasionally collaborated, and the distant and isolated *baillis* of Avranches and the Cotentin also joined forces at times.[16] In contrast to the teamwork in the northeast and the wide intermingling within the Capetian domain, such instances of collaboration were rare among the Normans. Styling themselves as *baillis* of Gisors, Verneuil, Rouen, Caux, Caen, Bayeux-Avranches, and Cotentin, they initiated a general pattern of holding assizes, conducting inquests, and executing royal commands alone within their *bailliages*.[17] As their activities became exclusive, their numbers decreased. Around 1180 the duchy had contained as many as twenty-seven *bailliages*, which Richard and John had begun to consolidate.[18] When Philip Augustus surveyed the fiefs in 1207, thirteen *bailliages* were acknowledged. By the time of the comprehensive feudal inventory of Register E in 1220, the Norman *bailliages* were reduced to eight, all but two identified by the *bailli*'s name. In the budget of 1221, six principal *baillis* reported their revenues: Gisors, Rouen, Caux, Caen, Cotentin, and Verneuil.[19]

These Norman trends towards geographic delimitation, exclusive jurisdiction, and consolidation eventually influenced the evolution of the other *bailliages* throughout the royal domain. Most of the evidence for this influence comes from the reign of Louis IX, but a few suggestions appear in the second half of Philip's reign. For example, Nevelon the Marshal, the powerful *bailli* of Artois, cooperated with colleagues before 1205, but no evidence of further collaboration survives for the rest of the reign.[20] The chief evidence of Norman influence comes in the feudal inventory of Register E in 1220. After completing the surveys for the eight

Norman *bailliages*, the chancery scribe turned to four jurisdictions in the Capetian domain: Vermandois, Sens, Bourges, and Etampes.[21] The first omitted the name of *bailliage* and of *bailli*, because, in all likelihood, it was still administered by a team. Sens and Etampes were designated by the names of their officials, Etienne de Hautvilliers and Adam Héron. Bourges was identified by its geographic name, probably because a replacement for Gilbert de Minpinc had not yet been decided on. Although the 1220 survey did not include the entire Capetian domain, it attempted to delimit the jurisdictions of specific *bailliages* as far as it went. With the exception of Vermandois, responsibility was assigned exclusively to a single *bailli*.[22] In essence this was the Norman system, which became the Capetian practice of the future.

The Norman Administration of Justice

Under the Angevin duke-kings the efficient judicial institutions of Normandy had generated three series of documents: the local assize rolls, the records of the central exchequer, and compilations of customary law known as *coutumiers* (or customals). After reestablishing order in the duchy, Philip Augustus found it advantageous to perpetuate these records. Although no local assize rolls have survived from Philip's reign, sufficient references lie scattered in charters to testify that they were continued after the French conquest. More important, by Easter 1207 the clerks at the exchequer at Falaise began preserving brief notices of decisions made at the biannual sessions, which were written down on rolls or in registers. In extant form they are preceded by a title announcing their character: "In the reign of Philip, king of the French, after he acquired Normandy, these judgments were made at the Norman exchequer by the barons assembled there" (*Regnante Philippo, rege Francorum, post acquisitionem Normannie quam fecit, facta sunt hec judicia in scacariis Normannie a baronibus existentibus in ejusdem*). This collection precedes by a half-century the *Olim*, the first extant collection of the judicial records of the central Capetian court, and may have stimulated the development of the early rolls of the royal *parlement*.[23]

This Norman legal precocity is also illustrated by the appearance of the *coutumiers*, which were private collections of customary law. Since the duchy was part of the Anglo-Norman realm, the law enforced in Norman courts took account of English precedents, which had been well formulated and written down since the early twelfth century. It is not surprising, therefore, that the first customs to be codified in France appeared in two Norman *coutumiers* during the reign of Philip Augustus. The first of these is difficult to situate in place and time. It was probably written in the Evrecin, because most of the persons mentioned are from that region. Since King Richard appears to have died and the seneschal Guillaume fitz Ralph to be still alive, it can tentatively be placed between 6 April 1199 and 9 June 1200. One manuscript refers to the duke variously as king of England and of France, which suggests that it was written when the fate of the duchy was still undecided, perhaps as late as 1203–1204. Though such evidence is not firm, it seems clear that the treatise was composed on the eve of the French conquest, inasmuch as it makes no mention of that crucial event and reflects the time when justice was rendered by the duke and his seneschal. If it was indeed composed in the region of Evreux, on which Philip had had designs since 1194, it may well have been an attempt to define and formulate traditional customs with a view to eventual French takeover. The second Norman *coutumier* can be more assuredly dated between 15 April 1218 and 14 July 1223, because it refers to an ordinance of the former date and the king was evidently still alive. It was probably composed near Bayeux, because of the prevalence of local material relating to the city. A treatise entirely independent of the first *coutumier* (although the two frequently deal with the same subjects), the second was clearly an attempt to reformulate the law applied in the Norman courts after the French conquest.[24] Joined to the surviving court records, these two Norman *coutumiers* permit a view of the operation of Capetian justice not afforded elsewhere.

Brother Guérin and his lay colleague convoked the judicial sessions of the exchequer twice a year at Falaise and later at Caen, but judgments were also given elsewhere, as for example in the case of the celebrated decision concerning the inheritance of Raoul Tesson over which Barthélemy de Roye presided at Rouen in 1214 (later confirmed at the regular session at Falaise).[25] At first, the travelling *justiciarii* and later the *baillis* convoked assizes throughout the duchy.[26] According to the first *coutumier*, they were to be held in each *vicomté* once or twice a year, at which time pleas in baronial courts were to cease so that all could attend. After the conquest, four sessions a year were customary at Bonneville, and three at Sées.[27] Charters and exchequer records indicate that assizes were held in at least twenty-eight towns and regularly at Rouen, Bernai, Pont-Audemer, Arques, Gisors, Evreux, Sées, Caen, Falaise, Bayeux, Avranches, Coutances, Carentan, and Mortain.[28]

The exchequer presidents, justices, and *baillis* merely convoked and presided over their respective courts. They do not appear to have rendered decisions as judges. Because peers had to be judged by peers according to Norman custom, the first *coutumier* required that local assizes be held by three or four knights or barons of the neighborhood, who were placed under oath to do justice faithfully and to maintain the assize rolls. For this reason, notices of the assizes frequently mention not only the justices or *baillis*, but also "the barons of the assize," "the barons who were present," or "many other barons." It was the latter who actually rendered judgment.[29] In similar fashion, the collection of exchequer decisions states that "the judgments in the Norman exchequer were made by the barons present there," and each session's record was prefaced with explicit mention of "the presence of many prelates, knights and barons."[30] At the exchequer session of 1217, Guérin and Gautier the Young were assisted by five bishops, the count of Alençon, and twenty-five other barons and knights. Four *baillis*, and two clerics—one of whom was the scribe Guillaume Acarin—were also present, but probably did not participate in the decision. The judgment of 1214 at Rouen over Raoul Tesson's inheritance was made by four bishops and twenty-one barons and knights, with the assistance of eight *baillis*.[31] Philip Augustus undoubtedly retained the Norman procedure of judgment by peers both in the assizes and at the exchequer to reassure the duchy's inhabitants that they would be judged according to traditional custom.

The law that Philip inherited in Normandy closely followed English precedents. When Henry II came to the throne in 1154, one of his foremost objectives was to reform the common law to alleviate the endemic disorders inherited from King Stephen. Henry diagnosed those ills as stemming from three general conditions: the unwarranted freedom of churchmen, the increase in violent crime, and the growing tendency to usurp land. We shall defer discussion on the first two to a later chapter, and focus here on the latter phenomenon, in which the disintegration of public authority permitted strong men to dispossess weaker neighbors. To address this situation, Henry created the possessory remedy, by which a plaintiff purchased from the king's justices a writ of novel disseisin. The justices then ordered that a jury of twelve men from the neighborhood be empanelled to declare whether the plaintiff had been dispossessed (disseized) of the land unjustly and without judgment. If this jury of recognition decided in the plaintiff's favor, the latter regained immediate possession of the land. Only possession (seisin) was adjudicated, and the case could be further tried to decide who had greater right to the land, but violent dispossession was blocked by speedy and effective action. Henry also applied the possessory remedy to disputes over succession in which a more powerful claimant attempted to acquire an inheritance by force. In this case the plaintiff purchased a royal writ of mort d'ancestor, which caused the justices to empanel a jury of recognition to decide what lands the deceased had possessed at his death and who was the closest kin. Possession was granted immediately on the jury's verdict, and questions of right were adjudicated at a later date. The provisions of novel disseisin and mort d'ancestor in Anglo-Norman law were of particular advantage to minors, women, and handicapped persons less able to defend themselves.

Attempting to formulate the duchy's customs on the eve of the French conquest, the first Norman *coutumier* was neither complete nor systematic. Although at the end of the treatise the author did attempt a comprehensive coverage of cases that pertained exclusively to the duke (the pleas of the sword),[32] his main intention was to discuss protections afforded to the weaker members of free society. Devoting particular attention to inheritance, minors, widows, guardians, and dowries, he rehearses the remedies of mort d'ancestor and novel disseisin. In his view the chief protection of possession (seisin) by weaker people was the jury of recognition available through the local assizes. Referring to novel disseisin, he explains that: "If any strong man, confident in his riches and the strength of his champions, but not in the Lord, wishes to implead a weaker man or neighbor and to take away his land, the weaker possessor of that land will have a recognition of twelve knights or vavassors under oath as to which of them has a greater right to that land."[33] Again, alluding to mort d'ancestor, he specifies: "Lest the powerful can do harm to the powerless, it is decreed that the possession of the father on the day that he died shall be demonstrated through a jury of twelve legal men of the neighborhood."[34] To ensure protection for the weak, it was important that the jury be impartial. "The jury of men will be composed not of relatives or partisans of either party but of those in whom enmity has been eliminated."[35] The recognitions were a ducal monopoly, obtainable through the duke's writ, which commanded the *bailli* to assemble a jury at the next assize in the plaintiff's neighborhood.[36] Not only must all other feudal courts cease operations, but those who were refused judgment in their lord's courts could take their pleas to the duke's courts.[37] By offering possessory remedies to the weak, and by providing alternatives to the feudal courts, ducal justice sought to reduce the nobility's inclination to help themselves, and thereby to eliminate the private warfare endemic to feudal society.[38] Like the *baillis'* assizes in the Capetian domain, the sworn barons and knights of the Norman assizes were also commissioned to hear complaints about the malfeasance of ducal officers. The assize was empowered to assemble a jury of twelve men of the vicinity to investigate complaints about the *vicomtes* and their sergeants. If any poor person accused a *bailli* or *vicomte* of wrongdoing, the sworn judges were to render justice in both civil and criminal cases and to punish the guilty.[39]

At the end of the reign, when Guillaume le Breton embellished his narrative of the conquest in verse, he asserted that the king was careful to preserve all Norman customs and laws that did not harm the church or openly contradict equity. (As an example of the latter, Guillaume cites Philip's modification of the rules governing trial by battle.)[40] In roughly the same period, the second *coutumier* also testified to Philip's concern to retain the duchy's traditional customs. A more systematic compilation than the first, the second *coutumier* opens with a dossier of documents (including a list of the pleas of the sword) and then turns to a discussion of the possessory remedies. These chapters provide sample writs closely modelled on English examples for novel disseisin, mort d'ancestor, bastardy, and so forth.[41] In fact, the second *coutumier* provides a summation of the business actually dealt with in the judicial sessions of the Norman exchequer. Of the 326 recorded cases heard at the exchequer at Falaise and Caen from Easter 1207 to Easter 1223, only a small proportion (14, or 4 percent) involved criminal proceedings.[42] The remaining 312 were civil cases, of which a third (107) concerned disputes over inheritance, dowry, custody, and other matters relating to succession. Another 11 percent (37) involved questions of possession and dispossession of land. If these two broad categories are grouped together, at least 30 percent (40 cases) of the total involved dowry and marriage portions relevant to women. Another 26 percent (37 cases) involved minors. It is clear, therefore, that in matters of inheritance and land possession, over half of the litigants were disadvantaged women and minors. How most of the judgments were obtained is not revealed in the record, because the decisions are merely introduced with the phrase *judicatum est*, but 26 percent (37 cases) of the inheritance and possession cases were explicitly judged by juries of recognition. Although this figure can hardly be comprehensive, its importance is illustrated by contrasting it with the 5 percent (8 cases) that were judged by judicial duel, the customary method for deciding land disputes among the feudal classes.

How weaker persons defended their rights against stronger parties may be illustrated by a case heard at Falaise in 1209. Eustache Caillot, a minor, sought the seisin of his father's land at the manor of *Rosetot* through a writ of mort d'ancestor, claiming that his uncle, Richard Caillot, had forcibly occupied it. Two juries of recognition were assembled to consider the complex circumstances of the case. Unable to arrive at a decision, the local *bailli* brought the case to the attention of Gautier the Young, president of the exchequer at Rouen, who transmitted it to the full exchequer at Falaise, where possession was finally awarded to the young Eustache.[43] This illustrates both the *baillis'* activities in the local assizes and the relationship of the exchequer to the local courts. In Eustache's plea at least the second recognition was held by an unnamed *bailli* at the local assize near *Rosetot*.

In 1219, to cite another example, the exchequer barons ordered Miles de Lévis to hold a recognition by jury at the assize of Coutances in a case of novel disseisin.[44] Many other judgments made at the assizes of Bonneville, Caen, Avranches, and Coutances were also taken into account in the exchequer proceedings, and the names of the local jurors were duly noted.[45] The *baillis* were ordered to execute the exchequer's decisions and to conduct numerous inquests.[46] The *baillis* were not, therefore, present at the exchequer's sessions in the capacity of judges, but as liaisons between the central court and the local assizes.

The biannual sessions of the exchequer could clearly review the decisions in the assizes. In the case of Eustache Caillot, the *bailli* sought advice first from the president and then from the full exchequer on a doubtful point of law. In 1211 the exchequer overturned a decision of a jury under Barthélemy Droon as a *judicium falsum* and reassigned possession to the defendant. In 1220 the barons overruled a decision of the court of Miles de Lévis in the case of a dowry.[47] Though the exchequer acted as a court of review and appeal over the assizes and other courts of Normandy, that was by no means its sole function. The vast majority of cases were brought directly to the exchequer by the litigants themselves, although they could be referred back to the local courts. In a sense, therefore, the exchequer at Falaise operated as *primus inter pares* in the Norman judicial system.

The Administration of the Jews

The Norman propensity for keeping records also prompted Philip Augustus to perfect his administration relative to the Jews. As we have seen, the principal features of Capetian Jewish policy were already in operation before the conquest of the duchy. The residence of Jews in the royal domain was stabilized, their lending was supervised by officials, and their transactions were recorded and certified with seals—all for the purpose of financial exploitation. These measures, which reached back to the reign of Louis VII, were paralleled by Angevin policy in England and Normandy. Upon the death of Aaron of Lincoln, the wealthiest English Jew, Henry II created a special exchequer to collect Aaron's debts, an institution that evolved into the exchequer of the Jews, complete with its own rolls. Soon after this, Henry established registries of deeds to record lending transactions, called the *arche Judeorum*, thus enabling the government to keep track of Jewish wealth. Keepers or justices of Jews were eventually appointed to supervise their affairs. If on a smaller scale, a similar regime was in effect in Normandy by the time Richard de Villequier was appointed custodian of the Jews there in 1203.[48] When Philip acquired the duchy in 1204, these Norman practices merely reinforced existing Capetian policies.

After 1204 the king reconfirmed the policy of stabilization established in 1198 for the entire royal domain. He required oaths and pledges at Mantes from Norman Jews wishing to remain permanent residents of the duchy. The agreement of 1198 was renewed with Countess Blanche of Troyes in 1210, and extended to the counts of Saint-Pol and Nevers as well.[49] In an ordinance (*stabilimentum*) of 1206, in which Blanche and Guy de Dampierre concurred, Philip decreed that each town was to select two sworn men to take custody of a new seal for certifying Jewish contracts and a scribe for writing them down.[50] In later instructions addressed to the *baillis* of the Ile-de-France and Normandy, the king limited the seal to debts above three *livres* and required the custodians to retain copies of the transactions. Finally, in February 1219 Philip codified his Jewish policy in a general ordinance (*constitucio . . . de judeis*) in which the Norman Jews were commanded to enroll their transactions before the *bailli* and ten knights of the local assizes, where they were to be kept for future reference.[51]

These measures designed to supervise and record Jewish debts enabled the royal government to make an inventory of Jewish lending. Between 1208 and 1212 a scribe copied the results of an inquest into debts owed to Jews into Register A that listed the total figures according to *prévôté*, *bailliage*, and four leading lenders.[52] Moses of Sens was singled out as the Jew who had extended the greatest amount of credit (60,000 *livres*). Helie de Bray and his brother Dieudonné were the two most important lenders in Paris. When their debts of 30,000 *livres* were added to those of other Parisian Jews, the total Jewish credit at the capital amounted to 42,500 *livres*. By contrast, Dieudonné de Verneuil, the sole Norman Jew cited by name, claimed only 2,592 *livres*. These four individuals, however, accounted for almost half the debts owed to the king's Jews. Jewish credit totaled 251,900 *livres*, or a sum equivalent to 25 percent more than the ordinary royal revenues in 1221. This inquest could have resulted from normal administration or may have been prompted by special circumstances. The anonymous chronicler of Melrose in Scotland observes that in 1210, when King John was despoiling the Jews in England, the French king ordered his Jews to be imprisoned because he feared their widespread usurious practices. Such distant testimony would not be noteworthy except for the fact that Register A also contains a list of twenty-six French and fourteen Norman Jews "who will remain in the *châtelet* of the Petit-Pont" (recently rebuilt in 1209–1210). At the head of the list are the four names identified in the inquest. We may suspect, therefore, that Philip had once again been tempted to revert to his former policies of despoliation, which in fact provoked an immigration of Jews to Palestine in 1211.[53] Whatever his depredations in 1210, they did not last long, however, because he continued to supervise and record Jewish transactions in an effort to profit from their loans. In 1217 he realized about 7,550 *livres* from his Jews, a sixfold increase over 1202/03.[54]

Supervision and recording were also accompanied by regulation of lending practices. The ordinance of 1206 set the weekly rate of interest at two *deniers* per *livre* (43 percent annually if not compounded) and prohibited the compounding of interest during the first year. Further instructions to the French and Norman *baillis* prohibited Jews from compounding interest altogether. In addition, the 1206 ordinance placed restrictions on pledges for securing loans. (Ecclesiastical ornaments and objects suspected of being stolen were, for example, unacceptable.) The comprehensive ordinance of 1219 repeated these regulations and attempted to protect certain classes of borrowers. Echoing Rigord's earlier complaints that Jewish usury oppressed the weaker classes, the ordinance forbade demanding interest from those without property whose sole support was their manual labor and from monks and regular canons without the express permission of their superiors. Even the property of the landed classes was partially protected from depletion through interest.

These measures expressed an underlying ambivalence about the king's role in supervising, recording, regulating, and profiting from the usurious practices of Jews, which were totally forbidden to Christians. It is therefore not surprising that four months after Philip's death in November 1223, Louis VIII enacted an ordinance that began to eliminate governmental involvement in Jewish usury with a view to suppressing usury altogether in the future. This campaign against Jewish usury became one of the cherished reforms of Philip's grandson, Louis IX.[55]

Seneschals in the Loire Valley

In contrast to Normandy, when Philip acquired the counties of Anjou, Maine, Touraine, and Poitou, he received from his predecessors neither important concentrations of domain nor widespread and effective administration. In general, the territories of the Loire valley were dominated by a handful of middle-level baronies that surpassed the limits of local castellans but did not achieve countywide scope.[56] Faced with these obstacles, the previous counts had been content to center their administration on the seneschal of their household, who acted personally on their behalf. When Henry II assembled his vast holdings in England and France in 1154, he was obliged by frequent absences to govern his continental lands through seneschals. Though Henry tried to take more direct responsibility in the first half of his reign, by 1176, after the great revolt of his sons, he had decentralized his administration, creating a justiciar in Normandy, and delegating more authority to his sons in Poitou and Brittany and to his seneschal in Anjou. Even in Normandy, Poitou, and Brittany, however, the office of the seneschal survived these reforms.[57] When Philip Augustus annexed Henry's former lands from the Channel to the Loire, he therefore inherited a regime based on seneschals. Although he had suppressed this office at his own court and in Normandy, he was not able to circumvent it in the Loire fiefs.

After Normandy, Anjou ranked second among Philip's prizes. If Normandy provided the Capetians with access to the sea, Anjou offered them routes to the Loire and beyond. By the twelfth century Anjou was understood to comprise not only the county that straddled the Loire and took its name from the city of Angers, but also the counties of Maine (named from the city of Le Mans) to the north and Touraine (from the city of Tours) upstream to the east. This complex of lands included over a score of baronies, of which those of Sablé, Mayenne, Craon, and Laval were most noteworthy.[58] When Henry II's accumulated territories had been threatened by the disputed succession in 1199, the Angevin barons had by and large supported the claims of their neighbor, Arthur, count of Brittany. Since Arthur was not an Angevin himself and only a boy of twelve, he had also required a seneschal to champion his cause in Anjou. He therefore conferred the office as a hereditary fief upon one of the leading barons, Guillaume des Roches, lord of Sablé. To this were added gifts of land, distributed between Guillaume and another important baron, Juhel de Mayenne. Since it cost the king of France little to do so at the time, he was content to confirm them in royal charters.[59] After Philip Augustus had sided openly with Arthur against John in 1202, however, and received from the Breton prince homage for Anjou, Maine, Touraine, and Poitou (should it be taken),[60] he also acquired Guillaume des Roches's hereditary claims to the Anjou seneschalship, which were difficult to disavow.

Guillaume des Roches belonged to a group of royal agents who had assumed an increasingly prominent role in Angevin administration in the late twelfth century.[61] Of modest origins, he strikingly improved his position by loyal service to a prince and by marriage to a baronial heiress. Stemming from a family of lesser knights from Château-du-Loir, halfway between Le Mans and Tours, Guillaume entered Henry II's service and, like William the Marshal, loyally defended the king during his last days at Le Mans.[62] As with William the Marshal, his faithful service to the Angevin monarchy, which continued under Richard, undoubtedly elicited royal permission to marry a rich heiress—in Guillaume's case, the daughter of Robert of Sablé, a leading Angevin baron. When Robert and his son died in the 1190s, Guillaume des Roches succeeded to the lordship of Sablé. His wife not only brought him extensive lands, but also ties to the baronial families of Mayenne, Craon, and Laval. These four seigneuries formed a strategic bloc running along the western border of Maine and into the center of Anjou. After Arthur conferred the hereditary seneschalship on Guillaume, the new seneschal became the decisive figure in the military and political history of Anjou, as is illustrated by his role at Balon in 1199 and at Mirebeau in 1202. When Philip Augustus refused to follow Guillaume's advice at the former incident, Guillaume deserted the Capetian party, bringing important Angevin barons with him to John's side. When John similarly ignored the seneschal's counsel at Mirebeau, and it became clear that the king was responsible for Arthur's disappearance, Guillaume and the Angevins again returned to Philip's camp. By March 1203 the French king had received charters of homage from the ten leading barons of the Loire valley. At their head were Guillaume des Roches and his wife's kinsmen, the lords of Mayenne and Craon.[63] Guillaume led this baronial coalition in the conquest of Maine, Anjou, and Touraine, and was personally entrusted with the capture of Chinon, a key fortress of the Loire. After the Capetian victory, Guillaume continued to play a major military role in the region. He contributed to its defense between 1206 and 1208 and stood at Prince Louis's side at La Roche-au-Moine in 1214 (for which Guillaume le Breton acclaimed him "a vigorous man, steadfast in faith, and proven in war").[64] He took part in the Albigensian crusades in 1209 and 1219 before his death in 1222.

Whatever these military contributions, however, Guillaume's chief importance lay in the administrative responsibilities of seneschal. When he joined forces with John between 1199 and 1202, the English king was faced with a dilemma. He could not ignore the powerful baron's support, yet he was reluctant to acknowledge the hereditary seneschalship. John waited until December 1199 to designate Guillaume seneschal, and not until after the treaty of Le Goulet was signed was he formally confirmed to the hereditary office over Anjou, Maine, and Touraine.[65] Philip Augustus was faced with the same dilemma, because, even more than John, he sought to free himself from baronial influence and to resist the creation of hereditary offices. With victory within grasp, however, Philip finally had to come to terms with the lord of Sablé if he wished to secure the Loire lands. He was obliged to accept the hereditary title, which he himself had in any case already assented to by confirming Arthur's grant. Philip's solution was to negotiate a series of agreements in which the seneschal's authority and revenues were clearly defined and carefully recorded in registers and charters kept in the royal archives. At the beginning of the Loire campaign at Poitiers in August 1204, Philip reconfirmed the hereditary seneschalship of Anjou, Touraine, and Maine to Guillaume des Roches, but with two restrictions: that the heritability be limited to direct children and that the seneschal not have custody of royal castles and fortresses by customary, or feudal, tenure. All such castles were to be granted by explicit letters patent, with the stipulation that they be returned at the king's will.[66] Two years later the king specified the extent of Guillaume's authority in greater detail. In May 1206 Philip granted the custody of Angers, Loudun, Saumur, Brissac, Beaufort, and "all the land of Anjou" at the king's pleasure, but he retained for himself Tours, Chinon, and Langeais, comprising the Touraine from Langeais to Berry.[67] In a final distribution of January 1207 Philip definitively retained Touraine and Chinon, along with Bourgueil, Loudun, and Saumur, permitting to Guillaume Anjou, Baugé, and everything else granted in 1206.[68] To tighten the Loire defenses against John's countermeasures, Guillaume des Roches was, in effect, relieved of the Touraine seneschalship, but was permitted that of Maine and Anjou, with the latter deprived of its southeastern corner.

In addition to assigning jurisdictions, Philip also divided revenues with Guillaume des Roches. In August 1204 he granted the seneschal one mark of silver from every fifty *livres* of domanial revenues (about 1.3 percent of the total) and one-third of the profits of justice (*forefacta, expleta,* and *servitia*). For his part, the king received virtually all of the domanial income, two-thirds of the revenues of justice, all of the sales of the forests, and all of the *tailles* and other exactions (*demanda*) levied on Christians and Jews.[69] In 1206, when Guillaume's custodies over Anjou were specified, the king granted the seneschal all the domanial revenues and profits of justice (*expleta*) to recompense the custodial expenses. If the expense exceeded the revenues, the seneschal was to submit a proper accounting. Normally, the king was not responsible for expenses beyond the revenues except when the king of England personally threatened to invade from Poitou.[70] In effect, therefore, Guillaume's income was finally increased to all the domanial revenue and profits of justice of specified lands in Anjou assigned to his custody. It is virtually impossible to estimate how much these revenues enriched Guillaume beyond his baronial income. As we shall see, the counties of Anjou and Maine were not included in the budgets of 1221 and 1227, making it difficult to assess their revenues.[71] But Guillaume's income was undoubtedly substantial, and demonstrated the seneschal's independence. Unlike in the royal domain, all revenues passed through one man's hands and were exempt from accounting. The king was satisfied as long as he was assured that the seneschal was taking no more than his due. Only *tailles* levied on Christians and Jews, and later expenditures in excess of receipts, required explicit accounting (*per legitimum compotum et scriptum*).

The seneschal of Anjou's independence is further underscored by the men who served in his administration. In September 1204 the king authorized Guillaume to appoint *baillis* to aid in the necessary tasks of his office.[72] In fact, only one *bailli* of importance emerges clearly: Hamelin de Roorta, an associate of Guillaume des Roches's since 1201. Hamelin was almost invariably styled as "*bailli* of both the lord king and the seneschal of Anjou" or simply as acting in the place of Guillaume des Roches.[73] His distinctive role is seen when compared to the *baillis* of the Touraine. When Tours was held directly by the king after 1206, it was administered by Guillaume *de Azaio* (1209–1219), Robert de Crespières (1210–1217), and Thierry de Gallardon (1217–1219), who called themselves simply *baillis* or seneschals of Touraine and Poitou and not *baillis* of the seneschals. Since Robert had previously been *prévôt* of Saumur, it is possible that these men were professional administrators who had risen through the ranks.[74] As during Henry II's time, the seneschal of Anjou exercised unusual authority. In contrast to Normandy and the rest of the royal domain, Anjou was therefore cut off from the normal administrative machinery and entrusted to one person. This arrangement suggests that Philip Augustus still harbored doubts about the security of the Loire fiefs and their readiness to be assimilated permanently into the royal domain.

As the king's representatives, Guillaume des Roches and Hamelin de Roorta were involved chiefly in administering justice under the authority of the *curia regis*. For example, Philip Augustus instructed his seneschal to hear pleas between the abbot of La Couture and the abbey's men to prevent complaints of default of justice.[75] The seneschal arbitrated agreements, conducted inquests, inquired into the regalian rights of the bishop of Le Mans, and counselled the king on the marriage customs of Anjou, Maine, and Touraine.[76] The activities of the neighboring Touraine *baillis* closely resembled those of the Angevin seneschal.[77] The judicial duties of Guillaume des Roches and his neighboring colleagues differed little from those of the other *baillis* of the royal domain. The qualities that distinguished him were his military leadership and financial independence.

Although Guillaume des Roches held the seneschalship by hereditary fief, the office could only be inherited by his direct heirs. Having no sons and being about to depart on the Albigensian crusade in 1219, Guillaume nonetheless conferred the seneschalship and most of the lands of Sablé on Aimery de Craon, the husband of his eldest daughter. Why the king ratified this transaction and reconfirmed the same terms as in 1206 and 1207 to Aimery after Guillaume's death in 1222 escapes us. Although the seneschalship survived Philip's reign, it soon lost its original importance. Aimery was humiliated by Pierre de Dreux, count of Brittany, and died in 1226, leaving a minor heir.[78] Thereafter the seneschalship devolved upon a woman. When Louis VIII conferred Anjou and Maine as an appanage upon his third son in the testament of 1225, effective control over the counties passed to the royal family.

Poitou witnessed even more spectacular growth among regional baronies of the middle level than Anjou. From about fifty Poitevin castellan families at mid-twelfth century there emerged four major baronial families, which held almost half of the castles in the region from the 1190s to the 1230s. At their height, the Thouars had fourteen, and the Mauléons and Lusignans twelve each. The Archevêques of Parthenay retained only three, but their holdings were unusually concentrated, which increased their effectiveness. This process of accumulating castles was stimulated by the rivalry between the Angevin count-kings and the Capetians, who continually competed for baronial support. The Angevins, who had held fourteen castles in Poitou in 1189, alienated most of their resources under Richard, and their position was further weakened by John's marriage to Isabelle d'Angoulême. Although this gained John important allies in the Angoumois and Limousin, it provoked the enmity of the Lusignans in Poitou. By the opening of the thirteenth century, the Poitevin region was consolidated in the hands of these four families, and whoever wished to govern the county as a unit was obliged to woo their support.[79]

Young Arthur had also done homage for Poitou in 1202 in the event it should be wrested from John. The following year Philip Augustus competed for the support of the Poitevin baronage by offering Aimery, *vicomte* of Thouars, hereditary possession of the castle of Loudun and, most important, the hereditary seneschalship of Poitou and Aquitaine, whenever these territories should come into the king's hands.[80] Aimery had served John briefly as seneschal of Anjou and custodian of Chinon,[81] but he now became the target of Capetian blandishments. Not only did he head one of the great baronies, but his brother Guy was the third husband of Constance of Brittany, the mother of the now imprisoned Arthur, a marriage alliance that brought together Philip's agents in Brittany and Poitou.[82] When Guillaume des Roches was commissioned seneschal of Anjou, Philip accorded the Poitevin seneschalship to Aimery on virtually the same terms at Poitiers in August 1204. Although most of the domanial income was reserved for the king, including forest profits, *tailles*, and other exactions, the seneschal could collect 1.3 percent of the *prévôtés'* revenues and one-third of the profits of justice. As in Anjou, the seneschal exercised custody over castles and fortresses only at royal pleasure and through explicit letters patent.[83]

Philip Augustus had secured military control over most of Poitou in the summer of 1204, but in formulating these terms he lost his bid for the Thouars' loyalty. Aimery had rejoined John by 1206, thereby foiling Philip's first attempt to gain baronial support.[84] Not long thereafter the king tried again, this time approaching Raoul, count of Eu, a member of the Lusignan family. Philip offered him all of the domanial revenues of

Poitou for five years in addition to 4,000 *livres parisis*, 100 knights, and 1,000 foot-sergeants for three months of military duty. To avoid a repetition of the defection of Aimery de Thouars, the king stipulated that Raoul yield the Norman county of Eu as security.[85] Apparently the terms did not tempt Raoul, because nothing further is heard of the scheme. For his part, John conferred the seneschalship of Poitou on Savery of the Mauléon family, who held the post intermittently between 1205 and 1223.[86] Because of his failure to enlist a major baronial family, Philip Augustus's hold on the Poitevin region was tenuous. As Philip confessed to the count of Eu, Poitou was too remote for the king to attend to it personally. Only the city of Poitiers and a small strip of surrounding territory survived of the Capetian conquest of 1204. When Philip and John signed the truce at Chinon in September 1214, no important Poitevin barons supported Philip. Significantly, the terms of the truce specified that the seneschal be an Englishman, Hubert de Burgh.[87] Unlike in Anjou, Philip Augustus's plan for a regime based on seneschals was unrealized for Poitou. Occasionally the royal *baillis* in Touraine styled themselves *baillis* or seneschals of Poitou as well, but their activities in the region are only vaguely known.[88] The effective conquest and organization of Poitou was deferred to Louis VIII and his son Alphonse, who received the county as an appanage.

If Poitou escaped Philip's regime of seneschals, Brittany was even more remote and less susceptible to royal administration. As long as Philip's protégé Arthur was alive, Brittany was his responsibility. When his death was presumed in 1204, the county was entrusted to the husband of Arthur's mother, Guy de Thouars. But the Poitevin's position in Brittany was too weak for effective rule. As we have seen, Philip's eventual solution was to give the province in fief to a royal cousin, Pierre de Dreux, who married Alix, the daughter of Guy de Thouars and Constance of Brittany.[89]

Reckoning the Gains of the Conquests

When contemporary historians chronicled the great conquests of 1204–1206, they were apparently unconcerned with estimating the economic value of the new lands. The one numerical fact that impressed Rigord (and, following him, Guillaume le Breton and Robert d'Auxerre) was that Normandy had been repossessed by the French kings after more than three hundred years. Robert d'Auxerre adds that the duchy, with its seven bishoprics, and Aquitaine with Poitiers, were reintegrated into the body of the realm (*corpus regni*).[90] Modern historians have estimated that Philip Augustus increased his domain from two to four times, but these figures are merely rough guesses, presumably based on the size of the new provinces.[91] Fortunately, however, a way is open to calculate these gains in a more precise fashion, thanks to the recent discovery of the budget of 1221.[92] This document helps to repair the losses of the financial records of the Norman exchequer and the central accounting bureau where the finances of the new territories were recorded. The budget of 1221 is somewhat late and fragmentary, but these disadvantages can be compensated for. Even though it was drawn up more than a decade after the conquests, it reflects the state of the post-conquest domain, because no important territorial changes had intervened. Although it is truncated at the beginning, the last part survives, which happily contains an accounting of the new territories and recapitulative totals. These figures, joined with subsequent identical exercises, can help us to reconstruct the account as a whole and to compensate for its deficiencies. Moreover, the document of 1221 possesses the advantage of being a true budget—that is, an attempt to account for the monarchy's total finances.

In the earlier accounts of 1202/03, which were designed primarily to supervise and control local royal officials, the *prévôts* and *baillis* appeared before the central bureau three times a year, at All Saints', Purification of the Virgin, and Ascension, rendered detailed statements of receipts and expenditures, and deposited the balances in the Temple. Having determined the balances individually for each official, the audit bureau made no further attempt to add up the receipts and expenditures to arrive at a total estimation of royal finances, although the bureau possessed an abacus that technically could have performed such an operation. By contrast, the document of 1221 regrouped the income and expenses in large categories, added up the receipts of the *prévôts* and *baillis*, converted *livres tournois* into *parisis*, subtracted the total expenditures, and arrived at a final balance in the treasury. The account of 1221 may, therefore, be called the "first surviving budget of the French monarchy" more aptly than those of 1202/03.[93] Its new format was adopted by two subsequent budgets, those of Purification 1227 and Ascension 1238.[94] Although the first of these is also a fragment, the second is complete, and both accounts help to supply features missing in 1221. Since the budget of 1221 can be dated more precisely to All Saints' that year,[95] these three accounts provide examples from the three terms of the French fiscal year. The account of 1238 was entitled *Magna recepta et magna expensa* (major receipts and expenses), which appropriately expresses the purpose of these budgets.

The budget of Ascension 1238, which was responsible for reporting the Easter term of the Norman exchequer, comes too late to be reliable for details about the reign of Philip Augustus. (We shall use it only for supplying aggregate totals after its figures have been adjusted.) That of Purification 1227 is closer in time to the budget of 1221 and contains the accounts of six out of the seven Norman and Touraine *baillis* active in 1221. Since its date in February did not correspond to the biannual schedule of the Norman exchequer, it reports only odds and ends that cannot be taken as representative of the new territories. Fortunately, however, the budget of All Saints' 1221 reports an account in *tournois* money that is intact and deals with Normandy and the Loire fiefs. Since it closely follows the Norman exchequer's Michaelmas term, it provides details of both fiscal procedures and the sources of revenue from the newly conquered lands. The counties of Anjou and Maine are absent from the budgets of All Saints' 1221 and Purification 1227, however, which poses a problem that has not yet been resolved. Either the seneschal Guillaume des Roches, who was still alive in 1221, made a separate accounting outside the normal procedures, or he accounted in the Ascension term, as the *bailli* Hardouin de Maillé did in 1238. (The problem of the absence of Anjou and Maine in 1227 is further complicated by the fact that Guillaume's successor, Aimery de Craon, had just died, leaving a minor heir as seneschal.)[96] In 1221, however, the six principal Norman *baillis* and the one *bailli* of Touraine rendered full accounts of their revenues in *tournois* money, which are summarized in Table 7.

These *baillis'* receipts of 1221 fall into five major categories of ordinary revenues, three of which were collected with regularity. The most important, consisting of 20,480 *livres tournois*, or 40 percent of the total, may be designated income from the domain and justice. The *bailliage* of Rouen, covered by six different entries, delivered the largest income, with 7,675 *livres tournois*,[97] and Tours the smallest, with 933 *livres tournois*. Since these sums required no further accounting, they must have been lump categories made up of a variety of smaller amounts. Jean de la Porte and Geoffroi de la Chapelle reported round figures *pro compoto*, which represented balances carried over from the previous terms. (This was also done in the accounts of 1202/03, and at Purification in 1227, when the two *baillis* continued to carry over rounded balances, *de compoto*.) A sec-

TABLE 7. Ordinary Income from Normandy and Touraine:
Budget of All Saints', 1221

	Livres tournois	Percentage of Total
REGULAR SOURCES		
Domain and justice	20,480	40%
Forests	6,486	13%
Fouage	15,384	30%
OCCASIONAL SOURCES		
Feudal revenues	6,370	12%
Regalia	1,379	3%
Others	1,179	2%
Total	51,278	100%

SOURCE: Nortier and Baldwin, "Contributions" 16–21.

ond ordinary and regular source of income was the produce of the forests, which in 1221 brought in 6,486 *livres tournois*, or 13 percent of the total. Ranging from 550 *livres* (Eawiz and Arques) to 20 *livres* (Montaigu-les-Bois and Teillier), the forests contributed the greatest number of entries to the accounts. Frequently reported in figures rounded to one hundred, fifty, or ten, or in amounts divisible by three, these entries indicate that the forest income was often tax-farmed in the manner of the *prévôts'* farms.[98] The most striking item among the ordinary and regular revenues of the newly conquered lands was the Norman *fouage*, or money tax. Collected triennially, it fell due on the feast of St. John the Baptist (29 August) in 1221, was accounted at the Michaelmas exchequer (29 September), and was finally reported in the All Saints' budget (1 November). It profited the king 15,384 *livres tournois* in 1221, or 30 percent of total revenue, but it should be remembered that the *fouage* was paid only once every three years.[99]

Beyond those sources regularly producing revenue, the *baillis* reported ordinary income resulting from particular occasions. Chief among these were the feudal revenues from reliefs, wardships, and fines, which will be examined in greater detail in chapter 11. For example, in 1221 Alix, heiress to the county of Eu, and Richard the Marshal, son of William the Marshal, were still paying 1,250 and 828 *livres* respectively on reliefs to succeed to their patrimonies. Similarly, Robert Malet's "fine" of 800 *livres* probably resulted from his claims to succeed to the county of Alençon.[100]

At All Saints' 1221 these feudal revenues amounted to 6,370 *livres tournois*, or 12 percent of the total. Likewise, among the seven bishoprics, the see of Rouen was vacant in 1221, since Archbishop Robert Poulain had died in May of that year. In November the *baillis* of Rouen and Caux collected 1,379 *livres tournois* (3 percent of the total) from the regalia at Rouen and Dieppe. Apart from the five major sources, the *baillis* accounted for insignificant sums that are difficult to categorize. The townsmen of Caen and Falaise, for example, paid Renaud de Ville-Thierri 500 and 250 *livres* respectively for undesignated purposes. Equally enigmatic are the 125 *livres* and 66 *livres*, 13 *sous*, 4 *deniers* received from the archdeacon of Rouen and the treasurer of Tours. Since the latter was Pierre Charlot, Philip's bastard son and the holder of a prebend in the king's gift, he was apparently paying on an obligation of 200 *livres* in triannual installments.[101]

These items evidently constituted the total accounted for by the Norman and Touraine *baillis* at All Saints' 1221. No extraordinary sums accounted under separate categories such as are to be found in the accounts of 1227 and 1238 were registered here. Normandy contributed by far the greatest amount in the *tournois* account. The six Norman *baillis* brought in 48,304 *livres*, or 94 percent of the total. Thierry de Gallardon, the *bailli* of Touraine, accounted for only 2,856 *livres*, or the remaining 6 percent.

In the budget of 1221 the total ordinary revenues of Normandy and Touraine (51,278 *livres tournois*) were converted into *livres parisis* at the normal rate of 5 to 4 to yield a total of 41,022 *livres parisis*.[102] These were then added to 32,632 *livres parisis* of revenue from the *prévôtés* and *bailliages* of the pre-1204 domain to produce a grand total income of 73,657 *livres parisis*. In crude terms, therefore, the new territories increased the royal income by 126 percent. As evidence of total "ordinary" income, however, these figures are misleading because they include with the regular income (domanial farms and so on) more important seasonal and occasional revenues that skew the total figures. We have already noted that the *baillis'* accounts of 1202/03, which reported seasonal and occasional sources, differed by as much as 15,000 and 33,000 *livres* in one year.[103] In addition to the normal variations of the agricultural seasons, moreover, the triannual terms of the central accounting bureau had to be adapted to the biannual rhythm of the Norman exchequer: All Saints' and Ascension accounted for most of the Norman revenue. Occasional income, such as feudal reliefs and the regalia, cannot be satisfactorily projected over a short term, and the figures of 1221 are further skewed by the inclusion of

TABLE 8. Ordinary Income of the French Monarchy: Budget of All Saints', 1221

	All Saints' 1221 (1)	Purification 1227 (2)	Ascension 1238 (3)	Totals (4)	Totals adjusted to reflect 1221 (5)
Prévôtés	14,300[a,b]	18,456	15,672	48,428[a]	46,104[a]
Large receipts of *baillis* in *livres parisis*	18,332[a,b]	23,233[b]	25,211[b]	66,776[a]	68,526[a]
Sums of receipts of prévôts *and* baillis *in* livres parisis	32,632	41,689	40,883	115,204	114,630[a]
Large receipts of *baillis* in *livres tournois*					
Norman *fouage* (1)	15,384				
[Gisors] Guillaume de Ville-Thierri (1,2), Warno de Verberie (3), Guiard de Seuil (3)	1,640	317	3,821		
[Verneuil] Barthélemy Droon (1,2)	2,268	928	166		
[Rouen, Bonneville] Jean de la Porte (1,2), Jean des Vignes (3)	9,680	1,087	24,121[c]		
[Caux] Geoffroi de la Chapelle (1,2,3)	8,942	777	6,689		
[Bayeux, Caen] Renaud de Ville-Thierri (1,2)	7,089	574			
[Bayeux, Avranches, Cotentin] Jean des Maisons (3)			13,596		
[Cotentin] Miles de Lévis (1), Baudoin de Danemois (2)	3,597	500			
[Touraine, Anjou] Thierry de Gallardon (1,2), Pierre le Ber (3)	2,856	10	3,780		
[Poitou] Hardouin de Maillé (3)			1,629		
[Others]			2,943		
Sums of receipts in livres tournois	51,278	4,197	56,745	112,220	100,336[a]
Equivalent in livres parisis	41,022	3,357	45,396	89,775	80,268[a]

Other large receipts				194,898[a]
Sums from the Jews		8,682		
Relief of Thomas, count of Flanders			15,000	
Total sums of receipts in livres parisis	73,657	53,729	101,279	228,665
Large expenses	48,447	37,480	75,286	161,213
Balance	25,210	16,249	25,993	67,452
Balance remaining from previous term	131,826	107,651		
Total Balance	157,036	123,900		

SOURCE: Baldwin, "Contributions" 16–21; a preliminary version of this table appears in ibid. 26.

[a] Estimated.
[b] Details lost or omitted.
[c] The *vicomté* of Rouen has been included with the *bailliage* of Rouen as is found in the account of 1221.

the Norman *fouage*, collected every three years. If we wish to arrive at a representative estimate of how much Normandy and the Touraine increased Philip's ordinary income, we therefore have to expand upon and modify the figures of 1221. One way to compensate for the seasonal variations—particularly those introduced by the Norman exchequer—is to combine the account of All Saints' 1221 with the subsequent accounts of Purification 1227 and Ascension 1238. Not only do these three budgets together complete the fiscal year, but they also follow the same basic format, which makes them commensurate. Although those of 1221 and 1227 are fragmentary, the inclusion of final recapitulative totals permits the reconstruction of their essential figures. Because of their differing dates, some material is, in fact, incommensurate, and is thus not included, but Table 8 sets out comparable data for estimating the "ordinary" income of the French monarchy in 1221, which, in turn, enables us to assess the financial gain from acquiring Normandy and Touraine.

Except for the *prévôts'* and *baillis'* receipts in *livres parisis* at All Saints' 1221, all of the sums in columns 1, 2, and 3 of Table 8 are actual figures reported in the budgets of 1221, 1227, and 1238. To reconstitute the two lacunae we may rely on Nicolas Brussel's report that the *prévôts* brought in 43,000 *livres parisis* during the fiscal year 1217.[104] Since we know from the accounts of 1202/03 that the *prévôts'* income varied little from term to term, we can estimate the *prévôts'* contribution to have been roughly one-third of that sum (14,300 *livres parisis*) at All Saints' 1221. The *baillis'* income in *livres parisis* in 1221 may be estimated by deducting the *prévôts'* income from the total *livres parisis* figure given. Column 4, which gives the totals of the three budgets, represents an entire fiscal year, but since it is partly derived from the 1227 and 1238 terms, it cannot be valid for 1221 without further adjustments, which are provided in column 5. The chief differences between the later accounts and that of 1221 result from expansions and contractions in the royal domain. Some minor *prévôtés* were acquired between 1221 and 1238. Although the *prévôtés* are not enumerated individually in 1227 or 1238, they can be identified in the general account of Ascension 1234. At that time the new acquisitions reported a negligible income of 1,162 *livres parisis*.[105] The revenues of Poitou (1,629 *livres tournois* = 1,303 *livres parisis*) reported by Hardouin de Maillé at Ascension 1238 after the conquests of Louis VIII were not available to Philip Augustus in 1221. On the other hand, Artois, which Philip possessed in 1221, had been alienated to Robert de Artois in 1237 and was absent from the account in 1238. At Ascension 1234, however, it produced only 1,750 *livres parisis* of income.[106] In order to derive the state of the domain in 1221, therefore, we should subtract from the totals the new *prévôtés* (2 × 1,162) and Poitou (1,303) and add to them Artois (1,750). Furthermore, the budgets of 1227 and 1238 respectively include 8,682 *livres parisis* from the *taille* of the Jews and 15,000 *livres parisis* from half the relief of Thomas de Savoie, who had married Jeanne, countess of Flanders, in October 1237.[107] Since these large sums were listed under separate entries apart from the *parisis* and *tournois* accounts of the *prévôts* and *baillis*, they were evidently considered "extraordinary income." The closest parallel in the budget of 1221 to such entries was the Norman *fouage*, which headed the *tournois* account. Since its revenue of 15,384 *livres parisis* was collected every three years, its full yield cannot be considered part of a normal fiscal year. To arrive at the "ordinary" income of the fiscal year, therefore, we should further deduct from the totals the *taille* of the Jews (8,682 *livres parisis*) and the relief of Flanders (15,000 *livres parisis*) and two-thirds of the Norman *fouage* (10,255 *livres tournois* = 8,204 *livres parisis*).

Column 5 thus records adjusted totals for the ordinary income of 1221. The figures conceal some imponderables that could influence the results in both directions. They include, for example, 1,811 *livres tournois* (= 1,449 *livres parisis*) from Anjou and Maine in 1238. Although this figure seems reasonable when compared with 2,856 *livres tournois* from Touraine in 1221, we are ignorant as to why Anjou and Maine were absent from the account of 1221.[108] No effort, moreover, has been made to adjust for inflation and other factors of appreciation between 1221 and 1238. Despite these problems, column 5 provides estimates grounded in the actual accounting procedures of the Capetian monarchy at the end of Philip's reign and shows that the king realized an "ordinary" income of 194,898 *livres parisis* in 1221.

Working with the accounts of 1202/03, we estimated a total "ordinary" income of 115,136 *livres parisis* on the eve of the invasion. Philip Augustus therefore showed a gain of 79,362 *livres parisis* in 1221, or an increase of 69 percent. The royal income thus did not even double after the conquest of Normandy and the Loire region. When we examine these conclusions more closely, we see that the *prévôts* and *baillis* reporting in *livres parisis* in 1221 brought in 114,630 *livres*, a slight increase of 8,165 *livres* over the *prévôts'* and *baillis'* income in 1202/03 (106,465 *livres parisis*). But this was offset by a comparable sum (8,671 *livres parisis*) realized on the Norman marches in 1202/03.[109] In final terms, therefore, Philip's net gains in 1221 resulted basically from Normandy and the Loire fiefs, which brought him an estimated 80,268 *livres parisis*, or an increase of 70 percent over 1202/03. Once again, these figures show that Philip's conquests did not double his former income.

A comparison of royal income based on two specific years presents disadvantages, however, which should be acknowledged. Because of circumstantial variations, no two years can be fully representative of longer periods of time. For unexplained reasons, both accounts may have omitted important sources of revenues for those years.[110] Except for the *prisée des sergents* in 1202/03 and the Norman *fouage* in 1221, both accounts apparently report only "ordinary" income. King John's enormous relief of 20,000 marks sterling (36,230 *livres parisis*) in 1200, for example, did not leave traces in 1202, and neither did comparable windfalls appear in 1221. Extraordinary feudal revenues most certainly increased the royal income on occasion, as, for example, when Ferrand paid a relief of 50,000 *livres parisis* in 1212 for Flanders, even greater than John's or than the 30,000 *livres* of relief in 1238.[111] The fact that the accounts of 1202/03 and 1221 present the *prisée* and the *fouage* separately and indicate no other windfalls such as appeared in 1227 and 1238 suggests that they were, indeed, accounts of "ordinary" income and are therefore comparable. If the increased income after the conquests is unexpectedly small to our eyes, this may result from the fact that the royal domain was already larger before 1204 than has been appreciated. Judged by *prévôts'* income, the acquisition of Vermandois, Artois, and Evreux had already increased royal revenues by 72 percent between 1179 and 1203, but a creditable basis for comparing the royal income of 1221 with that of 1179 is unfortunately not available. If the rate of increase after 1204 was smaller in relative terms than has been anticipated by modern historians, in absolute terms the increase of "ordinary" income by 80,000 *livres parisis* each year was an impressive sum and rendered Philip financially secure by the end of the reign.

Inquests and Inventories: The Mentality of Taking Stock

When a territory whose wealth and institutions were unknown to royal officials was annexed, the normal procedure for investigating the newly acquired rights and resources was to order a series of inquests. The sworn inquest employing a group of men from the vicinity to render a decision under oath served not only to resolve judicial disputes but also to find facts.[112] When he inherited Artois in 1191, for example, Philip Augustus took over Bapaume, through which passed much of the commerce between Flanders and the rest of the kingdom. Its famous tolls were worth at least 1,400 *livres* a year. Between 1196 and 1202 Philip commanded Barthélemy de Roye, Pierre de Béthisy, *prévôt* of Amiens, and Nevelon the Marshal, *bailli* of Artois, to assemble citizens from the leading towns of the region and to inquire which merchants had owed customs at Bapaume under the counts of Flanders.[113] When Philip acquired Normandy a few years later, he inherited well-established procedures for conducting inquests. The Anglo-Norman kings had undertaken a monumental inquest into the resources of newly conquered England in the Domesday survey of 1086, and a century later they employed similar procedures to determine the number of knight's fiefs in Normandy.[114] Immediately after subduing the duchy, Philip himself began to make use of the sworn inquest. One of his earliest tasks in August or September 1204 was to effect a strategic exchange with Berengaria, Richard's dowager queen. Berengaria handed over the castles of Falaise, Domfront, and Bonneville-sur-Touques in exchange for the city of Le Mans, exclusive of the bishopric and its baronage. To make the transaction palatable, Philip promised the queen that she would realize the same income at Le Mans as she had enjoyed from the three castles in 1191, the moment of Richard's departure on the crusade. Philip gathered groups of twelve to fourteen men from the three castles who declared under oath how much Berengaria had received at that time and what her obligations in *fief-rentes* and alms had been.[115] By means of inquests the king therefore informed himself on the extent and value of his newly acquired resources.

Simultaneously with the conquest of Normandy (1204–1205), a scribe in the Capetian chancery undertook to transcribe a register of documents and information useful to royal government into a book now called Register A. Among his materials were a dozen inquests, including the Bapaume and Norman investigations. In following years other scribes added another nine inquests to Register A, sufficient to encourage the scribe who initiated Register C in 1212 to include a special chapter under the heading *Inquisitiones facte*.[116] Other inquests were recorded in rapid succession on blank pages, and by the end of the reign the chapter on *Inquisitiones* in Register E (the third and last register, written in 1220) included at least ninety-nine inquests. From this collection, two major preoccupations emerge clearly, as is shown by Table 9.

TABLE 9. Inquests Collected in the Registers

	Percentage of Total Inquests (99)
GEOGRAPHIC DISTRIBUTION	
Artois, Vermandois, Valois	40%
Old domain south of Paris	18%
Old domain north of Paris	5%
Normandy	
Pre-1204 lands	19%
Post-1204 lands	12%
Loire fiefs	2%
Others	4%
SUBJECTS TREATED	
Forests	50%
Feudal affairs	15%
Justice	11%
Clergy and regalia	6%
Servile classes (*hôtes, tailles*)	6%
Domanial revenues and *gîte*	5%
Tolls	3%
Administrative districts	3%
Miscellaneous	1%

SOURCE: *Registres* I, nos. 1–97, 102, 114.

Although the initial incentive for compiling the registers was undoubtedly the conquests following 1204, overwhelming attention (82 percent of the inquests) was directed to lands acquired before that date. Only 14 percent of the inquests investigated the territories of the great post-1204 conquests. Even among the Norman lands themselves, more inquests (19 percent) treated the smaller gains before 1204 than the vast post-1204 lands. What is even more significant is that within the older royal domain, the greatest attention was paid to the northeastern provinces of Artois, Vermandois, and Valois, thus illustrating the predominant role of these lands during the formative decade of the 1190s. The surprising absence of Normandy and the Loire lands may, in part, be explained by the well-functioning Norman exchequer, which was undoubtedly well informed about the duchy. Similarly, the seneschal Guillaume des Roches may not have needed to investigate Anjou because of his familiarity with the region, but this does not explain the virtual absence of Touraine, where royal *baillis* were directly responsible to the central court. What is clear is that the teams of *baillis* operating in the northeastern lands were the most active in collecting information required for accom-modating these lands in the royal domain. The other striking characteris-tic of the collected inquests is that despite diversified interests in feudal matters, justice, domanial affairs, and the regalia, the royal *baillis* were preoccupied with forests (50 percent of the total).

The information gathered by the Anglo-Norman–Angevin inquests was eventually compiled in massive inventories resembling the Domesday Book and the survey of fiefs of 1172. From the beginning of Philip's reign, the Capetian court may also have had at its disposal similar, but more modest, inventories, or *états*, kept to check on the *prévôts'* income as the king toured the royal domain.[117] Most of these were probably lost at Fréteval in 1194, but the chancery clerks once again began inserting ac-counts and inventories, or *états*, into the royal registers after 1204. We have already noted how the *census* account and the *gîte* list kept track of domanial revenue, and the *fief-rente* and alms accounts recorded the king's obligations.[118] In addition, there were inventories of jewels, arma-ments, forests, Jews, and churches, occasionally updated by the chancery. The most important group was the feudal inventories, which, as we shall see, continued Anglo-Norman precedents and occupied as much as 14–20 percent of the pages of the registers.[119] We shall further see that the church lists encompassed the whole kingdom, whereas the feudal inven-tories were largely, although not exclusively, concerned with the post-1204 conquests. But the remaining inventories, focusing on domanial concerns, were largely directed towards the pre-1204 territory. Although prompted by the expansion of the great conquests, these inventories, like the inquests, applied the techniques of investigating and inventorying to the old domain and particularly to the northeastern provinces. One con-cern that best exemplifies this mentality is the royal forests.

Forests

The close attention devoted to forests is demonstrated by the numer-ous forest entries in the budget of 1221 and the preponderant number of forest inquests in the royal registers. The importance of wooded regions to the pre-industrial economy of Capetian France cannot, of course, be overstated. They supplied not only the major sources of energy—dead wood for heating and charcoal for the rudiments of industry—but live wood for construction, including stone building, which required exten-sive scaffolding. In addition, forests furnished wood for agricultural im-

as well as other silvan products (honey, wax), pasturage for ani-
fly pigs), and hunting preserves for the amusement of the
ruling classes. The primary forest materials were both consumed directly
by their possessors and sold for cash as markets were developed. Demographic pressure not only accelerated such exploitation, but also promoted cutting down forests to provide space and food for more people.
The rapid growth of population in the twelfth and thirteenth centuries
therefore threatened the forests and engendered an impulse to protect
and conserve wooded resources. Those lords who held forests developed
policies of placing their woods in "reserve" (*defensum*), a protected area,
so that they could manage them by achieving a balance between exploitation and conservation.[120]

The royal domain inherited by Philip Augustus contained numerous
forests, with heavy concentrations around Compiègne in the north,
Saint-Germain-en-Laye in the west, and Fontainebleau and Orléans to
the south.[121] By 1203 new acquisitions were made on the Norman borders at Breteuil and Evreux. After the conquests of 1204 Philip acquired
all the great ducal forests (Lyon, Roumare, and Rouvray near Rouen, for
example) as well as Retz in Valois upon the death of Countess Aliénor in
1213. No complete list of forest reserves was compiled for Philip's reign,
however. Even the forty-nine inquests from the royal registers omit major
forests (Fontainebleau and Roumare, for example). Of those investigated, however, three major concentrations, Orléans, Evreux, and Retz,
attracted sustained attention from royal officials. Since the first two were
acquired before 1204 and the last after that date, these well-documented
cases may illustrate the evolution of Philip's forest policy before and after
the conquest of Normandy.

The most extensive forests Philip inherited from his father were those
called les Loges (*de Legio*) on the right bank of the Loire surrounding
Orléans to the north and east.[122] Typical of forest inquests, the seven
concerning les Loges preserved in the royal registers declare forest
"customs"—that is, the usage (*usuarium*) permitted to lords, churches,
and other inhabitants of the region encircling the forest.[123] Rights to dead
wood for burning, to live wood for repairing houses, to pasturage for pigs,
and to gathering for charcoal burners are listed in minute detail. These
meticulous surveys identify and delimit the jurisdictions where each party
had enjoyed forest "customs" at least since the time of Louis VI. In one
particularly extensive inquest, findings were declared from oral and written evidence for hundreds of individuals and churches organized into four

principal *baillia*.[124] Another inquest investigated the rights of a certain Pierre *griarius* (supervisor of forests), a prominent knight from the Or-léanais region who frequently participated in the other inquests and be-longed to a succession of *griarii* who had supervised the forest of Orléans for the king since 1113. His chief function was, in fact, the protection and preservation of the royal forests.[125] Since the road leading north from Or-léans to Paris had encouraged heavy deforestation west of the city, Philip Augustus was determined to conserve what remained by investigating, identifying, and circumscribing these wooded areas.

Although extensive in coverage and minute in detail, these inquests ignore hunting rights and say little about commercial exploitation. Ex-cept for occasional clauses forbidding individuals to give away or sell dead wood, the customs are virtually silent about cash revenues the king may have realized.[126] In February 1202, Etienne de Bransles and Jean Minctoire, the two forest agents who accounted for les Loges, collected no more than an annual farm of 520 *livres*.[127] From all appearances, there-fore, the forests of Orléans did not produce significant income be-fore 1204.

The four inquests reporting on the forests of Evreux acquired in 1200 show few differences with those of Orléans.[128] With more emphasis upon live wood for construction (*merrenum*), they nonetheless detail the usual customs of dead wood, pasturage, and so forth, and mention virtually no exploitation for cash sales. Similarly in 1202/03 the accounts of the *prévôts* and *baillis* record no forest income for Evreux. Summarizing domanial in-come, the *census* account simply states: "All the revenues of the forest of Evreux and all the fines [*expleta*] of the same produce 61 *livres*"—again, an insignificant sum. Totalled up in 1202/03, the forests brought the king 7,432 *livres*, 10 percent of the *baillis*' income or 7 percent of the total normal income for that year.[129]

Though the Evreux inquests may resemble those of Orléans in the Ca-petian domain, they do not show the importance of the Norman forests to the Anglo-Norman and Angevin rulers before 1204.[130] Not only did the dukes share the normal demand for wood, but in a maritime province with possessions overseas, they also required lumber for constructing ships—as the famous Bayeux tapestry graphically illustrates. In 1171 Henry II ordered a comprehensive inquest into the Norman forests at the death of his grandfather, and at the same time he began investigating his feudal and other domanial resources.[131] In the duchy, as in England, the Anglo-Norman and Angevin kings took particular interest in assarts (encroachments on the forests), in their hunting prerogatives, in the resulting forest fines, and especially in exploiting the woods for cash. The first Norman *coutumier* (1199–1200) states formally that "wood cannot be sold from the marches without the consent of the duke or his justice."[132] The exchequer roll of 1198 shows that such sales (*venta*) produced a total forest revenue of 7,866 *livres tournois*, which constituted 8 percent of the revenue for that year.[133] The duchy's forests contributed only slightly more (8 percent) to the duke's income in 1198 than the Capetian forests to Philip's in 1202/03 (7 percent). Despite this low yield, the Angevin kings were nonetheless conscious of their importance. As John prepared to defend the duchy, the English royal forests contributed heavily to his finances. The royal forester Hugh de Neville, for example, having loaned the English king 3,350 marks against future forest revenues, transferred another 40,000 marks in 1203.[134] Just before losing the duchy, John was in the process of creating a chief forester (*principalis forestarum in Normannia*) to run parallel to the office in England.[135]

The disappearance of financial records makes it difficult to examine Norman forest administration after Philip's conquest. The only two inquests pertaining to post-1204 Norman forests merely recite the customs.[136] Yet fragmentary evidence suggests that the license to sell remained in force. When Philip gave Robert de Courtenay the castles of Conches and Nonancourt with their forests in 1205, he also conceded the *licenciam vendendi* at Robert's discretion.[137] Most forests were granted, like fiefs, "according to the use and customs of Normandy," which in the case of the abbot of Mortemer in 1209 implied that "all rights in the sale of the woods" (*omne ius . . . in venditionibus ipsius nemoris*) pertained to the king.[138] More important, an undated notice in Register C states that "when the king sells wood from the royal domain, no one can sell in the Cotentin forests of Huome or from Huome to Cherbourg or from Barneville-sur-Mer to Saint-Sauveur." Although citing no further examples, this notice nonetheless expresses the Norman principle that placed the license to sell wood under royal authority.[139]

Since only two inquests were collected on Norman forests acquired after the conquest, we are obliged to turn elsewhere to examine forest policy after 1204. Judging by the royal registers, the greatest attention was paid to Retz, annexed to the royal domain in 1213. The chancery clerks transcribed into Register C at least thirteen inquests concerning Retz, three of which formed part of a special dossier devoted to the Valois region compiled by a single scribe and inserted into the register.[140]

This dossier and the other inquests in Register C attempted to establish the customary usage of churches and inhabitants surrounding the forest reaching back to the time of the counts of Vermandois, Raoul, Philippe (also of Flanders), and Aliénor. Although most of the inquests were concerned with standard customs, the jurors do uncover suggestions that the Countess Aliénor regulated the sale of wood. For example, the Hôtel-Dieu of Crépy could initially sell its firewood, but was prohibited from doing so by the countess after the third year, and the prior of Saint-Waast of Ferté-Milon could sell his wood through permission (*licentiam*) from the countess. Alongside the protected reserve (*defensum* and *saltum*), there were the *vendas*, areas set aside for sale.[141] As heir to the countess, Philip Augustus himself began to exercise control over the sale of wood in the forest of Retz. One inquest placed in the dossier concludes by saying that "no one can sell, give, or assart without the license [*licencia*] of the king."[142] In 1215 the jurors declared that although nothing could be given, sold, or assarted throughout the whole forest of Retz, "the king could sell [*facere vendas suas*] in his forest whenever and as often as he wished."[143] Reporting these findings in a charter, the king commanded that they be observed by his foresters.[144] Unlike the inquests at Orléans and Evreux, acquired before 1204, Philip's investigations into Retz therefore explicitly dealt with the sale of wood. Although these rights were founded on precedents deriving from Countess Aliénor, interest in them was most likely stimulated by acquisition of the Norman forests, where the dukes had long established similar control. If the well-documented instance of Retz may be taken as typical of Philip's policy after 1204, the king organized the cash exploitation of his forest reserves by exercising the *licentia vendendi* throughout his domain.

The financial yield of the new forest policy can be perceived in the scattered fragments of surviving accounts. The entire forests of Normandy produced 6,486 *livres tournois* at All Saints' in 1221. Our first glimpse of Retz does not come until Purification 1227, when it yielded 790 *livres parisis*. At the same time Evreux produced only 200 *livres tournois*. Orléans was the most productive of all the forests, with a revenue of 1,175 *livres parisis*, indicating that the king was paying attention to its exploitation. At Purification 1227 the forests of the old domain produced at least 6,153 *livres parisis* and those of Normandy 1,069 *livres tournois*. (The small Norman returns resulted from the fact that the Purification term did not correspond to one of the regular sessions of the exchequer.)[145]

Although vitiated by their fragmentary state, seasonal bias, and differing bases, these totals nonetheless demonstrate a remarkable increase in Philip Augustus's forest revenues after 1204. At first glance, it is apparent that in one triannual term in 1221 the Norman forests were yielding 6,486 *livres tournois*, almost as much as for the whole year 1198 (7,866 *livres tournois*). Similarly, the old royal domain produced at least 6,153 *livres parisis* in one term of 1227, whereas in 1202/03 it netted 7,432 *livres parisis* for the whole year. Many of the figures for 1221 and 1227 are, moreover, divisible by three, suggesting that they may be extrapolated to arrive at the annual total.[146] If, for example, the Purification figure of 6,153 *livres parisis* were multiplied by a factor of 2.5, it would produce at least 15,000 *livres parisis*, double that obtained from the old royal domain in 1202/03. Again, if the Norman figures for All Saints' 1221 (6,486 *livres tournois*) and Purification 1227 (1,069 *livres tournois*) were added to an estimate for Ascension (6,400 *livres tournois*), they would be almost double the annual product in 1198.[147] If this reckoning is followed, and if *livres tournois* are converted to *parisis*, the royal forests produced 26,000 *livres* annually at the end of the reign—3.5 times the amount on the eve of the conquests. Even allowing for exaggeration in this kind of speculation, we may conclude that forest revenues increased from two to three times.[148] Though some of the increase was due to the new Norman and Loire territories, most of it resulted from more profitable exploitation in both the new and the old domain. The forest inquests assembled in the royal registers were not explicitly concerned with income, but they were nonetheless part of a royal policy to protect and exploit an increasingly important resource.

The conservative impulse behind the inquests was vital to efficient exploitation. To implement this policy a chancery clerk copied a list of twelve royal forests into Register A before 1212 under the rubric: "In a single year so much can be sold from the king's forests" (*Singulis annis potest tantum vendi de forestis domini regis*).[149] At a later date Etienne de Gallardon revised the list, marking corrections over the original figures and adding seven new names. It is apparent that since the king controlled the *licentia vendendi* in these forests, he could limit the cutting of wood to prevent deforestation. The totals of 8,430 *livres* for the original list and 14,250 *livres* for the revised version declared the maximum annual profit.[150] The initial list included the major royal forests (Fontainebleau, Orléans, and Saint-Germain-en-Laye, for example), but it was certainly not complete for the old royal domain, and though the revisions added some Norman forests (Bur and Rouvray near Rouen, for example), it was even less complete in covering the duchy.[151] The total of 14,250 *livres* can therefore only represent a selected list of royal forests. The maximum

prices are, moreover, difficult to square with revenues found
accounts.[152] Nonetheless, the existence of the list is in itself e..
Philip's government envisaged a policy of limiting deforestation as necessary for effective management.

In the decade following the great conquests, Philip Augustus fashioned the elements of Capetian forest policy for the thirteenth century.
Through scores of inquests, duly preserved in the registers, major royal
forests were minutely investigated in an effort to conserve and protect
their resources. Boundaries were outlined, thousands of users were identified, and a myriad "customs and usages" were defined and confirmed.
Inspired by Norman precedent, the sale of wood was controlled by a system of licensing (*licentia vendendi*) increasingly controlled by the king.
Under this new commercial exploitation the royal forests yielded from
two to three times more revenue than before 1204. Such success further
created the necessity of setting limits on the cutting of wood, thus giving birth to a policy of forest management that balanced conservation
against exploitation. In the second half of the century Philip's successors
Louis IX and Philip IV coordinated these elements into a coherent program. Under Louis IX the Norman system of licensing evolved into the
famous "*tiers et danger*," whereby the king received one-third, and eventually an additional tenth, of forest revenues. Under Philip IV the *gruerie*
of Orléans, under which the king shared up to one-half of forest income,
was fully organized. By mid-century the rubric *vende boscorum* became a
standard heading in the royal accounts, and forest revenues contributed a
significant proportion (10–25 percent) to total income.[153] These were
the final fruits of a policy that first emerged with the copying of inquests
into the royal registers.

Forest management was just one of the ways in which Normandy
exerted an influence on the development of Capetian government. The
acquisition of wealthy and extensive lands such as the duchy and the
Loire territories was, of course, bound to have repercussions throughout
the royal domain. Anjou was kept separate through the regime of seneschals inherited from Henry II, and characteristically of the level of
administration, her wealth cannot be calculated. Possibly it was not significant. But Normandy was both wealthy and efficiently governed. Incorporated directly into the royal domain, the duchy bequeathed certain
novelties to its Capetian conquerors. Ducal control over licenses to sell

wood enabled Philip Augustus to preserve and manage the forests for increased profits. The Norman judicial exchequer transmitted its habits of record keeping to the central royal court. Norman legal customs extended protections to women and disadvantaged classes through the jury of recognition. And Norman *baillis* became stationary and delimited in their jurisdictions, characteristics inherited by their namesakes throughout the royal domain.

No matter what weight historians may attach to these specific contributions, it is no less true that Normandy's most important influence was to stimulate and reinforce comparable institutions, which had already been framed by the 1190s. The acquisition of the duchy merely increased the efficiency of the machinery already assembled to supervise and exploit the Jews. The biannual sessions of the Norman financial exchequer were coordinated with the triannual schedule of the French bureau of accounts established since 1190. The *vicomtes* performed comparable tasks to the *prévôts*, and the itinerant justices to the Capetian *baillis*. The assizes of the duchy fitted well into the existing system of local assizes in the domain. The Norman perfecting of the inquest and the inventory stimulated the Capetians to make better use of these instruments. Finally, Normandy and Touraine added 80,000 *livres* each year to the ordinary revenues of the crown—though this was at best only an increase of 70 percent and not the doubling or tripling estimated by some modern historians. If the conquest of Normandy did not revolutionize the French state, it was nonetheless a rich prize and constituted a well-earned reward for the governmental reforms of the previous decade.

The King as Seigneur

Up to this point Philip Augustus has been considered primarily as a king (*rex*) and landholder who managed his domain through efficient central organs and local officials and who extended his influence beyond the domain through regalian churches and towns. At the same time, however, he was a lord or seigneur (*dominus*) over numerous vassals both in the royal domain and throughout the entire realm (*regnum*), vassals ranging from simple knights to great barons. The bonds uniting lord and vassal could be both personal, involving homage and oaths of fealty, and territorial, consisting of fiefs. These relations will be designated *feudal*, a term that is intentionally imprecise because it covers bonds that varied greatly according to region. Normandy, for example, possessed an established regime of fiefs that was unusually well defined and systematized, but feudal ties in Vermandois and Artois were comparatively undeveloped.[1]

Although the feudal bonds between the king and his vassals extended back to Carolingian times, their precise definitions were rarely recorded in charters and other written documents. Feudal obligations, to be sure, can be inferred from the actions of the king and his men as reported by the chroniclers, but it was not until the reign of Philip Augustus that the royal chancery generated and preserved sufficient charters to constitute a corpus of documentation officially defining the king's feudal rights over his vassals.[2] Philip was also the first among the French kings to have his

259

chancery inventory the knight's fiefs of the royal domain systematically in order to exploit them more fully. The impetus prompting these new inventories was the conquest of Normandy. When Philip inherited the duchy's well-established regime of fiefs, he had the feudal inventories of the Norman dukes copied into his new register, and these precedents inspired the formulation of feudal relations throughout the rest of the domain. Although Philip had begun to define his feudal rights from the beginning of his reign, the appearance of the royal registers in 1204 provides an appropriate occasion to view the Capetian as a feudal seigneur.

Because feudal institutions originated in periods when central government was disintegrating, they have often been interpreted as disruptive to royal power. But the rights exercised by lords over their vassals could also be used by kings to reinforce their positions, so that modern historians have frequently termed kingship in the High Middle Ages "feudal monarchy."[3] Seen in this positive light, the feudal nexus had at least four functions in royal government. In the first place, vassals performed administrative tasks by collecting domanial revenues and serving in the courts. Secondly, fiefs provided means of coercion both as enticements to loyalty and as restraints on disaffection through the threat of their removal, subject to the judgment of the lord's court. Thirdly, the obligations of reliefs, marriages, and wardships could be converted into financial assets. And, finally, fiefs furnished military service by providing contingents of armed knights for warfare and for garrisoning castles. Demanded from baronial vassals and from knights of the royal domain, these military obligations could also be commuted into financial resources. By Philip's time the Capetians had, for the most part, abandoned the first function, since *prévôts* no longer held their positions in fief and *baillis* were salaried. Great barons such as Philippe of Flanders and Thibaut of Blois, who disappeared from the court by the 1190s, were the last who may be considered to have served the king's court by feudal tenure. Only in the newly acquired Loire fiefs was the half-feudalized seneschal retained. But Philip Augustus did make use of the remaining functions of coercion, exploitation, and military service. By examining these functions we shall see how Philip's rights as seigneur were used to enhance royal government.

The Hierarchy of Fiefs

Underlying all efforts to formulate and coordinate a regime of fiefs was the concept of hierarchy. During the first century and half after the Capetians came to the throne, little sense of organization can be detected among the lords and vassals of northern France. Developing their ties without the guidance of a dominant authority, these feudatories established a vast maze of multiple and complex allegiances that implicated the king as well. The first to suggest a concept of hierarchical order appears to have been Suger, abbot of Saint-Denis and efficient counsellor to Louis VI and Louis VII.[4] Suger introduced two notions implicit in the formation of a hierarchy of fiefs. In the first place, he proposed a gradation of vassals that separated inferiors from superiors, with connecting bonds of homage. For example, the duke of Aquitaine was described as the lower vassal of Louis VI, but the superior lord of the count of Auvergne, thus establishing an embryonic hierarchy and chain of homages.[5] For such a hierarchy to exist, it must, in the second place, have an apex—that is, a person superior to all others and inferior to none. Suger assigned the king to this position by suggesting that he could do homage to no one. Louis VI, for example, was also count of the Vexin, which was normally held as the vassal of the abbey of Saint-Denis. When the king received the banner of the Vexin from the abbey's altar to lead the Vexin's knights against the threatening German invasion in 1124, Louis declared that he could not do homage to the abbey because he was king. Royal dignity, therefore, rendered Louis different from other vassals and placed him *ex officio* at the summit of the feudal hierarchy.[6]

This second notion was mentioned only briefly by Suger, but it was implemented by Philip Augustus whenever the occasion presented itself. When, for example, the king obtained the county of Amiens in 1185, his first major territorial acquisition, he discovered that its former possessor, the count of Flanders, was vassal of the bishop of Amiens for the county. "Since the king cannot and ought not to do homage to anyone," the royal charter declared, the bishop should remit the king's obligation to do homage in exchange for the king's remission of the *gîte* normally furnished by the bishops. Shortly thereafter, Philip made the same agreement with the bishop of Soissons for the castle of Pierrefonds, although the general principle was not enunciated.[7] A similar arrangement was drawn up with a layman in 1192, when Baudouin d'Aubigny excused Philip from doing homage for the castle of Beauquesne in exchange for an annual rent.[8] By 1213, when Philip Augustus finally acquired the remaining portions of Vermandois, the principle that "our predecessors the kings of France were wont to do homage to no one" was declared to be the usage and custom of the kingdom. At that time the charter of 1185 concerning Amiens, the first official declaration of the principle, was copied into the royal register on the reverse side of the page containing the general statement of 1213.⁹ Thereafter, the king's place at the apex of the feudal pyramid was recognized as the custom of the realm.

The chancery clerks also proceeded to explore more fully the implications of the hierarchic notion implicit in feudal homage. Two inventories were inserted into Register A and recopied into Register C that attempted to provide comprehensive lists of the nobility not merely of the royal domain but of the entire kingdom. The first, which may be called *Milites ferentes banerias*, lists bannerets (men who led knights into battle) by region (Normandy, Brittany, Perche, Anjou, and so on) and includes the names of some 566 men, chiefly from north of the Loire valley.¹⁰ The other, although more comprehensive in geographic scope (including southern regions as well), was organized entirely on hierarchic principles. It lists 215 men, divided into descending ranks of the feudal hierarchy: (1) *comites et duces*, (2) *barones*, (3) *castellani*, and (4) *vavassores*.¹¹ This hierarchic inventory was no more than a sample. Though the criteria are not made explicit, the clerks of the royal chancery were nonetheless attempting to introduce elementary hierarchic principles among the disordered feudatories of the French kingdom.

These four categories implied a gradation of dignity, but not necessarily a chain of vassalage from lower to higher. Bonds of vassalage could be established in a bewildering variety of possible combinations, introducing confusion into the feudal structure. The only firm principle involved the king, who could not be a vassal. To prevent interminable subdivisions of fiefs among heirs and further proliferation of ties of vassalage, northern lords such as the Norman dukes encouraged primogeniture, which for the most part allowed the eldest son to inherit his father's fief intact. Following Henry II's policy in Normandy and Anjou, his son Count Geoffrey attempted to introduce the principle into Brittany in 1185. Philip Augustus expressed his interest by having Geoffrey's assize copied into Register C shortly before 1213, when Brittany was confided to Pierre de Dreux.¹² Philip was not as concerned with the division of fiefs, however, as with the extension of vassalage. At Villeneuve-sur-Yonne, with the concurrence of the duke of Burgundy, the counts of Nevers, Boulogne, and Saint-Pol, the lord of Dampierre, and others, the king publicly declared a new custom governing the inheritance of fiefs throughout the kingdom. Beginning on 1 May 1209, whenever a fief was divided (and no matter how it was divided), the new heirs were henceforth to hold their portions as direct vassals of the original lord like their predecessor, and not through any intermediary lord. Apparently this was to eliminate the practice of *parage*, by which the fief was divided among male heirs but the younger brothers became vassals of the eldest, who alone did homage to the original lord.[13] This decree therefore attempted to introduce the process of "immediatization" into the feudal structure from which the king, as well as other lords, benefited. Tending to flatten the feudal pyramid by eliminating intervening vassals, this custom consciously sought to augment the number of direct vassals. In practice, however, the ordinance's effect was limited chiefly to the king's vassals in the Ile-de-France. As vassal to none, but lord over growing numbers of vassals, Philip Augustus thereby presided over a hierarchic structure that permitted him increased vassal contact with both magnates and knights.

Homage and Fealty

As seigneur Philip Augustus received from his vassals homage and fealty. By the former the vassal became the lord's *homme* (man), a term that implied self-surrender. By the latter, which immediately followed, the vassal swore his *foi* (faith) to the lord and specified that he would refrain from all harmful deeds.[14] Such acts established bonds that enabled the lord to coerce his vassals in many ways. These constraints will be examined in greater detail below, but in general the oath of fealty rendered any breach of faith on the part of the vassal a crime equivalent to perjury. Whether or not the Capetians received homage from all the major feudatories of the kingdom from the beginning, as some scholars have argued,[15] a number of barons were accustomed to perform this act before Philip's reign. The most impressive was Henry of Anjou, whose entire continental possessions were assembled by ties of vassalage. As early as 1151, and thereafter, Henry and his sons regularly did homage to the French kings for Normandy, Aquitaine, and Anjou.[16] Because homage was performed by the symbolic acts of kneeling, placing one's hands within the lord's hands, and a ceremonial kiss performed publicly before witnesses, the proceedings were usually conducted orally, as when Richard defied his father in 1188 and knelt before Philip Augustus at Bonmoulins to do direct homage for his lands.[17] Only seldom were the obligations reduced to writing before Philip's reign.[18]

Although Philip, like his predecessors, received the symbolic acts of homage personally, he also began to have them recorded in writing from

...ct of his reign. Not only were the homages of the powerful Angevins transcribed in charters (for example, that with Henry II in 1180, and the abortive treaty with Richard at Messina in 1191), but lesser vassals, such as Renaud de Dammartin in 1192, recorded their homage in written instruments.[19] Apart from the Angevins, the first major vassal to be so recorded was Baudouin IX, count of Flanders and Hainaut, when he succeeded his father in June 1196.[20] Charters have survived for the homages thereafter of most of the major feudatories throughout the reign.[21] The survival of this written evidence depended, of course, on efforts to preserve the documents. The charter of Philip and Henry II of 1180 was copied by a contemporary English chronicler. The treaty of Messina survived in the English royal archives. The homage of Renaud of Dammartin of 1192 was recorded as a chirograph (a copy for each party, separated by tearing). The royal half was lost, but Renaud's reentered the royal archives after Boulogne reverted to the royal family. The establishment of the royal archives in 1194 (in which the first item to be retained was Count John's acknowledgment of vassalage) and the initiation of the registers in 1204 created means of preserving records of homage. Even records of temporary allegiances, such as those of the count of Angoulême and the *vicomte* of Limoges in 1199, were carefully collected.[22] Philip Augustus's chancery was, therefore, responsible for instituting a general policy of keeping track of the great vassals' homage and fealty.

The King's Court

If disputes arose between lord and vassal over the terms of homage, the vassal agreed to submit to the adjudication of the lord's court. This judicial function was made explicit as early as 1126, when the duke of Aquitaine, in the case already considered, promised to produce his vassal, the count of Auvergne, in the court of their overlord, King Louis VI, when summoned to answer for misdeeds.[23] Philip Augustus did not neglect to spell out his jurisdiction in the written formulations of homage. The treaty of Messina with Richard noted that the count of Toulouse was subject to the royal court. In the same year Renaud de Boulogne's charter of homage specified that if the duke of Louvain contested the arrangements, the dispute was to be adjudicated in the king's court. Baudouin of Flanders's charter of 1196 furnished the classic formula: the count promised that "he would never fail in providing service to the king as long as his lord wished to offer him justice in his court and to allow him to be judged in the royal court by those who ought to judge him."[24] Thereafter the inclusion of a clause pertaining to the jurisdiction of the royal court became routine for all major as well as minor vassals.[25]

Although the royal court's competency was long established and regularly asserted in Philip's time, little evidence survives of its actual enforcement of jurisdiction over the great vassals before the second half of the reign. Surviving cases involving lay barons pleading at the king's court invariably included a churchman as adversary.[26] The prelate's presence not only accounts for the survival of the charter before the appearance of royal archives and registers, but also obscures the grounds of the king's jurisdiction. Was it feudal lordship or regalian right over churches? Even if the French king claimed competency as seigneur, it was still doubtful whether he could enforce a decision of his court over a powerful vassal in a suit of consequence.

The transformation of theoretical jurisdiction into effective suzerainty over great vassals came in the celebrated case of 1202. Philip summoned John before his court as duke of Aquitaine, obtained a condemnation, and executed the sentence by seizing all of John's lands north of the Loire.[27] The jurisdiction of the royal court had been well prepared. In the first document preserved in the royal archives (1194), John as count had acknowledged his obligation to do service and to submit to Philip's court for the fiefs for which John's ancestors had performed such service. As king in 1200, John reaffirmed this position and received his French fiefs from Philip under the same terms as his brother and father.[28] Since no records of the case survive from the court, we are dependent on the chroniclers' reports for the specific charges against John. Ralph of Coggeshall, who gives the fullest account, cites neglect of service and disobedience of summons. Writing at the end of the reign, Guillaume le Breton develops the well-known charges of the Lusignans against John and emphasizes that Philip received an appeal from the Lusignans as supreme lord over John as vassal.[29] The sentence of confiscation was noted not only by Ralph of Coggeshall, but also by Arthur, whose homage Philip accepted in place of John's. Three months later Arthur referred to the day on which John's fealty was declared void (*diffiduciavit*) for breaches (*interceptiones*) committed by a vassal against his lord.[30] In terms of scope and execution, the judgment of 1202 was a significant landmark in royal jurisdiction. By vindicating authority over a great vassal, it extended the jurisdiction of the king's court beyond the royal domain. The underlying justification of this extension was the bonds between lord and vassal. That Philip was able to enforce a decision against the greatest of his vassals by arms rendered his court's jurisdiction supreme in fact as well as in theory.

The case of Renaud, count of Boulogne, the most unstable of all Philip's vassals, reinforced the transformation. When Renaud's homage for Boulogne was first received in 1191, it was carefully recorded in a chirograph charter. Although the royal copy was lost, subsequent renewals of 1196 were preserved in the archives.[31] These records, the furnishing of pledges, and the imposition of ecclesiastical sanctions did not hinder Renaud from joining forces against Philip with King Richard and the count of Flanders in 1197, and then regaining the king's favor in 1201 without penalty. When Renaud attempted to repeat this behavior a decade later, however, he encountered a new situation. Philip summoned the count before his court in 1211 and demanded the castle of Mortain as security for fealty. When Renaud neglected to comply immediately, he was judged in default, just as John had been a decade earlier. Philip was, moreover, now strong enough to take the castle from Renaud and to dispossess the count of his lands.[32] That the king was able once again to enforce his court's sentence against a powerful and favored vassal reaffirmed the supreme jurisdiction of his court over the great vassals, and thereby beyond the royal domain.

Pledges

Because of the lord's difficulties in summoning vassals to answer charges in his court, it is not surprising that other means were sought to reinforce the obligations of vassalage. A long-established technique was to require the vassal to produce pledges who guaranteed the vassal's oath by promising to oppose him if he broke the agreement. The pledge's responsibility could be further assured by demanding a stated sum of money if the vassal defaulted on his obligations. Most often the pledges were put forward by the vassal, but they could also be chosen by the lord.[33] The practice of requiring pledges had already been firmly established by the Capetians before Philip Augustus's reign. In Suger's account, when the duke of Aquitaine promised to produce the count of Auvergne in Louis VI's court in 1126, he also furnished "numerous and sufficient pledges."[34]

Philip Augustus employed pledges at all levels, but their presence is most evident in dealings with his highest vassals. We have already seen, for example, how the young king manipulated his father-in-law, Baudouin, count of Hainaut, by numbering him among his pledges without Baudouin's consent in a truce with the count of Flanders in 1184. Count Baudouin's well-known homage to the king of 1196 was secured by forty vassals chosen by the king from Flanders and Hainaut. Richard's concessions to Philip in the peace of Gaillon of the same year were guaranteed by the archbishop of Rouen, who pledged, in addition, 200 marks of silver. In 1203 Simon, lord of Beausart, promised to deliver his fortress at the king's request, a promise for which he furnished three pledges, each obligated for one hundred *livres*. These early examples, which could be multiplied by the hundreds, illustrate the importance of the obligations that the pledges secured. Their use among lesser men is obscured by lack of documentation; in 1203, however, Philip banned three inhabitants of Laon from the realm because they were unable to produce the pledges required by a judgment in the royal court.[35]

Philip Augustus's contribution to this traditional practice was to introduce better record keeping, thereby facilitating more systematic procedures. Soon after the archives were established, the chancery began to collect individual charters of those acting as pledges. The first examples resulted from the treaty of Gaillon in January 1196. Charters from three men who pledged 1,300 marks that Robert, earl of Leicester, would not make private war against Philip were duly preserved.[36]

Since it became increasingly difficult to locate hundreds of such charters in an expanding archives, the chancery began making lists in the royal registers. The first was a list of nine men who pledged 1,000 marks to insure the fidelity of Guillaume du Hommet, constable of Normandy, soon after 1204. Between that date and 1220, over eighty lists were copied into Registers A and C. Most were concerned with the nobility of the Loire fiefs after 1209 and the Flemish lords captured in the campaigns of 1214. These notations were made wherever space was available in the registers, but the scribes occasionally grouped the material according to time and place.[37]

Since these improved records enabled the central government to account for individual pledges and their obligations, they undoubtedly contributed to the creation of networks among pledges. Certain prominent and trusted feudatories, such as Robert, count of Dreux, the counts of Saint-Pol, and the butlers of Senlis, were frequently called upon to guarantee the engagements of vassals throughout the realm.[38] In certain regions lesser men also served on multiple occasions alongside the great lords. In securing the vassals of the Loire valley, magnates such as the seneschal Guillaume des Roches and Juhel de Mayenne were active as pledges, but the names of local lords such as Guy Sénébaud from the Touraine and Robert de Bommiers from the Berry appear even more frequently on the lists. The names of at least nine men from the region appear on three or more lists.[39] Occasionally, they reciprocated as pledges for each other.[40] Another group of lords were frequently called upon to guarantee engagements in the Flemish region, especially after 1214, following the reestablishment of royal control. They included not only the influential castellans of Saint-Omer and Lens but the constable of Flanders and lesser men such as Renaud de Croisilles, Hellin de Waverin, and Michel de Harnes. The last-named served for at least nine different lords between 1212 and 1217.[41] Obviously, it was to the central court's advantage to keep a list of feudatories who could serve as pledges. In all likelihood the inventory of bannerets arranged geographically (the so-called *Milites ferentes banerias*) answered that need since the overwhelming majority of pledges after 1204 appear on that list.[42] Feudal inventories undoubtedly facilitated the creation of such networks among the nobility.

Evidence has not yet come to light as to how, and with what success, the royal government collected the sums pledged when a vassal defaulted. Yet it may be presumed that the procedures worked, or at least were considered sufficiently persuasive, because the administration of pledges was perfected by the *baillis* during the second half of the reign. As early as 1203, Nevelon the Marshal, *bailli* of Arras, received gages for 100 marks pledged by Gautier d'Avesnes for the fidelity of Ivain de Brac, that he would not aid the English king.[43] Precisely how Nevelon operated is revealed after Bouvines, when the *bailli* was instructed to secure pledges for Flemish nobility about to be released from captivity. Alard de Bourghelles was taken at Lille in 1213 and held at Compiègne. In April 1217 Philip Augustus wrote Nevelon instructing him to find pledges for 300 marks of silver on behalf of Alard, to obtain sufficient witnesses to the transaction, and to report back in writing. The *bailli* replied to the king with five names (including that of Michel de Harnes) whose pledges totalled 300 marks, and with eight others who witnessed the affair. Nevelon's reply was preserved in the royal archives, along with the five charters of the pledges, and the names of the guarantors were listed in Register C.[44] Enough evidence has survived to show that Nevelon's procedures became standardized and were followed by Gilles de Versailles, Renaud de Béthisy and other *baillis*.[45]

Marriage

Another traditional device for reinforcing feudal ties was marriage. Royal daughters and younger sons were particularly valuable as marriage partners to insure the great barons' fidelity. After marrying Adèle de Champagne in 1160, for example, Louis VII further strengthened his bonds with the Troyes-Blois family by giving the two daughters Eleanor of Aquitaine had borne him, Marie (b. 1145) and Alix (b. 1150), as wives to the counts of Troyes and Blois respectively. His deployment of the two daughters borne by Constance of Castile to secure the co-operation of the house of Anjou was less successful. The marriage of Marguerite (b. 1158) to the young King Henry of England was terminated by his untimely death in 1183, and she was sent off in 1186 to be the bride of King Bela of Hungary. Alix (b. 1160) was affianced to Count Richard, but he stubbornly refused to marry her for political and personal reasons, among them the fact that his father had abused her.[46] After releasing Richard from this engagement in 1191, Philip Augustus finally wed his long-suffering sister to the count of Ponthieu in 1195–1196.[47]

In customary fashion Philip ratified the treaty with King John at Le Goulet in 1200 by marrying his only son and heir, Prince Louis (b. 1187), to John's niece, Blanche de Castile (b. 1188).[48] Philip's marital adventures with Agnès de Méran, however, furnished him with two more children with whom to play the game. After Innocent III legitimized Agnès's children in November 1201, the five-year-old Marie (b. after 1197) was affianced to young Arthur of Brittany in April 1202, barely three months before he disappeared into John's prison.[49] When Arthur was presumed dead, the girl was offered in 1206 to Philippe, marquis of Namur and regent for the orphaned heiresses of Flanders, in order to augment the king's influence in the Flemish succession.[50] When the marquis died in October 1212, after one year of marriage, Philip may have considered giving his daughter to the king of Aragon, but in April 1213 he married her to Henri, duke of Brabant, his former ally in imperial politics. By this final wedding the king strengthened his position in the Low Countries and enlisted a baron for the projected invasion of England.[51] Marie's younger brother Philip (b. after January 1201) not only strengthened the royal lineage, but was also assigned a role in the Flemish region. Scarcely a year old, the prince was affianced in 1201 to the only daughter of Renaud, count of Boulogne. When the vacillating count showed signs of rebelling for a second time, the king renewed the marriage agreement in 1209 and had the wedding performed the following year, although his son was barely nine years of age. Renaud did defect in 1211, but Philip Augustus's son was the legitimate heir to Boulogne.[52] The king's grandson Philip (b. September 1209), the eldest son of Prince Louis, was assigned a similar role with respect to another wavering baron. After Hervé, count of Nevers, contemplated marrying his only daughter to a son of King John's, Philip Augustus offered his grandson Philip (or in the case of his death, a second grandson, Louis [b. 1214]) to the heiress of Nevers, Auxerre, and Tonnerre in 1215. The young Philip died three or four years later, and the agreement was allowed to lapse.[53] Although the king took advantage of his children and grandsons, his persistent refusal to treat Ingeborg as wife nonetheless limited the scope of his marital politics. Two legitimate children[54] and one grandson besides the royal heir offered limited opportunities by comparison to the five daughters of his father and the dozen children of his son.

Such marriages not only enabled the king to secure the fidelity of great barons, they also offered the monarch a means of guiding the family destinies of his major vassals. Throughout France it was customary for lords to assert the right to approve their vassals' marriages. It is doubtful that this right was actually exercised over many male vassals, but it was more effectively claimed over heiresses.[55] It is difficult to determine the Capetians' success in regulating marriages in major fiefdoms before Philip Augustus, but it cannot be ignored that Louis VII was unable to prevent his repudiated wife Eleanor, duchess of Aquitaine, from marrying his archrival, Henry of Anjou, in 1152.

From the outset, however, Philip Augustus exercised approval over the marriages of heiresses to great fiefdoms. The counties of Nevers and Auxerre offered him the earliest and most repeated opportunities. After taking custody in 1181, Philip gave the heiress Agnès in marriage to his cousin Pierre de Courtenay in 1184.[56] When Pierre himself was discomfited by an unruly vassal in 1199, the king profited from the situation to give Pierre's sole heiress, Mathilde, in marriage to the vassal, Hervé de Donzy, specifying that Mathilde could not marry anyone else without royal permission.[57] When Hervé, as count of Nevers and Auxerre, was in turn survived by a sole heiress, Agnès, the king proposed his grandson in

1215, and even if the arrangement was not executed, the count promised not to marry her off without royal consent. After the prince's death, the count repeated the promise in 1219 and specifically excluded four barons, including the son of King John.[58] (By 1221 Agnès was married to Guy de Châtillon, the eldest son of the count of Saint-Pol.)[59] In practice as well as in theory, therefore, the heiresses to Nevers and Auxerre were married with royal approval.

The great baronies of Champagne, Flanders, Brittany, and Burgundy also submitted to royal jurisdiction over the marriages of heiresses. The unanticipated death of the count of Champagne in 1201, leaving a widow, an infant daughter, and an unborn male heir whose rights to the succession were contested, presented the king with another opportunity. Dependent upon royal support, the countess Blanche de Navarre agreed to submit not only her own remarriage to royal approval, but also the eventual marriage of her daughter.[60] The capture and eventual death of Baudouin, count of Flanders and Hainaut, in 1206, leaving two young daughters, placed Flanders in a similar position. Once again, Philip imposed on the Flemish regent the condition that the girls not be married without royal consent. The king took the girls into custody in 1208 and married Jeanne, the heiress, to Ferrand of Portugal in 1212.[61] Philip Augustus was present at an agreement in 1209 that affianced Alix, heiress of Brittany, to Henri of Tréguier. Although this union did not take place, the king took custody of the girl and gave her to his cousin Pierre de Dreux in 1212.[62] The Capetian dukes of Burgundy, who were normally docile throughout the reign, likewise submitted to the king's explicit jurisdiction. When the young Hugues IV became duke in 1218, his mother and regent, Alix de Vergy, promised not to remarry without royal permission.[63] By this time royal control of the marriage of heiresses was normally assumed over all major vassals.

The king's jurisdiction also provided him with opportunities to achieve political objectives by arranging marriage alliances among barons. Early in his reign (1181) the young king was not sufficiently strong to prevent a series of marriages between the houses of Troyes and Hainaut.[64] By 1193, however, Philip employed the family of Nevers to attach the house of Flanders, followed by that of Namurs (1196), and finally that of Saint-Pol (1221).[65] Similarly, the king strengthened his position in the Flemish region by arranging a marriage between the brother of Renaud, count of Boulogne, and the daughter of the count of Ponthieu in 1208, when Renaud was still loyal. According to the anonymous chronicler of the region, the boldness of this marriage provoked wonderment among contemporaries.[66] As has been amply seen, too, the king used his marriage rights to reward his *familiares*.[67]

Fief-Rentes

A fief was traditionally land given by a lord to a vassal in exchange for services and obligations. With the emergence of a currency economy at the turn of the eleventh and twelfth centuries, however, a fief could also be created out of money. Designated a *fief-rente* by scholars, such a fief usually consisted of annual or semi-annual payments in return for homage, fealty, and service.[68] Although normally paid in money from the central treasury, local revenues, or commercial tolls, it could also be paid in kind. Although it did not consist of land per se, its revenues could nonetheless be derived from land.[69] Although resembling wages, it was usually distinct from wages and did not exclude additional remuneration. In the words of its most recent historian, its chief function was "to set up a feudal obligation upon the part of the vassal" that "enabled the lord to enter into feudal relations with men of all ranks and stations."[70] Like a fief in land, the *fief-rente* created obligations that provided the lord with coercive measures against vassals. To the vassal, the *fief-rente* offered the inducement of extra remuneration, sometimes over and beyond landed fiefs. To the lord, it afforded multiple advantages. A seigneur possessing monied resources could quickly offer *fief-rentes* without having to find specific lands. More important, the *fief-rente* could easily be discontinued without having to dispossess the vassal of his lands. Flexible and responsive to the lord's immediate needs, it permitted the creation of a *réseaux* (or network) of vassals through direct feudal ties, without passing through subinfeudations.[71] By the turn of the twelfth and thirteenth centuries the *fief-rente* had become a prominent instrument in the competition between Angevins and Capetians.

The Anglo-Normans seem to have been the first to use *fief-rentes* in northwestern Europe. Certainly, from the eleventh through the thirteenth centuries, the English kings offered the most lucrative inducements. But the institution was most widespread and deeply rooted in the intensely commercial environment of the Low Countries, where numerous instances appear from the beginning of the twelfth century on.[72] The first unmistakable Capetian use occurred in 1155, when Louis VII gave his brother Robert, count of Dreux, a revenue of 50 *livres* from Poissy.[73]

Philip Augustus likewise made occasional grants assigned to *prévôtés*. By 1202/03 they numbered more than a score.[74] The laconic reporting of the fiscal accounts makes it difficult, however, to distinguish *fief-rentes* from wages and other forms of remuneration. Such grants had apparently increased sufficiently to encourage the compilation of an inventory. Sometime after 1204, a chancery clerk copied into Register A a list of 93 *fief-rentes*, amounting to 3,173 *livres* annually. Subsequent scribes working on Registers A and C increased the number to 126, paying out 5,187 *livres*.[75] The expansion of Philip Augustus's activities thus once again encouraged the chancery to take stock of an important instrument of royal policy. Though some recipients were lesser figures such as chamberlains, royal sergeants, and a group of Genoese citizens, the great majority were knights and barons.[76] From the pages of these registers the intense competition between the Capetians and the Angevins for the loyalty of their feudatories can be clearly perceived.

Benefiting from well-established finances and vast continental holdings, the kings of England led the way.[77] Although they scattered *fief-rentes* throughout their lands, the earliest and most ardent receivers of English money were to be found in the Low Countries. Perhaps as early as 1066, but certainly by 1103, the Flemish counts regularly accepted money fiefs from the English kings. Richard reaffirmed this policy in 1194, one day after his release from prison, by bestowing *fief-rentes* on ten princes in Germany and the Low Countries. John merely continued and intensified his brother's policy in this. A study of his reign has uncovered almost three hundred *fief-rentes*, of which 30 percent were used to defend Normandy prior to 1205, with 40 percent granted in Flanders during the intensive buildup between 1212 and 1214 preparatory to Bouvines.[78] Again, following long-established practices, a large number of these grants were concentrated in the Flemish region, where John sought support prior to Bouvines. Even the French king's immediate entourage was not immune to English money. At the signing of the peace of Le Goulet in May 1200, for example, John bestowed money fiefs on the royal cousin Robert de Dreux and on Barthélemy de Roye, both of whom served as pledges for Philip Augustus.[79]

The English employment of *fief-rentes* evoked a response from Philip Augustus. According to the terms of the treaty of Gaillon in 1196, the important Norman lord Richard de Vernon ceded to the French king his fiefs at Vernon, for which he was compensated by other lands. Complementing this exchange Philip also added a *fief-rente* to be paid from the *prévôté* of Pontoise.[80] After the fall of Normandy, Philip increased John's *fief-rente* to the counts of Dreux to 500 *livres*.[81] Register A reveals the extent of the Capetian response between 1204 and 1212. Not only did it include the counts of Dreux and Auxerre and the butlers of Senlis, who were faithful supporters, but also distinct groups for whose loyalty Philip competed. Along the Norman borders, for example, the *prévôtés* disbursed *fief-rentes* to important Norman lords. Later another group from the Loire valley was appended to the original list.[82]

To meet the Angevin challenge Philip concentrated his *fief-rentes* in Flanders. As early as 1185, the Capetian is reported to have offered one to Jacques d'Avesnes, an important Flemish baron and counsellor to the count, for using his influence on Philip's behalf to negotiate the treaty of Boves.[83] After 1204 seven *prévôtés* in Vermandois and Artois on the original inventory paid out 1,219 *livres* annually, or 38 percent of total expenditures, to Flemish feudatories. The *prévôté* of Roye-Montdidier alone was responsible for 558 *livres*, and that of Bapaume for 231 *livres*.[84] In 1206 Barthélemy de Roye was sent to Courtrai to negotiate with Philippe de Namur over the future of Flanders after Count Baudouin's death. Among his tasks was to secure the fealties of the barons and knights of Flanders and Hainaut.[85] It cannot be determined whether Barthélemy began distributing *fief-rentes* at that time, but certainly before 1212, Etienne de Gallardon added twenty-four names to Register A. At least fifteen can be identified as Flemish lords to whom the king obligated himself for an additional annual expenditure of 1,160 *livres*. By 1212, therefore, almost half (49 percent) of Philip's *fief-rentes* were directed towards the Low Countries.[86] The chancery inventories show that the Flemish region was as receptive to French inducements as to Angevin.

Philip's Flemish orientation can be demonstrated not only quantitatively but also qualitatively with respect to those whom he favored. When Count Baudouin left on the crusade in 1202, the actual administration of Hainaut was confided to his uncle Guillaume de Thy-le-Château (known as Guillaume the Uncle), and the governance of Flanders to another uncle, Gérard d'Alsace, assisted by two *baillis*, Gilbert I de Bourghelles and Guillaume, castellan of Saint-Omer. Of these key figures, Guillaume the Uncle was already enjoying a *fief-rente* from Philip Augustus in 1203, and Gilbert de Bourghelles and Guillaume V of Saint-Omer were included on the final list before 1212.[87] Like the royal court, the Flemish court also contained four traditional lay household offices, which by the early twelfth century had come into the hereditary possession of four leading families. By 1212 members of three of these families were holding *fief-rentes* from the French king: Sibyl, wife of Robert I de Wavrin, seneschal; Michel III de Harnes, uncle of Michel de Boelare, constable; and Raze V de Gavere, the butler of Flanders.[88] In addition, Philip bestowed money fiefs on neighboring barons, such as the duke of Brabant and the count of Saint-Pol, and on stalwart supporters of the Flemish count, such as Arnaud IV d'Oudenaarde, Gautier III de Voomezele, Gautier I de Zottegem, and Baudouin III de Comines, as well as on lesser figures such as Osto de Arbre.[89] Since Guillaume the Uncle and the lords of Saint-Omer, Gavere, Oudenaarde, Zottegem, and Comines had already received gifts from King John, it is clear that Philip Augustus was competing for the support of the most influential nobility of Flanders.[90]

After Count Baudouin's disappearance, Philip Augustus assigned the execution of his Flemish policy to Philippe, marquis of Namur, to whom the king gave his daughter Marie in marriage. As leader of the royal party, the marquis attracted those favorably inclined, and his entourage therefore reflected the growing attraction of the king's *fief-rentes*. When the marquis travelled to Paris in 1206 to negotiate the initial marriage agreement for Marie, he was accompanied by six noblemen, only one of whom, Guillaume the Uncle, was the recipient of a French *fief-rente*, though three of the others (the castellans of Bruges and Ghent and the *avoué* of Béthune) were traditional supporters of the king.[91] In 1210, however, when Philippe de Namur established a dowry for Princess Marie at Valenciennes, the seventeen lords present included not only the castellans of Bruges and Ghent, but also six who enjoyed royal *fief-rentes*.[92]

Unable to ignore the Capetian challenge, King John responded with counterproposals. In May 1212 he wrote to six Flemish nobles, including three who were already receiving French money (Arnaud IV d'Oudenaarde, Raze V de Gavere, and Gautier I de Zottegem) and promised to restore their *fief-rentes* in return for service. About the same time he was in correspondence with the duke of Brabant.[93] In June he commissioned his chief agent, Renaud, count of Boulogne, along with Hugues de Boves, to return to Flanders and treat with the nobility individually as to the amount of their *rentes*. Among the twenty-four mentioned by name in letters patent were eight who were in Philip's pay.[94] For his services, Renaud himself received a *fief-rente* of 1,000 *livres*.[95] The full results of these negotiations are not entirely clear, but by July and September 1212 at least three were being paid.[96] Among the lords who sided with Count Ferrand in 1213, the chroniclers note at least five who were formerly paid by the French king, of whom three accompanied Ferrand to England early in 1214.[97]

Bidding became spirited in 1212. In June, for example, Philip Augustus renewed Michel III de Harnes's *fief-rente*, formerly held by his father. In August John dispatched messengers to Michel and his companions, and in September offered him a gift through Hugues de Boves.[98] In the end, however, it became apparent that the French had lost out in the competition. While the inventory of *fief-rentes* in Register A was still in service, the names of Osto de Arbre and Hubert de Carency were crossed out, indicating that Philip knew they were receiving favors from John.[99] During the year 1212 a scribe recopied the inventory into Register C, but not long after, someone began deleting names. Of the seventeen names comprising the core to whom Philip Augustus had offered *fief-rentes*, all but Michel de Harnes were eliminated.[100] Loyalty to Count Ferrand and the lavishness of John's purse nullified Philip Augustus's efforts to form a French party held together by *fief-rentes* among the Flemish nobility.

The French procedures for disbursing money fiefs are not entirely clear. The original list in Register A was grouped according to *prévôtés*, presumably reflecting where the recipients obtained their payments. In the Vermandois and Artisan *prévôtés*, however, about a dozen were designated *in bursa*, but that term does not indicate a central treasury because one of them, Michel de Harnes, received his money directly from Péronne.[101] The duke of Brabant was paid at Paris, but the example is isolated and exceptional.[102] Although the normal procedures remain uncertain, the scope of Philip's policy is clear. He eventually lost out in the bidding, but he had not wagered much. An annual commitment of less than 5,000 *livres* in 1212 did not strain the royal finances, which realized at least 200,000 *livres* in ordinary revenues.[103] Philip's two largest grants, those to the count of Dreux (500 *livres tournois* = 400 *livres parisis*) and the duke of Brabant (200 marks = 420 *livres parisis*), did not compare with John's 1,000 pounds sterling (3,200 *livres parisis*) to the count of Boulogne. Thirty *livres* to the influential Guillaume the Uncle was a normal Capetian payment. Even after the competition heated up, the castellan of Saint-Omer received no more than 100 *livres* (John offered him 60 marks sterling = 128 *livres parisis* in 1212), and the leading Flemings, Arnaud d'Oudenaarde, Raze de Gavere, and Gautier de Zottegem, obtained no more than 80 *livres*. Philip Augustus was too calculating a king to be indifferent to invidious comparisons and too rich after 1204 to be excused by impoverishment. Though he was evidently willing to compete with John in principle, he did not think it necessary to match John's sums. Whatever his reasons, he could not have been surprised over the defections.

Relief and Wardship

Philip's position as feudal suzerain provided him not only with means of coercing his subjects but also with sources of income that could be profitably exploited. Prominent among the latter were the rights of relief and wardship. Relief was the lord's traditional right to receive compensation either in land or in money when a vassal's fief was inherited by his heir, but only those of the great vassals are reported by chroniclers or recorded in charters that have survived. Numerous occasions on which the king collected reliefs have already been noted, and this is an appropriate point to draw conclusions.

At the outset Philip seems to have preferred reliefs in land. From the counts of Nevers the king received Montargis in 1184 and Gien in 1199; from the count of Flanders and the countess of Vermandois, he obtained Amiens, Roye, and Montdidier in 1185 and Péronne in 1191; and from the count of Boulogne, Lens in 1191.[104] Although Philip showed a preference for money in succeeding decades, he continued to accept landed reliefs, such as Nogent l'Erembert from the countess of Blois and Chartres in 1219 and Pont-Sainte-Maxence from Guy de Saint-Pol, another aspirant to Nevers, in 1221.[105]

By the 1190s the financial burden of the military campaigns undoubtedly induced Philip to be more receptive to reliefs in money. His gains have been recapitulated in Table 10.[106] Since two figures are reported by a chronicler for Richard in 1189, they are difficult to interpret. According to Roger Howden, Richard promised Philip 4,000 marks sterling "for his expenses," in addition to 20,000 marks that Henry had promised. Whether these sums referred to reliefs or to a previous agreement over the crusade cannot be determined. Gislebert de Mons's mention of Baudouin of Flanders in 1192, however, indisputably refers to a relief, which the chronicler thought was equivalent to a year's income. Thereafter, details of reliefs are furnished by surviving charters. The succession to great fiefs provided the king with a series of magnificent reliefs after 1200. The reliefs for Troyes in 1198 and 1201 are unrecorded, but the greatest prize was Flanders, which reached 50,000 *livres* in the bidding between Enguerran de Coucy and Ferrand of Portugal.[107] Reliefs of lesser

TABLE 10. Reliefs Collected in Money from Major Barons

	Sum	Equivalent in *livres parisis*
Richard (1189)	4,000 marks sterling	7,246
	20,000 marks sterling	36,230
Baudouin, count of Flanders (1192)	5,000 marks of silver	10,500
Renaud, count of Boulogne (1192)	7,000 *livres* Arras	7,000
Hervé, count of Nevers (1199)	3,000 marks of silver	6,300
John (1200)	20,000 marks sterling	36,230
Renaud, count of Dammartin (1202)	3,000 marks of silver	6,300
Thibaut, count of Blois (1212)	5,000 *livres*	5,000
Ferrand, count of Flanders (1212)	50,000 *livres*	50,000

SOURCES: 1189, Howden II, 741; 1192, Gislebert de Mons, *Chronicon Hanoniense* 580, and *Actes* I, no. 398; 1199, Teulet I, no. 502; 1200, *Actes* II, no. 633; 1202, Teulet I, no. 601; 1212, *Actes* III, no. 1259, *Actes* III, no. 1227, *Registres* VI, no. 63, Teulet I, nos. 978–81.

fiefs were collected by the *baillis*. Among those recorded in the budget of 1221, for example, Thierry de Gallardon, the *bailli* of Touraine, received sums from Richard, heir to the *vicomte* of Sainte-Suzanne, and the relief of Amboise and Montrichard.[108] Since reliefs were collected sporadically, they are difficult to accommodate with estimations of Philip's total annual revenues. The relief of a great barony such as Flanders (50,000 *livres*) could, however, yield as much as a quarter of ordinary annual income. Although the gains were occasional, Philip's rights as feudal suzerain constituted a significant part of his finances.

Still more difficult to assess financially, but of comparable importance, was the right of wardship. When a fief passed to a woman or minor son unable to fulfill military obligations, the lord assumed its administration until the military duties could be performed by the son or the woman's husband. During the interval, of course, the lord had an opportunity to exploit the fief for financial advantage. When the county of Nevers was inherited by a girl in 1181, for example, the king took charge of the fiefs until she was married in 1184. After the death of the count of Flanders in 1191, the king exercised a kind of tutelage over the fiefs of the countess of Vermandois, because he considered himself her heir. In particular, he supervised her almsgiving.[109] Two more spectacular opportunities for wardship were presented when the counts of Troyes and Flanders departed on crusade and then died, leaving as heirs a minor son and daughter respectively. The abundant documentation surviving for Troyes affords the clearest picture of royal guardianship. Philip confided the regency to the Countess Blanche until her infant son Thibaut came of age in May 1222. In 1201 the king demanded the castles of Bray-sur-Seine and Montereau-faut-Yonne as securities during the count's minority. Although Blanche was allowed to administer the domains and collect the revenues, she paid the king 500 *livres provins* (375 *livres parisis*) for the castles' maintenance. When Thibaut's succession was contested, the king took personal custody of the boy in 1209 and exacted 15,000 *livres parisis* from Blanche. By 1213 the countess was further required to agree not to fortify the towns of Meaux, Lagny, Provins, and Coulommiers under penalty of a fine of 20,000 *livres*.[110] In addition to these political constraints and financial exactions, Philip also confirmed the countess's charters, regulated the relations between Jews in Champagne and the royal domain, supervised the movement of serfs, extended royal protection to the merchants of the county, and even reformed the procedure for judicial duels.[111]

Although Philip's guardianship over Flanders is not as clearly documented, the supervision was comparable. The king confided the regency to the deceased count's brother, Philippe, marquis of Namur, in 1206. By 1208 Philippe had taken personal custody of the young heiress, Jeanne, which he retained until she was married to Ferrand of Portugal in 1212. It may be assumed, therefore, that the king profited from his wardship as he had from Troyes, a suspicion corroborated by the large size of the relief.[112]

Feudal Military Service

Whatever their original functions, by the twelfth century, fiefs in northern France and England were allotted primarily for military service. The vassal received land in order to furnish knights to fight in the lord's army. By Philip Augustus's reign, however, royal armies were not composed exclusively of feudal knights, but contained other knights and sergeants (mounted and foot), who were paid wages. In fact, because of the *prisée des sergents* and the fiscal accounts of 1202/03, more information survives about mercenary soldiers than about the feudal host in the first half of the reign.[113] Not until the appearance of the royal registers in 1204 does precise documentation become available about knight service supplied to the king through feudal obligations. Until then we are limited to vague notions of who served, how many, and under what conditions.

Before 1200 we must rely chiefly on contemporary chroniclers, who for the most part assumed that their readers were familiar with the nature and composition of Philip's armies. Only the important vassals are named (especially if they were captured in battle), and when numbers are given, they differ widely. The Capetian chronicler Rigord, for example, is content to repeat the phrase *collecto exercitu* every time the king gathered his host, without specifying who was assembled, and only rarely how many. Rigord reports that Philip relieved Arques with 600 chosen knights in 1195 and entrusted 200 knights to Arthur in 1202, and that Henri Clément and Guillaume des Roches led 300 knights against Thouars in 1208. Guillaume le Breton usually follows the same pattern as his predecessor,[114] and the Hainois chronicler Gislebert de Mons pays close attention to those military campaigns in which the count of Hainaut took part and is exceptionally precise about the count's contributions of knights— particularly about the costs. Though his reports may be credible for the Hainaut contingents, his accuracy is less convincing with respect to the hosts of other lords. (Can he be believed when he says, for example, that the count of Flanders led 1,000 knights against the king in 1181, and that Philip Augustus raised 2,000 knights against Flanders in 1185?)[115]

The one striking exception to the general dearth of reports about Philip Augustus's armies concerns his defeat by Richard at Courcelles-lès-Gisors in September 1198, which was publicized by at least ten contemporaries. Although some disagreement lingered as to the size of the two contending forces (Philip's: 200–500 knights; Richard's: 1,500 knights), most of the chroniclers were impressed with the French captives taken by Richard. Not only are they in relative accord over the number (90–100), they even agree on the most noteworthy. After naming four, Rigord avers that he is too distressed to record the others, but Roger of Howden, a partisan of the victorious Richard, is not as inhibited. Among the most famous, he lists forty-three French knights, including four (Mathieu de Montmorency, Philippe de Nanteuil, Robert de Saint-Denis, and Renaud d'Ascy) who were subsequently listed in the royal registers as bannerets originating from the Vexin, one from Coucy (Alain de Roucy), and one from the southern domain (Ferry *de Brunai*). Roger's list may be trustworthy both because of its size and because its most noteworthy names agree with French testimony.[116] It shows that in 1198 Philip drew his feudal host mainly from the Vexin, where he was operating, and only occasionally from neighboring provinces. It also suggests that Philip's army was composed of bannerets and lesser knights supplied directly from the royal domain and did not contain others furnished by the great vassals. At Courcelles-lès-Gisors, therefore, Philip's army was purely a domanial affair. It would nonetheless be wrong to assume from this sample that the Capetian army never contained knights supplied by the great vassals. Gislebert de Mons notes contingents from the young King Henry who in 1181 fought with Philip Augustus against the count of Flanders, who was in turn aided by Hainaut and Brabant. The counts of Blois, Troyes, Dreux, Flanders, and Hainaut subsequently accompanied Philip into the Berry in 1187, but it is less certain that they contributed to the fighting, since they were unsympathetic to his aggression against the Angevins. Rigord asserts that the French king summoned counts, dukes, and great barons (*magistratus*) in the spring of 1205 for the final campaign against John's lands in the Loire valley.[117] Since the contemporary chroniclers are of little help in illuminating the magnates' military contributions, we must turn to other sources to examine their feudal service.

MILITARY SERVICE OF PRELATES AND BARONS

Because of the ecclesiastical bias in medieval documentation, the military obligations of prelates are better known than those of lay barons. It was customary for all regalian bishops, who swore oaths of fealty to the king, to owe knight service to the royal host (*exercitum*). When Philip began to renounce regalian rights over certain bishoprics in 1203, therefore, the question arose as to whether this included the military obligation. The issue was not raised at Langres, but at Arras the king specifically acquitted the bishop of his military service. The mounting confrontation with John in the interval between the conquest of Normandy and Bouvines apparently caused Philip to change his mind. Between 1207 and 1209, the king's renunciation of the regalia over Auxerre, Nevers, and Mâcon specifically retained the obligation to contribute to the royal host. In the case of Mâcon, however, the bishop's knights were not required to serve beyond Dijon, even when the royal host was commanded by the constable, seneschal, or marshal, or by the king himself or his son.[118] Yet some confusion remains over the king's policy. To compensate for the depredations of the royal sergeants during the interdict in 1200, Philip had granted his cousin, Eudes, bishop of Paris, personal and lifetime immunity to military service, although episcopal knight quotas were nonetheless retained. In 1211 the king exempted the bishops of the province of Sens from military service in exchange for their aid to the pope against Emperor Otto. (If Otto attacked France, of course, they also had to aid the king.)[119] But this concession seems to have been intended as a temporary quid pro quo rather than a permanent renunciation.

This uncertainty undoubtedly encouraged the bishops to test so ambiguous a policy. In 1210 the king summoned the royal host to Mantes, where the army was to be led by Juhel de Mayenne and the count of Saint-Pol against the Breton castle of Guesclin. According to Guillaume le Breton, all barons and bishops sent their knights except for Guillaume de Seignelay, the spirited bishop of Auxerre, and his brother Manassé, bishop of Orléans, who refused service, claiming that their obligations were limited to an army personally commanded by the king. Through a judgment of his court, Philip fined the two bishops for default of service, basing his case on the charter of 1207, which specifically preserved the royal rights of host and summons. When the bishops refused to pay the fine, the king confiscated the regalia on which their feudal obligations were based. The bishops responded with an interdict against the royal lands, and the dispute was appealed to the pope, whose registers record both royal and episcopal contentions. Whoever had the better argument, the episcopal brothers were unable to withstand royal pressure. The chapter of Orléans refused to support its bishop in enforcing the interdict, and the two bishops submitted to the king by August 1212. In the final settlement the king granted Guillaume personal lifetime immunity and renounced certain *gîtes* for which Manassé was liable, but he reestablished an important principle: the bishops of Auxerre and Orléans owed knight service to the royal host "just as [do] all other royal bishops and barons." The bishops had thus rightfully been judged in default and Philip kept the confiscated regalian revenues.[120] After this test case had been resolved in Philip's favor, no other bishop disputed his feudal obligations,[121] but uncertainty once again reappeared at the accession of Louis VIII. When the bishops of Angers, Le Mans, and Poitiers swore fealty to the new king in November 1223, they declared that they neither owed personal service in the royal host nor were obligated to pay for anyone in their place—liberties they had enjoyed under Kings Philip, Richard, and Henry.[122] When the Norman bishops of Coutances, Avranches, and Lisieux claimed the same principle at the assembly of the royal host at Tours in June 1224, however, they were judged in default and fined.[123]

Although Philip Augustus defended his rights with respect to regalian bishoprics whenever challenged, no attempt was made to inventory the total extent of this service until Register A. Between 1204 and 1211, but probably shortly after the conquest of Normandy, a chancery scribe copied into that register a list of thirty-four episcopal cities (*civitates*) under the rubric: "These are the episcopal cities that King Philip has in his domain." Including the Norman and Loire sees, this list corresponds closely to the list of regalian bishoprics after the conquests of 1204–1205. Sometime after its composition, Etienne de Gallardon added a series of notations, of which the most frequent was "host" (*exercitum*). Of the thirty-four sees, eighteen were designated as owing this service. (The seven Norman bishoprics were not annotated, probably because they were already included in the Norman inventories of fiefs.) In the eyes of the royal chancery, therefore, at best twenty-five bishoprics (including Auxerre, Orléans, and Châlons) were subject to feudal military obligations, but at least nine (including Arras) were free.[124]

The *civitates* inventory makes no mention of the number of knights owed by the bishoprics, and though a corresponding list of regalian abbeys was also included in Register A, it omits details of their military obligations. The *prisée des sergents* of 1194 and 1202 does, however, specify the quotas of sergeants, wagons, and money owed by royal monasteries. Two other lists in Register A inventory the obligation of thirty monasteries to provide pack horses (*summarii*) and of eight abbeys to furnish wagons,[125] but no account is given of their knight service.

The most glaring omission in the registers is the military service of the great barons. The hierarchic list of French nobility in Register A only identifies names and titles, and the list of bannerets merely groups them according to regions.[126] The sole exceptions to these omissions are the feudal inventories of Normandy, which will be investigated later in greater detail.[127] Suffice it to say here that between May 1204 and February 1205 the first scribe to compile Register A included a copy of Henry II's great survey of Norman knight service, made in 1172. In the duchy, where knight service had long been defined, imposed, and regulated, these quotas were considered traditional by the time of the French conquest. In 1172 Henry's officers had estimated that Normandy contained at least 1,500 knights, of whom 581 were owed in service to the duke by direct vassals. Of these totals the great vassals[128] contributed knight service as shown in Table 11. Thanks to his predecessor's diligence and administrative talents, Philip Augustus therefore had a remarkable summary of the knight service of an important province at his disposal in 1204. He could see that his magnates benefited from 90 percent of the total number of knights, but contributed only 65 percent to the ducal/royal army. Those who profited most from this arrangement were the lay baronage, who enjoyed 73 percent of the totals but contributed only 47 percent to their

TABLE 11. Knight Service of the Great Vassals in Normandy, 1172
(with percentages of the total knight service in the duchy)

	Knights Enfeoffed	Knights Owed
Bishops	191 (13%)	61 (10%)
Abbots	59 (4%)	48 (8%)
Lay baronage	1,091 (73%)	273 (47%)
Total of great vassals	1,341 (90%)	382 (65%)
Total in the duchy	1,500	581

SOURCE: *Registres* III, A.

overlord. The Norman situation, however, was a special case from which
the king could not generalize for the rest of his great vassals.

The nature and the extent of military service owed by the great vassals
were qualified by one final distinction, which is also obscured in the
chroniclers' accounts. Though service in the host (*exercitum*) at regular—
perhaps annual—intervals required only customary and limited numbers
of knights, a royal lord could call upon his vassals for unlimited service
when he was seriously threatened and compelled to fight a just war
(*bellum*). This distinction between a regular *exercitum* and an extraordinary *bellum* can be seen as early as 1182, when Philip granted to the inhabitants of Chevrières that they need go no farther in the *exercitum* than
they could return within a day, except when summoned in the name of
war (*in nomine belli*).[129] As we have seen, the classic case of *bellum*, when
the German emperor threatened to invade France with a large army in
1124, is described in Abbot Suger's *Life of Louis VI*. Though the king
himself could raise only a small force from Paris, Saint-Denis, Etampes,
and Orléans (his domain) on that occasion, he was joined at Reims by
the duke of Burgundy and the counts of Blois, Troyes, Nevers, Vermandois, and Flanders. Even the most distant duke of Aquitaine and counts
of Brittany and Anjou arrived, although short notice prevented them
from bringing large contingents.[130]

The archepiscopal city of Reims on the northeastern border of France
continued to serve as a rallying point against danger from England,
Flanders, and the Empire. To oppose Richard's coalition with Count
Baudouin of Flanders in 1197, Philip requested the chapter of Reims to
send all of its armed men to meet him in Péronne. Careful to explain the

count's wrongdoings, Philip justified this unprecedented request for aid above customary service as defense of the crown *in nomine belli*. Perhaps on this occasion, or more likely in 1200, the clergy at Reims were apparently negligent in providing military service, and responded by offering prayers rather than arms. Whatever the date, Guillaume le Breton reports that in 1201, when the church appealed to the king to stop its harassment by the count of Rethel and Roger de Rozoi, Philip, in turn, offered his prayers rather than his arms. The clergy got the point and quickly corrected their attitude, after which the king issued a charter renewing his protection. Once again in 1207, as the menace from Flanders and the Empire increased, the chapter of Reims acknowledged that it would answer a royal summons for the defense of the realm and the crown "like all the other chapters of France." In exchange Philip acquitted them of normal service. Two years later, on the occasion of strengthening the fortifications of the city, the archbishop, chapter, and abbey of Saint-Remy repeated the pledge.[131]

The long-awaited invasion from the east finally materialized in 1214 and was met at Bouvines. In mimesis of 1124 Philip turned back his enemies *in nomine belli*. Because of the celebrity of the victory the battle of Bouvines is better reported than any other military engagement of the reign. Narrated in detail by two major chroniclers (one an eyewitness), it also generated a muster-list of troops transcribed into Register C. With such intensive reportage we may be assured that few baronial participants have escaped notice.[132] The army under Prince Louis that blocked John at La Roche-au-Moine contained only two barons, Guillaume des Roches and Aimery de Craon.[133] In the north, however, Philip was accompanied by three bishops (Senlis, Beauvais, and Laon) and eleven major barons, of whom the duke of Burgundy and the count of Dreux were the most prominent. Since the count of Troyes was still a minor, the Champenois baronage was led by the count of Grandpré. The muster-list of Register C was devoted to recording the levies from the royal domain (Vermandois, Coucy, Vexin, and Normandy). Though noting only two bishops and two counts, it contains another fifty-five names, most of which are also found on the list of banneret knights in Register A.[134]

Since chroniclers' estimates normally provide unreliable battle statistics, the muster-list, although incomplete, furnishes a more solid basis for such calculations. It accounts for 763 knights, grouped in units of five under the leadership of bannerets, all drawn from the royal domain[135] in northern France and the neighboring territories. Since it does not inventory the contingents of the great vassals reported as present by the chroniclers, their contributions must be estimated by rough guesses, which suggest a total of 560.[136]

In the final count, therefore, Philip Augustus won the battle of Bouvines with a feudal host of about 1,300 knights. When to these are added the 800 knights entrusted to Louis for the southern defense (figures supplied by Guillaume le Breton), they total little more than 2,000 knights, a surprisingly small number summoned from Philip's entire feudal resources at the most critical moment of his reign.[137] Aside from the three bishops named, none of the other twenty-nine regalian bishops who owed service in the host, including the frequently admonished archbishop of Reims, came to the king's aid. But the feudal levies were sufficient to secure victory. Although comparable information is lacking for the allied army at Bouvines, it has been estimated at 1,300–1,500 knights from the chroniclers' reports.[138] It is likely, therefore, that the two armies were evenly matched in numbers.

MILITARY SERVICE IN THE DOMAIN: THE FINDINGS OF THE INVENTORIES

Although the French king evidently lacked the authority and the means to compile reliable information about the feudal contributions of his great vassals, he was better informed about knight service furnished by the royal domain after 1204. By the turn of the twelfth century, the Capetians were able to profit from techniques developed by contemporary rulers to inventory knight service. Between 1194 and 1196, for example, Ramon de Caldes compiled a *Liber feudorum major* for the count-king of Barcelona that preserved charters of settlement involving infeudated castles. The artist who embellished the extant copy with a miniature painting depicts the prince and his clerk selecting charters to be included in the book from a chest.[139] More ambitious were the efforts of the counts of Champagne to inventory their vassals in the *Feoda Campanie*. The first list, compiled ca. 1172 and revised until 1192, includes the names of about 1,900 knights organized in 26 castellanies. Although other miscellaneous information is appended, its major goal was to record liege allegiance and castleguard. Transcribed into books, one copy was kept in the count's treasury at the church of Saint-Etienne in Troyes, and another was taken by Count Henri in 1190 to the Holy Land, where it was lost. Between 1200 and 1234 six other inventories were compiled on the same format, but all are incomplete by comparison to the first register, which they were intended to complement.[140]

Those most expert in drawing up inventories, however, were the Normans, who had acquired long experience in defining and recording knight service throughout their far-flung possessions from England to Sicily, as well as in the duchy itself. As early as 1086 William the Conqueror ordered the compilation of the renowned Domesday Book, which, although not strictly a book of fiefs, was a monumental effort to record the landed resources in England on which fiefs were based. This information was organized by feudal baronies of the realm. In 1166 William's great-grandson, Henry II, undertook a survey of the knight's fiefs of England by addressing specific questions to his immediate vassals. The purpose of this survey was not to ascertain the service owed by the tenants-in-chief directly, but to compute the total number of enfeoffed knights in England. Since the knight's names were also required, Henry could thus demand liege allegiance of all enfeoffed knights, and in determining their totals, he undoubtedly had a financial goal in mind. This was suggested two years later, when he assessed aid for the marriage of his daughter on the basis of both the old and new enfeoffments. In all events, some 318 direct vassals responded to the survey, reporting 7,525 knight's fiefs for an owed service of about 5,000 knights. Their sealed letters, called the *carte baronum*, were stored in a chest in the exchequer, probably like that of the count of Barcelona. Only at a later date were they copied into books.[141]

Around 1150, when he was preparing to repel a combined threat from the German and Byzantine emperors, Henry's contemporary Roger II, the Norman king of Sicily, likewise undertook a survey of his feudal resources. As an extraordinary measure, he wished to inventory all who could contribute to his defense, both those who merely held property in his domain and those who owed feudal service. Like Henry II, Roger fully intended to benefit from increases in service. The original list was compiled from declarations of tenants, but was updated by Roger's successors in 1167 and 1168 with information supplied by royal chamberlains and constables and by consulting registers (*quaterniones*). Called the *Catalogus baronum* in its extant form, it notes over 1,440 men who responded to the survey and who are arranged according to constabulary, county, or other great lordship throughout Norman Italy.[142]

The Norman rulers were equally active in assessing and recording feudal service in their homeland. As early as 1133, at the death of Richard, bishop of Bayeux, King Henry I dispatched his son, Robert, earl of Gloucester, to Normandy to conduct an inquest into the knight fees owed by the episcopal barony based on the testimony of twelve jurors. The results of the Bayeux inquest were written down in a long version and summarized in a shorter version kept at the English exchequer. Henry I was interested both in the total number of knights and *vavassors* enfeoffed by the bishop and in the customary service due to the bishop's overlords. It was discovered that the bishop had enfeoffed about 120 knights, of whom he owed the duke of Normandy 20 and the king of France 10. Formulated another way, 5 of the bishop's knights would normally equip a knight for the duke's service (or pay 40 *sous* each) and 10 would equip a knight for the king's service (or pay 20 *sous* each). Though the proportions between enfeoffments and service owed in these two formulations are not entirely consistent, the numerical quotas to the duke and king (20 and 10) became customary and fixed.[143]

The Bayeux inquest set a pattern followed in subsequent Norman surveys. In 1171, according to the chronicler Robert de Torigni, abbot of Le Mont-Saint-Michel, Henry II decided to investigate the resources (land, forests, and other domains) that his grandfather had held, but that the great barons had subsequently usurped. The results of this inquest nearly doubled the duchy's revenues.[144] A survey of the knights and *vavassors* was undoubtedly part of this program. A brief notice in the cartulary of Le Mont-Saint-Michel casts light on the procedure. On 8 September 1172 the king convened his Norman barons at Caen, where, as in the Bayeux inquest, two basic questions were put to them under oath. They were required to recognize how many knights each owed to the king (*ad servitium regis*) and how many they had for their own service (*ad suum proprium servicium*). As in the English survey of 1166, the barons responded in writing.[145] Except for the report of Robert, abbot of Le Mont-Saint-Michel, none of the individual letters have survived, but the numerical responses to the two questions were compiled on a single roll and arranged in a hierarchical plan: (1) bishops and abbots, (2) counts, (3) great honors, (4) lesser knights grouped according to *bailliages*, (5) honors in the king's hand (Conches, Tosny, Montfort, and Mortain), and (6) those who did not respond to the summons. Although incomplete, the inquest of 1172 was a comprehensive attempt to inventory both knight service owed and enfeoffments throughout the duchy. We have seen that the scribes calculated that King Henry was due the service of 581 knights from about 1,500 enfeoffments.[146]

A copy of the results was undoubtedly kept at Caen and another at the exchequer in England. In 1206 the English clerk Alexander of Swereford compiled a handbook of useful information for the exchequer, called the

"Little Black Book," in which were included reasonably full copies of the baronial charters of 1166 arranged according to shires and major baronies. When this manual went out of date in the second quarter of the century, he made a more ambitious collection of such information, this time denoted the "Red Book of the Exchequer." In it were recopied not only the *Carte baronum* of 1166, but also the Norman inquest of 1172 and a summary of the Bayeux inquest of 1133.[147] Although Normandy was no longer in English hands, the duchy's records were still preserved in the English exchequer.

THE CAPETIAN INVENTORIES OF NORMANDY

By the time the Norman inquest of 1172 was inserted into the Red Book, it was of only antiquarian interest to the English, but its importance to Philip Augustus was undeniable. The conquest had bequeathed him not only the Anglo-Norman regime of fiefs, but also the means of controlling them, including the inventories. The ducal capital of Caen fell into his hands on 19 May 1204, and during that same month Scribe N began transcribing the first materials for Register A. By February 1205, or shortly thereafter, when N completed the initial transcription, he had made a fair copy of the inquest of 1172.[148] Incorporated into the Capetian registers, this comprehensive survey, now authoritative through long acceptance and custom, transmitted to the French chancery the Anglo-Norman format for future inventories. Thus the two basic inquiries (how many knights were owed the king and how many enfeoffed?) were made available to the Capetians.

By 1204, however, the inquest of 1172 was in need of updating, and Etienne de Gallardon applied himself to the task until 1207–1208. Since the *baillis* had changed, he inserted the names of Renaud de Cornillon, Cadoc, and Guillaume Pullus in the appropriate sections and included the names of *bailliages* for place-names unfamiliar to the French chancery. The names of deceased tenants were replaced by those of their heirs, and, most important, Etienne attempted to revise the inventory by indicating in the margins who presently held the fiefs confiscated during the conquest. Lands worth the service of at least 114 knights were assigned to the count of Boulogne, Guérin de Galopin, Renaud du Bois, and others. The king retained for himself baronies and fiefs totalling at least 117 knights (annotated *rex habet*), but this figure was grossly incomplete.[149] Emending the old inquest, however, was not sufficient in giving the new lord an accounting of feudal resources, because with the conquest a number of great baronies and their enfeoffed knights came directly into the king's hands. When Robert, earl of Leicester, died in October 1204, for example, his Norman honors of Breteuil and Grandmesnil escheated to the king.[150] Shortly thereafter a new survey of the enfeoffments of these two baronies was ordered, which was completed before Scribe N finished his transcription of Register A. The names and number of fiefs were recorded in detail. The king may have feared an attrition of enfeoffments because the new inquests showed a decrease of knights from 1172.[151]

The earl of Leicester's barony was only one of a dozen major fiefdoms confiscated by Philip Augustus during the conquest. In April 1205 the king notified his Norman tenants that he was adding to the royal domain the lands of the earls of Warenne, Arundel, Leicester, and Clare, the count of Meulan, the lord of Montfort-sur-Risle, and other specified barons, and the lands of all the Norman knights who were then in England, whose names would be listed on a roll. He warned that aids (*auxilia*) from these fiefs could no longer be taken by other barons and knights, as they had been in the past.[152]

In order to account for the great dislocations in the feudal landscape, another comprehensive survey was needed to replace that of 1172. A new inventory, called the *Feoda Normannie*, was quickly drawn up by 1207 and copied into Register A, but without the care and consistency of that of 1172 in distinguishing between the two categories of knight service owed to the king and total enfeoffments. Designed for immediate use, the new survey attempted to inventory all fiefs from which the king directly benefited. It was not hierarchically or logically organized as in 1172, but apparently drawn up as the returns came in, starting with the honors of Breteuil and Grandmesnil. Eventually, the inevitable exceptions, modifications, and *rex habet*'s were added as notations. Most of the confiscated baronies announced in 1205 were accounted for in the inventory of 1207.[153] In the baronies added directly to the royal domain, all enfeoffed knights were apparently listed. For the rest of the duchy the inventory followed the example of 1172 by listing by *bailliage* those who owed the king service. For the first two *bailliages* of Eximes and Sées it attempted to report two sets of figures (service owed and enfeoffment) as in 1172, but in all others (Caen, Falaise, Vire, Rouen, Caux, and so on) it apparently furnished only details of the knight service owed the king. Few clues emerge from the text to suggest precisely how the survey was accomplished, but following the precedents of 1172 and of 1204 at Breteuil and Grandmesnil, it was surely the result of an inquest.[154] Despite the confusion and the notable omission of the Cotentin, the *Feoda Normannie* indicates that Philip Augustus could theoretically count on the service of at least 847 knights in 1207. These consisted of 370 knights owed to him as overlord (*servitium debitum*) and 477 knights drawn from lands in his hands.[155]

The surveys of 1172 and 1207 were not entirely commensurate because each omitted areas included in the other. But if we merely compare the number of knights accounted as due to the king (*servitium debitum* plus those in royal hands) in both inventories, we see that in 1207 Philip had 266 more than Henry had in 1172 (581). This increase of almost 50 percent resulted mainly from the confiscation of the great baronies during the conquest. But these gains in feudal service in the duchy appear to have had little effect on Philip's armies. Of the 847 potential knights, only 158 arrived at Bouvines from the Vexin and Normandy. The duchy contributed only 55, including Etienne de Longchamps, who lost his life.[156]

The deficiencies and omissions of the *Feoda Normannie* of 1207 prompted the copying of other surveys of Norman knight service into Register C. As fragments, they were merely preparatory to the great comprehensive inventory transcribed into Register E by Etienne de Gallardon in 1220. After 1212, for example, two scribes in particular began revising former Norman inventories,[157] and began to fill in lacunae from the 1207 inventory. The fiefs of Jean de Gisors and of Nogent l'Erembert, both in the *bailliage* of Gisors, and the fiefs of the Cotentin, lacking in 1207, were given an extensive survey.[158] It is clear that by this time an inventorying pattern had been established, because the last-named surveys were directly incorporated into the comprehensive inventory of Register E.[159]

Building on the inquests of 1172 and 1207, and the partial inventories of Register C, the survey of Register E was the most comprehensive and detailed of all. It began with Normandy and grouped its findings according to the eight major *bailliages* of the duchy.[160] Since the larger baronies contained fiefs in several *bailliages*, cross-references were provided to the chief seat of the fiefdom.[161] A major undertaking, the inventory was undoubtedly compiled by the eight *baillis* named in the chapters between 1218 and 1220.[162] The procedures for gathering the information were, for the most part, left concealed in the final draft. Apparently, the *baillis* relied chiefly on direct testimony from feudatories and only occasionally on written evidence.[163]

Although information was gathered about castleguard, sergeantries, pleas, and other matters, the overwhelming concern of the Norman survey was knight service, formulated in the two traditional categories: service owed and enfeoffments made. As regards fiefdoms still held by vassals, the surveyors were naturally interested in knight service due. In *bailliages* such as the Cotentin, Bayeux, Rouen, and Caen, where these great baronies were still prominent, the *servitium debitum* was placed at the head of each section.[164] As in the *Feoda Normannie* of 1207, when the *baillis* dealt with escheated fiefs in the king's hands, they were interested in all enfeoffments and were careful to record the names of knights, amounts of service, and the location of fiefs.[165] In the eight jurisdictions the *baillis* recorded fiefs yielding 646 knights from owed service and baronies and fiefs yielding the service of 652 knights that were in the king's hands. The king therefore benefited from a total of 1,299 knights in 1220. Again, it is difficult to know whether the bases of comparison were commensurate with those of 1207. This increase of another 53 percent (452 knights over the 847 knights in 1207) was probably due in part to the improved reporting of the *baillis*, but its ultimate significance is obscured by the fact that no knight service was demanded at the end of the reign, since the king's lands were at peace.[166]

The great survey of 1220 differs from its predecessors in that it includes more detail. Like that of 1207, it recensed all subtenants of the baronies then in the king's hands (but furnished more information). Unlike the *Feoda Normannie*, however, which was concerned only with service immediately available to the king, it also carefully noted the number and location of fiefs belonging to the great barons responsible for *servitium debitum*. The feudal resources of most bishops, abbots, and prominent barons such as Robert Bertram, Richard de Vernon, Guillaume du Hommet, Pierre de Préaux, and the chamberlain of Tancarville were minutely recorded.[167] Just why the *baillis* attempted not only to count up but also to specify all the enfeoffments of the duchy is difficult to answer. In 1166 Henry II had demanded such information to increase his assessments of aid (*auxilium*). In 1205 Philip warned that aids from confiscated baronies would be reserved for the king. Scattered throughout the survey of 1220 are a few references to *auxilia* (normally 100 *sous*), but these rare occurrences may be remnants of pre-1204 assessments.[168] In any case there is no record that Philip attempted to levy a general aid on his Norman fiefs. Though the survey of 1220 could have served that purpose, it is more likely that the careful detailing of enfeoffments was due to a desire for better records and a more complete knowledge of feudal resources.[169]

Following the two traditional questions, the *baillis* were able to record their findings in a standardized format, but one, Guillaume de Ville-Thierri, reported in a different manner.[170] His inventory of the *bailliage* of Gisors-Vexin was organized chiefly according to castellanies (Gisors, Vernon, Pacy, Mantes, and so on). Although he made detailed inquiries into the names of all tenants and subtenants, and the numbers and locations of their fiefs, he was not explicitly concerned with the amount of their service, but rather concluded each inquiry with a general formula that the tenant owed the king host and *chevauchée* (*exercitum et equitatum*) at his own expense. In the castellanies of Gisors, Vernon, Pacy, Meulan, and Nogent (incorporating the preparatory inventory from Register C), the amount of time the tenant owed as castleguard in the king's castle was added. Apparently, therefore, feudal service in the Vexin differed from that in the rest of Normandy, and the fiefs in the five above-named castellanies were devoted to garrisoning the royal castles. Since the Vexin had been longest under Capetian control of all the Norman provinces, its feudal structure more closely resembled that of the old royal domain, as we shall see.

THE INVENTORIES OF THE OLD CAPETIAN DOMAIN

After the eight Norman *bailliages*, Etienne de Gallardon turned to transcribing in Register E the surveys of the older Capetian domain: Vermandois, Sens, Bourges, and Etampes.[171] His task was not finished by 1220 because the oldest sections of the royal domain, such as Paris and Orléans, were missing. Whereas the Anglo-Norman dukes had regimented and inventoried their feudatories for at least a century, evidence of Capetian supervision of their ancestral domain remains slight. The list of bannerets and the hierarchic grouping of feudatories in Register A naturally included names from the royal domain,[172] but no effort to survey these Capetian lands is indicated until Register C came into use between 1212 and 1220. Perhaps inspired by the Norman example, one scribe compiled two broad-ranging lists, but because of a differing regime of fiefs, his questions were not the Norman ones. His first list sorted the knights from over twenty castellanies in the old domain according to two criteria: whether their lands were worth 60 *livres* of annual revenues or more, and whether they held their fiefs directly from the king or from some other lord.[173] The second listed knights, widows, and valets, principally from the *bailliage* of Orléans, according to *prévôtés*.[174]

These two lists helped in the preparation of the comprehensive survey of Register E.[175] In addition, other scribes compiled lists in Register C that added to the inventory of Register E.[176] The best example of the multiple layers of preparation that preceded Register E is provided by the castellany of Montlhéry. One scribe compiled a preliminary list of fourteen knights that was adopted by another scribe in his inventory of fiefs worth more than 60 *livres*. A third scribe then used this material to make an elaborate survey of fiefs at Montlhéry, which Etienne de Gallardon finally recopied without change into Register E and appended to the survey of Adam Héron for the *bailliage* of Etampes.[177]

The *baillis* of Vermandois, Sens, Bourges, and Etampes who gathered information between 1218 and 1220 for the comprehensive survey employed both the inquest and written charters, as had their Norman colleagues.[178] If these *baillis* followed Norman procedures, however, they did not ask exactly the same questions. The imposition of feudal service was less ancient in Vermandois, for example, than in Normandy, and this conditioned the information the Vermandois *baillis* could collect.[179] Like their Norman colleagues, the *baillis* in the old domain were interested in uncovering all fiefs, both those held directly from the king and those held as subtenants. The five *baillis* were scrupulous in listing every tenant of the king's (designated as *homo* or *homo ligius*) with a careful and detailed inventory of the nature and location of his fiefs.[180] A similar effort was made to identify all subtenants either by name or by location of fief. On occasion, the subtenants of an entire barony were listed in detail.[181] These *baillis*, unlike their Norman colleagues, made little effort either to count the number of enfeoffments or to specify the knight service owed. The chief difference between the Norman inventories and those of the older Capetian domain was thus the absence of the *servitium debitum*, so characteristic of the Anglo-Norman regime. In the *bailliages* of Sens, Bourges, and Etampes (with the exception of Montlhéry) no service was recorded at all. In the Vermandois castellanies, it was merely summarized by the formula "and he owes host and *chevauchée*".[182] Like the Norman inventories, therefore, those of the old domain appear to have been motivated simply by a desire for increased knowledge of the complexity of the king's feudal resources. In any event, they do not appear to have been used for any military purposes by the end of the reign.

CASTLEGUARD AND CASTLES

Among the military services inventoried in Register E, castleguard (*stagium, estage*) received special attention. Guillaume de Ville-Thierri investigated it in the Vexin castellanies, the Vermandois *baillis* continued the survey for the Picard castellanies, and a similar inquest was made at Montlhéry in the south. As in Catalonia, Champagne, and the Vexin, the fiefs of Vermandois had long been grouped around castles to provide these strongholds with defenders. So well organized were these castellanies that inventories detailing *estage* duties survive from the 1190s at Picquigny and elsewhere, which may have inspired the royal surveys in Register E.[183] Among the Vexin castellanies, Pacy and Nogent were well organized. Twenty-two knights, for example, provided a total of 30 months of guard duty at Pacy, at the rate of forty days of service annually per fief. At Nogent, acquired in 1218–1219, thirty-four knights provided a total of 70 months each year, most serving one or two months.[184] Among the Vermandois castellanies, Crépy-en-Valois and Ribemont were best served. At the former twelve knights provided 17 months of annual duty, and at the latter, the same number of knights furnished 105 months.[185]

The best organized castellany was at Montlhéry, for which three preliminary inventories were made in Register C. The last of these, which was recopied into Register E, was prepared by twelve jurors who recorded the name of each tenant, his relation to the king (*homo regis* or *homo ligius regis*), a description of his fiefs, his subtenants, his obligations of host and *chevauchée*, and always how much guard duty (*custodiam*) he owed at the castle. Sixty-three knights owed a total of 110 months, with the most common term set at two months. So well organized was this castellany that changes of its boundaries dating from the turn of the century were meticulously noted in an inquest. Perched on a hill commanding the road between Paris and Orléans, Montlhéry, held by hostile castellans, had long disrupted communications in the royal domain. After futile attempts to take it by force, King Philip I finally acquired it in 1105. A century and half later, during the reign of Louis IX, the castle of Montlhéry "in the heart of France and a land of peace" came to symbolize the stability of the Capetian domain.[186] This transformation undoubtedly resulted from the system of garrisoning strongholds perfected by Philip Augustus.

Except for the celebrated battle at Bouvines, most of Philip Augustus's military activities revolved around castles, either as the objects of sieges or as the sites of skirmishes. As warfare evolved in the late twelfth century, the stone fortress with its towering donjon and surrounding walls became the key to defending and controlling territory. To secure and stabilize his annexations of Normandy and the Loire valley, Philip found it necessary to consolidate his hold on the castles. The great conquests therefore stimulated him both to take stock of his fortresses and to bring a policy of castle construction to perfection during the years 1203–1214.

The distribution of royal castles naturally grew out of strongholds that Philip inherited from his predecessors, such as Montlhéry. Like his father and grandfather, the young king sought to maintain control over them from the beginning of his reign. In 1181, for example, Philip followed Louis VII's policy of preventing the commune of Soissons from incorporating the fortress of Saint-Médard into the urban defenses in an effort to secure the royal castle's independence.[187] The acquisition of new territories required obtaining the fortresses that assured their control: Beauquesne (1192) in Artois; Montargis (1195) in the Gâtinais; Gisors, Vernon, and Pacy (by 1196) in the Vexin.[188] As the new master of Normandy, Philip entered into numerous exchanges and transactions to obtain the key strongholds. He received Falaise and Bonneville-sur-Touques, for example, from Queen Berengaria (Richard's widow), Breteuil from the sister of the count of Leicester, and Mortemer from Renaud, count of Boulogne.[189]

Sometime between 1206 and 1210, after the great conquests were completed, the chancery clerks compiled a list of 113 "castles and fortresses King Philip holds." (See Map 1.) These castles extended from Hesdin, Lens, and Hénin (Pas-de-Calais) in the north to Crépy, Bruyères, and Cerny around Laon (Aisne) in the east, to Ennezat and Nonnette (Puy-de-Dome) in the south, to Montreuil-Bonnin and Loudun (Vienne) in the southwest, and included all of Normandy to the west. Within these confines, three major concentrations can be discerned: (1) the old southern domain, forming a triangle between Paris, Orléans, and Sens; (2) the Seine valley between Paris and Rouen; and (3) the northern border between the Ile-de-France and Normandy.[190] Obviously these patterns of distribution were inherited from Philip's predecessors. Whereas the heavy concentrations in the Seine valley and on the Norman borders reflected the fighting that had taken place for centuries, the remaining distributions show that castles were implanted simply to control the countryside.[191] The concentration in the southern domain, as well as the more even dispersal throughout the rest of Normandy, demonstrates that castles played a decisive role in governing even the most secure parts of the royal domain. After the list was completed by 1210, Philip continued to acquire new castles in response to particular circumstances, but these additions were not sufficient to cause the compilation of a new inventory.[192]

The decade between 1203 and 1214 also witnessed the culmination of a construction campaign to strengthen the fortifications of cities and castles throughout the royal domain. Apparently Philip's preparations for the crusade first prompted him to turn his attention to his towns. By 1190 he had built a new tower at Bourges that in all likelihood completed the walls begun by Louis VII.[193] Rigord observes that in the same year the king ordered his townsmen of Paris to enclose the right bank with a wall furnished with turrets and gates. This command was extended to other cities and castles throughout the kingdom, and the chronicler notes further building activity in 1194.[194] To prepare against the threats of the Flemings and the Germans in 1209, Philip lent 4,000 *livres* to the archbishop of Reims for strengthening his city. The following year a loan of 2,000 *livres* was offered to Châlons-sur-Marne for similar purposes.[195]

The extent of Philip's program for urban fortifications can be seen from a series of building accounts copied into Register A between 1205 and 1212. Best characterized as instructions to master builders, these accounts specified the kinds, quantities, dimensions, and costs of construction to be performed on cities and castles. Six cities (Laon, Compiègne, Melun, Evreux, Corbeil, and Paris) received new walls, moats, turrets, gates protected by twin towers, drawbridges, and other defenses. The left bank of Paris was encompassed with 2,500 meters of walls built to the specifications of those on the right bank. Strengthened with turrets, parapets, and crenellations, and pierced with six gates, these constructions cost Philip 7,020 *livres*. Furthermore, the Châtelet, guarding the Petit-Pont on the left bank, was furnished with new fireplaces, gates, posterns, and a prison consisting of three floors, at an additional expense of 570 *livres*. In these accounts the king paid out close to 27,000 *livres* for the defense of his cities.[196] Somewhat later (1212–1220) in accounts copied into Register C, he expended an additional 6,700 *livres* for the fortifications of Compiègne and Montdidier.[197] According to Guillaume le Breton, the king continued rebuilding walls and towers at his own expense up until the time of his death.[198]

Castles, as well as cities, were included in Philip Augustus's program, which reached its peak in the decade following the great conquests. By the late twelfth century the old *motte* and bailey castle, consisting of a wooden stockade perched on a mound surrounded by a ditch, had been superseded by stone fortifications composed of a central donjon, or keep, protected by encircling walls and a moat.[199] When Philip turned to such matters in the 1190s, he was bequeathed three precedents on which to model the central stone donjon. Since the late eleventh century, the most widespread fashion had been to build the keep in the shape of a rectangle, usually twice as long as it was wide (*barlongue*). This kind was constructed by the counts of Anjou at Langeais and Loches in the Loire valley, by the counts of Flanders at Ghent, and, most extensively, by the Anglo-Norman king-dukes at London, Dover, Caen, Arques, Falaise, and Domfront.[200] Large structures with massive walls, these donjons served both for residence and defense, but their flat surfaces were increasingly vulnerable to improved siege engines, and their ninety-degree corners provided dead angles that sheltered attackers from the archery and crossbows of the defenders. To remedy this last defect, the donjon could be fashioned in the shape of a polygon, such as the Anglo-Normans built at Gisors (central tower) in the late eleventh century. (The giant fortifications at Gisors, whose walls and gates were improved by Henry II, elicited the admiration of Louis VII's entourage, but provoked defiance from the twelve-year-old Philip when he first saw them in 1177).[201] Greatest resistance to siege engines and the fewest dead angles were, however, afforded by curved surfaces, and this inspired a third series of structures, using rounded donjons. The lords of Montfort at Houdan and the Capetians at Etampes and Ambleny employed complicated patterns of converging cylinders to round the corners.[202] A simpler solution was to use a cylindrical plan and thicken the wall at its most exposed side with a kind of spur. This was adopted by the lord of La Roche-Guyon in the Vexin, by King Richard at Château-Gaillard, and by Philip himself at Issoudun in Berry.[203]

The simplest solution, however, and the one Philip Augustus put to greatest use, was the pure cylindrical pattern. He may have been inspired by the example of Châteaudun in the Dunois, or more likely by his grandfather's tower at the royal palace on the Ile-de-la-Cité at Paris. Round towers had been known since antiquity and came readily to mind, but the inspiration was less important than the decision to put this kind of donjon into production. The first example was the tower of Louvre at Paris, which was probably begun contemporaneously with the walls in 1190 and was completed by November 1202.[204] At that time a certain Abelin in the Berry was instructed to build a tower at Dun-le-Roi "according to the same measurements as the tower of Paris."[205] The building accounts in Register A (1205 to 1212) show the king building four more units at Villeneuve-sur-Yonne, Orléans, Laon, and Péronne.[206] According

Illustrations

Illustrations 1–6 represent a sample of scenes from the life of Philip Augustus drawn from illustrated copies of the *Grandes chroniques de France*. Rigord de Saint-Denis and Guillaume le Breton wrote the first semi-official and official histories of Philip Augustus in Latin during the king's lifetime. Philip's grandson, Louis IX (1226–1270), was undoubtedly responsible for having these accounts and preceding Latin chronicles translated into French, thus comprising the *Grandes chroniques de France*. In or shortly after 1274 Primat, a monk of Saint-Denis, presented a copy of the *Grandes chroniques* to Louis's son, Philip III. This manuscript, which survives as Bibliothèque Sainte-Geneviève 782 in Paris, was richly illustrated and initiated a tradition of pictorial editions of the *Grandes chroniques*. (See the frontispiece for a miniature from this manuscript.) In the 1370s Charles V ordered a continuation of the chronicle and commissioned a new manuscript (Paris, Bibliothèque Nationale fr. 2813) replete with new illustrations. By the late fourteenth and fifteenth centuries the *Grandes chroniques* were frequently recopied and embellished with miniatures for the Paris book trade. The Walters Art Gallery manuscripts 138 and 139 in Baltimore exemplify the popularity of this work. Although the later artists undoubtedly introduced anachronisms into their portrayals, they nonetheless presented the earliest depictions of the history Philip Augustus inspired by the writings of Rigord and Guillaume le Breton. (The most recent studies of the *Grandes chroniques de France* are Gabrielle M. Spiegel, *The Chronicle Tradition of Saint-Denis*, Medieval Classics: Texts and Studies [Brookline, Mass., and Leyden, 1978], and Anne Dawson Hedeman, "The Illustrations of the *Grandes chroniques de France* from 1274 to 1422," diss., The Johns Hopkins University, 1984.)

Illustration 7 is a miniature from one of two surviving manuscripts of Gilles de Paris's *Karolinus*.

Illustrations 8–14 depict cylindrical towers constructed by Philip Augustus.

1. Louis VII's dream of the young Philip offering a chalice of blood to his barons. Paris, Bibliothèque Nationale fr. 2813, fol. 223r.

2. The anointing of Philip Augustus. Baltimore, Walters Art Gallery 138, fol. 1v.

3. Vassals offering their swords to Philip Augustus in homage. Baltimore, Walters Art Gallery 138, fol. 15r.

4. Bouvines: Philip Augustus against Emperor Otto of Brunswick. Paris, Bibliothèque Nationale fr. 2813, fol. 253v.

5. Bouvines: Emperor Otto of Brunswick flees from Philip Augustus. Baltimore, Walters Art Gallery 139, fol. 285v.

6. After Bouvines: The counts Ferrand of Flanders and Renaud of Boulogne are led captive by Philip Augustus. Paris, Bibliothèque Nationale fr. 2813, fol. 258v.

7. The poet Gilles de Paris presents his book, the *Karolinus*, to Prince Louis. Paris, Bibliothèque Nationale lat. 6191, fol. vii^v.

8. Villeneuve-sur-Yonne (Yonne). Photo. H. Roger-Viollet.

9. Gisors, Tour du Prisonnier (Eure). Photo. CAP Roger-Viollet.

10. Verneuil, Tour Grise (Eure). Photo. HLIR Viollet.

11. Vernon, Tour des Archives (Eure). © Arch.
phot. Paris/S.P.A.D.E.M.

12. Rouen, Tour Jeanne d'Arc (Seine-
Maritime). Photo. N.D. Roger-Viollet.

13. Chinon, Tour du Coudray (Indre-et-Loire). © Arch. phot. Paris/S.P.A.D.E.M.

14. Falaise, Tour Talbot (Calvados). Photo. J. Feuillie/C.N.M.H.S./S.P.A.D.E.M.

to their specifications, the towers of Villeneuve and Orléans had identical measurements, but those at Laon and Péronne were slightly larger. These early examples have since disappeared, with the sole exception of Villeneuve-sur-Yonne. Enough remains of this last donjon, however, to show that it corresponded closely to the specifications in Register A.[207] The one extant example, then, helps identify seven other extant towers with similar characteristics that can be attributed to Philip: the Norman fortifications of Gisors (Tour du Prisonnier), Falaise (Tour Talbot), Rouen (Tour Jeanne d'Arc), Vernon (Tour des Archives), Verneuil (Tour grise), and Lillebonne, and the Loire castle of Chinon (Tour du Coudray).[208] (See Plates 8–14.) Diverse evidence produces seven more towers that have since disappeared: Beauvais, Bourges, Cappy, Compiègne (Tour de Beauregard), Corbeil, Montargis, and Montdidier. This brings the total number of cylindrical towers built during the reign of Philip Augustus to twenty.[209]

In addition to their cylindrical exteriors, these towers resembled one another in possessing comparable measurements. Although the placement of doors and windows varied according to location and purpose, all were furnished with at least two floors, vaulted in stone, and with circular staircases enclosed in the walls. In the surviving examples, one striking characteristic predominates. Unlike preceding donjons, where the quality and size of the stones varied between edifices and even within the same edifice, indicating that the masons worked with materials found on hand, Philip Augustus's towers were constructed of blocks uniformly cut from stone of comparable quality. Even the building costs were comparable.[210]

These similarities suggest that a concerted and unified building program was mounted on a large scale. The utilization of the same basic plans, the same materials, perhaps even the same scaffolding, also suggest that the king organized a corps of engineers to execute his program. In the accounts of 1202/03 artisans called "masters" are listed, of whom four (Hugues, Thomas, Christophe, and Richard) were involved in construction work, mainly on the Norman marches. In the *baillis'* accounts, however, the aforementioned Abelin was clearly responsible for Dun-le-Roi and Issoudun, for which he made a full statement of expenses.[211] In Registers A and C, the work was entrusted to a group of nineteen masters, including Hugues and Thomas, but also Abelin, who worked on Montreuil-Bellay.[212] A Master Garnier was specifically designated a mason (*cementarius*) and Master Gilbert "a moat excavator" (*fossator*). Obviously, not all were recruited locally, because Garnier worked on sites as

distant as Montreuil-sur-Mer and Montargis, and Guillaume de Flamenville at Montdidier and Orléans. At Paris, Melun, Compiègne, Montdidier, and Montreuil-sur-Mer, they worked in groups of two or more.
The king himself took an active interest in the projects. At Loudun, Montdidier, and Pont de l'Arche he helped to lay out (*divisit*) the construction.
At Compiègne he personally ordered thirteen turrets for the walls, and at
Melun he procured wood for the gates and drawbridges.[213]

Employing specialized engineers who followed standardized plans and
building techniques, Philip Augustus constructed a score of cylindrical
keeps with speed and economy. The king budgeted between 1,200 and
2,000 *livres* each to build the individual towers. Even at the higher rate,
Philip's total program amounted to no more than 40,000 *livres*, a sum
comparable to the 50,000 *livres angevins* (or 34,000 *livres parisis*) that
Richard expended on Château-Gaillard alone in 1197–1198.[214] Granted
that the fortifications at Gaillard extended beyond the central stone donjon, and that the site was particularly inaccessible and expensive to build
on, Richard nonetheless spent a good deal more on this one project than
Philip on the fourteen castles listed in the building accounts between
1205 and 1212 (which cost 21,500 *livres*). In fact, Richard's castle cost
two-thirds as much as Philip expended on fortifying cities and castles
(48,500 *livres*) in the period following the Norman conquest. A standardized and efficient building program undoubtedly afforded the Capetian maximum protection for minimum cost.

Philip Augustus's round towers emphasized defense over residence.
The cylindrical shape offered greatest external resistance and stone-vaulted
floors hindered attackers from burning out the interior. The massive
four-meter-thick walls allowed, at most, an interior diameter of only
eight meters. Although Villeneuve was provided with fireplaces on two
floors, some towers had less heating or none at all.[215] Towards the end of
the reign, Philip devised a quadrangular plan with round towers at the
four corners to achieve a more commodious fortification.[216] The central
keep of the Louvre was later surrounded by such an arrangement, which,
like the earlier tower, may have served as a model—in any event, the
square donjon at Caen was also encompassed by square walls and corner
towers. Montreuil-sur-Mer, which appears in the building accounts of
1205–1212, was designed as an irregular polygon. The two best preserved examples of this plan are found at Yèvre-le-Châtel (Loiret) and
Dourdan (Essonne). In the former, an irregular parallelogram encloses
an extensive loge. The large corner towers resemble the earlier cylindrical

products. At Dourdan, however, a large cylindrical stone keep was placed at the north corner and overshadows the other, smaller corner towers. Finished shortly before 1222, Dourdan was Philip's last major military construction, and best represents a concluding phase in which residential requirements once again took precedence over defense—an apt symbol of the stability of the last years of the reign.

Because of their strategic value, castles could serve as a medium of exchange in dealings with vassals. Not only did Philip acquire and build fortresses to consolidate the royal domain and his new acquisitions, he also gave them away when it best served his interests. In distant fiefs, for example, where it became impractical to hold castles directly, he conceded them to neighboring lords. As early as 1189, the king gave the castle of Montboissier in gage to the count of Auvergne. In this inaccessible region Bertrand de la Tour received three castles, the bishop of Clermont four, and the bishop of Le Puy five.[217] In 1192 the count of Toulouse received Najac and Posquières in the Rouergue, and in 1194 Hugues de Berzé-le-Châtel submitted his castle in the Mâconnais in fief to the king.[218] Other examples could be added from equally remote regions.

After the conquests of Normandy and the Loire valley, many more castles that could be used to treat with vassals came into the king's hands. When Philip received Falaise, Bonneville-sur-Touques, and Domfront from Queen Berengaria's dowry, for example, he gave Domfront to Renaud, count of Boulogne, in exchange for Mortemer. Château-du-Loir, also from the dowry, was assigned to the seneschal of Anjou in exchange for the seneschalship of Le Mans.[219] As might be expected, too, the king used Norman castles to reward loyal supporters.[220] Even during the last years of his reign, Philip continued to deal in castles. Having constructed a tower at Sully-sur-Loire, for example, he confided it in 1218 to the bishop of Orléans.[221]

In many of the above transactions, it was specifically stipulated that the receivers of castles must return them at the king's express request.[222] In fact, Philip's frequent practice was to allow vassals to hold their castles on condition that they furnish pledges to deliver the strongholds on royal demand. In 1200, for example, six Norman lords gave assurances that Robert d'Ivry would deliver the border fortresses of Ivry-la-Bataille and Avrilly, and in 1203 Simon de Beausart offered pledges to render his castle in Picardie.[223] This arrangement was particularly widespread in the Loire valley, where royal authority was less firm than in the old domain and Normandy. We have seen that it was explicitly written into the contracts defining the powers of the seneschals of Anjou and Poitou. Not only were Loches and Châtillon-sur-Indre to be surrendered on request, but local lords furnished pledges to hand back the nearby castles.[224] Most of these promises were exacted between 1206 and 1214 in preparation for the final struggle over the Loire valley.

As feudal seigneur Philip inherited an intricate web of customary rights and privileges over his vassals that reinforced his authority as monarch. Making few efforts to alter this traditional legacy, he was content to define more clearly and record more precisely the advantages offered to him. His position at the apex of the feudal pyramid was given official sanction; his rights over wardship and marriage were clearly asserted; and the authority of his court over vassals, even over the great barons such as John, was effectively enforced. His attempts to record were more impressive. The terms of homages, fealties, and countless pledges were spelled out in written charters, stored in archives, and recopied or listed in registers. More important, detailed surveys of fiefs were drawn up and inserted into the registers. Prompted by well-established precedents in Normandy, Philip not only had the duchy's inventories entered into his registers, but also continued investigations to record all enfeoffments in minute detail by the end of the reign. When he approached the old domain, where owed service was not as well defined, he was equally assiduous in inventorying all enfeoffments. Had the survey been completed, not only all Norman fiefs, but all fiefs throughout the royal domain would have been duly inscribed in Register E.

Such efforts to define and document them strengthened Philip's feudal bonds with his vassals. Homage, fealty, marriage, and wardship—and even the less successful policy of offering *fief-rentes*—provided means of gaining the loyalties and restraining the disaffection of his men. Feudal rights also presented opportunities for exploitation in terms of both military service and financial gain. The great efforts to inventory the fiefs of the domain were not, however, notably fruitful in generating service in Philip's armies. Though knight service owed to the king in Normandy increased from 581 before the conquest to 847 in 1207, according to the surveys, only 158 of those knights, at most, fought with Philip at Bouvines. In fact, the king's entire feudal resources produced only 2,000 knights to defend the Capetians in the crucial moments of 1214. Despite the exhaustive measures to record all enfeoffments at the end of the reign, no feudal army was subsequently based on this information, and neither has any attempt been uncovered to use the fief as the basis for an aid or military tax. More effective were the efforts to organize fiefs for the service of castleguard, which complemented Philip's program of constructing castles and town fortifications to stabilize the countryside in the royal domain. Castles were more appropriate to the king's strategy than the feudal host after the great conquests were completed. As the importance of military service decreased, Philip's most lucrative rights as seigneur were perhaps those of wardship and relief. When great vassals like John of England or Ferrand of Flanders succeeded to their fiefs, royal finances could be increased by as much as one-fourth to one-third, but this happened rarely. In the final analysis, therefore, Philip's advantages as seigneur were both sufficient to prevent him from ignoring his feudal rights and not enough to account for his eventual success.

12

Repossessing the Churches

As we have seen, while laying plans to seize John's continental fiefs, Philip Augustus was threatened in 1200 by a papal interdict imposed on his lands because of his unsuccessful attempt to divorce Ingeborg. To win friends among churchmen, the king decided to extend unusual liberties to the French church. He not only publicized to the Norman clergy the Capetian policy of allowing free elections to royal bishoprics and abbeys but even initiated a program of renouncing regalian rights altogether. He further improved the clergy's legal status by according them virtual immunity from the secular police, an extreme privilege claimed for Anglo-Norman churchmen by the sainted Thomas Becket.[1] After the conquest was accomplished, however, Philip appears to have had second thoughts about the more advanced of these freedoms. As lord of Normandy, he fell heir to the Anglo-Norman duke's well-established control over bishops and abbots. To profit from this precedent, Philip accordingly began to rescind or modify his former measures.

New Gains

The Capetian conquests, of course, greatly augmented the number of royal churches. To the twenty-three regalian bishoprics held by the king

304

in 1203,[2] Philip added the metropolitan see of Rouen with its six suffragan bishoprics (Evreux, Lisieux, Bayeux, Avranches, Coutances, and Sées) and the three Loire sees of Angers, Le Mans, and Poitiers—an increase of ten bishoprics. The archbishopric of Tours, which the Capetians had long claimed as regalian, had been under constant harassment and isolation in territory belonging to the kings of England. After the conquest, it was effectively restored to the French king. The relationship of the nine suffragan sees in Brittany to the French monarchy remained unresolved until 1212. The three easternmost sees, Saint-Malo, Dol, and Rennes, as well as the three southernmost, Quimper, Vannes, and Nantes, had been under the control of the Angevins as counts of Brittany. The remaining sees of Léon, Tréquier, and Saint-Brieux were dependent on local lords. As long as Arthur was presumed alive, he inherited the claims of the Breton counts over their churches. In the marriage treaty of 1209, however, Guy de Thouars, then count of Brittany, gave the eastern sees to Henri de Tréquier as part of the dowry of his heiress, Alix, and retained for himself the southern bishoprics. Both Guy and Henri were to hold their bishoprics in fief from the king, but the arrangement was never executed. When Pierre de Dreux finally became count in 1212 through marriage to Alix, he assumed responsibility for the eastern and southern bishoprics, which he presumably held, like the county, in fief from the king.[3] Although Philip Augustus lost direct supervision of the Breton sees, he nonetheless increased the total of his regalian bishoprics by 43 percent from Normandy and the Loire lands, and regained effective authority over Tours.

Philip's gains in royal monasteries are more difficult to estimate. Between 1204 and 1212 a chancery scribe drew up a list of royal monasteries in Register A, which was recopied with additions into Register C in 1212. From the Loire region the list names Marmoutier, Bourgueil, Saint-Maixent, and Saint-Pierre-le-Puellier of Poitiers, and from further south, Tournus, Saint-Gilles, Figeac, Seilhac, and Issoire.[4] This constitutes only a minimal listing, because it omits the best-known royal abbey in the Loire valley, Saint-Martin of Tours. At the end of the list in Register C, however, the scribe added the notation: "All the abbots of Normandy who are black monks." The duchy was rich in monastic foundations, and at least forty-three Benedictine houses were flourishing at the time of the Capetian conquest.[5] Philip's gains from these alone must, therefore, have equalled, or even exceeded, the number of royal monasteries in the old Capetian domain, although the latter figure is uncertain. Because the notation was limited to the Benedictine abbeys, we are not able to assess what other foundations may also have been considered royal. We may suspect that Philip Augustus at least doubled his regalian monasteries from Normandy alone, but the precise extent cannot be calculated.

Despite uncertainties about the overall monastic gains, Philip's conquest of the Touraine did resolve one problem that had long vexed the Capetians' largest regalian monastery, Saint-Martin of Tours. Although a long-established royal foundation, this house of regular canons, like the neighboring archbishopric of Tours, was situated deep in Angevin territory and owed services to both the kings of France and the counts of Anjou. As early as 1190, Philip Augustus and Richard had ordered an inquest into their respective jurisdictions and the abbey's rights, but such agreements had not protected Saint-Martin from the ensuing conflict. In 1194, to cite only one example, Richard forcibly ejected the canons from their church.[6] When John was driven out in 1204, the abbey was finally released from this dual allegiance and enjoyed a measure of security. In 1211 Philip reconfirmed the findings of the inquest of 1190 and ordered his *baillis* to protect the church's properties, because it belonged especially to the king. In 1215 he further commanded his *bailli* Robert de Crespières to render to the canons the lands of their vassals who had deserted to England.[7] Containing over 150 prebends, the chapter was immense—at least three times the size of a large cathedral chapter. Because these prebends had frequently been used to support royal clerics, the chapter was plagued with absenteeism, prompting a papal investigation in 1204.[8] Philip nonetheless continued to give the post of dean and treasurer to his *familiares*. Eudes Clément, from the family of royal marshals, was dean between 1211 and 1216, and he was succeeded by Nicolas de Roye, nephew of Barthélemy de Roye.[9] When the treasurer died in 1216, the king promised the chapter that he would not keep the post vacant for more than a year. He finally conferred it on his illegitimate son Pierre Charlot, whose presence there until 1235 exemplified the royal character of the abbey.[10]

Continuities: Freedom of Elections

After the conquests Philip Augustus held true to one Capetian policy—the maintenance of free ecclesiastical elections. His promise to the Norman sees, announced in 1200, that they were free to choose their bishops, "just as the other canons of French churches have the power to choose their bishops," was faithfully kept.[11] The papal registers, which by recording appeals to Rome were sensitive to disputed elections, contain virtually no indication of royal interference.[12] The only case in which Philip showed an interest occurred at Paris at the end of the reign. In 1220 the chapter of Notre-Dame elected as its dean Master Gautier Cornut, whose family was connected by marriage to the Cléments. When the chanter of the cathedral raised objections, Pope Honorius III annulled the election, not because of the candidate's unsuitability, but because of procedural irregularities. The pope then proceeded to translate the bishop of Auxerre, Guillaume de Seignelay, to Paris. If the first candidate, a royal cleric, was favorable to Philip, the second was persona non grata, not only because of his continual obstinacy, but also because he was objectionable to the masters of Paris, who went on strike for six months. Reluctant to face such concerted hostility, Guillaume de Seignelay braved the heat and pestilence of Rome to ask the pope personally for permission to remain at Auxerre. When the pope remained insistent, the king and scholars were forced to acquiesce, and Gautier Cornut had to wait three years before finding another suitable prelacy, this time the archbishopric of Sens.[13]

Philip Augustus's isolated and unsuccessful attempt to voice his will in this episcopal election contrasted with John's reputation for persistent and brutal interference. The English king violently opposed a candidate at Sées in 1202, and in the same year he forcibly imposed Guillaume de Beaumont on the see of Angers. By 1205 he was embroiled in the turbulent and celebrated dispute at Canterbury over Stephen Langton.[14] Whether in England, Normandy, or the Loire valley, the churches felt John's heavy hand. For that reason Philip Augustus's promise of free elections in 1200 must have influenced the Norman bishops to welcome the Capetians. Towards the end of 1204 or the beginning of 1205, the archbishop of Rouen and his suffragans of Avranches, Lisieux, Coutances, and Sées informed Pope Innocent III that Philip had subjugated the duchy and received the fealty of the lay baronage. When they inquired whether they, too, should offer fealty according to Norman custom, Innocent's reply of March 1205 did not directly answer their question. Pleading ignorance of the particular circumstances, he advised the bishops to follow their own judgment.[15] In the light of Innocent's support of John only a year earlier, this response can only be interpreted as acquiescence in the conquest. Left to their own counsel, the Norman bishops did offer fealty. None thereafter objected to a new master whose demonstrated support of free elections could only be welcomed with a sense of relief.[16]

The effect of Philip's policy on the chapters of his newly acquired lands was dramatic. In Normandy and the Loire, where the chapters had regularly chosen royal clerics or candidates from families closely allied with the king, these traditional types virtually disappeared. In 1201, to be sure, Evreux elected Robert de Roye, nephew of the royal familiar Barthélemy de Roye, shortly after receiving its charter of liberty. But two years later, and again in 1220, the canons turned to their dean.[17] In fact, of nine elections held in Normandy from the conquest to the end of the reign, not one resulted in a candidate who could be considered "royal." Only one bishop came from outside the duchy, and he was a papal appointee. All the others were either members of the chapter or from the immediate vicinity. Among five elections held during the same period in the Loire bishoprics, only the first at Tours in 1206 chose a "royal" candidate. He was Geoffroi de la Lande, formerly canon of Saint-Martin of Tours and archdeacon of Paris, who was recommended by Eudes de Sully, bishop of Paris. Thereafter, in 1208, the canons of Tours eventually decided on their dean, as did the canons of Le Mans in 1214. The only outsider in these sees was Maurice at Le Mans in 1216, who had formerly been archdeacon of Troyes and was apparently chosen for his reputed sanctity.[18] Elsewhere in the royal domain, the regalian chapters continued to elect royal clerics—sons of Gautier the Chamberlain and candidates related to the king. Eudes de Sully, Philip's ecclesiastical advisor, continued to recommend appointments. But the influence of electoral freedom in the new territories began to alter the overall complexion of the bishops elected to regalian sees, as Table 12 illustrates.[19] In the two

TABLE 12. Royal and Local Candidates Elected
to Regalian Bishoprics, 1179–1223

	Total Candidates	Royal Candidates	Local Candidates
1179–1190	17	6 (35%)	5 (29%)
1191–1203	18	8 (44%)	3 (17%)
1204–1214	25	8 (32%)	13 (52%)
1215–1223	22	4 (18%)	12 (55%)

SOURCE: Appendix C.

decades following the conquests, the percentage of bishops considered favorable to the king ("royal" candidates) therefore fell from 44 percent to 18 percent. Conversely, those elections that can be attributed exclusively to local influence ("local" candidates) increased from 17 percent to 55 percent. By the end of the reign it had become obvious that royal cathedral chapters were responding to local stimuli rather than finding candidates "useful to the kingdom," as Philip had urged in 1190.

A Halt to Renunciations of Regalia

In 1203, shortly after Philip Augustus offered free elections to the Norman sees, he also began renouncing the regalia themselves.[20] Unlike the election policy, however, this move was abruptly discontinued in 1209. Thereafter, despite numerous vacancies, no more renunciations were announced. The crucial decision may have been taken two years earlier, in November 1207, on the death of the leader of the Norman bishops, Walter of Coutances, archbishop of Rouen. At that time Vivien, bishop of Coutances, wrote the king asserting on the testimony of men of good faith that the archbishop's temporal and spiritual goods belonged to the chapter during vacancies, and that neither the English kings nor their servants had touched them.[21] In other words, Vivien contended that the privileges Philip had recently granted to the chapters of Auxerre and Troyes had been customary at Rouen under the Anglo-Norman dukes. Undoubtedly refusing to accept this improbable story, Philip commanded a formal inquest into the vacancy left by the death of Archbishop Rotrou in 1183 and the subsequent election of Walter. Thirty-six men, including knights, burghers of Rouen and Andelys, the abbots of Fécamp and Caen, and the bishop of Avranches, offered sworn testimony on three issues: the temporal regalia, the spiritual regalia, and the election of the archbishop. In general they were agreed that at the death of Rotrou, King Henry took the temporal properties (regalia) into his hands, appointed custodians, and returned them to Walter on his elevation to the archbishopric. As to the conferring of prebends during the vacancy (the spiritual regalia), they divided over whether the king had the right or even actually bestowed them. But they were certain that both Rotrou and Walter had been made archbishops at the will of King Henry. When the canons had proposed a rival candidate in Robert de Neufbourg, the king forced the chapter to accept his favorite, Walter of Coutances.[22]

Rejecting the letter of Vivien of Coutances, Philip accepted the evidence of the inquest and had it transcribed into the registers. Although he willingly abandoned the Anglo-Norman practice of imposing royal candidates, he nonetheless continued to enforce the Anglo-Norman tradition of enjoying the regalia, both spiritual and temporal. About the same time, his *bailli* Jean de Rouvrai took custody of the archepiscopal possessions at Dieppe without provoking protest from either the new prelate or the chapter.[23] By the end of the reign, it had become routine for the dean of the chapter, after announcing the results of a new election, to request in writing that the king return the archbishop's holdings.[24] Even the papacy acquiesced in the king's exercise of rights to the spiritual regalia. In 1210 Philip conferred a prebend from the vacant see of Laon on a royal cleric, Master Thomas d'Argenteuil. When this gift was contested by another cleric, the king sought confirmation from Innocent III. Although the pope personally favored the other candidate, he nonetheless refused to contest the king's rights over the gift, thus preserving the principle of the spiritual regalia.[25] After 1209, drawing support from Norman precedents, Philip Augustus defended his regalian rights over all royal sees that he had not yet renounced.

Philip's about-face as regards the regalia doubtless produced resistance and encouraged the bishops to exploit any ambiguity that might test the royal decision. Closely connected to the regalia was the king's requirement of an oath of fealty from his bishops to guarantee the military service due from their fiefs. As we have seen, certain bishops attempted to oppose this aspect of the regalia. Although Philip's charter of renunciation to Auxerre in 1207 explicitly reserved his right to summon the bishop for army service, Guillaume de Seignelay, bishop of Auxerre, and his brother Manassé, bishop of Orléans, refused to answer a royal summons in 1210 on the technicality that the army was not led personally by the king. After a protracted dispute involving interdicts, confiscations, and papal involvement, the bishops finally submitted to the king in 1212 and recognized their military obligations for the return of their regalia.[26] In 1214, upon the resignation of the bishop of Le Mans, Philip ordered an inquest into whether the bishop had ever owed fealty to Kings Henry, Richard, or John. Although Philip agreed to abide by Angevin precedents as to fealty, he nonetheless assumed that he held the regalia during the vacancy and would restore them at the bishop's confirmation.[27] When the question of fealty was finally decided in 1223, Louis VIII also assumed that the king enjoyed this inalienable right at Le Mans, Angers, and Poitiers.[28] Whatever the distinctions between fealty and military service, by 1209–1210, after the policy of renunciations was abolished, Philip Augustus required full regalian rights from the bishoprics of the old domain, Normandy, and the Loire fiefs.

Taking Stock of Ecclesiastical Resources

The territorial expansion of 1204 prompted the chancery not only to inventory the fiefs in the royal domain but also to take stock of the king's ecclesiastical resources, all of which were recorded in the registers. Two clerks set themselves the task of compiling lists of regalian bishoprics.[29] The first drew up a list of eight archbishops and forty-five bishops headed by the rubric: "Archbishops and bishops that are under [*sub*] the king of the French." He then identified with the notation *sb'* (*sub*) twenty-five sees that were subject to the king, two that were not (*non sunt*), and left the remaining twenty-six blank. The second scribe composed a list of thirty-four episcopal cities (*civitates*) captioned "These are the *civitates* that King Philip has in his domain." This second list corresponds closely to the first, except for the omission of nine southern and eastern sees and the nine Breton bishoprics—all obviously outside the royal domain.[30] To this second inventory the scribe Etienne de Gallardon added notations indicating *episcopus/archiepiscopus* (bishop, archbishop), *regalia*, *exercitus* (army), and *procuratio* (*gîte*). Since these notations designate regalian characteristics, it appears that Etienne, like the scribe who used the *sub* notation, was attempting to identify regalian sees.[31]

When the *sub* annotations of the first list are compared with the regalian notations of the second, the correspondence between the two is nearly complete. With two exceptions, the inventories agree on the regalian bishoprics of the provinces of Reims, Sens, and Lyon, the Capetian heartland.[32] The interpretation of these lists depends on their dates, however, because they were transcribed into Register A between 1204 and 1212, when the status of individual sees was changing. Although undated, they can be best accommodated to the years 1207–1208.[33] This date suggests that the inventories were initiated towards the end of an unsettled period, when Philip attempted to abandon his policy of renunciation and to reestablish control over his regalian sees. Despite this chronological approximation and the close agreement between the two lists, however, they do not always accord with the evidence of the charters, particularly in what they omit.[34] These difficulties suggest that the chancery was not quite sure of the identifications. Perhaps the scribe of Register C omitted the *sub* designations and the *civitates* inventory altogether for this reason. Recopying the first, he entitled it merely: "Archbishops and bishops of the kingdom of France." The two inventories nonetheless represent, however imperfectly, a concerted effort by the royal chancery to account for the royal bishoprics after 1207–1208. (See Map 1.)

At the turn of the century, Philip Augustus was too preoccupied with his regalian bishops and his designs on the Norman and Angevin sees to pay much attention to those south of the Loire valley. In November 1204 he received homage from the bishop of Limoges, who was being harried by King John. Although Philip took the see under his protection, promising never to let it depart from his hand, the Capetian had few means to enforce his promise.[35] For almost two decades, moreover, Philip allowed his father's policy of sending letters of protection to the southernmost bishoprics of the province of Narbonne to lapse. But the revival of the crusade against the Albigensians after the murder of the papal legate in 1208 recalled the south to the king's attention. In that year Philip reissued his father's and grandfather's charters confirming the bishop of Maguelonne's possessions, accorded them royal protection, and linked them inseparably to the crown.[36] In 1210 he renewed his former charter conceding the regalia to the bishop of Lodève and granted him protection and the right to bear the royal standard. Five years later he received the bishop's personal fealty. In 1211 he sent two charters to the bishop of Uzès that enlarged his father's confirmation of the church's possessions. Finally, in 1212, he renewed his former contacts with the Auvergnat see of Le Puy and later reconfirmed to his cousin, the bishop-elect, the possession of various castles.[37]

Though these letters may have had little practical effect in extending the royal presence into the Midi—a movement that awaited Philip's son and grandson—they nonetheless increased the royal chancery's awareness of the geography of the provinces of Narbonne and Auch. When Etienne de Gallardon completed the first episcopal inventory of Register A, which had attempted to identify bishoprics under (*sub*) the king, he added the archbishopric of Narbonne and twelve southern bishoprics, to which a third hand appended four more. This new information remained tenuous and incomplete.[38] Subsequent copies in the royal registers attempted to improve upon the initial list. In 1212 the scribe of Register C corrected several spellings and added three more southern bishoprics,[39] but when compared with a *Provincialis* copied by another scribe on the other side of the folio, his list still lacked seven bishoprics from Auch. This *Provincialis* was a compilation of sees arranged by metropolitan provinces (whence its name) and was probably based on an exemplar furnished by the papal court.[40] When in 1220 Etienne de Gallardon did insert into Register E a comprehensive *Provincialis* of all Christendom, which was in fact derived from a papal model, he finally possessed an inventory of all French bishoprics that was, apart from scribal slips, both accurate and complete.[41] These bishops lists preserved in the royal registers show the clerks of the royal chancery, whose travels were limited to northern France, groping towards a full understanding of the episcopal resources of the kingdom.

Provinciales maintained at the chancery also stimulated the king's interest in the provincial organization of the French church. Just as Philip had defended Tours's metropolitan jurisdiction over the Breton sees as part of his rights over the kingdom, so he later took up the cause of the primacy of the archbishop of Bourges. Although entailing little jurisdictional authority, primacy was an honorific claim to precedence among archbishops. Located in the Massif Central, Bourges was one of the poorest dioceses, but its archbishop nonetheless claimed to be the primate of Aquitaine. On this authority he called a council in 1210, which the archbishop of Bordeaux neglected to attend, failing also to send representatives. When Bourges reacted by suspending Bordeaux from its metropolitan dignity, the dispute was appealed to the papacy. Since the archbishop of Bordeaux was an English protégé and the spiritual leader of John's remaining bishops in Aquitaine, the controversy naturally bore political overtones. It is therefore not surprising that Philip wrote Innocent III in defense of Bourges's claims in 1211. Although Bourges possessed meagre resources, Philip declared, its primacy rendered it nobler than all other churches in the kingdom. Bordeaux's disobedience derogated the kingdom's honor, and Philip felt compelled to request the pope to enforce Bourges's jurisdiction.[42] The controversy with Bordeaux dragged out beyond Philip's reign, but in the process the archbishop of Bourges did obtain an intermediate objective. In 1218 Pope Honorius III confirmed Bourges's primacy over the archbishop of Auch, the other metropolitan in the English-dominated southwest.[43] As in the case of Tours, Philip here entered an ecclesiastical dispute to defend his kingdom's integrity.

If the chancery clerks experienced difficulties in identifying regalian bishoprics, they were even more at a loss to account for regalian abbeys. The inventory entitled *Abbates regales* inserted into Register A between 1204 and 1212 lists nineteen monasteries. When the scribe of Register C recopied it in 1212, he added ten more names, plus the notation about all the black abbots of Normandy. Limited almost exclusively to ancient Benedictine foundations, this list, even in its augmented version, was grossly incomplete. Two more inventories were subsequently inscribed in Register A, which identified regalian abbeys by their military obligations. One of these compiled a list of thirty monasteries owing pack-horses (*summarii*) to the king, and the other, the *Prisia servientum*, noted some twenty abbeys owing sergeants, wagons, or money to Philip's standing army in 1194. These various lists yield a total of forty-five monasteries, not including the unspecified Norman churches, that were of special interest to the royal court (only a small core of fifteen are common to all three). Since these compilations were singularly inadequate, the chancery was evidently unable to produce a satisfactory definition of a regalian house, and when the scribe of Register C recopied the *abbates regales* in 1212, he dropped the adjective *regales* from the title, just as he had ceased identifying those bishoprics that were under (*sub*) the king.[44]

Beyond taking stock, the chancery clerks noted royal obligations towards churches in the royal domain, as in the alms account in Register A. In this inventory, the domain consisted of holdings after the treaty of Le Goulet in 1200, including Artois, Vermandois, and Evreux, but excluding the great conquests in Normandy and the Loire valley. Within these limits, twenty-nine *prévôtés* paid out a total of 1,002 *livres parisis* in alms each year to some 133 religious establishments and individual clergymen. More than half of this sum (519 *livres parisis*) went to churches in the newly acquired regions of Vermandois and Evrecin, administered by the *prévôts* of Péronne-Bapaume and Pacy-Evreux. We have already seen that Philip was not doing much more by these expenditures than matching the alms of his predecessors. Since this account did not include the more recent obligations to the Norman and Loire churches, when Etienne de Gallardon recopied it into Register E in 1220, he entitled it "The annual alms of the lord king; certain ones, but not all."[45]

An effort was, however, made to recognize the king's Norman obligations when the scribe who began Register A in 1204–1205 copied two other accounts from Rouen. Captioned "Alms and wages at Rouen to be paid from the exchequer," the first consisted of excerpts taken from the

Norman exchequer rolls of 1180, 1195, and 1198, to which at least one item was added from the opening years of John's reign. Even when wages to secular persons are deducted, it still accounted for 2,157 *livres* to be paid each year in alms at Rouen. Although 1,000 *livres* of this went to the archbishop, Philip's new alms at Rouen alone more than doubled those for the entire royal domain prior to 1204.[46] The second account was entitled "Alms owed by whoever holds the *vicomté*." Since they were paid chiefly in kind, it is difficult to calculate their total value.[47] These two Rouenais inventories nonetheless confirm an observation that was only suggested by the previous alms accounts. When Philip Augustus acquired new lands, he inherited from his predecessors greater obligations to churches than he was accustomed to paying in the old domain. If the Rouen accounts were at all representative of other Norman obligations, the king's alms rose dramatically after 1204. Unfortunately, we are not able to estimate their full extent. When the Norman exchequer resumed normal operations, it undoubtedly resumed responsibility for accounting the royal alms in the duchy. Since neither the subsequent Norman financial records nor the general accounts at the Temple have survived, we are ignorant of Philip Augustus's alms after 1204.

Defining Boundaries Between King and Clergy

Normandy provided Philip Augustus with precedents for reestablishing regalian rights and, on a theoretical level, for defining the legal boundaries between the king and the clergy. Since the early twelfth century, when the influence of the reformed papacy began to permeate Latin Christendom, churchmen had set about constructing their own system of ecclesiastical justice, which put the clergy outside royal and local jurisdiction. On the institutional level, they established an ascending hierarchy of courts, through which appeals passed from archdeacon to bishop to archbishop and, finally, to the pope. At the same time, the popes dispatched judges delegated to act with full papal authority. To regulate this machinery, a jurisprudence of ecclesiastical or canon law was perfected. Though churchmen continued to participate in customary justice as local territorial lords, by mid-century they possessed both their own courts and their own law. Designed primarily to resolve the clergy's internal disputes, ecclesiastical justice could not avoid contact with laymen and secular justice, especially since popes and canon lawyers kept expanding the competence of church courts. Their jurisdiction was extended beyond the clergy to include crusaders, widows, and orphans. Their competence included not only purely spiritual matters, but also "mixed" affairs such as marriages, testaments, alms, oaths, and crimes such as heresy and usury, all of which implicated laymen. And to defend the church's material position, ecclesiastical courts claimed jurisdiction over clerical property. Since the courts of the French and English monarchs were undergoing comparable development, it was only a matter of time before this expanding ecclesiastical justice came into conflict with royal justice and required efforts to define the boundaries of each.

Up to the turn of the twelfth century, most conflicts between ecclesiastical and secular jurisdiction were resolved at the local level, often to be confirmed by a royal charter.[48] When Philip Augustus acquired Normandy, however, he fell heir to a long succession of attempts to delimit jurisdiction between the church and royal courts. This Norman tradition, reaching back into the eleventh century, and including English experience as well, finally enabled Philip to achieve a comprehensive definition of the boundaries between ecclesiastical and royal justice.[49]

Duke William of Normandy convoked an assembly at Lillebonne as early as 1080 to formulate the relations between the clergy and the duke. The contemporary chronicler Ordericus Vitalis included these customs in his history—because, he asserted, later men would wish to learn of Norman laws under King William—and thereby gave expression to a deep-seated Anglo-Norman habit of writing down legislation. (Philip Augustus displayed his interest in the document by preserving a sealed copy in the archives and having it transcribed in the chancery registers.)[50] Henry II likewise attempted to resolve conflicts between himself and the clergy by reducing to writing the customs governing royal-clerical relations during the time of his grandfather, Henry I. Although the results, the famous Constitutions of Clarendon of 1164, were envisaged primarily for the English church, they were nonetheless relevant to Normandy, because both kings were also Norman dukes.[51] When Richard, accompanied by Walter, archbishop of Rouen, departed on crusade in 1190, their representatives in the duchy, the seneschal Guillaume fitz Ralph and Jean, dean of Rouen, arrived at an agreement that was published by the suffragan bishops.[52] After their return, the king and archbishop met with other bishops at La Roche-d'Orival (probably in 1198) and settled five issues, three of which had been considered in 1190. Their decisions were preserved in the dossier of documents preceding the second Norman *coutumier*, composed late in Philip's reign.[53] The author of the first Norman *coutumier*, writing around 1200, was also sensitive to the clergy's rights, because he attempted to interpret Norman custom in a manner favorable to clerics.[54] Philip Augustus himself, however, brought these preceding efforts to culmination in the year following the conquest. Assembling twenty-two barons and knights at Rouen on 13 November 1205, and with the help of four former Anglo-Norman officials, he ordered an inquest into the rights of Henry II and Richard over the Norman clergy. The long and comprehensive testimony was carefully preserved in a sealed charter at the archives, and was also inserted into the registers.[55] At the inquest, the barons admitted that since certain of their number were absent, they could not remember all the provisions. If it pleased the king, they were agreed to continue their work in the future. Accordingly, further modifications were negotiated in 1207 and 1218.[56]

Shortly before the inquest, another group of western barons assembled at the siege of Chinon in June 1205. Two years earlier a similar group had urged the king to resist papal pressure to make peace with John. Now the French barons once again requested the king in writing to withstand the demands of the pope and the clergy. Although the precise nature of the demands (*exacta*) was not specified, they involved usages and customs (*usus et consuetudines*) long in practice. Both barons and king pledged mutual faith to make no agreement with the pope or clergy without common consent.[57] Whatever these specific complaints, during the same year the barons and the clergy did come to an agreement (*stabilimentum*) over their differences at Paris. This settlement, which we shall call the Paris accords, survives in two forms: first, a list of ten grievances against the clergy's infractions of temporal justice, redacted by the king, and second, an expanded version of thirteen points at issue, with the final resolutions, which was then transcribed into the chancery registers.[58] Although the settlement cannot be dated more precisely than between Easter 1205 and Easter 1206, it was most likely drawn up with knowledge of the Norman inquest of November 1205, because it follows Norman proposals at several points. The Norman inquest simply defined the boundaries between ecclesiastical and ducal/royal jurisdiction, whereas the Paris accords dealt more broadly with the relations between the clergy and the whole French baronage.

Like most medieval settlements, the Norman inquest and the Paris accords of 1205 were drafted with little logical distinction between important and minor matters. Apart from specific proprietary questions and

minor matters over which the clergy had special jurisdiction (tithes, testaments, usury, and Sunday observance),[59] the articles of the two documents may be grouped in two categories, which dealt with major issues
dividing royal and ecclesiastical justice: (1) Concurrent secular and ecclesiastical rights in property and (2) the maintenance of public order.[60]

SECULAR AND ECCLESIASTICAL PROPERTY RIGHTS

Of great concern to both king and churchmen was the delimitation of
property and rights (considered also as property) in which laymen and
clergy had concurrent interests, as, for example, when laymen nominated
priests to their churches or clerics held land by military service. Preeminent among these was the first, called presentation of churches, or advowson. The right to present a candidate for institution as curate of a
specific church to the bishop had been exercised by laymen since the early
Middle Ages. Although the bishop could judge the candidate's fitness, he
could not refuse the presentee except for good cause. Recognized in Normandy as early as the canons of Lillebonne, this right was considered customary in the first Norman *coutumier* and was reaffirmed in 1205.[61] According to long-established Norman custom, whoever had presented the
previous curate, he or his heirs possessed the advowson. But if a particular presentation was disputed, who had jurisdiction? Pope Alexander III
had affirmed in 1179–1180 that advowson cases belonged exclusively to
ecclesiastical judges, but in Normandy such disputes had been tried in
ducal courts since early in the reign of Henry II, a practice sanctioned by
the Constitutions of Clarendon.[62] Though on the eve of the French conquest, the first Norman *coutumier* simply restated the Norman practice,
the inquest of 1205 further elaborated that the candidate could not obtain the church until the dispute had been adjudicated in the royal or
feudal court and the bishop had received letters patent announcing the
decision. Following the possessory procedures instituted by Henry II,
the Norman courts summoned a jury of twelve men to render a collective
decision as to who had presented the previous curate to the church.[63]
Like the other possessory remedies, this action decided possession and
not the proprietory question of the right of advowson. The inquest of
1205 nonetheless vindicated a customary Anglo-Norman right in the
face of papal opposition.

The Norman clergy were apparently dissatisfied with these procedures
because in 1207 Walter, archbishop of Rouen, and his suffragans petitioned the king to institute reforms. Philip accepted the bishops' pro-

posal that disputes over presentations were to be decided by a panel of four priests and four knights, selected by the diocesan bishop and royal *bailli* respectively.[64] Each priest and knight was to be questioned individually under oath, and the majority determined who had the right of presentation. Reforming custom in two ways, the new procedure substituted the canonical inquest for the Norman collective decision by a jury, and it initially sought to determine right rather than possession. If the eight did not know who had the right, however, they nonetheless granted possession. As in 1205, the bishops promised not to institute the curate until the matter was decided in the royal court. Now it was affirmed that if six months had elapsed without a decision, the bishops could institute a candidate, although without prejudice to the ultimate right.[65]

Between 1207 and 1223 the exchequer at Falaise considered at least seventeen cases of advowson (or about 5 percent of its total business). Most of these employed the old jury of recognition, and it was not until 1216 that the new system surfaced in the records.[66] In 1207 the bishops had promised to expedite disputes quickly, but the king for his part complained about their lack of speed. In 1218, therefore, Robert Poulain, archbishop of Rouen, conceded that if the deans who summoned the four priests did not appear on the day assigned by the *bailli*, they were fined nine *livres* for each offense, payable to the lazar house of Rouen.[67]

Disputes between churchmen and laymen over property increased as more land was acquired by churches throughout Western Europe. In Normandy, as in Norman England, all litigation over land was decided in the secular courts, where trial by battle was the normal proof, but during the course of the twelfth century the church increasingly claimed jurisdiction over disputes involving ecclesiastical property. The practical question of who owned a specific piece of land was therefore transformed into a jurisdictional conflict as to which court was competent to judge. In 1164 King Henry II attempted to solve the problem in the Constitutions of Clarendon by adopting a distinction between alms (*elemosina*: land subject to ecclesiastical jurisdiction) and lay fief (*feodum*: property subject to the secular courts).[68] If a dispute arose between a layman and a cleric over a holding, the king decreed, it should be decided by twelve legal men (jurors) and the justiciar whether (*utrum*) the holding was alms or lay fief. If alms, the case proceeded to the church courts, but if lay fief, it was under the jurisdiction of the king or a common lord.[69] Making no initial decision about to whom the land belonged, Henry's constitution merely assigned jurisdiction. Although emphasizing competence, it nonetheless allowed the royal court to decide an important question that influenced the eventual proprietary decision. The assize *utrum*, as it was called, therefore gradually became proprietary, assigning ownership in specific cases. In thirteenth-century England it was the normal way for a curate to vindicate his holdings. The evidence for the assize *utrum* in Normandy is not clear before the Constitutions, but after 1164 it was known and practiced as a writ *de feodo et elemosina*. At the end of the century, the first Norman *coutumier* indicated that it decided not only competence but also proprietary rights.[70]

When Philip Augustus's inquest investigated the procedure in 1205, it was determined that in a dispute between a cleric and a layman, it would be decided in the royal courts through the oath of legal men of the realm whether the property was a lay fief or alms. Reflecting the Constitutions of Clarendon, the working of this formulation emphasized competency, but did not exclude the possibility of resolving proprietary questions as in contemporary practice. The exchequer at Falaise considered a writ of *utrum* in ten cases (or 3 percent of the recorded disputes) between 1207 and 1223. Of these most involved competency; only two assigned possession of land.[71] The distinction between lay fiefs and alms proposed by Henry II was eventually accepted by the papacy. Pope Alexander III ordered cases involving fiefs to be tried in secular courts, and Innocent III followed his lead. Protesting Philip's aggressions against Normandy, Innocent affirmed that he had no intention of judging matters concerning fiefs.[72]

Since the preliminary decision was assigned to royal justice, the secular courts enjoyed an initial advantage. To redress the balance, the Norman clergy revived a Carolingian device known as thirty years' prescription. In 1190 the ducal authority had conceded that ecclesiastical property was immune from secular jurisdiction if it could be shown that the ecclesiastics had held it for thirty years or more. Furthermore, if tenure by alms could be demonstrated by charter, jurisdiction also belonged to the church.[73] Charter or thirty years' prescription therefore exempted ecclesiastical property from the writ *de feodo et elemosina* in Normandy.

No such privilege was recognized in England, and Philip's inquest of 1205 ignored the provision, but the Norman clergy apparently insisted on reviving it, because it was later incorporated into the writ *de feodo et elemosina*. At the Easter exchequer of Falaise in 1218, the bishops and barons agreed that if disputes arose over alms and lay fiefs, they were to be settled in the royal court by twelve legal knights. If either the cleric or layman asserted possession for thirty years without contest, the legal men would investigate the claim and assign jurisdiction to the appropriate court. If thirty years' prescription could not be proved, however, the writ *de feodo et elemosina* applied.[74] Although belatedly, Philip Augustus not only recognized this important concession to the Norman clergy, but also extended its provisions to laymen.[75]

To what extent did the jurisdiction of secular courts over lay fiefs apply to clerics who also held lay fiefs? In practical terms, what remedies had a lay lord against a clerical vassal negligent in performing services owed from a lay fief? In twelfth-century England, lords customarily distrained or seized the chattels of negligent vassals until due service was restored.[76] Such action obviously conflicted with clerical privileges. Canon law asserted the immunity not only of a cleric's person but also of his goods from secular courts.[77] The Anglo-Norman monarchs ignored clerical privilege in practice and distrained the goods of churchmen who failed to perform their services,[78] but this right was not defined either in England or in Normandy. When Philip Augustus's inquest rendered its report, however, the situation was finally clarified: any lord who suffered loss from a cleric holding a fief by knight fee could seize the cleric's chattels found on the fief until feudal obligations were satisfied. In Normandy clerical immunity was not allowed to obstruct feudal service, and we have seen that Philip applied this rule to the bishops of Auxerre and Orléans.[79]

Although the Anglo-Norman remedy *de feodo et elemosina* was not available throughout the rest of France, laymen nonetheless faced comparable problems. In 1205 the barons at Paris therefore proposed a summary solution: if a cleric impleaded a layman over landed possessions, the case should not be heard in a church court but in the court of the lord who had justice over the land—unless, of course, justice actually fell to an ecclesiastic.[80] Although this Parisian proposal was not as refined as the Anglo-Norman remedies, the two nonetheless shared general goals, namely to bring to a halt clerical encroachment on secular jurisdiction and to insure that disputes pertaining to land and its services remained in the courts of the king and the barons.

Property rights were equally affected by the church's claim to jurisdiction over pledges of faith and oaths. In the twelfth century many contracts involving landed property and moveables contained a pledge of faith (*fides*), whereby the parties pledged by their Christianity to fulfill the agreement.[81] Parallel to this pledge, the parties might also swear an oath (*sacramentum, juramentum*) to guarantee the contract. Since both the pledge of faith and the oath were religious acts, churchmen claimed that contracts containing them fell under ecclesiastical jurisdiction, thus extending the competence of church courts over land and moveables. Obviously, such broad claims could be expected to elicit strong secular reaction. King Henry II decreed in the Constitutions of Clarendon that pleas of debt, whether involving the pledge of faith or not, belonged to the king.[82] Archbishop Becket's party interpreted the king as intending to deprive ecclesiastical courts of all jurisdiction over breaches of faith and perjury, though it is not entirely clear that this was so. After Pope Alexander III condemned the proposition, and Becket was murdered, Henry retracted his innovation. The final resolution was reported in Glanvill's authoritative treatise, which declared that although breach of faith fell under the church's jurisdiction, to be punished by penance and satisfaction, the pledge of faith did not impede concurrent royal jurisdiction over lay tenements and debts, since the Constitutions had assigned such competence to the king.[83] In subsequent years the English royal courts normally forbade ecclesiastical judges to try cases over lay fees and chattels, except in matrimonial and testamentary cases, which were reserved especially for the church.

When the Norman clergy met with the seneschal in 1190, they sought to regain their pre-1164 position by demanding that breaches of faith and oath be tried in ecclesiastical courts as a rule. In particular, cases of dowry and marriage gifts were claimed for the church when they concerned moveables. Jurisdiction over landed property in such cases was left unresolved and deferred to later consultation.[84] Fifteen years later, however, Philip's inquest refused to accept these concessions and returned to a position closer to that of Henry II. The barons declared that no ecclesiastic should judge anyone's faith or oath involving lay fiefs or chattels. If, however, the faith concerned the chattels of a marriage portion (*maritagium*), testament, clerics, or crusaders—cases considered peculiarly ecclesiastical—the church had jurisdiction. The second Norman *coutumier* reveals that practice in the early thirteenth century generally relegated moveables to the church and lands to the king.[85] The exchequer at Falaise enforced Philip's provisions in 1208 by forbidding the bishop of Avranches to compel Richard Peillevillain to answer charges in an ecclesiastical court over breach of faith in his lay fief.[86]

Simultaneously with the Norman inquest, Philip adopted Henry II's principle in the accords of Paris. The king complained that clerics drew cases involving fiefs into their courts by means of pledges of faith, thus depriving feudal lords of their right to do justice. Replying to the demands of the clergy in terms similar to those of Glanvill, the king and barons agreed to permit the ecclesiastical courts general competence over breaches of faith and perjury, but excluded fiefs. If anyone was convicted in a church court, he might be punished with suitable penance, but the feudal lord did not lose jurisdiction.[87] Despite clerical pretensions as to oaths, the Capetian monarch, like the English, retained jurisdiction over fiefs.[88] Following the principle of 1205, Philip prohibited the townsmen of Saint-Quentin from bringing suits concerning inheritance and lands before the church courts as long as the royal courts were prepared to do justice.[89]

MAINTENANCE OF PUBLIC ORDER

The second boundary between temporal and spiritual jurisdiction involved the maintenance of public order, of which the Norman inquest examined three aspects: the truce of God, the excommunication of ducal officials, and the prosecution of criminous clerics. The clergy and barons at Paris concentrated on the last two. The truce of God had been the church's contribution to public order in a prior age when secular authority was helpless to curb violence. Following Flemish precedents, the Norman clergy instituted the truce of God at the Council of Caen in 1042 by declaring certain periods sacrosanct against acts of vioence. If anyone killed or maimed during the holy days, he was to be excommunicated and sent into penitential exile.[90] Although original responsibility belonged to the church, the duke also had an evident interest in the success of the truce. William the Conqueror affirmed in the canons of Lillebonne that if the bishop was unable to enforce the truce, he could seek aid from feudal lords and the ducal *vicomtes*.[91] In time the Norman dukes developed measures for maintaining the ducal peace that eclipsed those of the ecclesiastical truce.[92] Since the effective enforcement was assumed by the duke, King Henry I was obliged by 1135 to assure the Norman bishops of their customary fines of nine *livres* collected for infractions.[93] Thereafter, the clergy's interest in the truce of God was purely financial. Philip's inquest summed up the situation in 1205. The truce was defined as lasting from Wednesday evening to Monday morning. If anyone lost life or limb during that period, jurisdiction belonged to the royal court, but the church was assured of its fine if the accused was convicted.[94] Enforcement belonged to the king; the church was content with its money. When the first Norman *coutumier* asserted on the eve of the French conquest that no man dared make war against another, but brought his complaints before the duke's justice,[95] it signified that public order was now a ducal responsibility.

If responsibility for peace was the king's, what recourse had churchmen against the encroachments of royal officials? The chief clerical defenses were, of course, excommunication and interdict, applicable to offending officials as to everyone else, but the Constitutions of Clarendon placed limitations on sanctions against those closest to the king. No tenant-in-chief or minister of the royal household could be excommunicated, or have his lands placed under interdict, without prior approval of the king or his justiciar.[96] Reflecting Norman practice, the first Norman *coutumier* reaffirmed this principle.[97] The inquest of 1205 preserved ministerial immunity for Philip Augustus by declaring that the archbishop, bishops, and lesser ecclesiastics could not pronounce sentences of excommunication against barons, *baillis*, servants, or clerics of the royal household without the permission of the king or his seneschal. As heirs of the Anglo-Norman household, Philip's Norman ministers thus possessed an important advantage not recognized elsewhere in the Capetian administration.

Once again, Philip achieved a similar outcome in the Paris accords, where he extended the restrictions on excommunication to benefit not only the king but also the barons. If any lord or his servant willingly or unknowingly harmed the church, he could not be excommunicated or his land placed under interdict until he or his *bailli* (in case of his absence) had been duly consulted (*requisitus*). Whereas Anglo-Norman custom protected only royal officials, the Paris accords thus restricted clerical excommunications of all temporal lords and their officials. Although the two customs were not identical, they both shared the goal of curbing clerical weapons against political authority.[98] The archbishop of Rouen renewed the Norman privilege to Philip in 1218, but restricted its application. Out of love for the king, he conceded, neither he nor his *officialis* would excommunicate the chief royal *baillis* without consulting the king, but this immunity would last only two weeks. If the *bailli* refused to render a tonsured cleric or his chattels to the bishop or his *officialis*, however, excommunication followed immediately.[99] This exception pointed to a final problem in maintaining public order, the policing of criminous clerics.

Since public order was the ducal responsibility in Normandy, the duke naturally claimed jurisdiction over crimes committed by the clergy, but the latter claimed immunity from secular authority. How was the discrepancy to be resolved? As early as 1080, Duke William had allowed clerics who committed serious crimes, such as rape, theft, murder, and arson, to be punished by their bishops with monetary fines, with no mention of ducal responsibility.[100] We have already seen that during the twelfth century the punishment of clerical crime was complicated by two sets of privileges formulated in canon law to protect the clergy. Under the *privilegium canonis* the clergy were immune from any form of physical coercion and under the *privilegium fori* they were subject exclusively to ecclesiastical jurisdiction. Henry II had attempted to devise procedures by which royal and church courts could cooperate to handle the problem of mounting clerical crime, but Archbishop Thomas Becket's opposition and martyrdom guaranteed all English clerics complete immunity from secular courts. Becket's position was adopted in Normandy in 1190 (reconfirmed in 1198) and at Paris in 1200 by Philip Augustus under pressure of a papal interdict. By the turn of the century, therefore, the clergy throughout the duchy and the royal domain were exempt from the authority of the royal police.[101]

After the French conquest, Philip was apparently determined to reopen the question of clerical crime in Normandy. When the barons and knights investigated the matter in 1205, they began with the provisions of 1190. If a cleric was arrested for serious cause, such as theft or murder, he should be handed over to churchmen at their request. If convicted, he would be degraded and required to abjure the realm. He could neither be punished again for that crime nor reenter the realm without the king's permission.

In contrast to 1190, the inquest of 1205 thus recognized a second penalty—abjuring the realm. It is difficult to tell whether abjuring implied outlawry or merely exile. If outlawry, it was punishment second only to death. Deprived of all legal protection, the cleric could be hunted down like a wild beast and killed by whoever found him.[102] Even if only exile, a new penalty was added to degradation. Becket had formerly suggested abjuring the realm as fit punishment for criminous clerics, but Henry II had refused to allow ecclesiastics to impose it because it belonged exclusively to royal authority.[103] Though only one instance of its use against clerics has been found in Normandy (1166),[104] it was the normal procedure in dealing with those who fled justice by seeking asylum in a sanctuary. For example, King Richard and the archbishop of Rouen agreed in 1198 that those who took refuge in a church to escape justice had eight days to choose between submitting to the royal court or abjuring the realm.[105] Underlying this provision was the theory that not submitting to the justice of the realm denied one residence therein. It is not inconceivable that the barons and knights of the inquest envisaged the punishment of criminal clerics in the context of asylum. Ecclesiastical judges had most likely degraded clerics within a sanctuary to give them benefit of asylum. In 1205, however, abjuring was explicitly linked to degradation. Whatever the circumstances, the solution of 1205 was a decided improvement over that of 1190. Now the duchy could be cleared of convicted clerics whose punishment had formerly ended with degradation.

If the clergy posed problems for Normandy, their unruly conduct was even more threatening at Paris, where, in addition to the urban clergy, clerical students and masters swelled the population. The situation at the royal capital was further exacerbated by Philip Augustus's celebrated charter of 1200 to the Parisian scholars, which fully incorporated Becket's interpretation of the *privilegium fori*. But Becket's solution—consistent refusal to deliver degraded clerics into secular hands—was too extreme even for the ecclesiastical authorities, who wished to inflict more than degradation on clerics committing crimes abhorred by the church. In the famous decretal *Ad abolendam* (1184), Pope Lucius III had allowed clerics, as well as laity, convicted of heresy to be punished by secular authority. Pope Celestine III (1191–1198) permitted similar sanctions against incorrigibly felonious and obstinately rebellious clerics, and in 1201 Pope Innocent III applied them to forgers (normally clerics) of papal bulls.[106] It is not surprising, therefore, that in the Paris accords of 1205 Philip and his barons were tempted to reexamine the question. The careful prescriptions regulating the *privilegium canonis* were allowed to stand,[107] but the unconditional jurisdiction of the *privilegium fori* was reopened for scrutiny.

Since Philip had recently added abjuration to degradation and restricted the right of asylum in Normandy, this solution suggested a new approach to the problem. The right of sanctuary was widely exercised throughout the Capetian domain. The customs of Senlis, which Philip approved for Tournai in 1200, for example, maintained that if anyone pursued for homicide or other crimes sought refuge in a church, the clergy were forbidden to deliver him to the secular authorities.[108] In 1205 the clergy and the barons debated a special instance of church asylum in which a person captured by the king or another lord submitted to imprisonment until he paid his ransom. The clergy contended that if the person later escaped to a church, he was thereby liberated and released of his obligation to redeem himself. The barons and king countered that the person should not be freed of his ransom if he fled to a church, but the clergy should deny him entrance to the edifice or the atrium, so that he could be retaken. After limiting the right of sanctuary in this special case, the king returned to the central issue. In the preliminary redaction, the king and barons clearly stated their objection to the present customs. When a cleric was arrested for a manifest crime for which he should lose life or limb, he was turned over to the bishop. Although the bishop should degrade him and return him to the *baillis* for punishment, in fact he liberated the degraded cleric. As a compromise the king and barons conceded that though the degraded cleric should not be handed over directly to the secular courts, neither should he be released in a place of asylum. Rather, he should be released outside a church or cemetery, where the justiciars could apprehend him and administer punishment without committing sacrilege.[109] Since asylum was no longer involved, the Norman solution of abjuring the realm was unnecessary. Instead, the degraded cleric was treated as a layman. The accords of Paris in 1205 thus renounced the Becket position of 1200 and devised a solution that improved upon Norman precedents by reaching back to the Constitutions of Clarendon. Where Henry II had failed because of Becket's martyrdom, Philip Augustus finally succeeded through patient negotiation.

The new solution to clerical crime was applied in 1210 to the heretics condemned at the councils of Sens and Paris. These members of the clergy were degraded, handed over to the king's court, and burned in the field of Champeaux.[110] Nor was the papacy slow in accepting Philip's solution. In 1209 Pope Innocent III addressed a decretal to the bishop of Paris that offered general approval for degrading criminous clerics in the presence of royal officials and permitted their delivery to secular justice.[111] When an inquest was made into royal justice in the *prévôté* of Orléans at the end of the reign, the jurors could recall at least three cases in which the bishop had turned over convicted and degraded clerics to royal officers for punishment.[112] The vexing problem of clerical crime was thus met through the cooperation of ecclesiastical and royal courts.[113]

In the Norman inquest and the Paris accords of 1205, Philip Augustus attempted to draw a line along the long frontier between royal and ecclesiastical authority. Throughout this exercise in map making, the duchy of Normandy played a leading role. By the Norman inquest procedure, Philip examined important issues such as electoral practices at Evreux in 1200, the delimitation of royal-clerical rights in 1205, and the regalia of Rouen in 1207–1208. Except in the first example, whose results were unanticipated, the French king reached back beyond the agreements of

Richard in the 1190s to recover rights formulated by Henry II in the Constitutions of Clarendon in 1164. In most cases Philip was successful. Disputes over presentation of churches and lands held by alms or lay fiefs remained in the royal courts. Excommunication of ducal officials still required prior approval of the royal government. Contracts involving lay fiefs and chattels were exempt from ecclesiastical jurisdiction over pledges of faith and oaths. The distraint of clerics negligent in their feudal service was confirmed. Only in the sensitive area of criminous clergy was Philip unable to recover the full position of the Constitutions. Here he had to be content with outlawry or exile of degraded clerics in place of corporal punishment decreed by the royal courts. With so many and such disparate issues, it is difficult to assess whether the Norman church gained or lost under its new Capetian lord. How can the gain of freedom of elections be weighed against the loss of unrestricted jurisdiction over contracts? Nonetheless, when one distinguishes between policies before and after the conquest, a clear impression of change emerges. The king was eager to display a beneficent side before 1204, but he became intent upon vindicating his traditional rights afterwards. From being a beguiling seducer, Philip became a stern master.

Normandy also served to introduce change and redefinition into Philip's relations with the rest of the French clergy. Just as the inquest into the regalia at Rouen most likely influenced the king to cease renouncing his regalia elsewhere, so the Norman inquest enabled him to come to a general agreement with the clergy in the accords of Paris of 1205. Here Philip was able to obtain concessions comparable to his Norman prerogatives in pledges of faith, secular jurisdiction over landed cases, and excommunication of government ministers, and to extend these rights to the French baronage as well. In the vital matter of criminal clerics, he was able to exceed the Norman inquest and recover advantages originally proposed by Henry II. The Paris accords of 1205 were therefore Philip Augustus's equivalent of Henry's Constitutions of Clarendon, but whereas the Constitutions were bitterly contested by Becket and his followers in England, Philip's accords came into force in France without serious controversy. Troublesome bishops like the Seignelay brothers and Anselme of Laon may have contested the king but they were concerned with temporal, not canonical, jurisdiction.[114] With only minor exceptions, the accords of 1205 stabilized the frontiers between king and clergy for the remainder of the reign.

Victory,

1214—1223

The Fruits of Victory

Philip's victory at Bouvines evoked waves of rejoicing throughout the realm. In Guillaume le Breton's exuberant tableau, the populace danced, the clergy chanted, and bells were rung. Flowers and branches festooned churches and houses and carpeted the streets of towns and villages. Regardless of estate, family, and sex, everyone converged on the route of the triumphant army. Peasants and harvesters shouldered their scythes and rakes (for the crops were ripe) and rushed to see Count Ferrand led to Paris in chains. His foreign-sounding name elicited puns and jeers from the rustic crowds. Jubilation was general, but at Paris the townsmen and scholars greeted the king with such enthusiasm that one day was not long enough to satisfy their celebrations. For an entire week the students feasted, danced, sang, and illuminated the nights with torches. When the royal chronicler embellished his account with the verse of the *Philippidos*, he emphasized that peace was the most welcomed fruit of victory. Favoring the clergy and his friends, and punishing the wicked, the king peacefully ruled his kingdom and people with paternal affection. King and people competed as to who loved the other the most.[1]

Guillaume le Breton's accent on peace undoubtedly caught the prevailing mood of the final decade of Philip's reign. During the king's lifetime his lands north of the Loire were never to be troubled again. This absence of armed conflict, however, tended to reduce the king's role in the narrative accounts. As Philip faded in the splendor of peace, Guillaume le Breton increasingly turned to the military deeds of Prince Louis. These consisted chiefly of the two unfinished enterprises assumed at Soissons in 1213: the aborted expedition against England and the crusade against the Albigensian heretics in the south.[2] Both may be considered as adventures, because neither achieved its goals—in the first case ever, in the second, by the reign's end. In both cases the king was either outwardly hostile or reluctant to provide support.

Narrative: Adventures in England and the South

Condemned to remain in England after the defeats of 1214, King John acceded to the demands of his rebellious barons at Runnymede and granted the Magna Carta in June 1215.[3] But the English king still retained the support of his feudal suzerain, Pope Innocent III, who annulled the charter, excommunicated the rebels, and suspended Archbishop Stephen Langton for having cooperated with the rebellious party. Since John's military position remained strong in England, the rebels revived their former plan to enlist Capetian aid. Negotiations to offer Prince Louis the English crown were confirmed by a delegation of leading barons. The English chronicler Roger of Wendover noted that in addition to military support from France, Louis might neutralize John's mercenaries, most of whom came from lands subject to the French king.[4] As he had done three years earlier, the pope fulminated against the projected invasion, asserting protection over John as a papal vassal and an avowed crusader. Once again, the papal legate Cardinal Guala arrived at the French court to obstruct the impending invasion. This time the papal objections were countered by an elaborate set of arguments, presented in three differing versions—to the legate at Melun in April 1216, to the pope himself in Rome in May, and forwarded to Canterbury in June. Among the three versions the Capetians contended that John had lost his right to the throne when he betrayed Richard in 1194, that the French court had convicted John of murdering his nephew Arthur, that John had unlawfully surrendered his kingdom to the papacy without baronial consent, and that according to French custom, Louis was the rightful heir to the English throne through his wife, Blanche of Castile.[5] Roger of Wendover maintains that Innocent and his legate were not persuaded by these specious propositions. Certainly they were no more convinced by them than modern historians. To vindicate a decision already taken, the Capetians nonetheless broadcast them widely.

Preceded by two contingents, Louis crossed the Channel in May 1216 with a sizeable force. By the end of July, he and the rebel barons were in control of most of eastern England, with London as center of operations. In this heartland only the royal castles of Windsor, Lincoln, and the troublesome Dover (endangering contact with the Continent) held firm for John. This astonishing success was abetted by several conditions. According to the Anonymous of Béthune, who accompanied the expedition, Louis brought with him 1,200 knights, including the counts of Nevers, Dreux, Brittany, and Perche, and effective warriors like Enguerran de Coucy and Guillaume des Barres.[6] His adherents among the rebel barons included over a half-dozen earls and members of most of the leading baronial families, joined by the king of Scotland and Welsh and Irish princes. Although Dover held out, the rest of the Cinq Ports of the Channel offered little resistance. Having long suffered under John's arbitrary hand, twelve out of twenty English bishops welcomed Louis as a defender of church liberties. In Louis's entourage there was a coterie of learned English clerics, including Master Simon of Langton, the archbishop's brother, and Master Elias of Dereham, the archbishop's clerk, who openly preached Louis's and the rebels' cause in the churches of London.[7] To oppose this broad-based coalition, John could muster only loyal familiars such as the justiciar Hubert de Burgh, seven bishops, among them Peter des Roches, the curialist bishop of Winchester, and a handful of barons, including the aging William the Marshal, earl of Pembroke. As foreseen, the Flemish mercenaries began to slip home or join the French side. John's chief and most effective supporter remained the papal legate, Guala, who kept up a barrage of excommunications. Perhaps, however, John's most telling weakness was the intense animosity he aroused among his enemies. When he unexpectedly died from massive indigestion at forty-eight on 19 October 1216, he in one stroke released this crucial bond uniting the opposition. Caprice was John's hallmark and may have saved the English monarchy.

Since Louis was under anathema and the archbishop of Canterbury was absent in Rome seeking to lift his suspension, the Capetian had not yet succeeded in securing recognition as legitimate king of England. John's supporters lost no time in having his nine-year-old son Henry crowned at Gloucester as rightful successor. The child was committed to the care of the bishop of Winchester, and the earl marshal ran the government as *rector* of the king and kingdom, seconded by the earl of Chester; but, as usual, the greatest responsibility was born by the papal legate. Innocent III had also died recently, but Honorius III kept perfect step with his predecessor as suzerain and defender of the young king. When Henry assented to a revised version of Magna Carta, he became the rallying point for the legitimist cause. Eleven of the twelve defecting bishops returned to the new king. Early in 1217 Louis obtained a truce to journey to France, undoubtedly in hopes of securing more support. When he returned in April with his principal barons but with fewer knights, the rebel party had eroded in England. Unwilling to leave Dover unsubdued at his back, Louis renewed the siege, while the rest of the French and rebels turned to other royal strongholds, among them Lincoln. The earl marshal and the bishop of Winchester learned that a reduced French-rebel force was outside Lincoln, and wagered on full battle to obtain a decisive victory. After solemn preparations and renewal of excommunications, the loyalists achieved their objective. In an almost bloodless engagement fought on 20 May 1217, the rebel army was completely routed, half made prisoner, and only one notable figure killed, the young count of Perche. With God's judgment so apparent, defections to the loyalists increased. Louis made a final effort to enlist aid from France, but when reinforcements obtained by his wife were lost in August in a naval battle off Sandwich, he had to concede that the divine decision had been confirmed. The most serious obstacle to the peace negotiations was the punishment allotted to the English clerics of Louis's entourage. The terms, first discussed in June, were finally agreed upon in September 1217. In exchange for a tenth of his revenues for two years, to be donated to the crusades, Louis received absolution from excommunication.[8] The peace was facilitated by paying Louis 10,000 marks of silver to ensure his definite departure, an indemnity not included in the formal terms. The size of this sum (ten times larger than John's annual tribute to the pope) demonstrates the regents' eagerness to be rid of the French. But it was effective, because the Capetians never returned.

Although a failure, Louis's expedition sought to realize an ardent ambition of his father's. The Anonymous of Béthune reports that Philip, awaking one morning in 1213, exclaimed, "Mon Dieu, what is keeping me from conquering England!" We have seen that Louis's role in the expedition Philip then proposed was closely defined and restricted in a charter issued at Soissons in April 1213 and carefully preserved in Register C.[9] In contrast, however, the royal archives, registers, and other official documents contain no trace of Philip's involvement in the invasion of 1216–1217. To discern the extent of Philip's responsibility for the latter enterprise, we must look to reports by contemporary chroniclers.

Undoubtedly expressing the official view of the Capetian court, Guillaume le Breton steadfastly disclaims any involvement on the king's part in the adventure. When Louis responded to the initial call of the barons and Londoners by sending a contingent of knights, the chronicler adds, his father utterly disagreed with the measure. Guillaume also claims that after the pope and Guala excommunicated Louis in 1216, Philip confiscated the lands of his son and the latter's followers because he did not wish to violate his truce with the king of England. When the plight of Louis's expedition became desperate after John's death, the French king, fearing papal excommunication, refused to answer his son's requests for aid. Even when Louis returned to France during the truce in 1217, Philip refused to communicate with him. Yet at an earlier date Innocent himself was not convinced of Philip's official position and commanded the archbishop of Sens and his suffragans to excommunicate the king for apparent complicity. Learning that the expedition had set sail, the pope composed stern letters to Philip, but they were never sent, inasmuch as Innocent took sick and died—divine punishment, in the royal historiographer's opinion, for having doubted the Capetian's good faith. When Guillaume takes up Louis's expedition in the *Philippidos*, he devotes only four lines to it—enough, however, to maintain that the father refused to favor his son because he did not wish to incur the supreme pontiff's enmity.[10]

The contemporary English chronicler Roger of Wendover, whose vivid imagination often colors the events he reports, asserts Philip's initial involvement. When the rebel barons offered the crown to Louis, Philip demanded at least twenty-four suitable hostages, Roger asserts, and when confronted by the papal legate Guala, the king personally argued the case against John. But Roger also records Philip protesting devotion to the papacy and renouncing any counsel or aid to his son. Nonetheless, the king was willing to listen to Louis's vindication of his rights to the English throne. After Louis's case had been presented by his *procurator*, the prince begged his father not to hinder the enterprise. "When the king saw his son's perseverance and determination," the chronicler reports, "he gave permission and dismissed him with his benediction." After the defeat at Lincoln, however, Philip feared to respond to the pleas of his excommunicated son because the pope had often rebuked the king's consent, and Louis therefore relied on Blanche, who quickly sent reinforcements.[11]

The contemporary observer closest to the expedition and yet not an official spokesman for the Capetians was the Anonymous of Béthune. Both versions of his account agree with points made by Guillaume le Breton. When Louis returned to France, for example, the king is portrayed as not speaking to his son. But the chronicler indicates Philip's true attitude when the baronial embassy presented their proposal to Louis: "And when Louis heard their words he sought advice from his counsellors and those of his father, who urged him to undertake the affair. His father, however, openly made it appear that he did not wish to be involved because of the truce he had granted, but privately it was believed that he had advised him."[12]

Despite differences, no significant discrepancies arise among contemporary assessments of Philip's role. Officially, the king refrained from openly supporting Louis's expedition, even to the point of avoiding contact with his excommunicated son. This public posture was gratefully acknowledged by Pope Honorius III in April 1217.[13] At the same time, however, Philip tacitly consented to his son's venture, which he most certainly could have prevented. (Guillaume le Breton may have exceeded the limits of truth in claiming that the king confiscated his son's lands, for which no corroborating evidence has appeared.) Consonant with Philip's political skill, the king's policy was astute. The father had everything to gain from the son's gamble to acquire a new kingdom. Louis's charter of 1213 was presumably still in effect, and Philip avoided the risks of defeat. In any event, thanks to the English indemnity, Louis's failure was hardly a disaster.

While Philip and Louis prepared for the confrontation of 1214, the crusade against the Albigensian heretics had evolved into a three-cornered competition for domination in the south.[14] Leadership in the crusade was assumed by Simon, count of Montfort l'Amaury in the Ile-de-France, who was accompanied by feudatories from north of the Loire. His goal was not only to direct the papal crusade against heresy but also to dispossess lords who openly or covertly gave aid to the heretics. Chief among these was Raymond VI, count of Toulouse, who defended his lands and vassals while protesting his innocence. The third party was Peter II, king of Aragon, who, as count of the neighboring principality of

Barcelona, also had territorial ambitions along the Mediterranean littoral. In 1212 Peter and the other Christian princes of Spain won a decisive victory against the Almohade Muslims at Las Navas de Tolosa. Encouraged by this, the king of Aragon decided also to oppose Simon de Montfort's intrusion into the south by joining forces with the count of Toulouse. But Peter's ambitions were cut short in September 1213 by Count Simon at the battle of Muret, which shattered the Aragonese army and took the king's life. The count of Montfort therefore became the leading contender in the south shortly before the Capetians won their victories at La Roche-au-Moine and Bouvines.

Returning from La Roche-au-Moine in 1214, Louis was finally free to discharge his crusading vow, contracted the previous year at Soissons before he undertook the expedition to England. In April 1215 he set out for the south to help the count of Montfort consolidate his victories. The two oversaw the dismantling of the fortifications of Narbonne and decreed similar measures for Toulouse. When the forty days of the crusading vow were completed, Louis returned home; his only gain was the acquisition of a relic of St. Vincent, which he donated to the abbey of Saint-Germain-des-Prés. The lands of the count of Toulouse were provisionally confided to Simon by Pope Innocent until the forthcoming general council of the church could decide upon their disposition. When the great council met at the Lateran palace in Rome in November 1215, it formally dispossessed the count of Toulouse and confirmed his lands to the count of Montfort. The following April Philip Augustus gave his assent to the transfer when he received Simon at the royal court and accepted his liege-homage for the lands acquired from the heretics in the duchy of Narbonne, the county of Toulouse, and the *vicomtés* of Beziers and Carcassonne, which the count of Toulouse had formerly held from the king.[15]

Although Simon and his followers were officially commissioned by the pope, the king himself also most certainly preferred a new count of Toulouse drawn from the loyal baronage of the Ile-de-France to one from an independent southern family with marriage ties to England. When the count of Montfort was killed in June 1218 while besieging Toulouse, which still resisted the crusaders, the goals of both the papacy and Philip Augustus therefore received a setback. Pope Honorius immediately substituted Amaury de Montfort in the place of his deceased father and called upon the French king to dispatch a new army under Louis's leadership. Even with the promise of papal protection, absolution from penance incurred as a result of the English expedition,[16] and the offer of half of the proceeds of a crusading tithe of one-twentieth, Philip was reluctant to renew the venture. But when the pope turned to Thibaut, the young count of Champagne, the king finally agreed. Louis departed in May 1219 in the company of bishops such as Guérin of Senlis and Etienne of Noyon, barons such as Pierre, count of Brittany, and the count of Guines, and royal officials such as Guillaume des Roches, seneschal of Anjou. The royal force joined Amaury at the siege of Marmande, which they took, massacring the inhabitants, but once again Toulouse withstood the attack of the crusading army. Unable to make further headway, Louis returned home after the obligatory forty days had expired. Philip dispatched another contingent in 1221 under the command of the archbishop of Bourges and the count of La Marche, but this force, like the former one, was unable to improve the situation. The final submission of the south was to remain the task of Louis as king, and of his son, Louis IX.

Louis's two perfunctory pilgrimages suggest that the king was reluctant to commit much to the southern venture. Guillaume le Breton, who offers the official version, describes its major phases without comment, except to blame the failure at Toulouse on the treasonable negligence of Louis's companions. One continuator of Guillaume's text also notes that the king received the papal request for a crusading tithe with minimal compliance.[17] And Pierre des Vaux-de-Cernay, a Cistercian from the Ile-de-France who chronicled the Albigensian crusade as a partisan of the count of Montfort's, is openly critical of Philip's reluctance to give full support. When Louis first took the cross in 1213, Philip was greatly distressed, Pierre reports, without going into the reasons. He expresses dismay that when Louis was finally ready to fulfill his vow in 1215, Philip did not furnish the requisite aid and counsel, although he was the liege lord of the south, had often been warned about the heresy, and was frequently called upon for help. He blames the poor French participation on the wars in the north, which distracted the king's attention, but clearly perceives that, as with the English adventure, Philip was not prepared to invest the full authority and resources of the French monarchy in the crusade against the Albigensians.[18]

The Albigensian crusade was only one of several in the papal program. Honorius III had also organized an expedition to liberate the Holy Land in 1218 that included numerous French barons and prelates. This army had attacked the Muslim base in Egypt but foundered on the siege of Damietta in 1219. The papal legate therefore summoned a new convocation of French prelates to meet at Sens in July 1223 to discuss measures for both crusades. The king's poor health caused the council to be moved to Paris to meet him there, but Philip never attended because he died on 14 July before reaching the capital.[19]

Peace

The major conflicts of the last decade of Philip's reign took place across the Channel and deep in the south, far removed from the Capetian domain. Peace north of the Loire depended chiefly on the willingness of the English king to respect the truce of Chinon of 1215, due to expire at Easter 1220. Actually, all parties had a stake in observing and even prolonging it. Although Louis's English expedition could be seen as a violation, Philip Augustus maintained official neutrality out of respect—so the chroniclers claim—for the truce. In addition, any major effort in the south could be hindered by English hostility. Because of his youth and the newness of his regime, King Henry III, for his part, had much to gain from respecting the truce, and might have had reason to fear that Louis's crusading venture would become a pretext for encroaching on English rights in Poitou and Gascony.[20] Finally, it was long-established papal policy to keep peace between the kings of France and England to promote holy wars against infidels and heretics. Because of these concurrent interests, it is not surprising that when Honorius III suggested a renewal of the truce, Philip quickly opened negotiations with the English early in 1219. By March 1220 terms were concluded that extended the truce until Easter 1224.[21]

The terms, which closely followed those of 1215, perpetuated the status quo in the Loire region. If anything, the Capetian's support south of the Loire had eroded since 1215. Whereas Henry was supported by Aimery, *vicomte* of Thouars, and Hugues de Lusignan, two important barons in Poitou, those who swore on Philip's side included only prelates, barons, and familiars from northern France.[22] But the negotiations clearly reflected the reversal of positions between the Capetian and the Angevins since the outset of the reign. In 1179 Philip had been the youth under tutelage of his barons confronting Henry II, the seasoned and successful statesman, but now the roles were neatly exchanged. In responding to the pope, Philip refused to swear personally to the terms because "John's child," as he called him, could not, as a minor, be held accountable for his oath. Instead, he offered as many barons in pledge as were provided by Henry. (In the final statement, five unnamed French barons matched five named barons for the English.) Furthermore, Philip promised to observe the truce, unless his lands were molested by the English king, who ought to protect them—although, Philip added maliciously, this child had neither the money nor the power to act as had his father John.[23]

The truce of 1220 explicitly declared that Louis, the firstborn and *fidelis* of the king, guaranteed the terms as long as his father held to them.[24] Since his knighting in 1209, Prince Louis had not played a conspicuous role in his father's routine administration; indeed, he had been notable by his absence. Apart from his mother's legacy of Artois, he had been assigned revenues from six *prévôtés* (chiefly in the Gâtinais) on his dubbing.[25] By 1213 his personal household was sufficiently organized to produce an accounting of its expenses, a fragment of which has survived. At Soissons in April of that year, Louis, now twenty-six, was entrusted with tasks outside the royal domain in England and the south that absorbed his energies until 1219, but we have seen that his independence was severely restricted by an agreement made with his father.[26] The prince was largely absent from regular affairs—missing, for example, the judgment over Champagne held at Melun in July 1216. After the conclusion of the truce in 1220, however, Louis became more closely associated with his father's court. He took an active part, for example, in the decisions between the king and the bishop of Paris in March 1221 and again in April 1223 over the inheritance of Beaumont-sur-Oise.[27] Louis's participation in these important cases marked the start of the transition to his own reign.

The peace that prevailed after Bouvines naturally facilitated the smooth operation of government. Officials who had worked effectively for over two decades continued to perform their accustomed tasks. The intelligence report received by Henry III in 1227, which identified Brother Guérin and Barthélemy de Roye as Philip's chief counsellors, undoubtedly reflects the last decade of the reign.[28] The only adjustment that can be discerned is an increased role assumed by Brother Guérin. Before his election to Senlis and his triumph at Bouvines, Guérin was already acknowledged as second only to the king. But during the last decade he becomes even more prominent in the records—certainly abetted by his new episcopal dignity, but also as a result of increased activity. Present at every important assembly, he participated more in the decisions of the royal court than anyone else did.[29]

Although always Philip's right-hand man, Guérin now operated more independently. Immediately after Bouvines, for example, Nevelon the Marshal dealt directly with Guérin in arranging pledges for the captives.[30]

After the bishop returned from the Albigensian crusade in 1219, he began to act in his own name. During the negotiations for the truce, he wrote directly to the justiciar Hubert de Burgh, his counterpart in the English government, to protest that his position had been misrepresented by an envoy.[31] In April 1221 the royal *baillis* and *prévôts* received a letter directly from Guérin, and in October the *prévôt* of Amiens conducted an inquest ordered by the bishop.[32] In March 1222 Guérin personally sent copies of royal commands to the commune of Tournai and the *bailli* Nevelon the Marshal because the originals had not been obeyed on the excuse that they had not been written with the king's consent. By April 1223 the dean and chapter of Beauvais wrote Guérin directly concerning a decision in the royal court over the succession of Beaumont-sur-Oise.[33] These examples, among many, suggest that the bishop was acting in the king's place during the last years of Philip's life. Philip had been ailing and was sick enough in September 1222 to draw up his testament, in which Guérin was named executor. As the king's health declined, the bishop of Senlis undoubtedly cooperated with Prince Louis to effect a smooth transition. Guérin was apparently too occupied with these increased duties to attend to more routine matters. He excused himself to the monks of Corbie for not performing the benediction of the newly installed abbot, for example, and delegated Master Geoffroi, his *officialis*, in his place.[34]

Although his conquests were completed, Philip Augustus nonetheless continued to acquire new lands by peaceful means. Whether the result of increased judicial activity or simply of better records, the royal court appears to have intervened more frequently in the inheritance of fiefs held directly from the king. If the succession contained a fault, such as the lack of a son, or was disputed by another party, the king was afforded an opportunity to acquire new lands. A celebrated judgment was rendered at Melun in July 1216, when the *curia regis* upheld the claims of the youthful Thibaut IV to the fiefs of Champagne against those of Erard de Brienne and his wife Philippa. Although the king actually gained no land in this case, he profited financially from his wardship both before and afterwards. The decision, whereby he merely refused to accept homage from any other lord as long as Thibaut was prepared to submit to the royal court, was not final until the count came of age in 1222. Nonetheless, Philip thereby asserted indisputable jurisdiction over succession to fiefs.[35] In other cases, Philip refrained from taking advantage. When the barony of Bourbon passed from Guy de Dampierre to his son Archambaud in 1221, for example, Philip made no gains, although it was contested.[36] Nor did the king exact a price for adjudicating the settlement when the fiefs of his *familiaris* Guillaume de Garlande passed to the husbands of Guillaume's three daughters in 1217.[37]

For the most part, however, Philip could not resist profiting from deficient inheritances. Sometimes he intervened to reclaim royal lands whose titles were unclear. Although the castle of Issoudun in Berry had been in royal hands since 1200, for example, the king did not possess the castellany. Philip adjudicated the succession of the Culan family in 1217 and obtained full rights over the castle by 1221.[38] Similarly, the king used Countess Alix's succession to Eu in 1219 as an opportunity to reassert his claims over the castles of Mortemer, Arques, and Driencourt, as well as to obtain the fief of Bully and a relief of 15,000 marks.[39]

At other times, Philip intervened to make major new acquisitions. Although the king had confirmed the testament of Robert, count of Alençon, in 1217, when the count died two years later, Philip extracted from three distant heirs the city, the surrounding county, and the fief of Essai.[40] We have already seen that the king obtained Nogent l'Erembert in 1218–1219, perhaps as a relief, but certainly as the price for Count Gautier's succession to Blois through his wife.[41] When the count of Clermont-en-Beauvaisis died childless in 1218, Philip bought out his heirs to acquire the county intact, to which he added the neighboring Creil.[42] Similarly, the death of the count of Beaumont-sur-Oise without direct heirs in 1223 gave the king the opportunity to buy out the heirs.[43] Finally, Marie, daughter and heiress to Guillaume, count of Ponthieu, had incurred the king's wrath because her husband, Simon de Dammartin, had joined his brother Renaud at Bouvines. When the count died in 1221, Philip therefore refused Marie's claims, confiscated the fief, and assigned custody to Robert, count of Dreux. The heiress did not regain Ponthieu until the following reign.[44] The monks of Saint-Denis recognized the importance of these territories when they noted that the king had acquired not only the better-known lands of Vermandois, Poitou, Anjou, Touraine, and Maine, but also Alençon, Clermont, Beaumont, and Ponthieu.[45] The chancery clerks also took note of these acquisitions, inserting into Register C an inventory of alms and *fief-rentes* owed at Clermont and Creil.[46]

Paris

The victory celebrations of 1214 may serve to recall Paris to our attention and provide an appropriate moment in which to take a closer look at the city's development. Many of the prisoners taken at Bouvines were entrusted to the *prévôts* of Paris for incarceration. Count Ferrand was assigned to the tower of the Louvre outside the walls and the others to the two *châtelets* guarding the bridges linking the Ile-de-la-Cité with both banks of the Seine. A list of thirty-four captives detained at the Grand-Châtelet on the right bank was inserted into Register C. (Unfortunately, three of the prisoners managed to escape shortly thereafter.)[47] The fortifications protecting Paris had been brought to completion not long before the townsmen and students gave themselves over to the revelries of July 1214. The walls encircling the right bank had been begun in 1190. Those on the left bank were nearly finished in 1209–1210, when the jail in the Petit-Châtelet on the left bank was enlarged. The donjon of the Louvre, whose dimensions were alluded to in 1202, was still designated a "new tower" in 1210.[48]

As exemplified by the growing encirclement of its walls, Paris was transformed into the true capital of the realm during the crucial decade of the 1190s, when the king established his archives and accounting bureau there, summoning his *prévôts* and *baillis* to the city three times a year. The expansion of the royal domain and the perfecting of the administration demanded a focal point, which required that Philip pay increasing attention to the royal city. Its facilities had to be improved, its populations provisioned, and their activities supervised. But the king was not, in fact, the only authority in the city. He shared jurisdiction with the bishop and abbots of important collegial churches, whose jurisdiction had to be defined and accommodated. Nor was he the sole celebrity at Paris. The growing renown of the university attracted masters and students from all across Christendom, whose privileges required recognition.

These divisions within Paris bred conflicts over jurisdiction that required resolution and were clearly reflected in the topography of the royal city. Circumscribed by its fortifications, Paris consisted of three distinct sections in 1214: *l'Université*, *la Cité*, and *la Ville*.[49] The university made its home on the left bank, dominated for over a century by the abbeys of Saint-Germain-des-Prés, Sainte-Geneviève, and Saint-Victor. Philip's new walls included only Sainte-Geneviève, however, leaving the others outside. When constructed, the walls enclosed fields and vineyards, but, according to Guillaume le Breton, the resulting security so stimulated building that the whole left bank was soon filled with houses. In 1210 the royal chronicler had noted that Paris rivaled Athens and Egypt as a center of learning, attracting scholars from all over the world. The basic curriculum was not limited to the seven liberal arts, but included the higher disciplines of Roman law, canon law, medicine, and theology as well. These studies were encouraged by the amenities of the site, the abundance of goods, and the special privileges guaranteed by the king.[50] Even as modified by the accords of 1205, Philip's famous charter of 1200 afforded masters and students unusual freedom and security.[51] Nourished by this propitious environment, the main features of the university emerged during the last decade of Philip's reign. By 1213 the various faculties had devised procedures for licensing masters to teach. The papal legate Robert de Courson formulated the curriculum (courses and textbooks) in August 1215. By that year the masters had achieved the full independence of a corporation, thus constituting a true university. By 1219 the masters of arts were so numerous that they began to group themselves into "nations." By 1221 the university possessed its own seal, emblem and instrument of its autonomy.[52]

The smallest and most densely settled section was the Ile-de-la-Cité in the river Seine, where the two lords of Paris were installed, one on each extremity. At the eastern end, appropriately connected with the clerical left bank by the Petit-Pont, was the cathedral of Notre-Dame, the seat of the lord-bishop. This edifice constructed in the new Gothic style had absorbed the energies of Bishop Maurice de Sully ever since 1163, when he laid the cornerstone. By 1182 the choir was completed and the main altar consecrated, and at his death in 1196 the transepts and nave were all but finished. When the king prepared to leave the country in 1190, he provided that should the bishop die, the construction would continue under the supervision of the dean and chanter of the chapter, because, as he affirmed, Notre-Dame had won his special affection.[53] Under Maurice's successors, Eudes de Sully (1196–1208) and Pierre de Nemours (1208–1219), work proceeded on the western façade and its sculpture. By the pontificate of Guillaume de Seignelay (1219–1224) the gallery of kings had been completed and the great western rose window begun. Stretched across the entire façade and commanding the recently enlarged *parvis* below, this gallery of twenty-eight kings was an overawing, if ambiguous, monument to the authority of monarchy. Until they were pulled down in the Revolution, these statues were seen as the kings both of France and of Israel. To the south of the cathedral was the bishop's palace, and to the east and north, the cloister of the chapter.

On the western end of the Ile-de-la-Cité was the palace of the lord-king, with a round stone tower and the chapel of Saint-Nicolas.[54] Whenever the royal entourage came to the capital, this was the residence of the king, his family, domestics, chamberlains, chaplains, chancery clerics, and *familiares*. The sessions of the royal court and the archives were located here. Three times a year, in November, February, and the spring, scores of *prévôts* and dozens of *baillis* presented their accounts at the Temple on the right bank. The *baillis* and perhaps the *prévôts*, too, also reported to the royal palace. As the two chief *domini* of Paris, the king and bishop shared jurisdiction over the city. Their unfinished business was to come to an agreement over mutual boundaries, particularly on the right bank, Paris's most productive and prosperous section.

The king's palace was linked with the right bank by the Grand-Pont, surmounted with houses for the most part occupied by money changers—an appropriate introduction to the commercial character of *la Ville*.[55] Philip's walls, which replaced an earlier and more restricted rampart, had the same demographic effect on the right bank as later on the left. In 1192, two years after the walls were begun, the king expressly noted the growth of the *villa* and its bourgeois in a charter regulating the wine trade.[56] Since its Celtic origins, the right bank had developed around two commercial nuclei, the Place de la Grève to the east and the Champeaux to the west, both sites of ancient markets. To the northeast was situated the fortified tower of the Knights Templars. The right bank's development was stimulated by collaboration between the king and "our bourgeois" (*burgenses nostri*), as he often called them.

From the beginning of the reign, Philip directed his attention to the Champeaux. In 1181 he acquired a fair that the lepers of Saint-Lazare held on the road to Saint-Denis and transferred it to the Champeaux.[57] Two years later he constructed two large sheds (*halles*) surrounded by walls to provide an indoor market held every Saturday that largely specialized in the sale of cloth and garments, and later in grain and other foodstuffs. Since the crowds attracted to Les Halles were destructive to the neighboring cemetery of the Saints-Innocents, Philip also enclosed the latter with walls. The popularity of the enhanced commercial center brought rapid development to the surrounding quarter, as evidenced by the geometric plan of the new streets laid out to the northeast of the Champeaux.[58] Around 1185, according to Rigord's often-told story, when the young king could no longer endure the nauseous odors of the mud streets, he ordered the bourgeois and the royal *prévôt* to pave all the streets and squares with solid masonry. At least four principal streets leading into *la Ville* were thus improved. Finally, in 1190, Philip leaned even more heavily on his bourgeois, whose leading members were to collaborate in the government during his absence. On the eve of his departure, he commanded the citizens to encircle the right bank with walls fitted with gates and turrets, which was quickly accomplished at their expense.[59] In effect, this construction united the two commercial nuclei of Champeaux and Place de la Grève within the same protection. The king's interest was well established at the former, but not at the latter. His old chamberlain Gautier held the nearby Monceau Saint-Gervais in fief from the bishop, however, and when Gautier's heir, Jean the Chamberlain, died in 1216, Philip was able to take possession of the property. With the king owning property near the Place de la Grève, the chancery clerics dutifully noted the obligations of Monceau in Register C.[60]

The king and the bishop were lodged at their palaces on the Ile-de-la-Cité, but the prelates, barons, and royal officials who were drawn periodically to the royal court and the Temple were hard pressed to find suitable residences. One can imagine that the *hôtel* crisis at Paris became severe at times.[61] Suger had solved the problem for the abbots of Saint-Denis in 1150 by acquiring a house outside the walls on the rue Saint-Martin. The archbishops of Reims had a house near the Louvre, later taken over by the bishops of Beauvais. By 1222 the bishops of Auxerre also possessed a permanent residence.[62]

Whereas the surface encompassed by the walls of Paris can be measured (about 250 hectares), modern demographers have not been able to calculate the number of inhabitants. Conservatively estimated, however, the population probably grew from 25,000 to 50,000 in Philip's reign, making the Capetian capital the largest city north of the Alps.[63] To assure the supply of essential goods and services in this urban conglomeration naturally required organization and regulation, and early in his reign Philip intervened to supervise the trade in basic foodstuffs such as meat, wine, and bread. In 1182 the corporation of butchers petitioned the king for a written and sealed statement of their ancient customs under his father and grandfather. According to these terms, the butchers could freely deal in meat and fresh- and saltwater fish without paying tolls when entering the city. They could also control membership in their corporation in exchange for payments to the king and fees to the *prévôt* for their stalls. The chief butcheries were located near the Grand-Pont, where the waters of the Seine evacuated their wastes. The butchers set up stalls in a house close by and possessed pasturage outside the city at Chelles.[64] Similarly, the bourgeois of Paris requested the king in 1192 to limit the selling of wine in Paris to certified residents of the city.[65] Although little information has emerged on the bakers, the king did intervene in a dispute with the royal *prévôts* and regulated the use of ovens.⁶⁶ Royal licensing of essential trades and crafts was undoubtedly practiced early in the reign, because Philip set the annual fees for such permits in 1201. At least a dozen trades were officially recognized during the reign, including not only the butchers and bakers but also the cloth merchants, *merciers*, cutlers, goldsmiths, used-clothes dealers, and water merchants.⁶⁷

Provisioning a large city like Paris stimulated both agriculture in the Seine valley and long-distance trade. The marsh lands of the Marais, the ancient riverbed that encircled Paris to the north, were increasingly devoted to the cultivation of vegetables for consumption in the capital.⁶⁸ Equally important was the *réseau* of commercial connections, which not only supplied the city but also permitted Parisian merchants to participate in the developing trade of the kingdom. The chief commercial routes to Paris followed the Seine, which connected the capital with the sea once Rouen was taken and also linked it to the Oise, the Marne, the Yerres, the Yonne, and their tributaries. Paris was saddled on the Seine as on a horse—and at times it proved an unruly steed. In 1196 the spring floods so threatened the *Cité* that Philip fled to higher ground at the Mont-Sainte-Geneviève and the bishop to Saint-Victor. It required holy processions, enlisting the king and the monks of Saint-Denis, to subdue the crest of the waters. Ten years later, the river reared up again and carried away three arches of the Petit-Pont.⁶⁹ Only the sandy soil along the right bank was high enough to escape normal floodings and firm enough to permit the discharging and loading of boats. The principal port of Paris was located upstream from the Grand-Pont and extended from Place de la Grève to the point where the walls met the river.⁷⁰

The king intervened up and down the network of rivers to promote the commercial interests of his bourgeois of Paris. In 1200, for example, he persuaded the count of Auxerre to remove a prohibition against unloading salt at Auxerre that was prejudicial to Parisians. In 1204 he set boundaries along the Oise in a dispute between merchants from Paris and Burgundy. Within these limits all commerce had to be conducted with the participation of a merchant resident and based (*hansato*) at Paris. About the time when Normandy was added to the royal domain, Philip decreed that wine from the Loire lands must be transported into the duchy by wagon. River transport was allowed only from the Ile-de-France and Burgundy.⁷¹ Philip encouraged the merchants of Paris and Rouen to come to an agreement in 1210 over commercial partnerships, and ordered an inquest into measurements of salt disputed between the two cities. In 1215 he intervened between the abbot of Saint-Denis and his Parisian merchants to draw up procedures for the major commercial fair of the region, that of Lendit.[72]

As Philip added to the royal domain or brought great fiefs under his tutelage, he also extended privileges to adjacent lands whose merchants he wished to attract. After acquiring Amiens in 1185, for example, he granted protection to merchants from Flanders, Ponthieu, and Vermandois attending the fairs at Compiègne. The annexation of Artois was accompanied in 1193 by grants of protection and favor to the merchants of Ypres, who were to be treated like the bourgeois of Paris. As guardian of Champagne, he accorded Italian merchants attending the celebrated fairs of the region the same protection as his own merchants.[73]

The *burgenses nostri* whom Philip favored were the merchants of Paris. Among their number, however, was a more restricted group called the *mercatores aque*, the "water merchants," who conducted river traffic with Paris and who used the quays along the right bank at the foot of the Place de la Grève. Appearing as early as 1121, they received confirmation of their customary practices in 1170 that granted them a virtual monopoly of the Seine traffic between the bridges of Paris and Mantes. In 1187 Philip Augustus recorded an agreement between them and Gathon de Poissy over tolls at Maisons-Lafitte and another with the count of Beaumont. In disputes over salt, the water merchants had access to the standard measure kept at the chapel of Saint-Leufroy near the Grand-Pont.[74] Their growing importance is evident by 1214, when the king entrusted them with the construction of new port facilities immediately downstream from the Grand-Pont, for which task they were granted tolls for one year. Finally, in 1220, in exchange for an annual payment, Philip granted to "our water merchants based [*hansatis*] at Paris" supervision over the street vendors (*criarie*) at Paris and the regulation of weights and measures, sales taxes (*laudes et vende*), and petty justice.[75]

At the end of the reign, therefore, the corporation of water merchants began to divide jurisdiction over the *Ville* of Paris with the king. To what extent they contributed leadership to the Parisian bourgeois in paving the streets or building the walls at the beginning of the reign can only be conjectured, but they increasingly assumed the responsibilities of municipal government under Philip's grandson, Louis IX. They later occupied the "Maison aux Piliers" on the Place de la Grève, purchased by Philip Augustus in 1212. It is not, therefore, unreasonable to believe that they furnished informal leadership during Philip's time. The water merchants may be regarded as the embryo of the municipal government recognized later in the century.

Unlike those of most towns in the royal domain, the bourgeois of Paris were permitted no semblance of autonomy under a commune, since such would undoubtedly have derogated the king's authority in his own capital. The chief royal administrators at Paris were the *prévôts* and *baillis* stationed in the two *châtelets* on the left and right banks, guarding the entrances to the Petit-Pont and Grand-Pont. Between 1217 and 1219 the two incumbents, Nicolas Arrode and Philippe Hamelin, merged the *prévôtal* and *baillis'* functions, so that thereafter they are better designated as the hyphenated *prévôt-baillis* of Paris. Although both originated from prominent bourgeois families of sufficient wealth to underwrite the farm of the city, their chief function was to defend the king's interests and execute his orders.[76] Like most French cities, however, Paris harbored a bewildering maze of interwoven and overlapping jurisdictions. Apart from the parish boundaries, temporal jurisdiction on the left bank was divided, for the most part, between the abbeys of Sainte-Geneviève and Saint-Germain-des-Prés. Yet the royal *prévôt* also had responsibility for keeping peace, which embroiled him in the famous student riots of 1200.[77] Though the Ile-de-la-Cité was normally divided between the king and bishop, the royal concierge also exercised justice on the Grand-Pont and in houses on the Place Saint-Michel and near the royal palace.[78] The water merchants claimed petty justice on the right bank, but the chief authorities there were the king and the bishop, whose spheres of jurisdiction were in urgent need of definition.

The peaceful conditions of Philip's last decade undoubtedly encouraged the royal court to intervene not only in disputed successions but also in jurisdictional conflicts. In 1221, for example, the king commanded Guérin to hold an inquest into royal rights over justice in the city, county, and duchy of Laon—an inquest in which the bishop of Laon refused to participate.[79] At the same time, Philip undertook measures to resolve conflicting jurisdictions with the bishop of Paris. Early in 1221 the royal court opened hearings against the bishop concerning the king's rights in the Clos-Brunel, located within the walls on the left bank. The bishop was none other than Guillaume de Seignelay, who as bishop of Auxerre had often opposed the king. Recently translated to the see of Paris much against the will of the king and the scholars, Guillaume countered the royal claims with intricate delaying tactics. He finally departed, like the bishop of Laon, refusing to acknowledge the jurisdiction of the royal court. In the end, the court, including the archbishop of Reims, the bishop of Senlis, seven barons, and the king's household, had to be satisfied with making a public record of the proceedings without coming to a final decision.[80] The king nonetheless persisted and held an inquest into the fertile and rapidly developing lands lying westward on the right bank from the city walls to the Marais, which were known variously as the Bourg-l'Evêque and the Culture-l'Evêque. Two dozen bourgeois of Paris, including former royal *prévôts*, rendered a detailed report on the division of jurisdiction between the king and bishop. They cited specific cases over three generations when the royal *prévôts* (Eudes Arrode and Philippe Hamelin, among them) had imprisoned malefactors in the Châtelet accused of murder, assault, *mêlée*, and rape on these lands. Beyond these major crimes, the king had jurisdiction over the roads outside Paris leading to the suburbs. In general the bishop's justice was limited to *mêlée*, bloodshed that did not result in death, and the hanging of robbers at Saint-Cloud. In the course of the inquest, information was divulged on the king's jurisdiction over detailed rights. It was emphasized that all crafts (*ministerelli*) were under exclusive royal jurisdiction, both in Bourg-l'Evêque and in Paris itself.[81]

After this barrage of litigation, Philip was finally able in December 1222 to come to a settlement (*forma pacis*) with Bishop Guillaume and Dean Gautier Cornut, which in precise detail resolved jurisdiction not only over the disputed areas of Clos-Brunel and the lands outside the walls, but also within the *Ville* of Paris itself.[82] To the episcopal territories of Bourg-Saint-Germain (formerly Bourg-l'Evêque), Culture-l'Evêque, and Clos-Brunel, Philip extended those rights of justice and revenue that he claimed within the walls on the right bank (*in communi ville Parisiensi*). These included the major crimes of murder and rape if the accused were caught outright or confessed. All other cases belonged to the bishop's court. In these areas the king also exacted host and *chevauchée*, watchguard (*guettum*), the three traditional *tailles*, the money tax, and jurisdiction over merchants, street vendors, and measures. The bishop had jurisdiction over weights and measures only every third week, the so-called "week of the bishop." Finally, the king had all justice on the two major highways leading northwest from the walls to the bridges over the Marais, "the royal road" (*strata regali*) and "the public road" (*strata publica*). Justice (except for murder and rape) on other roads between the walls and the Marais was reserved to the bishop.

Within the walls of the *Ville*, Philip exercised his normal rights,[83] but especially emphasized his claim to the two commercial centers. The bishop confirmed the king's acquisition of Monceau-Saint-Gervais, and renounced all future quarrels over Les Halles at Champeaux, retaining only his traditional "week" in which he collected customs.[84] Since the king retained jurisdiction over all artisans and tradesmen (*ministeriales*), the bishop was permitted one from each of the essential trades and a *prévôt*, who were exempt from royal authority and taxation. Finally, to indemnify the bishop and chapter for losses incurred in enlarging the Louvre and the *châtelet* of the Petit-Pont, and for their concessions on Les Halles, Philip granted an annual rent on the *prévôté* of Paris.[85]

Since the early Middle Ages, the bishops of Paris had contested the Frankish monarchs for authority over Paris, often resorting to forged charters and privileges. Faced with a redoubtable adversary in the person of Guillaume de Seignelay, Philip, like his predecessors, reacted against these encroachments. By judicial proceedings he was finally able to put a stop to them and achieve "peace" with the bishop. The agreement made concessions, but it stabilized the division of jurisdiction over the royal city and its expanding suburbs. Reconfirmed by Philip III and Philip IV at the end of the thirteenth century, it remained in force until the seventeenth century.[86] In the final analysis, the *forma pacis* of 1222 epitomized Philip Augustus's achievement of supremacy over the royal city and concluded a stage in Paris's evolution as capital of the realm.

Prosperity

The peace that accompanied the spoils of conquest after 1214 produced a marked surge of prosperity, which can be detected in the budget of 1221, the first such to survive from northern Europe. By that year improved accounting techniques enabled the central bureau to draft a document, *Magna recepta et magna expensa*, that listed receipts and expenses in broad categories and drew a balance. Undoubtedly, other medieval rulers needed to know the overall state of their finances too. Henry III, for example, was obliged to renounce a campaign against the Welsh in 1232 because of insufficient revenue. Nonetheless, the first English attempt to draw up such a balance did not come until the "Pell Rolls" of the 1240s. In any case, whether an innovation or not, a budget was produced by the French administration in 1221 and is a means of assessing its prosperity.[87]

At the same time the accounting bureau at the Temple continued to draw up the usual triannual accounts supervising the *prévôts* and *baillis*.[88] As in 1202/03, however, these listed only the detailed receipts and expenditures of local officials and not the expenses of the king's *hôtel* or the expenditures of the royal chamber for important purposes such as warfare. By contrast the budget of 1221 included not only receipts, but also total expenses and the resulting balance. Unfortunately, the parchment of 1221 is fragmentary and gives only the grand total of expenses. Presumably the details were noted on a parchment now lost, because the budget of 1227, which followed the format of 1221 closely, included standardized categories of expenses.[89] By 1227 the main expenses of the royal *hôtel* (travel, *itinera*; wages and gifts, *dona*; equipment, *hernesia*) were included in the budget accounts, and since the wages, gifts, and equipment expenses of Prince Louis's household have survived in a fragment from Purification 1213, we may deduce that the *hôtel* expenses also formed part of the total in 1221.[90] Equally regrettable, the fragment of Prince Louis's account does not shed much light on accounting techniques, but its existence makes for a strong presumption that Philip Augustus's household drew up similar documents that were included in the *magna expensa* of 1221.

In November 1221 Philip received a total of 73,657 *livres* in revenue and spent 48,447 *livres*, leaving a balance of 25,210 *livres* in the treasury. The percentage of total expenses to total receipts (66 percent) in 1221 was roughly duplicated in 1227 (70 percent), indicating that the government was saving about a third of its revenues. Unlike in 1202/03, this balance was not fictitious, because household and warfare expenses (minimal in 1221) were already accounted for. Moreover, in 1221 and 1227 important balances (131,826 *livres* and 107,651 *livres*), which nearly doubled the current income, were already in the treasury from the preceding term. In effect, therefore, the treasury possessed 157,036 *livres* in November 1221 and 123,900 *livres* in February 1227, ranging from 81 percent to 64 percent of the estimated total ordinary income (194,898 *livres*) for the French monarchy in 1221.[91] Requiring only two-thirds of annual income to meet the ordinary expenses, Philip's treasury was rapidly filling with surpluses.

These full coffers also help account for the unusual size of the bequests in Philip Augustus's testament, drawn up one year after the extant budget. Fearing death because of increasing illness, the king made a will in September 1222, which survives in an original sealed charter written in a hand unfamiliar from the chancery records.[92] His bequests to his heir, family, churches, charities, restitution, and the crusades totalled the impressive sum of 790,000 *livres parisis*, or almost four times the annual ordinary income. At the rate of savings in 1221, it would have required twelve years to have discharged these obligations. The stated terms of the will are clear enough, except for the sum assigned to Louis for the defense of the realm (380,000 *livres*), which was erased from the parchment, probably before the king's death, and restored only recently in the latest modern edition. The execution of the will, after the king's death on 14 July 1223 is, however, not at all clear. Like the testaments of many kings, Philip's attracted widespread notice from contemporaries, especially from those in a position to know its terms. Notable among these were the monks of Saint-Denis, who continued Guillaume le Breton's chronicle and were interested beneficiaries, and a certain Conon, provost of the church of Lausanne, who was studying at Paris and was present at the royal funeral.[93] When their figures are compared with the sums assigned to the items in the testament of 1221, there is little agreement, except for the important bequest of 300,000 *livres* for the crusade.[94] Several observers, moreover, add that the count of Montfort was to receive 20,000 to 30,000 *livres* for fighting the Albigensians, a legacy not found in the will.[95] In particular, Conon, who gives an unusually detailed report, not only cites different figures than the copy of 1221 (6,000 rather than 10,000 *livres* for Ingeborg, for example)[96] but also mentions many other bequests. The confusion can be explained either by Philip's changing his mind between September 1222 and July 1223—a right he expressly reserved in 1222—or by gross misinformation on the part of the contemporaries. Unfortunately, no convincing resolution of the problem has yet appeared.[97]

Conon of Lausanne's testimony is of particular interest because he explicitly claims to have been present at the funeral and to have heard about details of the testament from the king's *familiares* and from public report. In his account, Philip bequeathed not only 300,000 *livres* for the crusading movement, but also 1,400,000 *livres* to Louis for maintenance and the defense of the realm, producing a grand total of 2,062,000 *livres* in outright legacies—close to three times the bequests in 1222 and ten times the estimated annual ordinary income of the monarchy. At the rate of savings in 1221, it would have required thirty-one years to pay this off. Evidently Conon believed Philip to be a wealthy king, because he prefaces his report with the assertion that "he [Philip] was scarcely fifty-nine years old and reigned forty-five years; and he endowed the kingdom and increased it beyond what can be believed, because, although his father King Louis did not leave him more than 19,000 *livres* in revenues, as the officials of the realm reported, he himself left his son Louis a daily revenue of 1,200 *livres parisis*."[98]

As we have seen, the sum of 19,000 *livres* is a plausible figure for the annual farms of the *prévôts* at the beginning of the reign, but the final figure, equivalent to 438,000 *livres* a year, is perplexing. It doubles the income estimated from the budget of 1221, and it is not clear how, or to what purpose, the royal income could be estimated at a daily rate. What is noteworthy about Conon's report of the royal income and legacies, however, is Philip Augustus's reputation for great affluence at the time of his death. This reputation is supported by the anonymous monk of Saint-Denis, whose summary of the king's life declares that Philip greatly increased the royal treasury.[99] The budgets of 1221 and 1227 demonstrate conclusively that the government was accumulating large surpluses in the treasury. The testament of 1222, the authenticity of which is beyond dispute, shows Philip so confident in the prosperity and solvency of his government that he committed it to obligations equalling four times the revenues of the preceding year. That his confidence was fully vindicated is demonstrated by the size of the balance that remained in the treasury in 1227: 123,900 *livres*.

14

Philip, the Realm,
and the Emergence of
Royal Ideology

Philip's was the first Capetian government to make systematic efforts to preserve documents in periodic fiscal accounts, archives, registers, and judicial compilations. These collections were both the products of and witnesses to the emergence of a sophisticated administration. But though admirably illuminating the workings of governmental machinery, the charters, accounts, inventories, and court cases contained in these collections shed little light on other questions of interest to modern historians. Philip was a successful king, but what were the mainsprings of his motivation and the depths of his personality? The royal lands increased and the king's influence spread throughout France, but how were the domain, the realm, and the empire defined and conceived? Governmental institutions began to work efficiently, but what were the ideological foundations of royal authority? Philip himself left no writings that were not drafted, indeed composed, by his chancery clerks. He seems to have had little time, training, or even inclination to reflect on himself or the significance of his deeds. To approach these questions we must therefore turn to contemporary writers and poets, particularly those closest to the royal entourage, who were both inspired and paid by the king to express his point of view. Their reflections on these issues are few in number and not sustained, but they do reveal scattered elements of the story. No complete portrait of Philip is offered, but individual traits are sketched in. No comprehensive definition of royal jurisdiction is formulated, but the terminology of domain, realm, and empire is employed. No coherent and systematic ideology is generated, but discrete concepts are forged for the theorists of succeeding generations. Though in fragmentary and incomplete form, Philip's personality, the definition of his realm, and the emergence of royal ideology are all depicted in the writings of men closely associated with the king who reflected on the achievements of his government.

Philip

What kind of person was Philip? For medieval as well as modern writers the appropriate time to pose this question is at the king's funeral, when the span of his life can be viewed as a whole. The fullest contemporary account of Philip's personality is furnished by the chronicler of Tours, who took the occasion of the king's death to offer a long catalogue of traits in rapid succession:

> Agreeable appearance, well-formed body, cheerful face, a bald pate, ruddy complexion, given to drink and food, prone to sexual desire, generous to his friends, stingy to his foes, skilled in strategems, orthodox in belief, solicitous of counsel, holding to his word, a scrupulous and expeditious judge, fortunate in victory, fearful of his life, easily moved, easily assuaged, putting down the wicked of the realm by sowing discord among them, killing no one in prison, availing himself of the counsel of lesser men, bearing grudges only momentarily, subduing the proud, defending the church, and providing for the poor.[1]

Because modern historians have found this description strikingly apt, they have accorded it prominence in their accounts. A blend of both the particular and the general, it illustrates a temptation, implicit in such efforts, to sum up through characterization, and therefore to generate stereotypes. Serving as a eulogy, it was also shaped by an underlying idealization of what a good king should be. In contrast the attempt here is rather to uncover what was unique about Philip and to distinguish him from other good kings, deferring the idealized and conventional to a subsequent discussion of royal ideology.

The royal historians Rigord and Guillaume le Breton neglect to record the distinctive traits of Philip's physical appearance. He may well have had a "well-formed body, a cheerful face, and a ruddy complexion" as the Tours chronicler maintains, but these praiseworthy features were attributable to most kings. That Philip was bald when he died at fifty-eight is also not surprising, but this condition may have been the permanent effect of an illness contracted on the crusade at twenty-five. Called *arnoldia* by the English chroniclers, it has been diagnosed by modern clinicians as an early manifestation of the sweating sickness (*la suette*), which was accompanied by fever, chills, peeling of skin, the loss of nails and hair, and extreme nervous disorders.[2] At whatever age Philip became permanently bald, as a youth he was known as tousled (*le valet maupeigné*), one whose hair was always bristling.[3] His second son, Philip, born of Agnès, doubtlessly inherited this trait, because he similarly was called *hurepel* (bristling hide).

If, indeed, Philip was affected by the sweating sickness after the crusade, it would help to explain some of his extreme behavior as the result of nervous disorders. When he learned of the assassination of the marquis of Montferrat, for example, the king became greatly agitated and went into seclusion for days. Similarly, fearing that Richard had hired the "Old Man of the Mountain" to dispose of him, he abandoned his father's example of refusing personal protection and instituted a bodyguard to watch over him day and night.[4] Philip was remembered by the chronicler of Tours as being still "fearful of his life" at the end of his career.

Philip's sexual life may also have suffered as a result of the illness. He was married at fifteen to Isabelle de Hainaut when she was ten, and his sexual functions appear to have been normal when the couple reached maturity. Although he threatened to divorce Isabelle, apparently for political reasons, she produced a son when he was twenty-two and died three years later in a second pregnancy. His behavior towards his second wife, Ingeborg, however, was anything but normal. At best their sexual life lasted the wedding night of 14/15 August 1193. Thereafter, and for the rest of his life, he refused to readmit her to his bed, though at the risk of destroying his life's work.

Even when he became reconciled with her on the eve of Bouvines, it was as queen and not as wife. Whatever personal responsibility the Danish princess bore for the presumed difficulties of their wedding night, Philip remained adamant in refusing her sexually. Anxious to reinforce the royal lineage with a second son (since Louis was sickly), Philip may have been temporarily impotent on his wedding night, a condition exacerbated by his recent illness. Since obsessive phobia was one of the psychological consequences of the sweating sickness, it may help to explain Philip's behavior. But Philip's clerks did not raise the possibility of his impotence until 1201, when they charged that Ingeborg had impeded consummation through sorcery. However seriously we may take the arguments advanced for Philip's divorce (most of which fail to satisfy modern historians, just as they failed to convince contemporaries), Philip's hypothetical impotence had certainly been cured by Agnès de Méran by 1196, when she produced two children. After her death in 1201, Philip probably consoled himself with several liaisons, but only one, that with the *damoiselle* of Arras, has come to light, because the king acknowledged their son, Pierre Charlot, born between 1205 and 1209. At death Philip was still known for his propensity to sexual desire.[5]

Within the galaxy of virtues evoked by the Tours chronicler are an unusual proportion pertaining to political aptitudes that historians can gloss with examples. The Angevins could ruefully testify to his "mastery of stratagems" and "ability to sow discord." His "speed and exactitude as judge" help to explain his effectiveness in promoting royal justice. The prominence of Gautier the Young, Barthélemy de Roye, Henri Clément, and Brother Guérin in his entourage supports the chronicler's perception that he used the counsel of lesser men. That he was "easily moved" may indicate impetuosity, aggravated by sickness. When he cut down the venerable elm at Gisors, the English chroniclers were impressed by the quickness of his anger. Yet he could be easily assuaged, a trait amply illustrated by the oscillating career of Count Renaud de Boulogne. That Philip killed no one in prison may be a contrasting allusion to John's murder of Arthur.[6]

Although the royal historians seldom ventured beyond the conventional in characterizing Philip, they attempt to distinguish him from his Angevin rivals. Rigord comments on his aversion to swearing, for example, citing an incident that took place when the king overheard a knight let an oath escape while gambling. Philip had the careless offender dunked and published an edict inaugurating a Capetian tradition of hostility to profanity. Philip himself swore by the lance of St. James, but Gerald of Wales contrasts the mildness of Capetian oaths with those of the Angevins, who habitually swore on the bodily members of God.[7] Another distinctive trait was Philip's reluctance to expend gifts on jongleurs, troubadours, and other public entertainers. Rigord remarks that whereas contemporary kings (doubtless a reference to the Angevins) and princes lavished gold, silver, horses, and rich garments on public entertainers, King Philip, remembering the teaching of holy men that to give to actors was to sacrifice to demons, promised to distribute his garments to the poor. Philip's attitudes in these two matters coincided with those of Pierre the Chanter, a contemporary theologian at Paris.[8] But one final trait, the king's probable illiteracy in Latin, tended to impede this clerical influence. Although Philip was certainly functionally literate, in that he could conduct written business in Latin through clerks, he was probably unable to read and write Latin with great assurance, because his early accession cut short formal schooling. His deficiency was nonetheless apparent to Innocent III during the negotiations involving Ingeborg and support for Jean de Brienne in Jerusalem. On both occasions the pope complained that his letters were being misinterpreted (*minus fideliter exponantur*) to the king. Though the fault in this case may have lain more with the royal clerks than with the king, Philip's illiteracy was also observed by a contemporary writer describing the king for aristocratic circles, who contrasts Julius Caesar's ability to write with Philip's lack thereof.[9]

A balding king, psychologically scarred by illness contracted on the crusade; a remarkably capable, if nearly illiterate, ruler with an aversion to swearing and public entertainers—this is hardly a distinctive portrait of one of the great kings of medieval France. Perceptions of the depths of Philip's character that would render his personality convincing to us are unfortunately obscured by the reticence of the sources.

The Realm

If the mainsprings of Philip's motivation remain obscure, his two major achievements are clearly apparent. By expelling the Angevins and gaining supremacy over the barons, he enlarged the royal domain and expanded the monarchy's geographic influence. By overhauling the governmental machinery, he rendered kingship more effective and far-reaching. What effect did these practical achievements have on ideology? After the territorial conquests, how were the terms *kingdom* (*regnum*), *domain* (*domanium*) and *empire* (*imperium*) defined? After the administration was transformed, how was the monarchy conceptualized?

Philip inherited from his predecessors an ill-defined concept of *regnum* that usually restricted it to the king's direct holdings (the domain). Suger, for example, treats the subject only obliquely, but when he refers to *Francia* he equates it with the Ile-de-France, and on one occasion he describes Normandy as lying outside the *regnum*. Little evidence survives that the early Capetians thought of their *regnum* as anything more than their domain.[10]

This limited definition persisted throughout Philip's reign, both before and after the conquests of 1204. When the king banished three perjurers from Laon in 1202, for example, they were excluded from land that was designated both *terra nostra dominica* and *regnum nostrum* as synonymous terms.[11] Following the practice of his predecessors, Philip often declared to churches, towns, or baronies that they would not be separated from the *corona regni Francie*. Although the phrase "crown of the kingdom of France" might imply a larger view of the *regnum*, it was usually coupled with the domanial expression *de manu regia* (or *nostra*), "the royal hand."[12] Yet on one occasion in 1185 the royal chancery argued with the pope that the creation of the archbishopric of Dol threatened the *integritatem regni nostri*, thus envisaging the kingdom to include Breton sees, which were outside the royal domain.[13]

Similar ambiguity affected the conception of *Francia*, or France. From the early Middle Ages on, the term designated all territories governed by the Franks, including lands east as well as west of the Rhine and Rhône.[14] Rigord recognizes two interpretations of this *regnum Francorum*, however, a larger one that includes the German lands, and a more restricted one defining it as the lands between the Rhine, Mosel, and Loire, which, he says, modern men (*moderni*) call *Francia*.[15] Yet Philip Augustus, like his forebears, was always styled *rex Francorum* (king of the French) in official chancery charters and never *rex Francie* (king of France), which would betoken the more recent geographic conception of France.[16]

The formulaic language of the chancery that equated *regnum* with domain and retained *rex Francorum* as Philip's title was undoubtedly conservative and slow to respond to territorial expansion. The royal registers, however, which were prompted by the conquests of 1204, began to reflect an incipient distinction between the domain and the kingdom. When a scribe listed the episcopal cities and royal castles in Register A, he placed them under the rubric: "*Civitates* and *castra* that King Philip has in his *domanio*."[17] The castles were situated both in the old royal domain (including Vermandois and Artois) and in the newly acquired Normandy and Loire territories. As has been seen earlier, the *civitates* were limited to royal bishoprics in the royal domain after the conquests of 1204. The *domanium*, therefore, was still defined as territories that the king held directly. A previous scribe had listed bishoprics that included not only the royal sees (*qui sunt sub rege Francorum*) but also others in western and southern France. When this list was recopied into Register C in 1212, the scribe omitted the distinction of royal submission and provided the rubric *Archiepiscopi et episcopi regni Franc[ie]*.[18] Here it is clear that the *regnum Francie* was larger than, and distinct from, the king's *domanium*, and comprised what later was known as the kingdom of France. In a similar way the registers also designate the French kings as *reges Francie*. When Etienne de Gallardon recopied the king lists of Register C into Register E in 1220, he changed the ambiguous *nomina regum Franc'* (for *Francorum*) to the *nomina regum Francie*.[19] Register E was not an official document, however, and the royal charters continued to style the king as *rex Francorum*. Nor did the isolated use of *regnum* in the larger sense establish a pattern. Not until the time of Philip the Fair was the term *regnum Francie*, kingdom of France, to appear in the records of the Capetian chancery in a way clearly distinguished from the royal domain.[20] The concepts of *kingdom* and *France* therefore changed little during Philip's reign.

A *rex* ruled over a *regnum*, but two or more *regna* were subject to an *imperator* (emperor). Military success might have tempted Philip to claim imperial dignity, but the protocol of his charters displays little inclination to utilize imperial formulae. Only Rigord elucidates the epithet *Augustus* by likening Philip to the Caesars, who enlarged (*auge[bat]*) the *rempublicam* (in Philip's case by acquiring Vermandois).[21] Since Philip was ostensibly opposed to it, no imperial pretensions were orchestrated to justify Prince Louis's expedition against England before 1216, and certainly few were justified after its failure. The only allusion to French domination over England occurs in verses celebrating the birth of a son, Philip, to Prince Louis and Blanche in September 1209, jotted down in Register A before Bouvines. Blanche was depicted as bringing into the world a future lord of both the French and the English who would match his grandfather in character as well as in name.[22] Not until 1223 were Louis's claims to rights over the English revived by Guillaume le Breton in the concluding verses of the *Philippidos*, dedicated to Louis VIII. He reminded the new king that the scepter of the youthful Henry III had been taken from his father, John, and conferred on Louis by virtue of Blanche's claims and unanimous election by the English clergy, people, and magnates. When the poet urged the Capetian to prosecute his rights, however, it was not in England but in Aquitaine, where the intruder was still entrenched. Louis was charged to give Henry no peace until Henry had resigned his scepter and Louis ruled over the two realms, thus expelling the English from the last corner of France.[23] Despite poetic ambiguity, Guillaume le Breton's vision is not *imperium* over England, but undivided rule over France. Only Gerald of Wales, the perennially disappointed Angevin courtier, dared to venture a notion of empire. Bringing his *De Principis instructione* to a conclusion, perhaps during the years of Louis's expedition, he indulged a favorite penchant by contrasting Capetian virtue with Angevin foulness and expressed the hope that the two kingdoms (and even a third) might be joined under one French monarch.[24] But as with the definition of *regnum*, the writers of the French royal entourage failed to articulate a consistent theory of *imperium* that would justify Philip's military conquests.

The Emergence of Royal Ideology

The chief burden of articulating a royal ideology fell upon the shoulders of a handful of chroniclers and poets associated with the monarchy. In composing his biography of Louis VI, for example, Suger of Saint-Denis had formulated a hierarchical conception of society with the king in his divinely appointed place at its summit.[25] In similar fashion, Rigord, a monk of Saint-Denis, and the royal cleric Guillaume le Breton narrated Philip Augustus's deeds in their prose chronicles and attempted to picture the king as an exemplary figure.[26] By concentrating on the conventional and ideal, they began to formulate elements of a royal ideology— elements coordinated by later writers into a more coherent theory.

Guillaume le Breton not only wrote a prose continuation of Rigord's chronicle, however, but also transformed the whole work into poetry under the title of *Philippidos*. Animated by the elation that swept over France after Bouvines, and completed shortly after the king's death, the 9,000 verses of this epic became the most fully articulated statement of royal ideology of Philip's reign. Culminating in Guillaume, therefore, verse and not prose became the vehicle most apt for expressing ideology. As a poet, however, Guillaume was preceded by three others who can be associated with the French monarchy. The first of this group was Pierre Riga, who originated in Reims, where he later held prebends at the cathedral chapter and Saint-Denis de Reims. Early in his career Pierre began writing occasional verse, such as a piece rehearsing the arguments between Louis VII and Henry II over the dowry of Princess Marguerite in 1157. Shortly after 1165 he devoted another poem to the birth of Philip Augustus and the attendant celebrations, which he had witnessed while studying in Paris. Between 1170 and 1200 he turned to the major work of his career, *Aurora*, a verse paraphrase of the entire Bible accompanied by allegorical and moral commentary. Completed before his death in 1209, this work was one of the most widely circulated texts of Latin poetry in the high Middle Ages.[27]

To bring this arduous task to an end during his declining years, Pierre apparently enlisted the collaboration of a fellow poet, Gilles de Paris, who contributed two revisions between 1200 and 1208. Originating in the royal capital, as suggested by his name, Gilles travelled to Rome in the 1190s to represent local churches in litigation before the papal court. As Gilles himself testifies, his residence in Rome in 1196 lasted six months, and gave him the opportunity to begin a major poem, *Karolinus*, which was completed in time for Prince Louis's thirteenth birthday on 3 September 1200. Consisting of a prologue, five books, an epilogue, and a *capitatio* (celebrating the illustrious writers of Paris), the *Karolinus* attempted to instruct the young prince on French history in general and, in particular, to offer Charlemagne as an example for imitation. Each of the first four books is devoted to a cardinal virtue (prudence, justice, bravery, and temperance) practiced by the great emperor, and the last book discusses *utilitas* to show how Charlemagne's example is to be emulated.[28]

Pierre Riga, Gilles de Paris, and Guillaume le Breton formed a closely knit circle of poets. Gilles openly acknowledges Guillaume as a fellow student who has now become a master in his own right, although he chides his friend for travelling too often to Rome to negotiate the king's marital separation, of which he disapproved. In the opening lines of the *Philippidos*, Guillaume evokes the poetic skill of Pierre Riga in uncovering the meaning of divine law, and in his concluding section he calls for Gilles's talents to celebrate the military triumphs of Louis VIII.[29] But the strongest tie binding them together was the common example of Gautier de Châtillon, certainly the most celebrated Latin poet of twelfth-century France. Born in Lille and schooled at Paris, Reims, and Bologna, Gautier taught at Laon and Châtillon (whence his name). After returning to France from Bologna, he gained the friendship and support of the king's uncle, Guillaume of the White Hands, recently (1176) elevated to the archbishopric of Reims. As notary and spokesman of this influential patron, he wrote a great epic, *Alexandreis*, between 1176 and 1182 at the archbishop's request. His final reward was a canon prebend at Amiens, where he died of leprosy. An epic poem devoted to the deeds of Alexander of Macedon and aspiring to revive the traditions of Vergil, Lucan, Claudian, and other Latin poets, Gautier's work was an immediate success in the schools of liberal arts, where it was recopied hundreds of times and glossed throughout the thirteenth century.[30]

Both Gautier's craft and his hero well served the poets of Philip Augustus's court as models. Guillaume quotes Gautier's opening lines, invokes the poet's name, and calls for his presence, along with that of Gilles, to celebrate Louis VIII's military deeds.[31] Every page of Guillaume's and Gilles's poetry echoes the phrases and poetic techniques of the *Alexandreis*.[32] Even the prose writer Rigord had a copy open before him when he composed the first prologue to his chronicle.[33] In the *Philippidos* Guillaume adopts Gautier's ten-book format (later expanded to twelve),[34] his use of mythological figures such as Victory and Fate, his long geographical *excursi*, his insertion of speeches by the combatants into the battle narratives, and even his mechanical techniques.[35] The military victories of Alexander provided a fitting exemplar for epic poetry narrating the achievements of the great emperor Charles, not to speak of the conquering Philip, who bore the Macedonian name of Alexander's father.

Whether as prose chroniclers or as poets, these writers intended their works to serve as instruction for the future. "History is a mirror of life [*speculum vite*]" notes the *Historia regum Francorum*, repeating a medieval commonplace.[36] Since such works were intended as mirrors for princes (*specula principum*) who might profit from history's examples, they were appropriately dedicated to royal princes who could learn from their great father. Guillaume le Breton prefaced and followed the *Philippidos* with words addressed to the royal bastard, Pierre Charlot, whom he tutored, but both Guillaume and the others naturally dedicated their major works to the heir apparent, Prince Louis. Rigord and Gilles offered their writings to Louis in 1200, most likely spurred on by the prince's marriage to Blanche of Castile at Port-Mort in Normandy on 23 May 1200. One surviving manuscript of the *Karolinus*, furnished with an illumination depicting the author giving his poem to Louis, was either a presentation copy kept at court or closely followed the original presentation manuscript.[37] (See illustration no. 7.) Guillaume opened his *Philippidos* with an address to Prince Louis and concluded the second version with an exhortation to the new king.

The internal cohesion of this small band is evident, but the personal ties between them and the king who was the subject of their writings are more ambiguous. Although Rigord styles himself *chronographus Francorum regis*, as far as can be told, his only support came from Saint-Denis and not from Philip himself. No direct royal patronage can be uncovered for Pierre Riga and Gilles de Paris either. This lack of support may have been due to dissonance arising between the king and the writers in the 1190s. In 1200 the royal lands were under papal interdict because of the king's attempted separation from Ingeborg, a deed that Rigord and Gilles openly criticized. Both authors further blamed the king for oppressing the church with heavy exactions and taxation.[38] Sensitive to their criticism, Philip may have been unappreciative of their attempts to serve him with their pens. His deficient Latin may also have rendered him unsympathetic to Gilles's labored versification. His proverbial distaste for jongleurs and actors would not have made poets, even those composing in Latin, feel comfortable in his presence. Perhaps for that reason, Gilles frequently took care to distance himself from the entertainment profession (*mimi, mithmi*).[39] After the interdict was lifted in 1200, however, and more particularly after the royal couple were reconciled in 1213, the tension between the king and the clergy began to dissolve. Rigord and Pierre Riga were both dead by 1213, and Gilles de Paris had dropped from sight, but Guillaume le Breton, who was active after 1200, enjoyed the king's full patronage, receiving royal commissions and prebends from the chapter of Senlis. Guillaume reciprocated Philip's favor by suppressing criticism and lavishing praise on the king both in his prose chronicle and in its poetic embellishment. Within the small group of historians and poets who wrote directly about and for the king, Guillaume le Breton therefore stands alone as the "official" royal spokesman.

Although few in number, these chroniclers and poets surrounding the king nonetheless began to forge elements useful to royal ideology. As panegyrists their first task was to provide heroic models on which the king and the royal princes could pattern their lives. The closest candidate, of course, was the great Charles, who, if not a direct ancestor of the Capetians, was a worthy exemplar. After devoting over two thousand lines to Charlemagne, Gilles de Paris concluded with the hope that God would raise up another Charles in the present turbulent times. Addressing Louis as *Karoline* at the end of the poem, Gilles saw his vision fulfilled in the young prince.[40] Rigord and Guillaume le Breton ignore the Carolingian exemplar in their *Gesta*, but when Guillaume turned to the *Philippidos*, he revived the spell of Charles's name. In the opening dedication Philip is called *Karolide*, the living virtue (*vivida virtus*) of the great emperor. Despite the frequent resonance of the name, however, Guillaume supports the theme with only minimal illustrations, noting, for example, that when Henry II threatened the town of Mantes in 1188, Philip marched to the rescue, just as Charlemagne had hastened back to Spain to avenge Roland's death at Roncevaux.[41] Since the incident was certainly the best-known event of contemporary literature, the comparison was not unusual.

In extolling Philip's military glory, Guillaume links the Capetian with two earlier conquerors of the world. He observes that although the Macedonian Alexander was victorious for twelve years, and Julius Caesar subjugated the world in sixteen, Philip had prolonged his success for thirty-two years, finally overcoming the Germans, English, and Flemings at Bouvines.[42] The Capetian victory celebrations, he says, rivaled those of Pompey, Titus, and Vespasian, and even those held at Rome honoring Caesar's triumph in Gaul.[43] Alluring as was Caesar's example, Gautier de Châtillon's influence was even stronger in promoting Alexander as the ultimate model for the Capetian victor with the Macedonian name. Both at the beginning and at the end of the *Philippidos*, Guillaume summons Gautier's eloquence to do justice to a ruler whose deeds equalled those of Alexander, Antiochus, and the twelve commanders.[44] After Gautier has recounted the Macedonian victory over Darius at Arbela and Alexander's triumphal entry into Babylon, the poet is moved to ask whether divine mercy might raise up in France another king like Alexander, who by force of arms will impose the true faith on the world, so that even Parthians, Carthaginians, and Spaniards will seek baptism from the archbishop of Reims.[45]

The *Philippidos* was Guillaume le Breton's response to Gautier's question. In Guillaume's verse Philip resembles his Macedonian forebear in both character and achievement.[46] When the French king pursued Richard into Berry in 1195, he performed an eight-day journey in three, speed worthy of Alexander on the march against the successors of Darius in Bactria, or of Caesar, who travelled from Sens to Paris in one day. Like Alexander, the young Philip combined rapidity with rashness. At the stalemate at Boves in 1185, when the count of Flanders challenged the king to single combat at night, Philip, like the young Macedonian, was tempted to accept and was prevented only by experienced counsel. In 1188 when Philip found himself cut off from the castle of Gisors by Richard's superior force, the king wanted to fight his way back along the road, but a faithful knight, Manassé de Mauvoisin, warned him that not even

Alexander would have dared such a feat.[47] The attraction of Gautier de Châtillon's lines, and with them of Gautier's hero, pervades the *Philippidos*. Otto's and Philip's speeches before Bouvines echo the phrases of Darius and Alexander before the battle of Issus. Philip's triumphal entry into Paris resonates with the Macedonian's into Babylon.[48]

In medieval literature, Alexander was universally acknowledged as the supreme heroic model. His exemplary quality was *magnanimitas*, signifying greatness in diverse manifestations, and already in the *Gesta*, Guillaume le Breton had coined *magnanimus* as an exclusive epithet for Philip, which was sustained throughout the *Philippidos*.[49] We shall see that when Guillaume wished to underscore the Franks' independence from the Romans, warranted by their common but parallel origins from the Trojans, he replaced Rigord's term *Augustus*, resonating Roman imperial overtones, with one appropriate to the more ancient conqueror, who, like Philip, bore a Greek name.

In recounting Philip's deeds the historians and poets were led to speculate on four ideologically significant events in the king's life. Philip's birth in 1165 resolved a dynastic crisis and drew attention to the blood right to the French throne claimed by the Capetians. His consecration in 1179 pointed to the sacred character imputed to the French monarchy by churchmen and to the king's reciprocal responsibility to defend the church. His decisive victory at Bouvines in 1214 reaffirmed the major achievements of the reign. And his death and burial in 1223 provided signs of the king's success as a divinely appointed ruler, suggesting Philip's personal sanctity—even his candidacy for sainthood. Prompted by these four events, Rigord, Gilles de Paris, and Guillaume le Breton formulated the basic components of a royal ideology suitable to justify the French monarchy.

THE BIRTH OF THE KING AND HIS BLOOD RIGHT

Philip's birth resolved a crisis that had threatened the Capetians' claim to the French crown. Since 987, when Hugues Capet had established his family on the royal throne, the Capetians had not failed to produce a legitimate male heir for six generations. But this good record was jeopardized under Louis VII. At his accession in 1137, the king had married the headstrong Eleanor, duchess of Aquitaine. When, added to their incompatible temperaments, the queen gave birth only to girls, Louis divorced her in 1152 and married Constance, a Spanish princess, who also produced only girls. At the death of his second wife in 1160, the king waited barely a month before marrying Adèle, the youngest daughter of the count of Champagne. But five years elapsed before the new queen gave promise of an heir. When on the night of 21 August 1165 a male child was finally born at Paris, the royal city erupted with undoubted relief. Church bells pealed, bonfires were lit in the squares, crowds poured into the streets, and thanks were offered in the churches. That evening the old king was at Etampes, fifty kilometers to the south. Louis lavished presents on the queen's servant who had borne the good news, accompanied by a charter in which the king expressed his rejoicing and thanksgiving to God for having finally bestowed on him and the kingdom "an offspring of the better sex because we have been dismayed by the great number of our daughters."[50] Louis VII and Adèle had at last preserved Capetian dynastic continuity through a seventh generation.

The rejoicing inspired a considerable literature. Pierre Riga's poem testifies to the mounting anxiety over the infant's gender as the hour neared, dissipated when someone perceived through a crack in the door to the queen's chamber that the child was a boy.[51] At the same time, a monk at Saint-Germain-des-Prés was moved to refashion the notes left by Suger into a short biography of Louis VII. Recounting the king's marital history, the author extolls the Capetian's dynastic superiority over neighboring kingdoms. Whereas the Germans and the English have suffered greatly because their rulers had failed to produce heirs, he notes, the French enjoy a royal succession free from dispute.[52] Two decades later Rigord adopted this theme to open his chronicle:

> Philip, king of the French, was born A.D. 1165 in the month of August on the twenty-second day on the feast of St. Timothy and St. Symphorian. He should be called *a Deo datus* [*Dieudonné*] because his righteous father, having received so many daughters from three wives, had not been able to have a masculine successor to the kingdom. With the queen Adèle, all the clergy, and the people of the entire realm, he beseeched God in prayer and almsgiving for a son. . . . His supplications were heard, and God gave him a boy, Philip by name.[53] (See frontispiece.)

Yet anxiety was not entirely eliminated. When Philip was urged to take the cross in 1185, he refused on the grounds that his wife had not yet been delivered of a son. When the infant Louis (born 1187) fell desperately ill of dysentery in 1191 during the king's absence, Rigord recorded the prayers at Saint-Denis and the holy processions of the bishop, chapter, students, and people throughout Paris for the prince's recovery.[54]

Since his first wife had died, one of Philip's major concerns upon his return was to remarry and to reinforce the royal lineage with sons.

Engendering an heir depended on the royal couple's fertility, but establishing a hereditary right to the throne depended on the dynasty's ability to persuade the barons and churchmen of the realm to accept its claim.[55] From the beginning, the Capetians acted as a *Geschlecht*—that is, a dynastic family bound by vertical ties between parents and children. Like all baronial families, they had every intention of passing on their lands to their heirs. Royal authority had come to them through election by the magnates, however, and it could presumably be transferred to another family by the same procedure. Since Hugues Capet had naturally desired to attach royal authority to his patrimonial succession, he employed a device utilized by the Carolingian and Byzantine emperors, that of associating his son Robert to the throne by having him anointed and crowned during his father's lifetime. The Capetians had done this without fail for six generations by the time of the death of Louis VII.[56] Such "anticipatory association" was commonly resorted to by baronial families. It was invaluable for keeping patrimony intact, and equally effective in enabling a smooth transfer of royal authority to take place, especially when the father was aged and infirm, a factor that undoubtedly encouraged Louis VII's decision to have Philip crowned.[57] Despite the diverse motivations and circumstances at each transition—the historical conditions were frequently different—the practice of "anticipatory association" offered one major advantage for a dynasty attempting to establish claim to the monarchy: it facilitated the barons' acceptance.[58]

Though it may be presumed that the Capetians never doubted their right from the beginning, it would be impossible to set a precise date when the magnates accepted their claim without question. Since that point was undoubtedly long past after six successful transitions, however, it is not surprising that Philip neglected to crown Louis before he died. In practice, therefore, his reign marks a *tournant* in this. The Capetians had never failed to practice anticipatory succession before and never bothered afterwards. The turning point may be further fixed at the ordinance-testament of 1190, when Philip left the country on a hazardous mission and explicitly designated Louis his heir, but left him unconsecrated and uncrowned.[59]

The drama of Philip's birth drew attention to his sex, not to his blood right. All the contemporary writers who deal with his birth and early childhood assume that he was born to be king. No explicit discussion of dynastic right has surfaced in royal circles prior to Philip's reign. The early Capetians simply justified their rule by religious consecration. In their charters and seals they were kings of the French *Dei gratia*.[60]

Despite this silence on the subject in the king's entourage, other writers had formulated theories about dynastic right that were available to royal apologists. By Philip's reign, three in particular, the Valerian prophecy, the *reditus* doctrine, and the theory of Trojan origins, were acknowledged in royal circles. Only the last however, received serious attention. The Valerian prophecy was a response to a claim raised at Sens in the early eleventh century that the Capetians were usurpers of the throne.[61] Two authors from the northern monasteries of Saint-Valery and Saint-Riquier reported not long afterwards that St. Valery had appeared in visions to Hugues Capet. To reward Hugues for recovering his body from the Carolingians, the saint had promised that the kingdom would be delivered to Hugues's successors "until the seventh generation."[62] Studiously ambiguous like most prophecies, the pronouncement could be interpreted either symbolically or literally. To some writers the number seven represented eternity, but if taken literally, it signified the end of the Capetian dynasty after the death of Philip Augustus at the latest, depending on how the generations were counted. As long as seven generations stood in the distant future, the early Capetians could ignore the prophecy, but concern may have increased as Philip approached his last days. This may explain why Etienne de Gallardon copied a summary of the prophecy into Register E in 1220, but at the same time nullified its literal effect by assigning the saint's apparition to Hugues's father, Hugues the Great, thus implying that the date had already passed without consequence.[63] From antiquity prophets and soothsayers had habitually dealt with dynastic change in their predictions of the future.[64] Virtual silence until Etienne's brief reference at the end of the reign suggests that Philip's court paid scant attention to the Valerian pronouncement.

However and whenever the Capetians secured dynastic right to the French crown, they had clearly displaced the Carolingian family. Apologists for the Carolingians had claimed that when Pope Stephen II anointed their progenitor Pippin in 754, he had pronounced an anathema on any successor not a Carolingian. To efface this curse, an evident recourse open to the succeeding Capetians was to claim Carolingian descent. By the twelfth century, moreover, most major baronial families in France could in fact claim Carolingian blood through the female line, and the Capetians were no exception. Apart from Anna of Kiev, every Capetian spouse was linked to the Carolingians, including Isabelle de Hainaut,

Philip's first wife. Isabelle's brother was Count Baudouin of Hainaut, who was the patron of the monastery of Marchiennes. In 1196, to glorify the patron's family, the queen, and her royal son Louis, a monk of the monastery, André de Marchiennes, wrote a history of the deeds and succession of the French kings that traced Isabelle's and Louis's Carolingian descent and announced that in the person of Louis the Capetians had "returned" to the lineage of Charlemagne. Expressed under the formula *reditus regni ad stirpem Karoli Magni*, the doctrine was a baronial creation and received scant attention in royal circles.[65] Rigord in his short chronicle of Saint-Denis and Gilles de Paris in his *Karolinus* are aware of the papal anathema, but ignore the *reditus* doctrine. The *Historia regum Francorum* publicized the evident fact that Philip's mother, Adèle, also possessed Carolingian blood.[66]

Although interest arose over the distant ancestors of the Capetians, no attempt to connect the Capetians by blood with the Carolingians was made by anyone in Philip's entourage until the end of the reign. To be sure, Gilles de Paris, repeated by Guillaume le Breton, calls both Philip and Louis *Karolida* after the great emperor, but the epithet designated Charles's moral example rather than a dynastic connection.[67] In the closing lines of the *Philippidos*, written after Philip's death, however, Guillaume le Breton did attach Philip and Louis to the *stirps* of Pippin. At this point in the poem, it was too late to justify the assertion with a genealogical dossier, but at about the same time the chronicler of Saint-Martin of Tours attempted to fill in the lacuna. In a passage containing numerous fictions, the author has Hugues Capet defeat the Carolingian Louis V in battle, and when Louis afterwards dies without heir, Hugues is elected to succeed him. Some claimed at the time that Charlemagne's descendants had failed in France, the chronicler continues, but had they read the genealogies of the Empire, they would have seen how Hugues was related to the great emperor.[68] Like the Valerian prophecy, the elaborate fiction of the *reditus* doctrine was, however, apparently of little concern to Philip's entourage.

Despite the Tours chronicler, those closest to Philip were fully aware of the dynastic change that had taken place at Hugues Capet's accession. Rigord, Guillaume le Breton, and the compiler of one king-list in Register C are explicit that Louis V was the last ruler of Carolingian stock and that Hugues had been elected by the barons.[69] These writers take little note of the family origins of the Capetians before Hugues's accession.[70] In place of genealogies tracing blood descent, the Capetians compiled king-lists that recorded royal succession. Among their catalogues of emperors, bishops, and popes, the chancery clerks who transcribed Register C between 1212 and 1220 included two briefly annotated lists of French kings, both ending with Philip "who now reigns." By ascending through the lists Philip's predecessors could be traced through the Capetians, Carolingians, and Merovingians to the fount of the French monarchy, its Trojan ancestors. Both catalogues are captioned "These are the names of the kings of the Franks who came from Troy."[71]

The legends of the Trojan origins of various European peoples were foundation myths that Germanic tribes adopted early in the Middle Ages to explain and legitimize their presence in Latin Christendom. Since the Germans saw themselves as successors to the Romans, they were attracted to the myth of Rome's foundation by the Trojan Aeneas, so eloquently expressed in Vergil's *Aeneid*. Just as Aeneas had led his people from burning Troy to found the Roman *imperium* in Italy, so Widukin depicted the Saxons as descending from the Trojans in the tenth century, Dudon de Saint-Quentin the Normans in the eleventh, and Geoffrey of Monmouth the Britons in the twelfth. The initiators of the theory of Trojan origins were the Franks, however, who created two versions, one by Fredegar in the seventh century and the other by the anonymous author of the *Liber historiae Francorum* in the eighth. By a complex process the diverse elements of the legend were conflated and transmitted to the twelfth century, when the venerable tradition met with renewed interest among the historians and poets of Philip Augustus's court.[72] Rigord makes fullest use of the legend in a parenthetical etymology of the name Paris, although the diverse elements that he borrowed are not coherently integrated. (In his *Short Chronicle of the Kings of France*, he presents an abbreviated version of the tradition that suppresses some of the discrepancies.)[73] Guillaume le Breton put a more coherent version of Rigord's account at the beginning of his *Gesta*, where the story belongs chronologically. This was further reworked in poetic form in the first book of the *Philippidos*, to which Guillaume planned to append a genealogical diagram. Earlier, Gilles de Paris had also illustrated the theory of Trojan origins in a genealogical sketch. The royal registers simply acknowledge the myth in the lists of kings.[74]

The legend of the Trojan origins of the Frankish kings cannot be quickly told in all of its complexity, but the major contours were preserved by the French writers. Although careful to identify the Trojan founders of the major Germanic tribes, Rigord and Guillaume pay special attention to Francio, son of Hector and grandson of King Priam. Adopting the name of this progenitor, the *Franci* had wandered into the Danube valley, where they built a city at Sicambria. After two centuries a group of their descendants led by Duke Ibor migrated into Gaul, settled around the city of Lutetia (which they renamed Paris), and fell subject to the Romans. The rest remained at Sicambria for over a millennium and half, until they rebelled against the Roman emperor Valentinian. Travelling to the Rhine, they resisted the emperor's attacks and entered Gaul under the leadership of Marcomirus, bringing the whole country down to the Pyrenees under their control. When they reached Paris, they were received with honors by their distant kinsmen. After encircling the city with walls, Marcomirus had his son Pharamond crowned the first king of the Franks. The succession passed to his grandson, Meroveus, after whom the Merovingian dynasty was named, and the latter's grandson was Clovis, the first Christian king. Through the procession of Merovingians, Carolingians, and Capetians, Philip was therefore able to demonstrate his Trojan origins.

As a foundation myth, the legend of Trojan origins contained multiple layers of meaning and served different purposes. Like most myths, it explained nomenclature through eponymous heroes such as Francio and Meroveus and through historical etymologies. Because of their resistance to Valentinian, the Franks also derived their name from *ferancos*— that is, *feroces*.[75] Rigord opens his account by saying that Lutetia, which was named for its mud (*lutum*), was renamed by the Trojans for Paris Alexander, the son of King Priam, or from *parisia*, which meant boldness in Greek.[76]

The broadest and most significant service of the foundation myth was, however, to situate the French kings and their people in the mythological cosmology of the genesis of nations. Like the biblical tower of Babel, Troy's destruction was a point of differentiation of peoples. As direct descendants of the Trojans, the French took their place as peers among other peoples, including the Romans. Rigord takes special note of the Trojan origins of two neighbors with whom the Capetians were then engaged in combat, the Normans and the Britons, and Guillaume le Breton, partial to the latter, embroiders his account with further details from Geoffrey of Monmouth.[77] But the French were also held to have enjoyed unbroken continuity of rulership in their kings' descent from Pharamond. Rigord was well aware of the genealogical lapses in the dynastic lineage, but he nonetheless asserts something literally untrue: "We have thought that these stories should be inserted into our history without prejudice to others because we believe that all of the kings of the French have descended [*decendisse*] from this ancient root."[78] But *decendisse* could here only have been interpreted symbolically. Having ignored the possibility of Carolingian origins, Rigord reverts to a more ancient source, the Trojans.

THE CONSECRATION OF THE KING
AND HIS DEFENSE OF THE CHURCH

Neither Philip's blood right nor his alleged Trojan origins were as essential to his royal authority as his consecration by the archbishop of Reims on 1 November 1179. (See illustration no. 2) By this ancient ceremony Philip followed the example of Pippin's anointing by Pope Stephen in 754 and of Hugues Capet's consecration by Adelbéron, archbishop of Reims, in 987. Through such ceremonies medieval kings claimed to rule by the grace of God, claims repeated endlessly in charters and seals in the title *rex Dei gratia*. As new dynasties, both the Carolingians and Capetians owed their establishment to this ecclesiastical consecration, but more than others Hugues Capet had depended for his survival on the support of the French prelates.

Churchmen created the ceremonies by which kings were consecrated and crowned throughout the barbarian kingdoms during the early Middle Ages. Sharing elements in common, these coronation *ordines* cannot be satisfactorily divided into regional traditions. The first exclusively designated for the Capetians was the *ordo* of Reims, which was confected during Louis IX's reign, undoubtedly to be used at the coronation of Philip III in 1270. Yet it contained elements from an *ordo* devised around 980 by Fulrad, abbot of Saint-Vaast in Arras, which also was followed in the Anglo-Saxon kingdoms. Because Philip I used this earlier *ordo* in 1059, and Louis VI may have used it in 1108 as well, it may be conjectured that the Fulrad *ordo*, or one close to it, served the Capetians at least until the coronation of Philip Augustus in 1179. Since we cannot be certain, it would be rash to place full confidence in the surviving text of the 980 *ordo* for the details of Philip Augustus's coronation, but it does seem to embody the traditional ceremony and contains elements that survived in the later Reims *ordo*.[79]

If Guillaume, archbishop of Reims, followed this text, he opened the ceremony with the traditional *petitio-responsio* also used in 1059. At the bishop's request, Philip promised to respect canonical privileges, law, and justice and to defend the bishops and churches throughout his realm. After this response, he was consecrated with oil and invested with the royal insignia, consisting of the ring, sword, crown, scepter, and rod. Presenting the king to those assembled as the rightful heir designated by his father, the archbishop once again reformulated the king's original *responsio* in terms of three traditional precepts (*tria precepta*): to preserve through all time true peace for the church of God and all Christian people, to forbid rapine and iniquities of all sorts, and to enforce equity and mercy in all judgments. After the clergy and people had acclaimed him three times with *vive le roi*, the king received the eucharist in both kinds. Since Philip was not yet married, the remaining section, involving the queen, was omitted. Such were the principal steps in the traditional ceremony. Around 1200 a cleric in France compiled an *ordo* that included elements from German usage and innovations that had already made their appearance elsewhere. As in England, for example, the simple promise was transformed into an oath, and both the *responsio* and the *tria precepta*, now reinforced by oaths, preceded the anointing, thus obliging the king to swear to his duties before consecration. Both these features were retained by the Reims *ordo* of 1270.[80] The *ordo* of 1200 was most likely too unwieldy for application, and its innovations too recent to have been put in service by 1179, but, in any event, it underscored the importance of the promise/oath and anointing as the central features of royal consecration.

Reporting the ceremony at Reims in 1179, Rigord simply notes that Philip was crowned, acclaimed, and anointed. He makes no mention of the Reims tradition that the oil of consecration had been miraculously delivered from heaven to St. Remi, the bishop who baptized Clovis.[81] As a monk of Saint-Denis, Rigord pays more attention to Queen Isabelle's consecration, which took place at the royal abbey seven months later. While the queen was anointed, the king again wore his crown. So many people pressed into the church that a royal official assigned to restraining the crowd accidentally broke three lamps over the main altar. As in the heavenly miracle at Clovis's baptism, the oil flowed down upon the heads of the king and queen as a sign of the blessing of the Holy Spirit. Guillaume le Breton, however, under no obligation to promote Saint-Denis's claims, omits Rigord's story and returns to the Reims tradition,[82] also inserting the account of Clovis's baptism into Rigord's narrative of the Merovingian kings. As St. Remi was about to perform the rite, the vessel containing the oil was broken at the devil's instigation, thus providing the pagan party with an omen against Clovis's intended conversion.

But God confounded his opponents by sending an angel with celestial oil for the baptism. Thereafter all French kings were anointed with this heavenly chrism.[83] Guillaume integrated the Reims tradition into his narrative of the consecration of 1179 in the *Philippidos*. Philip was anointed by the archbishop of Reims, who alone dispensed the chrism prepared by angelic hands that rendered the French king a friend of the king of heaven and exalted him above all other monarchs.[84] According to the *ordines* of 1200 and of Reims, the king was anointed on the head, chest, shoulders, and wrists. Yet the implications of royal consecration amplified by the Reims claims could not be accepted by the reformed papacy without strong reservations. Innocent III attempted to distinguish the royal ceremony from the ecclesiastical sacrament of consecration. To reduce the significance of royal consecration, he declared in 1204 that kings should be anointed on the shoulders and that only bishops should be anointed on the head with consecrated chrism. His restrictions, however, had no apparent effect on Capetian practice.[85]

If the church of Reims had collaborated with Frankish royalty since Merovingian times, the ties between the king and the monastery of Saint-Denis were equally ancient and close. Coalescing under King Dagobert in the seventh century, they reached a peak during the reign of Louis VII, when Abbot Suger became regent of the realm during the king's absence on crusade. By Suger's time the monks of Saint-Denis had accumulated impressive claims. Their saint, the apostle of Gaul and the first bishop of Paris, was identified with Dionysius the Areopagite and the influential theological authority subsequently called Pseudo-Dionysius. He had also become the protector of the realm and the patron of the king. The abbey was the predominant mausoleum for French kings and the repository of royal insignia. When Philip I acquired the Vexin, the Capetians became vassals of the monks of Saint-Denis for that land. The abbey's banner of the Vexin became the king's standard, which he took from the altar of Saint-Denis before departing into battle. According to a charter forged in the twelfth century, Charlemagne himself had held his kingdom in fief from God and St. Denis. To commemorate his dependency, the emperor placed four gold bezants upon the saint's altar each year, just as a serf offered four pieces of money to his lord as token of subjection. Charles commanded his successors to follow his example.[86]

Philip Augustus was careful to continue these ceremonies linking the Capetian monarchy with the royal abbey. After his coronation in 1179 the king gave the monastery his crown, scepter, and royal garments. When he died he was interred in the abbey with full honors, and his testament bequeathed his crown and jewels to the monks, which his son later redeemed for 11,600 *livres parisis*.[87] During his lifetime the abbey's banner had become conflated with the Oriflamme, the flag traditionally attributed to Charlemagne. Philip bore this standard into battle at the two critical moments of his reign: in 1190 on the crusade and in 1214 at Bouvines.[88] The inventory of jewels in Register A shows that the king annually fulfilled his ceremonial obligation. Its last item provides: "Four bezants for the lord king when he goes to Saint-Denis."[89]

As a monk of the royal abbey, Rigord was naturally disposed to accentuate the connections between Saint-Denis and the king. His narrative attempts to integrate the monastery's history into that of the monarchy by inserting the elections of abbots and the authentication of relics.[90] Rigord shows the two parties working in close collaboration. When Philip returned safely from the east in 1192, he hastened to Saint-Denis to offer prayers of thanksgiving and to lay a fine silk pall upon the altar as a token of his love, a gesture he repeated in 1195 after signing the peace of Gaillon, and again in 1199 after Richard's death.[91] In 1205 the king personally conveyed to the monastery a number of important relics (including a piece of the true cross and a thorn from the Saviour's crown) sent from the imperial chapel in Constantinople by Count Baudouin of Flanders, then newly elected Latin emperor there.[92] As in the past, the saint's relics were called upon to invoke divine aid for the kingdom. During the anxious days of 1191, they were displayed for the success of the crusaders and the safety of the king. In 1196, and again in 1206, they were carried in procession throughout Paris to abate the flooding of the Seine.[93] The saint could also extend protection over the person of the king and the royal lineage. When as a boy Philip almost perished in the forest on the eve of his coronation, he prayed for help to God, the Blessed Virgin, and St. Denis, "the patron and defender of the French kings." His prayers were answered, as were those offered up in 1191, when the infant Louis and the king were delivered from serious illness.[94]

When Guillaume le Breton reedited and continued Rigord's chronicle, he eliminated all but the unavoidable references to Saint-Denis, except to note that the abbey's tower had been struck by lightning in 1220.[95] The only service permitted the royal saint was at Bouvines, performed through the display of the Oriflamme. But Guillaume divides responsibility for the victory between St. Denis and St. Germain, who was so occupied with the battle that he neglected to defend his church at Auxerre against robbers.[96] Guillaume, moreover, sets the record straight about Philip's hunting accident, which Rigord had obscured. Doubtless in order not to detract from his patron saint's prestige, the monk of Saint-Denis had neglected to mention that the infirm Louis VII, hearing of the danger to his son, had crossed the sea to Canterbury to implore the aid of his late friend Thomas Becket, then newly canonized. Guillaume acknowledges Louis's journey in his chronicle and assigns a major role in curing Philip to the English saint in the *Philippidos*. According to the latter version, at the saint's tomb Louis reminded Becket of the hospitality he had enjoyed during his exile in France, recalled his promise to come to Louis's aid, and confided Philip to his tutelage.[97] After his healing, the young Capetian was assigned the avenging of the saint's assassination. Adopting Rigord's earlier suggestion that God had used Philip to bridle Henry II, Guillaume argues that the premature deaths of the young Henry and Geoffrey, and finally the old Henry's fate, were divine retribution for the martyr's death.[98] Thomas Becket's patronage of the Capetians was neglected soon after the opening books of the *Philippidos*, however, undoubtedly because the English saint lacked institutional support comparable to that of St. Denis. Guillaume envisions St. Denis welcoming Philip to his sanctuary, after the king had been ceremoniously entombed in the royal abbey, and announcing to the pope in Italy that Philip now reigned with Christ in heaven.

Not long afterwards, an anonymous monk of Saint-Denis likewise noted Philip's special relationship to the abbey. In an obituary appended to Guillaume le Breton's chronicle, he characterizes the king as the *maximus* defender of churches, above all of Saint-Denis, which enjoyed his special love, favor, and protection.[99] The monk recalls the promise Philip Augustus had taken at his consecration. Before being anointed, Philip, like all his Capetian forebears and most medieval monarchs, solemnly promised to defend each bishop and church throughout his realm. Among the *tria precepta* he further promised to preserve true peace for the church of God and Christian people at all times.[100]

In the 990s writers at Reims had revised the "Testament of St. Remi" to claim that God had permitted the accession of the Capetians because the Carolingians had failed to protect the church. If the Capetians, in turn, oppressed the church, they, too, would be deposed.[101] The author of the *Historia gloriosi regis Ludovici VII* tells how Louis VII came to the aid of the monks of Cluny in Burgundy, who were threatened by the count of Chalon-sur-Saône, and concludes that Louis's avenging of Cluny was rewarded by God with the birth of a son. To demonstrate the causal connection, the author was obliged to reverse the chronology and to place Louis's expedition into Burgundy (1166) before the birth of Philip (1165).[102]

Rigord follows the *Historia*'s account of Philip's birth and also depicts the defense of the church as characteristic of the first year of the new reign. A few days after his consecration, Philip returned to Paris to punish the Jews for crimes against Christians. A month later he led his first expedition against Hebo de Charenton, who tyrannized over the churches and despoiled the clergy in Berry. At fifteen he again showed that he merited the sobriquet *a Deo datus* not only because of his birth but also because of his protection of the clergy. Like his father, he, too, later descended into Burgundy to protect the monks and clergy against the depredations of the count of Chalon and Humbert de Beaujeu. Rigord sums up Philip's first year by declaring that in fulfillment of his coronation promises, the king waged his first two battles for churches and the liberty of the clergy.[103]

Until 1190 Rigord cites Philip's further harassment of the Jews (1180–1183) and a second campaign into Burgundy (1186) as fresh evidence of the king's service to the church.[104] After his return from the crusade, however, Philip's repudiation of his wife in 1193, his depredations against Richard's churches, the taxation of his own clergy during the heavy fighting of 1194, his allowing the Jews to return to Paris in 1198, and, finally, the great interdict of 1200 undeniably tarnished Philip's image as an ecclesiastical defender.[105] Composing the *Karolinus* shortly before the interdict, Gilles de Paris could claim at best that the people and churches suffered less in France than from the exactions of Richard and the German kings.[106] For his part, Rigord allowed the theme of defender of the church to lapse after Philip's return from the crusade.

The crusade of 1190 was, however, the demonstration *par excellence* that the Capetian was the church's devoted protector, waging war against its enemies in the distant Holy Land.[107] Even though Philip abandoned the cause precipitously, the popes never gave up hope of reenlisting the king in the crusading program. After Philip was reconciled with his wife and defeated his enemies at Bouvines, Honorius III attempted to regain his support for the campaigns against the heretics in the south (1215, 1218) and against Egypt, but with minimal success.[108] In the ensuing negotiations the king requested, and the pope granted, special protection of the Apostolic See for his person, realm, *fideles*, and their lands.[109]

The French king's defense of the church earned him the title *rex christianissimus* ("most Christian king"), which had been bestowed on the

French kings since Carolingian times. Pope Stephen II accorded it to Pippin in 754, and in 1098 Pope Urban II, eager to enlist the French for the crusades, connected the title to the sacred oil of Clovis's consecration.[110] Rigord uses the title prominently in the first version of the *Gesta* from the time of Philip's consecration until he left for the Holy Land. After his return, however, to the end of the chronicle (1208), the designation is dropped—another indication of Rigord's dissatisfaction. Although Guillaume le Breton was disposed to overlook Philip's faults, he adopted Rigord's latter style and substituted his favorite *magnanimus* for *christianissimus* both where he was copying Rigord in the prose chronicle and in the *Philippidos*, where no praise was too extravagant.[111] Like "defender of the church," "most Christian king" was a title that summed up the churchmen's aspirations for the young king at the beginning of the reign, but as Philip fell into difficulties with ecclesiastics during the 1190s, even Rigord and Guillaume le Breton, his most partisan historians, permit these epithets to lapse.

THE MEANING OF BOUVINES

Philip's equivocal standing in the church was finally resolved in 1213 when he regularized his marital status with Ingeborg. With this impediment removed, he faced the king of England, the emperor of Germany, and the counts of Flanders and Boulogne on the fields of La Roche-au-Moine and Bouvines. His overwhelming victories annihilated his opponents, confirmed his territorial conquests, and demonstrated the justice of his cause. A true *bellum* waged for ultimate objectives and won with decisive results, Bouvines proved conclusively that God himself favored the Capetians. Within a decade the *éclat* of the victory caught the attention of chroniclers as far away as Bordeaux and Genoa. It was frequently recorded by scribes in the royal entourage. A chancery clerk composed a brief notice in Register C, for example, which Etienne de Gallardon expanded and inserted into the king-list of Register E in 1220. Another scribe jotted a note on the royal genealogy prefacing Gilles de Paris's *Karolinus* in a manuscript kept in royal circles, and a fourth, in attendance on Ingeborg, reported the victory on the appropriate day (27 July) of the calendar in the queen's psalter.[112]

The battle's chief literary impact, however, was to inspire Guillaume le Breton to compose the *Gesta Philippi* and to rewrite it in verse as the *Philippidos*. In the opening dedication of the latter, he evokes the living spirit of the *Karolide* who vanquished the Germans, English, and Flemings at Bouvines. Realizing by the end of book 9 that he would be unable to hold to his original format of ten books, he required two more to do justice to the triumph.[113] Both works provided opportunity to draw together and highlight themes formulated by his predecessors vindicating the Capetian monarch. In his pages Philip appears as the supreme lord over the barons of the realm, the true "Frank" descended from the Trojans and free from imperial rule, and the renewed defender and benefactor of the church. These themes converged and found their sanction at Bouvines.

Bouvines represented a decisive victory over baronial rebellion that vindicated the king's rights as feudal lord. Philip had worked to document, define, systematize, and exploit feudal ties with his vassals, including both the great barons and lesser knights—all in an effort to secure jurisdiction. When the judgment against John in 1202 was enforced by arms two years later, the king's authority over his vassals had become a reality.[114]

Except for the case of 1202, Rigord had paid scant attention to Philip's feudal relations, preferring to envisage the king primarily as defender of the church. Guillaume le Breton's prose chronicle follows this example except to add the judgment of Renaud of Boulogne in 1211.[115] At the end of the reign, however, when the significance of the victory over Flanders and Boulogne was fully apparent, Guillaume adopts the king's lordship as one of his leading themes in the *Philippidos* and sets about reinterpreting the reign from this perspective. The conspiracy of the house of Champagne in 1180 gives him his first opportunity to do so. By marching against Châtillon-sur-Loire, the sixteen-year-old monarch forced Etienne, count of Sancerre, to submit, and the latter's example was followed by others who had refused homage.[116] Thereafter, the major barons are pictured as explicitly recognizing homage. Although on one occasion (1187) Henry of Anjou unsuccessfully sought to hold back Richard's vassalage, he and his sons nonetheless frequently proffered homage. Henry refused to retaliate after Philip cut down the elm at Gisors (1188), for example, because, in the words attributed to Henry, "the king is my lord . . . against whom the law forbids me to make war."[117] Even the distant count of Toulouse was a subject under feudal law. When the duke of Burgundy (1186) and Henry and Richard (1187) made peace, Guillaume pictures them submitting as vassals, on bended knee.[118] (See illustration no. 3.)

Expanding upon the *Gesta*, the *Philippidos* tells at greater length of
Philip's decisive judgment of 1202 when the lords of Lusignan appealed

their complaint against John to him as their feudal overlord. Before detailing John's deception and obstruction of justice, Guillaume makes the English king confess openly that Philip has ultimate jurisdiction. In the *Philippidos*, therefore, Guillaume is the first chronicler to sense the full import of the decision of 1202.[119] Possessing competence over important disputes, Philip's court claimed jurisdiction over lesser complaints against Richard such as those from the lord of Vierzon and a peasant who discovered a treasure at Châlus.[120] By the end of the reign the count of Brittany, a powerful vassal, submitted his case against Aimery de Craon to the king's court.[121]

The prime example of recent memory to attract Guillaume's attention was Renaud, count of Boulogne. When Renaud was about to rebel for a second time, although he had been twice favored and once forgiven, Philip summoned him to his court and seized the castle of Mortain for noncompliance. In the *Philippidos* Guillaume has Renaud complain to John that the Capetian had exiled and despoiled him without judgment. Addressing the count directly, the poet declares that Philip has, on the contrary, taken Mortain precisely because Renaud refused to submit to the royal court. If the count had humbly sought peace from his overlord, he would have received restoration and rewards even greater than in the past. Renaud's obstinacy, however, drove him to oppose his lord on the battlefield where, despite knightly skill and French prowess, he was finally captured. To escape an ignominious death at the hands of mere sergeants, the count appealed to the bishop of Senlis to deliver him to the king's judgment for the last time. After upbraiding the rebel for innumerable treasons against an overlord who had bestowed on him five counties, a wife, and a son-in-law, among other benefits, Philip condemned Renaud to perpetual chains, although he merited death.[122] To Guillaume le Breton, Renaud de Boulogne's fate at Bouvines was the clearest vindication of the feudal jurisdiction of the royal court. (See illustration no. 6.)

Philip's supremacy over the great vassals was expressed with striking imagery by a scribe who interpolated a visionary tale into Rigord's history at the end of the reign. Reflecting contemporary traditions, this story relates that before the birth of his son, Louis VII dreamed of the young Philip serving a gold chalice filled with human blood to his assembled barons. This vision of the French magnates drinking blood from a cup held by the future king was a vivid figure of royal lordship.[123] (See illustration no. 1.)

Philip's most spectacular achievement at Bouvines was to have defeated in pitched battle an adversary whom Guillaume depicted as a Roman emperor. (See illustration nos. 4 and 5.) If not a Caesar, Otto of Brunswick was at least a Nero. Only the king of France stood between him and Rome's lust to dominate the world.[124] The Oriflamme, a simple banner of red silk designed for church processions, had demolished Otto's terrifying standard of a dragon surmounted by an eagle.[125]

Since Otto was the Roman emperor, Guillaume resisted the temptation to dress the French king in Vergilian garb and picture Philip locked in single combat with Otto like Aeneas with Turnus. In the end the royal chronicler rejected Roman literary inspiration for the anti-imperialistic theme embodied in the legend of the Trojan origins of the Franks.[126] Adopting elements transmitted by Rigord, Guillaume not only depicts the Franks as the descendants of Trojans, equals to Aeneas's lineage, but also as having long resisted Roman domination.

In tracing the two Trojan immigrations into Gaul, Rigord had noted that since the first movement under Duke Ibor had no kings, it became subject to the Romans, who appointed consuls over the newly arrived people. The second, in Sicambria, however, had rebelled against the emperor Valentinian because of the Trojans' refusal to pay tribute. After successfully resisting Valentinian and after victories over other Germanic tribes, these Franks finally subdued Gaul under King Marcomirus, thus joining forces with their cousins at Paris. In the prose chronicle Guillaume did not alter Rigord's narrative except to place the two elements in chronological order. In the *Philippidos*, however, Guillaume emphasized the Franks' invincibility, despite Valentinian's efforts to force them to submit. To amplify this point, Guillaume added an embellishment originating with Aimoin de Fleury and transmitted by Gilles de Paris. Valentinian had written Marcomirus promising the Franks remission of tribute for ten years in exchange for help against the rebellious Alans. The Franks slaughtered the Alans so thoroughly that their bravery won renown. When, however, the Romans sought to reinstitute tribute ten years later, the Franks preferred to go into exile rather than to sacrifice liberty purchased with their blood. This story added further meaning to the name *Frank*. They were called *Franci* not simply because they were *feranci* or *feroces* in battle, but because they had earned their freedom from Roman servitude. What Gilles de Paris and Guillaume suggest poetically, a later glossator states plainly: the *Franci* were *liberi* (free) from the Roman yoke, a status confirmed at Bouvines.[127] Alexander rather than Caesar therefore became the preferred exemplar of the Capetian monarchy because predating Roman domination he was thereby independent of the Empire.

Anti-imperialism could also be given less subtle expression by comparing longevity. Couched in biblical terms, the length of life or the duration of a reign signified divine favor. Wickedness produced quick deaths and short rules. When Jerusalem fell to the Saracens in 1187, Rigord laments, Pope Urban III died after a year and a half, and subsequently Pope Gregory VIII sat for only a month and a half. "Such a rapid rotation of supreme pontifs," the chronicler observes, "was explained by no other reason than their own faults and the rebellion of Christians against God's grace." Both Rigord and Guillaume le Breton were acutely aware of Philip's age and the years of his rule as they chronicled his life. Guillaume reminds readers that Alexander had ruled only twelve years and Caesar only sixteen, but Philip had already accomplished thirty-two before Bouvines.[128] Etienne de Gallardon expressed the chancery's opinion when he recopied the lists of French kings and Roman emperors from Register C to Register E. In the table of contents he explains that the names of French kings and the years of their reigns are noted so that one can observe the small number of kings and the great number of their days in contrast to the Roman *principes* and other rulers. From Pharamond to Philip, the French kings occupy one column, but the Romans require two to three columns, although the list is not complete. One can therefore see that God, in whose hands life and death are measured, cut in half the years of the Romans, but prolongs the French into ripe age because of their goodness, piety, and defense of the church.[129]

This rivalry with the Roman empire and preoccupation with its longevity may help to explain a perplexing document, the Tiburtine Sibyl, found at the end of Register E. At the express request of Bishop Guérin, Etienne de Gallardon compiled a *Provincialis* consisting of lists of popes, French kings, Roman emperors, and the *Provincialis* proper—that is, all the bishoprics of Christendom. These lists were then followed by a copy of the Tiburtine Sibyl,[130] a document that originated in Greek at the end of the. fourth century in response to the defeat of the Roman emperor Valens at the battle of Adrianople in 378. In the form copied by the French chancery, the Latin version was reworked and added to until the end of the tenth century or the beginning of the eleventh. It was a popular treatise surviving in more than 130 manuscripts, 30 of which date from before the thirteenth century. As the Latin version explains, the Sibyl was the Trojan daughter of Priam and Hecuba, who after centuries of wandering was invited to Rome by the Emperor Trajan. There she was commissioned to interpret a vision about nine suns, which a hundred senators had dreamed in common. In her view the nine suns stood for nine generations of Roman history leading to the Christian era. These generations were followed by a long succession of kings, identified chiefly by their initials, which were continually changed and revised in subsequent versions. In the chancery's text the two most clearly identified are Charlemagne (K) and Constantine (*Constans*). At the end of time there would appear the last world ruler, Constans, king of the Greeks, who would become king of both the Greeks and the Romans, rule for over a century, eradicate the pagans, convert the Jews, and promulgate the Christian faith. He would defeat Gog and Magog, the forces of the Antichrist, journey to Jerusalem, set aside his crown and royal garb, and hand over his kingdom to God and Christ. When the Roman empire had thus ceased, the Antichrist would reveal himself openly, occupy Jerusalem, and greatly persecute Christians. In the end, however, the Antichrist would be killed on the Mount of Olives by the Archangel Michael before the last coming of Christ. In characteristic prophetic fashion, the Tiburtine Sibyl conflates the historical Constantine with the apocalyptic last emperor. This vision of the last emperor was also included in the *Revelations of Pseudo-Methodius* (660–680) and Adso de Montier-en-Der's *Letter on the Origin and Life of the Antichrist* (950), both of which also circulated widely in the thirteenth century. The popularity of these prophetic treatises may be most readily explained by their clear emphasis on the last world emperor.[131]

If the message and popularity of the Tiburtine Sibyl were closely tied to imperial interests, why was this text selected by the Capetian chancery in 1220? In contrast to the Tiburtine Sibyl, Adso's version had transformed the last emperor from a Greek and Roman king into a king of the Franks. It would be a Frankish king who, having preserved the Empire, journeyed to Jerusalem, divested himself of his regalia, and consummated the Roman and Christian empire. During the reign of Louis VII, Otto of Freising, an imperial partisan, noted that the Sibylline prophecy had been applied to the French king. Adso's letter, which was better known (extant in 170 manuscripts) than the Tiburtine Sibyl, would have therefore generated greater interest in the Capetian chancery.[132] But instead the French chose an imperial text that made the last emperor Greek and diminished the role of the Franks.[133] The problem is further complicated by the fact that Etienne de Gallardon produced a garbled and mutilated version when he copied out the text. Apparently not comprehending its intrinsic message, he hurried to finish by abbreviating it heavily towards the end. Many crucial sentences were sacrificed, including the final one: "The Sibyl foretold these and many other future events to the Romans."[134]

Why the Capetians selected a text on the demise of the Roman empire addressed directly to the Romans may elude us. The chancery did insert a copy into the registers following a list of Roman emperors in 1220 after Philip Augustus had defeated an emperor at Bouvines. Whereas in the fourth century the Tiburtine prophecy had been created to preserve confidence in the Roman empire after the disaster of Adrianople, the French court turned to it after another imperial defeat to animate their meditations on the Empire's future end. Without further clues, it would be rash to speculate on what conclusions the Capetians drew from their mutilated version.[135] Even when quoted correctly, the Sibyl, like all ancient seers, was a mistress of obfuscation, not of clarification. Whoever claimed to understand her perfectly was surely deluded, as an earlier Anglo-Norman poet had warned:

> Ci est aukes obscure
> La Sibille escripture.[136]

Meditation on the demise of the Empire, however, was certainly not uncongenial to the Capetian court after the victory of Bouvines.

The third message of Bouvines was to reestablish the Capetian titles as defender of the church and *rex christianissimus*, tarnished after Philip's return from the crusade. Whatever the earlier ambiguities of Philip's policy towards the church, by 1214 he had returned to the responsibilities assumed at his consecration. Before the battle Guillaume saw the king enter the church of Saint-Pierre to pray. Standing directly behind Philip, the royal chaplain reported the king's harangue to his troops:

> In God we place our entire faith and trust. King Otto and his army have been excommunicated by the lord pope because they are enemies and destroyers of the goods of the holy church. The money they take as their wages has been acquired from the tears of the poor and the plunder of the churches of God and the clergy. We, however, are Christians and enjoy communion and peace with the holy church. Although we are sinners, we submit to the church of God and defend the liberties of the clergy with all our power. Therefore, we must presume faithfully upon God's mercy who will give to us sinners victory over our and his enemies.

"At the request of the knights," Guillaume adds, "the king pronounced a blessing of the Lord with his hand upraised, and immediately the trumpets were sounded."[137] This prose version may approximate Philip's actual speech, because victory is still anticipated in the future tense. When Guillaume transposes the king's words into verse, however, the optimistic note swells into triumphal certainty. Echoing Alexander's exhortation before the battle of Issus (as composed by Gautier de Châtillon), Philip exclaims: "*Ecce quod optabam* . . . Behold, what I have desired the Lord has granted. . . . He will be the prosecutor of the entire battle; we are his ministers. Neither do I ever doubt that victory will be given him . . . because he will triumph in us." After this opening paean, the poet summarizes the two principal arguments of Philip's speech: first, that Otto and his allies have been expressly anathematized by the pope, but the French forces are in communion with the church, and second, that whereas Otto has sought to despoil the church, the French have defended it and the rights of the clergy. To these points, Guillaume's poetic version adds a third: that Philip has hesitated to do battle on Sunday, the sacred day on which the shedding of blood is forbidden.[138] These three arguments are developed throughout Guillaume's prose and verse chronicles.

Of the year 1213 the royal historian notes that Renaud de Boulogne was excommunicated for his oppression of the church and had allied himself with Otto and John, both of whom had also been anathematized orally by the pope.[139] John had been personally banned in 1209 for opposition to the archbishop of Canterbury, and Otto twice in 1210 and 1211, for quarrels over Italy. Guillaume neglects to mention that John's sentence had been lifted in 1213, but it was true that Otto and Renaud remained under ban at Bouvines. Technically speaking, Philip had never been personally excommunicated, and the interdict on his lands was lifted in 1200. The royal chronicler pictures him as assiduously avoiding excommunicates, even his son, when the latter was anathematized for the English expedition of 1218.[140]

John and Otto, as well as Renaud, were notorious for despoiling churches. Guillaume pictures John as mercilessly plundering the lands of the English prelates after they fled the interdict of 1207, sparing not even the Cistercians and Cluniacs. He sees Otto as a second Nero, who has devastated Rome and the papal lands and systematically extorted ransoms from pilgrims to the papal city and even to the Holy Land.[141] But Guillaume waits until his narrative reaches the eve of Bouvines itself to unveil Otto's plan for subverting the entire world order. The allies not only plot to divide the Capetian possessions among themselves but propose fundamental reforms of the church as well—changes that will affect the clergy as fundamentally as the infamous spoliations of Charles Martel in the eighth century. The clergy and monks are to be reduced drastically by extermination or deportation. The few survivors are to be forced to be content with small tithes and voluntary offerings from the faithful. When he finally receives his imperial crown, Otto continues, he will issue a universal decree to confiscate the church's estates and large tithes and assign them to the knights and people responsible for keeping peace. Active and productive laymen will thus replace the decadent clergy, who have become fat, indolent, and useless, given over to excesses of Bacchus and Venus.[142]

Following French historiographic tradition, Guillaume le Breton's chronicle depicts Philip as protecting churches, intervening in Auvergne on behalf of the bishop of Clermont, and planning an invasion of England to restore worship.[143] In the *Philippidos*, however, the Capetian is represented at Bouvines as facing the most serious challenge of his career. As the leading supporter of the pope and the clergy, he alone stands in defense of the present order against Otto's scheme for world domination, which is fraught with revolutionary change. Since the allies seek nothing less than the death of their adversary, the ensuing battle is to be fought to the finish.[144]

Viewed in this ominous light, it was essential that the Capetian position be free from blemish. If in the *Gesta* Guillaume takes no note that the battle was, in fact, fought on Sunday, in the *Philippidos* the holy day itself acquires heightened significance. When Richard invaded Brittany in 1196, he had violated the sanctity of Friday, and Guillaume attributes Richard's death three years later to this disregard for the holy seasons.[145] At Bouvines Philip could not bring himself to believe that Otto would fight on Sunday. Before the king entered the church to pray, he remained hopeful that the conflict could be postponed, but when the allied attack against the rear guard was confirmed, he declared that God would permit the French to defend themselves on Sunday, just as he had allowed the Maccabees to fight on the sabbath. It would even be to their advantage to fight on a day when the whole church was at prayer for their cause. The battle was thus joined on the day pagans call Sunday but Christians designate the day of the Lord.[146]

Since prayers in Christian churches had been answered, it was appropriate that the Capetian acknowledge his debt to God. Prior to Bouvines, Philip had not distinguished himself by founding a new church. In 1206

Rigord, as a Benedictine monk sensitive to patronage, took note of the ancient foundations of the Merovingians, the establishment of the Cistercian house of Barbeau by Louis VII, of four new abbeys by Maurice, bishop of Paris, and of the Cistercian house of Pontigny by Thibaut, count of Blois, but Philip, despite occasions for gratitude, had not yet made an endowment. Guillaume le Breton claims that in 1202 the king had built the abbey of Saint-Corentin near Mantes to house 120 nuns in memory of his concubine Agnès, but the foundation was not new and the memorial was scarcely one to win clerical approval.[147] Although the victory at Bouvines called for grateful acknowledgement, nothing is mentioned by 1219–1220, when Guillaume finished his prose chronicle. At the end of the reign, however, when Guillaume began book 12 of the *Philippidos*, he depicts the king rendering thanks to God on the evening after Bouvines and founding a chapel outside of Senlis as a perpetual monument to the victory.[148] Construction did not begin until 1221, and the edifice was consecrated in 1225. The foundation is attributed to the king in the church's surviving charters and obituary, but on the advice of Guérin, bishop of Senlis, who continued to provide for its endowment after Philip's death. Served by twelve regular canons recruited from Saint-Victor in Paris, and dedicated to Mary "who is strong and powerful in battle," the church was named *Victoria* because of the "victory God had given at Bouvines."[149] *Victoria* was also a pagan numen, a great bird that Guillaume le Breton depicts both in prose and poetry as slowly circling the field of battle, hesitating where to alight until the decision is certain.[150] By its very name, therefore, Notre-Dame de la Victoire blended pagan images of triumph with Christian recognition of divine help in the poetic vision of the *Philippidos*.

THE BURIAL OF THE KING AND HIS PERSONAL SANCTITY

Death was the customary moment to look for signs and miracles signifying God's approbation of the life of the deceased. Philip had apparently been in failing health since September 1222, when he drew up his last will, and the end came ten months later. While at Pacy, the king, disregarding the advice of his doctors, decided to join the ecclesiastical convocation at Paris called to prepare for new crusades. The journey aggravated his condition, and he died en route at Mantes on 14 July 1214. His body was brought to Paris and ceremoniously buried the next day at Saint-Denis with the assembled prelates and magnates in attendance. Past funerals of Capetians had received scant notice—Louis VII's was virtually unreported—but Philip Augustus's attracted the attention not only of Guillaume le Breton but of English as well as subsequent French chroniclers. If the testimony of Philippe Mouskés, writing twenty years later, can be accepted, this Capetian was the first to be buried like the Angevin kings of England, *more regio*, garbed in full regalia. His body, dressed in a tunic and dalmatic, was covered with a gold cloth. His head was crowned, and he held a scepter in his hand. Because of the rapid burial, he was probably not eviscerated and his face was left exposed.[151]

While a king was living, the traditional demonstration of the sanctity of his consecration was his ability to cure a disease called scrofula by merely touching the afflicted. Philip I and Louis VI are reported to have "touched," but no such claims have been found for Louis VII, Philip Augustus, or Louis VIII. Only with Louis IX's reputation for unusual sanctity do reports of the practice appear once again. The intervening silence may be explained as deference to reforming churchmen who objected to the monarchy's claim to miraculous powers, or perhaps the practice had simply lapsed.[152]

Since miracles were regarded as part of everyday experience, especially by monks, Rigord did not hesitate to lace his narrative with tales of prodigies, wonders, and miraculous events. Among these were three wonders attributed to Philip during the first decade of his reign. The first and most spectacular occurred during the confrontation between the king and the count of Flanders in 1185. As their armies faced each other across the Somme at Boves, their protracted encampments naturally destroyed the crops ripening in the late summer. The canons of the cathedral of Amiens, who held property in the area, feared that their prebendal income had been lost, but after the French departure the fields miraculously revived and produced even more than normal, whereas the billeting of the Flemish troops obliterated the harvest. Philip likewise unearthed an abundant spring of water at the siege of Levroux in Berry in 1188, when his army was suffering from extreme drought, and in 1189 the king discovered an unknown ford across the Loire after the citizens of Tours had destroyed the bridge. Rigord ceases to attribute such miracles to the king after Philip's return from the crusade, however, and Guillaume le Breton was evidently not as taken with wonders as Rigord. He succinctly summarizes these three in the *Gesta*, but adds no more. Later, in the *Philippidos*, he embellishes them and further attributes two visions to the king during the first decade of the reign. In the first year the young Philip was permitted a vision of the Christ-child while attending mass at

Saint-Léger-en-Yvelines, and while caught in a storm at sea en route to Sicily, he saw the monks of Clairvaux at prayer for his safe journey.[153]

Guillaume had intended to complete book 12 of the *Philippidos* while Philip was alive, but his death offered the poet an appropriate occasion to scrutinize the king's demise for signs of personal sanctity. Like those of many important personages, Philip's departure was announced by a heavenly portent. A comet more ruddy and longer lasting than normal appeared a month before his last illness. Although it terrified and confounded the population, it was held to have proclaimed rejoicing in heaven over the king's imminent arrival.[154] When he received the eucharist and expired at Mantes, a great lamentation arose throughout the city. His body was anointed and carried on a bier through the gate towards Paris. When the cortege had proceeded three times the range of a crossbow bolt, the bier was set down to change pallbearers. The spot was marked with a cross and sheltered by four columns. Since miracles soon occurred there, a church was later erected to consecrate the site.[155] The procession continued to Saint-Denis, where the monks buried Philip next to their first royal patron, Dagobert. The requiem mass was attended not only by the cardinal-legate and the archbishop of Reims, who officiated, but also by the archbishops of Sens, Tours, Rouen, and Lyon, and nearly all the bishops of France. Assembling at Paris to discuss church affairs, they had not realized that God had called them to witness the great king's funeral.[156]

Finally at rest in Saint-Denis, Philip quickly benefited from the services of the patron saint. According to Guillaume le Breton, Pope Honorius III was residing at that time at Segni. In the same city a citizen named Jacques was on his deathbed, having received the last rites from the papal *penitentiarius*. St. Denis, clothed in red, accompanied by Philip Augustus dressed in white, and preceded by angels, appeared to the dying man and commanded him to go to the pope with instructions to absolve the king and celebrate a mass for his venial sins. In order to give credence to the apparition and its message, the citizen was healed of his mortal illness. Thus, through the intercession of St. Denis, the whole world knew that Philip now reigned with Christ in heaven.[157]

These reports of miraculous signs exemplifying the king's sanctity were echoed in other chronicles written after Philip's death. The celestial portents and the providential coincidence of the ecclesiastical council were widely noted.[158] The miracles at Mantes were matched by the monks of Saint-Denis, writing in the nearly contemporary *Vita et actus beati*

Dyonisii, who claimed that the lame and blind were healed at Philip's tomb. This last treatise contains an almost identical prose description of St. Denis's appearance to the citizen of Segni, and may have been its source.[159] Whoever the originators were, the account was widely disseminated, appearing in at least eight versions.[160] The campaign of Guillaume and the monks to transform Philip Augustus into a saint certified by miracles and visions was not easily sustained, however, while the faults of the historical personage remained fresh in memory. By mid-century St. Denis was pictured as rescuing the king from demons bent on dragging him to hell, and then conducting him through purgatory to salvation.[161] When the Capetians produced a more creditable and better-attested saint in Louis IX, interest in his grandfather's candidacy doubtlessly subsided.

However tenuous, Guillaume le Breton's interest in the king's sanctity nonetheless epitomizes Philip's role in the development of Capetian ideology. During his reign royal historians and poets elaborated discrete elements serving to legitimize Capetian kingship, but not yet sufficiently developed to coalesce into a comprehensive theory. Since Philip's son died after a rule of thirty months, it was left to the long and fruitful reign of his grandson, Louis IX, to elaborate them fully and coordinate their potential for the monarchy. Louis himself became a candidate for sainthood by force of character, demonstrating the sacred power of his consecration by touching for scrofula, and his consuming passion for the crusade earned him, more than all his forebears, the titles of defender of the church and *rex christianissimus*.[162] During his reign the ancient coronation *ordo* was thoroughly revised and adapted to suit the specific needs of the Capetians. His friend and protégé Vincent de Beauvais argued the legitimacy of the monarch on ancestral as well as religious grounds. Combining the Valerian prophecy with the *reditus* doctrine, Vincent perceived the expiration of the seventh generation with Philip Augustus and a return to the *stirps* of Charlemagne with the accession of Louis VIII, who claimed Carolingian blood through his mother. The Carolingians and Capetians were thus united in Louis VIII, a concept later publicized by the quasi-official *Grandes chroniques de France* at Saint-Denis.

Vincent's theory found artistic and iconographic expression at the royal abbey after the choir and nave were reconstructed in the new "Gothic Court Style" during Louis IX's reign. In the modernized church the tombs were completely rearranged to illustrate the dynastic synthesis. At the crossing of the choir and the transepts, the Carolingians were aligned along the south side and the Capetians along the north. Between them, forming the bar of an H and uniting the two dynasties, was Louis VIII, flanked by Philip Augustus towards the Capetians and a space reserved for Louis IX towards the Carolingians. The tombs of the Carolingians and Capetians were furnished with recumbent funerary statues in marble, and those of the three central kings were richly decorated with gold and silver. The statue of Philip was surrounded by images of forty-eight bishops, undoubtedly evoking the great ecclesiastical assembly attending his obsequies. With his son and saintly grandson, Philip Augustus was thus accorded a place of honor in the royal mausoleum.[163] In ideology as well as in the workings of administration, Philip had forged the essential components of royal government, which Louis IX and later Philip the Fair coordinated into a puissant policy that dominated Western Christendom throughout the thirteenth and fourteenth centuries.

Postscript:
Uncovering the Government
of Philip Augustus

The findings and conclusions of the foregoing study of the government of Philip Augustus naturally depend directly on the quality and quantity of the historical evidence. To assess the results historians must take full cognizance of the nature and extent of the sources available and be aware of their defects and limitations, so that the foundations are not required to support conclusions they cannot bear. Like an archaeologist the historian should uncover the sources of his study for full inspection. This evidence is not merely passive and innocent testimony to the past, but also the direct product of the institutions under study, and our sources must be viewed in interaction with the administrative organs that generated them. These sources in themselves provide evidence of the growth of Philip's government. As a mirror of institutional progress, they may serve as a summation to this study. The composition of chronicles and the drafting of royal charters reflect the primitive stage of Capetian government. The institutional creations of the 1190s generated fiscal accounts and archives. The extensive conquests following 1204 created the need for inventories and registers, and the precocious legal system of the Normans inspired the enrollment of judicial cases. Chronicles, royal charters, fiscal accounts, archives, registers, and judicial rolls constitute the major categories of sources that must be laid bare to evaluate the governmental achievements of Philip Augustus.

Chronicles

Chronicles are the most elementary of the written forms of history. As narratives composed by contemporaries or near-contemporaries for posterity, medieval chronicles record firsthand experience (albeit rarely), rehearse common report (sometimes drawn from competent informants), and incorporate written documentation (*instrumenta*). If they are not entirely reliable vehicles of information, their perspectives have nonetheless provided modern historians with comprehensive frameworks for understanding the past. Their points of view were almost always shaped by the vocations of their authors and by their patrons. Although the latter might have been almost any wealthy personage, they could include the king or someone close to the royal entourage who encouraged the chronicler to express the king's perspective. Such royal chroniclers were therefore sensitive to the development of monarchy.

The chroniclers associated with Philip's entourage derived inspiration from a distinguished model written by Suger, abbot of Saint-Denis, two generations earlier.[1] His *Vita Ludovici Grossi* and his notes for a biography of Louis VII established a royal historiographical tradition in France. Three aspects of his career and writing were decisive in shaping the course of French historical writing about the monarchy. In the first place he established history as the major intellectual activity of the monks of Saint-Denis. During his abbacy the monks began compiling brief chronicles such as the *Gesta gentis Francorum*, and his biography of Louis VI inaugurated a series of regnal histories that was revived late in the twelfth century and sustained throughout the thirteenth century in the *Grandes chroniques de France*. Secondly, his expertise in government and his intimacy with Louis VI and Louis VII created strong bonds between historians and the royal court. Lastly, his writings focused on the king as the organizing principle of the narrative. Though a royal panegyric, his life of Louis VI was not merely a hagiographic biography of the kind Helgaud had previously composed for Robert the Pious, but attempted to explain and legitimate the growth of royal authority as personified in the king. Suger found no immediate emulators in the following generation, however, and his exemplar had to await Philip Augustus's reign for its continuance, doubtless under the influence of Philip's governmental accomplishments.

Royal historiography was recommenced at Saint-Denis by Rigord, who identifies himself as a Goth (from Bas-Languedoc), a doctor of medicine, a monk of Saint-Denis, and chronicler of the kings of France.[2] He had, however, already begun writing the *Gesta Philippi Augusti*, his major accomplishment, before he became a monk—at least by 1186. (He had taken the religious habit by the time he was stationed at the priory of Argenteuil in 1189.)[3] And as he expressly avers, he wrote on his own initiative, not at the request of the monastery or of the king. Yet he twice entitles himself *chronographus Francorum regis*, and he tells us that he was persuaded by his abbot to present his history to the king "so that the king might transmit it to the 'public monuments.'" Since the passage containing the phrase *publica monumenta* was copied intact from Gautier de Châtillon, it is difficult to know whether it implied the royal archives or merely the collections of Saint-Denis, but it is evident that Rigord himself enjoyed access to the king's archives. He transcribed important government documents, such as the famous ordinance-testament of 1190, and he expressly notes many documents preserved in the royal archives since their establishment in 1194.[4]

Rigord's *Gesta Philippi Augusti*, which survives only in two manuscripts, underwent three recensions: (1) one preceded by a prologue dedicated to the king in 1196, (2) a continuation dedicated to Prince Louis around 1200, and (3) a continuation to 1206, which apparently was cut short by the author's death. Cast in the form of a regnal history like Suger's *Vita Ludovici*, Rigord's chronicle recounts those deeds of the king that the author deemed significant. In the beginning Rigord was favorably disposed towards his subject, but after 1190 the chronicler could not repress his criticism of Philip's despoiling of churches and his scandalous separation from his wife Ingeborg, matters offensive to churchmen. Although not official history in a technical sense, because it lacked an express royal commission, Rigord's *Gesta Philippi* may be considered a semi-official account of the reign.

About 1204, shortly before Rigord's chronicle was broken off, an anonymous monk, probably from the Parisian abbey of Saint-Germain-des-Prés, voiced complaints about the present state of royal historiography. Since the records were so voluminous and dispersed among scattered works, he reports, some Frenchmen mistakenly asserted that the

French kings had done nothing worthy of note except at Paris. To remedy this situation, the monk of Saint-Germain proposed to make succinct excerpts from standard authorities (which he cited) and to arrange them in three books according to the three royal dynasties. Designating himself a compiler rather than an author, this monk realized his modest ambition only in sketchy fashion.[5]

Rigord's self-imposed task of writing an account of Philip's deeds was continued by Guillaume le Breton, who, although not a monk at the abbey, nonetheless availed himself of historical writings found there and maintained close ties with the royal court.[6] Originating in Brittany, schooled at Mantes, and ordained a priest, Guillaume was first supported by a prebend from the Breton see of Saint-Pol de Léon. As a mature man, he joined the royal court around the turn of the century, when he was employed to negotiate with the pope over Philip's marital problems and was appointed tutor of Pierre Charlot, the king's bastard son. He also served as Philip's personal chaplain, which assured his presence at the major military engagements of the reign, such as the siege of Château-Gaillard and the battle of Bouvines. By 1219 he had had at least two major prebends from the chapter of Senlis conferred on him by the king's chief counsellor, Bishop Guérin.[7] A constant member of the royal entourage, therefore, enjoying the king's patronage, and inspired by the resounding victory at Bouvines, Guillaume le Breton became, to a greater extent than his predecessors, the first "official" historian of the Capetian monarchy.

Guillaume's *Gesta Philippi* was composed in four phases. Shortly after Bouvines he chronicled the years 1209 to 1214 to serve as a continuation to Rigord. Then, ascertaining that Rigord's history, which he had found in Saint-Denis's archives, was not widely known, he decided to preface his own account with a summary of Rigord that abbreviated and added to the monk's narrative. To this second version, which was completed between 1216 and 1220, Guillaume added a prologue that explained his intentions.[8] At a later date he continued the narrative to 1220, and after his death a final version was made with the use of his unfinished notes.

In the prologue to the second version of the *Gesta*, Guillaume le Breton says he will leave to others the task of transforming Philip's deeds into verse. Actually, he could not long refrain from the temptation, because, shortly after 1214, while still under the spell of Bouvines, he himself tried his hand at a poetic rendition. The result was the *Philippidos*, preserved in two recensions.[9] Reviewing his achievement at the end of the poem, Guillaume claims that it took him three years to compose and two to correct the work.[10] These figures are difficult to understand because the first recension was most likely not completed until 1222. The king's death the following year prompted him to continue the narrative through the funeral. The completed version was undoubtedly finished by Louis VIII's death in 1226. Prologues and epilogues were addressed to the two royal sons, Louis VIII and Pierre Charlot. Taking Gautier de Châtillon's popular *Alexandreis* as a model for both style and structure, Guillaume's *Philippidos* was originally planned in ten books, but, when he had only reached the Flemish campaign of 1213 by the end of book 9, he realized that at least two more books were necessary to cover the king's victory of Bouvines.[11] Philip's death and the revisions of the second recension required a twelfth and concluding book.

The prose *Gesta* provided the basic core of factual material to be translated into verse, but in the *Philippidos* Guillaume added significant amounts of new material and recast the entire work. Announcing his intention of recounting the "battles and famous deeds of the magnanimous Philip" in the opening line, he elevates the king's military engagements to a dominant theme, which gives him an opportunity to amplify the previous descriptions of Philip's warfare in the *Gesta*.[12] Above the clamor of battle he adds lengthy orations by Richard, John, Renaud de Boulogne, Otto of Brunswick, and other worthy adversaries, to which the Capetian hero answers with brevity. Descriptions of towns and landscapes, allusions from classical mythology, and other poetic devices further embellish this epic poem of more than 9,000 lines. Following the tastes of late antique poetry revived by the Latin versifiers of the twelfth century, Guillaume le Breton thus recast the deeds of Philip Augustus to glorify and sanctify the king's image as a mirror of instruction for Louis VIII and his successors. In the *Philippidos* Guillaume came closer to articulating a royal ideology than anyone else at Philip's court.

Stimulated by Philip Augustus's political achievements, Rigord, the anonymous monk of Saint-Germain-des-Prés, and Guillaume le Breton therefore reflect the three formative decades of the reign. In the 1190s Rigord brought out the first recension of his *Gesta*, inspired by the acquisition of Vermandois and Artois and benefiting from the establishment of the royal archives, which supplied him with important documents. After the great conquests of 1204, the monk of Saint-Germain responded (even if ineffectually) to the need for a historiography worthy of Philip's political achievements. After 1214, when Capetian success had been confirmed by the victory at Bouvines, Guillaume le Breton's *Gesta* and *Philippidos* provided an unrestrained panegyric to the glory of the French monarch.

Because of the political diversity of medieval France, the Capetians were not alone in patronizing historical writing. Numerous other chronicles were composed, sponsored by a variety of local lords, but few of these are overtly concerned with the growth of royal institutions. Those exceptional texts dealing with the history of the monarchy during Philip's reign may be divided into two geographical groups, originating to the northeast and the southeast of Paris. Among the first is the *Chronicon Hanoniense* of Gislebert de Mons. Canon and *prévôt* of Saint-Pierre de Namur and patronized by Count Baudouin V of Hainaut, for whom he served as chancellor, the chronicler presents a full narrative of the history of this county bordering Flanders up until 1195, a time when the king was actively interested in the region. During the second decade of the thirteenth century, Robert VII, lord of Béthune, commissioned an anonymous author to record the conflict between the Capetian and the Angevin kings, which impinged heavily upon his region. Writing in the vernacular, the author composed two versions, the *Histoire des ducs de Normandie et des rois d'Angleterre* (1213–1220), which was cast in the form of a universal chronicle, and the *Chronique des rois de France*, which relied on the *Historia regum Francorum* for the period 814–1185, but was original thereafter until 1217.[13]

The genre of the universal chronicle adopted in the *Histoire*, which began with the creation of the world and quickly proceeded to the present, was also employed by the southeastern group. Robert, Premonstratensian canon of Saint-Marien in Auxerre, wrote such a work at the request of his abbot, giving a firsthand account from 1181 to 1211. Although concentrating on the Burgundian region for the recent period, he was also aware of the activities of the Capetians. After 1227, a canon of the royal abbey of Saint-Martin de Tours, probably named Péan Gastineau, continued and revised Robert d'Auxerre's account, substituting the affairs of Touraine for those of Burgundy. Similarly, Alberic, a Cistercian from Trois-Fontaines in the diocese of Châlons-sur-Marne, continued Robert d'Auxerre's chronicle from 1227 to 1251, but oriented his focus more towards Champagne.[14] Finally, the cathedral chapter of Auxerre compiled a collection of biographies of bishops modelled on the papal *Liber pontificalis*, the *Gesta pontificum Autissiodorensium*, which began in the ninth century and is unusually informative for the reign of Philip

Augustus, when the king was often involved in the bishops' affairs.[15] These contemporary local French chroniclers each perceived the growth of royal government from their individual vantages.

During the opening years of Philip Augustus's reign, however, the most prolific and keenest observers of contemporary politics were found not in Capetian France but in the lands of the Angevin kings of England. Better than the royal French historians, these English chroniclers illustrate the intimate symbiosis between the sources and the subject. Stimulated by the genius of King Henry II and the *éclat* of his court, the golden age of medieval English historiography occurred during the last two decades of the twelfth century and lingered through the first half of the following one.[16] The judicial, administrative, and political reforms of the great justiciar king inspired a remarkable group of chroniclers who were primarily interested in governmental matters. They were cognizant of the details of the king's daily itinerary; they knew his chief administrators personally; they collected and transcribed important governmental documents; and, most important, they kept abreast of one another, so that their chronicles were, in effect, a collaborative enterprise.

The first of the group is traditionally called "Benedict" of Peterborough, although his precise identity eludes us. Chronicling the period from 1169 to 1192, he offers astute observations on Henry's government and interlaces his narrative with copies of official documents. His work was continued from 1192 to 1201 by Roger of Howden, perhaps the vicar of that place, but certainly a royal clerk who served the king frequently as diplomat, investigator, and itinerant justice. Whether or not Roger was actually the original author of "Benedict," whose work he revised, he nonetheless shared his predecessor's governmental preoccupations. Benefiting from administrative experience, his chronicle has been called a quasi-official record of the central government.

To these may be joined Ralph de Diceto (perhaps from Diss in Norfolk), a canon, archdeacon, and finally dean of St. Paul's in London. Although not a royal agent, Ralph was well situated in London to be the intimate of political figures such as Hubert Walter, William of Longchamp, and Walter of Coutances, and to be familiar with the operations and personnel of the exchequer at Westminster. His chronicle, the *Ymagines*, which breaks off in 1200, is especially informative about the church and kingdom, as well as about events across the Channel. Another contemporary who wrote from intimate experience of the court was Gerald of Wales, archdeacon of Brecon. Although he dedicated his profuse literary production to great patrons such as Kings Henry, Richard, and John, and Stephen Langton, archbishop of Canterbury, these efforts never obtained for him his life's goal, the Welsh see of St. David's. A *courtisan manqué*, he shaped the *De Principis instructione* (1192–1216) into a violent but knowledgeable diatribe against the Angevin dynasty and a corresponding panegyric to the virtues of the Capetians. Whatever Gerald's writing lacks in balance, it compensates for in color.

These writers are merely four chosen from a galaxy of historians writing at the turn of the century, and their governmental preoccupations were shared by chroniclers whose outlook was more ecclesiastical and parochial, such as the Benedictine Gervase of Canterbury, who wrote chronicles (to 1199) in defense of Christ Church, Canterbury, and Ralph of Coggeshall (to 1224), the abbot of a small Cistercian house in Essex. These English historiographic traditions converged in the thirteenth century at the Benedictine abbey of St. Albans outside of London, where Roger of Wendover and his more famous successor, Mathew Paris, benefited from excellent informants and access to documentation to produce lively, if opinionated, narratives about Kings John and Henry III.

Because of their fascination with the precocious government of the Angevin kings, and because the Angevins ruled more than half of France, the English chroniclers follow their monarchs across the Channel in their writings and sustain an informed interest in events on the Continent. Although most were out of sympathy with the goals and policies of the Capetians, they nonetheless contribute a valuable perspective on the development of the French monarchy, if only because their perceptions were sharpened by political rivalry.

Charters

Before the appearance of the documentary collections initiated by the Capetian government in the 1190s, the chronicles are the prime source of information about the opening decade of Philip's reign. Expressing contemporary observations, these writings were naturally colored by the particular interests of their Capetian, Flemish, English, and other authors. From the time of his accession, however, Philip Augustus issued a stream of *actes* drafted by his chancery that served strictly governmental purposes. Since these administrative documents were not expressly designed to interpret the present for the future, they furnish a less self-conscious perspective on the workings of government. Not until 1204, however, did the royal government make any effort to keep a record of these documents. Before that date, and even afterwards, the survival of royal *actes* depended on the archival policies of their recipients. These *actes* cannot be used as evidence regarding Philip's government, however, until their survival in medieval collections has been taken into consideration. Between 1916 and 1979 the Académie des Inscriptions et Belles-Lettres undertook a painstaking and exhaustive search to collect all originals, copies, and mentions of such *actes*. From the nearly 1,900 that have been uncovered, 1,839 authentic *actes* illustrate how these documents survived and how they may be evaluated as evidence in connection with Philip's government. Grouped by major medieval collections and by the chronological divisions of the present study, the statistical results are presented in Table 13.

It is clear that until the appearance of the chancery registers in 1204, over half the surviving *actes* (53 percent) were collected by the recipients in ecclesiastical and secular archives. The royal archives, which were inaugurated in 1194, were designed to collect incoming charters, not to preserve outgoing royal documents. The exceptional royal *actes* found in them originated in baronial collections added subsequent to the reign. In whatever way the great barons and other nobles collected their documents, however, most family archives did not outlive the Middle Ages (except the few acquired by the royal archives).[17] Only cathedrals, monasteries, and other churches succeeded in preserving original charters and, more important, copied large numbers into codices called cartularies. They collected 49 percent of the surviving royal *actes*, passing on their records as perpetual corporations until ecclesiastical property was nationalized during the French Revolution, when church archives and libraries were preserved as public property. This explains the high survival rate of *actes* with ecclesiastical rather than secular recipients.

Although it is nearly impossible to estimate how many royal *actes* have been lost, they must have far outnumbered those that remain. One slight indication of these losses, and another index of the higher survival in church collections, can be gained by comparing two inventories drawn up in Philip's reign with extant royal charters. Between 1205 and 1211 the chancery compiled a list of alms that the king owed to churches and of *fief-rentes* that he owed to barons and knights. For 133 ecclesiastical recipients on the inventory, charters for 49, or 37 percent, are still extant, whereas for 129 barons and knights, only 11, or 9 percent, of the charters have survived. (Of the latter, 7 were preserved in the royal registers.)[18]

TABLE 13. Medieval Sources for the *Actes* of Philip Augustus

	1180 to 1190	1191 to 1203	1204 to 1211	1204 to 1214	1212 to 1220	1215/20 to 1222	Total
Originals in the royal archives	4 (0.36)	7 (0.54)		11 (1.0)		11 (1.38)	33 (0.77)
Originals in church archives	115 (10.5)	109 (8.4)		128 (11.6)		86 (10.7)	438 (10.2)
Copies in church cartularies	129 (11.7)	109 (8.4)		117 (10.6)		42 (6)	397 (9.3)
Totals from church sources	202 (18.4)	188 (14.5)		207 (18.8)		109 (13.6)	706 (16.4)
Originals and copies in secular archives	11 (1)	20 (1.5)		27 (2.4)		19 (2.4)	77 (1.8)
Copies in Register A	24 (2.2)	65 (5.0)	142 (17.7)				231
Copies in Register C	9 (0.8)	11 (0.85)	4 (0.5)		149 (16.6)		173
Copies in Register E	3 (0.3)	6 (0.5)	14 (1.75)		11 (1.38)	85 (28.3)	119
Extant *Actes*	378 (34.4)	415 (31.9)		600 (54.5)		446 (55.7)	1,839 (42.8)

NOTE: The first figure given is the number of *actes*; the figure in parentheses is the average number of *actes* per year. Shaded areas represent periods in which registers were actively in use. All unauthentic *actes* have been eliminated, as have the calendar years of 1179 and 1223, which were not full years in Philip's reign. I have tabulated only medieval sources. Multiple originals and multiple copies have been counted only once in each category. Since a single *acte* may have survived both in original and in copies, categories may overlap. To eliminate duplication between originals in church archives and copies in church cartularies, a total from church sources has been compiled.

SOURCE: *Actes* I–IV, supplemented and corrected by *Actes* V.

When royal *actes* were collected only by the recipients (until 1204), the extant survivors reflect a heavy ecclesiastical bias. The survival rate of royal *actes* destined for churches does not vary much for the remainder of the reign (from 13.6 to 18.8 per annum), but the appearance of royal registers in the chancery during the second half of the reign changes the picture significantly. From 1204 to 1211 Register A began collecting royal *actes* at the rate of 17.7 *actes* each year; from 1212 to 1220 Register C at 16.6 *actes*; and from 1220 to 1222 Register E at the extraordinary rate of 28.5 *actes*.[19] In addition, Register A, and to a lesser extent Registers C and E, preserved royal *actes* from the first half of the reign. From

1180 to 1203, 49 percent of the extant documentation is from the ecclesiastical collections, and the three royal registers retrospectively contributed 15 percent. After 1204, however, when they were in current operation, they preserved 39 percent of the extant royal *actes*, as against 30 percent for the church collections. For the entire reign the royal registers preserved 28 percent of the king's extant *actes* and the church recipients 38 percent. Although the ecclesiastical bias remains strong throughout, after 1204 the royal registers thus began to preserve a significant number of the king's *actes* of interest to the chancery.

Philip inherited an informally organized chancery at his accession. During his grandfather's reign most royal *actes* were written down by the recipients who, as churchmen in most cases, possessed established *scriptoria*. The king merely validated the document with his seal. Louis VII followed this practice, and appears to have availed himself of scribes from the local churches of Saint-Denis, Notre-Dame, Saint-Victor, and Saint-Germain-des-Prés, who drafted royal charters destined for their own churches or for other parties. When Philip was crowned in 1179, Hugues du Puiset was the royal chancellor. After Hugues's death in 1185, the office was left vacant. Although Brother Guérin signed his name to royal *actes* between 1202 and 1210, neither he nor his titular predecessor had any marked influence on chancery practice.[20] A few of Philip's *actes* may have been written by recipients, but most were produced by at least seventeen nameless scribes working for the chancery, who can be identified only by their handwriting. Except in 1190 when a record eighty extant documents were drafted by six scribes in preparation for the crusade, they normally worked in groups of two or three. Sometime between 1195 and 1200 these chancery scribes achieved a standardized script that distinguished their writing from other *scriptoria*. It becomes more difficult to separate them after this period, and the scribal hands may conceal multiple individuals.[21]

The chancery clerks also achieved a similar standardization in diplomatics—that is, in the formulas employed for drafting different kinds of *actes* in the name of the king. On the eve of the crusade (1190) the formal phrasing was established for three kinds of royal documents, from which the chancery rarely departed thereafter. Borrowing terminology from a contemporary (1191) royal *acte* to the Templars regulating chancery practice, we may call these three categories diplomas (*privilegia*), charters (*carte*), and letters (*littere*).[22] Diplomas begin with an invocation of the Holy Trinity and end with witnesses from among the household officers, the years of the reign and of the Christian calendar (but not the month), and a royal monogram. Less formal, charters begin with the king's name and a universal address (*Noverint universi* . . .) and end with the Christian year and the month. Letters are distinguished by a salutation (*salutem*) to all people (*universis*) or to named individuals and conclude, like the charters, with the Christian year and the month. A *mandatum* is a specific form of a letter in which the addressee is commanded to perform a deed. When the royal *actes* are extant only in copies where the formulae have been abbreviated, such as in the royal registers, it is often difficult to differentiate between diplomas and charters.[23]

All three categories were present from the beginning, but formal diplomas predominate from the first decade on (70 percent). This is undoubtedly due to the ecclesiastical bias in the evidence, since churches preferred their privileges and concessions to be confirmed with the more prestigious diplomas. Although the chancery output became increasingly diversified, producing higher percentages of charters and letters as the reign progressed, no specialized use can be attributed to any one of the three categories. The chancery clerks had standardized the forms but not the deployment of official royal documents.

Fiscal Accounts

The chronicles and charters of the first decade of Philip's reign reveal a government that remained in the primitive state inherited from the early Capetians. Most royal business relied on the memories of the king's ambulatory entourage, reinforced by minimal records, perhaps informal and portable notes. Three changes, however, intervened in the 1190s to create a demand for better documentation. Expansion of the royal domain, culminating in the acquisition of Vermandois and Artois in 1191, encouraged the establishment of a stable central capital at Paris from which the king could better supervise his lands. The summons of the Third Crusade removed Philip temporarily from France for eighteen months in 1190–1191. And the mounting warfare following his return caused him to lose his baggage train to Richard at Fréteval in Vendôme in 1194. As we have seen, among the losses were documents as well as treasure.[24]

What precisely Philip lost at Fréteval remains a matter for conjecture, but the experience of other contemporary governments, such as that of the count-kings of Catalonia, suggests that the peripatetic courts of the day may well have carried with them inventories, or *états*, of domanial revenues and other governmental resources. Later specimens have survived in the Capetian registers. The *prisée des sergents* drawn up in 1194, for example, lists the military contributions of towns and abbeys in the royal domain, and the *Census* from 1206 to 1210 provides an inventory of domanial income. Since the latter is limited to territories added between 1185 and 1206, the implication is that a comparable list for the old royal domain had been lost. In any event, when Guillaume le Breton describes the documents lost at Fréteval in his prose chronicle, he calls them "tax account books" (*libellis computorum fisci*). Embellishing the account in the *Philippidos* at the end of the reign, he terms them "fiscal documents and domanial accounts" (*scripta tributorum fiscique cyrographa*), including both *tributa* and *census*. The lost documentation answered the following questions: What is owed to the treasury (*fisco*)—for example, what and how much payment (*tributa*), what *cens* (*census*), what tolls (*vectigalia*)? Who are held to pay by feudal law and how much? Who are exempt and who are condemned to exactions? Who are serfs (*servi*) of the glebe (*glebe*) or by status (*conditionis*)? To what patron is the freedman (*manumissus*) bound by law? Even when the poetic language is discounted, these questions suggest that Philip's court carried domanial *états* in its baggage.[25]

Whatever may be speculated about these lost documents, Philip's departure in 1190 did produce the first "constitution" of the Capetian monarchy. Rigord declares that Philip convoked his friends and *familiares* to Paris before leaving, drew up his *testamentum*, and published an *ordinatio* for the whole kingdom. Just as the frequent absences of the English kings from their island kingdom to govern their continental lands generated a precocious series of records, so Philip's absence required him to put into writing his delegation of authority to subordinates. The result was the ordinance-testament, which established a temporary regency, confirmed older procedures, and made judicial and financial innovations. Among the latter was a new series of fiscal records. The king commanded that when the revenues were brought to Paris three times a year, his clerk Adam was to be present to write them down.[26]

Of all the records produced by the French government in the Middle Ages, none have suffered greater damage than the financial ones. Whatever survived war, neglect, and pillaging by antiquarians was decimated by a fire that gutted the building of the Chambre des Comptes on the night of 26/27 October 1737. Further losses occurred during the French Revolution. These calamities were, however, mitigated by one stroke of good fortune. Ten years before the fire, Nicolas Brussel, "Conseiller du

Roy, Auditeur ordinaire de ses comptes," published in an appendix to a book on fiefs a transcription of an entire triannual account from 1202/03.[27] He knew of another complete account from 1217 and of an incomplete one from 1219, from which he made occasional extracts. A careful reading of his book suggests that these three accounts were all that he could find in the Chambre des Comptes dating from the reign of Philip Augustus and that he transcribed the full account of 1202/03 presumably because it was the earliest.[28] In the preceding century other erudites had alluded to accounts from February 1211, May 1220, and November 1222.[29]

These chance survivals, crowned by the complete account for the fiscal year 1202/03, demonstrate that the system inaugurated in 1190 was maintained throughout Philip's reign. The salient characteristics of the 1202/03 account—triannual terms and separation of the functions of *prévôts* and *baillis* into different chapters—fit the ordinance. Brussel describes the account as "a great roll from the Chambre des Comptes," so in physical appearance it resembled the Pipe Rolls of the Anglo-Norman kings.[30] Preceding the conquest of Normandy by one year, it illuminates in a brilliant, if momentary, flash the great innovative decade opened by the ordinance of 1190.

A recent discovery has further helped to repair the misfortunes of the French financial archives. In 1978 the Bibliothèque Nationale acquired a sheet of parchment roll containing a royal account from November 1221. Although only a fragment, it can be compared with a series of later accounts from 1227 and 1238 known as *Magna recepta et magna expensa.* Unlike the account of 1202/03 it was not designed to supervise local officials, but to give the central court an overall view of its major revenues and expenses. It not only testifies to improvements in fiscal administration but also permits an estimate of the increase in revenues resulting from the territorial conquests of 1204. Its importance to an understanding of the second half of the reign is comparable to the light shed on the 1190s by the accounts of 1202/03.[31] Undoubtedly the increase in the size of the domain generated the need for a comprehensive picture—indeed, a "budget"—of royal finances.

The Royal Archives (Trésor des Chartes)

Even the most primitive government finds advantage in retaining incoming charters, documents, and other correspondence for future reference. Little is known about how the ambulatory Capetian court collected these materials, but when Hugues de Champfleuri, bishop of Soissons, resigned the royal chancellorship in 1172 and retired to the abbey of Saint-Victor at Paris, he took with him a large collection of letters, which he had copied into a codex at the abbey. Amounting to nearly four hundred items, the great bulk were addressed to King Louis VII by popes, archbishops, bishops, cardinals, abbots, kings, dukes, counts, and lesser persons. Although the originals have since disappeared, Hugues's register indicates that the royal chancery made an effort to retain incoming letters as early as 1156. These letters were not, however, official *actes* or documents that had judicial authority.[32]

Such official *actes* or *titres* were, in fact, retained in a collection subsequently known as the Trésor des Chartes. During Louis IX's reign, when the organs of central government were better established at Paris, the king constructed a sacristy adjoining the Sainte-Chapelle at the royal palace, the top floor of which was designated to house the collection. Known as the "cupboards of the king" (*in almariis domini regis*) in the thirteenth century, it acquired its permanent name, the Trésor des Chartes, in the following century from the sacristy. It was originally limited to *actes* received by the king, but was enlarged during the second half of the thirteenth century to receive archives from the newly conquered lands in the south and from the great baronies of Toulouse and Champagne annexed to the royal domain. Little organization or systematization was imposed on the collection until the beginning of the fourteenth century, when, under pressure of massive infusions, the custodian, Pierre d'Etampes, compiled the first comprehensive inventory. By the fourteenth century the Trésor des Chartes had become the nucleus of the royal archives.[33]

At the end of Philip Augustus's reign, however, the royal chronicler Guillaume le Breton explained that the royal archives had come into existence as a result of the skirmish at Fréteval on 5 July 1194, when Philip lost his baggage train to King Richard. The losses included royal documents that later had to be restored, and the royal archives resulted. Actually, the engagement at Fréteval was noticed by four contemporary chroniclers: two English, Ralph de Diceto and Roger of Howden, and the two French, Rigord and Guillaume le Breton. Although all were impressed by the treasure or money that Richard captured, "whose value was immense," according to Ralph de Diceto, only two mention documents among the losses. Roger of Howden remarks that the English king seized not only Philip's great treasure and chapel but also "the charters of all the men who had given themselves to the king of France and to Count John against Richard." Obviously such information was useful to Richard in suppressing John's rebellion. Writing soon after the event, Rigord naturally found the incident embarrassing and passes over it quickly, mentioning only that Philip lost his pack horses, money, and household furnishings.[34]

When Guillaume le Breton reviewed Rigord's account, he added that the king had suffered the loss of his seal and his tax account books. But when he wrote about Fréteval in the *Philippidos*, he added details hitherto unknown. After marvelling over the lost gold and silver, he again noted the seal and the fiscal documents. Whereas the lost treasure could readily be replaced, the records could not be retrieved without great effort. The responsibility of reassembling the documents in their former state (*qui cuncta reduxit . . . in solitum rectumque statum*) was assumed by the royal chamberlain, Gautier the Young. Guillaume le Breton thus gave rise to the tradition of the origins of the royal archives following the losses at Fréteval.[35]

Although Guillaume's explanation did not appear until the end of the reign, it can be corroborated from evidence in the Trésor des Chartes itself. As far as can be ascertained, the Trésor has been kept intact and separate from other collections from Pierre d'Etampes's first inventory in 1318 through the definitive reorganization by Jacques Dupuy in the seventeenth century. Except for the inevitable casual attrition, the present collection therefore contains the materials of the original archives. But other archives from Louis IX's southern conquests (1269), the county of Toulouse (1271), and the county of Champagne (1361) were subsequently acquired, which added material contemporary with or antedating Philip's reign.[36]

The earliest and best-documented example of these infusions originated in 1223, when the county of Beaumont-sur-Oise escheated to the crown and the king divided it among three distant heirs. During the reign of Louis IX a chancery clerk copied into Register E a list of charters from the county of Beaumont that Adam the concierge held at Paris. Among the thirty-one items in this inventory, at least twenty are still extant in the Trésor des Chartes. (This sample thus demonstrates that at least two-thirds of the Beaumont archives survived after incorporation into the Trésor des Chartes. The Beaumont example also suggests that the archives were kept at the king's palace, because Adam was a royal concierge.)[37] Among these are charters antedating the alleged origin of the royal archives in 1194.

In addition to whole collections, individual pieces found their way back into the royal archives. For example, the charter of Louis VI to the nuns of Notre-Dame d'Orléans (1119), now the oldest original royal charter in the Trésor, is inscribed "Letter returned from the nuns of Orléans" on the back. And the presence of another charter (1183) is explained by a dorsal notation: "The letter of Agathe, lady of Pierrefonds, is returned to the lord king by the monks of Longpont."[38] With these collections and individual pieces added after 1223 omitted, the development of the royal archives during Philip's reign as illustrated in the Trésor des Chartes is depicted in the accompanying graph.

One striking fact is clearly demonstrated: the year 1194 was crucial in the development of the royal archives. Before that date the archives contain only 28 original pieces from the entire preceding history of the French monarchy.[39] (No year produced more than 5 charters.) After 1194 and for the remaining twenty-nine years of Philip's reign, the Trésor des Chartes preserves at least 556 original pieces. Although individual years oscillate greatly, the extant charters leap to 17 in 1195 and hit increasing peaks of 28 (in 1199), 38 (in 1211), 43 (in 1215), reaching a record 63 in 1217. The subsequent losses cannot be fully assessed, although the Beaumont collection suggests that a third have disappeared since 1223. Nor can all additions subsequent to 1223 be identified with certainty. Pre-1194 charters could have found their way back without leaving trace of their entry. For that matter, the traditional story does not require the king to have lost *all* of his archives at Fréteval. Some documents may have survived the debacle.

Three original documents from the Trésor also point to the archives' commencement in 1194. A treaty between Philip and Count John against Richard dated in January 1194 at Paris remained in the royal archives in the form of a letter patent issued by John. Two letters of homage to the French king from Richard's Poitevin vassals Bernard, *vicomte* de la Brosse, and Geoffroi de Rancon, dated at Sens in March 1194, also survive.[40] Although these names fit Roger of Howden's description of men who went over to the king of France against Richard, their letters were obviously not among the charters that fell into Richard's hands at Fréteval. (They remained in Philip's possession.) But John's and the two Poitevins' charters were the first documents of the Trésor des Chartes to be of immediate and vital concern to the French king. The dates in January and March 1194 suggest that Philip's chancery began retaining documents in that year. They were followed by the original sealed text of Richard's

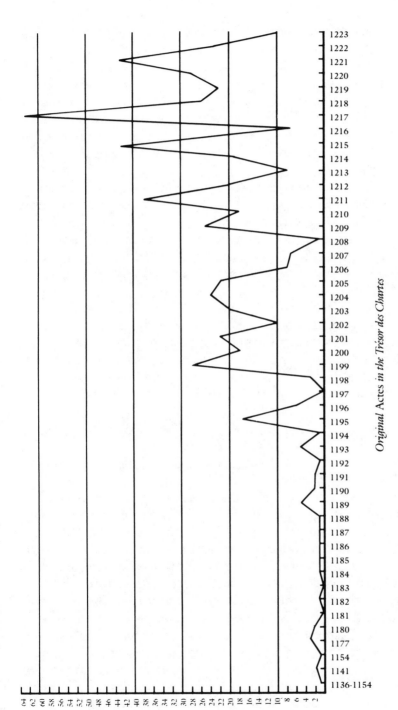

Original Actes in the Trésor des Chartes

NOTE: Years are calculated according to the system of the royal French chancery, beginning with Easter.

From all extant originals and notices of losses, *actes* from the following sources have been eliminated: southern conquests, Toulouse, Champagne, Templars, Beaumont, Valois, Boulogne, Gaucher de Châtillon, Guillaume, count of Ponthieu, and items explained by individual circumstances. Already in the fourteenth century the inventories of Pierre d'Etampes and Adam Boucher provided separate divisions for the collections of Toulouse, Champagne, Beaumont, Gaucher de Châtillon, and Guillaume, count of Ponthieu. See Teulet I, pp. xxvii-xxxv.

SOURCE: Teulet I.

treaty of Louviers, dated January 1196, and numerous accompanying charters.[41] Philip's agreements with important barons such as Renaud, count of Boulogne (1196), Baudouin, count of Flanders (1196), Guillaume, count of Ponthieu (1196), Thibaut, count of Troyes (1198), and Eudes, duke of Burgundy (1198), were collected in subsequent years.[42] The crucial treaty of Le Goulet in May 1200 was preserved in a sealed copy issued by John, now as king.[43] Most of these important political documents are noted by the chronicler Rigord, who apparently had access to the archives.[44]

Although it is difficult to confirm Guillaume le Breton's report about the role of Gautier the Young in establishing the archives, the surviving documents nonetheless show that Guillaume's chronology is correct. It is also difficult to determine precisely when the archives were located at Paris, but the experience at Fréteval must have encouraged this step soon afterwards. The year 1194 was therefore a *tournant* in the development of the royal archives. Nothing of importance has remained from before that date to indicate a previous royal collection. After that date the chancery began to preserve mounting quantities of documents, following a consistent and conscious archival policy. In the decade following the crusade, when Philip Augustus was busy reorganizing his government, the establishment of permanent archives along with an accounting bureau producing periodic fiscal records thus became integral parts of his program.

Registers

Collecting incoming documents required only passive receptivity and a restraint from discarding the most important, but recording outgoing charters, letters, and documents implied more active measures. The chancery was required to draft both the original document and a copy for preservation. The first extant effort to record and to assemble outgoing royal documents in a codex was undertaken during the spring of 1204, simultaneously with the conquest of Normandy. First an original transcription was made of a body of documents in a register by one or two scribes writing uniformly and continuously in a short time. To this other materials were added by diverse scribes in subsequent years. When these additions became too cumbersome, the whole register was quickly recopied under an improved organization. Once again additions were inserted throughout the register until it, too, became unwieldy and required recopying. This process produced the three royal Registers, A, C, and E.[45]

Since the registers were intimately connected with the work of the chancery, the person responsible for initiating the series was probably Brother Guérin, who had supervised this bureau since 1201.[46] The transcription of the original part of Register A was done by a scribe (designated N) between May 1204 and February 1205. Further *cahiers* of parchment, on which at least five scribes copied new material, were added both preceding and following the original nucleus between February 1205 and February 1212.[47] From February to August 1212, two or perhaps three scribes (designated α, β, and γ) recopied the contents of Register A into Register C, dividing the register into ten sections.[48] Until July/August 1220 at least nine scribes added new documents to Register C in spaces following the ten divisions.[49] As the book became encumbered, they abandoned all semblance of organization and copied wherever they found room.

By August/September 1220 Guérin, now bishop of Senlis and Philip Augustus's chief administrator, decided that once again it was time to wipe out the confusion with a clean copy. Doubtlessly mindful of the king's age (Philip died three years later), he knew that a new register would facilitate the transition between the king and Prince Louis. Guérin therefore commissioned his clerk Etienne de Gallardon, canon of Bourges, to execute Register E.[50] Etienne appears to have possessed long chancery experience because his distinctive hand made corrections and additions to Register A while the register was in use between 1205 and 1212. After resigning from royal service, he put his talents to further use by composing a well-organized cartulary for the chapter of Bourges (ca. 1230). Like Scribe α in Register C, Etienne both recopied and improved the organization of the former register, expanding the divisions to eighteen. In the margins of Register C, notations were made as to whether a document was to be, or had been, recopied and to what section it should be assigned. Completing his work in 1220, Etienne provided ample space between his divisions for succeeding additions. In the following years about a dozen hands can be distinguished, including Etienne's own, those of three or four scribes who worked on Register C, and over a half-dozen new hands.[51] Testifying to Guérin's foresight, Register E served the royal chancery as principal register during the reigns of Louis VIII and Louis IX, at least until 1247, when the latter had a copy (Register F) made to take on the crusade. New pieces were inserted throughout the second half of the thirteenth century.

The increased size of each register generated a greater incentive to refine the organization so that material could be located more rapidly. The only semblance of order in Register A, a small volume of ninety-six folios, occurs in the first two *cahiers* of the original transcription, where scribe N copied a block of royal charters relating to towns.[52] Interspersing urban charters with other matters in the remaining *cahiers* of the primitive section, he was followed by scribes who added documents with no respect to plan. Register A was apparently small enough to find one's way with little difficulty. When Scribe α copied Register C, he divided the material into ten groups headed by the following table of contents:

Incipiunt partes libri
   Feoda i   fol. 11r.
   Elemosine ii   fol. 13r.
   Servitia que feoda debent iii   fol. 14v.
   Servitia militum Normannie iiii   fol. 19bis r.
   Communie v   fol. 33r.
   Carte perpetue vi   fol. 64r.
   Carte non perpetue vii   fol. 78r.
   Inquisitiones facte viii   fol. 90r.
   Carte episcoporum et abbatum ix   fol. 99r.
   Census et statuti redditus x   fol. 106r.[53]

Even this plan was unsatisfactory to Etienne when he transcribed Register E. Categories such as alms (ii), inquests (viii), and domanial rents (*census*) (x) were retained, and the individual fief lists (ii and iiii) were replaced by comprehensive lists, but the divisions grouping all communes (v) and all churches (ix) together were too large, and the distinction between perpetual and non-perpetual charters (vi and vii) too vague. Etienne attempted to impose on this central core of charters a hierarchical scheme resembling that of Hugues de Champfleuri fifty years earlier. Placing the pope and king at the beginning, he arranged the prelates according to ecclesiastical dignity and the lay barons in order of social status. This central *corpus* of charters was preceded by fief lists and communal charters and followed by miscellaneous materials, producing the following plan of eighteen divisions:[54]

Incipiunt capitula registri compilati . . .
   1. Capitula feodorum domini regis   fol. 25r.
   2. Capitula cartarum communiarum civitatis   fol. 75r.
   3. Capitula communiarum castellorum   fol. 97r.

4. *Capitula litterarum domini pape* fol. 121r.
5. *Capitula cartarum regum* fol. 123r.
6. *Capitula cartarum sedium metropolitanorum* fol. 129r.
7. *Capitula sedium episcopalium et episcoporum* fol. 133r.
8. *Capitula abbaciarum et aliarum ecclesiarum que non sunt cathedrales* fol. 145r.
9. *Capitula cartarum reginarum* fol. 169r.[55]
10. *Capitula cartarum ducum* fol. 171r.
11. *Capitula cartarum comitum* fol. 173r.
12. *Capitula cartarum militum* fol. 209r.
13. *Capitula cartarum servientum* fol. 240r.
14. *Capitula inquisitionum* fol. 254r.
15. *Capitula quarundam elemosinarum* fol. 286r.
16. *Capitula generalium* fol. 292r.
17. *Capitula quorundam censuum* fol. 300r.
18. *Capitula provincialis* fol. 303r.

Within these broad divisions little effort was made to regroup individual documents. Scribe α recopied the block of town charters into the section *Communie* as he found them in Register A, abbreviating three and omitting one cancelled in Register A. The remaining charters were reproduced in the order of Register A. Etienne de Gallardon followed the order of Register C when he copied inquests into the equivalent chapter of Register E, with but few exceptions. The inquest into the regalia at Bourges, for example, was placed at the head of this chapter because he himself was a canon of that church. Other rearrangements can be explained by the interests of Bishop Guérin.[56]

The scribes of Register A provided no title for their chaotic collection. Scribe α called Register C by the amorphous term *liber* (codex). Not until Register E did Etienne de Gallardon apply the specific term *registrum* to his compilation. The word may have alluded to contemporary papal codices that recorded outgoing letters, but Etienne's preface announced a broader scope:

Incipiunt capitula registri compilati de feodis, elemosinis, concessionibus, munificenciis, et aliis negociis excellentissimi viri Philippi, Dei gratia Francorum regis illustrissimi . . .[57]

Outgoing letters and charters may have been implied in the phrase *concessionibus, munificenciis et aliis negociis* but *feodis et elemosinis* indicated other kinds of materials.

The three compilations of the royal chancery did, of course, serve as registers of outgoing communications. Well over half of their bulk consisted of diplomas, charters, and letters. Of these the overwhelming mass (ranging from 66 to 80 percent of the total) were issued by Philip himself or his royal predecessors.[58] Unlike the contemporary papal registers and the English rolls, which enregistered in chronological order, the French registers arranged charters topically according to category and recipient. We have seen that, while in operation, the registers preserved no more than 39 percent of the king's extant *actes* and only a bare fraction of the total output of the chancery.[59] In effect, therefore, these codices provided the royal government with a small selection of documents considered to be important, which were arranged topically for quick reference.

Precisely how the chancery performed the operation of enregistering is not entirely clear, but two alternative procedures suggest themselves: (1) The original was drawn up, sealed, and then copied into the register. When these originals and their copies are compared, however, it is frequently discoverd that the original version is more correct in grammar and spelling than the copy. Mistakes may perhaps be attributed to scribal negligence, but a second procedure remains a possibility. (2) A preliminary draft could have been composed that was both copied into the register in its rough form and copied with correct diplomatic formulae to be sealed and sent out as the original. This second hypothesis would explain why the month is often included in the rough drafts of the registers, characteristic of the more informal charters and letters, but is omitted in the original version when the charters or letters are transformed into diplomas.[60]

The first procedure of enregistering could only have been followed after 1204, when the registers came into operation. Register A contains eighty-nine royal *actes* from before that date, however, and the other two also include documents that antedate the composition of the registers. Three possible procedures can account for this material: (1) The chancery clearly possessed dossiers of documents later incorporated into the registers. Most of the pre-1204 charters in Register A, for example, pertain to towns and provided the original nucleus of the primitive part.[61] (2) In addition to these collective dossiers, the chancery could have kept the rough drafts of individual *actes* that were later copied into the registers when their importance became apparent. When the principle that the king could do homage to no one was enunciated in 1213, for example, the chancery transcribed an early mention of the policy from 1185 into Register C.[62] (3) The most common circumstance was when the recipient of a royal *acte* brought it to the chancery at a later date and requested that it be enregistered. When Brother Guérin became bishop of Senlis in 1214, for example, he had a royal charter of 1185 favoring the bishops of his see inscribed into Register C.[63] Except possibly for the last, all of these procedures suggest that the chancery was accustomed to making rough drafts before the originals were drawn up and copies were made in the registers.

Those sections devoted to charters contained incoming communications as well. In the papal chapter of Register E, for example, although only one letter from Philip Augustus to Innocent III was copied, five from the popes to the king were collected. But this tiny chapter was exceptional. In most chapters letters addressed to the king were in the minority (ranging from 1 to 26 percent of the total) by comparison with the royal charters with which they were mixed.[64] It is difficult to distinguish a regular policy for recording incoming materials, and thus to determine the relationship between the register copies and the royal archives.[65] Without contradictory evidence, it would be safe to assume that the scribes selected items considered relevant and important that permitted them to transcribe charters from English kings and French magnates and prelates addressed to third parties.

Only slightly more than half the pages of the three royal registers contain diplomas, charters, and letters issued by the king and other parties. As the tables of contents suggest, a great profusion of other kinds of information was also included. Of comparable utility was a collection of inquests that reported on royal rights and income from forests, tolls, justice, churches, fiefs, and other domanial resources. The scribes of Register A transcribed twenty-two inquests, which Scribe α assembled into a separate chapter in Register C. By the time Etienne de Gallardon and his successors had completed the collection in Register E, it recorded over a hundred inquests. Inventories of royal resources were another concern of the registers. In the original part of Register A, scribe N made a copy of the famous survey of Norman knight service ordered by King Henry II in 1172. Scores of other feudal inventories were added to Registers A and C until Etienne de Gallardon compiled a comprehensive survey filling over forty-five folios in Register E. Other lists provided information about castles, fortifications, armaments, and the mustering of sergeants. In addition there were lists of archbishops, bishops, royal abbeys, cardinals, and popes. Some inventories took on a fiscal character, such as those of forest revenues, debts owed to Jews, obligations of hospitality, and domanial revenues (*census*). Two inventories from Register A list the alms that the king owed to churches and the money rents paid to knights. Although copied by chancery clerks, they directly relate to the fiscal administration at the Temple and can be compared with the roll of 1202/ 03. Miscellaneous lists of prisoners of war, hostages, pledges for individual agreements, and genealogies were also included.

By now the organization and the contents of the chancery registers should be sufficiently clear to demonstrate that they were manuals of information useful to the routine operation of government. Unlike the royal archives, which accumulated chestfuls of parchment over the years, the registers were small in size and easily transportable as the chancery followed the king in his displacements. Arranged in a semblance of order and brought up to date every eight years, they offered the king and his counsellors a source of ready reference. They became indispensable tools for meeting the increased demands of administering the great territories acquired after the conquests of 1204–1206.

Norman Exchequer Judgments

Since the king's decisions and acts were the basis of further action, it was necessary to have permanent records accessible for consultation— particularly in courts of law where past judgments became the basis of future decisions. Although Philip's registers were fashioned for immediate administrative needs, they could have served as public records as well. In the beginning the chancery apparently experimented with this function. While scribe N was transcribing the original part of Register A in May 1204, he copied the *Etablissements* of Rouen, in which the king confirmed the customs of the newly captured Norman city. A few days later the king granted customs to Falaise, another Norman city, "just as contained in our roll, which was read to us and was transcribed in our register," and similar grants were made to Caen and Pont-Audemer in June and to Niort in August. These confirmations with accompanying references to the registers were copied into the original part of Register A by scribe N.[66] The chronicler of Saint-Martiale of Limoges recounts how in the same year the bishop of Limoges with the help of his barons quelled insurrections provoked by the king of England and returned his territory to the French king's rule. As a reward, the chronicler continues, King Philip had it inscribed in his register that the bishopric would never be separated from the royal domain. Scribe N copied the appropriate royal charter into the register in November 1204 or shortly thereafter.[67]

In the latter half of 1204, therefore, when the original part of Register

A was completed, the king referred to his register as a public record, but the practice appears to have been abandoned soon after, because the registers are rarely mentioned thereafter in official royal acts. When the king issued an important decree concerning the treatment of criminal clerics in 1210, he ordered his *baillis* and communes to copy the letter and store it safely, and he himself had a summary noted in Register A.[68] In 1218 he confirmed to the canons of Valséry forest usage "as he had recognized in a judicial inquest that he had transcribed in his register."[69] But not until the reign of Louis IX were Philip's registers consulted in the royal courts to decide cases of law.[70] Despite the initial experiment, the registers were apparently too closely bound up with the needs of daily administration in the chancery to serve as records accessible to a larger public.

Although Philip had not achieved a system of public records in the old Capetian domain, when he acquired Normandy he inherited well-established practices of maintaining judicial rolls both in the exchequer and in the courts. As in England, the Norman exchequer was established as a place for recording judgments at least as early as the reign of Richard. A Norman roll dating from the opening years of King John's reign provided public record of private agreements.[71] By the time of the *Trés ancien coutumier* (1199–1200), it was affirmed that recognitions and decisions of the judicial assizes be transcribed on rolls "for silencing disputes over affairs decided in the assizes."[72] Although these rolls have since disappeared, it may be inferred that on the eve of the French conquest the assizes periodically held throughout Normandy systematically produced records of judicial decisions for the benefit of future litigants.

After the French conquest of Normandy the rolls were continued. As early as May 1204 the *Etablissements* of Rouen were copied not only into the royal register but also onto a roll at Rouen, where they were read to the king. Scattered references indicate that assize rolls were kept throughout the duchy during Philip's reign, and the exchequer continued to be a place of enrollment.[73] Though the assize rolls have been lost, the Norman exchequer collection has survived in copies, bearing the title *Judicia in scacariis Normannie*.[74] Although the original no longer exists, some idea of its character and scope may be gained from three extant unofficial compilations taken from it by the end of the thirteenth century. These collections contain short notices of judgments, rendered by judges who are named, at the biannual sessions of the Norman exchequer held at Falaise (and later at Caen) from 1207 until 1243. Although the extant compilations were copied into books, the original collection is referred to as both a register and a roll. The notices bear the marks of official and public reports by clerks assigned to the regular sessions of the Norman court.[75]

The rolls of the Norman local assizes have all disappeared. Although the ordinance of 1190 commanded the *baillis* to record their fines (*forefacta*) at the monthly assizes throughout the old Capetian domain, no written evidence has survived of these operations.[76] Even the central court of the king produced no consecutive records until the reign of Louis IX. Dating from 1207, the *Judicia in scacariis Normannie* is thus the earliest surviving judicial roll of the Capetian monarchy. Although its extant copies may have been written down as private collections, they were presumably based on official rolls or collections now lost. Successors to the Anglo-Norman tradition, these judicial rolls were the sole public records of the French kings until the *parlement* of Louis IX began writing decisions in the *Olim*.

In general, the efforts of the Capetians to collect and preserve their records lagged behind their neighbors'. Already by the second decade of the twelfth century the Anglo-Norman kings—undoubtedly encouraged by lengthy absences on either side of the Channel—had created an exchequer in England that each year produced a record called the Pipe Roll. The first extant example from 1130 reveals sophisticated accounting techniques unparalleled in western Europe. Their Angevin successors continued these Pipe Rolls in an unbroken series, generated similar rolls in the Norman exchequer, and commissioned a manual that described the regular operation of an accounting bureau, the *Dialogue of the Exchequer* (1179). Since the 1150s the count-kings of Barcelona had produced and collected a series of *états* for their domains, and the counts of Flanders created an accounting bureau for their lands of which the first surviving record appeared in 1187. That it was not until 1190 that Philip Augustus established a fiscal bureau with accompanying accounts illustrates the French lag in accounting. Even the Capetian establishment of archives in 1194, which probably antedated comparable papal and English collections, was preceded by the similar policy of the count-kings of Barcelona, who had been collecting letters and memoranda since 1177–1178.[77]

In copying and preserving outgoing acts both the papacy and the English kings were well in advance of the French. Because of the ecclesiastical monopoly over literacy, the papal chancery had led the way since the early Middle Ages. As early as the fifth century, it created registers in the form of *codices* containing copies of outgoing letters. Although some earlier fragments have survived, the first continuous series, known as the *Registra Vaticana*, appeared under the pontificate of Innocent III (1198–1216) and reveals a regularized chancery procedure for enregistering letters. Simultaneously, the English monarchy attacked the problem by enrollment—the copying of outgoing royal charters and letters on skins of parchment sewn head to head and rolled up for storage. Although Richard may have inaugurated the policy, the first extant charter roll appeared at John's accession in 1199, and rolls of letters patent and close (sealed open or shut) followed soon after. The papal and English clerks transcribed a greater proportion of the chancery output than the French and arranged the documents in approximate chronological order.[78] Along with these papal and English advances, the appearance of the Capetian registers coincided with a general movement in western Europe to make a regular record of official acts.

Whereas the papal registers and the English rolls were limited to outgoing communications, the Capetian registers also contained incoming materials, inquests, inventories, accounts, and lists. As handbooks of useful information, they resemble the papal *Liber censuum*, compiled in 1192 by Cardinal Censius, chamberlain to Popes Clement III and Celestine III. Consisting of a cartulary of charters and a list of churches that owed taxes or *cens* to the pope, this had blank pages at the end of each section for additional information. In a similar manner, Alexander of Swereford, clerk of the English exchequer, composed the "Little Black Book of the Exchequer" (*Liber niger parvus*) around 1206, which contained important charters and a survey of knights' service taken in 1166. Between 1212 and 1230 he reedited it as the "Red Book of the Exchequer" (*Liber rubeus*) and added the Norman feudal survey of 1172 (also transcribed in Register A), abstracts from the Pipe Rolls, lists of scutage, returns from inquests, and other information useful to the exchequer. Early in the fourteenth century the French Chambre des Comptes drew up similar handbooks called *Libri memoriales*, most of which were destroyed in the fire of 1737.[79] Like these manuals, the registers of Philip Augustus were born from the practical demands of administration.

The papal registers and the English chancery rolls may also have served as public records to be consulted in the future, because the recipients of documents often paid to have their letters preserved. Whatever their function, the English monarchy provided public records as early as the opening decades of the twelfth century, when the Domesday Book, the famous land survey of 1086, was kept in the exchequer as a reference book for litigation. By Henry II's reign the exchequer also collected the Cartae Antiquae, a roll of charters, and copied documents on the Pipe Rolls to serve as public records. At the same time "assize rolls" appeared in the royal courts that noted past judgments for the purpose of facilitating future decisions.[80] The Norman exchequer at Caen maintained similar judicial rolls, just as it also produced fiscal accounts. In May 1204, when King John assessed his position in Normandy to be precarious, he ordered his rolls and charters transported from Caen to London.[81] When Philip Augustus began collecting the Norman *Judicia* in 1207, he merely perpetuated a tradition of public records inherited from the Anglo-Norman dukes.

The emergence of these accounts, archives, registers, and judicial rolls, despite their fragmentary condition, presents historians with new opportunities for investigating the development of governmental institutions. No longer are we dependent on contemporary chroniclers rehearsing the opinions of their patrons and at the mercy of chance or the bias of ecclesiastical recipients for the survival of royal charters. Because these collections were both witnesses to and products of royal government, the historian can begin to perceive Capetian government as it saw itself—from the inside.

The inauguration of the four major governmental collections between 1190 and 1207 also suggests that the Capetians were pulling abreast of their neighbors, especially the powerful Angevin kings of England. The accounts, archives, registers, and judicial rolls attest the creation of new fiscal, secretarial, and judicial institutions. Except for the judicial rolls, none were borrowed intact from adjoining lands. Propelled by similar needs, the Capetians rehearsed the development of their neighbors but followed their own traditions. Before 1190 a primitive and ambulatory monarchy was satisfied with the memories of the king's entourage, perhaps aided by domanial *états* and other expendable records. The king's acts were reported by chroniclers, for the most part English and Flemish, made sensitive to the affairs of government by the precocity of their successful patrons. His charters were collected by the recipients, for the most part ecclesiastics. The creative decade following the call for a crusade in 1190, however, produced the first constitution outlining the structure of government and established stationary organs at Paris adapted to administering a growing domain. The bureau of audit at the Temple began producing regular fiscal accounts, and the archives began retaining important documents in a permanent collection. Although Rigord began writing on his own initiative shortly before the crusade, he sensed the importance of these creations of the 1190s by transcribing the ordinance-testament, by availing himself of the archives, and by dedicating his chronicle to the king. The stunning military triumphs between 1204 and 1214, which drove the English king south of the Loire, made Philip heir to Normandy and to the needs and problems of the Angevin kings. Subject to the same pressures, he began to step up his efforts to investigate his lands, to inventory his resources, and to record his findings in convenient manuals called registers. His judicial rolls merely revived those of his predecessors at the Norman exchequer, but his new "budget" of 1221 improved upon the records of his predecessors by providing a comprehensive view of royal finances. The victory at Bouvines, which ensured the kingdom peace and prosperity during the final decade of Philip's reign, provided inspiration and leisure for Guillaume le Breton not only to continue Rigord's work but also to undertake a panegyric to the king in prose and verse that, in the end, fashioned the elements of a nascent royal ideology. The new records and the writings of the historians converged to signal a *tournant* and new maturity achieved by Capetian government during the reign of Philip Augustus. The French king was no longer merely reacting to his great vassals, chief among them the king of England. He was now able to seize the initiative to win supremacy in France and eventually achieve the supremacy of France in Latin Christendom. Benefiting from the resources of a rich kingdom, Philip laid the foundations of French royal power in the Middle Ages.

Appendices

Appendix A
Personnel of the Central Government

	1180[a]	1185[b]	1187[c]	1189[d]	1190[e]	1191[f]	1191[g]	1193[h]	1194[i]	1194[j]	1195[k]	1196[l]	1196[m]	1198[n]	1198[o]	1200[p]	1200[q]	1201[r]	1202[s]	1204[t]	1205[u]	1206[v]	1207[w]	1208[x]	1209[y]	1214[z]	1215[aa]	1215[bb]	1216[cc]	1216[dd]	1220[ee]	1223[ff]
Thibaut, count of Blois	x	x	x																													
Robert(s), count(s) of Dreux	x	x	x	x	x	x		x			x	x		x	x	x	x	x	x	x				x						x	x	
Guillaume, archb. of Reims			x	x	x	x		x	x	x	x		x																			
Philippe, bish. of Beauvais		x						x			x					x	x		x											x		
Philippe, count of Flanders	x	x	x	x																												
Gautier the Chamberlain	x	x	x					x			x			x	x	x	x		x	x												
Hugues, duke of Burgundy				x			x																									
Eudes, duke of Burgundy																		x							x				x			
Pierre, count of Nevers														x											x				x			
Hervé, count of Nevers									x	x	x					x	x	x		x	x				x		x					
Anselme, dean of Tours									x	x																						
Ours the Chamberlain								x	x		x			x	x	x	x	x		x		x		x		x					x	x
Dreu de Mello									x	x	x		x	x		x								x								x
Guillaume(s) de Garlande					x										x	x	x	x	x	x								x				
Barthélemy de Roye														x	x	x	x	x	x	x	x	x		x		x	x	x	x		x	x
Philippe de Lévis														x	x	x	x		x													
Gautier the Young														x	x	x				x		x		x			x					
Philippe de Nanteuil														x														x	x			x

Brother Bernard de Vincennes							x																								
Mathieu de Montmorency						x						x								x					x	x					
Guillaume(s) des Barres						x	x			x										x					x						
Mathieu, count of Beaumont						x			x																						
Jean, count of Beaumont																				x	x					x					
Guy de Dampierre					x x x	x			x x x																x					
Henri Clément, marshal					x	x			x																						
Albert de Hangest					x	x																			x	x					
Brother Haimard						x			x																	x					
Brother Guérin, bish. of Senlis					x				x																x	x	x				

NOTE: This chart identifies personnel most frequently in attendance at Philip's court by compiling information from sources, both chronicles and charters, that provide multiple names of men acting in the royal court. Names occurring only occasionally are omitted.

a Mediators chosen by Philip to negotiate with Henry II. 28 June 1180. Benedict I, 247. *Actes* I, no. 7; b Witnesses in behalf of Marguerite, Philip's sister, in the presence of Philip. 11 March 1185. Delisle, *Catalogue* no. 124, p. 497; c Negotiators for Philip in truce with Henry. 1187. Gervase of Canterbury II, 371; d Negotiators for Philip in peace with Henry. 1189. Benedict II, 69; e Ordinance-testament. 1190. *Actes* I, no. 345; f Philip's agents at Péronne. June 1191. *Actes* I, no. 383; g Philip's negotiators with Richard. 1191. Benedict II, 182; h Those who swore in behalf of Philip in the divorce proceedings against Ingeborg. 1193. Howden III, 224; i Philip's negotiators with Richard. 1194. Howden III, 254; j Philip's guarantors in a truce with Richard. 23 July 1194. Howden III, 257–60; k Those who swore to the consanguinity between Philip and Ingeborg in the divorce proceedings. 1195. Howden III, 307; l Philip's agents at the treaty of Gaillon. 15 January 1196. Teulet I, no. 431. *Actes* II, no. 517; m Witnesses to Renaud, count of Boulogne, swearing homage to Philip. June 1196. Teulet I, no. 448; n Supported Philip in receiving the homage of Thibaut, count of Troyes. April 1198. Teulet I, no. 473. *Actes* II, no. 581; o Represented Philip when Eudes, duke of Burgundy, promised not to ally with Richard. November 1198. Teulet I, no. 482; p Philip's pledges in the treaty of Le Goulet. May 1200. Teulet I, no. 578. q Witnesses to Amaury, earl of Gloucester, conceding Evreux to Philip. May 1200. Teulet I, no. 588; r Swore in behalf of Philip in receiving the homage of Blanche, countess of Troyes. May 1201. *Actes* II, no. 678; s Present at the judgment of the regalia of Châlons-sur-Marne. 1202. *Actes* II, no. 727; t Present at the surrender of Rouen. 1 June 1204. Teulet I, no. 716; u Supported Philip in his complaints against the pope and clergy. June 1205. Teulet I, nos. 762–67; v Present when Simon, count of Montfort, exchanged Breteuil with Philip. 1206. Teulet I, no. 815; w Present when Gaucher, count of Saint-Pol, recognized his holdings from Philip. November 1207. Teulet I, no. 829; x Witnesses to the homage of the count of Eu. 1208. Delisle, *Catalogue* no. 1182, p. 515; y Witnesses to Philip's ordinance on the succession of fiefs. 1 May 1209. Teulet I, no. 873; z Subscribers to Philip's truce with John. 18 September 1214. Teulet I, no. 1082; aa Witnesses to Jean de Beaugency confirming the lands that Aliénor, countess of Vermandois, gave to Philip. July 1215. Teulet I, no. 1126; bb Present at Raoul, count of Soissons's, recognition of forest rights to the bishop of Senlis. September 1215. *Actes* III, no. 1396; cc Summoned Blanche, countess of Troyes, to the royal court. July 1216. Teulet I, no. 1182; dd Present at the judgment over the succession of Champagne. July 1216. Teulet I, no. 1182; ee Present at the judgment of the bishop of Paris's rights over Clos Brunel. 1220–1221. Teulet I, no. 1439; ff Present at the judgment over the county of Beaumont-sur-Oise. 1223. E. Boutaric, *Actes du Parlement de Paris* (Paris, 1863) I, ccci.

Appendix B
Prévôts *and* Baillis

Identified Prévôts *During the Reign of Philip Augustus*

Amiens

  Aubert
  Pierre de Béthisy, 1186–1216?
  Richard, 1213
  Thibaut, 1214
  Jean de Fricamps, 1220–

Auxerre

  Jean
  Renaud
  Colin de Châtillon, 1219

Bourges

  Eudes *de Feuchicort*, 1192
  Pierre de Pavillon, 1211

Compiègne

  Henri Voiderue
  P[ierre?] 1198
  Pierre *Provinart*, 1215

Corbeil

  Bertraud, 1223

Evreux

  Nicolas Feron
  Gautier of Spain
  Nicolas de Vilers
  Robert d'Etampes
  Pierre d'Etampes

Etampes

  Mainier, 1188

Issoudun

  Arbert, 1190

Janville

  Laurent *Rotarius*, 1216
  Raoul *Clavel*, before 1216

Laon

  Geoffroi de Senlis, 1195
  Gilles de Valaureni, 1212
  Guy de Béthisy, ca. 1214
  Robert *de Lega*, 1217
  Geoffroi, 1217

Ingelrannus dictus Galfridus,
   1214, 1217–1225
Robert de Parigny, 1223
Geoffroi de Valavergny, 1223

Melun

   Everadus

Montdidier

   Rogo de Tornella, 1195
   Foulques *de Tanes*
   Roger fitz Ralph
   Roger *Pedagiarius*

Montlhéry

   Geoffroi, ca. 1220

Orléans

   Renaud, ca. 1210
   Etienne Botet, 1216
   Nicolas *de Clariaco*, 1216

Pacy

   Pierre

Péronne

   Renaud Bota, 1193
   Baudouin Pasté, 1193

Poissy

   Gérard, 1186

Senlis

   Geoffroi, 1183–1197
   Jean des Vignes, ca. 1220

Sens

   Baudouin de Gron, 1220

Vernon

   Nicolas *Bocellus*

Villeneuve-le-Roi

   Pierre, 1184

Identified Baillis *(with Titles in Latin) During the Reign of Philip Augustus*

Paris Region—Prévôt-baillis

Hugues de Meulan (1196)
   Prepositus Parisiensis
Jean (ca. 1198)
   Prepositus Parisiensis
Thomas (1200)
   Prepositus
Pierre du Thillai (1200)
   Prepositus Parisiensis (see also
   below, Southern Domain, Or-
léans region, and Normandy,
Caen region)
Robert de Meulan
   (1200–1203)
   Prepositus Parisiensis (1200)
Renaud de Cornillon (1202)
   Prepositus Parisiensis (see also
   below, Normandy, Contentin
   region)
Eudes Popin (1205)
   Prepositus Parisiensis

Eudes Arrode (1205)
Prepositus Parisiensis

Hugues de Bastons (1207, 1209)
Ballivus domini regis et miles (1207)

Philippe Hamelin (1207, 1217–1219)
Prepositus Parisiensis (1207)

Nicolas Arrode (1217–1219)
Prepositus Parisiensis

Southern Domain—Etampes Region

Guy Bernouvin (1202/03)

Hugues de Gravelle (1192–1203)
Domini regis assessor (1192)

Guillaume Menier (1203–1235)
Castellanus Stampensis, Stamparum assessor (1204), *Ballivus domini regis et miles* (1207)

Barthélemy Droon (1204)
Stamparum assessor (see also below, Normandy, Verneuil region)

Adam Héron (1204–1226)
Stamparum assessor (1204), *ballivus domini regis* (1211), *miles domini regis Francorum et ballivus* (1213)

Nicolas *de Chevanvilla* (1216)
miles et ballivus

Renaud l'Archer (1219–1222)
Ballivus domini regis (1219), *serviens domini regis* (1222)

Southern Domain—Orléans Region

Guillaume de la Chapelle (1201–1217)
Officialis domini regis (1201), *ballivus noster* (1201), *serviens*

noster (1201) (see also below, Normandy, Caux region)

Pierre du Thillai (1203)
Domini regis ballivus, assessor Aurelianensis (see also above, Paris region, and below, Normandy, Caen region)

Roger le Péager (1216, 1218)
Ballivus noster (1217)

Hugues *Breto* (1219)

Southern Domain—Bourges Region

Bertrand de Tournel (ca. 1190)
Ballivus Bituricensis

Eudes de Fulchecourt (ca. 1190)
Ballivus Bituricensis

Hugues de la Chapelle (1199–1209)
Ballivus domini regis (1199)

Abelin (1202/03)

J. de Perruche (1208)
Ballivus domini regis

Gilbert *de Minpinc* (1208–1217)
Ballivus domini regis (1208)

Gilbert de Chanceaux (1213)
Ballivia vestra

Mathieu Dreux (1213)
Ballivia vestra

Colin de la Chapelle (1221)
Castellanus Bituricensis

Pierre de Rouci
Castellanus Bituricensis

Southern Domain—Sens Region

Thierry de Corbeil (1202/03)

Etienne de Hautvilliers (1205–1227)
Ballivus (1205), *ballivus domini regis* (1216)

Garnier du Pré (1207)
Ballivus noster

Thomas *Scutifer* (1219)
Ballivus domini regis

Berruyer de Bourron (1221, 1224)
Ballivus domini regis (1222)

Nicolas de Hautvilliers
(1222–1245)
Miles et baillivus domini regis
(1222)

*Northeastern Domain—Vermandois
Region*

Pierre de Béthisy (1196–1205)
Prévôt of Amiens
(1186–1211), *Ballivus in
terra Petrefontis* (1196), *domini
regis ballivus* (1197)

Renaud de Béthisy
(1196–1221)
Ballivus in terra Petrefontis
(1196), *ballivus domini regis*
(1203)

Pierre de Villevoudée
(1197–1200)
Domini regis ballivus (1197)

Guy de Béthisy (1200–1210)
Ballivus domini regis (1200)

Guillaume Pastez (1200–1217)
Ballivus regis (1200)

Nicolas *Catus* (1202–1205)
Ballivus regis (1204)

Gilles de Versailles
(1207–1233)
Ballivus domini regis et miles
(1207)

Guillaume de Châtelliers
(1214–1227)
Regis Francie ballivus (1216)

Soibert de Laon (1216–ca. 1230)
Regis Francie ballivus (1216),
burgensis Laudunensis (1210)

Renaud de Beron (1223–1234)
Domini regis miles et ballivus
(1223)

*Northeastern Domain—Artois
Region*

Nevelon the Marshal
(1201–1222)
*Marescallus domini regis, bal-
livus Attrebatensis* (1201),
Ballivus noster [Ludovici]
(1219)

*Northeastern Domain—Incidental
Occurrences*

Renaud d'Aire (1193)
Ballivus domini regis

Joscelin (1193)
Ballivus domini regis

Nicolas du Castel (1212)
*De Aria et de Sancto Audomaro
baillivus*

Adam de Neuilly (ca. 1215)
Baillivus de Aria

Hugues du Fresne
(1215–1218)
Ballivus de Aria

Richard de Beauquesne (1216)
Ballivus Hisdinii

Jean (1220)
Baillivus de Hisdinio

Normandy—Vexin, Gisors

Gautier de Courcelles (1186,
1187)
Constabularius Vulcassini

Hugues de Maudétour (1193)
Constabularius Vulcassini

Pierre de Neuilly (1196)
Miles et justicius Vilcassinorum

Eustache de Hadencourt (1196)
Miles et justicius Vilcassinorum

Mathieu Pisdoë (1202/03)

Eudes the Chamberlain
(1202/03)

Eudes Plastras (1202/03, 1212)

Nicolas Harchepin (1203)

Aleaume Hescelin (1202–1217)
*Castellanus Gisorcii et baillivus
domini regis* (1209)

Jean Azon (1209)
Baillivus domini regis

Hugues de Bouconvillers (1212)
Domini regis ballivus

Thibaut le Maigre (ca.
1208–1228)
Ballivus domini regis (ca.
1210)

Guillaume de Ville-Thierri
(1219–1227)
*Castellanus Gisortii, domini
regis miles et ballivus* (1219)

Normandy—Verneuil Region

Nicolas Bocel (1202–1207)

Barthélemy Droon
(1209–1227)
Baillivus de Belismo (1212),
ballivus domini regis (1212)
ballivus de Vernoil (1213) (see
also above, Southern Domain,
Etampes region)

Folques Karrel (1212–1214)
Baillivus de Belismo (1212)

Normandy—Rouen Region

Guillaume Poucin (1202–1207)
*Castellanus de turre Ro-
thomagensi* (1204)

Guillaume Escuacol
(1208–1220)
Castellanus (1209)

Jean de la Porte (1219–1228)
*Baillivus domini regis de Ber-
naio* (1219), *castellanus Rothomagensis* (1220)

Normandy—Pont-Audemer Region

Cadoc (1202–1219/20)
Castellanus Gaillionis (1205),
baillivus Pontis Audomari
(1209)

Normandy—Caux Region

Jean de Rouvray (1204–1223)
*Justiciarius domini regis in Ca-
leto* (1204), *castellanus de Archis* (1205)

Guillaume de la Chapelle
(1209–1214)
Castellanus de Archiis (1210)
(see also above, southern domain, Orléans region)

Geoffroi de la Chapelle
(1212–1238)
*Miles, baillivus regis Francie et
castellanus de Archis* (1216)

Normandy—Caen Region

Pierre du Thillai (1205–1224)
Baillivus domini regis (1205),
baillivus Cadomensis (ca.
1205), *senescallus Normannie*
(1207), *senescallus Cadomi*
(1207), *justiciarius domini
regis* (1209), *ballivus domini
regis de Cadomo et Falesia*
(1211) (see also above, Paris
region, and southern domain,
Orléans region)

Normandy—Bayeux, Avranches Region

Garin Tirel (1206–1218)
Justiciarius domini regis (1206)

Renaud de Ville-Thierri
(1206–1227)
Justiciarius domini regis
(1206), *baillivus Baicarum et
Abrincarum* (1213), *senescallus*
(1217)

Eudes de Tremblay (1211,
1212)
Justiciarius domini regis
(1211), *castellanus* (1212)

Robert *de Waceo* (1211–1212)
Justiciarius domini regis (1211)

Normandy—Cotentin Region

Renaud de Cornillon
(1202–1214)
*Baillivus domini regis in Con-
stantino* (see also above, Paris
region)

Miles de Lévis (1215–1223)
Baillivus domini regis (1215),
*ballivus domini regis in Costen-
tino* (1215), *conestabulus Cons-
tenciensis* (1217)

Anjou, Maine, Touraine, Poitou

Guillaume des Roches
(1199–1222)
*Senescallus Andegavie et
Cenomannie* (1199), *senescallus
Andegavie, Turonum, et
Cenomannie* (1204)

Aimery de Thouars
(1203–1206)

*Senescallus Pictavie et ducatus
Aquitanie* (1203)

Aimery de Craon (1222–1226)
Senescallus Andegavensis
(1222)

Hamelin de Roorte
(1208–1221)
*Ballivus domini regis et sene-
scalli Andegavensis* (1211)

Geoffroi Malchien (ca. 1208)
*Ballivus noster [senescalli
Andegavensis]*

Robert Lisiardi (1220)
Ballivus senescalli Andegavensis

Guillaume de Azaio
(1209–1219)
*Samuri, Pictavie et Turonie bal-
livus* (1209), *ballivus Turonie et
Pictavie* (1213), *miles, senescallus Turonensis* (1219)

Robert de Crespières
(1210–1217)
*Ballivus domini regis in Turonia
et Pictavia* (1214), *senescallus
Turonensis* (1216)

Robert des Loges (1217, 1218)
*Senescallus Turonensis et Pic-
tavensis* (1218)

Thierry de Gallardon
(1219–1227)
Senescallus Turonie (1219),
Turonie et Pictavie senescallus
(1220), *ballivus Turonie*
(1220)

SOURCE: Delisle, *RHF* XXIV,*.

Appendix C
Elections of Bishops to Regalian Sees, 1179–1223

These charts identify bishops who were incumbent at the beginning of Philip's reign and those who were subsequently elected to regalian sees. The latter are arranged in chronological order, taking into account the changes in regalian status. The first date that indicates the election can only be approximate because of the crudity of the evidence.

The bishops are classified with the following symbols:

d   disobeyed papal interdict of 1200
o   obeyed papal interdict of 1200
l   recruited from local chapter
m   formerly a monk
s   local seigneurial influence
q   papal influence
r   royal influence
c   royal clerk
f   royal family by blood or by marriage
fa   family of a royal agent
os   recommended by Eudes de Sully
p   position at Paris
t   position at Saint-Martin of Tours
u   insufficient evidence of influence
*   master

The information has been compiled from Marcel Pacaut, *Louis VII et les élections épiscopales dans le royaume de France* (Paris, 1957), B. Gams, *Series episcoporum ecclesie catholice quotquot innotuerunt a Beato Petro Apostolo* (Ratisbon, 1873), K. Eubel, *Hierarchia catholica medii aevi* (Münster, 1913), I, *Gall. christ.*, corrected and supplemented by local studies. The most important are indicated in the footnotes.

Incumbent Bishops in Regalian Sees on 1 November 1179

See	Name	Family	Former Position	Classification
Bourges	Guérin d. 1180	"de Gallardun"	abbot of Pontigny	m
Reims	Guillaume d. 1202	Champagne (King Philip's uncle)	bish. of Chartres, archb. of Sens	d, r, f
Sens	Guy d. 1193	Noyers (marriage connection with royal family)	archd. of Sens	r, f, l
Mâcon	Etienne d. 1184	Bagé	archd. of Mâcon	l
Langres	Gautier d. 1179	Burgundy, brother of Duke Eudes	archd. of Langres	l, s
Autun	Etienne d. 1189		canon of Auxerre	u
Nevers	Thibaut d. 1189		dean of Nevers	l
Troyes	Mathieu d. 1180	Saint-Loup	dean of Provins	u
Auxerre	Guillaume d. 1181	Toucy	treasurer of Auxerre archd. of Sens	l
Orléans	Manassé d. 1185	Garlande (son of Gilbert, royal butler)[a]		l, r, fa
Chartres	John d. 1180	Salisbury	master at Paris	p, *
Paris	Maurice d. 1196	Sully (not the noble family)	canon of Paris and Bourges, master at Paris	l, p, *
Meaux	Simon d. 1194		treasurer of Meaux archd. of Sens	l
Soissons	Nevelon d. 1207	Quierzy[b]	archd. and *prévôt* of Soissons	o, l, s
Noyon	Renaud d. 1188			u
Laon	Roger d. 1201?	Rozoy (related to the counts of Namur and Hainaut)	dean of Châlons-sur-Marne	d, s
Châlons-sur-Marne	Guy d. 1191	Joinville		s
Beauvais	Philippe d. 1217	Dreux (cousin of King Philip)		d, r, f
Amiens	Thibaut d. 1204		archd. of Amiens	o, l

Incumbent Bishops in Regalian Sees on 1 November 1179				
See	Name	Family	Former Position	Classification
Thérouanne	Désiré d. 1191	Courtrai	archd. of Tournai	s
Tournai	Evrard d. 1191	lords of Avesnes, castellans of Tournai	archd. of Tournai	l, s
Arras	Fromond d. 1183	archd. of Ostrevant, aided by Philippe of Flanders		o, s
Senlis	Henri d. 1185		abbot of Saint-Quentin of Beauvais, canon of Sainte-Geneviève, Paris	m, p
Tours	Barthélemy d. 1206	Vendôme	dean of Tours	l
Clermont	Pons d. 1189		abbot of Clairvaux	m

[a]Eric Bournazel, *Le Gouvernement capétien au XIIe siècle* (Limoges, 1975), table following p. 189. Cartellieri I, Beilagen 81.
[b]William M. Newman, *Les Seigneurs de Nesle en Picardie*, Memoirs of the American Philosophical Society, no. 91 (Philadelphia, 1971), I, 100.

Chronology of Elections to Regalian Sees, 1179–1223

See	Name	Family	Former Position	Classification
Langres 1180–93	Manassé	Bar-sur-Seine	dean of Langres	l
Troyes 1181–90	Manassé	Pougy	archd. of Troyes	l
Chartres 1181–82	Pierre		abbot of Saint-Remi de Reims	m
Bourges 1181–84	Pierre		bishop of Meaux?	u
Chartres 1182–1217	Renaud	Bar and Moucon (cousin of King Philip)	*prévôt* of Chartres, treasurer of Saint-Martin of Tours	d, l, r, f, t
Auxerre 1183–1206	Hugues	Noyers (marriage connection with royal family)	treasurer of Auxerre	d, l, r, f
Bourges 1183–1200	Henri	Sully (cousin of King Philip, brother of Eudes of Paris)	abbot of Chaalis	m, r, f
Senlis 1183–1213	Geoffroi		monk and treasurer of Saint-Denis de Reims	o, m
Arras 1184–1203	Pierre		abbot of Pontigny and Cîteaux	m
Mâcon 1185–98	Renaud	Vergy	chanter of Mâcon	l
Orléans 1186–98	Henri	Dreux (cousin of King Philip and brother of Philippe of Beauvais)	archd. of Brabant	r, f
Noyon 1188–1221	Etienne	son of Gautier the Chamberlain		d, r, fa
Autun 1189–1223	Gautier			u
Clermont 1190–95	Gilbert			u
Nevers 1190–96	Jean		dean of Nevers	l
Châlons-sur-Marne 1190–1200	Rotrou	Perche (cousin of King Philip, brother of Guillaume of Châlons)	archd. of Reims, treasurer of Saint-Martin of Tours	r, f, t

	Chronology of Elections to Regalian Sees, 1179–1223			
See	Name	Family	Former Position	Classification
Troyes 1190–93	Barthélemy		*prévôt* of Provins, chancellor of count of Champagne	s
Thérouanne 1191–1207	Lambert	Bruges	chancellor of Reims	d, u
Tournai 1193–1203	Etienne	Orléans	abbot of Sainte-Geneviève, Paris, royal cleric	d?, r, c, m, *
Troyes 1193–1205	Garnier	Trainel		d?, s
Langres 1193–98	Garnier	Rochefort	abbot of Clairvaux	m
Sens 1194–99	Michel		dean of Meaux, Laon, and Paris, master at Paris[a]	o, p, *
Clermont 1195–1227	Robert	counts of Auvergne (cousin of King Philip)	dean of Autun	r, f, s
Nevers 1196–1202	Gautier		archd. of Troyes	d?, u
Meaux 1197–1207	Anselme		royal cleric, jurisprudent, dean of Saint-Martin of Tours[b]	d, r, c, t, *
Paris 1197–1208	Eudes	Sully (cousin of King Philip, brother of Henri of Bourges)	chanter of Bourges	o, r, f
Orléans 1198–1206	Hugues	Garlande, son of Guy[c]	dean of Orléans	d, l, r, fa
Mâcon 1199–1221	Pons	Villers	chanter of Lyons	u
Langres 1200–03	Hilduin		dean of Langres	l
Bourges 1200–09	Guillaume	related to the counts of Nevers	canon of Soissons and Paris, abbot of Chaalis, recommended by Eudes de Sully	d, m, r, os
Sens 1200–22	Pierre	Corbeil (not a noble family)[d]	canon of Paris, master of Paris, bish. of Cambrai	o, q, p, *

Chronology of Elections to Regalian Sees, 1179–1223				
See	Name	Family	Former Position	Classification
Evreux 1201–03	Robert	Roye (nephew of Barthélemy de Roye)		r, fa
Nevers 1202–21	Guillaume	de Saint-Lazare	royal cleric[c]	r, c, *
Evreux 1202–20	Luc		archd. and dean of Evreux	l
Châlons-sur-Marne 1203–15	Gérard	de Douai	canon of Paris[f]	p, *
Reims 1204–06	Guy		abbot of Val-Notre-Dame, papal legate, cardinal	m, q
Tournai 1204–18	Gosselin		archd. of Tournai	l
Amiens 1205–10	Richard	*vidames* of Gerberoy	dean of Amiens	l
Tours 1206–08	Geoffroi	la Lande	canon of Saint-Martin, archd. of Paris	r, t, p, os
Bayeux 1206–31	Robert	Ableges	canon of Bayeux	l, *
Laon 1207–10	Renaud	Surdel	canon of Laon	l
Reims 1207–18	Alberic		archd. of Paris, recommended by Eudes de Sully	r, p, os, *
Troyes 1207–23	Hervé		master at Paris, recommended by Eudes de Sully	r, p, os, *
Auxerre 1207–20	Guillaume	Seignelay (brother of Manassé of Orléans)	dean of Auxerre	l
Orléans 1207–21	Manassé	Seignelay (brother of Guillaume of Auxerre)	archd. of Auxerre and Sens	l
Meaux 1207–14	Geoffroi	Tressy (Poissy)	master at Paris[g] and treasurer of Meaux	l, *
Soissons 1208–19	Haimard		chanter of Reims, recommended by Eudes de Sully	r, os
Rouen 1208–22	Robert	Poulain	canon of Rouen	l, *
Thérouanne 1208–13	Jean		archd. of Thérouanne	l

Chronology of Elections to Regalian Sees, 1179–1223				
See	Name	Family	Former Position	Classification
Coutances 1208–38	Hugues	Morville	archd. of Coutances	l, *
Tours 1208–28	Jean	Faye	dean of Tours	l
Paris 1208–19	Pierre	son of Gautier the Chamberlain	treasurer of Saint-Martin of Tours	r, fa, t
Bourges 1209–18	Girard		archd. of Clermont	u
Laon 1210–15	Robert	Châtillon (cousin of King Philip)[h]	treasurer and archd. of Beauvais	r, f
Amiens 1212–22	Evvard	Fouilly	canon of Amiens, chanter of Arras	l
Avranches 1212–36	Guillaume	Ostilly		l
Thérouanne 1213–29	Adam	de Montreuil at Paris[i]	archd. of Paris, canon of Lilliers	p
Senlis 1213–27	Guérin		hospitaler, royal cleric	r, c, q
Meaux 1214–21	Guillaume	son of Gautier the Chamberlain	chanter and archd. of Paris	r, fa, p
Le Mans 1214–16	Nicolas		dean of Le Mans	l
Châlons-sur-Marne 1215–26	Guillaume	Perche (cousin of King Philip, brother of Rotrou of Châlons)	*prévôt* of Saint-Martin of Tours, archd. of Brussels	r, f, t
Laon 1215–38	Anselme	Mauny	canon	l
Le Mans 1216–31	Maurice		archd. of Troyes	u
Poitiers 1217–24	Guillaume	Prévôt		u
Beauvais 1218–34	Milon	Nanteuil-la-Fossé (related to the Dreux)	archd. of Beauvais	l, r, f
Bourges 1218–32	Simon	Sully (cousin of King Philip)	chanter of Bourges	l, r, f
Lisieux 1218–50	Guillaume	Pont de l'Arche	proctor of Lisieux, master at Paris	l, p, *
Tournai 1219–51	Gautier	Tournai	master at Tournai	l, *
Chartres 1219–34	Gautier	Chambli	abbot of Pontigny	m

Chronology of Elections to Regalian Sees, 1179–1223

See	Name	Family	Former Position	Classification
Reims 1219–26	Guillaume	Joinville	bish. of Langres	s
Soissons 1219–42	Jacques	Bazoches (brother of Gérard of Noyon)[i]	treasurer of Soissons	l, s
Paris 1220–23	Guillaume	Seignelay	bish. of Auxerre	q
Sées 1220–28	Gervais	English	abbot of Premontré, confessor of Honorius III, master at Paris	m, q, p, *
Evreux 1220–23	Raoul	Cierry	dean of Evreaux	l
Meaux 1221–22	Amaury		archd. of Meaux	l
Noyon 1221–28	Gérard	Bazoches (brother of Jacques of Soissons)	canon of Noyon, treasurer of Soissons	l, s
Orléans 1221–34	Philippe	Joui (nephew of Guillaume of Bourges)	canon of Orléans, archd. of Bourges	l
Rouen 1222–29	Thibaut	Amiens	treasurer of Rouen	l
Amiens 1223–36	Geoffroi	Eu	canon of Saint-Nicolas d'Amiens	l
Evreux 1223–36	Richard	Saint-Léger (Bellevue)	abbot of Bec	m
Sens 1223–41	Gautier	Cornu (Clément)	royal cleric, dean of Paris, master at Paris	r, c, f, p, *
Meaux 1223–55	Pons	Cuisy	archd. of Meaux	l

[a] Baldwin, *Masters, Princes and Merchants* I, 44, 45.
[b] The sole evidence for his learning comes from Gilles de Paris. See M. L. Colker, "The *Karolinus* of Egidius Parisiensis," *Traditio* 29 (1973): 319. Anselme was not designated as *magister* in his episcopal charters. Cartellieri (III, 92, n. 3) identifies him as the former dean of Saint-Martin of Tours.
[c] Bournazel, *Le Gouvernement capétien*, table after p. 189.
[d] Baldwin, *Masters, Princes and Merchants* I, 46.
[e] See chap. 6, at n. 187.
[f] Innocent III (*Regesta, PL* 214: 962; Potthast I, no. 1648) identified him by this title in 1202. See also Alberic de Trois-Fontaines 882.
[g] *Obituaires de la province de Sens*, ed. A. Molinier (Paris, 1902), I (1), 540.
[h] Newman, *Seigneurs de Nesle* I, 204, 207.
[i] Anne Lombard-Jourdan, *Paris—Genèse de la "Ville": La Rive droite de la Seine des origines à 1223* (Paris, 1976), 108.
[j] Newman, *Seigneurs de Nesle* I, 228, 247.

Appendix D
Archbishoprics, Bishoprics, and Abbeys

Archbishoprics and Bishoprics of France					
	Inventory				
	(1)	(2)	(3) (4) (5)		Qualifications
ARCHBISHOPS					
Lyon	x		x x x		
Bourges	x [q]	x	x x x		undoubtedly regalian
Reims	sb	ex, pr	x x x		
Tours	x [q]	pr	x x x		undoubtedly regalian
Sens	sb	ar, ex	x x x		
Rouen	x [q]	x	x x x		regalia confirmed in 1208
Bordeaux	ns		x x x		
Auch	ns		x x x		
Narbonne	[a]		x x x		
BISHOPS					
Le Puy	x		x x x		
Mâcon	sb [q]	r	x x x		regalia confirmed in 1202, renounced in 1209
Clermont	x [q]	ex	x x x		regalia confirmed in 1205 and 1220
Chalon-sur-Saône	x		x x x		
Langres	sb [q]	ex	x x x		regalia renounced in 1203
Autun	sb [q]	ex	x x x		regalia renounced in 1189
Nevers	sb [q]		x x x		regalia renounced in 1208
Troyes	sb [q]	ex	x x x		spiritual regalia renounced in 1207
Auxerre	sb [q]	ex, pr	x x x		regalia renounced in 1207
Orléans	sb	ep, ex	x x x		
Chartres	sb	ex, pr	x x x		
Paris	sb	ep, ex	x x x		
Meaux	sb	ex	x x x		
Soissons	sb	ep, ex	x x x		
Noyon	sb	ep, ex, pr	x x x		
Laon	sb	ep, ex	x x x		

Archbishoprics and Bishoprics of France

| | Inventory | | | | | |
	(1)	(2)	(3)	(4)	(5)	Qualifications
Châlons-sur-Marne	sb	ex, pr	x	x	x	
Senlis	x [q]	x	x	x	x	undoubtedly regalian
Beauvais	sb	ep, ex, pr	x	x	x	
Amiens	sb	ep, ex	x	x	x	
Arras	x [q]	x	x	x	x	regalia renounced in 1203
Thérouanne	sb	ex, pr	x	x	x	
Tournai	x [q]	x	x	x	x	undoubtedly regalian
Evreux	sb	x	x	x	x	
Lisieux	sb	x	x	x	x	
Bayeux	sb	x	x	x	x	
Avranches	sb	x	x	x	x	
Coutances	sb	x	x	x	x	
Sées	sb	x	x	x	x	
Rennes	x		x	x	x	
Nantes	x		x	x	x	
Vannes	x		x	x	x	
Quimper	x		x	x	x	
Léon	x		x	x	x	
Tréguier	x		x	x	x	
Saint-Brieux	x		x	x	x	
Saint-Malo	x		x	x	x	
Dol	x		x	x	x	
Angers	x [q]	x	x	x	x	regalia confirmed by 1223
Le Mans	x [q]	x	x	x	x	regalia confirmed by 1223, probably by 1214
Poitiers	x [q]	x	x	x	x	regalia confirmed by 1223
Limoges	x		x	x	x	
Périgueux	x		x	x	x	
Elne			x	x	x	
Angoulême	x		x	x	x	
Cahors	x		x	x	x	
Portaclusa			x	x		
Saintes	[a]		x	x	x	
Toulouse	[a]		x	x	x	
Mende	[a]		x	x	x	
Nîmes	[a]		x	x	x	
Agde	[a]		x	x	x	
Agen	[a]		x	x	x	
Albi	[a]		x	x	x	
Rodez	[a, a]		x	x	x	
Comminges			x	x	x	
Maguelonne	[a]		x	x	x	
Lodève	[a]		x	x	x	
Bayonne	[a]		x	x	x	
Bazas	[a]		x	x	x	

Archbishoprics and Bishoprics of France

	Inventory					Qualifications
	(1)	(2)	(3)	(4)	(5)	
Uzès	[a]		x	x	x	
Béziers	[a]		x	x	x	
Carcassonne	[a]		x	x	x	
Dax				x	x	
Lectoure				x	x	
Cousérans				x	x	
Tarbes				x	x	
Oloron				x	x	
Aire				x	x	
Lescar				x	x	

NOTE: This tabulation coordinates the information provided by five inventories of archbishoprics and bishoprics found in the royal registers with a view to determining the regalian status of the sees. The inventories, together with their sources of publication, are (1) "Archbishops and bishops that are under (*sb*) the king of France." Register A. *Registres* III, H; (2) "*Civitates* that the king has in his domain." Register A. *Registres* III, O; (3) "Archbishops and bishops in the kingdom of France." Register C. *Registres* III, H; (4)*Provincialis*. Register C. *Registres* IV, B; and (5) *Provincialis*. Register E. *Registres* IV, C.

The information is classified by the following symbols, provided in the inventories:

x	name listed without further indication	ep	bishop
sb	"under" the king	pr	*gîte*
[a]	additional hands	r	regalia
ns	not "under" the king	ar	archbishop
ex	army	[q]	qualification from other sources

Abbeys

	Regalian abbots REG. A. (1)	Abbots REG. C. (2)	Summarii REG. A. (3)	Prisée des sergents REG. A (4)	Prisée des sergents 1202 (5)	Accounts of 1202/03 (6)
Saint-Denis[a]	x	x	x	x	x	
Saint-Germain-des-Prés[b]	x	x	x	x	x	
Sainte-Geneviève[c]	x	x	x	x	x	
Ferrières-en-Gâtinais[d]	x	x	x	x	x	x
Saint-Benoît-sur-Loire[e]	x	x	x	x	x	x
Saint-Mesmin de Micy	x	x	x	x	x	x
Morigny	x	x	x	x	x	x
Saint-Maixent[f]	x	x				
Bourgueil-en-Vallée	x	x				
Marmoutier	x	x				
Saint-Gilles	x	x				
Tournus	x	x				
Sainte-Columbe-lès-Sens	x	x	x	x		
Sainte-Corneille de Compiègne	x	x	x	x	x	
Saint-Médard de Soissons	x	x	x	x	x	
Saint-Crépin-le-Grand de Soissons	x	x	x	x		
Saint-Remy de Reims[g]	x	x	x	x		x
Corbie	x	x	x	x	x	
Saint-Riquier[h]	x	x	x			x
Figeac[i]		x				
Seilhac[j]		x				
Notre-Dame de Soissons[k]		x	x	x	x	
Chelles		x		x	x	x
Faremoutiers		x				
Issoire[l]		x				
Mont-Martre		x		x	x	
Saint-Jean de Laon		x	x	x	x	
Saint-Josse-sur-Mer		x				
All Norman abbots who are black monks (see below)		x				
Abbas sancti Petri Pictavensis		x				
Massay (? *Abbas Mathaii*)			x			
Saint-Sulpice de Bourges			x			
Saint-Séverin de Château-Landon			x	x	x	x
Saint-Magloire de Paris[m]			x	x	x	x
Saint-Martin-des-Champs			x	x	x	
Saint-Père de Chartres			x			x
Sancta Maria Columbensis			x			
Saint-Maur-des-Fossés[n]			x	x	x	
Sanctus Baolus Remensis			(x)			
Saint-Thierry de Reims			(x)			

	Abbeys					
	Regalian abbots REG. A. (1)	Abbots REG. C. (2)	Sum-marii REG. A. (3)	Prisée des sergents REG. A (4)	Prisée des sergents 1202 (5)	Accounts of 1202/03 (6)
Montreuil-sur-Mer			x			
Saint-Vaast d'Arras			x			
Prior Messe (?)			(x)			
Saint-Valery-sur-Somme°			x			
Saint-Sanson d'Orleans				x	x	x
Saint-Victor de Paris				x	x	

NOTE: This tabulation coordinates information provided by six inventories of abbeys found in the royal registers and the fiscal accounts of 1202/03 with a view to determining the regalian status of the abbeys. Corroborating charters are listed in the footnotes, and the information is classified in the table by the following symbols:

    x   name listed

   (x)   name cancelled

SOURCES: (1) *Registres* III, I; (2) Ibid.; (3) *Registres* II, S; (4) *Registres* II, R; (5) *Budget* CXLVIII(1)–CXLIX(1); (6) *Budget* passim. [a]*Actes* III, no. 1143. [b]*Actes* III, no. 1143. [c]*Actes* I, no. 334. [d]*Actes* I, no. 156. [e]*Actes* III, no. 1143. [f]*Actes* II, no. 810. [g]*Actes* IV, no. 1559. [h]Teulet I, no. 451. [i]*Actes* I, no. 376. [j]*Actes* I, no. 376. [k]*Actes* I, no. 45. [l]AN *R 1143, fol. 209. [m]*Actes* I, no. 58. [n]*Actes* III, no. 1143. [o]Teulet I, no. 451.

"All Norman Abbots Who Are Black Monks"

This list of Benedictine abbeys in Normandy from the time of Philip Augustus expands on the note in Register C (see chap. 12, at n. 44): "All Norman abbots who are black monks." The information is drawn from *Gall. christ.* XI.

Diocese of Rouen

Saint-Ouen
Saint-Wandrille
Jumièges
Fécamp
Bec
Tréport
Saint-Victor-en-Caux
Saint-Georges de Boscherville
Saint-Martin d'Aumale
Valmont
Sainte-Catherine de Rouen
Montivilliers
Saint-Amand de Rouen

Diocese of Bayeux

Cerisy-la-Forêt
Fontenay
Troarn
Saint-Etienne de Caen
Longues
Sainte-Trinité de Caen

Diocese of Avranches

Mont-Saint-Michel
Moutons

Diocese of Evreux

Saint-Taurin
La Croix-Saint-Leufroy

Conches
Lire
Ivry
Saint-Sauveur

Diocese of Sées

Saint-Martin de Sées
Saint-Pierre-sur-Dive
Almenesches

Diocese of Lisieux

Saint-Evroult-en-Ouche
Bernay
Préaux
Grestain
Cormeilles
Saint-Léger-de-Préaux
Saint-Désir
Beaumont-en-Auge

Diocese of Coutances

Saint-Sever
Lessay
Saint-Sauveur-le-Vicomte
Montebourg
Hambye

Protected Monasteries

This list contains names of monasteries that received royal charters of protection and the dates of the charters. Sources are *Actes* I–V, cited in each listing.

Regalian

Morigny (1182) I, no. 70

Bec (1189, 1204) I, no. 283, II, no. 820

Saint-Benoît-sur-Loire (1196) II, no. 533

Saint-Maxient (1204) II, no. 810

Saint-Wandrille (1205) II, no. 874

Fécamp (1207) III, no. 1014

Saint-Mesmin de Micy (1214, 1217, 1223) III, no. 1320, IV, nos. 1498, 1809

Corbie (1214) III, no. 1339

Other Benedictines

Charlieu (1180) I, no. 20

Sarlat (1181) I, no. 22

Saint-Pierre-le-Vif (1182) I, no. 57

Saint-Nicaise de Meulan (1182) I, no. 60

Saint-Cyr-au-Val de Gallie (1190) V, no. 1839

Nant (1192) I, no. 415

Saint-Germer-de-Flay (1202) II, nos. 724 (?), 725

Notre-Dame-Saintes (1204) II, no. 832

Mosac (1217) IV, no. 1503

Regular Canons

Saint-Josse-au-Bois (1185, 1186, 1196) I, nos. 137, 161, II, no. 518

Saint-Jean d'Amiens (1185) I, no. 153

Saint-Jean-en-Vallée (1188) I, no. 244

Saint-André-au-Bois (1190), I, no. 302

Saint-Satur (1194) I, no. 469

Saint-Jean de Sens (1201) II, no. 668; (1220–1221) IV, no. 1635

Mont-aux-Malades de Rouen (1207) III, no. 1006

Others

Haute-Bruyère (1190) I, no. 339

Norman Templars (1205) II, no. 873

Saint-Martin de Tours (1211) III, no. 1222

Cistercians

Pontigny (1181, 1221) I, no. 24, IV, no. 1757

All Cistercians (1187) I, no. 215

Val-Notre-Dame (1187, 1190, 1221) I, nos. 216, 347, IV, no. 1757

Vaux-de-Cernay (1190) I, no. 340

Twelve Cistercian houses named, listed below with additional charters (1190) I, no. 347:

Cour-Dieu (1210) III, no. 1129

Lorroy

Ceranceaux (1221) IV, no. 1757

Barbeaux

Chaalis (1221) IV, no. 1757

Longpont (1221) IV, no. 1757

Valloires (1221) IV, no. 1757

Gard (1192, 1221) V, no. 1841, IV, no. 1757

Ourscamp (1195, 1221) II, no. 489, IV, no. 1757

Lannoy (1221) IV, no. 1757

Beaupré (1200, 1221) II, no. 636, IV, no. 1757

Froidmont (1221) IV, no. 1757

Valuisant (1190) I, no. 352

Beaubec (1194) I, no. 466

Billon (1194) V, no. 1847

Foucarmont (1196, 1221) II, no. 541, IV, no. 1757

Vauclair (1191) II, no. 597

Bohéries (1200) II, no. 632

Breuil-Benoît (1200) II, no. 652

Bonport (1200) II, no. 653

Preuilly (1203) II, no. 747

La Couronne (ca. 1210) III, no. 1161

Saint-André de Gouffern (1212) III, no. 1248

Savigny (1212) III, no. 1249

Fifteen Cistercian houses named, adding Clairvaux, Vaucelles, and Longvilliers to twelve above (1221) IV, no. 1757

Appendix E
Knight Service at Bouvines

	Register C (1)	Modern Estimates (2)	Guillaume le Breton (3)	Anonymous of Béthune (4)	Bannerets List (5)
BISHOPS					
Philippe, bishop of Beauvais	x 20		x		
Robert, bishop-elect of Laon	x 10		x		
Brother Guérin, bishop-elect of Senlis			x	x	
BARONS					
Jean, count of Beaumont	x 20		x	x	Coucy
Gaucher, count of Saint-Pol	x 30		x	x	St.-P.
Eudes, duke of Burgundy		(180)	x	x	Bur.
Pierre, count of Auxerre		(30)	x		Aux.
Robert, count of Dreux		(40)	x		Dreux
Henri, count of Bar-le-Duc		(30)	x	x	Misc.
Henri, count of Grandpré (the Champenois)		(180)			
Guillaume, count of Ponthieu (see below)				x	Pont.
Arnaud, count of Guines		(20)		x	Flan.
Raoul, count of Soissons		(30)		x	Misc.
Adam, *vicomte* of Melun		(25)	x	x	Misc.

450

	Register C (1)	Modern Estimates (2)	Guillaume le Breton (3)	Anonymous of Béthune (4)	Bannerets List (5)
VERMANDOIS, VALOIS					
Jean de Saint-Simon	x				
Clarembaud de Montchalons	x				Coucy
Knights of Saint-Quentin	40				
Aubert de Hangest	x				Verm.
Jean de Montgobert	x				Coucy
Raoul *Flamenc*	x				Verm.
Gilles de Plessis	x				Verm.
Raoul de Clermont	x				
Robert de la Tournelle	x				Verm.
Knights of Montdidier	50				
Hellin de Wavrin	x				Verm.
Gilles de Marquaix	x				Verm.
Knights of Péronne	50				
Philippe de Nanteuil	x				Verm.
Guy *Cocus*	x				
Knights of Chauny, Valois, and Senlis	50				
Knights of Pierrefonds	20				
Enguerran de Boves	x 10				Verm.
Guy de Choisy	x 5				
Guy de Thourotte	x 5				
Raoul d'Estrées	x 5				
Baudouin *de Rom* [*Rem?*]	x 5				Verm.
Barthélemy de Roye			x		Verm.
Galon de Montigni			x	x	
COUCY AND LAONNOIS					
Anseau de Ronqueroles	x 40				Coucy
Manassé de Mello	x 10				Coucy
Jean de Pierrepont	x 10				Coucy
Florence *Ville*	x 5				Coucy
Roger de Rozoi	x 10			x	Coucy
Vidame of Laon	x 5				
Gérard d'Ecri	x 5		x		Coucy
Quesnes de Condun			x		
Jean de Condun			x		
Enguerran de Coucy				x	
PONTHIEU AND ARTOIS					
Knights of Ponthieu	60				
Jean de Nesle	x 40		x		Flan.

	Register C (1)	Modern Estimates (2)	Guillaume le Breton (3)	Anonymous of Béthune (4)	Bannerets List (5)
His brother					Flan.
Thomas de Saint-Valery	x 20		x		Pont.
Renaud d'Amiens	x 20				Pont.
Hugues de Fontaines	x 5		x		Pont.
Gautier de Fontaines			x		
Isembard de Fontaines	x 5				
Pierre de Caieu	x 5				Pont.
Michel de Harnes		(5)	x		Arras
Hugues de Malaunoi		(5)	x	x	Arras
VEXIN					
Mathieu de Montmorency	x 20		x	x	Vex.
Guy de la Roche	x 10		x		Vex.
Knights of the Vexin	30				
Robert de Pinquigni	x 5				Vex.
Pierre de Richebourg	x 5				Vex.
Castellan of Néaufle	x 5				Vex.
Gilles d'Aci	x 5				Vex.
Guy the butler	x 10				Vex.
Robert de Poissy, le riche	x 5				Vex.
Amaury, his brother	x 3				
Guillaume des Barres		(10)	x	x	Vex.
NORMANDY					
Dreu de Moui	x 5				
Jean de Rouvrai	x 10		x		Nor.
Nicolas de Montigni	x 5				Nor.
Jean des Prés	x 10				Nor.
Etienne de Longchamps	x 5		x		Nor.
Geoffroi du Bois	x				Nor.
Renaud, his brother	x 10				Nor.
Robert d'Ivri	x 5				Nor.
Pierre Mauvoisin	x 5		x		Nor.
Robert de Harcanville (?)	x 5				
Guillaume de Mortemer		(5)	x		Nor.
OTHERS					
Guillaume de Garlande	x 20		x		Misc.

	Register C (1)	Modern Estimates (2)	Guillaume le Breton (3)	Anonymous of Béthune (4)	Bannerets List (5)
Renaud de Mangny	x 5				
Knights of Dammartin		10			
Etienne de Sancerre	x 10		x		Misc.
Gautier the Young			x		Misc.
Hugues de Mareuil			x		
Jean, his brother			x		
Pierre Tristan			x		
Garcio Comotus			x		
Michel d'Auchi, a bachelor				x	
Flamand de Créplaine				x	
Brother Thomas				x	
Brother Robert				x	
Totals of knights contingents	763	(560)			

NOTE: This tabulation correlates the evidence provided by the inventory in Register C, Guillaume le Breton, and the Anonymous of Béthune to identify the names of bishops, barons, and knights and the numbers of knights participating on Philip's side at Bouvines. Column 2 gives modern estimates of contingents drawn from outside the royal domain and not included in Register C. Column 5 identifies the geographical location (given by abbreviation) of the names from the list of bannerets in Register A. Code:

x   named by the source

Misc. miscellaneous category

The correlations between Register C and the two chroniclers, not only among the magnates but also among the lesser figures, suggest that the inventory in Register C was indeed drawn up preparatory to the battle.

SOURCES: (1) *Scripta de feodis* nos. 415, 416. (2) J. F. Verbruggen, *The Art of Warfare in Western Europe During the Middle Ages* (Amsterdam, 1977), 224–26. (3) Guillaume le Breton, *Gesta* and *Philippidos*. (4) Anonymous of Béthune, *Chronique des rois*. (5) "Etat par région des chevaliers bannerets" in *Registres* III, G (identified by region).

Abbreviations

Actes
> *Recueil des actes de Philippe Auguste.* Ed. H.-F. Delaborde, Ch. Petit-Dutaillis, J. Boussard, and M. Nortier. 4 vols. Paris, 1916–1979. Vol. V, additions and corrections, ed. M. Nortier, to be published.

Alberic de Trois-Fontaines
> *Chronica Alberici monachi Trium Fontium.* Ed. P. Scheffer-Boichorst. *MGH SS* XXIII, 631–950.

AN
> Manuscript. Paris, Archives Nationales.

Anonymous of Béthune, *Histoire des ducs*
> *Histoire des ducs de Normandie et des rois d'Angleterre.* Ed. F. Michel. Paris, 1840.

Anonymous of Béthune, *Chronique des rois*
> *Extrait d'une chronique française des rois de France par un anonyme de Béthune.* Ed. L. Delisle. *RHF* XXIV, 750–75.

Audouin, *Essai sur l'armée*
> Edouard Audouin. *Essai sur l'armée royale au temps de Philippe Auguste.* Paris, 1913.

Baldwin, "Contributions"
> See Nortier and Baldwin, "Contributions."

Baldwin, *Masters, Princes and Merchants*
> John W. Baldwin, *Masters, Princes and Merchants: The Social Views of Peter the Chanter and His Circle.* 2 vols. Princeton, 1970.

BEC
> *Bibliothèque de l'Ecole des Chartes*

Benedict
> Benedict of Peterborough. *The Chronicle of the Reigns of Henry II and Richard I.* Ed. W. Stubbs. 2 vols. London, 1867.

Borrelli de Serres, *Recherches*
> Léon Louis Borrelli de Serres. *Recherches sur divers services publics du XIIIe au XVIIe siècle.* 3 vols. Paris, 1895–1909.

Brussel, *Nouvel examen*
   Nicolas Brussel. *Nouvel examen de l'usage général des fiefs en France pendant le XIe, le XIIe, le XIIIe, et le XIVe siècle.* 2 vols. Paris, 1727.

Budget
   Le Premier budget de la monarchie française: Le Compte général de 1202–1203. Ed. Ferdinand Lot and Robert Fawtier. Bibliothèque de l'Ecole des Hautes Etudes, Sciences historiques et philologiques, no. 259. Paris, 1932. (Pagination of the photostatic edition of the account of 1202/03 is in roman numerals.)

Cartellieri
   Alexander Cartellieri. *Philipp II. August, König von Frankreich.* 4 vols. Leipzig, 1899–1922.

Coggeshall
   Radulphi de Coggeshall Chronicon Anglicanum. Ed. J. Stevenson. London, 1875.

Delaborde, *Layettes* V
   Vol. V of Teulet.

Delisle, *Catalogue*
   Léopold Delisle. *Catalogue des actes de Philippe Auguste.* Paris, 1856.

Delisle, *RHF* XXIV
   Léopold Delisle. "Chronologie des baillis et des sénéchaux royaux depuis les origines jusqu'à l'avènement de Philippe de Valois." *RHF* XXIV, * 15– * 385. (Numeration preceded by asterisks designates the preface.)

Diceto
   Ymagines historiarum. In *Radulfi de Diceto: Opera historica,* ed. W. Stubbs. 2 vols. London, 1876.

EHR
   English Historical Review.

La France de Philippe Auguste
   La France de Philippe Auguste: Le Temps des mutations. Ed. R.-H. Bautier. Colloques internationaux du Centre National de la Recherche Scientifique 602. Paris, 1982.

Gall. christ.
   Gallia christiana in provincias ecclesiasticas distributa. 16 vols. Paris, 1739–1877.

Gerald of Wales, *De Principis instructione*
   In *Giraldi Cambrensis opera,* ed. G. F. Warner, VIII. London, 1891.

Gervase of Canterbury
   Gervase, monk of Canterbury. *The Chronicles of the Reigns of Stephen, Henry II, and Richard I.* Ed. W. Stubbs. 2 vols. London, 1879–1880.

Gislebert de Mons, *Chronicon Hanoniense*
   Gisleberti chronicon Hanoniense. Ed. W. Arndt. *MGH SS* XXI, 481–601.

Guillaume le Breton, *Gesta*
> In *Oeuvres de Rigord et de Guillaume le Breton*, ed. H.-F. Delaborde, I, 168–333. Paris, 1882.

Guillaume le Breton, *Philippidos*
> In *Oeuvres de Rigord et de Guillaume le Breton*, ed. H.-F. Delaborde, II. Paris, 1885.

Honorius III, *Regesta*
> Honorius III, *Opera omnia*. In *Medii aevi biblioteca patristica*, ed. C.-A. Horoy. 4 vols. Paris, 1879–1880; calendared in Petrus Pressutti, *Registra Honorii papae III*. 2 vols. Rome, 1888–1895.

Howden
> *Chronica magistri Rogeri de Hovedene*. Ed. W. Stubbs. 4 vols. London, 1868–1871.

Innocent III, *Regesta*
> In *PL*, vols. 214–17; Vienna ed. in *Die Register Innocenz' III*, ed. O. Hageneder and A. Haidacher. 2 vols. Graz and Cologne, 1964, 1979.

JL
> P. Jaffé, G. Wattenbach, S. Loewenfeld et al. *Regesta pontificum Romanorum*. 2 vols. Leipzig, 1888.

Jugements
> *Recueil des jugements de l'échiquier de Normandie au XIIIe siècle (1207– 1270)*. Ed. L. Delisle. Paris, 1864.

Luchaire, *Actes de Louis VII*
> Achille Luchaire. *Etudes sur les actes de Louis VII*. Paris, 1885.

MGH SS
> *Monumenta Germaniae historica, Scriptores*.

Monuments historiques
> *Monuments historiques*. Ed. Jules Tardif. Paris, 1866.

Nortier and Baldwin, "Contributions."
> Michel Nortier and John W. Baldwin. "Contributions à l'étude des finances de Philippe Auguste." *BEC* 138 (1980): 5–33. The separate contributions of the two authors are distinguished by citing them under their respective names.

Pacaut, *Louis VII*
> Marcel Pacaut. *Louis VII et son royaume*. Paris, 1964.

Paris, BN lat.
> Manuscript. Paris, Bibliothèque Nationale, fonds latins.

Petit-Dutaillis, *Louis VIII*
> Charles Petit-Dutaillis. *Etude sur la vie et le règne de Louis VIII (1187– 1226)*. Bibliothèque de l'Ecole des Hautes Etudes, Sciences philologiques et historiques, no. 101. Paris, 1894.

PL
>   *Patrologiae cursus completus . . . series Latina.* Ed. J. P. Migne. 221 vols.
>   Paris, 1844–1903.

Potthast
>   Augustus Potthast. *Regesta pontificum Romanorum.* 2 vols. Berlin, 1874.

Powicke, *Loss of Normandy*
>   Maurice Powicke. *The Loss of Normandy, 1189–1204: Studies in the His-
>   tory of the Angevin Empire.* 2nd ed. Manchester, 1961.

Reg. A
>   Manuscript. Vatican. Ottoboni lat. 2796.

Reg. C
>   Manuscript. Paris, AN, JJ 7.

Reg. E
>   Manuscript. Paris, AN, JJ 26.

Registres
>   *Les Registres de Philippe Auguste.* Ed. J. W. Baldwin, with the assistance of
>   F. Gasparri, M. Nortier, and E. Lalou. Recueil des historiens de la France,
>   Documents financières et administratives, VI. Paris, in press. (Citations
>   refer to sections by roman numerals, to accounts and inventories by capi-
>   tal letters, and to individual inquests, charters, pledges, and items within
>   the accounts by arabic numerals.)

RHF
>   *Recueil des historiens des Gaules et de la France.* 24 vols. Paris, 1734–1904.

Rigord
>   In *Oeuvres de Rigord et de Guillaume le Breton,* ed. H.-F. Delaborde, I,
>   1–167. Paris, 1882.

Robert d'Auxerre
>   *Roberti canonici S. Mariani Autissiodorensis chronicon.* Ed. O. Holder-
>   Egger. *MGH SS* XXVI, 216–87.

Scripta de feodis
>   *Scripta de feodis ad regem spectantibus et de militibus ad exercitum vocandis e
>   Philippi Augusti registis excerpta.* Ed. L. Delisle. *RHF* XXIII, 605–723.

Suger, *Vie de Louis VI*
>   Suger. *Vie de Louis VI le Gros.* Ed. H. Waquet. Paris, 1964.

Teulet
>   *Layettes du Trésor des Chartes.* Ed. Alexandre Teulet, Henri-François De-
>   laborde, and Elie Berger. 5 vols. Paris, 1863–1909.

Wendover
>   Roger of Wendover. *The Flowers of History.* Ed. H. G. Hewlett. 3 vols.
>   London, 1886–1889.

Notes

1. Narrative: The Struggle for Survival

1. Delisle, *Catalogue* p. lxix.

2. For evidence of Louis's and Philip's gratitude, see *Actes* I, no. 2, and V, no. 1835.

3. Cartellieri I, 29–36, 41–48. For more details see chap. 14.

4. Chiefly: Rigord 8; Howden II, 193, 194; Diceto I, 438, 439; Gislebert de Mons, *Chronicon Hanoniense* 528; *Historia regum Francorum*, *RHF* XII, 221; *Chronicon anonymum Laudunense*, *RHF* XIII, 683.

5. For the transport of these presents, see *Magni rotuli scaccarii Normanniae sub regibus Anglie*, ed. Thomas Stapleton (London, 1840), I, 71.

6. See François-Louis Ganshof, "La Flandre," in *Histoire des institutions françaises au moyen âge*, ed. Ferdinand Lot and Robert Fawtier (Paris, 1957–62), I, 343–426.

7. See Jean Longnon, "La Champagne," in ibid. 123–36, and Michel Bur, *La Formation du comté de Champagne* (Nancy, 1977).

8. See Peter Munz, *Frederick Barbarossa: A Study in Medieval Politics* (Ithaca, N.Y., 1969).

9. See Jacques Boussard, *Le Gouvernement d'Henri II Plantegenêt* (Paris, 1956).

10. William M. Newman, *Le Domaine royal sous les premiers Capétiens (987–1180)* (Paris, 1937), 161–201.

11. On the royal consecration, see chap. 14.

12. Newman, *Le Domaine royal* 202–24; Marcel Pacaut, *Louis VII et les élections épiscopales dans le royaume de France* (Paris, 1957), 59–82; Pacaut, *Louis VII* 91–117.

13. Rigord 7, 11; Cartellieri I, 1–10. On Philip's birth and the practice of anticipatory association, see chap. 14.

14. Powicke, *Loss of Normandy* 12–17.

15. Cartellieri I, 25.

16. Ibid. I, 23–28; Pacaut, *Louis VII* 189.

17. Cartellieri I, 37–41.

18. Ibid. I, 48–55, 63–71.

19. Gerald of Wales, *De Principis instructione* 229. Cartellieri I, 59–60.

20. *Actes* I, no. 7; *RHF* XVIII, 133. See, too, Cartellieri I, Beilagen 68.

21. Cartellieri I, 71, 72, 82.

22. Ibid. I, 88–90.

23. Ibid. I, 95–115.

24. Ibid. 116–29.

25. Ibid. I, 136–39.

26. Ibid. I, 142–66.

27. Ibid. I, 167–82.

28. Ibid. I, 203–12.

29. Ibid. I, 212–28.

30. Gerald of Wales, *De Principis instructione* 176. Philip instituted masses for Geoffrey. *Actes* V, no. 1832.

31. Cartellieri I, 230–37.

32. Ibid. I, 230–32.

33. Ibid. I, 251–59, 276–81. See also Jean Hubert, "Le Miracle de Déols et la trêve conclue en 1187 entre les rois de France et d'Angleterre," *BEC* 96 (1935): 285–300.

34. Cartellieri I, 239–41, 286, 287.

35. Ibid. I, 281–84.

36. Howden II, 7.

37. Gervase of Canterbury I, 435, 436; Howden II, 50. Diceto II, 58; Cartellieri I, 291–94.

38. Cartellieri I, 294–316.

39. Delisle, *Catalogue* no. 124 and pp. 497, 498; Cartellieri I, 226.

40. Cartellieri I, 255.

41. Ibid. I, 242.

42. Ibid. I, 264, 297, 308, 310.

43. Sidney Painter, "The Third Crusade: Richard the Lionhearted and Philip Augustus," in *A History of the Crusades*, ed. Kenneth M. Setton (Philadelphia, 1962), II, 45–48. Cartellieri II, 26–52.

44. Cartellieri II, 43–74.

45. Howden I, 67.

46. Cartellieri II, 83–100, 106–10.

47. The authoritative studies on the acquisition of the northeastern territories are Léon-Louis Borrelli de Serres, *La Réunion des provinces septentrionales à la couronne par Philippe Auguste: Amiénois, Artois, Vermandois, Valois* (Paris, 1899), and Cartellieri.

48. Borrelli de Serres, *La Réunion* 6–13.

49. Ibid. 22, 23. Cartellieri I, 52–54.

50. Borrelli de Serres, *La Réunion* 27–35. Cartellieri I, 121–24, Beilagen 83–86.

51. Cartellieri I, 127–31.

52. Borrelli de Serres, *La Réunion* 35–39. Cartellieri I, 178–81.

53. Cartellieri I, 261, II, 96–97.

54. Ibid. I, 258, 312, 316, 322.

55. Ibid. I, 82–88.

56. Ibid. I, 195–202.

57. *Actes* I, no. 106. Cartellieri I, 110, 111, 236. René de Lespinasse, *Le Nivernais et les comtes de Nevers* (Paris, 1909–11), 396–98.

58. Cartellieri I, 236, 237.

59. *RHF* XVII, 425, repeated in Anonymous of Béthune, *Chronique des rois* 754. See also Cartellieri I, 105–13.

2. The King and His Men

1. Rigord 67. For other examples, see ibid. 40, 41, 53, 99.

2. Gervase of Canterbury I, 331, 373. See the comments of Antonia Grandsen, *Historical Writings in England, c. 550 to c. 1307* (Ithaca, N.Y., 1974), 258.

3. Benedict I, 244–46; Gervase of Canterbury I, 294; Gislebert de Mons, *Chronicon Hanoniense* 529.

4. Diceto II, 4, 9.

5. Benedict I, 284.

6. Diceto II, 7, 8, repeated in Wendover I, 126.

7. Gislebert de Mons, *Chronicon Hanoniense* 537.

8. Rigord 15, 30.

9. Benedict II, 6, 48, 49, 69.

10. Ibid. II, 67. See chap. 1 at n. 45.

11. Gervase of Canterbury I, 371, 372.

12. Ibid. I, 370, 371.

13. Ibid. I, 433, 434.

14. Eric Bournazel, *Le Gouvernement capétien au XIIe siècle, 1108–1180* (Limoges, 1975), 8.

15. See the observations of Cartellieri I, 83.

16. Bournazel, *Le Gouvernement capétien* 22, 157–61, 176, 177. On the rise of the *conseil*, see 151–73 and Pacaut, *Louis VII* 174.

17. Cartellieri I, 226, 242, 255, 308, 310, and Appendix A.

18. Cartellieri I, 68, 77, 226, and Appendix A.

19. Benedict II, 92, 93.

20. Cartellieri I, 226, 242, 255, 264, and Appendix A.

21. See the comment of Cartellieri I, 140, and Appendix A.

22. *Actes* I, no. 109.

23. *RHF* XVIII, 766.

24. *Actes* I, no. 345.

25. *Actes* I, no. 109. For other letters that Etienne wrote for the king, see ibid. I, nos. 136, 148, and 149. The abbot of Cercanceau was a royal emissary in 1185. Ibid. I, no. 136. The abbot of Saint-Denis represented Philip at Richard's coronation in 1189. Benedict II, 80.

26. Delisle, *Catalogue* pp. lxxxi–lxxxviii.

27. Their pensions were recorded in the accounts of 1202/03. *Budget* CXLVII (1), CLXXIV (2), CLXXXIX (1), and CLII (1).

28. *Actes* I, no. 401. In 1202 he was present at the royal judgment on the regalian rights of the bishopric of Châlons-sur-Marne. Ibid. II, no. 727.

29. Bournazel, *Le Gouvernement capétian* 111–18.

30. On the chancellor Hugues, see Cartellieri I, Beilagen 40–44.

31. Benedict I, 284. Gislebert de Mons, *Chronicon Hanoniense* 529, 531, 537. Cartellieri I, 41, 49, 51, 81, 107, 110.

32. *Actes* I, no. 8.

33. Bournazel, *Le Gouvernement capétien* 15, 31.

34. Ibid. 65, 176.

35. On Robert and Gilles, see *Monuments historiques* no. 678, and Robert d'Auxerre 246, whose picture was later confirmed by Innocent III, *Regesta*, PL 215:1170; Potthast I, no. 3107; and *Actes* I, no. 219. On Alberic, see *Actes* I, nos. 219, 365; Benedict II, 173; and Rigord 115.

On the Clément family, see Cartellieri I, 13, 40, 48, 49, 99, 100, Beilagen 16, 17; E. Richemond, *Recherches généalogiques sur la famille des seigneurs de Nemours de XIIe au XIVe siècle* (Fontainebleau and Bourges, 1907–8), I, 187–96; and J. Depoin, "Recherches sur quelques maréchaux de Philippe Auguste et de Saint Louis," *Bulletin historique et philologique du Comité des Travaux Historiques et Scientifiques* (1912): 188–94.

36. Diceto II, 43. Cartellieri I, 238.

37. They are identified as scribes A through G in the paleographical analysis of the chancery of Philip Augustus by Françoise Gasparri, *L'Ecriture des actes de Louis VI, Louis VII, et Philippe Auguste* (Geneva and Paris, 1973), 74, 75.

38. They include Magister Berterus (*Actes* I, nos. 218, 259) who may also be the poet who composed a lament over the fall of Jerusalem found in Benedict II, 26, and Howden II, 330 (see Cartellieri II, 47; John R. Williams, "William of the White Hands and Men of Letters," *Anniversary Essays in Medieval History by Students of Charles Homer Haskins* [Boston, 1929], 372–74; and chap. 14, n. 30); Eudes, who became abbot of Notre-Dame d'Etampes (*Actes* I, no. 273); Magister P. (*Actes* I, no. 136); and Adam, canon of Noyon (*Actes* I, no. 263).

39. Rigord I, 25. See also *Actes* I, no. 212; Richemond, *Recherches* I, 45; and Jean Bequet, "La Première crise de l'ordre de Grandmont," *Bulletin de la Société Archéologique et Historique du Limousin* 87 (1960): 304.

40. M. R. de Lasteyrie, *Cartulaire général de Paris* (Paris, 1887), I, no. 562, and Benedict II, 149. There was also a certain Philippe, *Actes* I, no. 298.

41. On Gautier in general, see Richemond, *Recherches* I, 9–53, and Bournazel, *Le Gouvernement capétien* 74–76, 89, 90, 100.

42. Delisle, *Catalogue* p. 497, and Rigord I, 64. See also Richemond, *Recherches* I, 42.

43. Alberic de Trois-Fontaines 884.

44. *Actes* I, no. 173, *Budget* CXLVI (2), and *Registres* II, D, no. 20. For his family affairs, see *Actes* I, nos. 173, 307–9, 328, 392; II, nos. 587, 613.

45. On the careers of his sons see chap. 6.

46. Delisle, *Catalogue* p. 497.

47. Compare, for example, those present at the charter of Queen Adèle at Paris in 1178. *Monuments historiques* no. 678.

48. On the early *prévôt*, see Jean-François Lemarignier, *Le Gouvernement royale aux premiers temps capétiens (987–1108)* (Paris, 1965), 157–59.

49. See chap. 3 at nn. 34, 35.

50. For a few examples from many, see (Poissy) *Actes* I, nos. 146, 234, 283; (Sens) 88, 171, 280; (Bourges) 40, 46, 187, 285.

51. See Appendix B.

52. Delisle, *Catalogue* p. 497, and Rigord 64.

53. For some examples of chaplains, see *Actes* I, nos. 97, 115, 154, 176, 178, 278, 285. For some early examples of sergeants, see ibid. I, nos. 55, 84, 232. Over thirty sergeants are known through charters providing them with gifts from the king. These charters accumulated so rapidly towards the end of the reign that a special chapter, *Capitula cartarum servientum*, was created in Reg. E, fols. 240r–244v, to contain them. In 1208 Philip made plans for establishing at Paris a house with a chapel and cemetery exempt from the authority of the bishop of Paris for retired royal sergeants (Innocent III, *Regesta, PL* 215 : 1382; Potthast I, no. 3586). By the end of the reign, they were buried at Sainte-Geneviève (Honorius III, *Regesta*, in Horoy, *Opera* IV, 528; Pressutti, II, no. 4741). In his testament the king bequeathed them 2,000 *livres* (Teulet I, no. 1546, *Actes* IV, no. 1796). Only one royal sergeant is known to have performed administrative service. After 1219 Renaud l'Archer, sergeant of the king, collaborated with the *bailli* Guillaume Menier in four judicial decisions. In one of them he attested an agreement for the abbey of Saint-Denis, but since he lacked a seal, he borrowed one from Geoffroi de la Chapelle, another royal *bailli* (*Registres* I, no. 59; Delisle, *Catalogue* no. 2047; Delisle, *RHF* XXIV, *50, *287). In 1219 he also participated with Barthélemy de Roye in surveying the royal lands at Melun (Delisle, *RHF* XXIV, *285). Like the other royal sergeants, he benefited from royal gifts and was also designated as the king's cupbearer (*Actes* IV, nos. 1462, 1626, 1820).

3. Justice and Finance:
The Chief Business of Government

1. This process is illustrated by an example from 1185, when Philip ordered the *prévôts* and *dispensatores* of his lands to minister to the needs of messengers from the Holy Land who were travelling through the royal domain. Rigord 47.

2. The following sketch of justice under the early Capetians is drawn from the standard studies: Achille Luchaire, *Histoire des institutions monarchiques de la France sous les premiers Capétiens* (Paris, 1891), I, 277–336; Yvonne Bongert, *Recherches sur les cours laïques du Xe au XIIIe siècle* (Paris, 1949), 55–111; and Pacaut, *Louis VII* 166–72.

3. These sources include chronicles and letters collected by royal servants. See the cases collected by Suger and Hugues de Champfleuri found in Luchaire, *Histoire des institutions* I, 281.

4. *Actes* I, nos. 206 and 305 are the exceptions. See Table 2 for the statistics.

5. *Actes* I, no. 52. Another example occurred at Corbie in 1209. *Actes* III, no. 1101.

6. *Actes* IV, no. 1436. See chap. 13 at n. 35.

7. The major exception to this rule occurred during the regency of 1190–1191. See chap. 7 at n. 7.

8. *Actes* I, nos. 8, 17, 65, 212, 343.

9. *Actes* I, no. 65, and Cartulary of Braisne, AN, LL 1583, pp. 186, 187 (1183).

10. *Actes* II, no. 727, IV, no. 1436, and Teulet I, no. 1439.

11. *Actes* I, nos. 116, 273, 447, II, nos. 727, 945, III, nos. 1101, 1311.

12. *Actes* I, no. 273.

13. *Actes* II, no. 727. The lesser clerics were Lothaire of Cremona; Rannulf, archdeacon of Bourges; Master Geoffroi de Poissy; and Master Nicolas de Chartres. Master Geoffroi de Poissy, Master Nicolas, and Master Lothaire all witnessed charters of Eudes, bishop of Paris, in June 1202 concerning the parochial jurisdiction of Sainte-Geneviève (*Gall. christ.* VII, instru. 226, 228, *PL* 214:1187, 1188). Master Geoffroi de Poissy also witnessed a charter of Thibaut, abbot of Saint-Maur, in 1187 (Cartulary of Saint-Maur-des-Fossées, AN, LL 46, fol. 114v). Master Nicolas was also identified as master Nicolas de Chartres (*Gall. christ.* VII, instru. 226). Master Lothaire may have been from Cremona. Innocent III addressed him as canon of Paris in 1202 (*PL* 214: 1094). None of these indications points to royal connections but rather to associations with the bishop of Paris.

14. *Actes* I, no. 179.

15. For example, *Actes* I, nos. 246, 443, II, nos. 592, 744.

16. *Actes* I, nos. 369, 370, 418, 458, II, nos. 684, 730, III, no. 1053.

17. *Actes* I, no. 341. See also *Actes* I, nos. 273, 274, 384. For delegations to royal officials, see *Actes* I, no. 362, II, nos. 622, 689, 943, IV, nos. 1606, 1689.

18. *Actes* II, no. 727, IV, no. 1436, and *Registres* VI, nos. 90, 91.

19. See Bongert, *Les Cours laïques* 159–82.

20. *Actes* I, no. 447. See also *Actes* II, nos. 619, 641, III, nos. 1081, 1142, 1298.

21. *Actes* II, no. 773, III, nos. 967, 1193, IV, nos. 1440, 1733, 1822.

22. *Actes* I, no. 201.

23. *Actes* I, nos. 145, 206. On Gatho de Poissy, a royal emissary, see chap. 2 at n. 36.

24. *Actes* II, nos. 753, 945, III, nos. 1101, 1144, 1278, 1311.

25. *Actes* I, no. 259, III, nos. 1002, 1378.

26. *Actes* IV, no. 1415.

27. Doris M. Stenton, *English Justice Between the Norman Conquest and the Great Charter, 1066–1215*, Memoirs of the American Philosophical Society, no. 60 (Philadelphia, 1964), 8, 51, 52, 76.

28. Reg. E. fol. 317r. *Registres* I, no. 72. This case was a letter to the king from three *baillis* announcing their judgment at Montdidier over the inheritance of Jean de Préaux.

29. As a legacy from Louis VI and Louis VII, the royal charters continued to assert that the king's seneschal participated in the exercise of justice, particularly in cases situated to the northeast of Paris. No evidence survives, however, that the incumbent seneschal, Thibaut de Blois, availed himself of these rights; moreover, it appears that they were abandoned after his death in 1191. The seneschal's rights with respect to justice are illustrated mainly in the charters of the Soissons family: Soissons, 1181 (*Actes* I, no. 35); Beauvais, 1182 (*Actes* I, no. 53); Vailly et al., 1185 (*Actes* I, no. 159); Compiègne, 1186 (*Actes* I, no. 169); Sens, 1189 (*Actes* I, no. 280); Villeneuve-en-Beauvaisis, 1200 (*Actes* II, no. 642); and Senlis, 1202 (*Actes* II, no. 706). See chap. 4 at n. 7. That they were probably abandoned after Thibaut's death is inferred from the *senescalcia* in the *Budget*. See ibid., p. 12 and chap. 7, n. 133.

30. Charles-Victor Langlois, "Formulaires de lettres du XII᷎, du XIII᷎, et du XIV᷎ siècle," *Notices et extraits des manuscrits de la Bibliothèque Nationale*, XXXIV, 1 (Paris, 1891), 13, 14. On the *prévôts'* justice under the early Capetians, see Luchaire, *Histoire des institutions* I, 226–34.

31. For example, when the king entered into *pariages* (sharing of jurisdiction) with other parties, the *prévôts* administered justice. *Actes* I, nos. 188, 189.

32. For some examples during the first decade, see *Actes* I, nos. 78, 161, 187, 216, 283.

33. Painstaking studies on the extent and nature of the royal domain of Louis VII were conducted by William M. Newman, *Le Domaine royal sous les premiers Capétiens (987–1180)* (Paris, 1937), 161–201, and Pacaut, *Louis VII* 119–160.

34. Pacaut (*Louis VII* 149, 150) has calculated the number of *prévôtés* by 1179 as thirty-seven or thirty-eight. Working with the accounts of 1202/03, I arrive at a total of forty-one by substracting the *prévôtés* added between 1179 and 1203. In 1179 they were Sens, Orléans, Châteauneuf-sur-Loire, Chécy, Fay-aux-Loges, Grez-sur-Loing, La Chapelle, Neuville-aux-Bois, Vitry-aux-Loges, Lorris-en-Gâtinais, Cépoy, Janville, Dixmont, Château-Landon, Dourdan, Pontoise, Yèvre-le-Châtel, Courcy-aux-Loges, Boësses, Moret, Samois, Poissy, Saint-Léger-en-Yvelines, Annemond, Chaumont-en-Vexin, Bourges, Etampes, Compiègne, Senlis, Villeneuve-le-Roi, Béthisy, Verberie, Laon, Montlhéry, Wacquemoulin,

Aubigny, Paris, Dun, Mantes, Fresnoy-en-Thelle, and Bray-sur-Somme. The accounts of 1202/03 omitted the lands in the dowry of Queen Adèle, but the dowry would also have been outside royal administration in 1179. In 1202/03 sixty-three *prévôtés* were administered by about forty-five *prévôts* (not counting the plural *prévôts* who administered one place). The application of the same proportion produces thirty to thirty-five *prévôts* for 1179.

35. These include Montargis (1184), Amiens, Ponthieu, Beauquesne, Montreuil-sur-Mer, Roie, Montdidier, Choisy, Thourotte (1185), and Issoudun (1187).

36. This material has been studied intensively by Newman, *Le Domaine royal* 1–66, and Pacaut, *Louis VII* 133–37.

37. Edited in *Registres* II, H. The thirty-five *prévôtés* fall into three general groups: (1) the Norman border territories acquired before the conquest of the duchy: Bréval (escheated in 1192), Anet (1193?), Pacy, Vernon, and Gisors (treaty of Issoudun, 1196), and Evreux (treaty of Le Goulet, 1200); (2) the territories of Artois, Picardie, and Vermandois acquired in the marriage negotiations with the counts of Flanders: Amiens, Roye, and Montdidier (1185), Bapaume, Péronne, and Hesdin (1191); and (3) the dowry of the queen mother Adèle: Lixy, Chesi, and Voulx, held in *pariage* with the abbey of Saint-Jean de Sens, and Corbeil, Melun, and Villeneuve-en-Senonais. In all likelihood the *Census* was inscribed into Reg. A after the death of Adèle in 1206 and before 1210, when the village of Boucly (listed in the accounts) was conceded to Gautier, castellan of Péronne (*Actes* III, no. 1128). For fuller discussion of the *Census*, see chap. 7 at nn. 95–99.

38. Totals were provided for Bapaume, Amiens, Beauquesne, Hesdin, Montreuil, Choisy, Corbeil, and Melun.

39. A. Verhulst and M. Gysseling, *Le Compte général de 1187 connu sous le nom de "Gros Brief," et les institutions financières du comte de Flandre au XIIᵉ siècle* (Brussels, 1962), and Thomas N. Bisson, *Fiscal Accounts of Catalonia* (Berkeley and Los Angeles, 1985). For fuller discussion of the *états*, see chap. 15 at n. 25.

40. AN J 1034ᴬ, no. 25. Wheat and oats accounts for Lens, Bapaume, Fampoux, Coullemont, and Avesnes. Wine accounts for Paris, Melun, Bourges, Lorris, Hesdin, Nogent, Anet, Vernon, Montargis, Saint-Germain, Pacy, Pont-de-l'Arche, Mantes, Crèpy, Béthisy, Saligny, Etampes, and Bois-Commun. The Paris account is entitled and dated: *Compotus vinorum MᵒCCᵒ vicesimo septimo mense mayo*. See Borelli de Serres, *Recherches* I, 39, and Bryce Lyon and A. E. Verhulst, *Medieval Finance: A Comparison of Financial Institutions in Northwestern Europe* (Providence, R. I., 1967), 46.

41. For the earliest example (1181), see *Actes* I, no. 31.

42. Edited in *Registres* II, C. The original list was compiled after November 1200, when the king made a donation—the latest that can be dated—to his chaplain at Sens (*Actes* II, no. 659). It was completed before February 1205, when a donation from Poissy found on the list was annulled (*Actes* II, no. 878).

Most of the alms in this account are also found in the *Budget* of 1202/03. See the cross-references in *Registres* II, C.

43. See the references in *Registres* II, C.

44. Eric Bournazel, *Le Gouvernement capétien au XIIe siècle, 1108–1180* (Limoges, 1975), 105–108.

45. *Actes* I, no. 306. He later enjoyed a *fief-rente* of twenty *livres* from the *prévôté* of Paris.

46. Edited in *Registres* II, D. Some of the *fief-rentes* may also be found in the *Budget* of 1202/03. See the cross-references in *Registres* II, D. On *fief-rentes*, see chap. 11.

47. See the conclusions of Luchaire, *Histoire des institutions*, I, 226.

48. *The Course of the Exchequer by Richard, Son of Nigel*, ed. Charles Johnson (London, 1950), 40, 41.

49. Luchaire, *Actes de Louis VII* no. 754; Luchaire, *Histoire des institutions* II, 347; *Actes* I, no. 168.

50. Poissy, *Actes* I, nos. 233, 234; Sens, *Actes* I, no. 280.

51. The authoritative study is Carlrichard Brühl, *Fodrum, Gistum, Servitium Regis: Studien zu den wirtschaftlichen Grundlagen des Königtums im Frankenreich und in den fränkischen Nachfolgestaaten Deutschland, Frankreich und Italien vom 6. bis zur Mitte des 14. Jahrhunderts* (Cologne, 1968), I, 220–309, especially 272–309.

52. *Registres* II, N (I).

53. Brienon in 1192. *Actes* I, no. 439.

54. For example, Chelles, 1189 (*Actes* I, no. 272); Flavigny, 1192 (ibid. I, no. 421); Saint-Julien-du-Sault, 1192 (ibid. I, no. 439); Senlis, 1202 (ibid. II, no. 706, and p. 272, n. 2; compare the versions in Regs. A and C).

55. Amiens, 1185 (*Actes* I, no. 139); Soissons, 1185 (*Actes* I, no. 155); Thérouanne, 1193 (*Actes* I, no. 445); and Auxerre, 1204 (*Actes* II, no. 860). See Brühl, *Fodrum* I, 294.

56. Dietrich Lohrmann, *Papsturkunden in Frankreich*, Neue Folge, 7 Band, Abhandlungen der Akademie der Wissenschaften in Göttingen, Philologisch-historische Klasse, 95 (1967), 590, and *Actes* I, no. 279, and JL no. 15, 864. Other such examples were Chelles, 1189 (*Actes* I, no. 272); Noyon, 1192 (*Actes* I, no. 406); Meung-sur-Loire and Pithiviers, 1212 (*Actes* III, no. 1258). See Brühl, *Fodrum* I, 280, and also 292, 293, for some examples from Louis VII.

57. See chap. 7 at n. 102.

58. *Registres* II, N (II).

59. Reg. E, fols. 311v–313r, 314v. These include the years 1223 to 1269.

60. On regalian rights, see Newman, *Le Domaine royale* 67–69, 216; Marcel Pacaut, *Louis VII et les élections épiscopales dans le royaume de France* (Paris, 1957), 59–72; Pacaut, *Louis VII* 91–107; and Jean Gaudement, *La Collation par le roi de France des bénéfices vacants en régale des origines à la fin du XIVe siècle*, Bibliothèque de l'Ecole des Hautes Etudes, Sciences religieuses, no. 51 (1935), 1–24.

61. On the significance of the consecration in returning the regalia, see chap. 8 at nn. 37, 38.

62. *Actes* I, no. 345.

63. William Stubbs, ed., *Select Charters of English Constitutional History* (Oxford, 1913), 166.

64. See the varying estimates of Newman, *Le Domaine royal* 202–4, 216, Pacaut, *Louis VII* 94–107, and Appendix C. Newman's is based exclusively on the survival of documentary evidence, and Pacaut's on a practical definition of *effectivement royale*. Appendix C, which relies on subsequent evidence, represents a minimum.

65. Appendix C.

66. J. D. Mansi, *Sacrorum conciliorum nova et amplissima collectio* (Florence and Venice, 1767), XXI, 533; statute renewed in 1215 (ibid. XXII, 1011). Of eighteen vacancies during the reign of Philip Augustus that can be measured in months, only five fell within the limit of three months.

67. From 27 February 1182 to 13 March 1183.

68. Luchaire, *Actes de Louis VII* no. 20 (1147), no. 383 (1157), and no. 773 (1179).

69. Mâcon, 1180 (*Actes* I, no. 8); Sens, 1183 (*Actes* I, no. 88); Paris, 1190 (*Actes* I, nos. 322, 323); Reims, 1190 (*Actes* I, no. 358); Bourges, 1190 (*Actes* II, no. 604); Châlons-sur-Marne, 1202 (*Actes* I, no. 727); Troyes, 1207 (*Actes* III, no. 982); Paris, 1207 (*Actes* III, no. 991); Meaux, 1222 (*Actes* IV, no. 1806).

70. Châlons-sur-Marne, 1147 (Reg. A, fol. 55v); Chartres, 1155, confirming grants of Henri, count of Blois, and Philip I (Reg. C, 61v); Orléans, 1157 (Reg. E, fol. 138r); Laon, 1158 (Reg. C, fol. 61v); Bourges, 1159 (Reg. C, fol. 120r); Mâcon, 1166 (Reg. C, fol. 19r).

71. *Actes* II, no. 604; *Registres* I, no. 46.

72. *Actes* II, no. 727; *Registres* I, no. 4. The *vidame*, who was the bishop's temporal agent, was fined for despoiling the bishop's house (*Actes* II, no. 726).

73. *Actes* III, no. 991.

74. Among the despoliations, two prebends were assigned to the king's clerks (Robert d'Auxerre 271; *De Gestis episcoporum Autissiodorensium*, *PL* 138:329; Innocent III, *Regesta*, *PL* 215:1169; Potthast I, no. 3107). See also Constance Bouchard, *Spirituality and Administration: The Role of the Bishop in Twelfth-Century Auxerre* (Cambridge, Mass., 1979), 132, 133.

75. For a fuller discussion of feudal reliefs, see chap. 11.

76. *Actes* I, no. 345.

77. On the administration of the Jews in the French royal domain, see Robert Chazan, *Medieval Jewry in Northern France: A Political and Social History* (Baltimore, 1973), 30–108.

78. Rigord 15, 16, 24–33; Guillaume le Breton, *Philippidos* 22; Chazan, *Medieval Jewry* 64–67.

79. Diceto II, 4.

80. Computed in terms of the early thirteenth century, such a policy would have realized more than 50,000 *livres*. See chap. 10 at n. 52 for an inquest into Jewish debts (1202–1212).

81. *Actes* I, nos. 90, 94, 95, 99, 133, 134, 166, 223, 263, 402; Rigord 30–32.

82. On the crusading taxes see Cartellieri II, 5–18, 58–74, 82–85, and Sydney Knox Mitchell, *Taxation in Medieval England* (New Haven, 1951), 5, 6, 12, 13, 64, 65, 114–23, 168–71.

83. *Actes* I, no. 123. On the date and details of this tax see Fred A. Cazel, Jr., "The Tax of 1185 in Aid of the Holy Land," *Speculum* 30 (1955): 385–92.

84. *Actes* I, no. 229, for the French version.

85. *Actes* I, no. 237.

86. *Actes* I, no. 252. The authenticity of this *acte* has been recently doubted on diplomatic grounds by Michel Nortier in "Les Actes faussement attribués à la chancellerie de Philippe Auguste," *Académie des Inscriptions et Belles-Lettres, Comptes rendus* (1981), 664–67.

87. The king also stipulated that if he died, the renunciation of *tallia* would remain in effect until his son was of age to make his own decisions (*Actes* I, no. 345). See Cartellieri II, 104, 105.

88. *Actes* I, no. 228.

89. *Actes* I, no. 345.

90. What was probably the autograph manuscript of Conan's *Note* was defectively read by G. Waitz in *MGH SS* XXIV, 782, as *mense 19 milia librarum*. John F. Benton, "The Revenues of Louis VII," *Speculum* 42 (1967): 89–90, has corrected the reading to *nisi. ixx. m. librarum* and has discussed its relevance to royal finances.

91. Pacaut, *Louis VII* 150–60, has attempted to estimate the annual income of Louis VII from the scattered documentary evidence. He proceeds in three stages and his results are pure speculation—almost an exercise in numerology. He first totals the documented evidence for the more or less fixed revenues and arrives at a figure of 20,270 *livres*. He then estimates that the occasional revenues were twice the fixed revenues (40,000 *livres*), giving a total of 60,000 *livres*. Finally, since his figure represents a grossly underreported sum, he multiplies it by 2.5 or 3 to arrive at 150,000 or 180,000 *livres* total annual income. Pacaut wished to attain the large figure because he accepted the misreading of Conan's testimony ("19,000 *livres* monthly") that resulted in 228,000 *livres* yearly income. See the criticism of Benton, "Revenues of Louis VII," 84–91. Afterwards, Marcel Pacaut, "Conon de Lausanne et les revenus de Louis VII," *Revue historique* 239 (1968): 29–32, revised his estimate downward to 110,000–120,000 *livres* yearly income for Louis VII, but his justification remains speculative. The estimate of 20,270 *livres* of documented fixed revenues (stage one above), however, approximates Conan's figure of 19,000 *livres* and supports the conjecture that this represents the fixed revenues of the *prévôtés*.

92. The *prévôtés* of 1179 are listed in chap. 3, n. 34. The farms are computed

from the *Budget* by eliminating balances carried forward, money transfers, and treasury transfers.

93. Pierre Dupuy, *Histoire du differend d'entre le Pape Boniface VIII et Philippe le Bel* (Paris, 1655), 77.

94. The *prévôtés* added between 1179 and 1190 are listed in chap. 3, n. 35. The farms are computed from the *Budget* as in chap. 7, n. 94.

95. For example, Benedict I, 321, II, 47.

96. See Cartellieri I, 58.

97. This can be deduced from the payment of the *senescalcia* by the *prévôts* to the royal seneschal in the account of 1202/03 (*Budget* p. 12). See also Luchaire, *Histoire des institutions* I, 179, and Henri Gravier, "Essai sur les prévôts royaux du XIe au XIVe siècle," *Nouvelle revue historique de droit français et étranger* 37 (1903): 565, 566.

98. Luchaire, *Histoire des institutions* I, 172–75.

99. *Registres* II, I (I–IV).

100. Borelli de Serres, *Recherches* II, 215, 216.

101. Lyon and Verhulst, *Medieval Finance* 15–17, 41, 42, 55–58.

102. On the English chamber, see F. T. Tout, *Chapters in the Administrative History of Mediaeval England* (Manchester, 1920), I, 67–119; J. E. A. Jolliffe, "The *Camera Regis* under Henry II," *EHR* 68 (1953): 1–21; J. E. A. Jolliffe, *Angevin Kingship* (London, 1963), 226–76; and H. G. Richardson and G. O. Sayles, *The Governance of Mediaeval England from the Conquest to Magna Carta* (Edinburgh, 1963), 229–39.

103. See chap. 5 at n. 34 and chap. 15 at nn. 34, 35.

104. Guillaume le Breton, *Gesta* 197; *Philippidos* 119, 120.

105. *Course of the Exchequer* 62.

106. This is the same analogy employed by Richard fitz Nigel in his *Course of the Exchequer* when he recounts the efforts of Nigel, bishop of Ely, to restore the operations of the English exchequer after its disruption during the anarchy of King Stephen's reign (ibid. 50). The evoking of Ezra's rediscovery of the scriptures as a type of reform was not unusual at the time. See Baldwin, *Masters, Princes and Merchants* I, 315.

107. Lyon and Verhulst, *Medieval Finance* 12–17, 41, 42, 61–63. Geoffrey H. White, "Financial Administration under Henry I," *Transactions of the Royal Historical Society*, 4th ser., 8 (1925): 56–78. Charles H. Haskins, *Norman Institutions* (Cambridge, Mass., 1918), 40, 41, 176, 177.

108. Suger also transferred money to Louis VII in 1149 through the services of the Templars. The standard study on the subject is Léopold Delisle, "Mémoire sur les opérations financières des Templiers," *Mémoires de l'Académie des Inscriptions* 33, part 2 (1889). See especially 20, 40.

109. *Actes* I, no. 345.

110. *Budget* passim; *Actes* II, no. 743; Brussel, *Nouvel examen* I, 428, note *a*. Haimard was one of the executors of Philip Augustus's will (*Actes* IV, no. 1796).

111. For the *prévôt* of Paris, see *Budget* CLXXV (1), CLXXXIX (2); for the *prévôt* of Lorris, who also carried money to Orléans, see ibid. CXCIII (2). The *prévôts* of Sens and Anet do not specify the destination of their money: see ibid. CXXXIX (2), CXCIV (2).

112. The English and Flemish treasuries developed elaborate processes for assaying coins to determine their debasement. See *Course of the Exchequer* 40–42 and Lyon and Verhulst, *Medieval Finance* 66, 67. We cannot tell how the French treasury dealt with this problem.

4. Towns and Churches:
The Extension of Royal Influence

1. The fundamental works on the Capetians and towns are Achille Luchaire, *Les Communes françaises à l'époque des Capétiens directs* (Paris, 1911); Charles Petit-Dutaillis, *Les Communes françaises: Caractères et évolution des origines au XVIII*ᵉ *siècle* (Paris, 1947); Albert Vermeesch, *Essai sur les origines et la signification de la commune dans le nord de la France (XI*ᵉ *et XII*ᵉ *siècles)*, Etudes présentées à la Commission Internationale pour l'Histoire des Assemblées d'États (Heule, 1966); and Susan J. Kupper, "Town and Crown: Philip Augustus and the Towns of France" (diss., The Johns Hopkins University, 1976).

2. On this point I follow the definition of Petit-Dutaillis, *Les Communes françaises* 27–36.

3. These include the following charters to towns, listed chronologically and cited according to their number in *Actes* I: Corbie (1180), 10; Tonnerre (1180), 19; Châteauneuf de Tours (1181), 30; Soissons (1181), 35; Bourges and Dun (1181–1182), 40; Noyon (1181–1182), 43; Corbie (1182), 52; Beauvais (1182), 53; Chaumont-en-Vexin (1182), 59; Reims (1182–1183), 73; Charité-sur-Loire (1182–1183), 75; Orléans (1183), 84; Dijon (1183–1184), 101; Châteauneuf de Tours (1184–1185), 122; Amiens (1185), 137A (see also *Actes* V, no. 1831); Compiègne (1186), 168, 169; Lorris (1187), 202; Dijon (1187), 210; Tournai (1188), 224; Pontoise (1188), 233; Poissy (ca. 1188), 234; Montreuil-sur-Mer (1188), 236; Saint-Riquier (1189–1190), 271; Chelles (1189–1190), 272; Laon (1189–1190), 279; Sens (1189–1190), 280; Amiens (1190), 319; Corbie (1190–1191), 368. These charters will not be repeated in the notes hereafter in this section.

4. See the comment of Guillaume le Breton, *Philippidos* 77–80, and Cartellieri I, 286, 287.

5. See Petit-Dutaillis, *Les Communes françaises* 86, 87, for a fuller discussion, and chap. 1, at n. 56.

6. The numbers in *Actes* I are Boiscommun (1186), 174; Voisines (1187), 208; Nonette (1188), 241; and Dixmont (1190), 303.

7. The charter for the rural association of Vailly and its surroundings is found in *Actes* I, no. 159. Although the Soissons charter was derived from an earlier charter of Beauvais, Soissons seems still to have had the dominant influence in the group. See Kupper, "Town and Crown" 84–86.

8. The numbers in *Actes* I are: Cerny (1184), 110; Crépy-en-Laonnois (1184–1185), 129; and Bruyères (1186–1187), 197.

9. Robert, count of Meulan, gave a commune to nearby Meulan (presumably after 1188) "according to the form of the commune decreed by the French king for Pontoise," as he puts it. The charter resembles that of Mantes more than that of Pontoise and was inscribed in Reg. A (*Registres* VI, no. 22).

10. See the conclusions of Kupper, "Town and Crown" 225–28.

11. Corbie, 1180, 1182; Châteauneuf de Tours, 1181; Soissons, 1181; Noyon, 1181, 1182; Beauvais, 1182; Compiègne, 1186; and Laon, 1189–1190.

12. The only exception to this Flemish and Norman preoccupation was the establishment of the commune of Sens in 1189–1190, which was not located in these contested areas.

13. Cerny, 1184; Crépy-en-Laonnois, 1184–1185; and Bruyères, 1186–1187.

14. On the history of the commune of Châteauneuf de Tours, see Petit-Dutaillis, *Les Communes françaises* 31.

15. Bourges and Orléans received royal charters of customs in 1181–1182 and 1183 respectively, however.

16. Rigord 34, 53, 54, 70.

17. *Actes* II, no. 616.

18. Royal charters from 1191 to 1204 included the following towns, listed here with their numbers in *Actes* I and II: Hesdin (1192), 408; Aire (1192), 430; Arras (1194), 473; Saint-Quentin (1195), 491; Montdidier (1195), 495; Henin-Liétard (1196), 529; Roye (1196), 539, 540; Tournai (1200), 625; Villeneuve-en-Beauvaisis (1200), 642; Senlis (1202), 706. In addition, the following rural communities were added to existing communes: Crandelain et al. (1196), 532; Vendress et al. (1201), 681.

19. Royal charters from 1204 to 1214 included the following towns, listed with numbers in *Actes* II and III: Andely (1204), 782; Rouen (1204), 789; Falaise (1204), 790; Caen (1204), 806; Pont-Audemer (1204), 809; Niort (1204), 828; Saint-Jean d'Angély (1204), 847, 859; Poitiers (1204), 857, 858; Nonancourt (1205), 877; Verneuil (1205), 879, 880; Fillièvres (1205), 893; Falaise (1205), 905A; Péronne (1207), 977; Hesdin (1207), 983; Cappy (1207), 984; Rouen (1207), 1000; Péronne (1209), 1067; Amiens (1209), 1072; Compiègne (1209–1210), 1100; Bray-sur-Somme (1210), 1117; Tournai (1211), 1176; Athies (1211–1212), 1212; Athies (1212), 1237; Châteauneuf de Tours (1212), 1241; Chauny (1213), 1295. In addition, the following rural community was added to a commune: Pancy and Corillon (1210), 1113.

20. Georges Espinas, ed., *Recueil des documents relatifs à l'histoire du droit municipal en France des origines à la Révolution: Artois* (Paris, 1934–43), II, no. 248 (Bapaume); II, no. 498, III, no. 577 (Lens); I, no. 111 (Arras); I, nos. 22–24 (Aire).

21. Royal charters from 1214 to 1223 included the following towns, listed here with numbers in *Actes* III and IV: Crépy-en-Valois (1215), 1389; Miraumont (1217), 1473; Caen (1220), 1665; Falaise (1221), 1693; Poitiers (1222), 1803; Beaumont-sur-Oise (1223), 1811; Chambly (1223), 1812. Prince Louis confirmed the grant to Hesdin in 1215 (Espinas, *Recueil* II, no. 498). In addition, the king confirmed the charters of the count of Ponthieu for a number of communes in 1221–1222 (*Actes* IV, nos. 1743–53, 1755).

22. Reg. A, fols. 11r–26v. The most recent was Poitiers (November 1204).

23. Subsequent additions were made in Reg. C beginning at fol. 33r. When Etienne de Gallardon compiled Reg. E, he placed the town charters under the heading of either *Civitates* (fol. 75) or *Castella* (fol. 97).

24. Edited in *Registres* III, N. For a discussion of the date see Petit-Dutaillis, *Les Communes françaises* 287.

25. The conclusions about filiations are derived from Kupper, "Town and Crown" 84–107. Montdidier belonged to the old family grouping of Laon, Andely to that of Mantes, and Crépy-en-Valois drew half its customs from the Soissons charter. In Artois and Vermandois, Péronne's charter inspired those of Hesdin, Cappy, Fillièvres, and Athies. Péronne undoubtedly possessed customs antedating its 1207 charter that were the source for Hesdin, Fillièvres, and perhaps Tournai. Saint-Quentin was the model for Roye, Chauny, and the rest of Crépy-en-Valois's customs. In 1195 Saint-Quentin was not yet in the royal domain, but the king was to inherit it if Countess Aliénor died without heir. In this capacity the king confirmed Aliénor's charter of customs and promised to abide by them if the city came into his hands. See Petit-Dutaillis, *Les Communes françaises* 55–70. In addition to the two principal families of Péronne and Saint-Quentin, there were the following groupings: Arras-Lens, Amiens–cities of Ponthieu, and Beaumont-Chambly.

26. These included Rouen, Falaise, Caen, Pont-Audemer, Poitiers, Niort, and Saint-Jean d'Angély. According to the list of *communie* in Reg. A, Verneuil belonged to this group (*Registres* III, N) and the charter of Nonancourt (*Actes* II, no. 877) professed to follow the model of Verneuil.

27. See chap. 3 at nn. 49, 50. Examples after 1191 included Montdidier (1193), Villeneuve-en-Beauvaisis (1200), Senlis (1202), Andely (1204), Athies (1212), and Crépy-en-Valois (1215). Similarly, towns such as Laon commuted their hospitality obligations for a fixed sum.

28. Examples were Chaumont (1182), Pontoise (1188), Poissy (1188), Henin-Liétard (1196), and Andely (1204).

29. The one exception to this defensive limitation before 1191 was Tournai (1188). See chap. 4, n. 3, and at n. 5.

30. On the rules of electing prelates formulated by the reign of Louis VII, see Marcel Pacaut, *Louis VII et les élections épiscopales dans le royaume de France* (Paris, 1957), 33–57, 147, 148.

31. *Actes* I, no. 345. The Constitutions of Clarendon are in William Stubbs, ed., *Select Charters of English Constitutional History* (Oxford, 1913), 166.

32. *De Gestis episcoporum Autissiodorensium, PL* 138:307.

33. For example, Teulet I, no. 1414, for the chapter of Evreux. A *licentia eligendi* for Châlons-sur-Marne for September 1215 survives in *Actes* V, no. 1872.

34. *Actes* II, nos. 772, 774, III, no. 1066. These chapters were also exempted from the regalia. See chap. 8, at nn. 30–36.

35. For an example from Louis VII, see A. Lecoy de la Marche, ed., *Oeuvres complètes de Suger* (Paris, 1867), 257. On the French practices, see Robert L. Benson, *The Bishop Elect* (Princeton, 1968), 365–69.

36. For an example from Louis VII, see above n. 35.

37. *Actes* II, no. 774. See also ibid. II, no. 772; III, no. 1066.

38. *Actes* III, no. 1337. In 1223 Louis VIII declared that the bishops of Le Mans, Angers, and Poitiers offered an oath of fealty like the other bishops of the realm. Teulet II, 1617, 1624; Reg. E, fol. 140r.

39. Ordinance (1190): *Actes* I, no. 345. Louis VII to Suger (1150): *RHF* XV, 525. *Licentia eligendi* to Châlons-sur-Marne (1215): see above chap. 4, n. 33.

40. Pacaut, *Louis VII* 67–69.

41. The election of Garmundus, abbot of Pontigny and brother of Gilles Clément, to Auxerre can be pieced together from Robert d'Auxerre 246 and Innocent III, *Regesta, PL* 215: 1169; Potthast I, no. 3107. Innocent III called the counsellor Gilo de Torneello, which was another name for Gilles Clément. See Alberic de Trois-Fontaines 900. On the event, see Cartellieri I, Beilagen 77–82. In a dispute with the chapter of Auxerre in 1180 the king also confiscated the episcopal revenues (Robert d'Auxerre 244).

42. *Les Lettres d'Etienne de Tournai*, ed. J. Deslive (Valenciennes and Paris, 1893), 225–27. See Baldwin, *Masters, Princes and Merchants* I, 9, 10 and chap. 8, at n. 5.

43. Pacaut, *Louis VII et les élections épiscopales* 143–48 and Pacaut, *Louis VII* 115–17.

44. See Appendix C, and chap. 4 at n. 47 for the number and determination of regalian bishoprics.

45. A category of bishops more difficult to evaluate includes John of Salisbury, bishop of Chartres, Maurice de Sully, bishop of Paris, and Henri, bishop of Senlis. All three may have formed ties with Louis at Paris, where John and Maurice were in the schools, and where Henri was canon of the royal abbey of Sainte-Geneviève. An old man at the time of his election, John was celebrated for his association with the martyred Thomas Becket, which may explain his successful candidacy. The election of Maurice de Sully (of a humble family, not to be

confused with the royal cousins) is also ambiguous. Two anecdotes circulated in the early thirteenth century on how Master Maurice was elected to the see of Paris. Caesar of Heisterbach (*Dialogus miraculorum*, ed. Joseph Strange [Cologne, 1851], I, 371) indicates that Maurice manipulated his own election. Jacques de Vitry (*Exempla*, ed. Goswin Fenken [Quellen und Untersuchungen zur lateinischen Philologie des Mittelalters, 15, 1, 1914] 123) claims that two candidates, Master Pierre Comestor and Master Maurice, were presented for royal approval. Louis VII inquired of the canons who the better cleric (teacher) was. When it was acknowledged that Pierre was the better, the king chose Maurice. This story illustrates the royal role in the election, but unfortunately for our purposes it does not demonstrate that the king knew the two Parisian candidates very well. See Baldwin, *Masters, Princes and Merchants* I, 156, II, 108.

46. See Appendix C.

47. I have identified the following as regalian bishoprics at the opening of Philip Augustus's reign:

Reims	Mâcon
Thérouanne	Sens
Tournai	Paris
Arras	Meaux
Amiens	Chartres
Noyon	Auxerre
Laon	Orléans
Soissons	Troyes
Beauvais	Nevers
Senlis	Bourges
Châlons-sur-Marne	Clermont
(Province of Lyon)	Tours
Langres	
Autun	

Though substantial consensus has been achieved among scholars in identifying most regalian bishoprics, the agreement has not been total. For the reign of Louis VII, William M. Newman, *Le Domaine royal sous les premiers Capétiens (987–1180)* (Paris, 1937), 216–17, has identified eighteen, but his figure, based exclusively on extant documentary evidence, is conservative. Pacaut, *Louis VII et les élections épiscopales* 63–72 and *Louis VII* 91–102, using a broader definition of "*effectivement royale*," has identified twenty-six regalian bishoprics. For the opening of the reign of Philip Augustus, I have attempted to use evidence supplied by the royal chancery in Reg. A. Two lists would appear to provide the names of regalian bishops: (1) *Archiepiscopi et episcopi qui sunt sub rege Francie*, edited in *Registres* III, H, and (2) *Hee sunt civitates que rex Philippus habet in domanio suo*, edited in *Registres* III, O. The first contains too many anomalies and contradictions with charter evidence to be entirely trustworthy. The second corresponds more closely with Pacaut's results and with the charter evidence. After substracting the Norman, Angevin, and Poitevin sees acquired in 1204, I have added only one name, Nevers, which is found on list (1) and is supported by charter evidence (*Actes* III, no. 1052). See Appendix D. My list agrees with Pacaut's except for adding Troyes and Nevers and rejecting Chalon-sur-Saône, Le Puy, and Mende. On the difficult case of Le Puy, see chap. 4, n. 50.

48. Pacaut, *Louis VII et les élections épiscopales* 72–77.

49. *Actes* I, no. 242.

50. *Actes* I, no. 239, renewed in 1192, no. 425. A charter of 1158 of Louis VII was copied into Reg. A. fol. 43r. See also Cartellieri I, 273, 274. It is difficult to determine whether *ad regiam jurisdictionem pertinere* implies a regalian jurisdiction. The sense of the lost charter (*Actes* I, no. 432) is also difficult to interpret.

51. A *provincialis*, listing bishoprics by provinces, was copied into Reg. C and Reg. E. Edited in *Registres* IV, B, C.

52. *RHF* XIX, 327. JL 15234.

53. *Actes* I, nos. 136, 148, 149.

54. *RHF* XIX, 329. JL 15914. *RHF* XIX, 291.

55. Innocent III, *Regesta*, Vienna ed. I, nos. 168, 169; Potthast I, nos. 176, 187.

56. Howden IV, 100–102.

57. Innocent III, *Regesta*, *PL* 214:625; Potthast I, no. 726.

58. Innocent III, *Regesta*, *PL* 214:635; Potthast I, no. 721. The English chronicler Wendover (I, 291–93) agrees with Innocent's interpretation.

59. *Actes* I, no. 345. See also the election at Saint-Denis in 1186. Rigord 65.

60. *Actes* I, no. 142. See also Rigord 66.

61. Saint-Médard de Soissons (1219), Teulet I, no. 1367; Sainte-Austreberte de Montreuil (ca. 1220), Teulet I, no. 1420 (the relationship of this nunnery to the Benedictine abbey of Saint-Saulve de Montreuil is not clear); Corbie (1221), *Actes* IV, no. 1737; Sainte-Geneviève de Paris (1222), Teulet I, nos. 1532, 1533, *Actes* IV, no. 1782; Cerisy (ca. 1220), Teulet I, no. 1417; Préaux (ca. 1218), Teulet I, no. 1421; Lire (1221), Teulet I, no. 1464, *Actes* IV, no. 1729; Cormeilles (1221), Teulet I, no. 1475; Lessay (ca. 1222), Teulet I, nos. 1560, 1561.

62. Notre-Dame-du-Val (ca. 1220), Teulet I, no. 1418; Massay (ca. 1222), Teulet I, nos. 1558, 1559; Sainte-Geneviève de Paris (1223), Teulet I, no. 1570.

63. See Henry II's formulation in the Constitutions of Clarendon (1164). *Select Charters*, ed. Stubbs, 166.

64. *Actes* I, no. 345. For other examples from charters, see *Actes* I, nos. 142, 334, III, no. 1143.

65. See Newman, *Le Domaine royal* 69–84, 202–4, and Pacaut, *Louis VII* 102–7, for their discussion of the difficulties and their respective conclusions. As with the bishoprics, Newman's estimates are conservative since they are limited to extant documentary evidence. Pacaut's take into consideration inferential evidence as well.

66. Edited in *Registres* III, I.

67. Although Sainte-Geneviève was at the time a house of regular canons, and Marmoutier was Cluniac, they were both ancient Benedictine foundations.

68. For example, Saint-Maur-des-Fossés, Saint-Magloire de Paris, Nemours, Saint-Pierre-le-Vif de Sens, Saint-Martin de Pontoise, Saint-Pierre de Chaumont, Liancourt, Coulombs, Saint-Laurent de Bourges, Massay, Saint-Julien de Tours, Montreuil-sur-Mer, Manglieu, Notre-Dame de Laon, Saint-Jean de Cuise, and Saint-Paul de Beauvais.

69. For example, Ferrières-en-Gâtinais, Saint-Maixent, Bourgueil-en-Vallée, Marmoutier, Saint-Gilles, Saint-Médard de Soissons, Saint-Crépin-le-Grand de Soissons, Saint-Remy de Reims, Corbie, Chelles, Issoire, and Saint-Pierre-le-Puellier.

70. For a full list and comparison with the findings of Newman and Pacaut see Appendix D.

71. 1189: *Actes* I, no. 273, confirmed by Celestine III, JL 16756. 1190: *Actes* I, no. 334. On the early history of this privilege, see Newman, *Le Domaine royal* 76.

72. For this paragraph see Appendix D.

5. Narrative: The Ill Fortunes of War

1. The most detailed and authoritative study of Philip's role in the Third Crusade remains Cartellieri II. See also Sidney Painter, "The Third Crusade: Richard the Lionhearted and Philip Augustus," in *A History of the Crusades*, ed. Kenneth M. Setton (Philadelphia, 1962), II, 45–85. The main arguments of Part 2 of the present study were outlined in my "La Décennie décisive: Les Années 1190–1203 dans le règne de Philippe Auguste," *Revue historique* 266 (1981): 311–37.

2. *Actes* I, no. 376.

3. Cartellieri II, 115–69.

4. Ibid. II, 180–205.

5. Ibid. II, 205–32.

6. Ibid. II, 232–58. See the lament of Guillaume le Breton, *Philippidos* 108, 109.

7. For the precedents to the Flemish succession, see chap. 1.

8. *Actes* I, no. 383.

9. For the details of the settlements and the events leading to them, see Cartellieri III, 5–13, and Léon-Louis Borrelli de Serres, *La Réunion des provinces septentrionales à la couronne par Philippe Auguste: Amiénois, Artois, Vermandois, Valois* (Paris, 1899), 45–52.

10. *Actes* I, no. 399. In addition the king confirmed her rights to Valois, Chauny, Ressons, Lassigny, Ribemont, and Origny; as far as can be told, she already had possession of these places.

11. Mathilde of Portugal, Count Philippe's second wife and widow, claimed an expanded dower that included Saint-Omer and Aire in Artois. But Baudouin, count of Flanders and Hainaut, was able to eliminate the expansions in an agreement of 1191. *Registres* VI, no. 29. *RHF* XVIII, 408, note *b*. See Cartellieri III, 5, 6, 8.

12. *Actes* I, no. 398. *Registres* VI, no. 31. See Cartellieri III, 11, and Henri Malo, *Un Grand feudataire, Renaud de Dammartin, et la coalition de Bouvines: Contribution à l'étude du règne de Philippe Auguste* (Paris, 1898), 29–43.

13. The fundamental and unexcelled study of the matrimonial relations between Philip and Ingeborg remains Robert Davidsohn, *Philipp II August von Frankreich und Ingeborg* (Stuttgart, 1888), from which Cartellieri draws his own account. See also Hercule Géraud, "Ingeburge de Danemark, Reine de France," *BEC* (1844): 3–27, 93–118.

14. William of Newburgh, *Historia rerum Anglicarum*, in *Chronicles of the Reigns of Stephen, Henry II, and Richard I*, ed. Richard Howlett (London, 1884), I, 367–69. Howden III, 224; Gervase of Canterbury I, 529; and Mathew Paris, *Historia Anglorum*, ed. Frederic Madden (London, 1866) II, 46, briefly echo this conclusion. Powicke, *Loss of Normandy* 91, 92 accepts these explanations.

15. Davidsohn, *Philipp II* 13–32. Cartellieri III, 57–63.

16. See the recent study of Georges Duby, *Medieval Marriage: Two Models from Twelfth-Century France* (Baltimore, 1978), 54–62, 73–80. Marie-Bernadette Bruguière, ignoring German scholarship on the subject, attempts to show that Philip and Ingeborg were in fact related by affinity of the second kind to the fourth degree, and that Ingeborg and Isabelle de Hainaut were related by affinity of the second kind to the second or third degrees ("Le Mariage de Philippe Auguste et d'Isambour de Danemark: Aspects canoniques et politiques," in *Mélanges offerts à Jean Dauvillier* [Toulouse, 1979], 135–56). But these relationships were beyond the confines of what churchmen normally investigated, and Philip's chancery itself seems to have been unaware of them.

17. Genealogies were copied into Reg. C at fols. 1v–2v. A false genealogy (*Balduinus comes Flandrie quatuor generavit filias . . .*) was cancelled and a correction was added (*Daci dicunt quod . . .*). For the texts see *Registres* VII, 5, *MGH SS* XIII, 257–59, *RHF* XIII, 415–17, and Davidsohn, *Philipp II* 297–306. For opposing genealogies from the Danes see *RHF* XIX, 307–10. See Davidsohn,

Philipp II 42, 307–9 for schematic depictions of the genealogies. On the marriage and divorce of Ingeborg, see ibid. 32–46, and Cartellieri III, 63–68.

18. Rigord 125.

19. Davidsohn, *Philipp II* 46–68. Cartellieri III, 68, 129–32.

20. Innocent III, *Regesta*, Vienna ed. I, nos. 171, 347, 348; Potthast I, nos. 199, 361, 362.

21. Davidsohn, *Philipp II* 68–96, Cartellieri III, 166, 167, IV, 24–28.

22. *Gesta Innocentii III*, *PL* 214: xcix, c.

23. Davidsohn, *Philipp II* 114–43. Cartellieri IV, 55–63. A letter (Potthast I, no. 983) from the lost papal register of 1200 has been recovered by C. R. Cheney; see "An Annotator of Durham Cathedral MS C.III.3, and Unpublished Decretals of Innocent III," *Studia Gratiani* 9 (1967): 50, 51, 65–68.

24. Davidsohn, *Philipp II* 159–70. Cartellieri IV, 63–71.

25. Innocent III, *Regesta*, *PL* 214:1191. *RHF* XIX, 504. Potthast I, no. 1499. Copied into Reg. A, fols. 8r, 51v. See also the letters of fourteen bishops supporting the action, preserved in the royal archives, Teulet I, nos. 625–38. On the death of Agnès and the legitimation of her children, see Davidsohn, *Philipp II* 170–80, and Cartellieri IV, 82–88.

26. For some examples: Coggeshall 76; Diceto II, 120; Robert d'Auxerre 256; Rigord 128, 130, 132, 140, 141; Guillaume le Breton, *Gesta* 197, 199; Cartellieri III, 99, 117, 118, 210; Powicke, *Loss of Normandy* 129.

27. Cartellieri III, 21–30, 34–42.

28. Ibid. III, 50–53, 69–72.

29. Ibid. III, 32, 33.

30. Teulet I, no. 412. Cartellieri III, 73–74.

31. In January 1192 Philip did demand that Richard's Norman vassals turn over Gisors according to the treaty of Messina, but when the Normans refused, Philip did not follow up with military action. Cartellieri III, 14–16. Powicke, *Loss of Normandy* 83, 95 n. 1.

32. Cartellieri III, 45–47.

33. Ibid. III, 74–77. Powicke, *Loss of Normandy* 96–98.

34. For details on the military skirmish at Fréteval based on topography, see R. Barré de Saint-Venant, *Nouveau aperçus sur le combat de Fréteval* (Vendôme, 1905). On the significance of this incident for the French royal archives, see chap. 15, at nn. 34, 35.

35. Cartellieri III, 85–98, 108–10. Powicke, *Loss of Normandy* 99–104.

36. *Actes* II, no. 517. Teulet I, no. 431. Cartellieri III, 118–22. Powicke, *Loss of Normandy* 107–10.

37. Cartellieri III, 127–29, 132–36, 142–46. Powicke, *Loss of Normandy* 111, 119.

38. Cartellieri III, 120–25, 138–42. Powicke, *Loss of Normandy* 114–17.

39. Cartellieri III, 127–29.

40. Ibid. III, 147–52. Teulet I, no. 450.

41. *Actes* II, no. 508. Cartellieri III, 114. In June 1196 the dowry of Eu and Arques was replaced with Villiers, Rue, Abbeville, Saint-Valery, and Saint-Riquier, without the regalia of the last two abbeys. Teulet, I, no. 451.

42. *Actes* II, no. 598. Teulet I, no. 493. Cartellieri III, 188. On the dating and the significance of this alliance, see John Gillingham, "The Unromantic Death of Richard I," *Speculum* 54 (1979): 37–39. Philip was still subsidizing the *vicomte* in 1202. *Budget* CLVI (1).

43. Cartellieri III, 17, 90.

44. Ibid. III, 137.

45. Ibid. III, 155.

46. Rigord 137, 138. Cartellieri III, 152–55, 164.

47. Cartellieri III, 156–62, 192, 193.

48. Ibid. III, 188–91. Powicke, *Loss of Normandy* 121–22.

49. *Registres* VI, no. 35. *RHF* XVII, 49. For the imperial background, see Cartellieri III, 165, 166, 171–79.

50. Cartellieri III, 166–68, 193, 194.

51. Ibid. III, 196–204. Powicke, *Loss of Normandy* 120, 122–24.

52. Cartellieri III, 207, 208. Powicke, *Loss of Normandy* 122–26.

53. On John's disputed succession, see Cartellieri IV, 3–14, Powicke, *Loss of Normandy* 127–33, and Sidney Painter, *The Reign of King John* (Baltimore, 1949), 1–16.

54. *Actes* II, nos. 607, 608. Cartellieri IV, 9.

55. Cartellieri IV, 18–20.

56. Ibid. IV, 16–18.

57. See chap. 5, at nn. 21, 22.

58. Cartellieri IV, 12–16.

59. *Actes* II, no. 621. Cartellieri IV, 34–36.

60. Teulet I, no. 613, copied into Reg. A, fol. 28r. Cartellieri IV, 83–85.

61. Cartellieri IV, 38, 39, 75–78.

62. During this period Innocent also attempted to promulgate legislation over French crusaders. When Philip consulted his barons over the legality of these ordinances, Eudes, duke of Burgundy, advised the king to resist such legislation unless it was approved by the king and his barons. Teulet, I, no. 768. Cartellieri IV, 77, 78.

63. Cartellieri IV, 9, 13, 14.

64. Ibid. IV, 24, 25.

65. These were conceded as Blanche of Castile's dowry.

66. *Actes* II, no. 633. Teulet, I, no. 578. Cartellieri IV, 36–49. Powicke, *Loss of Normandy* 134–38.

67. Cartellieri IV, 78, 79.

68. Teulet I, nos. 492, 494. Cartellieri IV, 3.

69. Cartellieri IV, 54, 98, 99.

70. Ibid. IV, 49–54, 71–73, 93–96. Powicke, *Loss of Normandy* 140–45. Sidney Painter and Fred A. Cazel, Jr., "The Marriage of Isabelle d'Angoulême," *EHR* 63 (1948): 83–89 and *EHR* 67 (1952): 233–35.

71. Cartellieri IV, 98.

72. *Actes* II, no. 709. Cartellieri IV, 103.

73. For the pledges, see Guillaume le Breton, *Gesta* 207. Cartellieri IV, 95.

74. Coggeshall 135, 136. See also Rigord 151, 152, Guillaume le Breton, *Gesta* 207, Cartellieri IV, 99–108, and Powicke, *Loss of Normandy* 145–49. I have adopted the interpretation of this judgment of Charles Petit-Dutaillis, *Le Déshéritement de Jean sans Terre et le meurtre d'Arthur de Bretagne: Etude critique sur la formation et la fortune d'une légende* (Paris, 1925), 4–18.

75. The castellanies of Longchamps, Lyons-la-Forêt, Ferté, Gaillefontaine, Mortemer, Gournay, and Driencourt were captured during the early summer of 1202, immediately after John's condemnation, and were included in the Marches accounts. See chap. 7, at nn. 153, 154.

76. *Actes* II, no. 488. Cartellieri III, 48, 49. See chap. 1, at n. 57.

77. Teulet I, nos. 502 (copied in Reg. C, fol. 117r), 503. Delisle, *Catalogue* nos. 574–77. Cartellieri III, 205, IV, 22–24. René de Lespinasse, *Le Nivernais et les comtes de Nevers* (Paris, 1909), I, 406–9.

78. These statistics are compiled from the *Budget*. The figure for 1203 is low because it does not include the domanial revenue of 8,671 *livres* collected by the war treasurers from the castellanies of Bray acquired in the summer of 1202. See chap. 7, at nn. 85, 92. I have excluded this last figure because it can not be readily divided into income collected by the *prévôts* and *baillis* and because it was produced at the outset of Philip's great campaign against Normandy.

6. The King's New Men

1. Among the sixty or more individuals inventoried as giving or receiving gems, the following categories can be found: (1) royal family: the king; the queen mother, Adèle de Champagne (recently deceased); Prince Louis; Blanche of Castile; Alix, countess of Blois (the king's half sister); Pierre, count of Dreux; and Robert de Courtenay (the latter two royal cousins), (2) great barons: Guy de Thouars, count of Brittany; Renaud, count of Boulogne; and the countess of Crépy, (3) prelates: the pope; the archbishops of Reims, Tours, and Treves; the bishops of Soissons, Chartres, Autun, Troyes, and Nantes; the abbot of Cluny; and the abbess of Préaux, (4) royal *familiares*: Brother Guérin; Barthélemy de Roye; Aubert de Hangest; and the chamberlains Gautier the Young, Ours, Eudes, and the wife of the recently deceased Malcio, (5) *baillis*: Pierre de Béthisy; Miles de Lévis; Nevelon the Marshal; Guillaume de la Chapelle; Guillaume Menier; Cadoc; and Hugues de Boutigny, (6) bourgeois from Arras, Amiens, and Noyon, (7) others: sergeant and butler Guillaume du Puy; the wife of Pierre

Choiseau, a forester; and Roger the Falconer. *Registres* II, I (II–IV). For a fuller discussion of the documentation, see chap. 3 at nn. 99 and 100.

2. A preparatory sketch for this chapter may be found in my "L'Entourage de Philippe Auguste et la famille royale," in *La France de Philippe Auguste* 59–73.

3. Rigord 100–105. *Actes* I, no. 345.

4. Rigord 99.

5. Edgard Boutaric, *Actes du Parlement de Paris* (Paris, 1863), I, ccxcvii, viii (referred to also in *Gall. christ.* IV, 397). *Actes* I, nos. 366, 370, 371, 375, 381, 382, 390–93. Although *Actes* V, no. 1840 reflects the terminology of regency charters, it was drafted too early (May 1190) and contains only one of the bourgeois.

6. See the tabulation of the personnel in Delisle, *Catalogue* p. lxii.

7. *Actes* I, no. 370. On the seal, see Delisle, *Catalogue* p. lxiii.

8. *Actes* I, no. 366.

9. For Saint-Ouen: *Actes* I, nos. 366, 370, 381; elsewhere outside of Paris: ibid. I, nos. 382, 392.

10. Eric Bournazel, *Le Gouvernement capétien au XIIe siècle, 1108–1180* (Limoges, 1975), 15, 35–40, 52–53, genealogical table.

11. See chap. 2, at n. 39, and chap. 3, at nn. 77, 78.

12. *Actes* I, no. 263.

13. M. R. de Lasteyrie, *Cartulaire général de Paris* (Paris, 1887), I, no. 562.

14. Delisle, *Catalogue* p. lxiii. The remaining two initials may indicate Baudouin Bruneau and Nicolas Boisseau.

15. Bournazel (*Le Gouvernement capétien* 75, 76, n. 90) speculates that Thibaut belonged to the Le Riche family. Detailed studies on the family have, however, failed to document the connection. See A. Longnon, "Recherches sur une famille noble dite de Paris aux XIe, XIIe, et XIIIe siècles," *Bulletin de la Société de l'Histoire de Paris et de l'Ile-de-France* (1879): 137, and J. Depoin, "Sur la famille Le Riche," in *Cartulaire de l'abbaye de Saint-Martin de Pontoise* (Pontoise, 1895), 270–305. The royal charters (see chap. 6, n. 16) definitely designated Thibaut as bourgeois, and contemporary anecdotes circulated about a notorious usurer called Thibaut the Rich. See Baldwin, *Masters, Princes and Merchants* I, 308, 309.

16. Gautier held properties on the Petit-Pont, Cité, Grand-Pont, Châtelet, Place de la Grève, and Saint-Merry, and at least three mills. *Actes* I, nos. 307, 308, II, nos. 587, 613, V, no. 1840. In 1173–1174 Brother Bernard and Thibaut the Rich aided Gautier in a land exchange. E. Richemond, *Recherches généalogiques sur la famille des seigneurs de Nemours du XIIe au XIVe siècle* (Fontainebleau, 1907), I, xxi. Gautier later abandoned his claims to a donation at Paris that Thibaut had made to the brothers of Vincennes. *Actes* II, no. 613. Thibaut often witnessed the charters of Gautier because he had married the chamberlain's sister. Since Thibaut's children all died before their father, Gautier was also Thibaut's heir. Richemond, *Seigneurs de Nemours* I, 73. Even the otherwise obscure Pierre the Marshal can be found on a charter of Gautier the Chamberlain's in 1179. See n. 13 above.

17. See chap. 6, at n. 113.

18. Cartellieri III, 61, 126, 195, IV, 60. He also attested a charter for Saint-Lazare in 1200. Cartulary of Saint-Lazare, AN, MM 210, fol. 45v.

19. Adam may have been one of the "*assessores domini regis*" at Etampes in 1192. Delisle, *RHF* XXIV, *49. See chap. 7, at n. 3. For his obituary, see *Obituaires de la province de Sens*, ed. A. Molinier (Paris, 1902), I (1), 108.

20. On successions to and vacancies in the household officers, see Delisle, *Catalogue* p. lxxxi–lxxxv.

21. Appendix A.

22. Delisle, *RHF* XXIV, *271.

23. René de Lespinasse, *Le Nivernais et les comtes de Nevers* (Paris, 1901), I, 472–74. Rigord, *Gesta* I, 162.

24. See *Registres* III, L. Though the grand chamberlain Mathieu was listed among the higher rank of the *comites* and the butler Guy among the *barones*, neither was active in royal service (ibid. III, J, K). Dreu de Mello was succeeded as constable in 1218 by another castellan from the Vexin, Mathieu de Montmorency. Mathieu gained dubious notoriety in 1198 when he was personally captured by Richard at Courcelles-lès-Gisors (see chap. 11, at n. 116), but he had a record of loyal service at Bouvines and with Prince Louis on the crusade. Since his administrative service was minimal, it appears that he held his office as a reward for military service.

25. Cartellieri III, 67. Robert Davidsohn, *Philipp II August von Frankreich und Ingeborg* (Stuttgart, 1888), 43–45.

26. *Actes* II, no. 633. Teulet I, no. 588.

27. See chap. 5, at n. 17.

28. *Actes* II, no. 727.

29. Cartellieri III, 10.

30. Cartellieri III, 63, 178. Davidsohn, *Philipp II* 59.

31. Guillaume le Breton, *Gesta* 205. Cartellieri IV, 55.

32. Cartellieri III, 19, 25, 50, 116, 143, IV, 24. Teulet I, no. 588. Appendix A.

33. Cartellieri III, 8, 10, 52, 64, 66, 93, 114, 116, 134, 148, 151, 182, 199, IV, 56. Appendix A. He last appears in a royal *acte* in 1201 (probably in December). *Actes* V, no. 1854.

34. See chap. 6, at nn. 207, 208.

35. See chap. 2, at n. 28.

36. *Actes* II, no. 587. Richemond, *Seigneurs de Nemours* I, 76. Appendix A.

37. *Actes* II, no. 644. See chap. 8, at n. 46.

38. Guillaume le Breton, *Gesta* 257. Alberic de Trois-Fontaines 884.

39. Richemond, *Seigneurs de Nemours* I, 103–50. See chap. 5, at n. 17, and Appendix C.

40. Richemond, *Seigneurs de Nemours* I, 153–58.

41. Howden III, 257–60. See also Richemond, *Seigneurs de Nemours* II, 3–15, and Appendix A.

42. *Actes* II, no. 520.

43. *Budget* CLXVII (1) and CLXXXVI (2). See chap. 6, at n. 271.

44. *Registres* II, I (III, IV). *Actes* II, no. 928.

45. He appears in the household account of Prince Louis in 1213. See Robert Fawtier, "Un Fragment du compte de l'hôtel de Prince Louis de France pour le terme de la Purification 1213," *Le Moyen Age*, 3rd ser., 4 (1933): 241.

46. Anonymous of Béthune, *Histoire des ducs* 166, 188.

47. On Gautier the Young, see Richemond, *Seigneurs de Nemours* II, 59–71, and Appendix A. Gautier is first mentioned in a royal charter in 1197 (*Actes* II, no. 554) "Gautier the Father" first appears in 1199 (ibid. II, no. 613). The obituary of the cathedral of Chartres designates the latter: "qui inter ceteros preminentes in aula regia regisque lateri familiaris adherentis" (sic). *Obituaires de la province de Sens*, ed. Molinier, II, 82.

48. See chap. 15, at n. 34.

49. Appendix A. His name is found on the back of a royal mandate of June 1200 to *baillis* and *prévôts* attesting to the king: "T[este] G. juvene." *Actes* II, no. 636. (See Nortier's corrections in vol. V.)

50. *Budget* CL (2), CCII (1), CCIII (1).

51. Ibid. CLVIII (2), CLXV (2), CLXXXVII (1), and *Registres* II, I (II–IV).

52. Teulet I, no. 613.

53. *Actes* II, no. 726. Speculation about Gautier's trip to Rome is based on a conjecture that identifies him with a certain knight "Gautier" named in the papal correspondence. See Davidsohn, *Philipp II* 117, Cartellieri IV, 55.

54. *Registres* I, no. 42.

55. Guillaume le Breton, *Gesta* 272.

56. *Jugements*, passim. At Easter 1213 Guillaume de la Chapelle presided in Gautier's place. In 1212 and at Michaelmas in 1213 there are no names for the presiding judges.

57. Delisle, *RHF* XXIII, *275. *Jugements* no. 49.

58. *Registres* III, P. *Actes* IV, no. 1516.

59. *Actes* II, no. 888.

60. These were a certain Renaud, who received money for wine (*Budget* CXLVII [1, 2]), Jean de Betefort, who was in charge of the royal wardrobe (ibid. CLVI [1], CLXXXIII [1], CC [2]; see also chap. 7, at n. 149 below), and Christophe Malcio (ibid. CLXXXIII [1]), who also appears in *Actes* II, no. 627, and *Registres* II, I (II–IV), and whose testament has survived. See Henri Stein, "Testament d'un chambellan de Philippe Auguste, 1205," *Bulletin de la Société de l'Histoire de Paris et de l'Ile de France* 30 (1903): 156, 157. See also *Actes* V (gifts not datable).

61. *Budget* CXLVII (2), CCII (2), CLXXXVII (1), CLIX (1), CLXI (1), CLXIV (1). It is not entirely clear that the "*Odo camerarius*" and the "*Odo cambellanus*" of these entries are the same person.

62. *Registres* II, I (I–IV). See chap. 3, at nn. 99–100.

63. *Actes* II, 783. A *"Stephanus cambellanus domini Ludovici"* also appears in 1219 in the Cartulaire blanc de Saint-Denis, AN, LL 1157, p. 304.

64. Henri Stein, "Pierre Tristan chambellan de Philippe Auguste et sa famille," *BEC* 78 (1917): 135–53.

65. Guillaume le Breton, *Gesta* 282, 283. *Actes* III, no. 1396; IV, no. 1639; V, no. 1873, and gifts not datable.

66. *"Radulfus de Nivernis cambellanus regis"* (1192), Teulet I, 400. *"Bricius cambellanus,"* *Actes* II, no. 761. *"Henricus consergius cambellanus noster,"* ibid. IV, nos. 1433, 1568, and 1720.

67. See chap. 6, at n. 276.

68. *Registres* I, no. 69. He was probably the same as the *"Thibaudus panetarius"* in *Actes* II, no. 624, *Actes* III, no. 1310, and *Budget* CL (2).

69. *Actes* III, no. 1035.

70. See chap. 6, at nn. 72, 73 and 278.

71. Teulet I, no. 412.

72. *Actes* II, no. 542.

73. Delisle, *Catalogue* p. lxxxiii.

74. See Appendix A.

75. On Barthélemy's career in general, see Pierre Daon, "Barthélemy de Roye, chambrier de France (v. 1160–1237)," in *Positions de thèses: Ecole des Chartes* (Paris, 1943), 49–54. See also his eulogy, written after his death in 1237, in Léopold Delisle, *Littérature latine et histoire du moyen âge* (Paris, 1890), 65–67.

76. Delisle, *Catalogue* no. 936. *Actes* II, no. 905, III, nos. 1348, 1376.

77. *Actes* II, no. 542. Gautier was employed by the *prévôt* of Paris. See *Budget* CXLVI (2), CLXXIV (2), CLXXXIX (2).

78. Ibid. CLVI (2), CXCIV (2), CCIII (2). *Registres* II, I, (III, IV).

79. Teulet I, no. 803. Cartulary of Ourscamp, Paris BN lat. 5473, fols. 47r, 58v. *Actes* II, no. 623. He was a vassal of Jean de Nesle. *Scripta de feodis* no. 224.

80. On the rue Saint-Germain l'Auxerrois, near Saint-Denis la Châtre, at Poissy, and at Gonesse. *Actes* III, no. 1346, V, no. 1869, II, no. 583A, IV, no. 1787. Delisle, *RHF* XXIV, *278.

81. *Actes* II, nos. 745, 886, III, no. 959.

82. See chap. 11, at n. 79.

83. *Budget* CLXIV (1), CLXVII (1).

84. Guillaume le Breton, *Philippidos* 270, 271.

85. Guillaume le Breton, *Gesta* 272, 284. *Registres* VII, no. 13. *MGH SS*, XXVI, 393.

86. For example, he was the king's guarantor against Count John in 1194, at Le Goulet in 1200, and with Renaud, count of Boulogne, in 1201. See Appendix A and Teulet I, no. 613. On the system of pledges, see chap. 11.

87. *Actes* II, no. 952.

88. Ibid. II, no. 727.

89. *RHF* XVIII, 359.

90. *Jugements* no. 137 and p. 35. *Registres* I, no. 41.

91. *Jugements* nos. 231–351.

92. *Actes* III, no. 1396.

93. *Registres* I, nos. 1 and 8.

94. Ibid. I, nos. 46 and 60. Also with Guérin, he participated in a number of forest inquests. Ibid. I, nos. 42, 78, 96.

95. *Scripta de feodis* no. 308. Appendix A. See Richemond, *Seigneurs de Nemours* II, 241, and Auguste Moutié, "Notes historiques et généalogiques sur les seigneurs de Lévis et leur famille," in *Cartulaire de l'abbaye de Notre-Dame de la Roche* (Paris, 1862), 313–428.

96. Moutié, "Seigneurs de Lévis" 431. Delisle, *RHF* XXIV, *49.

97. *Actes* II, no. 622.

98. *Actes* II, no. 644. See chap. 8, at n. 46.

99. *Actes* II, no. 727. His widow appears in the account of that date. *Budget* CLXXXII (1).

100. See chap. 10, at n. 8. Another son became archdeacon of Poissy and a third distinguished himself on the crusade against the Albigensians.

101. *Scripta de feodis* nos. 203, 227, 351, 363, 509.

102. Ibid., nos. 350, 363. The *domina de Hangest*, for example, was provided with a *fief-rente* of forty *livres* annually from the *prévôté* of Roye and Montdidier. *Registres* II, D, no. 63. The charters containing the name of the Hangests are numerous.

103. Appendix A. *Actes* II, no. 854. Guillaume le Breton, *Philippidos* 265.

104. *Budget* CLXIX (2). *Registres* II, I (IV).

105. Teulet I, no. 1049. Achille Peigné-Delacourt, *Cartulaire de l'abbaye de Notre-Dame d'Ourscamp* (Amiens, 1865), 545. Delisle, *Catalogue* no. 1522. Delisle, *RHF* XXIV, *279. Appendix A.

106. *Registres* I, nos. 1, 8, 40, 43, 44, 54, 56, 57, 63, 64. *Actes* III, nos. 1387, 1388.

107. Philippe de Nanteuil originated from the Soissonais and was listed among the *vavassores* of the Vexin in the royal feudal inventories (*Registres* III, G, M; *Scripta de feodis*, *RHF* XXIII, nos. 351, 365). Two inquests were made into his justice, forest, and hunting rights (*Registres* I, nos. 49 and 50). He was captured fighting for the king in 1198 and was present in the royal entourage at decisions made in 1198, 1215, and 1220 (Rigord 142 and Appendix A). Pierre du Mesnil was an agent of Philippe, count of Flanders, before he accompanied his lord on the crusade in 1190 (Louis M. de Gryse, "Some Observations on the Origin of the Flemish Bailiff (*Bailli*): The Reign of Philip of Alsace," *Viator: Medieval and Renaissance Studies* 7 [1976]: 280, 281. He served Philip Augustus in taking possession of Artois and in swearing to the king's divorce at Compiègne (Cartellieri III, 8, 67; Davidsohn, *Philipp II*, 44). Among other scattered examples of Philip's employment of knights, Michel, a knight, and Nicolas, a nobleman, were sent on missions to the pope regarding the interdict and

Ingeborg in 1200 (Cartellieri IV, 55). Guillaume *de Valle Gloris*, a knight, was part of a legation to King Henry III of England in 1220 (Teulet I, nos. 1388, 1389).

108. See chap. 2, at n. 35, and chap. 5, at n. 5.

109. *Budget* CLXVII (1, 2). Appendix A. *Actes* II, no. 807, renewed in 1207; *Actes* III, no. 986.

110. Rigord 165.

111. Guillaume le Breton, *Gesta* 264, 265. *Philippidos* 295.

112. *Registres* I, no. 42.

113. Guillaume le Breton, *Philippidos* 74, 77. Cartellieri I, 283, 286. See chap. 6, at n. 4.

114. Cartellieri II, 182, III, 22. Following Joseph Despoint's "Une Famille seigneuriale au XIIe et XIIIe siècles, la famille Garlande (Thèse manuscript de l'Ecole des Chartes, 1924), Bournazel (*Le gouvernement capétien*, genealogical table) postulates a Guillaume II who died in 1186–1187 and his son Guillaume III who died in 1216. The date of Guillaume II's death poses some difficulties because two Guillaumes were alive in 1190, one at Paris and the other on the crusade. The problem may be caused by the widespread use of the name Garlande, as Despoint indicates (p. 19).

115. *Budget* CLX (2), CLXV (2), CLXXVI (1), CCVII (2). Guillaume le Breton, *Gesta* 272, 284.

116. See Appendix A.

117. *Budget* CCI (1). *Actes* I, no. 451, II, nos. 501, 763.

118. *Actes* I, no. 451. Teulet I, nos. 1235–37.

119. Reg. C, fol. 116r, recopied in Reg. E, fol. 216r, v. Teulet I, nos. 1235–37.

120. *Scripta de feodis* no. 365. Holding lands at Mont-Saint-Gervais in Paris, the family took its name from the defensive wall (*barres*) around the right bank. Anne Lombard-Jourdan, *Paris—Genèse de la "Ville": La Rive droite de la Seine des origines à 1223* (Paris, 1976), 107. Guillaume le Breton made a pun on this meaning of the name (*Philippidos* 85).

121. *Actes* II, no. 669. This was the same family into which Barthélemy de Roye married.

122. *Actes* II, no. 669. This item was cancelled in the *fief-rente* accounts by the time of Register C. *Registres* II, D, no. 48. Guillaume also held a *fief-rente* from John in 1200–1201. Sidney R. Packard, *Miscellaneous Records of the Norman Exchequer*, Smith College Studies in History, no. 12 (Northampton, Mass., 1927), 10.

123. See "Guillaume des Barres" in the index to Rigord and Guillaume le Breton. Rigord identifies him as count of Rochefort (83) and Guillaume le Breton devotes especial praise to him in *Philippidos* 81.

124. See, for example, Cartellieri I, 201, 278, 287, III, 135, IV, 9.

125. Benedict II, 155. See also Cartellieri II, 155, 156.

126. Appendix A.

127. *Registres* I, no. 88.

128. *Actes* II, no. 688, dated between 1 November 1201 and 13 April 1202. *Actes* V, no. 1854, which carries the identical dating, may be more precisely limited to December 1201, when the king was at Reims.

129. Brother Guérin may have appeared at the royal court as early as 1197. According to the *Chronique de Flandre*, the king was at Saint-Pol in that year when a fight broke out between Renaud, count of Boulogne, and Hugues, count of Saint-Pol. The count of Boulogne left the court, and the king sent after him "Brother Guérin his counsellor" (Brussels, Bibl. Roy. 10232, fol. 29r, in *Chronique de Flandre anciennement composée par auteur incertain*, ed. Denis Sauvage [Lyon, 1562], 20, and Kervyn de Lettenhove, *Istoire et Chroniques de Flandre* [Brussels, 1879] I, 79). The incident is undated, but Cartellieri (III, 154, n. 5) places it in the context of the great defections of 1197, although with difficulty. The *Chronique de Flandre* is a late compilation from the mid–fourteenth century, drawn mainly from the Anonymous of Béthune and Baudouin d'Avesnes. See Henri Pirenne, "Les Sources de la chronique de Flandre jusqu'en 1342," in *Etudes d'histoire du moyen âge dédiées à Gabriel Monod* [Paris, 1896], 360–64, and Auguste Molinier, *Les Sources de l'histoire de France* (Paris, 1903), III, no. 2891. This particular passage cannot, however, be located in the latter sources. I am grateful to Gabrielle M. Spiegel for examining the manuscripts concerning this problem.

130. See Appendix A.

131. Guérin was with Philip at Reims (probably in December 1201), when the king confirmed a donation of Archbishop Guillaume's before the archbishop died on 7 September 1202. *Actes* V, no. 1854.

132. Guillaume le Breton, *Gesta* 256, 257. Innocent III, *Regesta*, PL 216: 618; Potthast I, no. 4530. For the details of this incident see chap. 9, at n. 75.

133. Guillaume le Breton, *Gesta* 256, 268. The necrology of Noyon calls him canon of Saint-Quentin (*Gall. christ.* X, 1414), but the sources of this notice are late and sometimes in error.

134. See chap. 6, at n. 209. There is no contemporary support for the attempts of eighteenth-century antiquarians to link Guérin with the family of Montaigu in Auvergne (Louis Archon, *Histoire de la chapelle des rois de France* [Paris, 1711], II, and *Gall. christ.* VII, 229, 230 and X, 1409). According to A. Vattier ("L'Abbaye de la Victoire: Notice historique," *Comité archéologique de Senlis: Comptes rendus et mémoires*, 3rd ser., 2 [1887]), Guérin should not be confused with Guérin de Montaigu, grand master of the Hospitalers; Guérin, grand prior of the Hospitalers in France; or Guérin, royal chaplain and almoner under Philip Augustus (after 1221), Louis VIII, and Louis IX. Canon Afforty reports an eighteenth-century tradition at Senlis that Guérin came from Châteauneuf Landon: "Mr. de Roquelaure, évêque de Senlis [1754–1801], m'a dit que la maison de Guérin, évêque de Senlis et chancelier de France, étoit fondu dans celle de Châteauneuf Landon" (Collection Afforty, MS Senlis Bibl. mun., XV,

287). His relatives included a nephew, Pierre (*Actes* III, no. 1031); "Magister Guillermus de Moreto clericus nepos venerabilis fratris nostri G. Silvanectensis episcopi" (Cartulary of Saint-Pierre de Lisieux, Paris BN lat. 5288, fol. 73v [1226]); a certain Nicolas; and "Fulco prior beati Arnulphi Crespiacensis" ([Canon Deslyons, annotated by Canon Afforty], "Le Chancelier Guérin," *Comité archéologique de Senlis: Comptes rendus et mémoires*, 3rd ser., 2 [1887], 73); and a niece, Esemburgis (*Actes* IV, no. 1715). He was buried at the monastery of Chaalis (Collection Afforty, MS Senlis, Bibl. mun. XI, 6041). For the Gaignières drawing of his tomb, see Jean Adhémar, *Les Tombeaux de la collection Gaignières: Dessins d'archéologie du XVIIe siècle* (Paris, 1974), I, no. 118.

135. *Budget* CXLII (2), CXCIII (2), XCXI (1), and CXCIII (1). See also Pierre Héliot, "Montreuil-sur-Mer et Montreuil-Bellay: Deux énigmes du premier registre de Philippe Auguste," *BEC* 127 (1969): 113–15.

136. *Budget* CLXXXII (1, 2).

137. *Actes* III, nos. 1292, 1308, 1324, 1344, 1395, IV, nos. 1590, 1648, Teulet I, no. 1052. Guérin's own gifts to the church of Senlis are recorded in the obituary of the cathedral of Senlis. Paris BN lat. 9975, fol. 33r, v.

138. *Actes* II, no. 688 to III, no. 1120.

139. Guérin's activities in the chancery left virtually no trace on the fiscal accounts of 1202/03. The single reference to twenty *livres* expended by Robert de Meulan "*pro i carta fratris Garini*" is scarcely sufficient to explain his chancery duties. *Budget* CLXXXII (1). The two clerks of Guérin to whom wages were paid may have served him in the chancery. See chap. 7, at n. 150.

140. *RHF* XVIII, 359. The attribution of "vicescancellarius" to Guérin in the letter of Innocent III of 5 June 1212 may be found only in a rubric supplied by the editors of *RHF* XIX, 554.

141. For example, the king's reconfirmation in 1185 of the bishop of Senlis's exclusive right to install royal abbots was transcribed into Reg. C, fol. 125v, undoubtedly at the request of Guérin after he became bishop of Senlis. *Actes* I, no. 142.

142. See chap. 15, at n. 50.

143. Petit-Dutaillis, *Louis VIII* 335, 336.

144. *Jugements* nos. 1–351.

145. In 1208 he was at the exchequer at Rouen when Nicolas *de Monteigneio* made a bequest to the abbey of Bonport. Delisle, *RHF* XXIV, *275. In 1214 he presided over the famous judgment of Guillaume Painel at Rouen. *Jugements* p. 35. *Registres* I, no. 41.

146. *Actes* III, 1378, and Appendix A.

147. For some examples of arbitrations: *Actes* III, no. 1193, IV, nos. 1733, 1759, 1789, 1822. For inquests: *Registres* I, nos. 41, 42, 46, 70, 71, 78, 95, 96.

148. *Budget* CLVIII (2), CLXIX (1), CLXXIX (2), CCX (2).

149. Ibid. CLI (1), CLXXX (1), CLXXXIII (2).

150. Ibid. CLIII (1), CLV (1). Etienne de Gallardon and Master Nicolas were

his clerks towards the end of his career. See chap. 6, at n. 220, and Pierre Chaplais, *Diplomatic Documents Preserved in the Public Record Office* (London, 1964), 139, 140.

151. *Registres* II, I (I–IV).

152. Delisle, *RHF* XXIV, *274, 275. *RHF* XVIII, 359.

153. Innocent III, *Regesta*, PL 216:618; Potthast I, no. 4530. See chap. 6, at n. 132, and chap. 9, at n. 75.

154. *Monuments historiques* no. 777. Delisle, *Catalogue* p. 520.

155. Anonymous of Béthune, *Chronique des rois* 766. Guillaume le Breton, *Gesta* 267; *Philippidos* 271, 278.

156. Guillaume le Breton, *Gesta* 269–88. *Actes* III, no. 1395.

157. Guillaume le Breton, *Gesta* 319.

158. For example, ibid. 232. *Actes* III, nos. 1360 and 1193 confirmed by Honorius III in Presutti I, no. 552. The cathedral of Soissons claimed him as their special advocate: *in curia domini regis et alibi in negociis nostre ecclesie gratuiter et utiliter pluries laboravit.* Obituary of Soissons, Paris BN Baluze, XLVI, 461.

159. Apparently he replaced the abbot of Saint-Germain-des-Prés in exercising this function. *Actes* IV, no. 1483. In the last years of the reign he was too busy to attend to this service. See chap. 13, at n. 34.

160. See chap. 13, at nn. 31–33.

161. Guillaume le Breton, *Gesta* 256; *Philippidos* 311, 312. Anonymous of Béthune, *Histoire des ducs* 120. The *Chronique des rois* 764 renders the phrase "qui trop ert sire de lui." See chap. 6, at n. 209.

162. The chief study on Haimard remains Léopold Delisle, "Mémoire sur les operations financières de Templiers," *Mémoires de l'Académie des Inscriptions* 33, no. 2 (1889): 61–64.

163. Brussel, *Nouvel Examen* I, 428, note *a*.

164. Appendix A. *Jugements* nos. 109, 134. In 1207 he was one of four arbitrators in a dispute between Jean Palée and Guillaume Escuacol and the abbey of Saint-Denis. Cartulaire blanc de Saint-Denis, AN, LL 1157, p. 542.

165. *Actes* II, no. 844.

166. For example, *Actes* II, nos. 743, 957.

167. Teulet I, nos. 1327, 1333.

168. See chap. 6, n. 154, and at n. 213. Delisle, "Templiers" 99.

169. Delisle, "Templiers" 62, 63. See also Thomas N. Bisson, *Conservation of Coinage* (Oxford, 1979) 164, 165.

170. *Gall. christ.* XIV, 177, 178. Cartellieri III, 90. *RHF* XVIII, 293.

171. Howden III, 254, 257–60. Appendix A.

172. *Actes* II, no. 520, from Diceto II, 139. Cartellieri III, 93, 97, 125. For Anselme's election to Meaux in 1197, see Cartellieri III, 92, n. 1.

173. Another example was Guy de Châlons, a cleric of Saint-Martin, for whose service the king recompensed the church. *Actes* II, no. 781.

174. Richemond, *Seigneurs de Nemours* I, 196–201.

175. *Registres* VI, no. 44.

176. *Budget* CLXXXIX (1). The reference to a disbursement of nine *livres* from the *prévôté* of Anet to *Odo Clemens* probably concerns him as well. Ibid. CXCIV (2).

177. Delisle, *RHF* XXIV, *275.

178. *Jugements* no. 114.

179. On Pierre Charlot, see chap. 9, at n. 62, and chap. 12, at n. 10.

180. *Budget* CLII (2), CLXIX (2).

181. *Actes* III, nos. 1051, 1061.

182. *Actes* III, no. 1337. Delaborde, *Layettes* V, no. 203.

183. See Petit-Dutaillis, *Louis VIII*, 116, 156, 208, 511.

184. Innocent III, *Regesta, PL* 214: 1014, 1015; Potthast I, nos. 1712, 1713.

185. Innocent III, *Regesta*, Vienna ed., I, no. 230; Potthast I, no. 235. Since Guillaume was elected bishop of Nevers in 1202, it is unlikely that he would have been paid in 1203 for a recent trip to Germany.

186. *Actes* II, no. 726.

187. Innocent III, *Regesta, PL* 215:16; Potthast I, no. 1841. See chap. 8, at n. 28.

188. Cartellieri IV, 55. Innocent III, *Regesta, PL* 216:617; Potthast I, no. 4529.

189. Teulet I, no. 1030.

190. Honorius III in Presutti I, no. 524. The same year the pope protested the king's granting Master B, "clerk of King Philip's," a prebend from Amiens that had originally been designated for a cardinal's nephew. Ibid. I, no. 852.

191. Teulet I, nos. 1388, 1389. In November 1224 at Catane, he and Guillaume de Bagneux were *legati regis Francorum* in a treaty between Frederick II and Louis VIII. Reg. E, fol. 168v. *RHF* XVII, 307n. Petit-Dutaillis, *Louis VIII* 263, 264, 474.

192. Teulet I, no. 819.

193. *Budget* CXLIX (2). In the next year he attested contracts of private parties as clerk of the king. Delisle, *RHF* XXIV, *45.

194. *Actes* III, no. 1374.

195. Paul Quesvers, "Notes sur les Cornu, seigneurs de Villeneuve-la-Cornue, la Chapelle-Rablais, et Fontenailles," *Bulletin de la Société d'archéologie . . . de Seine et Marne* (1893): 3–8. Henri Bouvier, *Histoire de l'église et de l'ancien diocèse de Sens* (Paris and Sens, 1911), II, 201, 202.

196. *Actes* IV, no. 1559. *Registres* VI, no. 82.

197. *Ego magister Bouo domini regis clericus custos regalium Belvacensium* (24 March 1220). Cartulary of Beaupré, Paris BN lat. 9973, fol. 98ra. *Magister Bovo custos ecclesie Sancti Quintini* (December 1221). Cartulary A of Saint-Remi de Reims, Arch. dép. Marne, H 1413, fol. 71v.

198. *Actes* III, no. 1089.

199. Teulet I, no. 934.

200. *Rotuli Normanniae*, ed. Thomas Duffus Hardy (London, 1835), I, 29. Cartellieri IV, 47.

201. *Rotuli litterarum patentium*, ed. Thomas Duffus Hardy (London, 1835), I (1), 122.

202. *Registres* VI, no. 77. He was present at the chapter of Laon in 1217. Auguste Bouxin, *Les Prévôtés du chapitre de la cathedrale de Laon au XIIIe siècle* (Laon, 1899), 22. He may also be the "Magister W. de Argent" who recounted to Ralph of Coggeshall a story of Philip Augustus's justice. Coggeshall 200. The following are scattered examples of royal clerics: *Magister Hugo Grandisputeis* (1197), Paris BN fr. 28400, fol. 42; *Ivo de Lauduno clericus* (1208), *Registres* V, no. 4; *Nicholaus clericus noster* (1217–1218), *Actes* IV, no. 1479; *Garinus clericus regis*, *Obituaires de la province de Sens*, ed. A. Molinier (Paris, 1906), II, 389.

203. On Saint-Martin see chap. 12, at nn. 6–10. On Saint-Frambaud: "*Ego Hermerus . . . Beati Frambaldi decanus totumque . . . capitulum notum facimus . . . quod bonie memorie Gauffrido Philippi illustris Francorum regis quondam cappellano et nostre ecclesie thesaurario viam carnis . . . ingresso, Willelemus nepos ejus qui prefato Gaufrido in capellania regia successit . . .*" (1195), Archives de Saint-Frambourg, Collection Afforty, MS Bibl. mun. Senlis, XIV, 889. Also ibid. XI, 7131.

204. *Gall. christ*. X, instru. 449.

205. On the comparison of France and England, see John W. Baldwin, "*Studium et regnum*: The Penetration of University Personnel into French and English Administration at the Turn of the Twelfth and Thirteenth Centuries," *Revue des études islamiques* 44 (1976): 204–6, 210, and "Masters at Paris from 1179 to 1215: A Social Perspective," in *Renaissance and Renewal in the Twelfth Century*, ed. Robert L. Benson and Giles Constable (Cambridge, Mass., 1982), 151–58.

206. The figure of five includes Etienne, elected to Tournai in 1191 (see chap. 4, at n. 42) and Anselme, who was perhaps the dean of Saint-Martin, elected to Meaux in 1197. (See chap. 6, at nn. 170–72, and chap. 8, at n. 5).

207. Howden III, 257–60. Guillaume le Breton, *Gesta* 232. Rigord (165) also records the role of Henri the Marshal in the Poitevin campaign of 1208.

208. *RHF* XVIII, 359.

209. Anonymous of Béthune, *Histoire des ducs* 120; *Chronique des rois* 764.

210. *Recueil des monuments inédits de l'histoire du tiers état*, ed. Augustin Thierry (Paris, 1850), I, 118.

211. Teulet I, no. 815. *Registres* V, nos. 4, 61. The latter charter, which was dated at Paris in March 1216, was based on a charter of Guy de Dampierre from ca. 1213. See chap. 9, n. 34. Cartellieri IV, 395, 396.

212. Guillaume le Breton, *Philippidos* 271, 304.

213. Teulet I, no. 1546. *Actes* IV, no. 1796.

214. For some English examples, see C. Warren Hollister and John W. Baldwin, "The Rise of Administrative Kingship: Henry I and Philip Augustus," *American Historical Review* 83 (1978): 887–90, 904.

215. See chap. 2, at n. 1.

216. See Bournazel, *Le Gouvernement capétien* 129–173 for a discussion of *conseil* in the preceding reigns.

217. Guillaume le Breton, *Gesta* 232, 256. *RHF* XVIII, 359. Anonymous of Béthune, *Histoire des ducs*, 120; *Chronique des rois*, 764.

218. Hollister and Baldwin, "Rise of Administrative Kingship" 890.

219. M. L. Colker, "The 'Karolinus' of Egidius Parisiensis," *Traditio* 29 (1973): 306. *Chronicon Sancti Martini Turonensis* in *RHF* XVIII, 304.

220. Chaplais, *Diplomatic Documents* 139, 140. Guillaume le Breton also observed this habit in Philip. At Bouvines, for example, when Philip changed his battle plans, he only informed a few so as not to alert Otto. *Philippidos* 310.

221. *Actes* I, no. 345.

222. See chap. 7, at n. 94.

223. The operation of the ordinance of 1190 is suggested when Renaud, the second *prévôt* of Orléans, who had abused the cathedral chapter, paid an amend to the church in 1210 in the presence of two *baillis*. Delisle, *RHF* XXIV, *277.

224. Although the term *ballivus* was known in local royal administration before Philip's reign, its appearances were sparse and it was never clearly defined. See the example of 1157 provided by Pacaut, *Louis VII* 177. A. Margry, "Nouvelles recherches sur les origines des grandes baillies royales," *Comité archéologique de Senlis: Comptes rendus et mémoires*, 4th ser., 2 (1897–98): 122–32.

225. *Actes* I, no. 108.

226. For example, *Actes* I, nos. 152, 153 (1185), 215, 216 (1187), 244 (1188), 266 (1189).

227. *Actes* I, nos. 294, 310, 324, 337, 339, 340, 345, 347–50, 352, 361, 362, 366.

228. *Actes* I, nos. 371 (1191), 375 (1191), 385 (1191).

229. For example, *Actes* I, nos. 407 (1192), 408 (1192), 430–38 (1192), 471 (1194), II, nos. 489 (1195), 522 (1196), 574 (1197), etc.

230. For example, *Actes* I, nos. 411 (1192), II, nos. 518 (1196), 541 (1196), 583 (1198), 632 (1200), 636 (1200), V, no. 1847 (1194).

231. Cartulary of Saint-Jean d'Amiens, Amiens Bibl. mun. 781, fol. 34r. On Pierre de Béthisy in general, see Delisle, *RHF* XXIV, *77.

232. Cartulary of Saint-Jean d'Amiens, fol. 28r. *Actes* I, no. 319.

233. Joseph Estienne, "Trois baillis du roi en Vermandois: Pierre de Villevaudé, Pierre de Béthisy, Guillaume Paté (1197–1200)," *BEC* 97 (1936): 87, 89, 90. Cartulary of Prémontré, Soissons Bibl. mun. 7, fol. 99v. *Registres* I, nos. 1 and 17.

234. *Budget* CLXIX (2).

235. *Budget* CLXIX (2), CXCIV (1).

236. *Budget* CLIII (1), CLXXVII (1), CXCIX (1). See the comment on p. 183.

237. Towards the end of the reign, Jean des Vignes, *prévôt* of Senlis, and Jean de Fricamps, *prévôt* of Amiens, also became *baillis*.

238. Every study of *baillis* must rely on the fundamental work of Léopold Delisle, "Chronologie des baillis et des sénéchaux royaux depuis les origines jusqu'à l'avénement de Philippe de Valois," *RHF* XXIV *15–*205, *271–*290. I shall cite only those references I wish to emphasize or those rare cases where I can add to his information. For a list of identified *baillis*, see Appendix B.

239. Delisle, *RHF* XXIV, *49. Ibid. *272. In 1204 Guillaume Menier was also styled "castellan of Etampes." Pierre du Thillai was both *bailli* and assessor of Orléans in 1203. Ibid. *247.

240. Ibid. *44. *Actes* II, no. 689.

241. Delisle, *RHF* XXIV, *116.

242. Eudes de Tremblay and Robert *de Waceo* called themselves *justiciarii domini regis* at the assizes of Mortain in 1211. Ibid. *156, *157. Jean de Rouvray also used the title from 1204 to 1208, as did Garin Tirel (1206), Renaud de Ville-Thierri (1206) and Pierre du Thillai (1209–1215), although the latter two were more frequently known as *baillis*. Ibid. *109, *144, *276, *134.

243. Ibid. *54. Estienne, "Trois baillis du roi en Vermandois," 87.

244. This can be readily seen in the collection of Delisle, *RHF* XXIV.

245. *Actes* I, no. 345.

246. *Actes* I, nos. 385, 426, 471. In 1202 the *bailli* of Sens, Thierry de Corbeil, was still executing the last order. *Budget* CL (2).

247. Delisle, *RHF* XXIV, *84, *86, *89–*91.

248. Here "active" will be defined as appearing more than once.

249. *Actes* II, no. 644.

250. The *bailliage* of Paris appeared as early as 1192. *Actes* I, no. 426.

251. *Budget* CXC (1), CCII (1). *Archives de l' Hôtel-Dieu de Paris*, ed. Léon Brièle (Paris, 1894), 24.

252. Brussel, *Nouvel examen* I, 482–84.

253. Although the *prévôt-baillis* of Paris invariably worked in pairs, fewer names have survived than from any other region. See Appendix B.

254. See Appendix B. Collegiality was probably practiced at other important *prévôtés* such as Orléans, where the farms were large. See, for example, *Actes* II, no. 661.

255. Delisle, *RHF* XXIV *272, *277.

256. Teulet I, nos. 1159, 1161. *Actes* IV, no. 1793.

257. These patterns of collaboration are drawn from the data provided by Delisle, *RHF* XXIV, *53–*59, *76, *77, supplemented by my own findings.

258. *Registres* I, nos. 1 and 8.

259. Delisle, *RHF* XXIV, * 277.

260. *Actes* III, no. 1396. Delisle, *RHF* XXIV, * 118.

261. Delisle, *RHF* XXIV, * 274, * 278.

262. Ibid. * 17, * 45, * 134–* 136.

263. Ibid. * 272, * 124–* 126.

264. Ibid. * 17, * 18, * 146.

265. Ibid. * 17, * 146, * 147. Delisle, *Catalogue* no. 1472.

266. *Rotuli Chartarum*, ed. Thomas Duffus Hardy (London, 1837), 97. See also Powicke, *Loss of Normandy* 172, and Delisle, *RHF* XXIV, * 44.

267. Delisle, *RHF* XXIV, * 110. *Jugements* nos. 109, 162.

268. A.-P. Floquet, *Histoire du privilège de Saint-Romain* (Rouen, 1833), II, 601.

269. Delisle, *RHF* XXIV * 279. *Actes* III, nos. 1388, 1396. *Registres* I, nos. 42 and 43.

270. Joseph R. Strayer, *Administration of Normandy under Saint Louis* (Cambridge, Mass., 1932), 96, 97.

271. Robert de Meulan received 121 *livres*, 5 *sous pro se ipso* (perhaps for the first third of the year) and 240 *livres* (perhaps for the last two-thirds). *Budget* CLXXXII (1) and CLXXXIII (2). Mathieu Pisdoë received 45 *livres* for 60 days and 166 *livres* 10 *sous* for 222 days. Ibid. CXLIX (2) and CC (2). Hugues de Gravelle's wage was specified at 10 *sous* a day. Ibid. CXLIII (2), CLXXI (1), and CXCII (2). See also Audouin, *Essai sur l'armée* 55.

272. Audouin, *Essai sur l'armée* 39. For representative artisan wages, see the account of the *prévôté* of Paris, *Budget* CXLVI (1, 2).

273. *Budget* CLVI (2), CC (2), CLXXVI (2), CXCI (1).

274. They were Pierre de Béthisy (*Prepositus Ambianensis*), Nevelon the Marshal, Guillaume de la Chapelle, and Guillaume Menier. *Registres* II, I (II–IV).

275. Those who were explictly identified as knights were: Guillaume Menier, Adam Héron, Nicolas de Chevanville, Nicolas *Catus*, Guillaume de la Chapelle, Renaud de Béthisy, Guillaume Pastez, Gilles de Versailles, Guillaume de Castelièrs, Renaud de Béron, Jean de Rouvray, Geoffroi de la Chapelle, Renaud de Cornillon, and Renaud de Ville-Thierri. Guillaume de Ville-Thierri and Geoffroi de la Chapelle called themselves "knights of the king." Cartulaire blanc de Saint-Denis, AN, LL 1157, p. 634 and p. 546.

276. *Actes* II, no. 697. (Guillaume was later called a knight; see Delisle, *RHF* XXIV, * 279.) *Actes* III, no. 1075. *Actes* IV, no. 1655. Cartulaire blanc de Saint-Denis, AN, LL 1157, p. 546. (Renaud the Archer was also a royal *échanson*. *Actes* IV, nos. 1462, 1626, 1820.)

277. Among numerous references, *persolvit Soiberto civi Laudunensi baillivo domini regis*. Petit-Cartulaire de l'évêché de Laon, Arch. dép., Aisne, G 1, fol. 29v.

278. *Actes* II, nos. 549, 815.

279. See chap. 6, at n. 231.

280. Delisle, *RHF* XXIV, * 58. At one point Renaud de Béthisy was desig-

nated as *prévôt* of Roye. *Registres* I, no. 89. Similarly Guillaume Pastez was also added to the *prévôts*, but this may have been a confusion with Pierre de Béthisy: *Ego Willelmus Pastes et Petrus Ambianensis et Renaldus de Bestesi prepositi et ballivi domini regis omnibus.* Cartulaire de Prémontré, Bibl. mun. Soissons 7, fol. 99v.

281. Delisle, *RHF* XXIV, *97, *110, *112, *278.

282. Auguste Moutié, "Notes historiques et généalogiques sur les seigneurs de Lévis et leur famille," in *Cartulaire de l'abbaye de Notre-Dame de la Roche* (Paris, 1862), 319–27.

283. Delisle, *RHF* XXIV, *99.

284. *Registres* I, no. 17, which identifies Pierre and Renaud as brothers, also refers to Guy de Béthisy, but without further comment.

285. A. Verhulst and M. Gysseling, *Le Compte général de 1187 connu sous le nom de "Gros Brief," et les institutions financières du comté de Flandre au XII*ᵉ *siècle* (Brussels, 1962), 113, and De Gryse, "Observations on the Origin of the Flemish Bailiff," 256. A *Willelmus Pasted* was a vassal of the bishop of Paris at the turn of the century. B. Guérard, *Cartulaire de Notre-Dame de Paris* (Paris, 1850), I, 9. Delisle, *RHF* XXIV, *57, n. 15.

286. *Actes* I, no. 410. Delisle, *RHF* XXIV, *136, *109.

287. Delisle, *RHF* XXIV, *43, *144, *145.

288. See chap. 6, at n. 95.

289. See chap. 10, at n. 12 for the career of Cadoc, *bailli* of Pont-Audemer.

290. Anonymous of Béthune, *Chronique des rois* 770. Delisle, *RHF* XXIV, *84–*86. Gerald of Wales, *De Jure et statu Menevensis ecclesie*, ed. J. S. Brewer (London, 1863), III, 240.

291. Richer de Sénones, *Gesta Senoniensis ecclesie*, *MGH SS* XXV, 288–90. A shorter version is in Coggeshall 197–99.

292. W. L. Warren, *Henry II* (Berkeley and Los Angeles, 1973), 294–300.

293. The standard work on Flemish *baillis* is Henri Ernest Adolphe Nowé, *Les Baillis comtaux de Flandre: Des origines à la fin du XIV*ᵉ *siècle* (Brussels, 1929), but pp. 17–22 on the early *baillis* should now be reconsidered in the light of De Gryse, "Observations on the Origin of the Flemish Bailiff," 243–94.

294. *Actes* I, no. 287.

7. The Reorganization of Justice and Finance

1. *Actes* I, no. 345.

2. In 1190 Philip also confirmed a charter to the commune of Amiens that provided for holding general pleas (*in placito generali*) by the royal *prévôt* at Christmas, Easter, and Whitsun, an arrangement similar to the royal assizes. *Actes* I, no. 319. Pierre de Béthisy, the royal *prévôt* of Amiens, heard these pleas with the mayor of Amiens at Christmas 1191 and in January 1192. Cartulary of Saint-Jean d'Amiens, Amiens Bibl. mun. 781, fol. 28r, and *Recueil des monuments inédits de l'histoire du tiers état*, ed. Augustin Thierry (Paris, 1850), I, 117.

3. Delisle, *RHF* XXIV, *49, *45, *272. In 1209 those who held assizes at Orléans were still designated as *assissiarii*. *Actes* III, no. 1105.

4. Delisle, *RHF* XXIV, *272.

5. Chauny: 1216 (ibid. *55); Compiègne: 1218 (E. Morel, *Cartulaire de l'abbaye de Saint-Corneille de Compiègne* [Compiègne, 1904], II, 6); Senlis: 1218 (Delisle, *RHF* XXIV, *283), ca. 1220 (ibid. *56), 1212–1220 (*Registres* I, no. 31); Montdidier: 1219 (Delisle, *RHF* XXIV, *284); Clermont: 1219 (ibid. *285); Péronne: 1219 (*Actes* IV, no. 1582); Laon: 1220 (Delisle, *RHF* XXIV, *286); Amiens: 1221 (*Actes* IV, no. 1694).

6. See chap. 10, at nn. 26–28.

7. During Louis VII's absence on the crusade the regent, Abbot Suger, may also have attempted to hold regular pleas exclusively at Paris. See the letter of Pierre, archbishop of Bourges, to Suger in 1148, which supported Renaud de Monfaucon's refusal to answer a summons to court at Paris. *RHF* XV, 703. This system, if instituted, did not survive the king's return to France, as was also the case with that of Philip Augustus.

8. *Actes* I, no. 345.

9. E. Boutaric, *Actes du parlement de Paris* (Paris, 1863), I, ccxcviii.

10. See chap. 6, at nn. 5–9.

11. See chap. 6, at n. 223.

12. *Actes* II, no. 727. See chap. 7, at nn. 34–36, for further details.

13. By the third hearing Ponce had submitted letters that denied jurisdiction to the French king in favor of the king of Aragon. *Actes* II, no. 867. For an earlier example of setting the date, see the case between the duke of Burgundy and the bishop of Langres in 1153. Charles Victor Langlois, *Textes relatifs à l'histoire du parlement* (Paris, 1888), 20.

14. For other examples of assigning times, see: *Actes* III, no. 1256 (1212); IV, nos. 1436 (1216), 1499 (1217); Teulet I, no. 1439 (1221).

15. *Actes* III, nos. 977, 1105.

16. On default of justice, see *Histoire des institutions françaises au moyen âge*, ed. Ferdinand Lot and Robert Fawtier (Paris, 1958), II, 302–14. The procedure was not fully defined until the mid–thirteenth century.

17. *Si vero de judicio faciendo quatuor aut tres concordare nequiverint, ad curiam domini regis discordiam referent, et juxta predicte curie consilium querele sine duello per illos quatuor ad ulmum terminabuntur.* (Saint-Denis, 1200) Cartulaire Blanc de Saint-Denis, AN, LL 1157 pp. 387–88.

18. *Actes* III, no. 1200.

19. *Actes* III, no. 1277.

20. For other examples, see *Registres* VI, no. 68, and *Actes* IV, no. 1570. In 1211 the king refused to hear a dispute between the abbey of la Couture and its men in which the royal seneschal had intervened because of default of justice. *Actes* III, no. 1219.

21. *Actes* I, no. 145. This act has not been noticed by those who have discussed the "*appels volages du Laonnois*."

22. *Registres* I, no. 95. *Histoire des institutions*, ed. Lot and Fawtier, II, 328–29, does not consider this to be, strictly speaking, a default of justice.

23. Maurice Jusselin, "Le Droit d'appel dénommé 'appel volage' et 'appel frivole,'" *BEC* 71 (1910): 527–87, and *Histoire des institutions*, ed. Lot and Fawtier II, 324–31.

24. On Frankish, Norman, Angevin, and Capetian inquests, see the studies of Robert Besnier, "*Inquisitiones* et *Recognitiones*: Le Nouveau Système des preuves à l'époque des Coutumiers normands," *Revue historique de droit français et étranger*, 4th ser., 28 (1950): 183–212; Josèphe Chartrou, *L'Anjou de 1109 à 1151* (Paris, 1928), 132–57; and Yvonne Bongert, *Recherches sur les cours laïques du Xe au XIIIe siècle* (Paris, 1949), 261–76.

25. See Table 2 for the details. The proportions of inquests by decade were 1179–1190: 13 percent; 1191–1203: 17 percent; 1204–1214: 29 percent; 1215–1223: 24 percent. Total for reign: 22 percent.

26. For example, *Actes* II, no. 641 (1200). See also *Actes* II, no. 689 and *Actes* III, no. 1148.

27. For example, *Actes* I, no. 305 (1190). See also *Actes* II, nos. 644 and 744.

28. Delisle, *RHF* XXIV, *277.

29. *Convocatis tam clericis quam burgensibus antiquioribus, ex hiis electi honestiores jurarent quod veritatem dicerent super hiis que viderant.* Teulet I, no. 371.

30. *De inquisitione facienda, et nos eam per legittimos homines terre fieri fecimus. Actes* II, no. 641. *Inquisivit et comperit per juramenta hominum patrie. Actes* II, no. 689.

31. For other inquests of the Norman type held in the *curia regis*, see Cartulary of the Chapter of Evreux, Paris BN n.a.l. 296, fol. 1v; *Actes* III, nos. 1092, 1148; Delisle, *RHF* XXIV, *277; *Actes* III, nos. 1286, 1300, 1359; *Actes* IV, nos. 1659, 1689.

32. *Per assertiones hominum utriusque antiquorum et juratorum terminata et sopita fuit contentio. Actes* I, no. 357. A decision between Philip Augustus and the canons of Sens over justice at Pont-sur-Yonne in 1190 was probably also resolved by a canonical inquest, because the king took testimony from his own sergeants: *Didicimus a servientibus nostris, quorum juramentum ad cognitionem rei recepimus, quod tota justicia. Actes* I, no. 359.

33. *A testibus, scilicet Masticonense et Cabilonense episcopis et Cluniacense et Sancti Petri Cabilonensis abbatibus ex utraque parte evocatis rei veritatem duximus inquirendam.* Boutaric, *Actes du parlement* I, ccxcviii.

34. *Actes* II, no. 727. See Appendix A for the participating judges. See chap. 3, at n. 72, and chap. 7, at nn. 125–26, for the ecclesiastical implications of the decision.

35. Hence the presence among the *litterati* of a certain Lothair of Cremona, who was probably an Italian Roman lawyer.

36. *Registres* I, no. 4.

37. For other inquests of the canonical type held in the *curia regis*, see *Actes* III, no. 1163, IV, nos. 1415, 1465.

38. *Actes* IV, no. 1445.

39. The first extant case (1200) called upon the *prévôts* of Paris. *Archives de l' Hôtel-Dieu de Paris (1157–1300)*, ed. Léon Brièle (Paris, 1894), 24. See also *Actes* II, no. 689, III, no. 967; Delisle, *RHF* XXIV, *277, *278; *Actes* III, nos. 1286, 1300, 1370; IV, nos. 1415, 1500, 1506, 1591; Delisle, *RHF* XXIV, *282, *287.

40. *Actes* I, nos. 357, 359, 443; II, no. 727; Teulet I, nos. 371, 1439.

41. Abbot Suger's regency during Louis VII's absence on the crusade may also have generated an accounting bureau. See Raoul de Vermandois's letter to Suger of 1149 in which royal sergeants were summoned *ad computandum. RHF* XV, 517. But there is no evidence of this procedure surviving after Louis's return.

42. *Quod de reddititbus nostris non ibunt extra Compendium. Actes* I, no. 168.

43. Nor have the restorations made by Gautier the Young survived. See chap. 3, at n. 106.

44. *Actes* I, no. 345.

45. For a description of these accounts see chap. 15, at nn. 28, 29, and 31.

46. In the ordinance of 1190, the first term was set at Saint Remy (1 October), but by 1202 it had been moved forward to All Saints', where it remained throughout the thirteenth century.

47. Poissy, Meulan, Dordan, and Dun, for example, accounted twice a year; Mantes once a year. For a general discussion of the different terms that may be found throughout the accounts, see *Budget* 5–10.

48. In the November and February terms, the *Marchie* accounts are actually called *Ballivie*, which is an evident error, because they are of the same nature as the *Marchie* account of May 1203. *Budget* CLVII (2), CLXXXIV (1), and CCIV (1).

49. *Budget* CXLVIII (1).

50. See chap. 7, at nn. 154 and 188–95.

51. See, for example, the accounts of 1234 and 1248, *RHF* XXII, 566–67, and XXI, 261–63.

52. *Budget* CXLVI (1), CLXXIV (1), and CLXXXIX (1). The following discussion of the *prévôt* of Paris's account represents a composite of these three terms.

53. See chap. 3, at nn. 41–46.

54. Twenty-two out of forty-four *prévôtés*. The *prévôté* of Bapaume and Péronne was also included in the *baillis'* chapters for no apparent reason.

55. See the tabulations in *Budget* and Appendices.

56. *Budget* CLV (2), CLXXXII (1), CCI (2).

57. See, for example, the Evreux account. *Budget* CXCVI (1).

58. These transfers were normally indicated by listing identical sums and proper names in both the receipts and the expenditures. In February 1203, for example, Robert de Meulan received money from nine persons, three of whom reappear among the expenses. Another striking example occurs in the account of

Renaud de Béthisy, who received sums from thirty-four individuals, twenty-six of which were charged in the expenditures. *Budget* CLXXVII (2). In these instances the *baillis*' accounts served merely to transfer funds.

59. On the Norman exchequer, see Charles H. Haskins, *Norman Institutions* (Cambridge, Mass., 1918), 174–78. The Norman rolls have been edited by Thomas Stapleton in *Magni rotuli scaccarii Normannie sub regibus Anglie* (London, 1840–44), 2 vols. The *Gros Brief* was edited by A. Verhulst and M. Gysseling, *Le Compte général de 1187, connu sous le nom de "Gros Brief," et les institutions financières du comté de Flandre au XII* siècle (Brussels, 1962). A comprehensive discussion of Flemish financial institutions is contained in Bryce Lyon and A. E. Verhulst, *Medieval Finance: A Comparison of Financial Institutions in Northwestern Europe* (Providence, R.I., 1967), 12–40. On Barcelona, see Thomas N. Bisson, *Fiscal Accounts of Catalonia* (Berkeley and Los Angeles, 1985).

60. Verhulst and Gysseling, *Compte général* 159, 160, to be compared with *Budget* CLII (2), CLXXVI (2), CXCVIII (2). In 1202/03 Bapaume was joined with Péronne, and for reasons that elude us was placed in the *baillis*' chapters for the three terms of November, February, and May. The editors (*Budget* 175) explain that the *prévôt* arrived too late for it to be included in the *prévôts*' chapter, but this would not explain why it remained in the *baillis*' chapter. Despite its position, it was actually a *prévôt*'s account, because it was listed by the place-name of the *prévôté* and not by the personal name of a *bailli*. More important, all three accounts report the farm and list the expenses characteristic of *prévôtés*.

61. *Magni rotuli*, ed. Stapleton II, 462–63, clxx–clxxii, to be compared with *Budget* CLXXIII (2), CLXXX (2), CXCIV (1), and CXCVI (1). See also the summary of the Norman account for military purposes in Powicke, *Loss of Normandy* 206–8.

62. Guillaume Pastez is noted as receiving a robe. *Budget* CLXXVI (2). Concerning him and Pierre de Béthisy, see chap. 6, at n. 257.

63. Neither *prévôts*' account mentions Nicolas Harchepin, but his name is suggested in the *baillis*' accounts. *Budget* CLXXX (2) and CXCVI (1). In 1202 Philip Augustus gave Richard d'Argences the fief of Brétignolles. *Actes* II, no. 734.

64. Evreux in 1198: 560 *livres angevins* = 384 *livres parisis*; Evreux in 1202/03: 900 *livres parisis*; Bapaume-Péronne in 1202/03: 3,636 *livres parisis*.

65. Seventeen churches in all received alms, some of which were in Péronne. They were also listed in the alms accounts. *Registres* II, C. For correlations between the *Gros Brief*, the accounts of 1202/03, and charter evidence, see chap. 8, at n. 51.

66. See also *Registres* II, C for a list in the alms account.

67. Ibid. II, H.

68. For examples of *fief-rentes*, compare *Magni rotuli*, ed. Stapleton II, 462, with *Budget* CLXXIV (1). For examples of grain supplies, compare *Magni rotuli*, ed. Stapleton II, 464, with *Budget* CLXXX (2).

69. *Magni rotuli*, ed. Stapleton II, 463. According to Richard fitz Nigel, it was standard procedure at the English exchequer for the sheriff to produce writs at each session, where they were verified and collected by the chancellor's clerk and duly noted on the Pipe Roll. *The Course of the Exchequer by Richard, son of Nigel*, ed. Charles Johnson (London, 1950), 32–34.

70. Only three mentions of royal letters appear in the *Budget*: CLXIV (1), CCV (2), and CLXVII (1). See the observation of Borelli de Serres, *Recherches* I, 17, 18. The ordinance of 1190 decreed that treasure was to be dispatched to the king in the east on the command of royal letters. *Actes* I, no. 345. For examples of such kinds of letters, see *Actes* II, nos. 870, 883. For another difference between the Norman and Capetian fiscal regimes, see the comparison of procedures for accounting fixed alms, chap. 8, at nn. 55–56.

71. The triannual payments were demonstrated by Lyon and Verhulst, *Medieval Finance* 38, in contradiction to Verhulst and Gysseling, *Compte général* 58–60.

72. Evreux is missing in both the *baillis'* and *prévôts'* chapters of the November 1202 term, but the *prévôt's* account of the February 1203 term speaks of the farm as *de secondo tertio*, and the *bailli's* account of February 1203 refers to revenues of justice accounted before and after the previous November. Both of these indications suggest that three terms were expected in the Evreux account.

73. For the anomalous position of the Bapaume account in the *baillis'* chapters, see chap. 7, n. 60. It also included a few items that were appropriate for the *bailli's* chapter.

74. *Course of the Exchequer* 29, 84–92.

75. These matters occupy the entire treatise. *Course of the Exchequer*, passim.

76. Lyon and Verhulst, *Medieval Finance* 39, 40.

77. *Actes* I, no. 345.

78. For Haimard's and Guérin's activities, see chap. 6, at nn. 128–69.

79. Edited in *Budget*. In their introduction to the edition, Ferdinand Lot and Robert Fawtier have performed two important services. They have subjected the entire account to a new audit, in which they have verified and corrected the figures, and have also categorized and totalled the receipts and expenditures throughout the account. I have availed myself of such of their computations as served my purposes and have relied on their figures except in the instances noted.

80. Reginald Lane Poole, *The Exchequer in the Twelfth Century* (Oxford, 1912), 3. James H. Ramsay, *A History of the Revenues of the Kings of England* (Oxford, 1925), I, 184. H. G. Richardson and G. O. Sayles, *The Governance of Mediaeval England* (Edinburgh, 1963), 261–65, 297ff.

81. This appears to have been the goal of accounting since antiquity. C. E. M. de Ste. Croix, "Greek and Roman Accounting," in *Studies in the History of Accounting*, ed. A. C. Littleton and B. S. Yamey (Homewood, Ill., 1956), 38.

82. Lot and Fawtier, *Budget* 51–53, argue that the account is complete in its

coverage of the domain, but they do not consider whether it includes "extraordinary" revenues such as large feudal reliefs.

83. Lot and Fawtier furnish these calculations: *prévôts*, 34,014; sergeants, 26,453; *baillis*, 83,301; marches, 67,998; yielding a total of 211,766 *livres*. Ibid. 32. These totals differ slightly from those on p. 26.

84. Ibid. 28–53, in which Lot and Fawtier reaudit the account for duplications and balances carried over.

85. Ibid. 25, 27. See chap. 7, at n. 92.

86. Revenue "that has been utilized": *prévôts*, 31,061; *baillis*, 64,996; marches (actual income), 8,671; yielding a total ordinary income of 104,728 *livres*. When the sergeants' 26,453 *livres* are added, the total annual income accounted amounts to 131,181 *livres*. Ibid. 48. Although an improvement over the crude figures, these adjusted figures for the royal income "that has been utilized" are also approximations. As long as the May 1202 account is lacking, we cannot be certain about the receipts of November 1202.

87. Ibid. 49–51. Lot and Fawtier have reduced these figures with two further refinements, whose results are, however, negligible. The sum of 8,671 *livres* for the marches is too low because it neglects revenues collected in kind.

88. 29,117 (farms)/31,781 (*prévôts'* receipts) = 92 percent. Ibid. 11.

89. Ibid. 12, 13. See chap. 7, n. 54.

90. See chap. 5, at n. 66.

91. The *baillis'* accounts do, however, report income from the regalia of bishoprics. See chap. 7, at nn. 124–31.

92. *Budget* CLVII (2), CLXI (1), CLXXXIV (1), CLXXXVII (1), CCV (2), 25, 27. On the conquest of these territories, see chap. 7, at nn. 153–54.

93. See chap. 3, at nn. 92–94, and chap. 5, at n. 78.

94. The total of sixty-two *prévôtés* is made up of the fifty-eight recorded in the *prévôts'* chapters and four that appear in the *baillis'* chapters (see *Budget* 76, 77 for the latter). The number of *prévôts* is derived from the number of accounts, with the understanding that more than one *prévôt* could have accounted for the larger *prévôtés*. The figure 33,164 *livres* consists of 29,117 accounted in the *prévôts'* chapters, plus 3,636 for Bapaume and 411 for minor *prévôtés*, which for unexplained reasons were placed in the *baillis'* chapters. *Budget* 7–11, 76, 77. The slight difference between the *prévôts'* farms (29,117 *livres*) and the *prévôts'* receipts (31,781 *livres*, see Table 3) is accounted for by the minor revenues the *prévôts* also received in addition to their farms.

95. Athies and Clary were included with Péronne-Bapaume in 1202 (*Budget* CLIII [1]), but Cappy's inclusion is only conjectural. Boucly was given to the castellan of Péronne in 1210. See chap. 7, at n. 97.

96. The price of grain is calculated from the sales recorded in May 1203 at Bapaume (*Budget* CXCVIII [2]): 1 *muid* of wheat = 4.47 *livres* (the most advantageous of two prices) and 1 *muid* of oats = 2.78 *livres*. The data summarized in Table A are drawn from *Registres* II, H.

TABLE A. Estimation of the Farm of Péronne–Bapaume

	Livres	Wheat	Oats
Bapaume	1,600	50	10
Péronne	52	141	3
Athies	87	100	10
Boucly	11	84	19
Clary	61	15	13
Cappy	2	14	4
Totals	1,813	404	59
		× 4.47 *livres*	× 2.78 *livres*
	1,813 *livres* +	1,805 *livres* +	164 *livres* = 3,782 *livres*

NOTE: These estimates do not include 1,529 chickens and 44¼ *mancaldi* of uncultivated land.

TABLE B. Revenue of Bapaume and Hesdin
in 1187 and 1206–1210

	Livres	Wheat	Oats
BAPAUME			
Gros Brief (1187)	120	118	49
Census (1206–1210)	1,600	50	10
HESDIN			
Gros Brief (1187)	639	60	69
Census (1206–1210)	498	25	22

97. *Actes* III, no. 1128, Teulet I, no. 924. *Registres* II, H. The rent consisted of 120 *livres* plus two former rents of 2 *livres* each. The revenues may be estimated as 84 *muids* of wheat × 4.47 = 375; 19 *muids* of oats × 2.78 = 53; revenue received in *livres* = 11. Total: 439 *livres*.

98. *Registres* II, H. Verhulst and Gysseling, *Compte général* 159, 160, 164, 165. The totals of Bapaume and Hesdin may be compared as shown in Table B. The higher numerical income at Bapaume in the *Census* is due to the inclusion of the tolls of Bapaume (1,400 *livres*), which were excluded in the *Gros Brief*. On the strength of royal money as opposed to the local currencies in Artois and Vermandois, see Thomas N. Bisson, *Conservation of Coinage* (Oxford, 1979), 144–56.

99. See chap. 8, at nn. 49–51.

100. For produce not converted to money, see *Budget* CLX (2), CLXI (2), and CLXXXVII (2).

TABLE C. *Gîte* Collected in 1202/03

	Budget (ref.)	Actes (nos.)	Livres
IDENTIFIED AS *GÎTE* IN THE ACCOUNTS			
Laon (commune)	CXLV (1)	I, 279	200
Noyon (commune)	CXLIV (1)	I, 406	160
Abbot of Ferrières	CLXXXI (2)		43
IDENTIFIED AS *GÎTE* FROM CHARTERS			
Les Bruyères	CL (2)	I, 471	20
Saint-Julien-du-Sault	CL (2)	I, 439	5
Abbess of Chelles	CLXXX (1)	I, 272	9
Montdidier (commune)	CXLIV (1), CLXX (1), CXCII (2)	II, 495	600
POSSIBLE IDENTIFICATIONS FROM *GÎTE* LIST			
Fresnoy	CXCVII (2)		125
Larchant	CLIV (1)		13
Blandy	CLI (1)		40
Total			1,215

101. The total of 10,353 *livres* is made up as follows: *baillis*, 2,510; *tensamenta*, 211; *prévôts*, 174; marches, 7,458 (8,671 minus 1,212 for *expleta*, or justice). *Budget* 13, 25, 27, 54, 55, 72.

102. For *gîte*, see chap. 3, at nn. 51–59, and Table C.

103. *Baillis*, 7,282 *livres*; *prévôts*, 150. *Budget* 13, 14, 55–57. The *prévôts'* sum includes 120 *livres* collected by Jean Minctoire from the forest of Orléans. *Budget* CLXVIII (2), CXC (1).

104. I prefer to interpret *de bosco de Loia* as Saint-Germain-en-Laye rather than Lognes. In the forest account of Reg. A (*Registres* II, M, no. 6) it was designated as *foresta Laie*.

105. *Course of the Exchequer* 30, 31, 103, 104.

106. On the *taille*, see Carl Stephenson, "The Origin and Nature of the 'Taille,'" *Revue belge de philologie et d'histoire* 5 (1926): 801–70, and "Les Aides de villes françaises au XIIᵉ et XIIIᵉ siècles," *Le Moyen Age*, 2nd ser., 24 (1922): 274–328, translated and reprinted in *Medieval Institutions: Selected Essays*, ed. Bryce D. Lyon (Ithaca, N.Y., 1954), 1–103. Theodore Evergates, *Feudal Society in the Bailliage of Troyes under the Counts of Champagne* (Baltimore, 1975), 16–30, confirms this picture for Champagne.

107. *Budget* 60, 61. This figure excludes 450 *livres* from the *taille* of bread and wine at Orléans, which will be accounted for separately. See chap. 7, at n. 117.

108. Brussel, *Nouvel examen* I, 528, 529.

109. In 1200 Philip regulated the method of assessment of the *taille* by the officials of Bapaume. *Actes* II, no. 638. It produced 200 *livres* in 1202/03. *Budget* CXCIX (1).

110. *Actes* III, no. 1148 and *Registres* I, no. 52.

111. *Budget* CXLV (1), CL (2). In February 1218 Thierry de Corbeil again received a payment. *De burgensibus Altisiodori C libros*. Brussel, *Nouvel examen* I, 514.

112. *Budget* CLXXX (1), CLXXIX (2).

113. *Budget* 61–63. The figure is 200 *livres* less than that of the *Budget* 63, because the *taille* of Bapaume has been repeated here.

114. *Actes* II, no. 657. *Budget* CLIV (1). The Easter payment does not appear in the accounts.

115. This total is made up as follows: 150 (*Budget* 72) + 84 (ibid. 76) + 12 (= 20 *livres* Gien, ibid. CLXXXI [2]).

116. William M. Newman, *Le Domaine royal sous les premiers Capétiens* (Paris, 1937), 27. *Budget* 72. *Actes* II, nos. 710, 711.

117. *Budget* CL (1), CLXXXIX (1), CLXXIV (1). See Bisson, *Conservation of Coinage* 29–44, on the Capetian money taxes.

118. *Budget* CXCVII (2), CCIII (1). Linking *fraagium* with *foagium* was the conjecture of Charles DuCange, followed by Lot and Fawtier, ibid. 71. The definitive study of the Norman *fouage* is now Bisson, *Conservation of Coinage* 14–28. On Philip's later profit from this money tax, see chap. 10, at n. 99.

119. Rigord I, 141. On Philip's earlier policies, see chap. 3, at nn. 77–81.

120. Teulet I, no. 479. *Actes* II, nos. 582, 583. The agreement was renewed with the Countess Blanche in 1203 (*Actes* II, no. 776), but an exception was permitted to the Jew Cresselin to lend in the royal domain.

121. *Budget* 59, 171. For the royal seal of the Jews at Pontoise, see Brigitte Bedos, "Les Sceaux," *Art et archéologie des juifs en France médiévale*, ed. B. Blumenkranz (Toulouse, 1980), 218. A Robert de Baan' was *prévôt* of the Jews at Pontoise in 1204. Cartulaire blanc de Saint-Denis, AN, LL 1157, p. 594. See also Robert Chazan, *Medieval Jewry in Northern France* (Baltimore, 1973), 90.

122. *Prévôts*, 26 *livres*; *baillis* 1,224. *Budget* 13, 58. This total included 466 *livres*, which, for some unexplained reason, were still collected from the Champenois Jews, and sums of 60 and 40 *livres* from named Jews, which were probably loans. Brussel, *Nouvel examen* I, 581, arrives at a total of 1,200 *livres* for income from Jews in 1202/03.

123. Only one abbey (the priory of Charité) paid a figure as high as 200 marks (420 *livres*). All others paid 200 *livres* or under. *Budget* 65, 66. These small sums make it difficult to believe that regalia from the royal abbeys were being paid here.

124. See Appendix C. Two other bishoprics that may have been vacant in 1202/03 were Nevers and Evreux. Gautier, bishop of Nevers, died on 11 January 1202. He was eventually succeeded by Master Guillaume de Saint-Lazare, the royal cleric. *Gall. christ.* XII, 641, 642. Pope Innocent III addressed letters to the bishop of Nevers dated 16 March 1202, 1 December 1202, and 3 January 1203 (Innocent III, *Regesta, PL* 214: 961, 1137, 1154; Potthast I, nos. 1637, 1783, 1808), but whether these were intended for Guillaume is not clear. Since the vacancy does not appear in the accounts of 1202/03, it was probably short. Neither is the situation clear at Evreux. Guérin, bishop of Evreux, died on 14 August 1201 and was succeeded by Robert de Roye, who died in 1203. He in turn was followed by Luc, who was consecrated by 16 February 1203. This quick succession of bishops between 1201 and 1203 did not permit long vacancies. *Gall. christ.* XI, 581, 582. Moreover, when Philip acquired the bishopric in 1200, he granted it freedom of elections as an example to the other Norman sees. *Actes* II, no. 637. It is not likely that he would have demanded heavy regalian exactions so soon thereafter. See chap. 8, at nn. 20–23.

125. Innocent III, *Regesta, PL* 214:976; Potthast I, no. 1666. Alberic de Trois-Fontaines 882.

126. *Registres* I, no. 4. *Actes* II, no. 727. The *vidame* was also fined for his despoiling of the deceased bishop's goods. *Actes* II, no. 726. See chap. 3, at n. 72. *Budget* CLII (1), 64.

127. For the disputed election, see chap. 8, at nn. 28–29. Guy de Béthisy appears to have been responsible for this account. It was recorded immediately preceding his own account and he assumed the balance in May 1203. *Budget* CLXXVIII (2), 64, 187. Relying on the figures of p. 187, I count only the net, not the gross profit as do Lot and Fawtier. Actually there are twenty weeks between 7 September 1202 and 2 February 1203.

128. *Budget* CLXXIX (1), 64. The designation *de Conilla et de Rione* is not clear.

129. *Budget* CLXXX (1), 64.

130. Extrapolating from the figure of 2,620 *livres* for the first twenty weeks (or 131 *livres* per week) over a year and ten months (or ninety-two weeks) gives 12,052 *livres*.

131. See chap. 3, at nn. 68–73 and chap. 8, at nn. 18–19.

132. *Actes* I, no. 345. *Budget* CLXXIX (2), CXCIX (1).

133. Made up as follows: 5,142 (*expleta*) + 168 (murders, "mellays," etc.) + 70 (charters, seals) + 1,213 (judicial revenues in the marches) + 194 (*senescalcia*) + 20 (judicial revenues in the *prévôtés*). *Budget* 12, 13, 27, 57, 58, 70, 76.

134. Cartulaire blanc de Saint-Denis, AN 1157, pp. 387–89. *Budget* CLVI (1), carried over to February 1202, CLXXXII (1).

135. *Budget* CLV (2). *Actes* II, no. 720.

136. *Actes* II, no. 753. *Budget* CL (1). Jean de Santilly's payment (53 *livres*) also included that of the mayoress of Ruan and the mayor of Tillai. In another example, the *bailli* Renaud de Béthisy received 100 *livres* from a place called

Rully, probably a proffer for a royal charter of franchises granted to the men of this place. *Budget* CLXXVII (2), CLXXVIII (1). *Actes* II, no. 728.

137. *Baillis*, 11,327 *livres*; *prévôts*, 306. This figure consists of adding the totals of cathedral chapters, abbeys, and feudal aids computed by Lot and Fawtier. *Budget* 13, 64–70.

138. *Baillis*, 750; *prévôts*, 20. *Budget* 13, 59. *Registres* III, M.

139. *Prévôts*, 604; *baillis*, 433. *Budget* 13, 60.

140. *Budget* CLXXVII (1), CXCIX (1).

141. *Budget* CLIV (2), CLII (1).

142. Lot and Fawtier, *Budget*, 66–71, consider all sums contributed by lay personages to be "feudal aids." Since it excludes churches and includes revenues from justice, loans, and other income, this category is of little use.

143. These figures are drawn from *Budget* 72–79. A number of items that Lot and Fawtier discuss here I have included elsewhere. I have indicated where I have changed their figures.

144. Guillaume Poucin's 100 *livres de prestito* should be changed to 1,000 *livres*. *Budget* 73.

145. *Baillis*, 1,034; *prévôts*, 7. *Budget* 13, 73.

146. See chap. 7, at nn. 55–58, and the discussion of Lot and Fawtier in *Budget* 83–129.

147. *Budget* 101–10, 117–21.

148. *Budget* CLXXVI (1), CXLV (2), and CLXIX (2).

149. *Budget* CLVI (1), CLXXXIII (1), CC (2). In the *prévôts'* chapters, the household of Prince Louis received 1,840 *livres* and the children of Poissy 10 *livres*. Ibid. 110, 111. But neither of these sums pertain to the central court.

150. Borelli de Serres, *Recherches* I, 183. *Budget* 131–33.

151. *Budget* 129. Appendix A.

152. The figure of 77,000 *livres* is calculated as follows: 31,781 (*prévôts'* receipts) + 74,684 (*baillis'* receipts) − 29,500 (*prévôts'* and *baillis'* expenses) = 76,965. I have not included the domanial revenues collected by the marches' treasurers (8,671) in the calculations because they were already designated for the war.

153. Cartellieri IV, 116–24, 126, 141, 146, 147, 152. Powicke, *Loss of Normandy* 148–60.

154. *Budget* CLVII (2), CLXXXIV (1), and CCIV (2). In the first terms these two chapters are called *ballivie*. Only in May 1203 are they entitled *marchie*.

155. *Budget* CLXI (1) to CLXXII (2).

156. Ibid. CLXVI (2), CLXXVII (2).

157. *Actes* II, no. 501. *Budget* CLXV (2), CCVII (2).

158. *Budget* CCV (1). Cartellieri IV, 132, n. 6, argues that the *comes Robertus* is Count Robert of Dreux.

159. For example, in November 1202, ten mounted sergeants were kept at Gaillefontaine and twenty-one were moved to Ferté. *Budget* CLIX (2).

160. For the statistics of the marches' accounts see Audouin, *Essai sur l'armée*

116, 117. These figures are based on Audouin's computations of the average number of troops during the year. Vernon, Evreux, Pacy, Le Goulet, and Grossoeuvre contained 117 knights and 598 foot-sergeants as compared with 67 knights and 302 foot-sergeants in Gisors, Neufmarché, Longchamps, and Lyons-la-Forêt.

161. *Budget* CLXVI (1), CLXXXVI (2).

162. Statistics furnished by Audouin, *Essai sur l'armée* 84–91.

163. Ibid. 40–50.

164. In November 1202 a payment was recorded for a wagon destined for Tours. *Budget* CLXVIII (1). This is the only explicit reference to travel to the Loire valley.

165. These figures are based on Audouin's totals of the average number of troops stationed at the different castles. From them I have deducted the footmen stationed at Sens, Bray, and Montereau included in Audouin's totals and have added his estimate of foot-sergeants for Driencourt, Pacy, and Grossoeuvre. Audouin, *Essai sur l'armée* 116–18.

166. See ibid. 98–109.

167. *Budget* CCV (1). Audouin, *Essai sur l'armée* 111, 112. The romance of Eustache le Moine asserts that Cadoc had 300 sergeants, which, according to Audouin, is a reasonable figure. In all events, Guillaume le Breton's figure of 1,000 *livres* a day clearly seems an exaggeration. *Philippidos* 192.

168. Howden IV, 40. On this well-known scheme and its failure see A. L. Poole, *From Domesday to Magna Carta* (London, 1951), 370, 371.

169. In November Guillaume spent 832 livres for Gaillefontaine, 800 for Gournay, and 721 for Ferté. *Budget* CLIX (1). For other examples, see CLXXXV (2) and CCVI (2).

170. *Budget* CLX (2) and CCVII (1).

171. *Budget* CLXVI (2). See the similar outlays by the castellan of Vernon, ibid. CLXXXVI (1), and the castellan of Lyons-la-Fôret, ibid. CLXXXVII (2).

172. Only in November 1202 does the *prévôt* of Vernon pay for the transport of money and crossbow bolts. Ibid. CLXVI (1).

173. *Registres* II, P. This inventory lists those castles acquired between 1200 and the campaign of the summer of 1202, with Mortemer, acquired at that time, added in a second hand.

174. From the statistics assembled by Audouin, *Essai sur l'armée* 51, 63, 74, 81, 92, 93 and summarized on 113, 114.

175. In 1203 the Norman *bailli* Richard de Fontenay paid 72 *d. angevins* to knights, 24 *d.* to mounted sergeants, and 8 *d.* to foot-sergeants in the west of Normandy. (The *livre angevin* = .68–.71 *livre parisis*.) *Magni rotuli*, ed. Stapleton, II, 547, 548. For additional information on wages paid by the English in Normandy, see Audouin, *Essai sur l'armée*. See note 174 above.

176. These totals are based on Audouin, *Essai sur l'armée* 118, but with the expenses of Sens, Bray, and Montereau deducted at the exchange rate between Paris and Provins currency. Ibid. 80, 81, 92, 93. The outlay of 27,370 *livres* did not support the estimated force of 2,282 men (see chap. 7, at n. 165) for an

entire year of 365 days. At the normal wages (see chap. 7, at n. 174) this would have cost 68,144 *livres*. Computed differently, the assignment of 9,512 *livres* for knights would have maintained 257 knights for only 123 days at the normal rate, or 10,092 *livres* would have supported 1,608 sergeants for only 188 days.

177. *Budget* 128.

178. *Budget* 129.

179. Rigord 105. That the Louvre was completed by 1202 is suggested by the mention that the tower of Dun was to be made according to the measurements of the tower of Paris. See chap. 11, at n. 204, and Jean Vallery-Radot, "Quelques donjons de Philippe Auguste," *Bulletin de la Société des Antiquaires de France* (1964), 159. The completion of the walls on the left bank of Paris cost 7,020 *livres* in the first decade of the thirteenth century. See chap. 11, at n. 196.

180. *Budget* CLIII (2). In addition, Abelin paid 193 *livres* for the fortifications of Issoudun.

181. *Budget* 22–27. See chap. 7, at n. 85.

182. For example: *Budget* CLXXVI (1) (see CLXXX [2]); CLXXXVII (1) (see CLXXVI [1]); CCVII (2) (see CXCI [2]); and CCVIII (1) (see CXCVI [1]).

183. For some examples: Chaumont: *Budget* CLXI (1); Vernon: CLXVII (1); Guérin: CLVIII (2). Guérin appears at least eleven times in the marches' accounts. For his receipts from the *baillis'* chapters see appendix A in ibid.

184. For some examples: Chaumont: *Budget* CCIV (2); Gautier: CLVIII (2); Robert: CLXXXIV (1, 2), CCX (1).

185. See chap. 7, at n. 152, for the treasury balance.

186. See chap. 7, at nn. 90–91. Comparable sums do not appear in the accounts of 1202/03, but we do not know whether any were forthcoming that year. In May 1238 the relief of the count of Flanders was accounted separately from the ordinary revenues. See chap. 10, at n. 107.

187. Rigord 147. Coggeshall 112. For Philip's effectiveness in despoiling the bishoprics of Auxerre and Orléans at a later date, see chap. 3, at n. 74, and chap. 12, at n. 26.

188. For the communes' limited military contributions between 1179 and 1190, see chap. 4, at nn. 28–29. In the subsequent period broader obligations were imposed on Saint-Quentin 1195, (*Actes* II, no. 491); Henin-Liétard 1196, (II, no. 529); Wacquemoulin 1196, (II, no. 530); Crandelain et al. 1196, (II, no. 532) Roye 1196, (II, nos. 539, 540); Etampes 1199–1200, (II, no. 616); Fillièvres 1205, (II, no. 893); Bray-sur-Somme 1210, (III, no. 1117); Athies 1211–1212, (III, no. 1212); Crépy-en-Valois 1215, (III, no. 1389); Caen 1220, (IV, no. 1665); Falaise 1221, (IV, no. 1693); Doullens 1221–1222, (IV, no. 1755); Poitiers 1222, (IV, no. 1803); Beaumont-sur-Oise 1223, (IV, no. 1811); and Chambly 1223, (IV, no. 1812). A few retained the limitation to local warfare: Villeneuve–Saint-Melon 1196, (II, no. 531); Dizy 1196–1197, (II, no. 545); Cléry 1201–1202, (II, no. 691); and Saint-Germain des Bois 1202, (II, no. 716).

189. *Registres* II, R. The *prisée des sergents* has been studied intensively by

Borrelli de Serres, *Recherches* I, 467–527, Audouin, *Essai sur l'armée* 7–34, and Lot and Fawtier, *Budget* 15–20. My conclusions are based on these studies.

190. Rigord 129.

191. Audouin, *Essai sur l'armée* 19–28. He estimates that the income of 26,453 *livres* represented the equivalent of 8,055 sergeants and 170 wagons.

192. If the assessments of 1194 are converted into money (at the rates of 1202), the *prisée* was worth 36,776 *livres* as compared with the 26,453 *livres* accounted in 1202. Ibid. 11. The figure 36,776 *livres* is arrived at by adding: 16,463 *livres* (cash) + (3 *livres* × 6,195 sergeants =) 18,585 *livres* + (13.5 *livres* × 128 wagons =) 1,728 *livres*. These figures credit Arras and Beauvais with money and not with sergeants.

193. The total of 1,037 *livres* is computed from items specifically designated as for sergeants: 604 (*prévôts*) + 433 (*baillis*). See *Budget* 19, 13, 60. By comparing the *Prisia* of 1194 with individual items in the *baillis'* and *prévôts'* chapters, Lot and Fawtier claim to have raised the total of the tax to 41,077 *livres*, but most of their additions are speculative. Ibid. 15–20.

194. Audouin, *Essai sur l'armée* 29–31.

195. See Table 6.

196. *Course of the Exchequer* 52.

8. The Blessings of Ecclesiastical Liberties

1. See chap. 4, at nn. 30–31 and at n. 39.

2. For the case of Tournai, see chap. 4, at n. 42. The most abundant source of information about disputed elections comes from the papal registers, which commenced at the accession of Innocent III in 1198. See chap. 8, at n. 26.

3. *Actes* I, nos. 457, 464. Of the some twenty-five disputed monastic elections in France that appear in the papal registers from 1198 to 1223, none gives hint of royal interference.

4. See Appendix C.

5. For the Garlandes, see chap. 6, at nn. 113–19; for Etienne of Tournai and Anselme of Meaux, see chap. 4, at n. 42, and chap. 6, at nn. 170–74.

6. Robert d'Auxerre 272. Alberic de Trois-Fontaines 887. The other candidates suggested to regalian sees by Eudes de Sully were Geoffroi to Tours (1206), Master Hervé to Troyes (1207), Master Alberic to Reims (1208), and Haimard to Soissons (1208).

7. These included Reims, Beauvais, Chartres, and Châlons-sur-Marne, who were related to the king, and Noyon, related to Gautier the Chamberlain. See Appendix C.

8. Teulet I, nos. 448–50. See chap. 5, at nn. 70–71.

9. Howden IV, 4. See above for the treaty of Gaillon, chap. 5, at n. 36. La Charité was a priory of Cluny that also served as a pledge for Philip Augustus.

10. Data from Audouin, *Essai sur l'armée* 11, 123–29. In 1202 twenty monasteries contributed 6,781 *livres*, or 26 percent, to the war tax. Ibid. 28, 135–40.

11. Cartellieri IV, 24–33. Augustino Theiner, *Vetera monumenta slavorum meridianalium historiam illustrantia* (Rome, 1863), I, 48. Because only the rubrics to these letters to the archbishops of Rouen and Lyon survive, their full content cannot be known.

12. *Decretales Gregorii IX*, 1.5.1, ed. E. Friedberg (Leipzig, 1879), II, 41–43; Potthast I, no. 1403. On the conflicting reports, see Cartellieri IV, 28, n. 7.

13. These include Châlons-sur-Marne, Langres, Autun, Mâcon, Clermont, and Tours.

14. Data on those bishops who obeyed or disobeyed the interdict have been compiled from *Gesta Innocentii III*, *PL* 214: xcviii, xcix, ciii, and the papal registers for the years 1200–1201, for which only the rubrics survive. They are printed in Theiner, *Vetera monumenta* I, 48–63. The cases of Troyes, Nevers and Tournai are less clear than the others, because the rubrics do not specify that the reconciliation was for disobedience of the interdict, but the dates (1200–1201) make it likely. Nevers was not absolved until 1202. Innocent III, *Regesta, PL* 214:961; Potthast I, no. 1637.

15. See also *Annales Aquicinctensis monasterii*, *MGH SS* VI, 436. Renaud, archbishop of Lyon, who was persecuted by the king, was also a royal cousin. See Appendix C.

16. Innocent III, *Regesta, PL* 214:931; Potthast I, no. 1249. The *vite* produced by his canonization are naturally silent over the affair. *Acta sanctorum*, Jan., I (Antwerp, 1643), 627–39.

17. Theiner, *Vetera monumenta* I, 63. The pope nonetheless permitted Saint-Denis to recite the office in low voice and with doors closed despite the interdict. AN, L 236, no. 30. See Germaine Lebel, *Catalogue des actes de l'abbaye de Saint-Denis* (Paris, 1935), no. 131.

18. Rigord 147. Coggeshall 112. See Theiner, *Vetera monumenta* I, 48, for the rubrics of Innocent's letter to the bishop of Senlis.

19. *Actes* II, no. 650. The king exempted Eudes from personal military service, although retaining the due service from the bishopric.

20. *Actes* II, no. 637. The papal confirmation dated 30 April 1201 is found in the cartulary of Evreux, Arch. dép. Eure G 122, p. 5. It was enrolled in the papal registers for the fourth year of Innocent III, which are now lost but for the rubrics. Potthast I, no. 1363. Theiner, *Vetera monumenta* I, 57. On the royal charter to Evreux, see John W. Baldwin, "Philip Augustus and the Norman Church," *French Historical Studies* 6 (1969): 4–6.

21. Léopold Delisle, *Recueil des actes d' Henri II* (Paris, 1909), I, 395. I. P. Shaw, "The Ecclesiastical Policy of Henry II on the Continent," *Church Quarterly Review* 151 (1951): 151–54.

22. The incumbent, Guarin de Cierry, did not die until 14 August 1201.

23. The Sées incident has been recounted by Sidney R. Packard, "King John and the Norman Church," *Harvard Theological Review* 15 (1922): 20–24, and H. G. Richardson and G. O. Sayles, *The Governance of Mediaeval England* (Edinburgh, 1963), 339, 340.

24. Guillaume le Breton, *Philippidos* 219, 220. The theme is also rehearsed in the *Normanniae nova chronica*, ed. A. Chéruel, *Mémoires de la Société des Antiquaires de Normandie* 18 (1851): 19.

25. Appendix C. The family relationship of Robert de Roye and Barthélemy de Roye was discovered by Fernando Pico, "The Cathedral Chapter of Laon, 1155–1318," (Unpublished manuscript) nos. 480, 624. The bishop of Evreux is not to be confused with Robert de Roye, archdeacon of Evreux and of Senlis and treasurer of Noyon. Because of his connections with the Roye family, who were well represented in the Laon chapter, Robert, bishop of Evreux, was named in the Laon obituaries. Paris BN lat. 9226, fol. 12v and Laon Bibl. mun. 341, p. 316.

26. For the fourth disputed election that concerned the king, that of Paris in 1220, see chap. 12, at n. 13.

27. Innocent III, *Regesta* for 1200. Rubrics in Theiner, *Vetera monumenta*, I, 49. *Decretales Gregorii IX*, 1.5.1, II, 41–43. Potthast I, no. 1043. *Gesta Innocentii III*, PL 214: cii, ciii. The partisan chronicle *De Gestis episcoporum Autissiodorensium*, PL 138: 320, 327, omits the reasons for Hugues's rejection. Pierre's good relations with the king were noticed by Geoffroi de Courlon, *Chronique de l'abbaye de Saint-Pierre-le-Vif de Sens*, ed. G. Julliot (Sens, 1876), 502, 504. For his royal service see chap. 6, at n. 31.

28. Innocent III, *Regesta*, PL 215: 16, 224, 398; Potthast I, nos. 1841, 2085, 2269. *Chronicon Laudunensis canonici*, RHF XVIII, 712, 713. Alberic de Trois-Fontaines 884. Robert de Courson, *Summa*, Paris BN lat. 14524, fol. 38v, in Marcel and Christiane Dickson, "Le Cardinal Robert de Courson, sa vie," *Archives d'histoire doctrinale et littéraire du moyen âge* 9 (1934): 75.

29. Innocent III, *Regesta*, PL 215: 1228, 1230, 1271, 1419; Potthast I, nos. 3190, 3191, 3194, 3429. *Chronicon Laudunensis canonici*, RHF XVIII, 713.

30. *Actes* II, 727. See chap. 7, at nn. 125–26.

31. *Registres* VI, no. 44. *Actes* II, no. 708. In 1166 Louis VII had denied the count of Vienne the regalia of Mâcon.

32. In 1189 Philip Augustus admitted that he wrongly held the regalia of Autun after the death of Bishop Etienne, and recognized the right of the archbishop of Lyon to hold the royal regalia of Autun during its vacancy and that of Autun to hold the regalia of Lyon. This arrangement was peculiar to the two churches and does not seem to have had broader import. *Actes* I, no. 254, renewed in 1222, ibid. IV, no. 1773. See also Jean Gaudemet, "Les Origines de la régale réciproque entre Lyon et Autun," *Mémoires de la Société pour l'Histoire du*

Droit et Institutions des Anciens Pays Bourgignons, Comtois, et Romands 5 (1938): 22–26.

33. *Actes* II, nos. 772, 774. See chap. 4, at n. 34. Already during the vacancy of 1198–1200, caused by a disputed election, the regalia of Langres were administered by Hugues, bishop of Auxerre, because Langres was on the confines of the kingdom and the Empire. *De Gestis episcoporum Autissiodorensium, PL* 138:320.

34. *Actes* III, no. 968 (confirmed by Innocent III, *Regesta, PL* 215:1300; Potthast I, no. 3276). *Actes* III, nos. 1052 and 1066. Richard de Gerberoi, bishop of Amiens (1205–1210), requested by letter that the king allow the *vidame* of Amiens the exercise of the regalia, just as Louis VII had permitted it to the *vidame* Girard at the death of Bishop Thierry in 1164. Brussel, *Nouvel examen* II, 766. Delisle, *Catalogue* no. 1013. Such a request reflected the claims of the house of Gerberoi, former *vidames* of Amiens, to which Richard belonged, more than a desire to be rid of the royal exercise of rights over regalia. On Richard's background, see *Gall. christ.* X, 1180.

35. *Actes* III, no. 982 (confirmed by Innocent III, *Regesta PL* 215:1324, 1326; Potthast I, nos. 3288, 3292). The renunciation of the spiritual regalia to Amiens (*Actes* III, 1063) should be dated 1279. See the correction in *Actes* V. In all events, Philip Augustus continued to confer prebends. Henri Bouvier, *Histoire religieuse de la ville d'Amiens des origines au XIVe siècle* (Amiens, 1921), 276.

36. Robert d'Auxerre 271. *De Gestis episcoporum Autissiodorensium, PL* 138:329. *Actes* II, no. 835, III, no. 1106.

37. *Gall. christ.* IV, Instr. 196 suggests it for Langres in 1200. *Actes* II, no. 774 (Arras, 1203). See Robert L. Benson, *The Bishop Elect* (Princeton, 1968), 366–68.

38. Innocent III, *Regesta, PL* 215:1366; Potthast I, no. 3362 (Thérouanne, 1208); *Regesta, PL* 216:48; Potthast I, no. 3730 (Bourges, 1209); *Actes* III, no. 1066 (Mâcon, 1209); *Actes* III, no. 1337 (Le Mans, 1214); Teulet I, no. 1414 (Evreux); Teulet I, no. 1473 (Orléans, 1221); Teulet I, no. 1513 (Rouen, 1222); and Teulet I, no. 1565 (Nevers, 1223) merely announce the election without specifying confirmation.

196. *Registres* II, O (I). Guillaume le Breton, *Gesta* 240, 241, claims that the walls of Paris were completed by 1211–1212, but the accounts probably antedated their completion.

197. *Registres* II, O (III). The walls of Bourges were also the object of a fragmentary account (1212–1220) in Reg. C. *Registres* II, O (IV).

198. Guillaume le Breton, *Philippidos* 367.

199. For a general discussion of castles, see Gabriel Fournier, *Le Château dans la France médiévale: Essai de sociologie monumentale* (Paris, 1978), 65–225. For the fundamental study on donjons, see Pierre Héliot, "L'Evolution du donjon dans le nord-ouest de la France et en Angleterre au XIIe siècle," *Bulletin archéo-*

de France, ed. E. Laurière et al. (Paris, 1723–1849), XI 282–84. Although the royal charter may be dated as contemporary with or a little later than the interdict, the bishop of Senlis's charter must have been either before or after the interdict, because Geoffroi was persecuted by Philip for publishing the papal decree. See chap. 8, at n. 18.

40. For the *privilegium canonis*, see Baldwin, *Masters, Princes and Merchants* I, 141–45. On the *privilegium fori* the fundamental study is Robert Génestal, *Le Privilegium fori en France*, Bibliothèque de l'Ecole des Hautes Etudes, Sciences Religieuses, no. 39 (1924).

41. William Stubbs, ed., *Select Charters of English Constitutional History* (Oxford, 1913), 164, 165.

42. Pope Alexander III in *Decretales Gregorii IX*, 2.1.4, II, 240.

43. Cartulary of the Chapter of Rouen, Rouen, Bibl. mun. 1193, fol. 142rb–vb, printed in *Concilia Rotomagensis provinciae*, ed. Guillaume Bessin (Rouen, 1717), I, 100. Also in Diceto II, 87. Mathew of Paris, *Chronica majora*, ed. R. Luard (London, 1874), II, 368, also reports this solution.

44. Second Norman *coutumier* in *Coutumiers de Normandie*, ed. Joseph Tardif (Rouen, 1881, 1896), I, 68, 69. See also Baldwin, "Philip Augustus and the Norman Church," 25.

45. This statement appears in a sermon of a Dominican of Saint-Jacques preached at Paris 6 April 1231. *Les Sermons universitaires Parisiens de 1230–31*, ed. M. M. Davy, Etudes de philosophie médiévale, no. 15 (1931), 337, 338.

46. Howden IV, 120, 121. *Actes* II, no. 644.

47. Ten years later in letters to the principal communes of the royal domain, the king reiterated these principles and specified the serious crimes for which a cleric could be arrested: murder, homicide, adultery, rape, and assaults that shed blood. *Actes* III, nos. 1125, 1125[bis].

48. Baldwin, *Masters, Princes and Merchants* I, 146–48, and "A Debate at Paris over Thomas Becket between Master Roger and Master Peter the Chanter," *Collectanea Stephan Kuttner, Studia Gratiana* 11 (1967): 119–32.

49. Since these royal charters were valuable to the churches of Artois, a significant proportion were preserved in cartularies. See for example: *Actes* I, nos. 407, 409, 412, 414, 416, 431, 433–38. Compare these samples with the list of alms in *Registres* II, C.

50. *Actes* I, no. 399, the limitations of which were imposed in *Actes* II, nos. 496, 497, 595, 596.

51. Compare A. Verhulst and M. Gysseling, *Le Compte général de 1187, connu sous le nom de "Gros Brief," et les institutions financières du comté de Flandre au XIIe siècle* (Brussels, 1962), 159, with *Budget* CLII (2) and *Registres* II, C. Unfortunately, the account of Hesdin is incomplete for 1187 (Verhulst and Gysseling, *Le Compte général* 164, 165) and cannot be compared with the royal accounts. The royal accounts group Bapaume and Péronne together, so that their totals cannot be compared with that of 1187, where Bapaume is alone. On the relationship

between royal money and local coinage in Picardie, see Thomas N. Bisson, *Conservation of Coinage* (Oxford, 1979), 144–54.

52. Luchaire, *Actes de Louis VII*, nos. 5, 713 (Bec); 282, 416, 557, 665 (Jumièges); 515 (Fécamp); 572, 729 (Saint-Wandrille); 772 (Vallasse).

53. See, for example: *Actes* I, nos. 33 (Valasse), 172 (Jumièges), 283 (Bec), II, nos. 674 (Bec), 541 (Foucarmont), 653 (Bonport), 655 (Sainte-Catherine de Rouen), and 719 (Mortemer).

54. *Actes* II, nos. 646, 760.

55. This paragraph presents the conclusions of the comparison drawn from *Magni rotuli scaccarii Normannie sub regibus Angliae*, ed. Thomas Stapleton (London, 1844), II, 462, 463; *Budget* CLXXIII (2), CLXXIV (1); and *Registres* II, C. One *livre parisis* equaled 1.46 *livres angevins* in the accounts of 1202/03. These figures for the alms at Evreux supersede my rough calculations in "Philip Augustus and the Norman Church," 3.

56. *Actes* II, no. 675. In the alms account it was expected to bring 3.3 *livres parisis* annually. For the yields and prices in 1198 and 1203, see the references in chap. 8, n. 55.

9. Narrative: The Great Conquests and the Victory at Bouvines

1. Cartellieri IV, 116–19. Powicke, *Loss of Normandy* 149, 150. See chap. 5, at nn. 73–74.

2. Teulet I, no. 647. *Actes* II, no. 723.

3. Cartellieri IV, 120–24. Powicke, *Loss of Normandy* 150–52.

4. Cartellieri IV, 125, 126.

5. Ibid. IV, 142. Powicke, *Loss of Normandy* 157, 158. In May 1203 Philip made gifts to the count of Alençon. *Budget* CCII (2).

6. Cartellieri IV, 136–39, 148–51, 179–82. On the date of Arthur's death, see Charles Petit-Dutaillis, *Le Déshéritement de Jean sans Terre et le meurtre d'Arthur de Bretagne: Etude critique sur la formation et la fortune d'une légende* (Paris, 1925), 18–29.

7. *Registres* VI, no. 45. On these and other defections see Cartellieri IV, 142, 143, 146–50.

8. See chap. 7, at nn. 160–61.

9. Wendover I, 316, 317. Cartellieri IV, 162. Powicke, *Loss of Normandy* 158.

10. On the taking of Château-Gaillard and its preparations, see Cartellieri IV, 153–60, 166–70, 173–79, Powicke, *Loss of Normandy* 160–69, 253–56, and Raymond Quenedey, "Le Siège du Château-Gaillard en 1203–1204," *Bulletin de la Société des Amis des Monuments Rouennais* (1913): 53–89.

11. Cartellieri IV, 190–99. Powicke, *Loss of Normandy* 256–64. The Anony-

mous of Béthune (*Histoire des ducs* 99) says that Pierre de Préaux surrendered Rouen on the advice of the archbishop.

12. Innocent III, *Regesta, PL* 214: 984; Potthast I, no. 1673.

13. Innocent III, *Regesta, PL* 215:64; 176–80, 325; Potthast I, nos. 1921, 2009, 2181.

14. Teulet I, nos. 678, 683–92.

15. On the papal interventions, see Cartellieri IV, 160–66, 170–73, 202–5.

16. On the Loire campaign, see ibid. IV, 206–11, 217–24, 228–37, and Arthur J. Lyons, "The Capetian Conquest of Anjou" (diss., The Johns Hopkins University, 1976), 43–77.

17. *Registres* VI, no. 51. Cartellieri IV, 243–49.

18. Anonymous of Béthune, *Histoire des ducs* 109. Wendover II, 8. Mathew Paris, *Historia Anglorum*, ed. F. Madden (London, 1866), II, 101. Mathew Paris, *Chronica majora*, ed. H. R. Luard (London, 1874), II, 489.

19. See chap. 1. On the subsequent relations between Philip Augustus and Champagne, see Henry Arbois de Jubainville, *Histoire des ducs et des comtes de Champagne* (Paris, 1859–69), IV (1), 24–121, and Michel Bur, "Rôle et place de la Champagne dans le royaume de France au temps de Philippe Auguste," in *La France de Philippe Auguste* 248–54.

20. *Actes* II, no. 581. Teulet I, no. 474.

21. This summary of the agreement represents a conflation between the charter of Blanche (*Registres* VI, no. 41) and that of Philip Augustus (*Actes* II, no. 678), which differ in detail.

22. Only Blanche's charter survives, Teulet I, no. 878. For the concurrence of Prince Louis and Eudes, duke of Burgundy, see ibid. I, nos. 879, 880. For receipts of Blanche's payments, see *Actes* III, nos. 1132, 1154.

23. *Actes* III, nos. 1306, 1313, 1314. For the guarantees by the barons named in the agreement, see Teulet I, nos. 1054, 1055, 1057–60. Blanche's fine is noted in Delisle, *Catalogue* no. 1466.

24. On the Breton succession, see Cartellieri IV, 291–93, 334–36, and Sidney Painter, *The Scourge of the Clergy: Peter of Dreux, Duke of Brittany* (Baltimore, 1937), 4–8.

25. *Actes* II, nos. 764, 765. Philip alluded to Arthur's acts as late as 1206. Ibid. III, no. 960.

26. For example, Philip exchanged fiefs with Guy. *Actes* II, no. 950.

27. *Registres* VI, no. 56.

28. Teulet I, nos. 601 (misdated by Teulet), 1026, 1027, 1033.

29. Rigord 165, 166. For the dating of this campaign, see Cartellieri IV, 268–71.

30. Cartellieri IV, 264–68. *Actes* III, no. 1021.

31. On the fiefs of Auvergne, see Cartellieri IV, 20–22, and André Bossuat, "L'Auvergne," in *Histoire des institutions françaises au moyen âge*, ed. Ferdinand Lot and Robert Fawtier (Paris, 1957), I, 104–6.

32. See chap. 1, at n. 54. Cartellieri I, 312. Diceto II, 168 claims that John accepted this renunciation in the treaty of Le Goulet in 1200, but it is not included in the text. Cartellieri IV, 41, n. 3.

33. Teulet I, no. 501. In 1212 Philip confirmed Guillaume's assignment of dowry to his wife. Ibid. I, no. 1016. *Actes* III, no. 1254. Cartellieri IV, 394, 395.

34. Guy de Dampierre sent the king inventories of the military supplies captured at these strongholds. *Registres* VI, nos. 74–76. In March 1216 Guy offered pledges to surrender the Auvergnat fortresses at the king's command. Later Archembald's name was substituted for his. Ibid. V, nos. 61, 62.

35. Guillaume le Breton, *Gesta* 233–36. Cartellieri IV, 393–97. Guy de Dampierre may have had interest in the region of Auvergne as early as ca. 1205, as is shown by *Registres* V, no. 2.

36. Léon-Louis Borrelli de Serres, *La Réunion des provinces septentrionales à la couronne par Philippe Auguste: Amiénois, Artois, Vermandois, Valois* (Paris, 1899), 79–83. See chap. 1, at nn. 47–53, and chap. 5, at nn. 7–12, for their assimilation.

37. For these early actions see chap. 5 and Henri Malo, *Un Grand Feudataire, Renaud de Dammartin, et la coalition de Bouvines: Contribution à l'étude du règne de Philippe Auguste* (Paris, 1898), 33–41, 55–69. On his relations with John, see Cartellieri IV, 85.

38. The complicated terms of the agreement attempted to foresee all eventualities. Should the infants Philip and Mathilde be married and survive Renaud, they were to inherit the entire lands of the count and his wife. After their marriage they were to receive one-third of Renaud's present possessions and one-half of any future acquisitions. Should Philip die, Mathilde was to be remarried only with the king's consent. Teulet I, no. 601. Cartellieri IV, 84. Malo, *Un Grand Feudataire* 71, 72.

39. *Actes* II, nos. 770, 862, 863. Teulet I, no. 733. Cartellieri IV, 211. Malo, *Un Grand Feudataire* 80.

40. *Actes* III, nos. 1043, 1044. Cartellieri IV, 275, 276, 283, 284. Malo, *Un Grand Feudataire* 98, 99, 103, 104.

41. See chap. 9, at n. 14, and *Actes* III, no. 1035.

42. *Registres* VI, no. 62. Cartellieri IV, 285, 291.

43. *Registres* V, no. 13. Cartellieri IV, 286.

44. *Actes* III, no. 1133. Teulet I, no. 925. Cartellieri IV, 290.

45. *Actes* III, nos. 1202, 1203. Cartellieri IV, 300–303. Malo, *Un Grand Feudataire* 139–43.

46. Teulet I, nos. 972, 974, 976.

47. Cartellieri IV, 39, 108, 237, 238.

48. Nine French and Flemish lords guaranteed this future marriage, to take place in January 1211, with pledges of 10,000 marks. For the pledges, see *Actes* II, nos. 952, 953; Cartellieri IV, 238–40. For the marriage, see the assignment

of dower in 1210 by Philippe of Namur in Teulet I, no. 952; Cartellieri IV, 303, 304.

49. If the girls themselves opposed the king's candidates, they were to be returned to the marquis's custody on the condition that they not be married without the king's consent, a guarantee of royal service, and the payment of relief. *Actes* III, no. 1042. Cartellieri IV, 276.

50. *Actes* III, no. 1227. *Registres* VI, no. 65. Cartellieri IV, 304–7.

51. Among the pledges supporting Enguerran was Philippe, bishop of Beauvais, who was hostile to Renaud, count of Boulogne. See *Registres* V, no. 20, and chap. 9, at n. 45.

52. Teulet I, nos. 978–81. Cartellieri IV, 307, 308.

53. Delaborde, *Layettes* V, no. 189. Cartellieri IV, 308–10.

54. Cartellieri IV, 81, 99, 212.

55. Ibid. IV, 213.

56. Ibid. IV, 259–61.

57. Ibid. IV, 286–90, 294–98.

58. *Registres* V, no. 5, VI, nos. 48, 53. Cartellieri IV, 213, 271–74.

59. Cartellieri IV, 295, 296.

60. *Registres* VI, no. 67. Cartellieri IV, 330–34.

61. Robert Davidsohn, *Philipp II. August von Frankreich und Ingeborg* (Stuttgart, 1888), 205–8.

62. Estimates of the birth date of Pierre Charlot vary between 1205 and 1209. See ibid. 211, 212; Williston Walker, *On the Increase of Royal Power in France under Philip Augustus* (Leipzig, 1888), 32; and Cartellieri IV, 278.

63. Innocent III, *Regesta*, PL 214:1014; Potthast I, no. 1712. Davidsohn, *Philipp II* 189, 190.

64. Davidsohn, *Philipp II* 209. Cartellieri IV, 228.

65. Reg. C, fols. 1v–2v, published in *Registres* VII, no. 5, *RHF* XIII, 415–17, *MGH SS* XIII, 257–59, and Davidsohn, *Philipp II* 298–304. See the discussion in Davidsohn, *Philipp II* 220–22, and Cartellieri IV, 277–79.

66. Davidsohn, *Philipp II* 228.

67. Ibid. 217, 218.

68. Ibid. 228–38. Cartellieri IV, 279–81.

69. *Actes* III, no. 1152. Davidsohn, *Philipp II* 240, 241. Cartellieri IV, 296, 297.

70. Guillaume le Breton, *Gesta* 245.

71. Cartellieri IV, 310–16.

72. For example, in 1209 Philip was negotiating with John de Lacy and in 1212 with the Welsh prince Llywelyn. *Actes* III, no. 1079 and Teulet I, no. 1032.

73. Whether Innocent actually deposed John and whether the pope actually commissioned Philip to invade England remain disputed points among historians. See C. R. Cheney, "The Alleged Deposition of King John," in *Studies in*

Medieval History Presented to Frederick Maurice Powicke (Oxford, 1948), 100–16, Sidney Painter, *The Reign of King John* (Baltimore, 1949), 190–92, and Cartellieri IV, 341–43.

74. Cartellieri IV, 343, 344. Petit-Dutaillis, *Louis VIII* 186, 187.

75. *Registres* VI, no. 71.

76. Ibid. VI, no. 70. Cartellieri IV, 346–52. Petit-Dutaillis, *Louis VIII* 35–37.

77. Davidsohn, *Philipp II* 250–56. Cartellieri IV, 352, 353. On Guérin's responsibility for this decision, see chap. 6, at n. 132. Ingeborg's daily expenses and livery appear in the financial accounts of 1217, which illustrate her restoration as queen. Brussel, *Nouvel examen* I, 552.

78. Cartellieri IV, 359–64. Painter, *The Reign of King John* 192–94.

79. Cartellieri IV, 363–74. F. W. Brooks, "The Battle of Damme—1213," *Mariners' Mirror* 16 (1930): 263–71.

80. Cartellieri IV, 380, 398.

81. Ibid. IV, 382.

82. Ibid. IV, 375–77. A list of the hostages was transcribed in Reg. C. *Registres* VII, no. 12.

83. Cartellieri IV, 378, 379.

84. Ibid. IV, 386–91.

85. Anonymous of Béthune, *Chronique des rois* 766. Cartellieri IV, 399, 400.

86. Cartellieri IV, 391, 392, 406, 407, 413, 414, 421.

87. Ibid. IV, 407.

88. Ibid. IV, 400, 401, 411, 412.

89. Ibid. IV, 420.

90. Ibid. IV, 381–86, 402–24.

91. *Registres* V, nos. 33–35, 38. Cartellieri IV, 410, 411. Shortly thereafter Guillaume de La Guierche deserted Philip. Cartellieri IV, 424.

92. Our chief source for the events at Châteauroux and La Roche-au-Moine is Guillaume le Breton, *Philippidos* 286–95 and *Gesta* 260–64. See also Cartellieri IV, 411, 424–28.

93. A French chronicler claimed that John wrote Otto that he could easily vanquish Philip because Louis's army contained all the young knights, leaving Philip only with the old. *Historia regum Francorum* in *MGH SS* XXVI, 395, 396.

94. On the distinction between *guerra* and *bellum*, see the summary in Georges Duby, *Le Dimanche de Bouvines* (Paris, 1973), 145–59, and chap. 14, at n. 112.

95. Guillaume le Breton, *Gesta* 265–99, embellished and further elaborated in *Philippidos* 296–347. For the fullest and most recent discussion of Bouvines, on which my discussion is based, see Cartellieri IV, 433–73, and J. F. Verbruggen, *Krijgskunst in West-Europa in de Middeleeuwen, IXe tot begin XIVe eeuw* (Brussels, 1954), 399–435, trans. Sumner Willard, and S. C. M. Southern, *The Art of Warfare in Western Europe during the Middle Ages: From the Eighth Century to 1340* (Amsterdam, 1977), 220–37.

96. After the battle was over Guillaume le Breton reported this division in

Gesta 295 and expanded on it in *Philippidos* 306. The count of Flanders was to have Paris; the count of Boulogne, Péronne; the count of Salisbury, Dreux; Hugues de Boves, Beauvais; the count of Nevers, Sens; and German barons, Château-Landon and Mantes.

97. Guillaume le Breton reports this counsel when discussing Renaud de Boulogne at the end of his description of the battle. *Gesta* 287; *Philippidos* 341–43. See also Cartellieri IV, 449–51.

98. Reported at a later point in his description of the battle by Guillaume le Breton. *Gesta* 286.

99. Reported only in Guillaume le Breton, *Philippidos* 340.

100. On tactics and numbers, see Verbruggen, *Art of Warfare* 220–23, 236, 237, and chap. 11, at nn. 32–38.

101. *Registres* VII, no. 13. Cartellieri IV, 621–33.

102. *Actes* III, no. 1340. Teulet I, no. 1083. Cartellieri IV, 480–90. Guillaume le Breton, *Gesta* 294, also notes Philip's weakness in the Loire valley. On the truce of Thouars, see chap. 9, at n. 17.

10. Baillis *and Seneschals:* Justice and Finance in the New Domain

1. *Actes* II, no. 723. Teulet I, no. 647.

2. For a survey of Norman administration on the eve of the Capetian conquest, see Charles H. Haskins, *Norman Institutions* (Cambridge, Mass., 1918), 164–69, 174–87; Powicke, *Loss of Normandy* 50–67; Sidney R. Packard, "The Judicial Organization of Normandy, 1189–1204," *Law Quarterly Review* 40 (1924): 442–64; and R. de Fréville, "Etude sur l'organisation judiciaire en Normandie au XIIe et XIIIe siècles," *Revue historique de droit français et étranger* 36 (1912): 681–736.

3. *Actes* II, no. 793, 802. Powicke, *Loss of Normandy* 173, 174, 271, 272. Occasionally, important *baillis* such as Pierre du Thillai and Renaud de Ville-Thierri were called *senescallus Normannie, senescallus Cadomi,* or *senescallus,* but these titles were not consistent, and neither did the *baillis* fulfill the duties of the great seneschal. For their titles, see Appendix B. See also the conclusions of Lucien Musset, "Quelques problèmes posés par l'annexion de la Normandie au domaine royal français," in *La France de Philippe Auguste* 300, 301.

4. *Jugements* pp. 4–90.

5. For example, see *Actes* IV, nos. 1403, 1441, 1501, 1558, 1592, 1663, 1684, 1741, and 1810. The accounts of 1221, 1227, and 1238 also reflect the biannual sessions of the Norman exchequer. Nortier and Baldwin, "Contributions" 25–27.

6. For early evidence of the *vicomtes,* see Delisle, XXIV *97 (Caux, 1204),

*97 (Saukeville, 1205), *97 (Vaudreuil, 1205), *97, *273, *274 (Sées, 1207), *97 (Caux, 1207).

7. See chap. 6, at nn. 242–43. The financial functions are revealed in the account of 1221.

8. For a list of Norman *baillis*, see Appendix B. On their previous background, see chap. 6, at nn. 275–88. On Robert *de Waceo*, see *Jugements* p. 130. On clerical participation in Angevin justice, see Ralph V. Turner, "The Judges of King John: Their Background and Training," *Speculum* 51 (1976): 447–61. See also Musset, "Quelques problèmes," in *La France de Philippe Auguste* 303, 304.

9. Joseph R. Strayer, *Administration of Normandy under Saint Louis* (Cambridge, Mass., 1932), 96, 97, 119, 120.

10. For the king's grants of fiefs to *baillis* and the yearly revenues that they yielded, see: Cadoc, *Actes* II, no. 887 (this fief was to be returned after his death; see *Registres* III, P). Cadoc et al., *Actes* IV, no. 1441. Jean de Rouvray (140 *livres*), *Actes* II, no. 797, 944 (Jean received a fief before the conquest; see *Actes* II, no. 556). Guillaume Poucin (100 *livres*), *Actes* II, no. 815 (until his marriage; he also received a fief before the conquest; see *Actes* II, no. 549). Pierre du Thillai (70 *livres*), *Actes* II, no. 927, and III, no. 1023. Renaud de Cornillon (60 *livres*), *Actes* III, no. 1075. Geoffroi de la Chapelle (60 *livres*), *Actes* III, no. 1078. Miles de Lévis (54 *livres*), *Actes* IV, no. 1549. For the *baillis'* salaries, see chap. 6, at nn. 270–74.

11. MS Gonesse, Archives Hospitalières. This register has survived because it became part of the archives of the Hôtel-Dieu of Gonesse, to which Pierre du Thillai made donations beginning in 1208. The archives have remained intact at the hospital to this day. For a description of and extracts from the register, see Léopold Delisle, "Fragments de l'histoire de Gonesse principalement tirés des archives hospitalières de cette commune," *BEC* (1859): 113–52, 247–77, especially at 115, 116, 120, 259–67. Another sign of Pierre's success was the extent of his ecclesiastical foundations. See, for example, *Actes* IV, nos. 1576, 1577, 1584.

12. Delisle, *RHF* XXIV, *130–33.

13. See Appendix B. Often the *bailli* was identified as the *castellanus* of the place.

14. Delisle, *RHF* XXIV, *116, *144, *157.

15. Teulet I, nos. 1415, 1416.

16. Delisle, *RHF* XXIV, *97, *110, *112, *281, *285. *Jugements* no. 233, Delisle, *Catalogue* no. 2017, pp. 521, 522.

17. For a sample, drawn from the records of the exchequer, of *baillis* holding assizes and conducting inquests alone, see chap. 10, at nn. 43–46. These examples could be multiplied many times. See the observations of Strayer, *Administration of Normandy* 21, and de Fréville, "Etude sur l'organisation judiciaire," 728, 729. Strayer dates the change around 1209.

18. The survey of fiefs of 1172 reports about twenty *bailliages*. *Registres* III A. Powicke, *Loss of Normandy* 68–78, 272, counted twenty-seven. See also Strayer, *Administration of Normandy* 7, 8.

19. *Registres* III C. *Scripta de feodis* nos. 1–177, in 1220 contained Coutances, Bayeux, Rouen, Verneuil, Caen, Gisors, Bonneville, and Caux. Nortier and Baldwin, "Contributions," 8.

20. *Registres* I, nos. 1, 8. See chap. 6, at n. 258.

21. *Scripta de feodis* nos. 178–312. The castellany of Montlhéry (ibid. nos. 300–313) was prepared separately.

22. About the same time that the inventory of Etampes was being prepared (1217), the *bailli* Adam Héron conducted an inquest into the limits of royal rights at Melun. *Registres* I, no. 60. The survey of the fiefs of Montlhéry was likewise accompanied by an inquest into the limits of the castellany. Ibid. no. 92. *Scripta de feodis* no. 313.

23. For a discussion of the Norman judicial documents, see chap. 15.

24. The two *coutumiers* are edited by Ernest-Joseph Tardif in *Coutumiers de Normandie* I (1) (Rouen, 1881): (first *coutumier* in Latin), 1–57; (second *coutumier* in Latin), 59–101; I (2) (Rouen, 1903) (both *coutumiers* in old French), 1–93. They have both been called the *Très ancien coutumier de Normandie* because they were translated together as one treatise in old French in the thirteenth century. For discussion of their background, see Tardif, *Coutumiers* I (1), xii–xciv, and Paul Viollet, "Les Coutumiers de Normandie," in *Histoire littéraire de la France* 33 (1906), 43–65. Tardif (pp. lxv–lxxii) argues for the date 1199–1200 and Viollet (pp. 48, 49) for 1203–1204. The ordinance referred to in the second *coutumier* is in *Jugements* no. 230. See chap. 12, at n. 74.

25. *Registres* I, no. 41, confirmed in *Jugements* nos. 137, 138.

26. For some examples of justices holding assizes, see chap. 6, at nn. 241–42. For examples (among many) of *baillis* holding assizes: Barthélemy Droon at Sées, 1217 (Delisle, *RHF* XXIV, *282), at Verneuil, 1220 (ibid. *125); Pierre du Thillai in 1211 (Delisle, *BEC* [1859]: 118), at Argentan, 1216 (Delisle, *RHF* XXIV, *280); Renaud de Ville-Thierri at Bayeux, 1214 (Delisle, *RHF* XXIV *279), at Avranches, 1221 (*Jugements* no. 302); Renaud de Cornillon at Coutances (Delisle, *RHF* XXIV, *146); Miles de Lévis at Coutances, 1219 (*Jugements* no. 244), in 1220 (*Jugements* no. 275).

27. Tardif, *Coutumiers* I, 37, 44. *Jugements* no. 98. Delisle, *RHF* XXIV, *273, 274.

28. Data gathered principally from Delisle *RHF* XXIV and *Jugements*. They were also held at Saint-Wandrille, Lillebonne, Vaudreuil, Caudebec, Fécamp, Neufchâtel, Bec, Grandmesnil, Verneuil, Argentan, Vire, Bonne, Valonges, and Bellême.

29. Tardif, *Coutumiers* I, 24, 25. For examples of the barons on the assizes, see Delisle, *RHF* XXIV, *273, *274, *276. De Fréville ("Etude sur l'organisation judiciaire," 681–736, especially at 714–26) has argued that the presence of the

barons was a French innovation and was contrary to preceding Anglo-Norman and Angevin usage. Though students of the Anglo-Norman–Angevin period do not accept his conclusions (see Haskins, *Norman Institutions* 184, n. 160), they nonetheless remain valid for the Capetian era. The Norman pattern of the barons of the assizes is reminiscent of the four *prud'hommes* who were to aid the *prévôts* in the Capetian domain decreed by the ordinance of 1190. See chap. 7, at n. 1.

30. *Jugements* p. 4ff. See chap. 10, at n. 23.

31. *Jugements* pp. 53, 54. *Registres* I, no. 41. *Jugements* p. 35. The Easter session of 1213 under the presidency of Brother Haimard and Guillaume de la Chapelle included four *baillis*, the *justiciarii* Robert *de Waceo*, a prelate, a townsman of Sées, and Robert Crassus, an *assessor* of the justices. *Jugements* p. 30.

32. Tardif, *Coutumiers* I, 43.

33. Ibid. I, 18, 19.

34. Ibid. I, 7.

35. Ibid. I, 7, 25.

36. Ibid. I, 27.

37. Ibid. I, 26.

38. Ibid. I, 27.

39. Ibid. I, 44, 45.

40. Guillaume le Breton, *Philippidos* 218, 219. Unlike Norman law, which decreed only monetary penalties for the accuser who failed in battle (see the first *coutumier*, in Tardif, *Coutumiers* I, 41), Philip ordered that the accuser, like the defendant who failed in battle, was liable to corporal penalties.

41. Tardif, *Coutumiers* I, 70, 72, 73.

42. This and the following statistics are derived from *Jugements*. Their accuracy can only be approximate because of the problems of overlapping categories and the difficulty of identifying actions from the summary notices.

43. Ibid. no. 49.

44. Ibid. no. 244. Barthélemy Droon, Pierre du Thillai, and Renaud de Ville-Thierri held numerous recognitions to determine the seizin of land. Ibid. nos. 107, 168, 309.

45. For example, Bonneville: ibid. nos. 70, 98; Caen: nos. 108, 137, 241; Avranches: nos. 166, 302; Coutances: nos. 168, 262. In 1212 the exchequer referred to the prior decisions of Pierre du Thillai, the bishop of Avranches (over bastardy), and Renaud de Ville-Thierri. Ibid. no. 108. For other examples of transfer of bastardy cases to the bishops' courts, see ibid. nos. 22, 89. On the writ of bastardy see the second *coutumier* in Tardif, *Coutumiers* I, 73.

46. *Jugements* nos. 95, 233. The following *baillis* were ordered to hold inquests: Renaud de Ville-Thierri: ibid. nos. 157, 180, 233, 316, 339; Pierre du Thillai: nos. 185, 188, 232; Miles de Lévis: nos. 154, 233, 317; Cadoc: nos. 200, 204.

47. Ibid. nos. 79, 275. The exchequer judgment of 1214 over Raoul Tesson's inheritance at Falaise in effect reviewed a decision at Rouen. *Registres* I, no. 41.

Jugements nos. 137, 138, 212, 298. On the division of the Tesson inheritance, see Powicke, *Loss of Normandy* 352, 353.

48. On Angevin Jewish policy in England and Normandy, see H. G. Richardson, *The English Jewry under Angevin Kings* (London, 1960), 109–70 and 201–12. For Capetian policy, see chap. 7, at nn. 119–22 and, in general, Robert Chazan, *Medieval Jewry in Northern France* (Baltimore, 1973), 63–99.

49. *Registres* V, no. 1. Philip continued to vindicate ducal rights over the Jews in Normandy. See, for example, *Actes* III, no. 1200, Teulet I, nos. 977, 1282, 1353, 1360. For Troyes, Saint-Pol, and Nevers, see *Actes* III, no. 1127, and Teulet I, nos. 922, 923.

50. *Actes* II, no. 955. A seal for the Jews of Paris has survived from the same year. If it represents the new seal, it differs from the old seal only by the addition of the counter-seal. Brigitte Bedos, "Les Sceaux," in *Art et archéologie des juifs en France médiévale*, ed. B. Blumenkranz (Toulouse, 1980), 218, and Chazan, *Medieval Jewry* 88, 89.

51. *Actes* IV, nos. 1555, 1554. The constitution of 1219 was noted by the chronicler Robert d'Auxerre 283.

52. *Registres* II, L. The scribe Etienne de Gallardon added the last item and a new total. On the four individuals, see Chazan, *Medieval Jewry* 93–95.

53. *Chronicon de Mailros*, ed. J. Stevenson (Edinburgh, 1835), 109, 110. *Registres* VII, no. 17. In this list Dieudonné de Verneuil is grouped with the French Jews. See Chazan, *Medieval Jewry* 79, 80, 86, 87 for evidence on the migration of 1211. Two other lists of French and Norman Jews in Reg. A and C (*Registres* VII, nos. 16, 18) have not yet found an explicable context.

54. The calculation was made by Brussel, *Nouvel examen* I, 581, and is probably reliable because his total for 1202/03 agrees with the modern editors. See chap. 7, n. 122. He includes a number of excerpts of Jewish revenues from the accounts of 1217. For example, see ibid. I, 515, 573, 581. In 1227, 8,682 *livres* were entered into the Budget as the *Summa judeorum*. Borrelli de Serres, *Recherches* I, 183. The meaning of this sum is difficult to interpret in light of the shift in the royal policy towards Jews in November 1223.

55. Teulet II, no. 1610. For a recent discussion of the better-known policies of Louis VIII and Louis IX towards the Jews, see Chazan, *Medieval Jewry* 100–53.

56. See the analysis of Poitou in Robert Hajdu, "Castles, Castellans and the Structure of Politics in Poitou, 1152–1271," *Journal of Medieval History* 4 (1978): 27–53.

57. Jacques Boussard, *Le Gouvernement d'Henri Plantegenêt* (Paris, 1956), 352–60, 510–15.

58. Ibid. 99–103 for a summary account. The baronial structure of Anjou deserves fuller study.

59. *Actes* II, nos. 607, 608.

60. *Actes* II, no. 723. Teulet I, no. 647. See chap. 9, at n. 2. The king bolstered the agreement by affiancing his daughter Marie to Arthur. *Actes* II, no. 709.

61. On the career of Guillaume des Roches, see Gaston Dubois, "Recherches sur la vie de Guillaume des Roches, sénéchal d'Anjou, du Maine, et de Touraine," *BEC* 30 (1869): 377–424; 32 (1871): 88–145; and 34 (1873): 502–41. Now updated by Arthur J. Lyons, "The Capetian Conquest of Anjou" (diss., The Johns Hopkins University, 1976), 112–31.

62. *Histoire de Guillaume le Maréchal*, ed. Paul Meyer (Paris, 1891, 1901) I, 318, 319, III, 108–10.

63. *Registres* VI, no. 45. For these events, see chap. 9.

64. Guillaume le Breton, *Gesta* 260.

65. *Rotuli chartarum*, ed. T. D. Hardy (London, 1837), I, i, 23, 25, 32, 34, 59, 70–72. The confirmation is at p. 72.

66. *Actes* II, no. 829. Teulet I, no. 723. About the same time the king negotiated an exchange between Guillaume des Roches and Berengaria, the widow of King Richard. Berengaria renounced her rights over Château-du-Loir, Guillaume's family seat, and Guillaume gave up his rights of seneschalship over the city of Le Mans, the dowry of Berengaria. *Actes* II, nos. 840, 841.

67. *Actes* II, no. 948. Teulet I, no. 808. Delaborde, *Layettes* V, no. 163. Guillaume did not receive the seneschalship of Bourges and the Touraine from Langeais to Berry, as stated by the editors of *Actes* II, no. 948. C. J. Beautemps-Beaupré, *Coutumes et institutions de l'Anjou et du Maine* (Paris, 1890), II, i, 170.

68. *Actes* III, no. 963.

69. *Actes* II, no. 829. Teulet I, no. 723. One month later Philip allowed Guillaume to apply to his lands and fiefs the rates of remuneration allowed in royal lands. *Actes* II, no. 838.

70. *Actes* II, no. 948. Teulet I, no. 808. Delaborde, *Layettes* V, no. 163.

71. See chap. 10, at n. 108.

72. *Actes* II, no. 838.

73. *Ballivus domini regis et senescalli Andegavensis* or *in Andegavia vice fungens domini Guillelmi de Ruppibus*. Delisle, *RHF* XXIV, * 157, * 158. In 1201 he had custody of Tours for Guillaume des Roches as *prévôt* and constable. Dubois, "Recherches," *BEC* 34 (1873): 507. Two other figures who rarely appear in the sources were also *baillis* of the seneschal: *coram Gaufrido Malchien ballivo nostro constituto* (ca. 1208) and *Robertus Lisiardi baillivus senescalli Andegavensis* (1220). Célestin Port, *Cartulaire de l'hôpital Saint-Jean d'Angers* (Paris, 1870), no. 41, and Delisle, *RHF* XXIV, * 157.

74. Delisle, *RHF* XXIV * 159, * 160.

75. *Actes* III, no. 1219. *Cartulaires des abbayes de Saint-Pierre de la Couture et de Saint-Pierre de Solesmes* (Le Mans, 1881), 169.

76. *Actes* III, nos. 1080, 1286, 1337, IV, no. 1456. Teulet I, no. 1062.

77. For some examples: Guillaume *de Azaio*: Teulet I, nos. 1159, 1161, *Registres* I, no. 27; Robert de Crespières: *Actes* IV, no. 1407; Thierry de Gallardon: *Actes* IV, no. 1606, Teulet I, no. 1391, *Registres* I, no. 103.

78. *Actes* IV, nos. 1563–65, 1790. Charles Victor Langlois, "Formulaires de

lettres du XIIe, du XIIIe, et du XIVe siècle," *Notices et extraits des manuscrits de la Bibliothèque Nationale*, 34, 2 (Paris, 1895), 17.

79. For the growth of regional baronies, see Hajdu, "Castles, Castellans, and the Structure of Politics in Poitou, 1152–1271," especially pp. 34–36. On John's problems with the Lusignans, see chap. 5, at nn. 68–74.

80. *Actes* II, nos. 765, 775. Guillaume le Breton, *Gesta* 223. On Aimery de Thouars and the administration of Poitou, see Philip Knachel, "The Conquest and Pacification of Poitou" (diss., The Johns Hopkins University, 1954), 12–38.

81. *Rotuli chartarum*, ed. Hardy, I, 31. Howden, IV, 96, 97.

82. Guillaume le Breton, *Gesta* 223. Howden IV, 97.

83. *Actes* II, no. 830. Teulet I, nos. 724, 725.

84. *Rotuli litterarum patentium*, ed. T. D. Hardy (London, 1835), I, i, 67. Rigord, 164.

85. *Actes* II, no. 926.

86. Hajdu, "Castles, Castellans, and the Structure of Politics in Poitou, 1152–1271," 36.

87. *Actes* III, no. 1340.

88. Delisle, *RHF* XXIV, *159, *160.

89. See chap. 9, at n. 28.

90. Rigord, *Gesta* 161. Guillaume le Breton, *Gesta* 221. Robert d'Auxerre 267, who, in turn, was followed by Alberic de Trois-Fontaines 882.

91. For example, Williston Walker, *On the Increase of Royal Power under Philip Augustus* (Leipzig, 1888), 118 (twice); Achille Luchaire in *Histoire de France*, ed. E. Lavisse (Paris, 1901), III (1) 204 (2.4 times); Auguste Longnon, *La Formation de l'unité française* (Paris, 1922), 110 (3 times); Charles Petit-Dutaillis, *La Monarchie féodale en France et en Angleterre* (Paris, 1933), 257 (twice), 271 (4 times); Joseph R. Strayer, *Western Europe in the Middle Ages* (New York, 1955), 124 (3 times). Because of the impressionistic nature of these estimates, the base of comparison is not always clear.

92. For an edition of the budget and a preparatory study of its contents and importance, see Nortier and Baldwin, "Contributions," 5–30.

93. For the accounts of 1202/03, see chap. 7. They were called "le premier budget de la monarchie française" by their editors, Ferdinand Lot and Robert Fawtier.

94. The budget of 1227 was edited by Borrelli de Serres, *Recherches* I, 176–83; that of 1238 in *RHF* XXI, 256–60.

95. The chief elements for dating the budget are the vacancy of the archbishopric of Rouen (4 May 1221–5 March 1222) and the presence of the Norman *fouage*. For a full discussion, see Nortier, "Contributions" 14–16. The date of Ascension 1222 is not likely.

96. On the fiscal arrangements of the seneschal of Anjou, see chap. 10, at nn. 69–71. Aimery de Craon, who died in May 1226, left his minor son Maurice as heir. Arthur Bertrand de Broussillon, *La Maison de Craon, 1050–1480* (Paris, 1893), I, 148, 151, 170.

97. These entries listed the *vicomté* of Rouen, the *bailliages* of Vascoeuil, Rouen, Bonneville, and Pont-Audemer, and the balance of Jean de la Porte. See the discussion of Nortier, "Contributions" 9, 10.

98. See the discussion of ibid. 10, 11. Many of these forests continue to appear in the budgets of 1227 and 1238.

99. See the discussion of ibid. 12, 14. Brussel, *Nouvel examen* I, 528, 529, reports that in 1217 the *taille* of bread and wine (also a money tax) brought in 1,500 *livres* at Paris.

100. On the affairs of Alix, countess of Eu, see Teulet I, no. 1360; of Richard the Marshal, see ibid. I, no. 1397, *Actes* IV, no. 1641; of Robert Malet, see Teulet I, nos. 1415, 1416, 1426. The reference to the son of the chamberlain of Tancarville may also involve a relief. For a discussion, see Nortier, "Contributions" 10, 11. For feudal reliefs see chap. 11.

101. See the discussion of Nortier, "Contributions" 11, 12. On Pierre Charlot, see chap. 9, at n. 62, and chap. 12, at n. 10.

102. For a preparatory study to the interpretation of the budget of 1221, see Baldwin, "Contributions" 21–30 and table on p. 28, the conclusions of which have been slightly modified here.

103. See Table 3.

104. Brussel, *Nouvel examen* I, 465.

105. *Prévôtés* included in the account of Ascension 1234 that were added after 1221 were Beaumont, Chambly, Asnières, Champagne (766 *livres*); Pont-Saint-Maxence (166 *livres*); Boiscommun (35 *livres*); Bourgneuf de Loury (3 *livres*); and Brai [-sur-Somme or -sur-Loire?] (192 *livres*). *RHF* XXII, 566–72.

106. Ibid. XXI, 568.

107. The account of 1221 lists minor sums for the old debts of the Jews (137 *livres tournois*) and for the Jew of Archembaud de Bourbon (100 *livres tournois*). On the marriage of Thomas de Savoie, see Elie Berger, *Histoire de Blanche de Castille, reine de France* (Paris, 1895), 330, 331, and Teulet II, nos. 2583, 2584.

108. Since the seneschal shared the revenues with the king in Anjou and Maine, we would expect the revenues to be less than those of Touraine, which were administered directly by *baillis*. As yet it is difficult to understand why Anjou and Maine were absent in 1221, but present in 1238. Their absence in 1227 may be explained by the fact that, like Normandy, they accounted on a biannual schedule.

109. The estimate of 114,630 *livres* is reasonably certain because it is based on figures taken directly from the three accounts. What proportions of this estimate are due to the *prévôts* and *baillis* is less certain because we lack the *prévôtés'* figures from 1221. Accepting the estimate of 14,300 *livres* from 1217 allows only 18,332 *livres* for the *baillis* during that term. On this basis the revenues of the *baillis* in the old domain in 1221 (68,526 *livres*) fell below those of the *baillis* in 1202/03 (74,684 *livres*), but these losses were compensated by the gains among the *prévôts* (from 31,781 *livres* in 1202/03 to 46,104 *livres* in 1221). The reasons for the losses among the *baillis* are not clear, but the gains among the *prévôts* may

be explained by the *prévôtés* recovered in Queen Adèle's dowry in 1206, by the new *prévôtés* added with the acquisition of the rest of Vermandois and Valois in 1213, and by increases in the farms. For example, the farm of the *prévôté* of Paris rose from 3,700 *livres* in 1202/03 (*Budget* 9) to 5,500 *livres* in 1219 (Brussel, *Nouvel examen* I, 483).

110. For example, Thomas Bisson ("Les Comptes des domaines au temps de Philippe Auguste: Essai comparatif," in *La France de Philippe Auguste* 524, 525) concludes that the *Magna recepta* accounts cannot be complete because they omit *monnayage/seigneuriage*, which he estimates to have constituted between 5 and 10 percent of the total revenue. In the accounts of 1202/03, however, *seigneuriage* does appear (*Budget* CLIV [1]), but it is insignificant (10 *livres*). See chap. 7, at n. 114.

111. On the reliefs of John and Ferrand, see chap. 5, at n. 66, and chap. 9, at n. 52.

112. On the judicial use of inquests, see chap. 7.

113. *Registres* I, no. 8. The value of the tolls was recorded in ibid. II, H, no. 105.

114. See chap. 11, at nn. 143–47.

115. Berengaria's charter announcing the exchange and the three inquests was copied into Reg. A. See *Actes* II, no. 837 n. 2, and *Registres* I, nos. 11–12. To complete the transaction Berengaria exchanged Château-du-Loir for the seneschalship of Le Mans with Guillaume des Roches. *Actes* II, no. 840. See chap. 10, n. 66. The French chancery apparently took special interest in Berengaria's dowry because it transcribed into the registers copies of Richard's charters of 1191 assigning her lands in France (*Registres* VI, no. 28) and in England (*Registres* VI, no. 30), as well as John's charter of 1201, which proposed a series of changes (*Registres* VI, no. 42). On Berengaria's difficulties with John over her dowry, see Cartellieri IV, 193, and *Dictionary of National Biography* (Oxford, 1921), II, 325, 326.

116. Those collected in the primitive part of Reg. A were *Registres* I, nos. 1, 2, 4–13; those added between 1205 and 1212 were: nos. 14, 18, 20–25, 27.

117. See chap. 3, at nn. 36–39.

118. See chap. 3, at nn. 37, 42, 44, and 52.

119. My estimates of the proportion of pages devoted to feudal inventories are Reg. A, 39/192 = 20 percent; Reg. C, 40/290 = 14 percent; and Reg. E, 95/620 = 16 percent.

120. French forests in the early modern period and the Middle Ages have been carefully studied by Michel Devèze, *La Vie de la forêt française au XVI siècle*, Ecole Pratique des Hautes Etudes, Centre des Recherches Historiques, Les Hommes et la terre, 6 (Paris, 1961), 2 vols., and by Heinrich Rubner, *Untersuchungen zur Forstverfassung des mittelalterlichen Frankreichs*, Vierteljahrschrift für Sozial- und Wirtschaftsgeschichte, Beiheft 49 (Wiesbaden, 1965), whose conclusions were summarized in "Recherches sur la réorganisation forestière en

France (XIIᵉ et XIIIᵉ siècles)," *Bulletin philologique et historique du Comité des Travaux Historiques et Scientifiques*, année 1963 (Paris, 1966), I, 271–79. Unfortunately, the useful work of Rubner did not take into account the forest inquests of the registers of Philip Augustus.

121. For surveys of the forest before Philip Augustus, see William H. Newman, *Le Domaine royal sous les premiers Capétiens (987–1180)* (Paris, 1937), passim; Pacaut, *Louis VII* 134; and Rubner, *Untersuchungen* 8.

122. Rubner, *Untersuchungen* 20–29, has also focused attention on the forest of Orléans.

123. For extensive definitions of forest customs based on early modern evidence, see Devèze, *La Vie* I, 83–119. The inquests detailing the customs in the forests of Orléans are in *Registres* I, nos. 2, 3, 6, 59, 61, 77, 117.

124. Philip Augustus reconfirmed to the townsmen their forest customs in 1187 after the original charters of Louis VI and Louis VII were destroyed in a fire. *Actes* I, no. 202. The royal chancery possessed a copy of the customs from a charter of Louis VII in Reg. A, fol. 58r. *Registres* I, no. 3. For other examples of delimitation, see *Registres* I, nos. 59 and 77. That these *defensa* were maintained from the beginning of the reign is seen in *Actes* I, nos. 221 and 344.

125. *Registres* I, no. 117. Although copied into Reg. E during the reign of Louis VIII, this inquest may be contemporary to no. 3 because its jurors are identical. Pierre's feudal position may be seen in *Scripta de feodis* nos. 375, 408, 553–56. He was listed among the knights holding fiefs from the king and having more than sixty *livres* of annual income. On the origins of the *griarius*, see Rubner, *Untersuchungen* 22, 36, 37.

126. In 1201 Philip permitted the canons of Saint-Liphard de Meung to sell their wood at Bucy for three years in exchange for half the price, but this does not seem to be a general practice. This agreement gained the king twenty-five *livres* in 1202. *Actes* II, no. 698. *Budget* CLXXVII (1). (Bucy is to the west of les Loges.) The king made a similar concession to the prior of Flottin. *Actes* II, no. 736.

127. *Budget* CLXVIII (2), CLXXVII (1), CXC (1). That Jean paid 40 *livres* each term and that Etienne paid 133 *livres*, 6 *sous*, 8 *deniers* (× 3 = 400 *livres*) for "one-third of the woods of Orléans" suggests that the forest income was farmed.

128. *Registres* I, nos. 15, 16, 20, 78, 79, 80.

129. Ibid. II, H, no. 58. See chap. 7, at nn. 103–5, for the forest income in 1202/03.

130. On the Norman forests, see Rubner, *Untersuchungen* 63–78, and Strayer, *Administration of Normandy* 76–79.

131. Robert de Torigny, in *RHF* XIII, 315.

132. Tardif, *Coutumiers* I, 28. In 1180, for example, Thomas de Tornebu paid ten *livres tournois* for a *licentia vendendi*. *Magni rotuli scaccarii Normannie sub regibus Anglie*, ed. Thomas Stapleton (London, 1840), I, 41.

133. Sales (5,697 *livres*) plus farming (1,157 *livres*) plus a minor income

equals 7,886 *livres tournois*. Statistics gathered by Rubner, *Untersuchungen* 74, from *Magni rotuli*, ed. Stapleton, II. For the comparisons of these figures, see chap. 10, at nn. 146–48.

134. Charles R. Young, *The Royal Forests of Medieval England* (Philadelphia, 1979), 50. This is the most recent study of the administration of the English forests.

135. Rubner, *Untersuchungen* 106.

136. *Registres* I, nos. 38 and 82, for the forests of Bonneville and Lyons.

137. *Actes* II, no. 875.

138. Teulet I, no. 872, printed in *Cartulaire Normand de Philippe Auguste, Louis VIII, Saint Louis, et Philippe le Hardi*, ed. Léopold Delisle (Caen, 1852), no. 169. This interpretation was later supported by a charter of Louis IX. Delisle, *Cartulaire Normand* no. 1147. For other examples of charters that may fit this interpretation, see Strayer, *Administration of Normandy* 76, nn. 5, 6; 77, n. 2. See also Rubner, *Untersuchungen* 82.

139. *Registres* I, no. 37. Robert, archbishop of Rouen, also restated the principle in 1218. Teulet I, 1282. In 1219 the canons of Notre-Dame d'Eu were forbidden to sell their wood in the forest of Parc when the king sold in the county of Eu. *Actes* IV, no. 1562.

140. The dossier included fifteen charters from the lords of the region (including the king) in favor of churches adjacent to the forest. It was compiled in a gathering of four folios in Reg. C. (fols. 134r–137v) by scribe γ and consisted of the following charters: *Registres* VI: no. 11 (1157), no. 16 (1169), no. 18 (1174), no. 10 (1155), no. 8 (1144–1150), no. 5 (1137), no. 12 (1163), no. 21 (1188), no. 20 (1187), no. 6 (1134–1145); Luchaire, *Actes de Louis VII* no. 36 (1139), p. 355, no. 13 (1163), no. 14 (1164), no. 17 (1169); *Actes* II, no. 496, and three inquests: *Registres* I, nos. 73–75. Outside of the dossier, Register C contains the following inquests concerning the forest of Retz: *Registres* I: nos. 50 (undated), 17 (before 1207), 42 (before 1214), 36 (undated), 43 (May 1215), 44 (May 1215), 65 (undated), 54 (undated), 76 (undated), 91 (undated). To these Reg. E added two more: nos. 70 (undated), 71 (undated).

141. *Registres* I, no. 73. The use of the term *vendas* to signify reserved areas may also be found in ibid. nos. 63, 64, and 75. For other examples of the *licentia*, see ibid. no. 54. In a similar way the countess exercised the *licentia vendendi* as lady of Chauny. She refused to accord it when requested until she acceded to the intercession of the bishop of Noyon. Ibid. nos. 63 and 65, repeated in *Actes* III, no. 1388, and V, no. 1871. In the charter of Philip Augustus *venditiones* was substituted for the unusual *vendas*. The countess also exercised the right to license sales in the neighboring forests of Chauny. See *Registres* I, nos. 56, 57.

142. *Registres* I, no. 74. An exception was made for *hôtes* (settlers), who had been explicitly granted the right to give away wood. In 1221 the king gave Hugues de Béthisy the woods of *Lumenout* but reserved the license to sell. *Actes* IV, no. 1709.

143. *Registres* I, no. 43, repeated in *Actes* III, no. 1387.

144. Another forest concern of the inquests after 1204 was hunting preroga-tives. See the inquiries into the rights of the count of Soissons, Philippe de Nan-teuil, and Eudes le Turc in the forest of Retz. *Registres* I, nos. 42, 50 and 71. Although the interest of French royalty in hunting was long-standing, it may have been stimulated anew by the acquisition of Normandy, where royal preroga-tives were effectively enforced.

145. For the budget of 1221, see chap. 10, at nn. 94–95. The figures from the Purification account of 1227 are from Borrelli de Serres, *Recherches* I, 176–83. The total of 6,153 *livres parisis* is a minimal figure because the begin-ning of the account is missing. It differs somewhat from that of Rubner, *Unter-suchungen* 110, 111, who has also compiled total figures for forest revenues.

146. For examples from 1221, see chap. 10, at n. 98. For some examples from 1227: Hesdin, 266 *l.* 13 *s.* 4 *d.* × 3 = 800 *l*; Ponthieu, 433 *l.* 6 *s.* 8 *d.* × 3 = 1,300 *l*; Compiègne, 783 *l.* 6 *s.* 8 *d.* × 3 = 2,400 *l.*

147. This estimate does not seem unreasonable when Norman forests yielded 10,800 *livres tournois* at Ascension 1238. Rubner, *Untersuchungen* 111.

148. Individual cases also illustrate this great increase: Evreux, from 61 to 200 *livres*; Orléans from 520 to 1,175 *livres* (for one term). I have not attempted to create a composite year for forest income from the budgets of 1221, 1227, and 1238 as I have done earlier for total income. This seems less feasible because the 1221 budget lacks the details for the *livres parisis* accounts and the 1238 budget probably reflects changes in forest management instituted by Louis IX.

149. *Registres* II, M. Each forest is listed with two figures, a large sum (rang-ing from 250 to 2,000 *livres*) and a smaller price per arpent of forest (ranging from 4 to 24 *livres*). Although the relation of the second to the first figure is not entirely clear, the large sum indicates the maximum that could be sold during the year. The first item begins *De Bierra singulis annis LX arpenni M et V^c lb., arpen-num XXIIII lb.* If one multiplies the price per arpent (24 *livres*) by the number of arpents (60), one arrives at 1,440 *livres* (approximately 1,500 *livres*), which may explain how the large figures were computed. But the number of arpents is omit-ted for the remaining items. That the list contained maximum limits for cutting wood was suggested by Léopold Delisle, *Etudes sur la condition de la classe agri-cole et l'état de l'agriculture en Normandie au moyen âge* (Evreux, 1851), 363.

150. My totals are 8,730 *livres* and 14,370 *livres* respectively.

151. Significant omissions from the old domain: Compiègne, Ponthieu, and Hesdin, all accounted for in 1227; from Normandy: Lyon, Londe, Gouffern, Exmes, Bonneville, Eawy, Arques, accounted for in 1221 and 1227.

152. For example, the incomes of Saint-Germain-en-Laye (1,300 *livres*) and Vincennes (3,200 *livres*) in 1202/03 greatly exceeded the maximums allowed in Reg. A (800–1,000 and 1,200 *livres* respectively). Similarly, Fontainebleau and Poocour were farmed for 2,545 and 1,300 *livres* in 1226, although their respec-tive limits were 1,500 and 360–700 *livres*. Only Rouvray (present Bois de

Boulogne) and Breteuil seem to have conformed to the restrictions. From figures rescued from the *baillis'* accounts in 1217 and 1219 by Brussel, *Nouvel examen* I, 483, notes *a* and *b*, Rouvray appears to have produced 600 *livres* annually, which agrees with the maximum limit. In 1221 Breteuil produced 336 *livres* for one term and had a limit of 400 *livres*. Quite possibly, however, the accounts included more than the sale of wood and are incommensurate with the maximum sale figures for that reason.

153. For the forest policy of Louis IX and Philip IV, see Borrelli de Serres, *Recherches* I, 393–464; Strayer, *Administration of Normandy* 76–79; and, most recently, Rubner, *Untersuchungen*, who concentrates on these two reigns—see especially 22, 23, 92, 93, 105, 127, 185, 186. Strayer and Rubner (especially pp. 64–93) envisage the origins of the *tiers et danger* in the period preceding the Capetian conquest, and reject Borrelli de Serre's placing of its origins during the reign of Louis IX. Though the *tiers* was undoubtedly related to the earlier *licentia vendendi*, evidence for a systematic tax of one-third of the forest revenues does not appear before the 1230s.

11. The King as Seigneur

1. Compare the conclusions of Charles H. Haskins, *Norman Institutions* (Cambridge, Mass., 1918), 5, 6, and Robert Fossier, *La Terre et les hommes en Picardie jusqu'à la fin du XIIIe siècle* (Paris, 1968), II, 668, 669.

2. On the efforts of Ferdinand Lot, *Fidèles ou vassaux? Essai sur la nature juridique du lien qui unissait les grands vassaux à la royauté depuis le milieu du IXe jusqu'à la fin du XIIe siècle* (Paris, 1904), to find early evidence of the great barons rendering homage to the French kings, see the criticism of Jean-François Lemarignier, *Le Gouvernement royal aux premiers temps capétiens (987–1108)* (Paris, 1965), 172, 173, and Thomas N. Bisson, "The Problem of Feudal Monarchy: Aragon, Catalonia and France," *Speculum* 53 (1978): 470, 471.

3. The classic statement may be found in Charles Petit-Dutaillis, *La Monarchie féodale en France et en Angleterre* (Paris, 1933).

4. Lemarignier, *Le Gouvernement royal* 170–76. See also the discussion of Eric Bournazel and Jean-Pierre Poly, "Couronne et mouvance: Institutions et représentations mentales," in *La France de Philippe Auguste* 218–24.

5. Although Louis VI never succeeded in eliciting the performance of vassalage and homage from Henry I as duke of Normandy, he continued to claim superiority as feudal lord. Suger, *Vie de Louis VI* 238–41 (for Aquitaine); 106, 107, 184, 185 (for Normandy). For the Norman theory that rejected French superiority, see C. Warren Hollister, "Normandy, France and the Anglo-Norman *Regnum*," *Speculum* 51 (1976): 229–31.

6. Suger changed his mind about the king doing homage between his *Vie de Louis VI*, 220, 221 (for homage), and his *De Rebus in administratione gestis*, in

Suger, *Oeuvres*, ed. A. Lecoy de la Marche (Paris, 1867), 161, 162 (against homage). See Louis Halphen, "La Place de la royauté dans le système féodale," in *A travers l'histoire du moyen âge* (Paris, 1950), 266–71.

7. If, however, the king should ever give the county of Amiens to someone else who could do homage, the former rights would be resumed. *Actes* I, nos. 139, 155. In 1204 the king similarly received the castle of Gien from the bishop of Auxerre. Teulet I, no. 739. In April 1223, when the king acquired the county of Beaumont-sur-Oise, the bishop of Beauvais remitted the homage formerly due from the count in exchange for a tithe. Teulet I, no. 1571.

8. *Actes* I, no. 422. For other examples, see Bournazel and Poly, "Couronne et mouvance," in *La France de Philippe Auguste* 222, 223.

9. Teulet I, no. 1053. *Actes* III, no. 1309, copied on Reg. C, fol. 56r. *Actes* I, no. 139 is copied on Reg. C, fol. 56v.

10. *Registres* III, G. It may be dated between 1204 and 1207–1208 and probably followed the hierarchic inventory (see chap. 11, at n. 11) because the items of *Radulfus de Roia* and *Guido Malevicini* in the hierarchic list are noted as *heres Radulfi de Roja* and *heres Guidonis Malevicini* in the geographic list. The geographic divisions may be grouped with total number of names as follows: Normandy-Vexin (102); the western fiefs (Brittany, Perche, Anjou, and Touraine, 139); the northeastern fiefs (Flanders, Boulogne, Ponthieu, Saint-Pol, Artois, Vermandois, and Coucy, 151); southern domain (Corbeil, Orléans, Gâtinais, Auxerre, Nevers, and Berry, 80); Dreux (8); Champagne (56); and Burgundy (30).

11. The first category contained thirty counts and two dukes (Burgundy and Brittany). The second category included sixty-one great lords, who usually bore the titles of *domini* or *vicescomes*. The third included seventy-nine castellans, who called themselves *castellani* or *domini* and only occasionally *vicescomes*. The lowest level of *vavassores* comprised forty-three knights without further title. *Registres* III, J–M. The sections of lay vassals of this inventory (I have here omitted the ecclesiastical sections containing archbishops, bishops, and abbots, and the communes) may be dated between October 1203 and January 1206. The section of *comites et duces* was recopied into Register E, to which were added the dukes of Toulouse, Narbonne, Aquitaine, and Normandy. On the use of the term *vavassor* as an equivalent of *miles*, see P. Guilhiermoz, *Essai sur l'origine de la noblesse en France au moyen âge* (Paris, 1902), 165–69.

12. The charter was transcribed after 1212, when Reg. C was begun, and before April 1213, when a royal letter of that date was copied on the page. *Actes* III, no. 1287. For the enfeoffment of Brittany to Pierre de Dreux, see chap. 9, at n. 28.

13. *Actes* III, no. 1083. On the custom of *parage*, see Robert Boutruche, *Seigneurie et féodalité* (Paris, 1970), II, 237–39. On the ordinance of 1209 and its effect, see Pierre Petot, "L'Ordonnance du 1er mai 1209," in *Recueil de travaux offert à M. Clovis Brunel*, Mémoires et documents publiés par la Société de l'Ecole

des Chartes, no. 12 (Paris, 1955), II, 371–80. Paul Ourliac, "Législation, coutumes et coutumiers au temps de Philippe Auguste," in *La France de Philippe Auguste* 473–75, emphasizes the difficulty of enforcing the custom outside the Ile-de-France.

14. For these definitions, see F. L. Ganshof, *Feudalism* (New York, 1961), 72–78, 84–86. On Philip's strategy of enfeoffments, see Josette Metman, "Les Inféodations royales d'après le 'Recueil des actes de Philippe Auguste,'" in *La France de Philippe Auguste* 503–17.

15. Lot, *Fidèles ou vassaux?* has been the principal advocate of this position.

16. On the feudal basis of the Angevin holdings, see ibid. 80–86, 204–18 and, most recently, Hollister, "Normandy," 236–41.

17. See chap. 1, at n. 37.

18. An early example was the charter recording the homage of the count of Flanders to the king of England in 1101 and incidentally the count's liege-fealty to the French king. *Regesta regum Anglo-Normannorum, 1100–1135*, ed. C. Johnson and H. A. Cronne (Oxford, 1956), no. 515.

19. *Actes* I, nos. 7, 376, 398.

20. W. Prevenier, *De oorkonden der graven van Vlaanderen (1191–aanvang 1206)* (Brussels, 1962), II, no. 52.

21. The following are the more important charters of homage: Thibaut III, count of Troyes, 1198, *Actes* II, no. 581; Dauphin, count of Auvergne, 1199, Teulet I, no. 501; King John, 1200, Teulet I, no. 578, *Actes* II, no. 633; Blanche, countess of Troyes, 1201, *Actes* II, 678, *Registres* VI, no. 41; Arthur, count of Brittany, 1202, Teulet I, no. 647, *Actes* II, no. 723; the Angevin barons in 1203, *Registres* VI, no. 45; Ferrand, count of Flanders, 1212, Teulet I, no. 978; Pierre, count of Brittany, 1212, Teulet I, no. 601.

22. Teulet I, nos. 492–94, which were invalidated by the treaty of Le Goulet in 1200, *Actes* II, no. 633.

23. Suger, *Vie de Louis VI* 240. The anonymous *Histoire du roi Louis VII*, ed. A. Molinier in *Vie de Louis le Gros par Suger* (Paris, 1887), 162, asserts similar jurisdiction by Louis VII over Henry of Anjou in 1152. See Lot, *Fidèles ou vassaux?* 205, 206.

24. See chap. 11, at n. 20.

25. For some examples of major vassals: Angoulême, 1199, Teulet I, no. 494; Auvergne, 1199, Teulet I, no. 501; Arthur, 1202, Teulet I, no. 647; Toulouse, 1208, *Actes* III, no. 1021; Flanders, 1212, Teulet I, no. 978; Champagne, 1222, *Registres* V, no. 76. For minor vassals: *Actes* II, nos. 719, 788, 823, 867, Teulet I, no. 668. These examples could be multiplied many times.

26. Two examples: bishop of Langres vs. the duke of Burgundy in 1153, Charles V. Langlois, *Textes relatifs à l'histoire du parlement* (Paris, 1888), 18–21, Luchaire, *Actes de Louis VII* no. 296; and Mont-Saint-Martin vs. the countess of Saint-Quentin in 1200, *Actes* II, 641. Again, many more examples could be found. For a rare exception of a recorded case between two non-ecclesiastical parties, see chap. 11, n. 34.

27. See chap. 9.

28. Teulet I, nos. 412 and 578. *Actes* II, no. 633.

29. Coggeshall 135, 136. Guillaume le Breton, *Philippidos* 155–59. See chap. 5, at n. 74, and chap. 14, at n. 119. That John was also accused of the murder of Arthur was a conflation produced by Capetian propaganda in 1216. See chap. 13, at n. 5.

30. Teulet I, no. 647. *Actes* I, no. 723.

31. *Actes* I, no. 398 (see chap. 5). For the fealty of 1196, see Teulet I, no. 448. For references to it in April 1198, see Delisle, *Catalogue* no. 529, and *Actes* II, no. 580.

32. *Actes* III, nos. 1202, 1203. Guillaume le Breton, *Gesta* 242, 243; *Philippidos* 252, 253. Cartellieri IV, 300–303. Henri Malo, *Un Grand Feudataire, Renaud de Dammartin* (Paris, 1898), 139–43. See chap. 9, at nn. 45–46.

33. In the absence of monographic studies on the pledge, see Achille Luchaire, *Manuel des institutions françaises* (Paris, 1892), 193; Charles Petit-Dutaillis, *La Monarchie féodale en France et en Angleterre* (Paris, 1933), 339, 340; and Josette Metman, "Les Inféodations royales d'après le 'Recueil des actes de Philippe Auguste,'" in *La France de Philippe Auguste* 515–17. Luchaire claims that the practice originated in the eleventh century in the south of France.

34. Suger, *Vie de Louis VI* 240. When Louis VII decided a dispute between the count of Mâcon and the lord of Beaujeu in 1173, pledges guaranteed the decision. Luchaire, *Actes de Louis VII*, no. 628.

35. For the incident of 1184, see chap. 1, at n. 25; 1191: *Actes* I, no. 376; 1196: Teulet I, no. 432; 1203, Beausart: Teulet I, nos. 680–82; 1203, Laon: *Actes* II, no. 737.

36. Teulet I, nos. 438–40.

37. *Registres* V, no. 3. The pledges copied into the registers have been collected in *Registres* V. For example, Reg. A, fols. 72v and 74v, listed the vassals of Touraine and Berry in 1209–1210. Reg. C, fol. 109r, dealt with the same area in 1214–1215. Reg. C, fols. 3r, 30v–31v, contained the Flemish pledges after Bouvines.

38. Dreux: Teulet I, nos. 668, 742, 1523; *Registres* V, nos. 17, 66, 76. Saint-Pol: *Actes* II, nos. 580, 953; *Registres* V, nos. 16, 17, 19, 20, 60, 66. Senlis: Teulet I, nos. 681, 742, 1453; *Registres* V, nos. 13, 66. These and the following citations of pledges do not pretend to be exhaustive.

39. Roches: *Actes* II, no. 788; *Registres* V, nos. 18, 21; Teulet I, no. 1201. Mayenne: Teulet I, no. 805; *Registres* V, nos. 14, 19, 21, 33. Sénébaud: Teulet I, nos. 774, 955: *Registres* V, nos. 7, 10, 11. Bommiers: Teulet I, nos. 771, 1041; *Registres* V, nos. 8, 10. In addition to the above, the following were involved in at least three transactions: Robert, count of Alençon, Geoffroi de Preuilli, Guillaume de Sillé, Jollain *de Bloto*, and Rotrou de Montfort.

40. For example, the lord of Passavant and Jollain *de Bloto*. *Registres* V, nos. 25 and 34.

41. Saint-Omer: Teulet I, no. 1005; *Registres* V, nos. 37, 46, 52, 63. Lens:

Teulet I, nos. 980, 983; *Registres* V, nos. 46, 63, 65. Constable: *Registres* V, nos. 56, 60, 65. Croisilles: Teulet I, no. 985; *Registres* V, nos. 46, 56. Waverin (uncle and nephew): *Registres* V, nos. 46, 44, 56, 57, 60, 63. Harnes: Teulet I, no. 982; *Registres* V, nos. 44, 46, 49, 56, 60, 63–65.

42. *Registres* III, G.

43. Teulet I, no. 666.

44. *Actes* IV, no. 1486. Teulet I, nos. 1211–17. *Registres* V, no. 64. The king's letter must also have been returned with the others, because it was also preserved in the archives. On the background of the incident, see Cartellieri IV, 381, 625, and *Registres* VII, no. 13.

45. Nevelon followed the same procedures for Gautier de Vormezele. *Actes* IV, no. 1487. Teulet I, nos. 1219–28. *Registres* V, no. 63. See also his treatment of Baudouin de Lens in 1215 (*Registres* V, no. 55) and Gérard de Grimberge in 1216 (Teulet I, nos. 1162–73 and *Registres* V, no. 60). For Versailles and Béthisy, see *Actes* IV, no. 1445.

46. Philip's fifth sister, Agnès (b. after 1166 of Adèle de Champagne), was married in 1180 to Alexius Comnenus, emperor of Byzantium. For the daughters of Louis VII, see Cartellieri I, genealogical table 1.

47. See chap. 5, at n. 2 and n. 41. In August 1195 Philip assigned the counties of Eu and Arques as her dowry (*Actes* II, no. 508) but in June 1196 replaced them with Viliers, Rue, Abbeville, Saint-Valery, and Saint-Riquier, retaining the regalia of the last two abbeys (Teulet I, no. 451).

48. See chap. 5, at n. 66.

49. See chap. 5, at n. 72. *Actes* II, no. 709.

50. See chap. 9, at n. 48. *Actes* II, nos. 952, 953, and Teulet I, no. 952, contain the dowry agreements.

51. See chap. 9, at n. 74 and n. 76. *Actes* III, no. 1287, and *Registres* VI, no. 70, contain the mutual terms of the marriage agreement. See also Cartellieri IV, 344, 350, 351.

52. See chap. 9, at nn. 38–40. Teulet I, nos. 601, 925. *Registres* V, no. 13, and *Actes* III, no. 1133, contain the terms of the marriage agreements.

53. *Registres* VI, no. 81. The prince was still alive in 1218 (see Teulet I, no. 1302), but by 1219 the count was promising not to marry Agnès to designated suitors. *Registres* V, no. 69. In 1221 Agnès married Guy, the son of Gaucher, count of Saint-Pol (Teulet I, no. 1447). See Petit-Dutaillis, *Louis VIII* 97, 98, and Cartellieri IV, 490.

54. Philip's illegitimate son, Pierre Charlot, was assigned a career in the church. See chap. 12, at n. 10.

55. After the Capetian conquest, for example, Guillaume des Roches wrote the king advising him about his rights as regards heiresses according to the customs of Anjou, Maine, and Touraine. Teulet I, no. 1062. In the absence of a general study on the feudal prerogatives with respect to marriage, see Achille Luchaire, *Manuel des institutions françaises: Période des Capétiens directs* (Paris, 1892), 203.

56. See chap. 1, at n. 57. *Actes* I, no. 106.

57. See chap. 5, at n. 76. *Actes* II, no. 612. Teulet I, no. 502. Count Pierre promised specifically to exclude Philippe, marquis of Namur, who in 1199 was out of royal favor. Delisle, *Catalogue* nos. 575–77.

58. See chap. 11, at n. 53, and *Registres* V, no. 69. Thibaut of Champagne, Enguerran de Coucy, and the son of the duke of Burgundy were excluded in addition to the son of King John.

59. Teulet I, no. 1447. The following year the dowager countess Mathilde again promised not to marry without royal consent. Ibid. I, no. 1502.

60. *Registres* VI, no. 41. *Actes* II, no. 678. See chap. 9.

61. *Actes* II, no. 952, III, no. 1042. See chap. 9. In 1195 the king exacted a promise not to marry without royal consent from Mathilde, the dowager widow of count Philippe of Flanders, but she was no longer in the line of succession. Paris, BN lat. 9015, fol. 3. Teulet I, no. 428.

62. *Registres* VI, no. 58. Teulet I, no. 601. See chap. 9, at n. 27.

63. Teulet I, nos. 1305, 1314. See Jean Richard, *Les Ducs de Bourgogne et la formation du duché du XIᵉ au XIVᵉ siècle* (Dijon, 1954), 188, 189. For other examples, see the charters of Isabelle, lady of Amboise, in 1215 (*Registres* VI, no. 80) and Alix, countess of Eu, in 1219 (Teulet I, nos. 1353, 1360).

64. See chap. 1, at n. 23.

65. See *Actes* I, no. 453, and Delisle, *Catalogue* no. 399, for 1193; see chap. 5, at n. 40, for 1196; see chap. 11, at n. 59, for 1221.

66. *Actes* III, nos. 1043, 1044, Teulet I, no. 902, and Anonymous of Béthune, *Chronique des rois* 763.

67. See, for example, Guillaume de Garlande, who married the sister of Gaucher de Châtillon in 1193 (*Actes* I, no. 451, II, no. 500); the marriage between the children of Nevelon the Marshal and Girard, lord of Equancourt, in 1209 (*Actes* III, no. 1062); and the marriage of the daughter of Barthélemy de Roye to the brother of the castellan of Bruges in 1214 (*Actes* III, no. 1348).

68. The two fundamental studies on the *fief-rente* are Michel Sczaniecki, *Essai sur les fiefs-rentes* (Paris, 1946), which defines the institution for France, and Bryce D. Lyon, *From Fief to Indenture: The Transition from Feudal to Non-Feudal Contract in Western Europe* (Cambridge, Mass., 1957), which expands the scope to include England, the Low Countries, and Germany. For their respective definitions, see pp. 7 and 5 of these volumes.

69. Sczaniecki (*Essai* 7) insists that a *fief-rente* cannot be assigned on land, but Lyon (*From Fief to Indenture* 133–35) distinguishes between revenues assigned *on* lands, in which the lord retains possession of the land (which are true *fief-rentes*), and revenues assigned *in* lands, where the vassal has the lands as well (which are not *fief-rentes*). It is not always possible to distinguish the two cases from the documents, however, and it is less certain whether contemporaries always made the distinction.

70. Lyon, *From Fief to Indenture* 243.

71. Ibid. 66–68. Sczaniecki, *Essai* 97, 98.

72. Lyon, *From Fief to Indenture* 29–39.

73. The king permitted Robert to alienate 30 *livres* of the revenue to other vassals, and this portion eventually returned to the king. Louis finally conferred the 30 *livres* on his butler, Guy de Senlis, who was permitted to collect it at Montméliant or Senlis. Luchaire, *Actes de Louis VII* no. 353, p. 401. By 1202 this revenue was collected at Paris. See *Budget* CXLVII (1), CLXXIV (2), CLXXXIX (1), and *Registres* II, D, no. 23. Count Robert's remaining *fief-rente* at Poissy had apparently increased, because in 1185 he alienated another 30 *livres* to the Hôtel-Dieu. *Actes* I, no. 146, *Budget* CXLII (2), and *Registres* II, C, n. 111. The examples from the time of Suger (1147–1149) cited by Eric Bournazel, *Le Gouvernement capétien au XIIe siècle* (Limoges, 1975), 105, 106, are more doubtful. They may have been wages or other forms of remuneration without vassalic obligations.

74. For example, the king's grants to Jean *Nigrus* in 1192 (*Actes* I, no. 403), Richard de Vernon in 1196 (*Actes* II, no. 519), Raoul Goujon in 1200 (*Actes* II, no. 664, III, no. 1280), Roger de Maule in 1200 (Delisle, *Catalogue* no. 646A) and Raoul de Louvain in 1203 (*Actes* II, no. 768). For a summary and an example of the difficulty of identifying the *fief-rentes* in the accounts of 1202/03, see *Budget* 93, 94, 121.

75. Although most names were grouped according to the *prévôtés* from which the revenues were paid, the last twenty-one in the first redaction were merely appended to the *prévôté* at Mantes. Between February 1205 and 1212, Etienne de Gallardon added another twenty-four names, worth 1,674 *livres* annually. When the whole inventory was recopied into Reg. C in 1212, four names were added (totalling 140 *livres*), and a second scribe added five more names (totalling 200 *livres*) probably before 1220. *Registres* II, D. Gaston Dept, *Les Influences anglaises et françaises dans le comté de Flandre au début du XIIIeme siècle*, Université de Gand, Recueil de travaux publiés par la Faculté de Philosophie et Lettres, 59 (Ghent, 1928), 196–98, dates the second hand in Reg. A to ca. 1208, but his evidence is purely circumstantial.

76. Chamberlains: Eudes, *Poetellus*, Gautier the Father, and Renaud; sergeants: Roger *Pice*, Martin *Andolle*, and Jean Latimer; Genoese: Rubeus de Wolta, Nicolas de Aurea (replaced by Manuel), Guillaume de Spina, and Heliot de Genoa (replaced by Jacobus Helioti). In 1226 Louis VIII confirmed to Guillaume *Spinula* the *fief-rente* given him by his father. Reg. E, fol. 226v. Delisle, *Catalogue* no. 2231.

77. On the English deployment of *fief-rentes*, see Bryce Lyon, "The Money Fief under the English Kings, 1066–1485," *EHR* 66 (1951): 161–93, summarized in *From Fief to Indenture* 32–39, 169, 170, 202–6.

78. Lyon, "Money Fief," and *From Fief to Indenture* 206.

79. Robert de Dreux's *fief-rente* (400 *livres angevins*) had originated with Henry II. *Rotuli chartarum in Turri Londonensi asservati*, ed. Thomas D. Hardy (London, 1837), I (1), 58. For Barthélemy de Roye (60 *livres angevins*), ibid. I

(1) 64. Barthélemy also held *fief-rentes* from the count of Champagne in 1200 and 1221. Auguste Longnon, *Documents relatifs au comté de Champagne et de Brie, 1172–1361* (Paris, 1901), I, 86. Sczaniecki, *Essai* 99, 128.

80. *Actes* II, no. 519. Lyon (*From Fief to Indenture* 27) interprets the amount of the *fief-rente* as 800 *livres*, but this was the value of the lands for which Richard de Vernon owed the service of five knights. The *fief-rente* was 15 *livres*, 15 *sous*, as is confirmed by *Budget* CXLI (2) and *Registres* II, D, no. 45.

81. *Actes* II, no. 827. *Registres* II, D, no. 96. Apparently, Barthélemy de Roye was already sufficiently indebted to the king not to require a *fief-rente*.

82. Normans: Robert de Poissy, Philippe de Blaru, Pierre de Mauvoisin, Robert de Meulan, Richard de Vernon, and the castellan of Néaufle. Loire: Guy de *Monte Dulceto*, Gervais de Pruillé, Robert Karrell, and Hervé de *Bello Mortario*. *Registres* II, D.

83. Gislebert de Mons, *Chronicon Hanoniense* 548. Sczaniecki, *Essai* 33. Lyon, *From Fief to Indenture* 27, 165. The term 100 *libratas terre* casts doubt on whether this was a true *fief-rente*. In the beginning it may have been such, but at the end the king gave Jacques land worth 100 *livres* at Crépy-en-Laonnois. The fundamental study on the competition between the Angevins and the Capetians over Flanders is Dept, *Influences*.

84. *Registres* II, D.

85. *Actes* II, no. 952. See chap. 9, at n. 48.

86. Dept, *Influences* 39–45. *Registres* II, D.

87. Guillaume the Uncle's *fief-rente* from the *prévôté* of Laon was recorded as early as February 1203. *Budget* CLXXI (2). For the identification of the Flemish nobility, I have relied on E. Warlop, *The Flemish Nobility before 1300* (Kortrijk, 1975), 4 vols. See II, no. 192/22, for Guillaume V, castellan of Saint-Omer, and II, no. 134/4, for Gilbert I de Bourghelles, who was also castellan of Lille (1200–ca. 1208) before the majority of his son.

88. *Registres* II, D, nos. 22, 94, and 126. I have identified the Sibyl who held a *fief-rente* from the *prévôté* of Paris after November 1202 (*Budget* CXLVI [2]) as Sibyl of Alsace, wife of Robert I de Wavrin, seneschal of Flanders, who died ca. 1197. Sibyl held the seneschalship during the minority of her son Hellin II until he was knighted at Bouvines. Warlop, *Flemish Nobility* II, no. 227/16, 22. The identification of the family of Harnes presents some difficulties. In November 1202 a Michel de Harnes (probably Michel II and also Constable) received a *fief-rente* from the *prévôté* of Péronne-Bapaume. *Budget* CLII (2). In June 1212 the king renewed this *fief-rente* to Michel de Harnes (probably Michel III), who was uncle of Michel the Constable. *Actes* III, no. 1245. See also *Actes* IV, no. 1473. Warlop, *Flemish Nobility* II, no. 103/4, 7, and no. 28/18. Raze V de Gavere: Warlop, *Flemish Nobility* II, no. 86/11.

89. *Registres* II, D. The duke of Brabant's (called here the duke of Louvain) *fief-rente* (200 marks) was conferred on him in February 1205 (ibid., VI, no. 48) and renewed in April 1213 (*Actes* III, no. 1287). See chap. 9, at n. 58. It

was also noticed by the chronicler Ralph of Coggeshall 148. On the important Flemish families see Warlop, *Flemish Nobility* II, nos. 167/17 (Oudenaarde), 220/18 (Voormezele), 336/8 (Zottengem), 49/4 (Comines). Osto de Arbre appeared in the charter of Philippe, marquis of Namur, in 1210. Teulet I, no. 952. See chap. 11, at n. 92. Other lesser Flemish figures include Gérard de Saint-Aubert (Warlop, *Flemish Nobility* I, 506), Hubert de Carency (ibid. II, no. 45), Nicolas and Gérard de Condé (-sur-l'Escaut) (Dept, *Influences*, 83, 85), Gilles d'Aigremont (Warlop, *Flemish Nobility* II, no. 2/5), and Guillaume de Beaumont (Dept, *Influences* 83, 84). A number of these served as pledges for Philip. Those who served frequently as pledges and received *fief-rentes* include the butler of Senlis; Robert, count of Dreux; the count of Saint-Pol, the castellan of Saint-Omer; Michel de Harnes; Robert de Bommiers; and Guillaume de Lignières. See chap. 11, at n. 41. In 1205 Robert de Bommiers received a *fief-rente* from Saumur. *Actes* II, no. 912.

90. Dept, *Influences* 56–59, 61, 62.

91. See chap. 9, at n. 48. *Actes* II, no. 953. Dept, *Influences* 82–84. The company also included Gautier from the traditionally favorable family of Avesnes.

92. Teulet I, no. 952. The six were Arnaud IV d'Oudenaarde, Gérard de Saint-Aubert, Guillaume the Uncle, Nicolas and Gérard de Condé, and Osto de Arbre.

93. *Rotuli litterarum clausarum*, ed. Thomas D. Hardy (London, 1833), I, 130. *Foedera*, ed. Thomas Rymer (London, 1816), I (1), 106. Cartellieri IV, 314, n. 3.

94. *Rotuli litterarum patentium*, ed. Thomas D. Hardy (London, 1835), I (1), 93. The eight were Gilbert I de Bourghelles, Arnaud IV d'Oudenaarde, Raze V de Gavare, Gautier III de Voormezele, Gérard and Nicolas de Condé, Baudouin III de Comines, and Guillaume the Uncle.

95. *Rotuli chartarum*, ed. Hardy, I (1), 186.

96. The three who were paid were: Guillaume V, castellan of Saint-Omer (ibid. I, 119); Hugues de Boves for the fief of Osto de Arbre (*Rotulus mise* in *Documents Illustrative of English History in the XIIIth and XIVth Centuries*, ed. Henry Cole [London, 1844], 238, other gifts on 249, 253); and Gautier de Zottegem (*Documents*, ed. Cole, 240, 241). For this final name I interpret the name *Walterius de Subrigh'* or *de Subringham* as Gautier de Zottegem. See also Dept, *Influences* 115.

97. The three who went to England were Arnaud IV de Oudenaarde, Raze V de Gavere, and Gilbert I de Bourghelles. Anonymous of Béthune, *Chronique des rois* 707–13; *Histoire des ducs* 139. See Warlop, *Flemish Nobility* I, 308, and Dept, *Influences* 128.

98. *Actes* III, no. 1245. *Rotulus mise* in *Documents*, ed. Cole, 239, 242.

99. *Registres* II, D, nos. 106, 109. Hubert de Carency's name was also deleted from the list of *vavassores*.

100. Ibid. The seventeen do not include the two above (n. 99) who were

struck off from Register A. They do include Gautier I de Zottegem, whose name was not transferred from Register A to C and was therefore eliminated by the scribe who made the second copy.

101. *Budget* CLII (2). *Actes* III, no. 1245. Sczaniecki, *Essai* 4–6, suggests that *in bursa* implies a central treasury. In Reg. E the entire inventory was entitled *Feoda in bursa*.

102. *Registres* VI, no. 48.

103. On Philip's ordinary finances after the conquest of Normandy, see Table 8.

104. Nevers, 1184: *Actes* I, no. 106; Flanders, Vermandois, 1185: see chap. 1, at n. 52; Vermandois, 1191: *Actes* I, no. 399 (in addition, the king paid the countess 13,000 *livres*); Boulogne, 1191: *Actes* I, no. 398.

105. Teulet I, no. 1337, and *Actes* IV, no. 1711.

106. See Table 10 for the references.

107. The royal charter (*Actes* II, no. 678) of 1201 for Troyes mentioned that a relief would be paid when the heir came of age, but no indication of that relief when Thibaut was declared a major in 1222 has survived.

108. Nortier and Baldwin, "Contributions," 20. Delisle, *Catalogue* no. 2048. Also Teulet I, no. 1445. For other reliefs collected in 1221, see chap. 10, at n. 100.

109. Philip also attempted to assume custody of Brittany in 1186 on the death of Count Geoffrey, but was prevented by Henry II. See chap. 1, at n. 31. Nevers: *Actes* I, no. 106; Vermandois: *Actes* II, nos. 496, 497, 595, 596.

110. For 1201, see *Actes* II, no. 678, and *Registres* VI, no. 41; for 1209, Teulet I, no. 878; for 1213, Teulet I, no. 1054, and *Actes* III, nos. 1313, 1314. As an exception, the king allowed the walls of Provins to be repaired in 1216. *Actes* IV, no. 1422. On the wardship of Champagne, see chap. 9.

111. Charters: *Actes* II, no. 688, III, no. 1217; Jews: *Actes* III, no. 1127, Teulet I, no. 479, *Actes* II, nos. 678, 776, 955, III, no. 1127; serfs: *Actes* II, no. 921, III, no. 1094, Teulet I, nos. 939, 940, *Actes* III, no. 1138; merchants: *Actes* III, no. 1107; duels: *Actes* III, no. 1394.

112. See chap. 9, at nn. 48–49.

113. See chap. 7.

114. For examples of *collecto exercitu* until 1195, see Rigord 17, 41, 49, 78, 94, 123, 125, 127, 131. For his citation of figures, see Rigord 131 (1195), 152 (1202), 165 (1208). For examples of Guillaume le Breton's figures, see *Gesta* 220 (1204), 251 (1213).

115. Gislebert de Mons, *Chronicon Hanoniense* 531–33, 547. J. F. Verbruggen (*The Art of Warfare in Western Europe During the Middle Ages* [Amsterdam, 1977], 8) believes that Gislebert is generally reliable (but not infallible) in his figures for knights but cannot be trusted concerning sergeants.

116. See chap. 5, at n. 48. In particular, see Howden IV, 56, 57, for the English list of captives. Richard's letter recounting the battle (found in Howden IV, 58, and Coggeshall 84, 85) declares that he personally captured Mathieu de

Montmorency, Alain de Roucy, and Foulques *de Gilerval*. Rigord 141, 142 names the following captives: Alain de Roucy, Mathieu de *Marli* (*sic* for Montmorency), Guillaume de Merlou, Jr., and Philippe de Nanteuil.

117. Gislebert de Mons 531–33; Cartellieri I, 255; and Rigord 161, 162.

118. Langres: *Actes* II, no. 772; Arras: *Actes* II, no. 774; Auxerre: *Actes* III, no. 968; Nevers: *Actes* III, no. 1052; Mâcon: *Actes* III, no. 1066. See chap. 8, at nn. 30–36.

119. *Actes* II, no. 650 (see chap. 8, at n. 19). *Actes* III, no. 1169.

120. Guillaume le Breton, *Gesta* 229, 230. The local chronicle, *De Gestis episcoporum Autissiodorensium*, is strangely silent about the dispute over military service, possibly because the bishops lost their case. In vague terms the chronicler does state that the bishop of Orléans did partially liberate his vassals from royal service. *PL* 138: 332. Innocent III, *Regesta*, *PL* 216: 357, 417, 570, 571, 619, 620, 635; Potthast I, nos. 4145, 4747, 4245, 4443, 4444, 4531, 4532, 4543. *Actes* III, nos. 1155, 1257, 1258. Teulet I, nos. 1017, 1018. See also the account in Constance Brittain Bouchard, *Spirituality and Administration: The Role of the Bishop in Twelfth-Century Auxerre* (Cambridge, Mass., 1979), 132–34.

121. When the aged Gérard de Douai, bishop of Châlons-sur-Marne, resigned his see, he was required to maintain his military obligations because the bishopric was located in a troubled region between the borders of France and the Empire. Honorius III, *Regesta*, in Presutti I, no. 316; text in Horoy, *Opera* II, 249.

122. Teulet II, nos. 1617, 1624. Reg. E, fol. 140r.

123. *Scripta de feodis* no. 133. Petit-Dutaillis, *Louis VIII* 408, 409.

124. See *Registres* III, O, and Appendix D for the details. Nevers, which was subject to the host, was omitted, probably by oversight. Mâcon, which was subject to limited host duty, was annotated only with "*regalia*."

125. Appendix D, and *Registres* II, S, T.

126. *Registres* III, G.

127. For a fuller treatment of the inventory of 1172 see chap. 11, at nn. 145–47.

128. The figures for the bishops, abbots, and lay baronage are more easily obtained than the totals for the entire duchy, which include numerous indeterminate factors among the lower vassals. I have therefore adopted the totals arrived at in 1172 by the compilers of the survey (1,500 and 581) to calculate the percentages. Working with the version found in the *Red Book of the Exchequer* and attempting to refine these figures, Thomas K. Keefe has arrived at two sets of totals for enfeoffments and knights owed: 1,846/575 and 1,500/458. *Feudal Assessments and the Political Community under Henry II and His Sons* (Berkeley and Los Angeles, 1983). (I am grateful to the author for allowing me to consult his study before publication.) Working with the version in Reg. A, I calculate enfeoffments and knights owed as 1,812/556.

129. *Actes* I, no. 51. The same distinction appeared in an agreement between

Philip and Richard over Saint-Martin of Tours in 1190. *Actes* I, no. 361. On the distinction between *guerra* and *bellum*, see Georges Duby, *Le Dimanche de Bouvines* (Paris, 1973), 145, 146.

130. Suger, *Vie de Louis VI* 218–30. When Suger states that the count of Flanders brought 10,000 knights, which he could have trebled if he wished, his statistics cannot be trusted.

131. For 1197, see *Actes* II, no. 566. For 1200–1201, Guillaume le Breton, *Gesta* 206, and *Actes* II, no. 700. For 1207, Teulet I, no. 827[bis], p. 567. For 1209, Teulet I, no. 903. On the concept of the defense of the realm, see Joseph R. Strayer, "Defense of the Realm and Royal Power in France," in *Studi in onore di Gino Luzzatto* (Milan, 1949), IV, 289–96, reprinted in Joseph R. Strayer, *Medieval Statecraft and the Perspectives of History* (Princeton, 1971), 294.

132. The following conclusions are drawn from Appendix E, which is compiled from Guillaume le Breton, Anonymous of Béthune, and the muster-list in Reg. C.

133. Guillaume le Breton, *Philippidos* 290.

134. Bishops: Beauvais and Laon. Counts: Beaumont and Saint-Pol. Of the fifty-five names, forty-one were found on the banneret list. Guillaume le Breton added thirteen names and the Anonymous of Béthune another five.

135. Vermandois and Valois, the inheritance of Countess Aliénor (280); Ponthieu and Artois (185); Coucy and Laonnois (95); the Vexin (103); and Normandy (55). The total from Vermandois includes 20 from the bishop of Beauvais and 20 from the count of Beaumont; that of Coucy includes 10 from the bishop of Laon; that of Ponthieu includes 30 from the count of Saint-Pol. The sole exception to the multiple of five was Amaury de Poissy, who accounted for three.

136. Burgundy (180), Champagne (180), Dreux (40), Auxerre (30), Bar-le-Duc (30), Soissons (30), Melun (25), Guines (20), and lesser bannerets (25). Most likely their totals did equal those of the muster-list. These estimates are drawn from Verbruggen, *Art of Warfare* 224–26, with the following modifications: I have eliminated the count of Sancerre, whom Verbruggen seems to have confused with Etienne de Sancerre. I have disregarded 70 knights from Etienne de Longchamps (a figure given by Guillaume le Breton) as being included in the Vexin and Norman totals. I have considered Enguerran de Coucy's contingent as included in the Coucy totals, probably in Ansoldus de Ronquerolis's figure. On Verbruggen's p. 226, the contingents of Normandy and Coucy are already accounted in the muster-list of Reg. C. My general estimates are nonetheless commensurate with Verbruggen's.

137. Guillaume le Breton, *Philippidos* 286. The figure of 800 does not seem unreasonable, since it was half of Philip's force at Bouvines and enough to scare off John. Actually, when Philip reunited his army from Bouvines with that of Louis, he had more than 2,000 knights for the Poitevin campaign, according to Guillaume le Breton, *Gesta* 298. See Verbruggen, *Art of War* 223, 226.

138. Verbruggen, *Art of War* 227, 228. See the summary of evidence in Cartellieri IV, 611, 612: Chronicle of Tours (1,500), Chronique de Saint-Denis (1,500), *Annales Sanctae Columbae Senonensis* (1,300), André de Marchiennes (1,500).

139. *Liber feudorum major*, ed. Francisco Miquel Rosell (Barcelona, 1945–47), 2 vols. See Thomas N. Bisson, "The Problem of Feudal Monarchy: Aragon, Catalonia, and France," *Speculum* 53 (1978): 468, 469, and "Ramon de Caldes (c. 1135–c. 1200): Dean of Barcelona and King's Minister," in *Law, Church, and Society: Essays in Honor of Stephan Kuttner*, ed. Kenneth Pennington and Robert Somerville (Philadelphia, 1977), 281, 286, 287.

140. *Documents relatifs au comté de Champagne et de Brie, 1172–1361*, ed. Auguste Longnon (Paris, 1901), I. See Theodore Evergates, *Feudal Society in the Bailliage of Troyes under the Counts of Champagne, 1152–1284* (Baltimore, 1975), 9, 10, 61.

141. Three questions were asked: (1) How many knights had been enfeoffed before the death of Henry I (1130); (2) how many had been enfeoffed since then; and (3) how many knights did they support directly from their domain to fulfill their owed service? Owed service could only be computed, in certain cases, by adding items (1) and (3). The totals of enfeoffed knights were furnished by (1) and (2). *Liber niger scaccarii*, ed. Thomas Hearne (Oxford, 1728), I, 49–340, and *The Red Book of the Exchequer*, ed. Hubert Hall (London, 1896), I, 186–445. The three questions were repeated in the charter of the archbishop of York, as well as the request for liege allegiance. *Red Book of the Exchequer* I, 412, 413. See also *Red Book of the Exchequer* II, ccxvi–ccxx; Sidney Painter, *Studies in the History of the English Feudal Barony* (Baltimore, 1943), 32–35; C. Warren Hollister, *The Military Organization of Norman England* (Oxford, 1965), 30–32; and Keefe, *Feudal Assessments*.

142. *Catalogus baronum*, ed. Evelyn Jamison, in *Fonti per la storia d'Italia* (Rome, 1972), 101. See also ibid. xv–xxii and C. H. Haskins, "England and Sicily in the Twelfth Century," *EHR* 26 (1911): 655–65.

143. In *Scripta de feodis* nos. 435–51, and H. Navel, "L'Enquête de 1133 sur les fiefs de l'évêché de Bayeux," *Bulletin de la Société des Antiquaires de Normandie* 42 (1934): 13–38. The short version was also published in *Red Book of the Exchequer*, II, 645–47. See, too, Charles H. Haskins, *Norman Institutions* (Cambridge, Mass., 1918), 15–20, and Hollister, *Military Organization* 75–80.

144. *The Chronicle of Robert of Torigni*, in *Chronicles of the Reigns of Stephen, Henry II, and Richard I*, ed. Richard Howlett (London, 1889), IV, 251. Apparently, the findings of this inquest have survived for the Avranchin. Léopold Delisle, *Recueil des actes de Henri II* (Paris, 1909), introduction, pp. 345–47. See also Haskins, *Norman Institutions* 338ff.

145. The barons provided two letters each to be deposited in the royal treasury. The first was sealed and gave the number of names owed the king; the second, unsealed, indicated the names and therefore also the numbers of knights

enfeoffed. *Vavassors* were listed after the knights. Howlett, *Chronicles* IV 349–53, and *Scripta de feodis* nos. 452–61. The notice was attributed to Abbot Robert de Torigni.

146. Published in *Red Book of the Exchequer* II, 624–45, *Scripta de feodis* nos. 417–34, and *Registres* III A. An indication to a roll is found in *Red Book of the Exchequer* II, 643. See the discussion of Jacques Boussard, "L'Enquête de 1172 sur les services de chevalier en Normandie," in *Recueil de Travaux offert à M. Clovis Brunel*, Mémoires et documents publiés par la Société de l'Ecole des Chartes, 12 (Paris, 1955), 193–208. The totals do not correspond exactly to the findings of the French version. See chap. 11, n. 128.

147. See chap. 15, at n. 79. On Alexander of Swereford, see *Red Book of the Exchequer* I, lxii. On contemporary attempts in Germany to compile feudal registers, see Waldemar Lippert, *Die deutschen Lehnbücher: Beitrag zum Registerwesen und Lehnrecht des Mittelalters* (Leipzig, 1903), 9, 10, 130, 131, 152, 176.

148. See chap. 15, at n. 47.

149. For examples of these annotations, see *Registres* III, A.

150. *Actes* II, no. 861. Teulet I, no. 738. See Powicke, *Loss of Normandy* 343, 344. Pacy-sur-Eure was ceded to the French king in 1194.

151. Breteuil decreased from eighty-one to fifty-two, Grandmesnil from forty to twenty-six. Apparently the inquest stirred up controversy because seven fiefs were denied at Breteuil and four at Grandmesnil. At the end of each survey was appended a list of knights doing homage directly to the king. *Registres* III, B.

152. *Actes* II, no. 901. Other baronies or barons named in the letter were Gravenchon-en-Caux, Geoffroi de Sai, Robert Bertram (his fiefs were restored by 1207, however), Moutiers-Hubert, and Saint-Jean-le-Thomas. The roll listing knights in England has apparently disappeared. On the transfer of fiefs, see the conclusions of Lucien Musset, "Quelques problèmes posés par l'annexion de la Normandie au domaine royal français," in *La France de Philippe Auguste* 296–300.

153. Confiscated baronies were those of the earl of Leicester (Breteuil, Grandmesnil, and Pacy), the earl of Warenne (Belcombre and Mortemer), the earl of Clare, the count of Meulan (Beaumont-le-Roger and Pont-Audemer), and the lord of Montfort-sur-Risle. The inventory also noted the confiscated lands of the earl of Chester and the earlier acquisitions of Evreux (Evreux and Gravenchon-en-Caux) and Vaudreuil. *Registres* III, C. The earls of Gloucester and Chester, whose fiefs were added to the royal domain, were included together thus producing confusion in the rubric. The fiefs of Auge belonging to Robert Bertram are listed under two categories because by 1207 they had been restored. Evreux was acquired in 1200 and Vaudreuil in 1203. The fiefs of Geoffroi de Sai are scattered throughout the inventory. Powicke, *Loss of Normandy* 351. I have not been able to locate the honors of Arundel, Moutiers-Hubert, and Saint-Jean in the survey of 1207. The survey concludes with miscellaneous lists—for example, fiefs in the French and Norman Vexin, escheats, the fiefs of Meulan in the king's

hand, and the fiefs and subtenants of Néaufle. In the middle, it includes a list of Breton bannerets found in *Registres* III, G.

154. The phrase *sed dicunt quod . . . viderunt* in the item on the bishop of Avranches suggests an inquest. *Registres* III, C.

155. These are my calculations from ibid. III, C.

156. Before 1212, when Reg. A was superseded by Reg. C in the royal chancery, one final feudal inventory was included in its pages. The names of thirty-eight knights were listed as "those who give fealty to the lord king for the honor and county of Mortain." Although not dated, this survey most likely followed the seizure of Mortain from Renaud, count of Boulogne, after the judgment of September 1211. At the same time, the king was seeking oaths of fealty from the *vidame* of Picquigni and Renaud d'Amiens against the count of Boulogne, the German emperor, and the English king. The demand for fealty from the knights of Mortain therefore facilitated the eventual transfer of the barony to the king's son, Philip Hurepel. The date of the survey is suggested by its place in Reg. A. It was written by Scribe P (fol. 85v), who wrote other charters in the same gathering (no. 9) in 1210 and 1211. The king's letters to Renaud were copied in the same gathering on fol. 82r. For the surrounding events, see Delisle, *Catalogue* nos. 1301–4, and Cartellieri IV, 303.

157. For example, on fols. 24–26, immediately following the *Feoda Normannie*, scribe ζ copied new inventories of the often-surveyed baronies of Breteuil and Grandmesnil, as well as Sainte-Scolasse, which had returned to the king in 1207–1208. This survey was most likely made by Barthélemy Droon, the *bailli* of Verneuil, whose name appears in the heading. To it scribe ζ appended new inventories of Evreux and Vaudreuil and of the fiefs of Longchamps. *Bailliage* of Barthélemy Droon: Reg. C, fol. 24r, v, *Scripta de feodis* nos. 518–24; Evreux and Vaudreuil: Reg. C, fol. 24v, *Scripta* nos. 526–29; Longchamps: Reg. C, fol. 24v, *Scripta* no. 530. Scribe ε completed the Longchamps survey and added another of the *vicomté* of Meulan. Longchamps: Reg. C, fol. 25v, *Scripta* nos. 531, 532; *vicomté* of Meulan: fol. 26r, *Scripta* nos. 533–35. Scribe ε also added an inventory of the *vicomté* at fol. 9r. *Registres* III, E. Elsewhere scribe ζ included inventories of Robert de Poissy: Reg. C, fol. 9r, *Scripta* no. 104, n. 8; and Guy de la Roche-Guyon: fol. 127r, *Registres* III, F.

158. Jean de Gisors: Reg. C, fol. 8v, recopied in Reg. E, fol. 37r, v, *Scripta de feodis* nos. 98–103, after the version of E; Nogent: Reg. C, fol. 122v, recopied in Reg. E, fols. 35v–36r, *Scripta* nos. 84–91, after the version of E (another list of knights of Nogent who did homage to the king was copied in Reg. C, fol. 10v, *Scripta* no. 536); Cotentin: Reg. C, fols. 126r–127r, recopied in E, fols. 25r–26r, *Scripta* nos. 2–16.

159. The Longchamps survey was taken after Etienne de Longchamps's death at Bouvines in 1214 and that of Nogent after the fief was acquired in 1218–1219. Although difficult to date precisely, these preparatory inventories were com-

pleted before 1220, when they were included in Reg. E. Etienne de Long-champs's fiefs were inherited by his son Baudry. Powicke, *Loss of Normandy* 334, 335. On the acquisition of Nogent l'Erembert, see chap. 13, at n. 41. The survey in Reg. C, fol. 122v, may have been made prior to the death of the count of Blois, because the word *defuncti* was added to the version in Reg. E.

160. Cotentin, Bayeux-Avranches, Rouen, Verneuil, Caen, Gisors-Vexin, Bon-neville, and Caux. The survey of Reg. E is edited in *Scripta de feodis* nos. 1–313.

161. Under the *bailliage* of Bonneville, for example, it was noted that the knight fiefs pertaining to baronies outside the *bailliage* of Lisieux answered for service at Breteuil, Beaumont, Montfort, etc. Since they had been recorded else-where, they were not repeated at Bonneville. Ibid. no. 131. For other examples of cross-references, see nos. 12 and 132.

162. The items that can be dated most recently in the survey are ibid. nos. 19, 144, 166, Fontaine-Guérard given to Gautier the Young in 1218 (*Actes* IV, no. 1516); *Scripta de feodis* no. 49, a donation to the abbey of Belle-Etoile in 1218–1219 (*Actes* IV, no. 1544); *Scripta* nos. 84–91, the incorporation of Nogent l'Erembert into the royal domain from December 1218 to February 1219 (see chap. 13, at n. 41); *Scripta* no. 195, the gift of Bonneuil-en-Valois to Robert de la Tournelle in 1218 (*Actes* IV, no. 1531).

163. At times, the respondents expressed their ignorance over questions and opposed allegations of the *baillis* and other barons. Examples of direct testi-mony: "*ut dicit*," *Scripta de feodis* no. 48; "*Robertus Bertram cognoscit*," ibid. no. 48; "*Rogerus dicit*," ibid. no. 113; examples of writing: "*domina cognovit per litteras suas*," ibid. no. 51; of ignorance: ibid. nos. 7, 48; of opposition: nos. 18, 113, 132, 169.

164. Ibid. nos. 1, 17, 18, 19–27, 48, 49.

165. Barthélemy Droon, *bailli* of Verneuil, surveyed Sainte-Scolasse as well as the reoccurring baronies of Grandmesnil and Breteuil, and Pierre du Thillai, *bailli* of Caen, included the baronies of Montbrai, Chester, Cleville, as well as Nonant, Sainte-Scolasse, and Montpinçon, which had escheated from Guérin de Glapion in 1207–1208. Grandmesnil, *Scripta de feodis* nos. 34–36; Breteuil, nos. 37–39; Sainte-Scolasse, nos. 44, 45; Montbrai, no. 52; Nonant, no. 54; Sainte-Scolasse, no. 55; Montpinçon, no. 56; Chester, nos. 57, 58; Cleville, no. 59. Barthélemy Droon's survey of Grandmesnil, etc., was not copied directly from the preparatory survey in Reg. C. See chap. 11, n. 157.

166. These are my calculations, drawn from *Scripta de feodis* nos. 1–177, which naturally contain a number of assumptions in interpreting the evidence.

167. Bertram, ibid. no. 2; Vernon, no. 4; Hommet, no. 5; Préaux, no. 28; Tancarville, nos. 169–175. Other examples can be added to these.

168. *Scripta de feodis* nos. 7, 20, 22, 62, 115, 117, 118, 122, 126, 146, 149, 158, 160. Ibid. no. 63 notes *escuagium*. See chap. 11, at n. 141 and at n. 152.

169. Along with the preceding surveys, the inventory of 1220 contains a

wealth of information about the structure of fiefs. Both the Norman sections and those of the old domain deserve fuller investigation, which is excluded by the limits of this study.

170. *Scripta de feodis* nos. 61–109.

171. Ibid. nos. 178–313.

172. See chap. 11, at nn. 10, 11.

173. Scribe η, Reg. C, fol. 4r–5v. *Scripta de feodis* nos. 369–92. Those castellanies included were Melun, Corbeil, Senlis, Béthisy, Orléans, Lorris, Grez and Chapelle-la-Reine, Montargis, Yèvre, Courcy, Moret, Château-Landon, Gien, Poissy, Mantes, Anet, Bréval, Dammartin, Paris, Montlhéry, and Etampes. In 1217 two *baillis* conducted an inquest into the value of fiefs of the castellany of Poissy that elaborated the above survey. Copied into Reg. E, fol. 38r. *Registres* I, no. 55 and *Scripta de feodis* nos. 110, 111.

174. Reg. C, fol. 6v–7v, *Scripta de feodis* nos. 394–414. Although called *balliva*, the groupings consisted of the following *prévôtés* or castellanies: Lorris, Gien, Montargis, Château-Landon, Orléans, Chécy, Châteauneuf-sur-Loire, Vitry-aux-Loges, Courcy, Yèvre, Grez and Chapelle-la-Reine, Boësse, and Janville. Scribe ε copied the sections on Grez and Chapelle and Boësse.

175. The Vexin castellanies of Mantes, Bréval, and Anet found in the 60 *livres* list, for example, were also included in Guillaume de Ville-Thierri's *bailliage* in Reg. E. *Scripta de feodis* nos. 68–71, 80–83. Both lists provided names in the castellany of Gien that were finally included in the comprehensive survey by Etienne de Hautvilliers for the *bailliage* of Sens. Ibid. nos. 247–51.

176. Two lists of those owing castleguard at Ribemont were eventually included in a comprehensive survey of Vermandois in Reg. E, for example, as was a brief notice of Alain de Roucy. Ribemont: *Scripta de feodis* nos. 542, 541, and 212–19; Roucy: ibid. nos. 393, 211. On Alain de Roucy's capture at Gisors in 1198, see chap. 11, at n. 116.

177. Scribe α, Reg. C, fol. 24r, *Scripta de feodis* no. 551; scribe η, Reg. C, fol. 4r, *Scripta de feodis* no. 391; scribe ε began on Reg. C, fol. 25v, but perhaps for lack of space began over again on fols. 142r–143v. Edited from the version of Reg. E in *Scripta de feodis* nos. 300–313. Other feudal inventories in Reg. C that did not contribute directly to Reg. E are: (1) the countess of Vermandois's holdings from the bishop of Senlis, fol. 1r, *Scripta de feodis* no. 543; the county of Clermont-en-Beauvaisis, fol. 6r, *Scripta de feodis* nos. 544–46; the lord of Saint-Valery, fol. 27v, *Scripta de feodis* nos. 537, 538; Etienne de Feins, fol. 28r, *Scripta de feodis* nos. 547–49.

178. Vermandois: *Scripta de feodis* nos. 178–233 (for an addition to the castellany of Ferté-Milon made in 1221 at Reg. E, fol. 68r, see *Actes* IV, no. 1728); Sens: *Scripta de feodis* nos. 238–69; Bourges: *Scripta de feodis* nos. 270–88; Etampes: *Scripta de feodis* nos. 289–312. Only the *baillis* of Sens (Etienne de Hautevilliers) and Etampes (Adam Héron) are explicitly named. The most re-

cent item that can be dated is the gift of Bonneuil-en-Valois to Robert de la Tournelle in July 1218, *Scripta de feodis* no. 195. See *Actes* IV, no. 1531.

A knight designated as *juratus* made the opening statement at Saint-Quentin. The section on Montdidier was assembled *per juramentum militum*, who often confessed to ignorance about their fiefs. The twelve jurors who collected testimony on the castellany of Montlhéry were named at the end. It was simpler to transcribe in full Jean de Nesle's French charter than to rework it into the Latin format of the preceding surveys. Saint-Quentin: *Scripta de feodis* no. 178; Montdidier: *Scripta de feodis* nos. 227–35 (for other acknowledgments of ignorance see *Scripta de feodis* nos. 241, 247); Jean de Nesle: *Scripta de feodis* nos. 223–25. William M. Newman (*Les Seigneurs de Nesle en Picardie [XIIᵉ–XIIIᵉ siècle]*, Memoirs of the American Philosophical Society, no. 91 [Philadelphia, 1971], I, 44–48) dates this charter before March 1215.

179. On the general character of feudalism in Vermandois, see Robert Fossier, *La Terre et les hommes en Picardie jusqu'à la fin du XIIIᵉ siècle* (Paris and Louvain, 1969), II, 546–48.

180. Etienne de Hautvilliers even tried to estimate their value in monetary terms. *Scripta de feodis* nos. 240, 241.

181. For example, the lords of Buno-Bonnevaux (Sens), *Scripta de feodis* nos. 265–69, and Issoudun (Bourges), ibid. nos. 279–88.

182. No service was recorded for the castellany of Péronne. *Scripta de feodis* nos. 184–93.

183. AN R 1 (34, 35). See Fossier, *La Terre et les hommes en Picardie* II, 668–72.

184. *Scripta de feodis* nos. 65–67 (Pacy) and nos. 84–89 (Nogent). A preliminary survey for Nogent was made in Reg. C, ibid. no. 536.

185. *Scripta de feodis* nos. 194–200 (Crépy), nos. 212–19 (Ribemont), nos. 227–35 (Montdidier). Montdidier was garrisoned by ten knights, but most of their service was unknown at the inquest.

186. For the three surveys, see *Scripta de feodis* nos. 551, 391, and 300–301. For the inquest, see ibid. no. 308. A more detailed statement of this inquest is found in Reg. C, fol. 143v, and printed in *Scripta de feodis* no. 313 and *Registres* I, no. 92. It refers to the time of the *baillis* Philippe de Lévis and Hugues de Gravelle (1192–1204). On Philip I's acquisition of Montlhéry, see Suger, *Vie de Louis VI* 38. On Louis IX's opinion, see Jean de Joinville, *Histoire de Saint Louis*, ed. Natalis de Wailly (Paris, 1874), 29.

187. *Actes* I, no. 44.

188. Beauquesne: *Actes* I, no. 422; Montargis: *Actes* II, no. 488; Vernon: Teulet I, no. 441; and Pacy: Teulet I, nos. 433–37.

189. Falaise and Bonneville-sur-Touques: *Actes* II, no. 837; Breteuil: *Actes* II, no. 861, Teulet I, no. 738; Mortemer: *Actes* II, no. 862, Teulet I, no. 733.

190. *Registres* III, P. This list was compiled after January 1206, because it con-

tains Beaumont-le-Roger, which was returned to the king at that date. Teulet I, no. 799. It was probably completed by April 1210, when the king purchased Brai-sur-Somme, which was added to the list by a second hand. Teulet I, no. 919. As examples of these concentrations: (1) Montlhéry, Dourdan, Etampes, Yèvre-le-Châtel, Montargis, Moret, and Corbeil; (2) Pontoise, Meulan, Poissy, Mantes, Vernon, Le Goulet, Gaillon, Gaillard, Vaudreuil, Pont de l'Arche, and Molineaux; and (3) Gisors, Gournay, Ferté-Saint-Simon, Gaillefontaine, and Mortemer.

191. See a summary of the discussion of the distribution of English castles in Hollister, *Military Organization in Norman England* 161–66.

192. Lillebonne in 1211 after the defection of Renaud, count of Boulogne; Issoudun in 1213 with the submission of Guillaume de Chauvigny; Ribemont, Chauny, and Ferté-Milon in 1213 with the death of Aliénor, countess of Vermandois; and Nogent l'Erembert in 1218–1219 in exchange with the countess of Blois. Lillebonne: see chap. 9, at n. 45; Issoudun: Teulet I, nos. 1040–43. See Guy Devailly, *Le Berry du Xe siècle au milieu du XIIIe* (Paris, 1973), 433–35. Ribemont, Chauny, Ferté-Milon, and Nogent-le-Roi, see chap. 9, at n. 36.

193. The "new tower" first appears in Philip's charters in 1189 (*Actes* I, nos. 257, 285), but there were still claims for damages caused by its construction in 1190 (*Actes* I, no. 360). The walls are mentioned as early as 1181. *Actes* I, no. 40. On these fortifications, see Hippolyte Boyer, "Les Enceintes de Bourges," *Mémoires de la Société Historique, Littéraire, Artistique et Scientifique du Cher*, 4th ser., 5, (1888–89): 107, 137, 138, and, most recently, Carlrichard Brühl, *Palatium und Civitas: Studien zur Profantopographie spätantiker Civitates vom 3. bis zum 13. Jahrhundert* (Cologne, 1975), I, 165, 166.

194. Rigord 105, 129. Guillaume le Breton, *Gesta* 191.

195. Teulet I, no. 903. *Actes* III, no. 1130. See chap. 11, at n. 131.

196. *Registres* II, O (I). Guillaume le Breton, *Gesta* 240, 241, claims that the walls of Paris were completed by 1211–1212, but the accounts probably antedated their completion.

197. *Registres* II, O (III). The walls of Bourges were also the object of a fragmentary account (1212–1220) in Reg. C. *Registres* II, O (IV).

198. Guillaume le Breton, *Philippidos* 367.

199. For a general discussion of castles, see Gabriel Fournier, *Le Château dans la France médiévale: Essai de sociologie monumentale* (Paris, 1978), 65–225. For the fundamental study on donjons, see Pierre Héliot, "L'Evolution du donjon dans le nord-ouest de la France et en Angleterre au XIIe siècle," *Bulletin archéologique du Comité des Travaux Historiques et Scientifiques*, n.s., 5 (1969): 141–94. For the identification of castles I have used *L'Atlas des châteaux forts en France*, ed. Charles-Laurent Salch (Strasbourg, 1977).

200. In addition to the work of Héliot (above n. 199), see the particular studies of Marcel Deyres, "Le Donjon de Langeais," *Bulletin monumental* 128 (1970): 179–93; F. Lesueur, "Le Château de Langeais," *Congrès archéologique de France*

106 (1948): 378–400; and Jean Vallery-Radot, "Loches," ibid. 106 (1948): 111–25.

201. For a summary on Gisors, see Yves Bruand, "Le Château de Gisors, principales campagnes de construction," *Bulletin monumental* 116 (1958): 243–65. For the report of the young Philip's reaction to Gisors, see Gerald of Wales, *De Principis instructione* 289.

202. Jacques Harmand, "Houdan et l'évolution des donjons au XII⁰ siècle," *Bulletin monumental* 127 (1969): 187–207; 130 (1972): 191–212, 347, 348. Pierre Héliot, "L'Age des donjons d'Etampes et de Provins," *Bulletin de la Société Nationale des Antiquaires de France* (1967): 289–309. E. Lefèvre-Pontalis, "Le Donjon quadrilobé d'Ambleny," *Bulletin monumental* 74 (1910): 69–74.

203. Pierre Héliot, "Le Château-Gaillard et les forteresses des XII⁰ et XIII⁰ siècles en Europe occidentale," in *Château-Gaillard*, Etudes de castellologie européene, no. 1 (Caen, 1964), 53–75, and Jean Vallery-Radot, "La Tour blanche d'Issoudun," in ibid. 149–60.

204. See the suggestive essay by Alain Erlande-Brandenburg, "L'Architecture militaire au temps de Philippe Auguste: Une Nouvelle Conception de la defense," in *La France de Philippe Auguste* 595–603. For the Louvre, see ibid. 601, 602.

205. *Budget* CLIII (2), CLIV (1). At the same time Abelin was working on the fortifications of Issoudun, although the castle was not yet formally in the king's hands. See chap. 11, n. 192.

206. *Registres* II, O (I). Jean Vallery-Radot, "Quelques donjons de Philippe Auguste," *Bulletin de la Société Nationale des Antiquaires de France* (1964): 155–60.

207. Jean Vallery-Radot, "Le Donjon de Philippe Auguste à Villeneuve-sur-Yonne et son devis," in *Château Gaillard*, Studien zur mittelalterlichen Wehrbau und Siedlungsforschung, no. 2 (Cologne, 1967), 106–112.

208. Gisors: Yves Bruand (see above n. 201); Francis Salet, "Verneuil," *Congrès archéologique de France* 111 (1953): 407–57; Jean Vallery-Radot, "Le Donjon de Lillebonne," in *Mélanges offerts à René Crozet* (Poitiers, 1966), II, 1105–13; René Crozet, "Chinon," *Congrès archéologique de France* 106 (1948): 342–63. Rigord 162 says that Philip rebuilt Chinon after taking it in 1205.

209. Compare the list of Erlande-Brandenburg, "L'Architecture" 598.

210. Comparable measurements: exterior diameter (13–18.6 meters), interior diameter (6–8 meters), thickness of walls (3.8–6.9 meters, with 4 meters most common) and height (more difficult to assess, 27–31 meters). Comparable costs: Dun-le-Roi 1,200 *livres* in 1202; Orléans 1,400 *livres*, Villeneuve 1,600 *livres*, Laon 1,900 *livres* and Péronne 2,000 *livres* in 1205–1212. Ibid. 598–601.

211. Hugues: *Budget* CXLVII (2), CLXIII (2), CCIX (1); Thomas: ibid. CLVIII (2), CLX (1); Christophe: ibid. CLXIX (1), CLXXIII (1), CXCIV

(2), CCIX (1); Richard: ibid. CLXX (2); Abelin: ibid. CLIII (2), CLIV (1), CLXXVIII (2).

212. They were Master Abelin, Master Adam, Master Alard, Master Amaury, Master Boso, Master Eudes, Master Garnier, Master Gautier, Gautier de Mullent, Geoffroi *Canoele*, Master Gilbert, Master Hugues, Guillaume de Flamenville, Master Guillaume, Master Mathieu, Master Raoul, Raoul *Brancel'*, Master Renaud, and Master Th[omas]. *Registres* III, O (I–III). Erlande-Brandenburg, "L'Architecture,"596, 597.

213. *Registres* II, O (I, III). Héliot, "Château-Gaillard," 69.

214. Powicke, *Loss of Normandy* 194.

215. On the deployment of fireplaces, see Jean Vallery-Radot, "Villeneuve-sur-Yonne" 106–12, and Héliot, "L'Evolution du donjon" 174.

216. Again, the fundamental study has been provided by Pierre Héliot, "La Genèse des châteaux de plan quadrangulaire en France et en Angleterre," *Bulletin de la Société Nationale des Antiquaires de France* (1965): 238–57. See also Héliot, "Château-Gaillard," 71, 72, and the particular studies of Jean Vallery-Radot, "Note sur l'enceinte quadrangulaire du château de Caen," *Bulletin monumental* 121 (1963): 69–73; Jean Vallery-Radot, "Yèvre-le-Châtel," *Congrès archéologique de France* 93 (1930): 401–13; and Denise Humbert, "Le Château de Dourdan," *Congrès archéologique de France* 103 (1944): 236–45. *Actes* IV, no. 1780 (1222) suggests that Dourdan had been recently completed.

217. Count of Auvergne (1189): *Actes* I, no. 286. Bertrand de la Tour (1212): Orcet, Montpeyroux, and Coudes, *Actes* III, no. 1251. Bishop of Clermont (1207): Mauzun, Delisle, *Catalogue* no. 1043; (1214): Lezoux, Antoingt, Dallet, *Actes* III, no. 1318. The bishop of Le Puy (1212, 1215): Chalencon, Rochebaron, Chapteuil, Glavenas, and Arzon, *Actes* III, nos. 1252, 1362.

218. *Actes* I, no. 413 (renewed in 1211, *Actes* III, no. 1201), and *Actes* II, no. 479.

219. *Actes* II, nos. 837, 840, 841, 862.

220. For example, Radepont to Pierre Moret (1203), *Actes* II, no. 761; Argentan to Henri Clément (1204), *Actes* II, no. 807 (reconfirmed in 1207, *Actes* III, no. 986); Nonancourt and Conches to Robert de Courtenay (1205), *Actes* II, no. 875, Teulet I, no. 747 (reconfirmed in 1217, Teulet I, no. 1262); Loches and Châtillon-sur-Indre to Dreu de Mello (1205), *Actes* II, no. 885, Teulet I, no. 804; Neuf-Marché had been given to Guillaume de Garlande in 1195, *Actes* II, no. 501; Gaillon to Cadoc, Fontaine-Guérard to Gautier the Young, and Formerie to Philippe, bishop of Beauvais, *Registres* III, P. Cadoc and Gautier the Young were probably granted their castles for life, just as Philip had granted Tosny to Cadoc in 1205, *Actes* II, no. 887. In 1217 and 1218 the king transformed these gifts in perpetuity, *Actes* IV, nos. 1509, 1516. The bishop of Beauvais received his castle in 1202 for a period of twenty-two years, *Actes* II, no. 714.

221. In 1219 the castle of Les Montils was exchanged for Nogent-le-Roi. *Registres* V, no. 67. Teulet I, nos. 1297, 1298, 1332, 1333.

222. These included Mauzun, Radepont, Nonancourt, Conches, Loches, Châtillon-sur-Indre, and Sully-sur-Loire.

223. Teulet I, nos. 594 and 680–82. See Robert Hajdu, "Castles, Castellans and the Structure of Politics in Poitou, 1152–1271," *Journal of Medieval History* 4 (1978): 41.

224. Gillemont (1205): Teulet I, no. 771; Montrésor (1205): no. 772; Mont-bazon (1206): no. 813; Argenton-Château (1209): nos. 892–96; Palluau (1211): no. 954; Marchainville (1211): no. 1008; Chamotocé (1212): nos. 988–94.

12. Repossessing the Churches

1. See chap. 8.

2. The twenty-five regalian bishoprics at the beginning of the reign minus Langres and Arras, whose regalian status was renounced in 1203. See above chap. 4, n. 47.

3. See chap. 9, at nn. 27–28.

4. Appendix D.

5. This estimation is computed from evidence in *Gall. christ.* IX. See Appendix D.

6. *Actes* I, no. 361.

7. *Actes* III, nos. 1214, 1222, IV, no. 1407. The king also gave them the lands of prisoners who had escaped if the abbey would pay the ransoms.

8. Innocent III, *Regesta, PL* 217: 109, 110; Potthast I, no. 2199. For the size of the abbey, see E.-R. Vaucelle, *La Collégiale de Saint-Martin de Tours des origines à l'avènement des Valois (397–1328)*, Mémoires de la Société Archéologique de Touraine, no. 46 (1907), 183.

9. Vaucelle, *Collégiale de Saint-Martin* 439. See chap. 6, at n. 174. Nicolas later became bishop of Noyon. He was succeeded at Saint-Martin in 1229 by Master Alberic Cornut, a nephew of Eudes Clément from the well-known family of royal *familiares*.

10. *Actes* IV, nos. 1450, 1493. On the papal dispensation for his illegitimacy, see *Actes* IV, no. 1483, and Honorius III in Horoy, *Opera* II, 373, Pressutti I, nos. 532–34, and *RHF* XIX, 631.

11. *Actes* II, no. 637. See chap. 8, at n. 20. See also John W. Baldwin, "Philip Augustus and the Norman Church," *French Historical Studies* 6 (1969): 1–30, for a study preparatory to this chapter.

12. In Normandy elections were contested at Bayeux (1205) and at Rouen (1221), but both disputes were due to local divisions in the chapters. Innocent III, *Regesta, PL* 215: 594, 595; Potthast I, no. 2472, for Bayeux. Honorius III in Horoy, *Opera*, IV, 34, 35; Pressutti, II, no. 3591; Potthast I, no. 6848, for Rouen. See Baldwin, "Philip Augustus and the Norman Church" 9. The chapter of Tours similarly divided in 1208, but both candidates were equally acceptable

to the king. Innocent III, *Regesta, PL* 215:1465, 1466; Potthast I, no. 3505. See Arthur J. Lyons, "The Capetian Conquest of Anjou," (diss., The Johns Hopkins University, 1976), 177, 178. The chapter of Le Mans also split in the election of 1216, but neither of the rival candidates, the provost and the dean, nor Maurice, archdeacon of Troyes, who was eventually elected, had royal connections. See the account in Thomas de Cantimpré, *Boni universalis de apibus* (Douai, 1627), I, i, 5–8.

13. Honorius III in Horoy, *Opera*, III, 361; Pressutti I, no. 2286. *Actes* IV, no. 1636. *De Gestis episcoporum Autissiodorensium, PL* 138:342. Guillaume le Breton, *Gesta* 329, 330.

14. For Sées, see chap. 8, at n. 23. For the lesser-known incident at Angers, see Innocent III, *Regesta, PL* 214:980, 981; Potthast I, no. 1669. *Rotuli litterarum patentium*, ed. Thomas D. Hardy (London, 1835), I, i, 4, 14, and Lyons, "Capetian Conquest of Anjou" 161–63. The dispute over Canterbury is well known.

15. Innocent III, *Regesta, PL* 215:564; Potthast I, no. 2434. When the bishop wrote, Henri, bishop of Bayeux, was either unsympathetic or, more likely, dying. (He died during the course of 1205.) The bishopric of Evreux had already been acceded to Philip. Baldwin, "Philip Augustus and the Norman Church" 1, 2. On Innocent's support of John, see chap. 9, at nn. 12–13.

16. The Anonymous of Béthune (*Histoire des ducs* 99) claims that Pierre de Préaux, John's commander at Rouen, surrendered the city to Philip Augustus on the advice of the archbishop of Rouen.

17. Baldwin, "Philip Augustus and the Norman Church" 7, 8. See chap. 8, at n. 25.

18. For the post-conquest elections in Normandy and the Loire region, see ibid. 7, 8; Lyons, "Capetian Conquest of Anjou" 170–81; and Appendix C.

19. Royal clerics: Guérin at Senlis (1213), Gautier Cornut at Sens (1223). Sons of Gautier the Chamberlain: Pierre at Paris (1208), Guillaume at Meaux (1214). Candidates related to the king: Robert de Châtillon at Laon (1210), Guillaume du Perche at Châlons (1215), Miles de Nanteuil at Beauvais (1218), Simon de Sully at Bourges (1218). Eudes de Sully's recommendations: Geoffroi at Tours (1206), Alberic at Reims (1207), Hervé at Troyes (1207), Haimard at Soissons (1208). The biographical information and statistics are derived from Appendix C.

20. See chap. 8, at nn. 32–36.

21. This interesting letter survives only in the edition of Guillaume Bessin, *Concilia Rotomagensis provinciae* (Rouen, 1717), II, 33. One would like to know more of its provenance. Although the letter is undated, it most likely preceded the inquest of 1207–1208 (see below n. 22) because Vivien died on 15 February 1208.

22. *Registres* I, no. 18. Although undated, it appears most appropriate during the vacancy between Walter of Coutances (died 16 November 1207) and Robert Poulain (elected 23 August 1208). It also contains testimony on the administra-

tion of specific properties such as at Andelys. See also Baldwin, "Philip Augustus and the Norman Church" 6, 7.

23. This was noted in an inquest made into the activities of Jean de Rouvrai in the *bailliage* of Arques in 1208. *Registres* I, no. 112.

24. See Teulet I, no. 1513, for a letter preserved in the royal archives from the election of Thibaut in 1222, and ibid. no. 1414, for a similar letter from Evreux in 1220.

25. Ibid. no. 934.

26. See chap. 11, at nn. 120–23, for this controversy.

27. *Actes* III, no. 1337.

28. Teulet II, nos. 1617, 1625. Reg. E, fol. 140r. See chap. 11, at n. 122, for the military implications of these charters.

29. The conclusions of this paragraph are drawn from *Registres* III, H, O, co-ordinated in Appendix D.

30. In addition to the nine Breton sees, Lyon, Bordeaux, Auch, Le Puy, Chalon-sur-Saône, Limoges, Périgueux, Angoulême, and Cahors were omitted. The omission of Nevers appears to be an oversight.

31. The *episcopus/archiepiscopus* notation is difficult to interpret in this context.

32. The two exceptions are the Norman bishoprics (excluding Rouen) that were designated *sub* in the first list and unannotated in the second, and Clermont, which was undesignated in the first list and marked as owing military service beyond the Loire in the second. For a discrepancy over Tours, see below n. 34.

33. The *sub* list appears to have been compiled before 1207 because Auxerre, Nevers, and Mâcon, which lost their regalian status in that year and afterwards, were still designated as subject to the king. In fact, 1207 is the best date for the list because Rouen, which was left undesignated, had not yet been officially adjudged regalian by the inquest of 1208. In the *civitates* list Etienne probably made his annotations before 1208, when the status of the Norman sees (left unannotated) was not yet official, or certainly before 1209, when Mâcon (designated regalian) was formally renounced. Additional evidence that the *civitates* list was composed after 1204 is the recognition that the king abandoned the *gîtes* of Auxerre and Varzay to the bishop of Auxerre in 1204 in exchange for the fief of Gien. See *Actes* II, no. 860, and Teulet I, no. 739.

34. The renunciation of Arras in 1203 was recognized in both lists, but that of Langres of the same year was not, nor that of Autun in 1189. See chap. 8, at n. 33. Sees such as Tours, Bourges, and Senlis, for which other evidence indicates long-established regalian status, were left undesignated in both. Undesignated in the *sub* list, Tours is annotated with *procuratio* in the *civitates* list. It is difficult to determine whether this constituted regalian status. The Loire bishoprics of Angers, Le Mans, and Poitiers were also left undesignated, probably because their regalian status was not confirmed until the inquest of 1214 at the earliest.

35. *Actes* II, no. 856.

36. At the same time, he ordered the count of Toulouse and other barons of Provence to preserve the rights of Maguelonne. *Actes* III, nos. 1037, 1038. For Philip's earlier policy, see chap. 4, at nn. 48–50, and for the Albigensian crusade, see chap. 13.

37. Lodève: *Actes* III, nos. 1119, 1139, 1392. See also *Actes* IV, no. 1420. Uzès: *Actes* III, nos. 1179, 1211. Le Puy: *Actes* III, nos. 1252, 1362, IV, no. 1612. In 1219 the king intervened in behalf of the bishop in a dispute with the town and confirmed his rights. *Actes* IV, nos. 1571–73.

38. The unusual orthography and double inclusion of Rodez, because of different spellings, suggests that the chancery was unclear about the south. *Registres* III, H. *Nerbona* for *Narbonensis* as in Reg. C; *Bisaciensis* for *Vasatensis* or *Bazas* (Bazas); *Rodanensis* and *Ruthinensis* for Rodez. (The first variant is omitted in Reg. C.)

39. He added Elne, Comminges, and the enigmatic *Porticlusa*, also found in the *Provincialis* of Reg. C under the province of Auch. He still omitted Lectoure, Dax, Cousérans, Tarbes, Oloron, Aire, and Lescar.

40. *Registres* IV, B. It corresponded closely to the *Provincialis* of Reg. E (IV, C), which was derived from a papal exemplar. The *Provincialis* of Reg. C also offered the following unusual spellings: *Aniensis* for *Aquensis* (Dax) and *Ariensis* for *Adurensis* (Aire).

41. *Registres* IV, C. For an example of a scribal slip, it listed the two spellings of Tarbes, *Bigorriensis* and *Tarmensis*, as two separate bishoprics.

42. Innocent III, *Regesta, PL* 216:644; Potthast I, no. 4559. *Actes* III, no. 1197. For the background, see L. de Lacger, "La Primatie et le pouvoir métropolitain de l'archevêque de Bourges au XIIIᵉ siècle," *Revue d'histoire ecclésiastique* 26 (1930): 43–65, and, most recently, Guy Devailly, *Le Berry du Xᵉ siècle au milieu de XIIIᵉ* (Paris, 1973), 493–503.

43. For a record of the dispute during Philip's reign, see Innocent III, *Regesta, PL* 216:867, 866; Potthast I, nos. 4745, 4750; Honorius III in *RHF* XIX, 655, 659; Pressutti I, nos. 1093, 1349. For the decision over Auch, see Honorius III in *RHF* XIX, 657; Pressutti I, no. 1216.

44. For this paragraph, see *Registres* III, I; II, R, S, T, which are tabulated in Appendix D. For a criticism of these lists, see nn. 32–34 above.

45. *Registres* II, C. Pacy-Evreux: 244 *livres*, 10 *sous parisis*; 76 *livres*, 4 *sous angevins*; 1 *livre*, 10 *sous chartrains*. Péronne-Bapaume: 222 *livres*, 17 *sous*, 1 *denier parisis*. Total alms: 938 *livres*, 16 *sous parisis*; 90 *livres*, 10 *sous angevins*; 1 *livre*, 10 *sous chartrains*. For the comparisons in the Bapaume and Evreux accounts, see chap. 8, at nn. 49–56.

46. *Registres* II, A. Total alms and wages: 2,457 *livres*. Wages to secular persons: 300 *livres*, 10 *sous*.

47. *Registres* II, B.

48. The customs of Arras, approved by Philip in 1194, for example, required that suits of clerics contesting lay properties be heard by municipal or royal judges and those involving fiefs by feudal overlords. *Actes* I, no. 473. When the

townsmen and clergy of Tournai fell into disagreement over their respective rights in 1200, the king and Guillaume, archbishop of Reims, proposed six different sets of customs drawn from the province to be used as models. The townsmen eventually settled on those of Senlis as most suitable for regulating matters concerning debts, taxes, crimes, etc. Apparently Philip was dissatisfied with this solution, because two years later he protested to the pope that the Tournai bourgeois were using the church courts to escape royal jurisdiction over moveables, debts, *tailles*, and like matters. *Actes* II, nos. 625, 662. The six models were Senlis, Amiens, Noyon, Beauvais, Soissons, and Laon. For the accompanying documents, including a description of the customs of Senlis, see *Ordonnances des roys de France de la troisième race*, ed. E Lauvière (Paris, 1769), XI, 282–84. Philip's complaint was recorded in Innocent III, *Regesta, PL* 214 : 1157; Potthast I, no. 1815.

49. For a preliminary study of the Norman precedents, see Baldwin, "Philip Augustus and the Norman Church" 11–30.

50. *The Ecclesiastical History of Orderic Vitalis*, ed. Marjorie Chibnall (Oxford, 1972), II, 24–26. Teulet I, no. 22. Reg. A, fol. 47r. The sealed charter was that of Henry II, probably issued on 25 February 1162. Pierre Chaplais, "Henry II's Reissue of the Canons of the Council of Lillebonne of Whitsun 1080 (? 25 February 1162)" *Journal of the Society of Archivists* 4 (1973): 627–32.

51. *Select Charters of English Constitutional History*, ed. William Stubbs (Oxford, 1913), 163–67.

52. Cartulary of the chapter of Rouen, Rouen Bibl. mun. 1193, fol. 142rb–142vb, printed in Bessin, *Concilia* I, 100. Also in Diceto II, 86–88, and Mathew Paris, *Chronica majora*, ed. H. R. Luard (London, 1874), II, 368.

53. E.-J. Tardif, *Coutumiers de Normandie* (Rouen, 1881), I, 68, 69.

54. See the interpretation of Paul Violet, "Les Coutumiers de Normandie," in *Histoire littéraire de la France* (Paris, 1906), XXXIII, 51–60.

55. Teulet I, no. 785. *Registres* I, no. 14.

56. Teulet I, no. 828. *Actes* III, no. 992. Teulet I, no. 1282.

57. The barons included the counts of Sancerre, Auxerre, Nevers, and Perche, as well as Robert de Courtenay and Guy de Dampierre. Teulet I, nos. 762–67. Cartellieri IV, 225, 226. On the baronial charters of 1203, see chap. 9, at n. 14.

58. *Actes* II, nos. 899, 900.

59. The proprietary questions concerned Lisieux, Gournay, Ferté, Gaillefontaine, and Louviers. The minor matters have been dealt with in Baldwin, "Philip Augustus and the Norman Church" 13, 15.

60. All mentions of the Norman inquest of 1205 refer to Teulet I, no. 785, and *Registres* I, no. 14. All mentions of the Paris accords of 1205 refer to *Actes* II, nos. 899, 900.

61. Teulet I, no. 22. Tardif, *Coutumiers* I, 23, 75.

62. *Decretales Gregorii IX* 2.1.3, ed. E. Friedberg (Leipzig, 1879). Haskins, *Norman Institutions* 171, 172. Stubbs, ed., *Select Charters* 164.

63. F. Soudet, "Les Brefs de patronage d'église," in *Travaux de la semaine d'his-*

toire de droit normand, summarized in *Revue historique de droit français et étranger* 4th ser., 4 (1925): 622.

64. Teulet I, no. 828. *Actes* III, no. 992. The royal reply is also included in the second *Norman coutumier* in Tardif, *Coutumiers* I, 77, 78. *Actes* III, no. 1041 (ca. 1208), elaborated the details of the procedure, and was copied into the royal registers. For the distinction between canonical and Norman inquests, see chap. 7, at nn. 26–37.

65. Canon 17 of the Lateran Council of 1179 set the limit of four months to decide disputes between laymen over advowson. *Sacrorum conciliorum nova et amplissima collectio,* ed. J. D. Mansi (Florence and Venice, 1759–93) XXII, 227. Six months were allowed to ecclesiastical patrons. *Decretales Gregorii IX,* 3.38.22.

66. *Jugements* no. 170. Another example of the new procedure may be found in the Cartulary of Le Mont-Saint-Michel (1219), *RHF* XXIV, 285. For the remaining cases at the Norman exchequer, see *Jugements* nos. 35, 55, 111, 112, 127, 129, 131, 201, 202, 233, 234, 253, 254, 258, 262, and 327.

67. Teulet I, no. 1282.

68. On alms and lay fiefs, see Frederick Pollock and Frederic William Maitland, *The History of English Law* (Cambridge, 1952), II, 240–51; E. Blum, "Les Origines du bref de fief et d'aumône," in *Travaux de la semaine d'histoire du droit normand . . . 1923* (Caen, 1925), 369–416; Elisabeth G. Kimball, "The Judicial Aspect of Frank Almoin Tenure," *EHR* 47 (1932): 1–11; Samuel E. Thorne, "The Assize *Utrum* and Canon Law in England," *Columbia Law Review* 33 (1933): 428–36; R. Besnier, "Le Procès petitoire dans le droit normand du XIIe et du XIIIe siècle," *Revue historique de droit français et étranger,* 4th ser., 30 (1952): 212–16; R. C. van Caenegem, *Royal Writs in England from the Conquest to Glanvill,* Seldon Society Publications, no. 77 (London, 1959), 325–30.

69. Stubbs, ed., *Select Charters* 165, 166.

70. Tardif, *Coutumiers* I, 19, 20, 46–48. See also the second *coutumier,* ibid. I, 98.

71. *Jugements* (adjudging competence): nos. 12, 23, 33, 48, 51, 59, 70, 325; (adjudging possession): nos. 60, 88. Not all of these cases are unmistakably clear from the summary record.

72. Alexander III, in *Decretales Gregorii IX,* 2.2.6 and 4.17.7. Innocent III, *Regesta PL* 215 : 176; Potthast I, no. 2181.

73. The versions of Diceto II, 87, and the Cartulary of the chapter of Rouen, Rouen Bibl. mun. 1193, fol. 143va, specify twenty in place of thirty years. This represents either an attempt of the clerical party to improve the terms of prescription or, more likely, a scribal error. The version of the second Norman *coutumier* in Tardif *Coutumiers* I, 69, has thirty years, which was the traditional Carolingian limit.

74. *Jugements* no. 230.

75. The second Norman *coutumier* in Tardif, *Coutumiers* I, 98, refers directly to the exchequer decision, as does a royal command to the Norman *baillis* in 1223. *Actes* IV, no. 1810.

76. Glanvill, *Tractatus de legibus*, IX, 8, ed. G. D. C. Hall (London, 1965), 112. Pollock and Maitland, *History of English Law* I, 353, 354.

77. According to the principle *mobilia sequuntur personam*. Paul Fournier, *Les Officialités au moyen âge* (Paris, 1880), 65, 77.

78. A notable example was William Rufus's seizure of the temporalities of Canterbury in 1097 when Archbishop Anselm's feudal levies were deficient. A. L. Poole, *From Domesday to Magna Carta* (Oxford, 1951), 176.

79. See chap. 11, at nn. 120–23, for the details.

80. The principle was illustrated by cases involving serfs and property bought or inherited by clerics. Specifically, the barons decreed that clerical sons of bourgeois and peasants should not inherit more than half of their parents' land if the parents had other children. Any land given to a cleric beyond half of the family patrimony owed service and aid to the lord of the land. After the death of the cleric, the land reverted to the nearest heirs. If a cleric bought land, he owed service to its lord. *Actes* II, nos. 899, 900.

81. Jean Yver, *Les Contrats dans le très ancien droit normand* (Domfront, 1926), 42–63. Fournier, *Les Officialités* 86, 87.

82. Stubbs, ed., *Select Charters* 167. Pollock and Maitland, *History of English Law* II, 197–200.

83. Glanvill, *Tractatus* X, 12, p. 126.

84. Diceto II, 87. Yver, *Les Contrats* 202–6.

85. Tardif, *Coutumiers* I, 83, 94. R. Génestal, "L'Inaliénabilité dotale normande," *Revue historique de droit français et étranger*, 4th ser., 4 (1925): 573.

86. *Jugements* no. 33. A similar case occurred in 1211. Ibid. no. 82. It was reaffirmed about 1223 against Robert, archbishop of Rouen. *Cartulaire normand de Philippe Auguste, Louis VIII, Saint Louis, et Philippe le Hardi*, ed. Léopold Delisle (Caen, 1852), no. 1130.

87. This principle was anticipated in 1194 in Philip's confirmation of the customs of Arras. *Actes* I, no. 473. The agreement of 1205 went on to specify that a widow could plead before either the king or the church as she wished over her dowry, if it did not concern a fief. If she chose the ecclesiastical jurisdiction, the church court could compel the defendant to respond. *Actes* II, no. 900. This choice between the two jurisdictions in cases of dowry was also permitted by Glanvill, *Tractatus* VIII, 18, p. 93, but under different circumstances.

88. In connection with oaths, the barons also protested against the custom of ecclesiastics who summoned laymen before their courts and compelled them to take an oath that they would obey the decision. *Actes* II, no. 900.

89. *Actes* III, no. 1317.

90. Bessin, *Concilia* I, 39. Haskins, *Norman Institutions* 37, 38. J. Yver, "L'Interdiction de la guerre privée dans le très ancien droit normand," in *Travaux de la semaine d'histoire du droit normand . . . 1927* (Caen, 1928), 313, 314.

91. Teulet I, no. 22. Yver, "L'Interdiction de la guerre privée," 315–23.

92. Tardif, *Coutumiers* I, 65–68. Yver, "L'Interdiction de la guerre privée," 331, 332.

93. Henry I's charter was reviewed by Richard and the agreement of 1190 reconfirmed the previous charters. Bessin, *Concilia* I, 99. Diceto II, 87.

94. In 1222 the exchequer at Caen again assured the bishops that they would receive their fines promised by Richard's charter. *Jugements* no. 329.

95. Tardif, *Coutumiers* I, 27.

96. Stubbs, ed., *Select Charters* 165.

97. Tardif, *Coutumiers* I, 1, 2. The *coutumier* then proceeded to outline how churchmen could receive redress in ducal justice for wrongs committed by ducal officials.

98. When, at the end of the reign or the beginning of the next, an inquest was taken into the rights of justice of the king and the bishop of Arras at Oppy and Bois-Bernard, the bishop recognized that he could not coerce the royal *bailli* by excommunication. *Registres* I, no. 106. See also the case at Orléans. Ibid. I, no. 98. These appear to be specific restrictions, however, and not the general principle enunciated in 1205.

99. Teulet I, no. 1282.

100. Ibid. I, no. 22.

101. For a fuller discussion of the issues of this paragraph, see chap. 8.

102. Austin Lane Poole, "Outlawry as a Punishment of Criminous Clerics," in *Historical Essays in Honour of James Tait*, ed. J. G. Edwards, V. H. Galbraith, and E. F. Jacobs (Manchester, 1933), 246.

103. Ibid. 239.

104. A case reported by Arnulph of Lisieux. Ibid. 244.

105. Tardif, *Coutumiers* I, 69. In the mid–thirteenth century this procedure was further elaborated in the *Summa de legibus* 81, in ibid. II, 195, 196.

106. *Decretales Gregorii IX* 5.7.9; 2.2.10; 5.2.7. JL nos. 15109, 17639. Potthast I, no. 1276.

107. They were reconfirmed in 1210 in letters to the principal communes of the royal domain. *Actes* III, nos. 1125, 1125 [bis].

108. See chap. 12, n. 48.

109. In addition to the criminous clerics, the king protested against the case of a man accused of rape whom the clergy did not want to be judged in a lay court but to purge himself with an oath in a church court. *Actes* II, no. 899. In the apparent response to this case, the man accused of rape has been changed to a cleric. The king and barons replied in terms similar to their solution for all criminous clerics. The cleric should be handed over to the church for degrading, after which the king or his justice could take him outside the church or atrium and punish him. *Actes* II, no. 900.

110. Guillaume le Breton, *Gesta* 233.

111. Innocent III, *Regesta PL* 215: 1562; Potthast I, no. 3656.

112. *Registres* I, no. 98.

113. Clerical privileges were confirmed for the household servants of the clergy as well. In an incident of March 1207 the king and his *baillis* vindicated

the clerical privileges of a servant of Master Gilbert de Marleiz, canon of Rouen, against the jurisdiction of the commune. During the course of the dispute, the commune was placed under interdict. See *Chronicon Rotomagense*, *RHF* XVIII, 359. A better text from Jumièges and Rouen manuscripts is printed by Bessin, *Concilia* II, 41. *Antiquus cartularius ecclesiae Baiocensis*, ed. V. Bourrienne (Paris, 1902), II, 26, 27. Robert Génestal, *Privilegium fori en France*, Bibliothèque de l'Ecole des Hautes Etudes, Sciences Religieuses, no. 39 (1924) I, 53, 54. In what appears to be a related incident judged at the Easter session of the Norman exchequer in 1207, three men of Master Raoul de Coutances, canon and colleague of Master Gilbert de Marleiz, were convicted of false accusation against the men of Rouen. *Jugements* no. 28. For a similar incident ca. 1210, the city of Orléans was placed under interdict when the *prévôt* arrested a *hôte* of the chapter of the cathedral. Delisle, *RHF* XXIV, *277. In 1200, however, the privileges of the chapter of Paris did not extend to their men. *Actes* II, no. 644.

114. *Actes* III, no. 1157. Teulet I, no. 1439. (This was probably the dispute to which Honorius III referred in 1221 and 1223. Pressutti I, nos. 3251, 3259, 4323; Horoy, *Opera*, IV, 333.) *Registres* I, no. 95. See chap. 11, at nn. 120–23, and chap. 13, at nn. 79–81.

13. The Fruits of Victory

1. Guillaume le Breton, *Gesta* 296, 297; *Philippidos* 357–59.

2. See chap. 9, at nn. 72–6.

3. The following account of the English expedition merely summarizes the definitive treatments in Petit-Dutaillis, *Louis VIII* 54–183, Sidney Painter, *The Reign of King John* (Baltimore, 1949), 349–77, and Maurice Powicke, *The Thirteenth Century, 1216–1307* (Oxford, 1953), 1–15, as well as Cartellieri IV, 505–38.

4. Roger of Wendover in Mathew Paris, *Chronica maiora*, ed. H. R. Luard (London, 1874), II, 647.

5. Full discussion of the various versions of and arguments for Capetian intervention may be found in Petit-Dutaillis, *Louis VIII* 72–87, and *Le Déshéritement de Jean sans Terre et le meurtre d'Arthur de Bretagne* (Paris, 1925), 29–67. A genealogy of the kings of England from William I demonstrating Blanche's claim was included in Reg. E. *Registres* VII, 7. See also a similar example in the St. Alban's manuscript of Mathew Paris, *Chronica maiora*, II, 661, at the appropriate point in the narrative.

6. See both versions of the Anonymous of Béthune: *Histoire des ducs* 162 and *Chronique des rois* 770.

7. On the circle of learned clerics, see F. M. Powicke, *Stephen Langton* (Oxford, 1928), 135–37.

8. The royal archives contained letters from the legate and the papal *peniten-*

tiarius giving the conditions for absolving the anathemas. Teulet I, nos. 1240, 1241.

9. Anonymous of Béthune, *Histoire des ducs* 119, 120, and *Chronique des rois* 764. *Registres* VI, no. 71. See chap. 9, at n. 75.

10. Guillaume le Breton, *Gesta* 305, 307–9, 312, *Philippidos* 359.

11. Roger of Wendover in Mathew Paris, *Chronica maiora* II, 648, 651–53, III, 25, 26.

12. Anonymous of Béthune, *Histoire des ducs* 187 and *Chronique des rois* 770.

13. Honorius III in *RHF* XIX, 629; Pressutti I, no. 524. See *Actes* IV, no. 1483.

14. The standard treatments of Louis's expeditions to the south, on which the following paragraphs rely, are Petit-Dutaillis, *Louis VIII* 184–202, and Cartellieri IV, 503, 504, 541, 542, 544–47, 556, 557. On the importance of the competition in Languedoc, see Yves Renouard, "1212–1216: Comment les traits durables de l'Europe occidentale moderne se sont définis au début du XIIIe siècle," *Annales de l'Université de Paris* 28 (1958): 5–21.

15. *Actes* IV, nos. 1418, 1419, and 1421. Among the three royal charters, two basic versions may be discerned. Although the wording is virtually identical, the arrangement of the phrases suggests two different emphases. The first (nos. 1418, 1421) suggests that Simon did liege-homage for the duchy of Narbonne, the county of Toulouse, and the *vicomtés* of Béziers and Carcassonne, held by the count of Toulouse from the king, which contained the lands of the heretics. The second (no. 1419) suggests that Simon did homage for the lands of the heretics in the duchy, county, etc., held by the count from the king. Since the first version was cancelled in Reg. C in favor of an abbreviation of the second, it appears that the second became the accepted formulation. It corresponds more closely to the judgment of the Lateran council, which assigned all lands conquered from the heretics to Simon, who would hold them from their rightful lord—that is, the king of France. For the Lateran decision, see *Sacrorum conciliorum nova et amplissima collectio*, ed. J. D. Mansi (Florence, 1767), XXII, 1069.

16. Honorius III in *RHF* XIX, 669, 670. If the clerics in Louis's entourage undertook the Albigensian crusade, they would be absolved from the penalties for the English expedition. Pressutti I, nos. 1891, 1892. Gervais, abbot of Prémontré and later bishop of Sées, had advised Innocent III in 1216 that those who were excommunicated for following Prince Louis into England should receive absolution if they spent as much time against the Albigensians. *Histoire littéraire de France* (Paris, 1835), XVIII, 45–48.

17. Guillaume le Breton, *Gesta* 300, 306, 316, 319, 329, 331.

18. Pierre des Vaux-de-Cernay, *Hystoria Albigensis*, ed. P. Guégin and E. Lyon (Paris, 1930), II, 109, 110, 134, 135, 242, 243, 245, 246. The chronicle breaks off with Louis's acceptance of the cross in November 1218.

19. Cartellieri IV, 556–65, 568, 569.

20. This fear was alluded to by Honorius III in a letter to the papal legate. *RHF* XIX, 687; Pressutti I, no. 2102.

21. The principal documents of the negotiations are contained in *Actes* IV, nos. 1553, 1574, 1601, 1602, 1619; Honorius III in *RHF* XIX, 680, 684; Pressutti, nos. 1989, 2056; and Teulet I, nos. 1387–89. Cartellieri IV, 539, 540, 546–54. For the truce of 1214, see chap. 9, at n. 102.

22. Teulet I, 1391. "Actes de Louis VIII," no. 21, in Petit-Dutaillis, *Louis VIII* 452. *Actes* IV, no. 1602.

23. *Actes* IV, no. 1574.

24. *Actes* IV, no. 1619. Also in the preliminary draft (*Actes* IV, no. 1602), where Louis swore for himself.

25. On his minimal administration of Artois, which remained for the most part in the hands of Nevelon the Marshal, see Petit-Dutaillis, *Louis VIII* 205–16. After Renaud, count of Boulogne, forfeited his fief in 1211, Louis took custody as its overlord. Guillaume le Breton, *Gesta* 243, and Guillaume d'Andres, *Chronica*, ed. J. Heller, *MGH SS* XXIV, 763. For the six *prévôtés* of Poissy, Lorris, Château-Landon, Fay-aux-Loges, Vitry-aux-Loges, and Boiscommun, see *Registres* VI, no. 55.

26. Edited by Robert Fawtier, "Un Fragment du compte de l'hôtel du prince Louis de France pour le terme de la Purification 1213," *Le Moyen Age*, 3rd ser., 4 (1933): 225–50. On the agreement in 1213, see chap. 9, at n. 75.

27. Teulet I, 1439, and *Registres* VI, no. 90.

28. *Diplomatic Documents Preserved in the Public Record Office*, ed. Pierre Chaplais (London, 1964), I, 139. See chap. 6, at n. 220.

29. Appendix A. *Actes* III, no. 1378, IV, nos. 1436, 1606, 1654, 1691, 1733, 1759, 1789, 1822. Teulet I, no. 1439. Delisle, *RHF* XXIV, *287. E. Boutaric, *Actes du parlement de Paris* (Paris, 1863), ccci. Cartulaire blanc de Saint-Denis AN, LL 1157, pp. 788, 789. Petit-livre blanc de l'évêché de Chartres, Paris BN lat. 11062, fol. 21r.

30. See chap. 11, at n. 44.

31. *Diplomatic Documents*, ed. Chaplais, I, 97, and Cartellieri IV, 646. See also 550.

32. Senlis, Bibl. mun. Col. Afforty XV, 380. Delisle, *RHF* XXIV, *288.

33. *Actes* IV, no. 1765. Teulet I, no. 1572. Other examples of Guérin acting in his own name include *Actes* IV, no. 1606 (1219); Senlis, Bibl. mun. Col. Afforty, 379, 380 (August 1220); Cartulary of the bishopric of Laon, Arch. dép. Aisne, G2, fol. 68v (24 November 1221, concerning *Registres* I, no. 95); Cartulaire blanc de Saint-Denis AN, LL 1157, pp. 788, 789 (18 December 1222).

34. January 1221. Cartulaire de Corbie, Paris BN lat. 17758, fol. 54v. Master Geoffroi, *canonicus et officialis Silvanectensis*, was active at Senlis from 1215 (*Actes* III, no. 1378) to 1223. He appears in scores of charters collected in Senlis, Bibl. mun. Col. Afforty, XIV, XV.

35. For the major statements of the judgment, see *Actes* IV, nos. 1436–39, 1454, 1467. Teulet I, nos. 1476–79. For the disputed succession and wardship, see chap. 9 and Henry Arbois de Jubainville, *Histoire des ducs et des comtes de Champagne* (Paris, 1859–69), IV (1), 135–98.

36. The king confirmed that Jocerand le Gros renounced his claims on the barony. *Actes* IV, no. 1758.

37. Teulet I, nos. 1235–37. Guérin, bishop of Senlis, who was the immediate overlord, also confirmed the settlement in 1221. Senlis, Bibl. mun. Col. Afforty, XV, 399, 400, and *Gall. christ.* X, instru. 450. The royal chancery profited from the occasion to compile a dossier on the family's holdings in Reg. C. For the dossier, see chap. 6, at n. 119.

38. The relevant documents are *Actes* IV, nos. 1491, 1627, 1723, 1725, 1726; Teulet I, nos. 1230, 1458, 1462. See also Guy Duvailly, *Le Berry du Xe siècle au milieu du XIIIe* (Paris, 1973), 433–35.

39. Teulet I, no. 1360. The matter was mentioned in a preliminary draft for the truce of 1220. *Actes* IV, no. 1553. Cartellieri IV, 548, 549.

40. *Actes* IV, nos. 1501, 1778. Teulet I, nos. 1415, 1416, 1426.

41. Teulet I, nos. 1332, 1333, 1337. Delisle, *Catalogue* nos. 1865, 1870.

42. *Actes* IV, nos. 1521, 1527, 1531, 1535. Teulet I, no. 1339.

43. *Registres* VI, nos. 90, 91; V, no. 78. Teulet I, nos. 1571, 1572. *Actes* IV, nos. 1813, 1815, 1818. Delisle, *Catalogue* nos. 2197, 2199, 2201–6.

44. Teulet I, no. 1480. Petit-Dutaillis, *Louis VIII* 360, 361.

45. "Chronicon Sancti Dionysii Recentius," ed. E. Berger, *BEC* 40 (1879): 289. Cartellieri IV, 595, 596.

46. *Registres* II, E.

47. Guillaume le Breton, *Gesta* 293, 294. *Registres* VII, no. 13. Cartellieri IV, 478–80.

48. One gate on the left bank was not yet finished in 1209 (*Actes* III, no. 1102), but Innocent III began to deal with the redistribution of parishes occasioned by the walls in 1210. Innocent III, *Regesta PL* 216: 284; Potthast I, no. 4028. See *Registres* II, O. On the Louvre: *Actes* III, no. 1109. Guillaume le Breton (*Gesta* 293) called the Louvre a "new tower" in 1214. The king was still compensating for damages caused by the construction at the Louvre and the Petit-Châtelet in 1222. *Actes* IV, no. 1805. For the construction of the fortifications, see chap. 11, at nn. 195–98.

49. From an abundant bibliography, see the most recent work, Jacques Boussard, *Nouvelle histoire de Paris: De la fin du siège de 885–886 à la mort de Philippe Auguste* (Paris, 1976), 282–381.

50. Guillaume le Breton, *Gesta* 230, 240, 241. On the schools of Paris during the reign of Philip Augustus, see Baldwin, *Masters, Princes and Merchants* I, 63–149, and "Masters at Paris from 1179 to 1215: A Social Perspective," in *Renaissance and Renewal in the Twelfth Century*, eds. Robert L. Benson and Giles Constable (Cambridge, Mass., 1982), 138–72.

51. See chaps. 8 and 12.

52. *Chartularium universitatis Parisiensis*, eds. Heinrich Denifle and Emile Châtelain (Paris, 1889), I, 75–79, 89, 98, 99. Gaines Post, "Parisian Masters as a Corporation, 1200–1246," *Speculum* 9 (1934): 421–45, reprinted in *Studies in Medieval Legal Thought: Public Law and the State, 1100–1322* (Princeton, 1964), 27–60.

53. *Actes* I, no. 346. On the king's questionable choice of the Chanter for the responsibility, see Baldwin, *Masters, Princes and Merchants* I, 65–69. For the chronology of the construction of Notre-Dame, see Allan Temko, *Notre-Dame of Paris* (New York, 1955), 310–12.

54. The definitive study on the royal palace is Jean Guérout, "Le Palais de la Cité à Paris," *Fédération des sociétés historiques et archéologiques de Paris et de l'Ile-de-France, Mémoires* 1 (1949): 146–57.

55. The most recent and definitive study of the right bank is Anne Lombard-Jourdan, *Paris—Genèse de la "Ville": La Rive droite de la Seine des origines à 1223* (Paris, 1976), especially pp. 97–160.

56. *Actes* I, no. 426.

57. *Actes* I, no. 31. Philip recompensed the lepers with an annual rent from the *prévôté* of 300 *livres*. In 1202/03, however, they were receiving only 240 *livres*. *Budget* CXLVII (1), CLXXIV (2), CLXXXIX (1).

58. Rigord, *Gesta* 33, 34, 70, 71. On Philip's interest in the quarter, see Lombard-Jourdan, *Paris* 108–110, and Boussard, *Nouvelle histoire* 317, 318.

59. Rigord, *Gesta* 53, 54, 105.

60. *Actes* II, no. 587, IV, nos. 1424, 1425. *Registres* II, F. On the intricacies of this exchange, see Lombard-Jourdan, *Paris* 106–8.

61. This appears to be the humorous point of a contemporary *chanson de geste*, the Narbonnais. Robert Dion, "La Leçon d'une chanson de geste: Le Narbonnais," *Fédération des sociétés historiques et archéologiques de Paris et de l'Ile-de-France, Mémoires* 1 (1949): 23–45.

62. Josef Semmler, "Die Residenzen der Fürsten und Prälaten im mittelalterlichen Paris (12–14 Jahrhundert)," in *Mélanges offerts à René Crozet* (Poitiers, 1966), II, 1220, 1222, 1228, 1229, and Lombard-Jourdan, *Paris* 230, n. 526, 246, n. 684.

63. See, for example, Carlrichard Brühl, *Palatium und Civitas: Studien zur Profantopographie spätantiker Civitates vom 3. bis zum 13. Jahrhundert* (Cologne, 1975), I, 19. For evidence of growth on the right bank, but without figures, see Lombard-Jourdan, *Paris* 135–41.

64. *Actes* I, no. 74, III, nos. 1121, 1238. A charter of Louis VII (1162) regulating the butchers at Paris was copied in Reg. A, fol. 22v. Lombard-Jourdan, *Paris* 126–30.

65. Outsiders who brought in wine by boat could not discharge it in the city, but their wine could be purchased by other outsiders for transport outside the *bailliage* by wagon, again, without discharging. *Actes* I, no. 426.

66. *Registres* I, no. 116.

67. *Actes* II, no. 670. The names of the streets around the Champeaux and Place de la Grève give evidence of numerous other trades. See *Le Livre des métiers d'Etienne Boileau*, ed. R. de Lespinasse and F. Bonnardot (Paris, 1879), iv—vii. Lombard-Jourdan, *Paris* 132, 133.

68. Lombard-Jourdain, *Paris* 142, 143.

69. Rigord, *Gesta* 134, 165. Diceto II, 142, 143. Reinerus, *Annales, MGH SS* XVI, 660.

70. Lombard-Jourdan, *Paris* 124, 125.

71. *Actes* II, nos. 640, 850, 865. Tolls on the Oise in the county of Beaumont and on the Seine between Melun, Corbeil, and Paris were set with the king's consent. *Registres* VI, no. 64. *Actes* IV, no. 1446. *Registres* VII, no. 11.

72. *Actes* III, no. 1108. Teulet I, no. 913. *Actes* III, no. 1385. By 1213 Philip's jurisdiction over the fairs had been recognized because of his regalian rights. *Actes* III, no. 1298.

73. *Actes* I, nos. 135, 448, II, no. 610, III, no. 1107, V, no. 1863.

74. *Actes* I, no. 206. *Registres* VI, no. 64. For the most recent work on the water merchants, see Lombard-Jourdan, *Paris* 146—54.

75. *Actes* III, no. 1316; IV, no. 1625. Jurisdiction over false measures, robbery, assaults, and high justice remained with the king. The standard work on the origins of the Paris municipality is A. Vidier, "Les origines de la municipalité parisienne," *Mémoires de la Société de l'Histoire de Paris et de l'Ile-de-France* 49 (1927): 250—91.

76. In the accounts of 1217 the two men rendered the *prévôts'* and *baillis'* accounts separately; in 1219 they were joined together. Brussel, *Nouvel examen* I, 482—84. On the prominent bourgeois families, see Boussard, *Nouvelle histoire* 305—13. The tower at the walls of the left bank facing the Louvre was named after Philippe Hamelin, or at least his family. *Actes* III, no. 1193. See chap. 6, at n. 253.

77. See, for example, *Actes* III, no. 1193, and chap. 8, at n. 46.

78. *Registres* I, no. 118.

79. *Registres* I, no. 95. See chap. 7, at n. 22.

80. Teulet I, no. 1439. Delisle, *Catalogue* no. 2034.

81. Specific royal rights were in respect to *tailles*, tolls, host and *chevauchée*, watchguard, street vendors, measures, merchants, and deceased usurers. *Registres* I, no. 100. Lombard-Jourdan, *Paris* 113, 114. Undated, the inquest may be placed shortly before the final agreement of 1222.

82. *Actes* IV, no. 1805. See the commentary of Lombard-Jourdan, *Paris* 114—20, and her edition of a contemporary translation into French, 161—66.

83. In 1220 he had granted jurisdiction over street vendors, measures, sales taxes, and petty justice to the water merchants. Apparently he considered this delegation dependent on his ultimate rights over these matters. See n. 81 above.

That a night watch was established by Philip Augustus is confirmed by *Le Livre des métiers d'Etienne Boileau* 66.

84. During this "week" the bishop could also collect customs from entering foreigners who resided outside, but nothing from foreigners who resided within the city or its suburbs. To safeguard the receipts from his "week," the bishop was allowed to keep strongboxes at the *châtelets* of the Grand- and Petit-Ponts, where the royal revenues were also received. The goods of ecclesiastical persons were exempt from the king's customs (*merellis*) upon declaration of the clerics' wagoners and sergeants.

85. The rent was 20 *livres*. Philip also gained the fief of Ferté-Alais, for which he indemnified the bishop. Jurisdiction over the recently opened rue Neuve-Notre-Dame leading into the *parvis* before the cathedral was divided between the king and bishop.

86. On the episcopal encroachments, see Lombard-Jourdan, *Paris* 110–13, 120, 121.

87. Nortier and Baldwin, "Contributions," 5–30. See chap. 10. On Henry III, see Roger of Wendover, *Historia Anglorum*, ed. F. Madden (London 1866), II, 341, 342. Before the Pell Rolls, balances may have been noted in the Wardrobe accounts. James H. Ramsay, *A History of the Revenues of the Kings of England* (Oxford, 1925), I, 261–65, 297.

88. Fragments from 1217 and 1219 have been preserved in Brussel, *Nouvel examen* I, 439, 447, 483, 484, 515, II, 1036.

89. For 1227: travel (*itinera*); wages, gifts, and equipment (*dona, hernesia*); horses (*equi, roncini*); crossbowmen and sergeants (*balistiarii, servientes*); marches and new castles (*marchie, turres nove*); forest wardens (*custodes forestarum*); expenses of *prévôts* and *baillis* (*expense prepositorum et ballivorum*); and expenses of individuals such as the queen regent and the counts of Champagne and Boulogne. Borrelli de Serres, *Recherches* I, 183. The budget of 1238 was even more detailed, containing some forty categories of *magna expensa*. RHF XXI, 259, 260.

90. At that time Louis's expenditures in wages, gifts, and equipment (3,392 *livres*) were about half those of young Louis IX in 1227. Fawtier, "Un Fragment du compte de l'hôtel de prince Louis," 233–46. For later examples of *hôtel* accounts, see RHF XXI, 226–51, and XXII, 583–615. Without corroborating evidence, however, we should not extrapolate the other categories of 1227, and certainly not those of 1238, into the budget of 1221.

91. Nortier and Baldwin, "Contributions," 26, 29. See Table 8. On the balances in 1202/03, see chap. 7, at n. 152.

92. Teulet I, no. 1546. *Actes* IV, no. 1796. Following the suggestion of the seventeenth-century erudite Peiresc, Nortier has been able to restore the erased figure from the long scribal strokes that remain. See also Nortier and Baldwin, "Contributions" 30–33.

93. The chief reports come from (1) Conon de Lausanne, *MGH SS* XXIV, 782; (2) monk of Saint-Denis in Guillaume le Breton, *Gesta* 325 (this version is also contained in the obituary of Chartres, *Obituaires de la province de Sens*, ed. A. Molinier [Paris, 1906], II, 74–76, and in the manuscript Paris, Mazarine 2017, published in Cartellieri IV, 653, 654); (3) *Chronicon Sancti Martini Turonensis*, *RHF* XVIII, 304; (4) Alberic de Trois-Fontaines 913; (5) Coggeshall 193. Cartellieri IV, 565–68, offers detailed comparisons of these sources.

94. Not only were most contemporaries agreed over the amount, but a charter was copied in Reg. E from the master of the Templars in August 1223 acknowledging the amount according to the terms of the bequest. *Registres* VI, no. 93.

95. Conon, monk of Saint-Denis, and Alberic de Trois-Fontaines.

96. In September 1218 Philip offered Ingeborg 10,000 *livres* (the same as in 1221) in exchange for her dower lands (*maritagium*). *Actes* IV, no. 1542. At the same time, Ingeborg made a will distributing this sum in similar ways to the king's will in 1221. Delisle, *Catalogue* pp. 520, 521. In August 1223 Louis VIII restored to Ingeborg some of her dower lands. *Registres* VI, no. 94.

97. See the differing conclusions of Cartellieri IV, 565–68, and Nortier, "Contributions" 32, 33.

98. *MGH SS* XXIV, 782, 783. See chap. 3, at n. 90, and Baldwin, "Contributions" 29, 30.

99. In Guillaume le Breton, *Gesta* 323.

14. Philip, the Realm, and the Emergence of Royal Ideology

1. *Chronicon Sancti Martini Turonensis* in *RHF* XVIII, 304. For modern use of this account, see the notable attempts to characterize Philip by Achille Luchaire in *Histoire de France depuis les origines jusqu'à la Révolution*, ed. Ernest Lavisse (Paris, 1901), III, 279–84, and by Cartellieri IV, 577–94. In contrast to the Tours Chronicler stands the more conventional catalogue of virtues in Rigord 31.

2. The fullest discussion of this disease as it pertained to Philip may be found in Auguste Brachet, *Pathologie mentale des rois de France, Louis XI et ses ascendants: Une Vie humaine étudiée à travers six siècles d'hérédité, 852–1483* (Paris, 1903), 253–91.

3. *Li Fet des Romains*, ed. L. F. Flutre and K. Sneyders de Vogel (Paris, 1935), 18, discussed most recently in Jeanette Beer, "French Nationalism under Philip Augustus—An Unexpected Source," *Mosaic* 7 (1974): 59. In Italian sources Philip was thought to be one-eyed, perhaps by association of his name with Philip of Macedon. Cartellieri IV, 577.

4. Rigord 120, 121, and Guillaume le Breton, *Gesta* 194. See the interpretation of Brachet, *Pathologie mentale* 300–306. Philip's sudden departure from Pal-

estine in 1191 need not be ascribed to his illness alone. For his other reasons, see chap. 5, at nn. 7–12.

5. For Philip's marital life see chap. 5 and 9 and the interpretation of Brachet, *Pathologie mentale* 307–31.

6. See chap. 9, at n. 6.

7. Rigord 14 and Guillaume le Breton, *Gesta* 181. Gerald of Wales, *Gemma ecclesiastica* in *Opera* II, 161, and *De Principis instructione* 318.

8. Rigord 71, 72. On the ecclesiastical influence, see Baldwin, *Masters, Princes and Merchants* I, 202 and 254.

9. Innocent III, *Regesta PL* 215: 1136 and 216: 37; Potthast I, nos. 3072 and 3715. *Li Fet des Romains* 18, 19, and Beer, "French Nationalism" 59.

10. Suger, *Vie de Louis VI*, 6, 8, 102, 110, 122, 180, 182, 184, 204, 222, 240, 250. See the discussion of Charles T. Wood, "*Regnum Francie*: A Problem in Capetian Administrative Usage," *Traditio* 23 (1967): 117, 118.

11. *Actes* II, no. 737.

12. For examples before 1204: *Actes* I, nos. 34, 71, 117, 188, 189, 194, 232, 240, 253, 330, 332, II, nos. 479, 524, 527, 531, and 555. After 1204: *Actes* II, nos. 800, 810, 856, 870, III, nos. 1037, 1116, 1201, 1262, 1268, 1283, 1284.

13. *Actes* I, no. 149. See chap. 4, at nn. 51–58, for the conflict over Dol.

14. Margret Lugge, *"Gallia" und "Francia" im Mittelalter: Untersuchungen über den Zusammengang zwischen geographisch-historischer Terminologie und politischem Denken vom 6.–15. Jahrhundert*, Bonner historische Forschungen, no. 15 (Bonn, 1960), is the most authoritative discussion.

15. Rigord xxv. Pierre the Chanter distinguished between a "francia particularis circa parisius" and a "francia generalis." Baldwin, *Masters, Princes and Merchants* II, 109, n. 1.

16. My own experience with the manuscripts of the royal registers confirms Delisle's (*Catalogue*, pp. lxiii, lxiv) observations on this practice. The major exception is the *successores nostri reges Francie* in *Actes* I, no. 330.

17. *Registres* III, O. See chap. 12, at n. 30, for the episcopal cities.

18. Ibid. III, H.

19. Ibid. IV, A (IV).

20. See the discussion of Wood, "*Regnum Francie*" 117–47, especially pp. 132, 133.

21. Rigord 6. Rigord also attributed the imperial *semper Augustus* title to Philip. Ibid. 1, 53.

22. *Registres* VII, no. 1.

23. Guillaume le Breton, *Philippidos* 380, 381.

24. Gerald of Wales, *De Principis instructione* 328.

25. See chap. 11, at nn. 4–6, and the interpretations of Georges Duby, *Les Trois Ordres ou l'imaginaire du féodalisme* (Paris, 1978), 277–81, and Gabrielle M. Spiegel, "History as Enlightenment: Suger and the *Mos Anagogicus*," in *Abbot Suger and Saint-Denis*, ed. Paula Gerson (New York, in press).

26. See chap. 15 for a fuller description of the royal historians. The *Historia regum Francorum*, composed by an anonymous monk of Saint-Germain-des-Prés, made few contributions to royal ideology.

27. The occasional verse is found in a collection known as the *Floridus aspectus*. The two relevant pieces here were edited by B. Hauréau, "Un Poème inédit de Pierre Riga," *BEC* 44 (1883): 5–11, and by H.-François Delaborde, "Un Poème inédit de Pierre Riga sur la naissance de Philippe Auguste," *Notices et documents publiés pour la Société de l'Histoire de France à l'occasion du cinquantième anniversaire* (Paris, 1884), 121–27. Pierre Riga may also be the author of a poem celebrating the consecration of Guillaume, archbishop of Reims, in 1176. See John R. Williams, "William of the White Hands and Men of Letters," *Anniversary Essays in Medieval History by Students of Charles Homer Haskins* (Boston, 1929), 382, 383, and *Aurora Petri Rigae: Biblia versificata*, ed. Paul E. Beichner, 2 vols. (Notre Dame, Ind., 1965), which contains a convenient introduction to Pierre's life and writings. On his death, see Alberic de Trois-Fontaines 889.

28. M. L. Colker, ed., "The *Karolinus* of Egidius Parisiensis," *Traditio* 34 (1973): 199–325, contains the most recent edition and introduction to his life and works. (References to the *Karolinus* in subsequent notes give the page numbers of this edition.) His gift to the Mathurins is found in the Cartulaire des Mathurins de Paris, AN, LL 1544, fol. 1r. See also JL 17374.

A poet and historian who circulated further out on the periphery of the royal entourage was Hélinand de Froidmont. As a young man Hélinand gained fame in northern France as a *trouvère* and won admittance to royal circles. His reputation as a *trouvère* is reflected in a line of the *Roman d'Alexandre*: "Quant li rois ot mangié, s'apiela Elinant," which shows that Hélinand's name came readily to mind as a well-known poet who entertained the king. Repenting of his worldly life, however, he converted to the Cistercians around 1185 and joined the monastery of Froidmont in the Beauvaisis, where he died around 1230.

Even as a monk, however, Hélinand marshalled his poetic talents to compose the *Vers de la mort*, a vernacular meditation on death. Inveighing against the vanities of the world, he reproached by name six contemporary prelates and one baron for their failings. Although the poem is susceptible to varying and overlapping interpretations, these figures suggest a pointed attack on Philip Augustus's attempted separation from Ingeborg, since all seven were involved in the fraudulent proceedings at Compiègne in 1193. See *Les Vers de la Mort par Hélinant, moine de Froidmont*, ed. F. Wulff and E. Walberg (Paris, 1905), and an English translation by William D. Paden, Jr., "The Verses on Death by Hélinant de Froidmont," *Allegorica* 3 (1978): 63–103. For the Ingeborg interpretation, see William D. Paden, Jr., "*De Monachis rithmos facientibus*: Hélinant de Froidmont, Bertran de Born, and the Cistercian General Chapter of 1199," *Speculum* 55 (1980): 669–80. For other interpretations, see G. S. Williams, "Against Court and School: Heinrich of Melk and Helinand of Froidmont as Critics of Twelfth-Century Society," *Neophilologus* 62 (1978): 513–26.

Hélinand also composed a universal chronicle in Latin from the beginning of the world to 1204. According to Vincent de Beauvais, writing in the 1240s, Hélinand lent certain *cahiers* of the work to his friend, Guérin, bishop of Senlis, who then lost them through forgetfulness or negligence. Vincent de Beauvais, *Bibliotheca mundi*, vol. IV, *Speculum historiale* (Douai, 1624), 1222. The reputedly lost sections may have been seen by Léopold Delisle in a manuscript of Beauvais, now lost again. See "La Chronique d'Hélinand, moine de Froidmont," *Notices et documents publiés pour la Société de l'Histoire de France à l'occasion du cinquantième anniversaire* (Paris, 1884), 141–54. The fullest published collection of excerpts may be found in Vincent de Beauvais, *Speculum historiale*, reprinted in *PL* 212:771–1082. For the most recent studies on Hélinand's historical work, see M. P. Arnaud-Cancel, "Le Huitième Livre de la chronique d'Hélinand de Froidmont," *Positions des thèses de l'Ecole des Chartes* (Paris, 1971), 9–14; Monique Paulmier-Foucart, "Ecrire l'histoire au XIIIᵉ siècle: Vincent de Beauvais et Hélinand de Froidmont," *Annales de l'Est* 33 (1981): 49–70; and E. R. Smits, "Helinand of Froidmont and the A-Text of Seneca's Tragedies," *Mnemosyne* 36 (1983): 324–58. To Vincent's well-known story, the [Canons Deslyons and Afforty] ("Le Chancelier Guérin," *Comité archéologique de Senlis: Comptes rendus et mémoires*, 3rd ser., 2 [1887]: 113) add that Guérin asked his clerk Etienne de Gallardon to write a short chronicle on the French kings from Pharamond to Philip Augustus, which was preserved in a manuscript from Saint-Germain-des-Prés. To aid Etienne, Guérin borrowed Hélinand's chronicle, which he lost. Unfortunately, I have not been able to verify this intriguing version.

Finally, Hélinand was responsible for the *De Bono Regimine principis*, a didactic mirror-of-princes text that loosely excerpted passages from John of Salisbury's *Policraticus* to explicate Deuteronomy 17:14–20 on the good king. Since it was undoubtedly written while Philip was alive, it was most probably intended for the Capetian monarch or for his son. It survives only in those excerpts collected by Vincent de Beauvais, *Speculum historiale* 1227–30, reprinted in *PL* 212:735–46. The manuscript Paris BN nouv. acq. lat. 3085, pp. 1–46, merely recopies Vincent's version. See S. Solente, *BEC* 112 (1954): 198. On Hélinand's treatise, see Wilhelm Berges, *Die Fürstenspiegel des hohen und späten Mittelalters*, MGH Schriften, no. 2 (Munich, 1938), 295, 296, and Philippe Delhaye, "La Morale politique de Hélinand de Froidmont," *Mélanges de sciences religieuses* 23, suppl. (1966): 107–17.

Michael Wilks ("Alain of Lille and the New Man," *Renaissance and Renewal in Christian History: Studies in Church History* 14 [1977]: 137–57) and Linda E. Marshall ("The Identity of the New Man in the 'Anticlaudianus' of Alain of Lille," *Viator: Medieval and Renaissance Studies* 10 [1979]: 77–94) have not yet made a sufficient case, in my opinion, to link Philip Augustus with Alain de Lille's *Anticlaudianus*. In all events, since Alain had no discernible ties with the Capetian court, it would be difficult to make him a patronized royal apologist.

29. *Karolinus* 305, 321. Guillaume le Breton, *Philippidos* 2, 382.

30. *Galteri de Castellione Alexandreis*, ed. Marvin L. Colker (Padua, 1978) is a recent and authoritative edition. In addition to the introduction to this edition, see the accounts of Max Manitius, *Geschichte der lateinischen Literatur des Mittelalters* (Munich, 1931), III, 920–27, and F. J. E. Raby, *A History of Secular Latin Poetry in the Middle Ages* (Oxford, 1957), II, 72–80, 190, 191. A thirteenth-century gloss claimed that the *Alexandreis* grew out of rivalry between Gautier and a royal clerk, Magister Berterus, for the favor of Archbishop Guillaume. *Alexandreis*, ed. Colker, p. xv, xvi. See the comments of John R. Williams, "William of the White Hands," in *Anniversary Essays . . . Haskins* 375–77. On Magister Berterus, see chap. 2, n. 38.

31. Guillaume le Breton, *Philippidos* 1, 382.

32. See the detailed studies of A. Pannenborg, *Zur Kritik der Philipis* (Aurich, 1880), 16–19, and *Karolinus* 211 and identification of sources in Colker's footnotes throughout.

33. Compare these excerpts from the two prologues:

Et mirum est, humanum genus a prima sui natura, secundum quam cuncta que fecit Deus valde bona creata sunt, ita esse deprauatum ut pronus sit ad condempnandum quam ad indulgendum et facilis sit ei ambigua deprauare quam in partem interpretari meliorem. Hoc ego reueritus diu te, o mea Alexandrei, in mente habui semper supprimere et opus quinquennio laboratum aut penitus delere aut certe quod uiuerem in occulto sepelire. Tandem apud me deliberatum est te in lucem esse proferendam ut demum auderes in publica venire monumenta.

Alexandreis 3, 4.

Et mirum est humanum genus a prima sui origine (secundum quem cuncta que fecit Deus valde bona creata sunt) ita esse depravatum ut promptius sit ad condemnandum quam indulgendum, et facilius sit ei ambigua depravare quam in partem interpretari meliorem . . . Hoc ego pertimescens, opus decennio elaboratum habui in voluntate supprimere aut penitus delere, vel certe, quantum viverem, in occulto sepelire. Tandem . . . hoc opus in lucem protuli et christianissimo regi humiliter obtuli, ut sic demum per manum ipsius regis in publica veniret monumenta.

Rigord, 5, 6.

On Rigord's borrowing from Gautier, see M. L. Colker, "Walter of Châtillon, Rigord of Saint-Denis, and an Alleged Quotation from Juvenal," *Classical Folio* 24 (1970): 89–95.

34. Guillaume le Breton, *Philippidos* 209, 280.

35. Where Gautier played with acrostics, inserting the letters of the name of his patron *Guillermus* into the opening initials of each book, Guillaume followed by spelling out *Philipus Rex E[st] Christ[ianissimus] Francorum* in the *Philippidos*.

On Pierre Riga's playing with acrostics, see Raby, *History of Secular Latin Poetry* II, 36. Gilles de Paris opened each of his books with the initial of the virtue discussed in the books. *Karolinus* 205, 323. All were obsessed with counting their lines of verse: 15,056 lines by Pierre Riga, and 1,632 added by Gilles de Paris (counted in Gilles's edition), *Aurora Petri Rigae* 17; 2,232 in *Karolinus* 316; 9,145 in Guillaume le Breton, *Philippidos* 384. For the difficulties experienced by critical editors in arriving at the same figures, thus suggesting interpolations, see M. L. Colker, "Stichometry That Does Not Tally," *Scriptorium* 16 (1962): 85–89, and *Karolinus* 218 and n. 102. All except Pierre recorded the time required to complete their poems: five years, *Alexandreis* 3; ten years, Rigord 5; two years in writing and correcting, *Karolinus* 301; written in three years and corrected in two, Guillaume le Breton, *Philippidos* 384.

36. *RHF* XVII, 423.

37. Berges (*Fürstenspiegel* 73–79) discusses these works in the context of the mirrors of princes. Guillaume le Breton, *Philippidos* 1, 4, 379, 383. Rigord 1. *Karolinus* 241, 301, 308, 315, 325. The possible presentation copy is Paris BN lat. 6191. Gilles mentions the wedding as having passed, and that he intends to present the work on Louis's thirteenth birthday (3 September), but the wedding was certainly the more festive occasion. Rigord acknowledges the wedding explicitly.

38. Rigord 125, 128, 129, 131, 147, 148, 150, 151. *Karolinus* 244, 306, 308, 324. For Hélinand's criticism, see n. 28 above.

39. *Karolinus* 289, 291, 302, 315, 323.

40. Ibid. 304, 316. The editor, Colker, has provided a synopsis of the books of the poem (206–9) and an edition of medieval glosses to the *Karolinus* that explicated the four virtues (234–36).

41. Guillaume le Breton, *Philippidos* 3, 80. Guillaume also refers to Charles's conquest of Saxony. Ibid. 310. Simon de Montfort evoked Charles, Roland, and Ogier as heroes at Muret. Ibid. 234.

42. Ibid. 2, 3. Actually, Bouvines was fought in the thirty-fifth year of Philip's reign. Hélinand, *De Bono Regimine principis*, PL 212:745, following John of Salisbury's *Policraticus*, also evokes the examples of Caesar and Alexander. See similar passages in Gerald of Wales, *De Principis instructione* 7, 27, 42.

43. Guillaume le Breton, *Philippidos* 355, 356.

44. Ibid. 1, 382, 383.

45. Gautier de Châtillon, *Alexandreis* 143, 144. Compare also Gilles de Paris, *Karolinus* 304.

46. The name Philip, and with it presumed Macedonian lineage, entered the Capetian dynasty through Anna of Kiev, the queen of Henry I. Andrew W. Lewis, *Royal Succession in Capetian France: Studies on Familial Order and the State* (Cambridge, Mass., 1981), 47.

47. Guillaume le Breton, *Philippidos* 125, 126 (Berry); 56 (Boves); 139, 140 (Gisors).

48. Compare *Philippidos* 305–9 with *Alexandreis* 52–54; 381 with 55; 313

574 NOTES TO CHAPTER 14

with 58; 357 with 141. See the discussion of Pannenborg, *Zur Kritik der Philipis* 18, 19.

49. Guillaume le Breton, *Gesta* 168, 176, 179, 227, and so on. *Philippidos* 4, 6, 20, 25, and so on. On the definition of *magnanimitas* as applied to Alexander, see George Cary, *The Medieval Alexander* (Cambridge, 1956), 197–200.

50. Cartellieri I, 1–10, Beilagen 49.

51. Delaborde, "Un Poème inédite de Pierre Riga," *Notices et documents* 123–27. See chap. 1, at n. 13, for the birth.

52. *De Glorioso Rege Ludovico* in *Vie de Louis le Gros par Suger*, ed. Auguste Molinier (Paris, 1887), 147, 149.

53. Rigord 7, 8.

54. Ibid. 48, 111, 112. See chap. 5 on Philip's marriage policy.

55. The most recent and exhaustive treatment of Capetian dynastic claims is Lewis, *Royal Succession in Capetian France*, which reduces the need for further study of the problem.

56. Louis VI was a partial exception to this. Although not crowned in his father's lifetime, he was nonetheless entitled *rex designatus*. Lewis, *Royal Succession in Capetian France*, 51.

57. Pope Alexander III had urged that Philip be associated as early as 1171. For a discussion of the circumstances, see ibid. 74–77.

58. Andrew W. Lewis, "Anticipatory Association of the Heir in Early Capetian France," *American Historical Review* 83 (1978): 906–27, restated in *Royal Succession in Capetian France*, has sought to modify the long-accepted "royalist" view of anticipatory association by demonstrating its widespread use among contemporary baronial families, arguing for advantages other than royal succession, and discussing in detail the circumstances attendant on each Capetian succession. But none of the factors that he suggests replace the underlying utility of anticipatory association for royal succession.

59. Lewis, "Anticipatory Association," 923, n. 63, and *Royal Succession in Capetian France* 92–94.

60. Pierre Riga calls Philip *regius puer*, and the monk of Saint-Germain characterizes him as *nobilissima proles* like his father. Lewis, *Royal Succession in Capetian France* 34.

61. *Historia Francorum Senonensis*, *MGH SS* IX, 364–69. This view was probably prompted by competition between the archbishops of Sens and Reims over the right to crown the king.

62. *Historia relationis corporis Sancti Walarici*, *RHF* IX, 147–49, and *Cronica Centulensi sive Sancti Richarii*, *RHF* VIII, 273–75. On the Valerian prophecy, see the studies of Gabrielle M. Spiegel, "The *Reditus regni ad stirpem Karoli Magni*: A New Look," *French Historical Studies* 7 (1971): 147–51, and Lewis, *Royal Succession in Capetian France* 36, 50.

63. *Registres* VII, no. 4. It is possible that the original version of the prophecy assigned the saint's apparition to Hugues the Great.

64. A contemporary example was the prophecy of Hugh, bishop of Lincoln, about the sons of Henry II. *The Life of St. Hugh of Lincoln*, ed. D. L. Douie and H. Farmer (London, 1961), II, 184, 185.

65. André de Marchiennes, *Historia succincta de gestis et successione regum Francorum*, partially edited in *MGH SS* XXVI, 204–15. On the doctrine, see Karl Ferdinand Werner, "Die Legitimät der Kapetinger und die Entstehung des 'Reditus regni Francorum ad stirpem Karoli,'" *Die Welt als Geschichte* 12 (1952): 203–25, and Spiegel, "The *Reditus regni*" 145–74.

66. Rigord, *Short Chronicle*, in Soissons, Bibl. mun. 129, fol. 136v. *Karolinus* 249–51. *Historia regum Francorum*, RHF XII, 220. Lewis, *Royal Succession in Capetian France* 119.

67. See chap. 14, at n. 113. That Philip called his bastard son (born 1209) Pierre Charlot is not conclusive in pointing to Carolingian connections.

68. Guillaume le Breton, *Philippidos* 384. *Chronicon magnum Turonense*, RHF X, 280, 281. Lewis, *Royal Succession in Capetian France* 111–13.

69. Rigord 61. Guillaume le Breton, *Gesta* 176. *Registres* IV, A (V). Gilles de Paris was also aware that there was no apparent link between the Carolingians and Capetians. See Andrew W. Lewis, "Dynastic Structures and Capetian Throne-Right: The Views of Giles of Paris," *Traditio* 33 (1977): 241. The royal genealogies of the eleventh century, which were well known in the twelfth and thirteenth centuries, were also clear about this rupture. See Bernard Guenée, "Les Généalogies entre l'histoire et la politique: La Fierté d'être Capétien, en France, au moyen âge," *Annales: Economies, Sociétés, Civilisations* 33 (1978): 343, 344, reprinted in *Politique et histoire au moyen âge: Recueil d'articles sur l'histoire politique et l'historiographie médiévale (1956–1981)* (Paris, 1981), 452, 453.

70. Only Gilles de Paris showed how Hugues was descended from Duke Robert the Strong, in a genealogical diagram illustrating the *Karolinus*. Paris BN lat. 6191, fol. 48v. Lewis, "Dynastic Structures," fig. 1, pp. 234, 241, 242. On the baronial genealogies, see Georges Duby, "Remarques sur la littérature généalogique en France aux XIᵉ et XIIᵉ siècles," *Académie des Inscriptions et Belles-Lettres: Comptes rendus* (1967): 335–45, reprinted in *Hommes et structures du moyen âge* (Paris, 1973), 287–98. The only true genealogies transcribed in the royal registers were those of Ingeborg and the dukes of Normandy and the kings of England. *Registres* VII, nos. 5 and 7. Gilles de Paris also included a genealogy of the kings of England. Lewis, "Dynastic Structures" 235.

71. *Registres* IV, A (IV, V). The second list entitled the kings the *Sarraceni reges Francorum*. On the distinction between genealogies and catalogues, see Guenée, "Les Généalogies" 341, 356, 357.

72. On the role of the Trojan origins as a foundation myth, see R. W. Southern, "Aspects of the European Tradition of Historical Writing: 1. The Classical Tradition from Einhard to Geoffrey of Monmouth," *Transactions of the Royal Historical Society*, 5th ser., 20 (1970): 188–95. The development of the Frankish tradition lacks a thoroughgoing study. For the specific texts: *Chronicarum quae*

dicitur Fredegarii Scholastii MGH SS Rer. Mer. II, 45, 46, 93, 95; *Liber historiae Francorum, MGH SS Rer. Mer.* II, 241; Aimoin de Fleury, *De Gestis Francorum, RHF* III, 29; Suger in Paris BN lat. 12710, fols. 34r–35r (see also Jules Lair, "Mémoire sur deux chroniques latines composées au XIIe siècle à l'abbaye de Saint-Denis," *BEC* 35 [1874]: 551–57). For a recent discussion of the manuscripts of Hugues de Saint-Victor's *Chronicon,* see Grover A. Zinn, "The Influence of Hugh of St. Victor's *Chronicon* on the *Abbreviationes chronicorum* by Ralph of Diceto," *Speculum* 52 (1972): 42–56. I am grateful for help from Gabrielle M. Spiegel in writing this section on the Trojan origins.

73. Soissons, Bibl. mun. 129. Excerpts published by Delaborde in Rigord pp. xix–xxvi.

74. Rigord 54–64. (Rigord drew explicitly on Aimoin de Fleury and Hugues de Saint-Victor. Ibid. 54, 55.) *Short Chronicle of the Kings of France,* Soissons Bibl. mun. 129, fols. 133r–135r (excerpts edited in Rigord, xxv). Guillaume le Breton, *Gesta* 169–72, *Philippidos* 9–15. Gilles de Paris in Paris BN lat. 6191, fols. 46v, 47r (see Lewis, "Dynastic Structures" 232, 233). *Registres* IV, A (IV, V).

75. Rigord 56. Guillaume le Breton, *Gesta* 171, *Philippidos* 11. The ultimate source for the etymology was Isidore of Seville, *Etymologiarum sive originum libri,* ed. W. M. Lindsay (Oxford, 1911), IX, 2, 101.

76. Rigord 54, 58. Guillaume le Breton, *Gesta* 170, *Philippidos* 11, 13. Rigord and his followers paid further attention to particular elements whose significance was heightened for their own times. When the royal domain had begun to expand, Rigord depicted Marcomires subjugating all of *Germania* and Gaul down to the Pyrenees (56). After the conquest of Normandy was a fact, Guillaume could be more precise about the kingdom's boundaries: "from the sea that separates us from England to the boundaries of Charlemagne [in the Pyrenees], so that what used to be called Gaul is now the land of the French" (*Philippidos* 13). As Philip encircled Paris with walls, Rigord noted that Marcomires had done the same (59). Guillaume observed that he had brought the Parisians together and made of them one people. Paris was then, as it had become since, the *caput* of the kingdom, the seedbed (*germina*) of kings, and the teacher of the whole world (*Gesta* 171, *Philippidos* 11, 13). As Guillaume drew his epic poem to a close, he could not resist allusions to Trojan heroes while recounting Philip's victories: When Simon de Montfort harangues his troops before the battle of Muret, he recalls their Trojan origins (*Philippidos* 234). The ships at Damme are likened to those at Troy (ibid. 260). After the victory at Tournai, the Trojans are once again evoked (ibid. 279). Philip's attempt to fight Otto single-handed at Bouvines is inspired by Aeneas's battle with Turnus (ibid. 334).

77. Rigord 57, 60, 61. Guillaume le Breton, *Gesta* 172, 174, 175.

78. Rigord 64.

79. The Fulrad *ordo* has most recently been edited by Paul L. Ward, "An Early

Version of the Anglo-Saxon Coronation Ceremony," *EHR* 57 (1942): 350–61. The account of the 1059 ceremony is in *RHF* XI, 32, 33, and that of 1108 in Suger, *Vie de Louis VI* 84–88. Percy E. Schramm's numerous contributions to the study of coronation *ordines*, on which these paragraphs are based, have been summarized in *Der König von Frankreich: Das Wesen der Monarchie vom 9. zum 16. Jahrhundert* (Darmstadt, 1960), I, 112–28, 145–62, 193–217. See his list in II, 4. See also the complementary study by Marcel David, "Le Serment du sacre du IXᵉ au XVᵉ siècle: Contribution à l'étude des limites juridiques de la souveraineté," *Revue du moyen âge latin* 6 (1950): 5–272.

80. David, "Le Serment du sacre" 202, 223, 224, 236–40. The acclamation disappears in the Reims *ordo*.

81. Rigord 13. Guillaume le Breton, *Gesta* 179. Gilles de Paris pays little attention to royal consecrations, but describes Charlemagne's imperial coronation in 800 in greater detail. *Karolinus* 279. For the Reims tradition, which originated in Carolingian times and was revived in 1131, see Schramm, *König von Frankreich* I, 147.

82. Rigord 20–22. Guillaume le Breton, *Gesta* 180.

83. Guillaume le Breton, *Gesta* 173, 174, *Philippidos* 14, 15.

84. Guillaume le Breton, *Philippidos* 20, 21.

85. Innocent III, *Regesta PL* 215: 282; Potthast I, no. 2138. Schramm, *König von Frankreich* I, 157.

86. For the relations between the Capetians and Saint-Denis, see Schramm, *König von Frankreich* I, 131–44, and Gabrielle M. Spiegel, "The Cult of Saint-Denis and Capetian Kingship," *Journal of Medieval History* 1 (1975): 43–69, and *The Chronicle Tradition of Saint-Denis: A Survey*, Medieval Classics: Texts and Studies, no. 10 (Brookline, Mass., and Leyden, 1978), 11–37.

87. Elie Berger, "Annales de Saint-Denis généralement connues sous le titre de *Chronicon Sancti Dionysii ad cyclos paschales*," *BEC* 40 (1879): 279. *Actes* IV, no. 1796. Teulet II, no. 1597. In 1261 Louis IX once again deposited his grandfather's crowns with Saint-Denis. *Registres* VI, no. 101.

88. Rigord 98. Guillaume le Breton, *Gesta* 271, *Philippidos* 319. The Fulrad *ordo* also provided a benediction for the royal banner (*vexillum*) at the conclusion of the coronation ceremony. Paul L. Ward, "An Early Version," *EHR* 57 (1942): 361.

89. *Registres* II, I (IV). Louis IX also performed this ceremony regularly. See Schramm, *König von Frankreich* I, 134, 135, 142–44. Spiegel, "Cult of Saint Denis" 59–61.

90. Rigord 65, 66, 114, 115, 138.

91. Ibid. 118, 133, 146.

92. Ibid. 162. The event was confirmed by a charter of 14 September 1205 in the Cartulaire blanc de Saint-Denis, AN, LL 1157, pp. 63, 64. In 1193 Philip restored the castle of Châteauneuf to the abbey. Rigord 123.

93. Rigord 113, 114, 134, 165.

94. Ibid. 11, 111, 112. In 1193–1194 Rigord recorded a number of miracles performed by the saint for individuals. Ibid. 124, 125, 127, 128.

95. Guillaume le Breton, *Gesta* 320. He also noted the coronation of Queen Isabelle in 1180 and the restoration of Châteauneuf. Ibid. 180, 195.

96. Ibid. 271, *Philippidos* 319, 378.

97. Guillaume le Breton, *Gesta* 178, *Philippidos* 18–20.

98. Rigord 96. Guillaume le Breton, *Philippidos* 20, 59, 93. Philip also freed the Norman church, a cause for which Becket died. *Philippidos* 219, 220.

99. Guillaume le Breton, *Philippidos* 371, 376, 379, and *Gesta* 323, 324. This addition to Guillaume le Breton was copied into the obituary of the cathedral of Chartres, omitting only the special reference to Saint-Denis. *Obituaires de la province de Sens*, ed. Auguste Molinier (Paris, 1906), II, 74.

100. Ward, "Early Version" 351, 357.

101. *Testamentum Sancti Remigii, MGH SS rer. mer.*, III, 345, 346. Lewis, *Royal Succession in Capetian France* 19, 35.

102. Molinier, *Vie de Louis de Gros* 172–74, 176. Lewis, *Royal Succession in Capetian France* 72.

103. Rigord 14–19. Guillaume le Breton, *Gesta* 180. Actually, there was a third expedition against the Blois conspiracy, which had also disturbed the peace of the church. It is most likely that Humbert de Beaujeu did not oppose the king at this time. For the complexity behind Rigord's simplistic account, see Georges Duby, *La Société aux XIe et XIIe siècles dans la région mâconnaise* (Paris, 1953), 535–42.

104. Rigord 24–31, 50–53.

105. Ibid. 124, 125, 128, 129, 141, and 147.

106. *Karolinus* 306, 307.

107. Philip's claims as a crusader were noticed in the obituaries of the anonymous monk of Saint-Denis (Guillaume le Breton, *Gesta* 324), recopied at Chartres (*Obituaires de Sens*, ed. Molinier, II, 74), and of Le Mans (G. Busson and A. Ledru, *Nécrologe-obituaire de la cathédral du Mans* [Le Mans, 1906], 171).

108. For Philip's crusading activities, see chap. 5.

109. *RHF* XIX, 671; Potthast I, no. 5900. It is too much to attribute to this letter the creation of a royal diocese personally dependent on the king as Louis Moreau argues in "Recherches sur l'origine et la formation du diocèse royal en France" (thesis, Université des Sciences Humaines de Strasbourg), 126, 127.

110. Jean de Pange, *Le Roi très chrétien: Essai sur la nature du pouvoir royal en France* (Paris, 1949), 31, 144. Berges, *Die Fürstenspiegel* 74, 75. Schramm, *König von Frankreich* I, 184, 185.

111. Rigord 4 (prologue), 15 (first mention), 98 (last mention). The only exception was in 1205 (p. 163) when Philip gives relics to the abbey. The only exception in Guillaume le Breton is in *Gesta* 312, where the chronicler calls Philip *vir christianissimus* because he refuses to communicate with his excom-

municated son. *Christianissimus* only appears in the acrostic to the *Philippidos*. *Christianissimus rex* was attributed to Philip by the obituary of Notre-Dame de Paris. *Obituaires de Sens*, ed. Molinier, I (1), 152. Rigord's employment of the sobriquet *Augustus* follows the same pattern as *christianissimus*: 4 (prologue), 12 (first use at consecration), 98 (last use in 1190), with one exception in 1205 (p. 162) when Philip returns victorious from the Loire campaign.

112. For the diffusion of the accounts of Bouvines among contemporary chroniclers, see Georges Duby, *Le Dimanche de Bouvines* (Paris, 1973), 238. The notice in Reg. C is accompanied by one from the battle of Muret. *Registres* VII, nos. 2 and 3, IV, A (IV). For the notice in Gilles de Paris, *Karolinus: Philippus iste habuit bellum in franchia contra othone imperatore, comite bolonie, comite flandrie. Othonem fugavit; comitem bolonie, comitem flandrie in vincula capta detinuit.* Paris BN lat. 6191, fol. 48v. For the psalter of Ingeborg: MS Chantilly, Musée Condé 1695, fol. 6v. Florens Deuchler, *Die Ingeborg-psalter* (Berlin, 1967), 6, 12. For the narrative of the battle, see chap. 9.

113. Guillaume le Breton, *Philippidos* 3, 280. At the beginning of book 6 he observes that the peace ushered in by the fall of Château-Gaillard lasted until Bouvines. Ibid. 151.

114. See chap. 11, at nn. 27–30.

115. Rigord 151. Guillaume le Breton, *Gesta* 207, 245.

116. Guillaume le Breton, *Philippidos* 29. Compare with the accounts of *Gesta* 180 and Rigord 18.

117. Henry: Guillaume le Breton, *Philippidos* 60, 70, 94; Richard: ibid. 95, 100, 126; John: ibid. 151. For the comparable accounts in the *Gesta*: 186, 189, 205.

118. Toulouse: Guillaume le Breton, *Philippidos* 66, 229; Burgundy: ibid. 35; Henry and Richard: ibid. 63.

119. Ibid. 155–59.

120. Ibid. 128, 145. Compare with *Gesta* 199, 200, 204.

121. Guillaume le Breton, *Philippidos* 362, 363. One continuation of the *Gesta* 333 breaks off at this point.

122. Guillaume le Breton, *Philippidos* 250, 252, 253, 342, 346, 352, 353. Between the last two episodes Renaud made yet another attempt to rebel. On Renaud's career, see chap. 9.

123. Rigord 8. The story probably postdates Guillaume le Breton, who, although partial to such visions, ignores it in both *Gesta* and *Philippidos*. The vision may also be found in Gerald of Wales, *De Principis instructione* 135, 227, composed between the 1190s and 1217.

124. Guillaume le Breton, *Philippidos* 245, 305.

125. Guillaume le Breton, *Gesta* 272, 284. *Philippidos* 318, 319, 350.

126. Guillaume le Breton, *Philippidos* 334.

127. Rigord 56, 58. The *Short Chronicle* (Soissons 129, fol. 133v) makes a brief allusion to the defeat of the Alans. Aimoin de Fleury, *De Gestis Francorum,*

RHF III, 29, 30. Gilles de Paris, *Karolinus* 268, with gloss on 239. Guillaume le Breton, *Gesta* 170, 171. *Philippidos* 11–13.

128. Rigord 82. Guillaume le Breton, *Philippidos* 3.

129. *Registres* IV, A (III), (IV and note *a*). The practice of recording the length of reigns was begun with the popes in the *Liber pontificalis*. Bernard Guenée, *Histoire et culture historique dans l'Occident médiéval* (Paris, 1980), 157. For the French registers, see *Registres* IV, A (I).

130. Reg. E, fols. 303r–309v. Edited in *Registres* IV, A (I), C, A (III), (IV), and VII, no. 4. For a useful collection of sources and a recent introduction to the abundant literature on the Tiburtine Sibyl and related apocalyptic treatises, see Bernard McGinn, *Visions of the End: Apocalyptic Traditions in the Middle Ages* (New York, 1979). Elizabeth A. R. Brown ("La Notion de la légitimité et la prophétie à la cour de Philippe Auguste," in *La France de Philippe Auguste* 77–110) also gives an extensive discussion of the documentation.

131. The Tiburtine text is edited by Ernst Sackur, *Sibyllinische Texte und Forschungen* (Halle, 1898), 180–87. Translations and discussion of the literature are found in McGinn, *Visions of the End*, 43–50, 70–76, 82–87.

132. Otto of Freising, *Gesta Frederici I Imperatoris* (Hannover, 1884) 8, 9. Benedict I, 154, and Howden III, 78, report that Richard was also acquainted with the Adso text.

133. Although the king "K" (Charlemagne) was called *Salicus rex de Francia* and several of his successors were identified as *Salici*, none of those kings who might be interpreted as Franks play roles comparable to the last Greek, Constans.

134. Etienne's copy begins abruptly in the middle of the fifth generation with the birth of Christ. The abbreviations increase markedly with the appearance of Constans, the last emperor. Among the important sentences excised was the crucial "*Et cum cessaverit imperium Romanum.*" For the omissions, see *Registres* VII, no. 4.

135. In "La Notion de la légitimité" 77–110, Elizabeth A. R. Brown proposes to interpret the Tiburtine prophecy by referring to the Valerian prophecy that was transcribed directly after the Tiburtine text in Reg. E. Although her documentation is admirable, I cannot follow her conclusions, despite the proximity of the two texts.

136. *Anglo-Norman Texts: Le Livre de Sibile by Philippe de Thaon*, ed. Hugh Shields (London, 1979), lines 507, 508.

137. Guillaume le Breton, *Gesta* 270, 273.

138. *Philippidos* 313, 314. Alexander's speech opens: "*Ecce dies optata. . . .*" Gautier de Châtillon, *Alexandreis* 58.

139. Guillaume le Breton, *Gesta* 244.

140. Ibid. 312.

141. *Philippidos* 244, 245.

142. Ibid. 305–8. Otto also had plans to take the lands around Rome promised to Frederick II by the pope. Only the plan to divide France was contained in the *Gesta* 295.

143. Guillaume le Breton, *Gesta* 234, 253.

144. *Philippidos* 305.

145. Ibid. 131, 142.

146. Ibid. 312, 315–17. For the importance of Sunday, see Duby, *Le Dimanche de Bouvines* 155, 156.

147. Rigord 50, 137, 164. Guillaume le Breton, *Gesta* 206. Louis VII had made a gift to the abbey in 1161. Luchaire, *Actes de Louis VII* no. 453.

148. *Philippidos* 350. It was also recorded in the continuation of the *Gesta* 321 by the monk of Saint-Denis.

149. The documentation has been collected by A. Vattier, "L'Abbaye de la Victoire: Notice historique," *Comité archéologique de Senlis: Comptes rendus et mémoires*, 3rd ser., 2 (1887): 1–60; *Gall. christ.* X, 1413; *Obituaires de Sens*, ed. Molinier, I (1) 5–70.

150. Guillaume le Breton, *Gesta* 281 (on the right wing of the battlefield) and *Philippidos* 340 (on the left wing).

151. The chief chroniclers reporting Philip's death are: Guillaume le Breton, *Philippidos* 365–79; Continuation of the monk of Saint-Denis in *Gesta* 322–27; *Chronicon Turonense*, *RHF* XVIII, 303, 304; Richer de Senones, *Gesta Senoniensis ecclesie*, *MGH SS* XXV, 296, 297; Coggeshall 195, 196; E. Berger, "*Chronicon Sancti Dionysii recentius*," *BEC* 40 (1879): 289; Philippe Mouskés, *Chronique rimée*, ed. F.-A.-F.-T. de Reiffenberg (Brussels, 1838), II, 431, 432. Cartellieri IV, 564–73, has coordinated the evidence. The authoritative study on the funerals, burials, and tombs of the French kings is Alain Erlande-Brandenburg, *Le Roi est mort: Etude sur les funerailles, les sépultures et les tombeaux des rois de France jusqu'à la fin du XIIIe siècle* (Geneva, 1975). See especially 14–16, 18, 30. Rigord 23 describes Louis VII's tomb at Barbeau, erected by Adèle de Champagne, but not his funeral.

152. See Marc Bloch, *Les Rois thaumaturges: Etude sur le caractère surnaturel attribué à la puissance royale particulièrement en France et en Angleterre* (Strasbourg, 1924), 30–36.

153. Rigord, everyday miracles: 119, 124, 125, 127, 128, 139, 140; royal miracles: 44, 45, 91, 95. Guillaume le Breton, *Gesta*, everyday miracles: 201; royal: 183, 187, 190. *Philippidos*, royal miracles: 57, 67, 91; two visions: 26, 97.

154. Guillaume le Breton, *Philippidos* 365, 366. Rigord frequently precedes the birth or death of important personages with heavenly portents. For examples: 81, 111, 120, 163.

155. *Philippidos* 369–71.

156. Ibid. 371–73.

157. Ibid. 371, 375–77.

158. Continuation of monk of Saint-Denis, *Gesta* 322, 324; *Chronicon Turonense*, *RHF* XVIII, 303; Wendover II, 271. Coggeshall 196.

159. The saint plays the leading role in the story, just as he had performed similar services for other royal patrons, reported in the *Vita* for Dagobert, Charlemagne, and Charles the Bald. *Vita* published in André Duchesne, *Historiae*

Francorum scriptores (Paris, 1649), V, 260. Charles J. Liebman, Jr., *Etude sur la vie en prose de Saint Denis* (Geneva, N.Y., 1942) xv, xxiv, xxv, dates this section of the *Vita* from 1223 and argues that Guillaume le Breton took the story from *Vita*, but the latter could also have borrowed from Guillaume. The *Vita* was completed in 1233. Based on similar practices at the funeral of Louis IX and other examples, Robert Branner ("The Montjoies of Saint Louis," in *Essays in the History of Architecture Presented to Rudolf Wittkower* [London, 1967] I, 13–15) sees the reporting of miracles at Philip's funeral as an "unsuccessful attempt to canonize Philip Augustus."

160. It is also found in *Chronicon Turonense*, *RHF* XVIII, 304; Paris Mazarine 2017 (published in Cartellieri IV, 654); Continuation of André de Marchiennes, *De Gestis MGH SS* XXVI, 213, 214; and Philippe Mouskés, *Chronique rimée* II, 431, 432. See also n. 161 below.

161. *Anecdotes historiques . . . tirés du recueil inédit d'Etienne de Bourbon*, ed. A. Lecoy de la Marche (Paris, 1877), 271, 272. Richer de Senonenses, *Gesta Senoniensis ecclesie*, *MGH SS* XXV, 297. See also Jacques Le Goff, "Philippe Auguste dans les 'exempla,'" in *La France de Philippe Auguste* 150, 151.

162. Most recently, see William Chester Jordan, *Louis IX and the Challenge of the Crusade* (Princeton, 1979), 182–213. For the ideological relationship between the reigns of Philip and Louis, see Berges, *Die Fürstenspiegel* 78–80.

163. On the tombs of Saint-Denis, see Erlande-Brandenburg, *Le Roi est mort* 81–83, 162; Georgia Sommers Wright, "A Royal Tomb Program in the Reign of St. Louis," *Art Bulletin* 56 (1971): 223–43; Lewis, *Royal Succession in Capetian France* 116, 117; Elizabeth A. R. Brown, "La notion de la légitimité" 95, 96.

15. Postscript: Uncovering the Government of Philip Augustus

1. For a recent assessment of Suger's contributions as a historian, see Gabrielle M. Spiegel, "History as Enlightenment: Suger and the *Mos Anagogicus*," in *Abbot Suger and Saint-Denis*, ed. Paula Gerson (New York, in press), and *The Chronicle Tradition of Saint-Denis: A Survey*, Medieval Classics: Texts and Studies, no. 10 (Brookline, Mass., and Leyden, 1978), 40–52. The latter work is the authoritative account of French royal historiography at Saint-Denis and the basis for this section.

2. Rigord pp. xx and 1. Henri-François Delaborde, "Notice sur les ouvrages et sur la vie de Rigord, moine de Saint-Denis," *BEC* 45 (1884): 600. On Rigord in general, see Delaborde's introduction to Rigord pp. iii–xxxiii, and Spiegel, *The Chronicle Tradition* 56–63.

3. Reference to Rigord may be found in the obituaries of both Saint-Denis

and its priory at Argenteuil. *Obituaires de la province de Sens*, ed. Auguste Molinier (Paris, 1902), I (1), 331, 351. In December 1193 *magister Rigort* and *magister Thomas* witnessed a charter of Abbot Hugues, found in the Cartulaire blanc de Saint-Denis, AN, LL 1157, p. 60.

4. *Actes* I, no. 345. Rigord's familiarity with the royal archives becomes apparent when the contents of the Trésor des Chartes are compared with his chronicle: treaty with Count John (1194), Teulet I, no. 412, with Rigord 126; peace with Richard (1196), Teulet I, no. 431, with Rigord 133, 134, *sicut in authentico utriusque continentur instrumento*; peace with King John (1200), Teulet I, no. 578, with Rigord 148, *in authenticis instrumentis ab ipsius confectis et sigillatis plenius continetur*; submission of the count of Rethel and the lord of Rozoi (1201), Teulet I, nos. 619, 620, and 624, with Rigord 151, *datis securitatibus cum juramentis et obsidibus*; Arthur's homage (1202), Teulet I, no. 647, with Rigord 152; Loches given to Dreu de Mello (1204), Teulet I, no. 804, with Rigord 162. On the exemplar for Rigord's preface, see chap. 14, n. 33.

5. Auguste Molinier, *Les Sources de l'histoire de France des origines aux guerres d'Italie* (Paris, 1903), III, 5. The preface is contained in the manuscripts Paris BN lat. 14663, fol. 194r, and 17008, fol. 2v, partially edited in *RHF* XVII, 423–24. That the work came from Saint-Germain-des-Prés is suggested by two of the sources cited: *a chronicis Hugonis Floriacensis . . . a quodem libello qui de gestis regum francorum loquitur qui apud Sanctum Germanum de Pratis juxta Parisius reperitur*. Another monk of Saint-Germain-des-Prés reworked Suger's notes on Louis VII to produce the *Historia gloriosi regis Ludovici Septimi* around 1165. See Spiegel, *Chronicle Tradition* 41–44, 48–52.

6. Delaborde's introduction to Guillaume le Breton, *Gesta* pp. xxxiv–lxxxii, and Spiegel, *Chronicle Tradition* 63–68.

7. Senlis, Bibl. mun., Collection Afforty, XV, reprinted in *Gall. christ.* X, instru. 449. That royal patronage was involved is suggested by the prebend to a certain Guillaume, nephew of Barthélemy de Roye.

8. Guillaume le Breton, *Gesta* 168, 169.

9. On the *Philippidos*, see A. Pannenborg, *Zur Kritik der Philipis* (Aurich, 1880), and Delaborde's introduction to Guillaume le Breton, *Gesta* pp. lxvii–lxxvii.

10. Guillaume le Breton, *Philippidos* 384, 385.

11. Ibid. 209, 280.

12. Ibid. 6. The recital of the battle of Bouvines, however, is reduced from that in the *Gesta*.

13. Molinier, *Les Sources* III, 5, 6, 24.

14. Ibid. III, 86–91.

15. Most recently, see Constance Brittain Bouchard, *Spirituality and Administration: The Role of the Bishop in Twelfth-Century Auxerre* (Cambridge, Mass., 1979), 5–12.

16. Medieval English historiography has been recently well treated by An-

tonia Grandsen, *Historical Writing in England c. 550 to c. 1307* (Ithaca, N.Y., 1974). This brief account merely summarizes her pp. 219–36, 242–46, 253–60, 321–31, 356–77. On Gerald of Wales, see Robert Bartlett, *Gerald of Wales, 1146–1223* (Oxford, 1982), 69–100.

17. Those rare secular collections that did survive consist, for example, of the cartularies of Champagne, Flanders, and Artois, plus registers and collections from towns such as Abbeville, Saint-Quentin, Eu, and Orléans from the thirteenth and fourteenth centuries.

18. These figures are based on data from *Registres* II, C, D.

19. For the royal registers, see chap. 15, at nn. 45–51.

20. On Hugues and Guérin, see chap. 2, at nn. 26 and 30, and chap. 6.

21. The conclusions of this paragraph are based on Françoise Gasparri, *L'Ecriture des actes de Louis VI, Louis VII et Philippe Auguste* (Geneva and Paris, 1973), especially 25, 26, 52, 73–78.

22. *Actes* I, no. 378.

23. The earlier diplomatic study of Philip's *actes* by Delisle, *Catalogue* pp. lv–lvi, should be replaced by Michel Nortier, "Les Actes de Philippe Auguste: Notes critiques sur les sources diplomatiques du règne," in *La France de Philippe Auguste* 442, 443, and "Les Actes faussement attribués à la chancellerie de Philippe Auguste," *Académie des Inscriptions et Belles-Lettres: Comptes rendus* (1981): 659, 660.

24. See chap. 5, at n. 34.

25. Guillaume le Breton, *Gesta* 197, *Philippidos* 118–21. The hypothesis of *états* lost at Fréteval was formulated by Thomas N. Bisson, "Les Comptes des domaines au temps de Philippe Auguste: Essai comparatif," in *La France de Philippe Auguste* 525–28. It is suggested by his edition and study of the Catalonia accounts: *Fiscal Accounts of Catalonia* (Berkeley and Los Angeles, 1985). Except for modifying his chronology, I have followed Bisson's hypothesis.

26. Rigord 100–105. *Actes* I, no. 345.

27. [Nicolas] Brussel, *Nouvel examen de l'usage général des fiefs en France pendant les onzième, douzième, treizième et quatorzième siècles: pour servir à l'intelligence des plus anciens titres du domaine de la couronne et de l'histoire*, 2 vols. (Paris: C. Prud'homme, 1727; reprint, Paris: J. de Nully, 1750), pp. CXXXVIII–CXXXIX. Modern reprint with introduction in *Budget*.

28. See, for example, Brussel, *Nouvel examen* I, XLIV, 486.

29. DuCange noted the title of Chandleur (February) 1211 in Paris, Arsenal 5259, fol. 164. Baluze extracted from May 1220 in Paris, BN Baluze 51, fol. 59v. D'Hérouval extracted from the account of Meulan dated November 1222 from a roll in the Chambre des Comptes, Paris, BN Vexin 3, p. 207, Vexin 14, fol. 121r. See Borrelli de Serres, *Recherches* I, 404.

30. Brussel, *Nouvel examen* I, 404.

31. The account was discovered by Michel Nortier. For an edition and discussion, see Nortier and Baldwin, "Contributions." For a further discussion, see

chap. 10. The household account of Prince Louis for 1213 was edited by Robert Fawtier, "Un Fragment du compte de l'hôtel du prince Louis de France pour le terme de la Purification 1213," *Le Moyen Age* 43 (1933): 225–50.

32. The Victorine manuscript, Vatican Reg. Lat. 179, edited in André Duchesne, *Historia Francorum scriptores* (Paris, 1641), IV, 557–762. For discussion, see Achille Luchaire, *Etude sur quelques manuscrits de Rome et de Paris* (Université de Paris, Bibliothéque de la Faculté de Lettres, 1899), VIII, 31–39, and Françoise Gasparri, "Manuscrit monastique ou registre de chancellerie? A propos d'un recueil épistolaire de l'abbaye de Saint-Victor," *Journal des savants* (1976): 131–40. The original disposition and groupings of the letters may be best seen in Andreas Wilmart, *Codices regienenses latini* (Vatican City, 1937), I, 419–30.

33. Delaborde, in *Layettes* V, pp. xxii–xlvii.

34. Diceto II, 117. Howden III, 255, 256. Rigord 129.

35. Guillaume le Breton, *Gesta* 196, 197, *Philippidos* 118–121.

36. Delaborde in *Layettes* V, pp. xvii–xx, xxvii–xxx.

37. Reg. E, fol. 15r. The edition of this list found in L. Douët d'Arcq, *Recherches historiques et critiques sur les anciens comtes de Beaumont-sur-Oise du XIe au XIIIe siècle* (Amiens, 1855) *Mémoires de la Société des Antiquaires de Picardie*, Documents inédits, IV, preuves, 225–227, is defective. After the item *Cartam Edeve de Monciaco super donatione quam fecit comitati de Bosco-Godardi* should be added *Cartam domini regis de sacramento quod Henricus de Sancto Dionisio fecit comiti super fortericia de Molleia*. The following item then continues, *Cartam domini regis de dono quod fecit comiti de feodo de Atheinvilla et de Fonqueroles*. The inventory also indicates that there is a repository of eight or nine Beaumont charters at Val-Notre-Dame, but the notices are not specific enough to permit identification with extant originals. Adam was concierge in 1231. Delaborde, *Layettes* V, no. 360.

38. *Littere reddite de hospicio monalium Aureliansium.* Teulet I, no. 47. *Littere Agathe domine Petrefontis reddite domino regi a monachis Longi Pontis donationibus sibi factis.* Ibid. I, no. 320. An example from 1201 is: *Littere reddite domino regi de rebus quas emit ab heredibus R. Falconarii apud Everam.* Ibid. I, no. 621.

39. Delaborde, in *Layettes* V, p. ii, found twenty-one originals in the Trésor des Chartes before 1194, but he has not specified the basis of his statistics.

40. Teulet, I, no. 412. Ibid. I, nos. 414, 415. Because the calendar year has been reckoned from Easter according to Capetian chancery usage, these three items fall in 1195 on the graph.

41. Ibid. I, nos. 431–41.

42. Ibid. I, nos. 448, 450, 451, 479, 482.

43. Ibid. I, no. 578. Its accompanying agreements may be found in ibid. I, nos. 579–89.

44. See chap. 15, n. 4.

45. So named by Léopold Delisle, the first scholar to study them seriously. *Catalogue* pp. vi–xxv. Delisle also designated the fourteenth-century copy of A

as Register B (AN JJ 8), the fourteenth-century copy of C as Register D (AN JJ 23), and Louis IX's copy of E, which he ordered executed in 1247 before departing on the crusade, as Register F (Paris BN lat. 9778).

46. In addition to the pioneer work of Delisle, the major studies on the registers have been Alexandre Tuetey, "Rapport sur la mission à Rome, en 1876, rélatif au cartulaire de Philippe-Auguste," *Archives des missions scientifiques et littéraires*, 3rd ser., 6 (1880): 313–94, and the introduction of Delaborde in *Actes* I, pp. v–xl. A paleographic and codicological analysis of Register A has been provided by Françoise Gasparri, "Note sur le *Registrum Veterius*: Le Plus Ancien Registre de la chancellerie de Philippe-Auguste," *Mélanges de l'Ecole française de Rome* 83 (1971): 363–88. This work on Registers C and E has been continued in an unpublished study, which the author has kindly allowed me to consult. This section is based on her conclusions.

On occasion, arguments have been advanced to hypothesize the existence of a "lost register" that preceded Register A. Delisle (*Catalogue* p. ix) merely conjectured its existence as the work of Gautier the Young between 1200 and 1204. Tuetey ("Rapport" pp. 318, 319) and Edouard Audouin ("Les Chartes communales de Poitiers et les Etablissements de Rouen," *Bulletin historique et philologique du Comité des Travaux Historiques* [1912]: 125–28) noted references to a *registrum* in Register A itself that suggested a prior work. But as Delaborde (*Actes* I, p. ix) noted, since all these references (see chap. 4, at n. 26) refer to the "Etablissements de Rouen" and follow it in the text, they could in fact refer to Register A.

More recently, Michel Nortier ("Les Actes de Philippe Auguste: Notes critiques sur les sources diplomatiques du règne," in *La France de Philippe Auguste* 437, 438) has noted a chronological order within the *actes* transcribed in Register A. Since those from May–June 1204 to January–February 1205 (fols. 30–40) appear to have been written at one time (because of uniformity of ink and hand), they could not have been copied as they were produced, but were transcribed at one time from a previous register. This argument is only compelling, however, if the originals were drafted first and then copied into the register. If, as Nortier himself maintains later (ibid. 438–42; see n. 60 below), the chancery produced a preliminary rough draft, which was later transcribed into the register and was also corrected and recopied as the "original," the preliminary rough drafts that remained in the chancery could have been gathered together and copied at one time in January–February 1205. These drafts need not have been bound in a codex, as would be required by a *registrum*. As yet, there is no compelling reason to hypothesize a lost register.

Since Gautier the Young was a chamberlain, and was only associated in the chronicle tradition with the restoration of financial documents lost in 1194, there is little evidence to link him to the register, which was a product of the chancery and appeared ten years after the loss. Since the only mention of his name in Register A records the possession of a castle, his personal imprint is minimal.

47. Designated as Scribes P, R, S, T, and U. P, R, and U are known from other work in the royal chancery. Gasparri, *L'Ecriture* 77, 78.

48. Scribe α performed the principal work, which was completed by β. The section copied by γ, Reg. C, fol. 134r–137v, concerns Vermandois and Valois. It is impossible to determine whether it was included in the original nucleus or added at a later date. Scribe α was scribe O of the chancery. Gasparri, *L'Ecriture* 77.

49. Scribes δ, ε, ζ, η, θ, κ, and λ. Scribes α and β also made additions. Scribe δ is Scribe R of Reg. A and the chancery. Scribe ζ is scribe Q of the chancery. Gasparri, *L'Ecriture* 77.

50. See the preface to Reg. E, fol. 16r in *Registres* VIII and *Actes* I, p. xxxi. On the career and hand of Etienne de Gallardon, see Léopold Delisle, "Etienne de Gallardon, clerc de la chancellerie de Philippe Auguste, chanoine de Bourges," *BEC* 40 (1899): 5–18. He is identified as scribe U in Reg. A. The cartulary of Bourges is contained in Paris BN nouv. acq. lat. 1274.

51. Scribes ε, ζ and λ found in Reg. C were also at work in Reg. E. Scribe δ' in Reg. E may be the same as Scribe δ in Reg. C. In Reg. A, C, and E the most active hands can be readily identified. The less frequent hands, however, may hide more than one different scribe. I am grateful for the comments of Jean Guérout, archivist at the Archives Nationales, who has made an independent study of the hands found in the Registers.

52. Reg. A, fols. 11r–26v. *Cahiers* 2 and 3 of the manuscript.

53. *Registres* VIII. Reg. C, fol. 10v.

54. *Registres* VIII. Reg. E, fols. 16r–22v. Etienne also employed the hierarchic principle in organizing the cartulary for Bourges. Delisle, "Etienne de Gallardon" 8.

55. Chapter 9 found in the text of Reg. E is lacking in the table of contents.

56. *Registres* I, no. 46. Documents relating to Bourges were placed at the head of sections devoted to communes, metropolitans, and inquests; two charters of Bishop Guérin were placed at the head of the section on bishoprics. *Registres* VIII.

57. Reg. E, fol. 16r., in *Registres* VIII, and *Actes* I, p. xxxi. *In extrema vero tocius registri parte continetur tractatus.* . . . Reg. E, fol. 22v in *Registres* VIII. *Hic incipit registrum domini illustrissimi Francorum regis Philippi.* . . . Reg. E, fol. 25r.

58. In samples taken from Reg. E the percentage of royal charters to the total was as follows: 80 percent in chapter 7 on bishops, 66 percent in chapter 8 on abbeys and other churches, and 73 percent in chapter 12 on knights.

59. See Table 13.

60. I have adopted the conclusions of Nortier, "Les Actes de Philippe Auguste," in *La France de Philippe Auguste* 438–42, which is the most recent study of the problem. His solution approaches that of Delisle in *Catalogue* p. vii, who postulated a preliminary "minute" before the final copies.

61. A dossier on the Garlande family was copied intact into Reg. C. For these dossiers, see chap. 6, at n. 119.

62. *Actes* I, no. 139, and III, no. 1309. See chap. 11, at n. 9.

63. *Actes* I, no. 142. When the churches of Autun and Lyon had their regalian rights reconfirmed in 1222, they had the original charter of 1189 transcribed into Register E. *Actes* I, no. 254, IV, no. 1773. For other examples of recipients, see *Actes* I, nos. 126, 284.

64. These have been edited in *Registres* VI. In samples taken from Reg. E the percentage of letters addressed to the king to the total was as follows: 17 percent in chapter 7 on bishops, 1.5 percent in chapter 8 on abbeys and other churches, and 26 percent in chapter 12 on knights.

65. All of the incoming letters in chapter 7 of Reg. E are still extant in the Trésor des Chartes. In chapter 12 a third can still be found in the Trésor des Chartes.

66. Rouen: *Actes* II, no. 789. Falaise: *sicut continetur in rotulo qui coram nobis lectus fuit et in registro nostro transcriptus. Actes* II, no. 790. Caen: *sicut in rotulo Rothomagensi continetur et in nostro similiter registro continetur. Actes* II, no. 806. Pont-Audemer: *ad consuetudines quas ipsi tenuerunt que continentur in registro nostro. Actes* II, no. 809. Niort: *ad puncta et consuetudines communie Rothomagensis que continentur in registro nostro. Actes* II, no. 828. The reference to the register occurs in the charter form but not in the letter form copied by Scribe N into Reg. A.

67. *RHF* XVIII, 239. *Actes* II, no. 856.

68. *Actes* III, nos. 1125, 1125bis. The command was obeyed by the chapters of Noyon, Tournai, and Saint-Omer. The register contained a copy of the letter addressed to the commune of Sens.

69. *Actes* IV, no. 1523. For the inquest, see *Registres* I, nos. 43, 44. When in 1221 the monks of La Charité wished to make new copies of their charters of 1181 and 1203, exemplars were not available in the royal registers, which had not yet been started. *Actes* IV, no. 1740, I, no. 34, and II, no. 741. Occasionally, references were made to the royal archives. *Actes* III, nos. 1313, 1314.

70. A. A. Beugnot, *Les Olim, ou registres des arrêts rendus par la cour du roi* (Paris, 1839), I, 613, 614 (found in *Actes* IV, no. 1594, from Regs. C and E) and I, 625, 626 (found in *Actes* II, no. 807, and III, no. 986, from Regs. A, C, E). In 1259 Louis IX acquitted the abbot of Saint-Denis of *gîte* owed the king, but only after deleting the record of the *gîte* in the Registers. Brussel, *Nouvel examen* I, 541, 542, and Guillaume de Saint-Pathus, *Vie et miracles de M. Saint-Louis*, ed. M. C. d'Espagne (Paris, 1971), 40, 41.

71. *Jugements* pp. 268–70. *Rotuli Normanniae*, ed. Thomas Duffus Hardy (London, 1835), I, 1–22.

72. *Omnes vero questiones et nomina juratorum scripta sunt in assisia in rotulis qui bene et fideliter conservantur. . . . Rotuli vero conservantur ad contentiones deprimendas de rebus in assisia diffinitis. Coutumiers de Normandie*, ed. Ernest-Joseph Tardif (Rouen, 1881), I, 24, 25.

73. For example: 1207, Caen, in Léopold Delisle, "Fragments de l'histoire de

Gonesse," *BEC* (1859): 248; Avranches, 1217, in Delisle, *RHF* XXIV, *280, *281; Bernai, 1219, in ibid., *284; and Avranches, 1222, in ibid., *287. See the general discussion in *Jugements* pp. 267–70.

74. Delisle's *mémoire* in *Jugements*, pp. 247–89, discusses the origin, nature and scope of the collection.

75. A judgment of 1225 refers to a decision of 1208: *sicut continetur in registro. Jugements* nos. 34, 367. A document of 1255 refers to a decision of 1218: *quod inventum fuit in rotulis domini regis.* Ibid. no. 242 and n. 1. One of the clerks may be identified as Guillaume Acarin, originally a clerk of the *bailli* Pierre du Thillai, who was active in the exchequer in 1217. After the judicial sessions were moved to Caen in 1220, he was regularly present, simultaneously holding the position of dean in the local church. Ibid. no. 205, n. 4, and pp. 272–76.

76. *Actes* I, no. 345.

77. See Bryce Lyon and A. E. Verhulst, *Medieval Finance: A Comparison of Financial Institutions in Northwestern Europe* (Providence, R.I., 1967), and Bisson, "Les Comptes des domaines," in *La France de Philippe Auguste* 527, and *Fiscal Accounts of Catalonia.*

78. Leonard E. Boyle, *A Survey of the Vatican Archives and of Its Medieval Holdings* (Toronto, 1972), 7, 103, 104. Geoffrey Elton, *England 1200–1660* (Ithaca, N.Y., 1969), 35–37, is a recent survey of the English medieval collections.

79. *Le Liber Censuum de l'Eglise Romaine,* ed. Paul Fabre and L. Duchesne, 3 vols., Bibliothèque des Ecoles Françaises d'Athènes et de Rome, 2nd ser., no. 5 (1889–1952). *Liber niger scaccarii,* ed. Thomas Hearne, 2 vols. (Oxford, 1728). *The Red Book of the Exchequer,* ed. Hubert Hall, 2 vols. (London, 1896). J. Petit et al., *Essai de restitution des plus anciens mémoriaux de la Chambre des Comptes de Paris,* Université de Paris, Bibliothèque de la Faculté des Lettres, no. 7 (Paris, 1899).

80. On public enrollments in England, see H. G. Richardson, *The Memoranda Roll . . . of King John,* Publications of the Pipe Roll Society, n.s., no. 21 (London, 1943), pp. li–lix.

81. *Rotuli de liberate ac de misis et praestitis,* ed. Thomas Duffus Hardy (London, 1844), 102.

Index

Aaron of Lincoln, 231
Abbeys: elections, 70; Norman, 447; protected, 72–73, 448–49; regalian, 70–72, 172–73, 314, 305–6; regalian list of, 445–47, 477nn.67–68
Abbots, 13, 70
Abelin, *bailli*, 130, 430
Abelin, mason, 98–99
Accounts, fiscal, 144–52, 405–7; for 1202/03, 57, 101, 106, 128, 145–50, 152–75, 240, 407; for 1221, 240–48, 351–52, 407; for 1227, 352, 354, 407; for 1238, 240–48, 407; lost at Fréteval, 56. *See also* Fréteval
Accounts, jewel, 55, 117, 377
Acre, 78
Adam, bp. of Thérouanne, 440
Adam, canon of Noyon, 102–3, 462n.38
Adam, chamberlain, 34, 55
Adam, cleric, 118, 145, 406
Adam, concierge, 409
Adam, son of Gautier the Young, 108
Adam, *vicomte* of Melun, 450
Adam Héron, 127, 131, 132, 138, 225, 294, 430, 522n.22, 548n.178
Adam de Neuilly, 431
Adélberon, archbp. of Reims, 374
Adèle, queen: absence at coronation of PA, 6; and birth of PA, 14, 368; dowry of, 44, 466n.37, 528n.109; marriage to Louis VII, 15; rebellion against PA, 16; as regent, 69, 102
Adèmar, ct. of Angoulême, 94, 97
Adèmar, *vicomte* of Limoges, 94, 97
Adso de Montier-en-Der, 385
Advowson, 318–19
Agathe, lady of Pierrefonds, 410

Agnès, daughter of Louis VII and Adèle of Champagne, 536n.46
Agnès de Méran, 165, 269, 357–58; death of, 86; marriage to PA, 84–86
Agnès de Nevers, 26, 270
Agreements, judicial, 38, 41–43
Aimery, constable of Auvergne, 200, 214, 219, 237, 241, 382, 433
Aimery, *vicomte* of Thouars, 92, 95, 195, 199, 214, 238, 339, 433
Aimery de Craon, 214, 219, 237, 241, 382, 433; at La Roche-au-Moine, 285
Aire, 81. *See also* Saint-Omer
Alain de Lille, writings of, 571n.27
Alain de Roucy, 280, 546n.176
Alard de Bourghelles, 268
Alberic, archbp. of Reims, 182, 439
Alberic Clément, 34, 113
Alberic Cornut, 553n.9
Alberic de Trois-Fontaines, writings of, 399
Albigensian crusade, 35, 199, 209, 235, 336–39
Aleaume Hescelin, 128, 133–34, 160, 432
Alexander the Great, 366–67, 383–84, 387
Alexander III, pope, 184, 318
Alexander of Swereford, 288, 421
Alexius Comnenus, emperor, 536n.46
Aliénor, countess of Vermandois and Saint-Quentin, 50, 187, 238, 255, 278, 473n.25, 534n.26, 550n.192; inheritance of, 24, 200; marriage to Mathieu, ct. of Boulogne, 15
Aliénor, sister of Arthur, 192
Alix, countess of Blois, 481n.1

591

Designer: Janet Wood
Compositor: G&S Typesetters, Inc.
Text: 10/12 Galliard
Display: Galliard
Printer: Maple-Vail Book Mfg. Group
Binder: Maple-Vail Book Mfg. Group

DATE DUE
